MW01252914

LIBRARY OF NEW TESTAMENT STUDIES
474

Formerly Journal for the Study of the New Testament Supplement Series

Editor

Mark Goodacre

JESUS, THE SABBATH
AND THE JEWISH DEBATE

Healing on the Sabbath
in the 1st and 2nd Centuries CE

Nina L. Collins

B L O O M S B U R Y
LONDON • NEW DELHI • NEW YORK • SYDNEY

Bloomsbury T&T Clark
An imprint of Bloomsbury Publishing Plc

50 Bedford Square	1385 Broadway
London	New York
WC1B 3DP	NY 10018
UK	USA

www.bloomsbury.com
Bloomsbury and the Diana logo are registered trademarks of Bloomsbury Publishing plc

First published 2014

British Library Cataloguing-in-Publication Data
A catalogue record for this book is available from the British Library.

ISBN:	HB:	978-0-56738-587-1
	ePDF:	978-0-56727-034-4

Library of Congress Cataloging-in-Publication Data
A catalog record for this book is available from the Library of Congress.

Typeset by Forthcoming Publications Ltd (www.forthpub.com)
Printed and bound in Great Britain

The Jewish high regard for life, life sacred, precious and blessed,
imposes the duty to preserve it under all circumstances,
regardless of material cost and human exertion.

Meyer S. Lew, *The Humanity of Jewish Law*
(London/New York: Soncino, 1985), 25

CONTENTS

Contents

PREFACE

The Hebrew phrase פיקוח נפש, *pikkuach nefesh*, has come to refer to the requirement in Judaism that all individuals must perform acts of healing and saving life even if it involves violating the law. This book began with a quest to discover the origins of this phrase. It soon became apparent that both the concept and its name were preceded by a significant history and the search for this history has resulted in this book.

There are many people to thank for their help in completing this research. Foremost is Professor Keith Elliott, who has encouraged me in every way. Then there is Professor John Rogerson and Professor Amy-Jill Levine, who read through early versions of the text. I must also thank Alec McAllister, of the University of Leeds, who monitored the software I have used. Other scholars who have also not hesitated to share their knowledge include Professor Nathan Aviezer, Professor Dan Bahat, Rabbi Dr Louis Jacobs ז"ל, Dr Lutz Doering, Father John Donahue, Dr Eva Frojmovic, Dr John Kahn, Professor Menahem Kahana, Dr Menahem Kister, Dr Ian Moxon and Dr Avihai Shivtiel. Their comments have often inspired new trains of thought. Many thanks also to Frances Harris and Dr Ruth Collins who read proofs of much of the material in this book. I am also grateful to my publishers, who have tolerated extended delays.

The greatest thanks however go to my family. This book is dedicated to my dear husband Leon for his constant encouragement and support, and to our children, Ruth, Paula and Simon, for whom the principle of *pikkuach nefesh* has always been a guiding light in their lives.

ABBREVIATIONS

Biblical Texts

These are cited in the usual way

Rabbinic Texts

b.	Babylonian Talmud
m.	Mishnah
t.	Tosefta
y.	Jerusalem Talmud

The tractates of the above works are abbreviated as below. Texts from the Mishnah are cited according to tractate, chapter and '*mishnah*', and similarly from the Tosefta, according to tractate, chapter and *halachah* (e.g. m. Ber 1.1 and t. Ber 1.1). The Jerusalem Talmud is cited according to its relationship with its comments on the Mishnah, meaning that, for example, y. Ber 1.1 refers to the comments of the Jerusalem Talmud on the text of m. Ber 1.1 The Babylonian Talmud is cited according to its folio page and side (a or b), as in the Vilna edition.

Arak	Arakhin
Avot	Avot
AZ	Avodah Zarah
BB	Baba Bathra
Bekh	Bekhorot
Ber	Berachot
Betz	Betzah
Bikk	Bikkurim
BK	Baba Kama
BM	Baba Metzia
Dem	Demai
Eduy	Eduyoth
Eruv	Eruvin
Gitt	Gittin
Hag	Hagigah

Hall	Hallah
Hor	Horayoth
Hull	Hullin
Kel	Kelim
Ker	Kerithoth
Ket	Ketuboth
Kidd	Kiddushin
Kil	Kilaim
Kinn	Kinnim
Maas	Maaseroth
Makk	Makkoth
Maksh	Makshirin
Meg	Megillah
Meil	Meilah
Men	Menachot
Midd	Middoth
Mikv	Mikvaoth
MK	Moed Katan
MSh	Maaser Sheni
Naz	Nazir
Neg	Negaim
Ned	Nedarim
Nidd	Niddah
Ohol	Oholoth
Orl	Orlah
Par	Parah
Peah	Peah
Pes	Pesahim
RH	Rosh haShanah
San	Sanhedrin
Shab	Shabbat
Shevi	Sheviith
Shevu	Shevuoth
Shek	Shekalim
Sot	Sotah
Sukk	Sukkah
Taan	Taanith
Tam	Tamid
Tem	Temurah
Ter	Terumoth
Toh	Tohoroth
TY	Tevul Yom

Uktz	Uktzin
Yad	Yadaim
Yeb	Yebamoth
Yom	Yoma
Zab	Zabim
Zev	Zevahim

Other Rabbinic Texts

Rab.	Rabbah

Texts from Qumran

CD	The [Cairo] Damascus Document
4Q265	Serek-Damesq (4QMiscRules)

Philo

Mos	*De Vita Mosis*
Ios	*De Iosepho*
Legat ad Gaius	*De Legatione ad Gaium*

Josephus

Ant	*The Jewish Antiquities*
Bel	*The Jewish War*

Other Abbreviations

b.	ben *or* bar (the Aramaic equivalent of the Hebrew 'ben'), 'the son of'
mss	manuscript(s)
R.	Rabbi *or* Rav[1]

---

1. The title 'Rabbi' was probably used from around and after 70 CE (see the comments below, Chapter 2, n. 1), when it was given by the Sanhedrin to tannaitic sages of the land of Israel, who thereby received authority to judge penal cases. The title 'Rav' (or 'Rab') was given to Babylonian sages, who received their ordination in their schools. See further the entry on 'Rabbi' in *The Jewish Encyclopedia*, vol. 10 (Jerusalem: Keter, 1971), 294.

Bibliographical Abbreviations

Abbreviated journal and series titles appearing in the footnotes are written out in full in the Bibliography.

BDB   Brown, F., S. R. Driver and C. A. Briggs, *A Hebrew and English Lexicon of the Old Testament* (Oxford: Clarendon, 1972)

Nestle–Aland   *Novum Testamentum Graece* (Stuttgart: Deutsche Bibel-gesellschaft, 1979)

OTP   Charlesworth, J. H., ed., *The Old Testament Pseudepigrapha* (2 vols.; London: Darton, Longman & Todd, 1985)

Chapter 1

THE PROBLEM OF HEALING IN JUDAISM

It can safely be said that all civilised societies allow acts of healing and saving life. It seems, however, that for many of the Jewish people in Hellenistic times, the laws in their ancient God-given texts often did not allow for these humanitarian deeds, especially when needed on the Sabbath day. This book will examine how the Jewish sages in post-biblical times debated and resolved the apparently irreconcilable pro-hibitions of Jewish written law with the overriding need for acts of healing and saving life. The first chapter in this book provides a brief background to the subject—how did Jewish law effectively prevent acts of healing and saving life, although without the express prohibition of such acts? The next three chapters evaluate the evidence for the Jewish debate preserved in the gospels of the New Testament. The following seven chapters then examine the evidence preserved in the early rabbinic texts, including the possible direct interaction between Rabbi Akiva and Matthew (in Chapter 6). The final chapter of this book briefly sum-marises the evidence that has been discussed. The facts that emerge will suggest that in spite of apparent violation of Jewish written law, there is no evidence in the early Jewish and Christian texts that the Jewish sages ever prevented or criticised actions of healing and saving life, but always allowed such actions to take place.

I. *The Sabbath Problem*

But why—it must be asked—should a deed of healing and/or saving life cause any problem in Jewish law? The answer to this question depends ultimately on the fact that according to ancient Jewish belief, all Jewish law is derived from the Jewish God by whom it was passed to Moses at Sinai.[1] In fact, according to ancient Jewish belief, God gave to Moses

---

1. Exod 19:16–20:26.

1

two types of law, the written law and the oral law. The written law is basically the Pentateuch, which Moses wrote down at the direction of God and which therefore records the actual words of God. In contrast, the oral law, which Moses also received, was the beginning of a tradition of interpretation of the written law, if, for example, the latter seems unclear or incomplete, or—as will be seen in pages of this book—if the deeper, underlying meaning of a text had not yet been revealed.[2]

The actual problem in Judaism regarding acts of healing and saving life arises from the fact that the written law in the Pentateuch makes no obvious provision for exceptional circumstances which might violate this law. This omission is particularly acute on the Sabbath day, when the holy written God-given Jewish law forbids any action which is classified as 'work'. Thus, because acts of healing and saving life are considered in Jewish law as acts of 'work', it seems that no act of healing and/or the saving of life is allowed to take place on the Sabbath day, a period of about twenty-four hours that regularly occurs every seven days.[3] Moreover, although of course work is permitted on other days of the week

2.   The historical transmission of the oral law is stated at m. Avot 1.1, probably a text from Persian times, which was followed by the period of the *zugot*, the pairs of Jewish sages listed in m. Avot 1.2, who continued the transmission of Jewish oral law. The earliest outright declaration of the Jewish belief in the existence of both written and oral Jewish law is found in the Babylonian Talmud, b. Shab 31a. For a traditional discussion on the relationship between the written and the oral Jewish law, see, e.g., Z. H. Chajes, *The Student's Guide Through the Talmud* (2nd edn; trans. J. Schachter; New York: Philipp Feldheim, 1960) 1-32. For brief modern discussions, see, e.g., E. N. Dorff and L. E. Newman, *Contemporary Jewish Ethics and Morality* (New York: Oxford University Press, 1995) 59-78, esp. 64-7, and J. P. Meier, *A Marginal Jew*. Vol. 3, *Companions and Competitors* (New York: Doubleday, 2001) 317-18. A short rational account of the development of Jewish oral law is provided by W. Sibley Towner, 'Hermeneutical Systems of Hillel and the Tannaim: A Fresh Look', *HUCA* 53 (1982) 101: 'Every community which regards as normative certain texts given by the worthies of old must develop a "hermeneutic", a means whereby these fixed standards can be kept in an effective relationship with the ever-changing frontier of day-to-day experience. In the two centuries surrounding the turn of the era, six factors impelled Rabbinic Judaism towards the elaboration of a hermeneutic far more self-conscious than anything previously known: the canon of the Scripture was fixed; a body of authoritative Torah not part of that canon had to be kept in fruitful relationship to it; the institutions of the *Bet-Knesset* and *Bet-Midrash* emerged as settings for carrying on the hermeneutical task; sectarian competition increased the urgency for an explicit hermeneutic; Hellenistic culture offered models from its own interpretive tradition; and the normative role of the Temple ceased.'
3.   For the prohibition of work on the Sabbath in Jewish written law, see Exod 20:10; 31:14; 35:2; Deut 5:14.

(providing of course that they are not festival days), the action that is needed for a particular act of healing or saving life may also once again cause a violation of Jewish law. For example, it may be necessary to feed an invalid on the day of a religious fast, or to administer an oral medicine containing an ingredient that is forbidden for consumption by Jewish law. This raises a basic question: Does the God-given origin of all Jewish law mean—on occasion—that sickness can be neglected and an individual left to die just because the act that is needed causes a violation of Jewish law, for example, because illness or danger may strike on the Sabbath day?

For the Jewish sages, therefore, the obvious necessity for acts of healing and saving life in spite of the uncompromising statements in Jewish written law, which make no obvious allowance for the performance of such deeds, could only mean that the Jewish *oral* law on this subject had not yet been revealed. The Jewish sages were thus challenged to reveal this oral law, and as far as our existing sources will allow, their early discussions are traced in this book.

II. *Are All Actions of Healing and/or the Saving of Life Considered as 'Work'?*

Is there any way to avoid the link in Judaism between 'work' and acts of healing and saving life? Is it possible, for example, to perform an act of healing and/or saving life on the Sabbath without also performing an act of 'work'? This question is especially important for readers of the gospels who note that Jesus was not criticised for two of his Sabbath cures, that of the mother-in-law of one of his disciples, and that of a man with an evil spirit.[4] It has therefore been suggested that these cures were performed in a way that was not classified as 'work', so that the action of Jesus did not violate Sabbath law, which would thus explain why Jesus was not criticised for performing these cures. This, however, cannot be the case. As is well known, the Mishnah (the earliest work of Jewish oral law, which was written down around 200 CE, but which contains much material from earlier times), provides a list of thirty-nine *main* classes of 'work' which are totally prohibited on the Sabbath day.[5] However, the term 'work' in Jewish oral law, especially in relation to acts of healing and/or saving life, has a far wider significance than these thirty-nine acts.

4. Mark 1:29-31; Luke 4:38-39 with Matt 8:14-15; and Mark 1:21-28 and Luke 4:31-37. These incidents are discussed in Chapter 3.
5. See m. Shab 7.2, cited below.

This is because in relation to acts of healing and/or saving life, 'work' is regarded as the *result* of an *intended* act, rather than the result of a particular action that may be performed. In other words, *any action* which is performed with the *intention* to heal or with the *intention* to save life is considered in Judaism as an act of 'work'. For example, even an act of speaking is considered as 'work', if the act of speaking is intended to heal. In fact, as was noted by the ancient Jewish sages themselves, God himself used only words when He worked in order to create the world, see Gen 1:3, 6 etc., so that the concept of words as actions of 'work' is not unknown in Jewish thought.[6] However, this of course does not mean that speech is prohibited on the Sabbath day. It is only when words or actions which are not usually associated with 'work'—for example, taking the hand of a sick person—are deliberately used for the purpose of healing and/or saving life that the actions of a healer are considered as 'work'.[7] Thus, when Jesus removed an evil spirit or cured on the Sabbath using merely words (Mark 1:25; Luke 4:39), or when he cured a sick woman on the Sabbath by merely raising her from her bed (Mark 1:31), he violated Sabbath law just as decisively as if he had performed any of the more familiar acts of 'work' which are specifically prohibited on the Sabbath day. In short, *however an act of healing and/or saving life is performed, it is regarded in Judaism as an act of 'work' which is strictly forbidden on the Sabbath day.* This simple principle is thus the basis for any hostility that was shown towards Jesus when he healed on the Sabbath, and which was undoubtedly shown to any other Jewish healer who also healed on the Sabbath day. The reason that Jesus was apparently not criticised for performing two of his Sabbath cures, in spite of the fact that he violated Jewish law, will be discussed in Chapter 3.

The indissoluble connection in Jewish law between an act of healing and 'work' thus means that it is fruitless to search the many ancient Jewish texts in order to discover which of the actions that are forbidden by Sabbath law were used by Jesus for the two Sabbath cures in which

---

6. Midrash Gen Rab. IV.6, on Gen 1:7.

7. The importance of *intention* in relation to *work* is implicitly recognised in m. Shab 14.4: 'One who has pain in his teeth may not suck vinegar through them, but he may take vinegar according to his usual way, and if he is healed, he is healed...'; similarly, t. Shab 12.9. In other words, the action of sucking wine and vinegar is allowed only if the *intention* was not to heal, although healing may accidentally occur through this act. Balsam and oil are similarly forbidden at t. Shab 12.8, 10, 11, 12. See also m. Shab 2.5, which recognises the link between *intention* and *work*: 'Goats may go out [with their udders] bound up if the [intention] is [thereby] to keep them dry, but *not* if [it is intended] to collect the milk'.

he was not criticised for performing these cures.[8] Similarly, neither can it be assumed that Jesus used a particular method for performing a Sabbath cure in order to avoid any criticism for this cure. In short, the lack of criticism when Jesus performed the above two Sabbath cures has no connection whatever with the methods that he used—Jesus violated the Sabbath when he was *not* criticised for his Sabbath cures just as surely as when he was criticised for these deeds. The lack of criticism of Jesus for these Sabbath cures must therefore be attributed to some other cause. This also means that actions of healing and saving life are only generally discussed in Jewish law because of the fact that they cause a violation of Jewish law.

III. *Acts of Healing Are Acts That Save Life*

The paragraphs above have referred briefly to the fact that acts of healing in Jewish law are also considered as acts that save life. This is due to the fact that, even with the help of modern medical aids, and as was certainly the case in ancient times, it is impossible to anticipate how an illness might progress. In other words, because any illness may lead to death, an act of healing is an act that saves life. 'Healing' in Jewish law is thus equivalent to an act that saves life. In addition, because danger to life and consequent death may result from causes other than illness—such as a fire or a fall into a pit or fighting, especially in a defensive war—this means that 'healing' in Jewish law also includes action in such circumstances which aims to prevent death. 'Healing' in Jewish law thus has the extended meaning of *any* action that is required in *any* situation of danger to life. This is perhaps best appreciated in amoraic texts (texts from the Talmuds) in which the simple term סכנה (*sakanah*), meaning 'danger', is used for all situations that require healing or saving life (see Chapter 8).

This wider understanding of the act of healing in Jewish law is clearly implied in the gospel texts. Thus one of the arguments used in the gospels to justify an act of healing on the Sabbath day claims that because it is permitted to *save the life* of a sheep that has fallen into a pit—a situation not caused by illness of any kind—it must also be permitted *to cure* a man with a withered hand (Matt 12:11-12). Similarly, Jesus notes that if it is permitted to *save the life* of an animal on the Sabbath by allowing it

---

8. For example, see the recent unsuccessful search in Jewish texts for the link between acts of healing and/or saving life and the violation of Sabbath law by J. P. Meier, *A Marginal Jew*. Vol. 4, *Law and Love* (New Haven: Yale University Press, 2009) 235-52.

to drink (and thus preventing its death from thirst), it must also be permitted to *cure* a woman with a bent back (Luke 14:1-6). A third example is implied by the story of Jesus in the Galilean fields, when the disciples of Jesus violate Sabbath law in order to 'cure' their starvation which is a threat to their lives (see the discussion on Mark 2:23-28 and the parallel texts in Chapter 3). The lack of understanding of this broader meaning of 'healing' within Jewish law has, however, often led to the exclusion of the latter Galilean event from the list of the Sabbath cures which Jesus performed, with a resulting loss of essential information that contributes to the history of the Jewish debate on acts of healing and the saving of life.[9]

Since, therefore, references to 'healing' in Jewish law refer in effect to any kind of action which helps to prevent death and thereby, it is hoped, helps to preserve life, references in the present study to acts of healing in Jewish law will always also refer to acts that save life, even when the latter is not explicitly declared. Similarly, of course, actions which save life in Jewish law must also be considered as actions which heal, and the same legal approach applies to them both.

IV. *What Evidence Connects Acts of Healing and/or Saving Life with Acts of 'Work'?*

Another aspect of this topic that must be clarified before the main discussion begins concerns the connection in Judaism between acts of 'work' and acts of healing and/or saving life. How do we know that acts of healing are considered as 'work' which is totally forbidden on the Sabbath day? The answer to this question is particularly important for scholars of the gospels who wish to know if the antagonism shown to Jesus when he cured on the Sabbath has any basis in Jewish law. However, in spite of the most extensive and exhaustive research, no simple statement of this link has ever been found in the early Jewish texts—not in the Hebrew Bible, nor in the books of the Apocrypha, nor in texts from Qumran, and neither in the Pseudepigrapha nor in the Jewish diaspora literature, such as the compositions of Aristobulus, Philo and Josephus, and neither in any of the rabbinic texts.[10] In fact, the earliest link between

9. See, e.g., J. P. Meier, *A Marginal Jew*. Vol. 1, *Rethinking the Historical Jesus: The Roots of the Problem and the Person* (New York: Doubleday, 1987), who mistakenly excludes this event from Jesus' Sabbath cures.

10. See, e.g., the fruitless search in the Jewish sources by Meier, *A Marginal Jew*, 4:235-52, who claims that restrictions on healing on the Sabbath were a 'rabbinic innovation' which was introduced after 70 CE and that the stories of

'healing' and 'work' does not occur in a Jewish source, but in the gospels of the New Testament, in the works of Luke and John.

John indicates this connection when he claims that Jesus justified his performance of Sabbath cures with the words *My father is still working and I am working* (John 5:17). As will be further discussed in Chapter 3, these words make sense only if we assume that they are based on the Hebrew (or Aramaic) text of Gen 2:2, which refers to 'work' on non-Sabbath days in the course of the statement that *on the seventh day God finished His work* (in Hebrew מלאכתו, literally, 'his work') *which He had done, and He rested on the seventh day from all His work...*[11] The Semitic versions of Gen 2:2 thus seem to declare that God both worked *and* rested on the seventh day of the week. (In contrast, the Septuagint version of Gen 2:2 states that God only *rested* on the Sabbath day.) Assuming therefore that when God 'worked' on the Sabbath, this 'work' consisted of acts of healing and/or the saving of life (although there is no hint that this is the case), Jesus thus justifies his Sabbath acts of healing by claiming that he, like God, could 'work' on the Sabbath by performing acts of healing and/or saving life. In other words, Jesus thus equates acts of healing and/or saving life with everyday secular 'work'. The gospel of John also implies this link by using the verb ἐργάζεσθαι to refer to working on non-Sabbath days and the related noun τὰ ἔργα for ordinary work.[12] John again defines healing as 'work' when Jesus in John refers to 'one work' of healing he performed on a Sabbath day (ἓν ἔργον, John 7:21). John thereby confirms, albeit indirectly and unintentionally, that acts of healing and/or saving life are regarded in Judaism as acts of 'work', which are totally prohibited on the Sabbath day.

The link between 'work' and acts of healing and/or saving life is even more clearly indicated in the gospel of Luke when the leader of a synagogue alludes to the Pentateuchal law of Exod 20:8-11 (or Deut 12:11-15) while rebuking his congregation for seeking Sabbath cures

---

healing on the Sabbath in the gospels 'must be judged unhistorical' and their present form reflects Christian polemics, rather than the historical Jesus' (p. 294). This, however, is probably incorrect, as will be shown in the pages of this book.

11. The terms 'literal' and 'literally' are used in this book as defined by J. A. Davila, '(How) Can We Tell if a Greek Apocryphon or Pseudepigraphon Has Been Translated from Hebrew or Aramaic?', *JSP* 15.1 (2005) 3-16. In translation circles, 'literal' is generally used in the sense of 'formal equivalence', in contrast to something along the lines of 'dynamic equivalence', and implies a one-to-one correspondence between all the grammatical and lexical elements in the original language and the target language, rather than a translation that expresses the equivalent sense naturally in the target language.

12. ἐργάζεσθαι, John 5:17; 6:27, 28, 30; 9:4 (×2); τὰ ἔργα, John 3:19, 20, 21 etc.

(Luke 13:14). The leader of the synagogue thus refers to texts which state that 'work' may be performed on non-Sabbath days. He thereby implies that 'work' is forbidden on the Sabbath day, and that acts of healing are considered as 'work', which must therefore not be performed on the Sabbath day. Thus: *There are six days on which it is necessary to work* (ἐργάζεσθαι). *Come on those days and be healed* (θεραπεύεσθε) *and not on the Sabbath day* (Luke 13:14). Acts of healing are thus connected with 'work'.

There are, however, no similar allusions or statements in the ancient Jewish texts. As a result, without using the evidence from the gospel texts, a direct connection between acts of healing and/or saving life and the concept of 'work' can only be surmised from the Jewish sources by the existence of the many permits in the early rabbinic texts, particularly in the Mishnah and Tosefta, which allow acts of healing and/or saving of life on the Sabbath day (which are listed in Chapter 11), since the very fact that it was necessary officially to permit the performance of such actions on the Sabbath can only denote that they were otherwise *not* allowed. This can only be explained on the basis of an assumption that the action that was necessary was considered as 'work'. In other words, the very existence of these directives in the Jewish texts indicates the link between 'healing' and 'work' which—apart from actions of healing and/or saving life—is otherwise forbidden on the Sabbath day. In fact, the lack of a specific, articulated verbal link is no surprise. As was noted by Josephus in the late first century CE, *the Pharisees passed on to the people certain regulations handed down by former generations and [which are] not recorded in the Laws of Moses.*[13] Josephus here refers to Jewish rabbinic oral law, which only began a process of transcription around 200 CE. The books of Jewish oral law that were subsequently produced do not however provide a complete record of Jewish law, and—among their omissions—none note specifically that 'healing' is 'work'.

V. *The Jewish Sources Used in This Book*

Before the main discussion begins, it may be useful to review some of the basic facts concerning the early written texts of rabbinic oral law which have preserved most of the Jewish evidence that will be discussed in this book. As its name suggests, rabbinic oral law was at first preserved only orally, and it seems that a written record of such law was

13. Josephus, Ant XIII.297.

officially forbidden by the oral law itself.[14] This attitude, however, changed after the devastation in biblical lands caused by the wars with Rome in the first and second centuries CE, which eventually inspired a process of transcription of rabbinic oral law. The first work produced was the Mishnah, which appeared towards the end of the second century. This was followed about thirty years later with the Tosefta, a work with the same arrangement of material as the Mishnah, but often including extra historical information and a more extensive collection of oral law. Other books which were also published around this time and which are relevant to the discussion here include two commentaries on a large section of Exodus, the *Mekilta de-Rabbi Ishmael*, a product of the school of R. Ishmael, and the *Mekhilta de-Rabbi Shimon bar Yochai*, a product of the school of R. Akiva, *Sifre baMidbar*, a commentary on *Numbers*, *Sifra*, a commentary on Leviticus, and *Sifre Devarim*, a commentary on Deuteronomy. These works record the opinions of the tannaitic Jewish sages from post-biblical times until around the end of the second century, collectively known as the *tannaim*. Subsequently, the oral commentaries of the Jewish sages on these tannaitic works, especially on the Mishnah and Tosefta, were published in the fourth century, in the Jerusalem Talmud, and in the Babylonian Talmud, which was probably published in the fifth century CE. These two later works record the debates of the amoraic sages, collectively known as the *amoraim*. Along with the gospels of the New Testament, which were written by those who were contemporaries of first-century tannaitic sages, these works of rabbinic oral law have preserved most of the evidence which is discussed in this book.

VI. *Attitudes to the Violation of Sabbath Law in Texts from Before the First Century CE*

As briefly noted in the discussion above, the written law of the Penta-teuch unequivocally states that all 'work' is prohibited on the Sabbath day, whose violation necessitates the penalty of death (see Exod 31:14). The uncompromising nature of this biblical law *may* be confirmed by the story of the unfortunate man who was sentenced to death for collecting sticks on the Sabbath, although there is no reason to assume that he was

---

14. The classic proof text is b. Tem 14b; see the discussion in H. L. Strack and G. Stemberger, *Introduction to the Talmud and Midrash* (trans. M. Boekmuehl; Edinburgh: T. & T. Clark, 1991) 36-42. It is interesting to note that this strict prohi-bition against the writing of oral law was not followed by the community who lived in Qumran, whose writings date from the second century BCE.

punished for an act of healing and/or saving life.[15] It is therefore strange that in spite of the frequent necessity for acts of healing and/or saving life in any society and at any time, and in spite of the fact that the ancient Jewish texts, especially the Pentateuch, include numerous laws and describe numerous events, there is no indication in any of this material that there was a problem connected with acts of healing and/or saving life. The earliest event when this problem was noted and was later recorded in writing involves the subject of war on the Sabbath, when Ptolemy Lagus conquered Jerusalem because—according to the historian Agatharchides of Cnidus who was active in the second century BCE— the Jews refused to fight on the Sabbath day. This event may have taken place in 320 BCE. In his *Jewish Antiquities* XII.6, Josephus records:

> [Agatharchides of Cnidus states that] there is a nation called Jews, who have a strong and great city called Jerusalem, which they allowed to fall into the hands of Ptolemy by refusing to take up arms [on the Sabbath] and, instead, through their untimely superstition submitted to having a hard master.[16]

It seems, however, that the first official attempt to deal with the problem of healing and/or saving life on the Sabbath day only occurred in Maccabean times. This also involved war on the Sabbath, when a group of about one thousand pious Jews again refused to fight on the Sabbath and were consequently all killed. This event probably took place in 167 BCE. As a result, Mattathias the Maccabean, the Jewish leader at that time, together with his 'friends', issued an edict which allowed fighting on the Sabbath, although only in self-defence. The most detailed of the two accounts of this event, 1 Macc 2:39-41, reads as follows:

> 2: [29]At that time many went down to dwell in the desert, seeking justice and vindication, [30]they and their children and their wives and their cattle, hard pressed by the persecution. [31]A report came to the King's men and to the forces in Jerusalem, the city of David, that men who had violated

---

15. Num 15:32-36. The rabbinic Jewish sages, however, imply surprise at the severity of the biblical punishment of the man collecting sticks and give different opinions concerning the nature of his offence—y. San 22.4 suggests that the man was 'uprooting', and b. Shab 96b suggests that he was 'carrying', both forbidden actions on the Sabbath.

16. Josephus himself apologetically claims that Ptolemy's Sabbath offensive succeeded because the Jews were enjoying their Sabbath rest, and did not suspect an attack, see Josephus, Ant XII.4. Other possible records of such deliberate Sabbath attacks on the Jews are discussed by A. F. Johns, 'The Military Strategy of Sabbath Attacks on the Jews', *VT* 13 (1963) 482-6.

the command of the King had gone down to the hiding places in the desert. [32]With a large force they pursued them and coming upon them, they encamped and formed in battle line against them on the Sabbath day, [33]saying to them, 'Come out and obey the word of the King and we shall let you live'. [34]They however replied, 'We shall neither come out nor obey the word of the King to violate the Sabbath day'. [35]Accordingly they advanced quickly upon them in battle line. [36]But the Jews neither replied to them nor hurled a stone at them nor blocked the entrances to their hiding places, [37]saying, 'Let us all die in our innocence. Heaven and earth bear witness over us, that you condemn us unjustly.' [38]They attacked them in battle line on the Sabbath. They were killed with their wives, their children, their cattle, to the number of one thousand human beings.

[39]When the news [of the total massacre of the Jews] reached Mattathias and his friends (Ματταθιας καὶ οἱ φίλοι αὐτοῦ) they were deeply grieved over the victims' fate. [40]They said to one another, 'If we all do as our brothers have done and do not fight against the gentiles for our lives and our laws, they will now quickly wipe us off the face of the earth'. [41]On that day they came to a decision: 'If any person comes against us in battle on the Sabbath day, we shall fight against him and not all die as our brothers died in their hiding places'.[17]

The following aspects of this story are relevant for this book:

(1) The decree of Mattathias allows a violation of Sabbath law only for the *specific* situation of fighting on the Sabbath. It is important to note that it is not a *general* permit for action in any situation of healing and/or saving life which might necessitate a violation of Jewish law.

(2) The decree limits the action that can be taken within the specific situation that is allowed to self-defence. Thus, as the text states, the permitted action is allowed only when 'any person comes against us in battle'.

(3) The decree is wholly pragmatic and does not justify the permitted violation of Sabbath law with any religious-based proof, namely, proof that was based on any of the Jewish holy, written texts. The text simply states that if the Jews refused on the Sabbath to fight in self-defence, they would quickly be conquered (because they would always be attacked on the Sabbath) and would thus cease to exist. Although obviously a rational and pragmatic decision, the lack of religious justification for a permitted major violation of Jewish law—in this case, Sabbath law—cannot have been comfortable for 'Mattathias and his friends'. It can therefore be assumed that at least from the time that this edict was

17. Trans. J. A. Goldstein, *1 Maccabees: A New Translation with Introduction and Commentary* (AB 41; New York: Doubleday, 1976) 63, 163. 2 Macc 6:11 preserves a shorter account of the same event.

issued, probably in 167 BCE, the Jewish sages sought a way to justify acts of healing and/or saving life within the tradition of Jewish law, especially on the Sabbath day.

(4) Although it might be expected that it was the Jewish leaders who insisted on the strict observance of Pentateuchal law, even with regard to acts of healing and/or saving life, while it was ordinary people who pressed for a relaxation of such callous law, the reverse is the case for the Maccabean event. In the story related in the text, it seems that it was ordinary pious Jews who adopted a strict, rigid attitude towards Pentateuchal law which resulted in their deaths, while it was the Jewish leaders of the time—Mattathias, a priest and his 'friends', presumably also priests—who attempted to prevent future similar and predictable disasters by allowing a violation of Jewish law.

(5) The *halachic* (legal) decision to allow a violation of Jewish law was not issued by one person, but by several, in this case by 'Mattathias and his friends'. A collective authority for the issue of such permits is also hinted in a directive in the Tosefta which notes that an individual in a position to violate Jewish law by an act of healing and/or saving life need not consult a 'Jewish court' (בית דין; see the discussion on t. Shab 15.11-13 in Chapter 11).

It seems, however, that the decree of Mattathias was not accepted by all. An outright rejection of any fighting on the Sabbath is one of approximately nine activities which are totally prohibited on the Sabbath in the sectarian book of *Jubilees*, perhaps composed by contemporaries of the Maccabees, as can be seen in *Jub.* 50:12-13:

> And [as for] any person who does work on it [= the Sabbath] or who goes on a journey or who ploughs a field either at home or any [other] place, or who kindles a fire, or who rides on any animal, or who travels the sea in a boat, and any person who slaughters or kills anything, or who slashes the throat of cattle or bird, or who snares any beast or bird or fish, or who fasts or makes war on the day of the Sabbath, let the person who does any of these on the day of the Sabbath die so that the children of Israel might keep the Sabbath according to the commands of the Sabbaths of the land, just as it was written in the tablets which he placed in my hands so that I might write for you the law of each time and according to each division of the days.

A similar, but more extensive list of thirty-nine—'forty minus one'—*main* prohibited acts of 'work' on the Sabbath is also preserved in a directive in the Mishnah. In m. Shab 7.2, translated below, the Hebrew terms that follow after the prohibited actions are featured in later discussions in this book:

The main classes of 'work' (אבות מלאכות, literally, 'fathers of works')
[which are prohibited on the Sabbath] are forty minus one: (1) sowing,
and (2) ploughing, and (3) reaping (הקוצר, that is, 'harvesting'), and
(4) binding sheaves, (5) threshing (הדש), and (6) winnowing (הזורה), and
(7) cleansing crops, (8) grinding, and (9) sifting, and (10) kneading, and
(11) baking, (12) shearing (הגוזז) the wool, (13) washing and (14) beat-
ing it and (15) dyeing it, and (16) spinning, and (17) weaving, and
(18) making two loops, and (19) weaving two threads, and (20)
separating two threads, and (21) tying (קושר) [a knot], (22) loosening [a
knot] and (23) sewing two stitches, (24) tearing in order to sew two
stitches, (25) hunting (הצד) a gazelle, and (26) slaughtering (השוחטו) it
and (27) flaying it (28) and salting it and (29) curing its skin, and
(30) scraping and (31) cutting it up (המחתך), (32) writing two letters,
and (33) erasing in order to write two letters, (34) building (הבונה), and
(35) pulling down (והסותר), (36) putting out a fire (המכבה) and (37) lighting a fire (המעביר), (38) striking with a hammer, (39) taking out anything
from one domain into another (המוציא מרשות לרשות). These are the main
classes of work (אבות מלאכות), [altogether] forty minus one.

When was this list in the Mishnah compiled? Its similarity with the list in
Jubilees (cited above) suggests that both were composed at around the
same time. The list in the Mishnah is however more extensive—thirty-
nine actions are listed in contrast with only about nine in *Jubilees*. It
is also more sophisticated in that it defines only the '*main* activities'
(אבות מלאכות, 'fathers of works') which are forbidden on the Sabbath
day. Assuming that greater sophistication implies later law, it is thus
probable that the list in the Mishnah was compiled at a later time. If then
the book of *Jubilees* was composed sometime between 161 and 140 BCE,
as many scholars assume,[18] it is probable that the list in the Mishnah was
compiled in later Hasmonean times.

A further attempt to settle at least one aspect of the problem of
fighting on the Sabbath can be dated around the turn of the millennium.
This can be seen in the directive of Shammai the Elder, who became the
president of the Sanhedrin after the death of Hillel (which occurred
around 10 CE), and who used Deut 20:19-20 to 'prove' that a siege may
be continued on the Sabbath day. This ruling of Shammai is the earliest
recorded directive relating to acts of healing and/or saving life that is
based on a proof text from Jewish written law, and thus marks a
significant milestone in the Jewish debate to justify such acts within
Jewish law. Tosefta Eruv 3.7/Sifre Devarim 203 reads:

18. For the date of composition and a translation of *Jubilees*, see O. S.
Wintermute, 'Jubilees', in *OTP* 2:35-142.

A camp that goes out to fight an optional war does not besiege a gentile town less than three days before the Sabbath. And if one begins [a siege, it may continue]. Even on the Sabbath we do not stop. And thus did Shammai the Elder interpret [Deut 20:19-20], *When thou shalt besiege a city...and you shall build siege works against the city that makes war with you until it falls*—[this means that you can fight] even on the Sabbath.[19]

Further early evidence of concern for saving life on the Sabbath can be seen in the following two directives from Qumran:

4Q265 Frag. 7, 1.5-9:

(5) on the Sabbath ... No [one] should [take out] of his tent an implement or foo[d]
(6) on the Sabbath ... day. ...No one should take out an animal (בהמה) that has fallen
(7) in [to] water on the Sabbath day. But if it is a person (נפש אדם) who has fallen
(8) in [to] water on the Sabbath [day], he may throw his garment to him to lift him out with it. No one should carry an implement (כלי)
(9) ...on the Sabbath [day]...

Damascus Document 11:16-17:

(13) No-one should help an animal (בהמה) give birth on the Sabbath day ... And if <it falls > into a pit
(14) or an opening, he should not take it out on the Sabbath. ...
(16) ... And any living man (נפש אדם) who falls into a place of water or into a <reservoir> [on the Sabbath],
(17) no one should take him out with a ladder, a rope or a utensil.[20]

19.   The Erfurt mss. attributes this interpretation to 'Hillel the Elder'. But the fact that this is a minority reading is evident from the Vienna, London and printed mss. which read 'Shammai the Elder'; see S. Leiberman, *Tosefet Rishonim*, vol. 1 (Jerusalem: Reuben Mass, 1999) 154. This is also the reading of Sifre Devarim 203 (Sifre on Deuteronomy 203), b. Shab 19a and Midrash ha-Gadol. According to M. D. Herr, 'The Problem of War on the Sabbath in the Days of the Second Temple and the Mishnah and Talmud', *Tarbiz* 30 (1961) 242-56, 341-56 (252), however, Shammai issued only the *halachah* based on Deut 21:19 that allowed a siege to begin three days before the Sabbath, while it was R. Yoshiah (יאשיה) (110–135 CE), who interpreted עד רדפה, 'until it (= the city) falls' (Deut 20:20), to mean that a siege may be continued, even on the Sabbath.
20.   Text and translation from F. García Martínez and E. J. C. Tigchelaar, eds., *The Dead Sea Scrolls: Study Edition* (Leiden: Brill, 1997) 548-9, translating 'utensil' instead of 'implement', according to L. Doering, 'Much Ado About Nothing? Jesus' Sabbath Healings and Their Halakhic Implications Revisited', in *Judaistik und Neu-testamtliche Wissenschaft* (L. Doering, H.-G. Waubke and F. Wilk, eds.; Göttingen:

Like the permits of Mattathias the Maccabean and Shammai (described above), these directives also limit the permitted violation of Sabbath law to a specific situation. In addition, they also restrict the methods that could be used for the rescue to be performed. For 4Q265, this is achieved positively by allowing (only) the garment of the rescuer to be used for rescuing an individual, presumably serving as a kind of rope. For the Damascus Document, this restriction is achieved negatively by forbidding the use of a ladder or rope or any utensil. In relation to the way that they limit the permitted action, each directive is thus a mirror image of the other and both attempt to pre-empt the carrying of any implement to the scene of the accident, an action which is specifically forbidden (earlier in lines 5 and 8 of 4Q265). This suggests that like the normative Jewish community from which they probably originally came, the community from Qumran also forbade carrying on the Sabbath between different domains.[21]

Unlike the permit of Shammai, however, although similar to the decree of Mattathias, the directives from Qumran also lack any religious proof to justify the permitted leniency in Sabbath law, which must surely have caused similar unease in the community at Qumran. The very existence of these directives, however, also suggests that, just as implied by the Maccabean decree, the specific leniency on the Sabbath which they allow was approved by the official leaders of this group, as it would not otherwise have been included into texts which (we must assume) were an official record of their law.

VII. *Significant Features of the Sources Discussed Above*

The texts discussed above preserve evidence of Jewish attitudes to Sabbath law in relation to acts of healing and/or saving life from before the first century CE. It seems that in the last three centuries of the first millennium BCE, both ordinary Jews and their leaders were consciously aware of the strict boundaries of Sabbath law in relation to acts of healing and/or saving life, and that among ordinary Jews, there were those

---

Vandenhoeck & Ruprecht, 2008) 230. See also J. Baumgarten et al., *Qumran Cave 4, XXV: Halakhic Texts* (DJD 35; Oxford: Oxford University Press, 1999) 68. The whole text is translated by G. Vermes, *The Complete Dead Sea Scrolls in English* (London: Allen Lane/Penguin, 1997) 155. For commentary on this text, see L. H. Schiffman, *Reclaiming the Dead Sea Scrolls* (Philadelphia: The Jewish Publication Society, 1994) 279-81.

21.   See m. Shab 7.2, cited above. Carrying on the Sabbath is first forbidden at Jer 17:22.

who chose death rather than violate this law. This strict religious attitude of some ordinary Jews to acts of healing and/or saving life that violate Jewish, especially Sabbath law, will be confirmed in Chapters 3 and 4 of this book. On the other hand, apart from the leaders of the sect by whom the book of *Jubilees* was produced, it seems that the Jewish leaders themselves opposed this extreme attitude to acts of healing and/or saving life, and thus in spite of the fact that they were permitting a violation of Jewish law, allowed such deeds to take place. These leaders include (1) Mattathias the Maccabean and his colleagues (called 'friends'), (2) the leaders of the community who resided in Qumran and (3) Shammai the Elder, in the late first century BCE.[22]

It can also be seen that the permits that were issued did not allow a general violation of Jewish law by any acts of healing and/or saving life, but granted permission only for specific situations. In addition, as is evident especially for the directives from Qumran, and also, to a lesser extent for the decree of Mattathias, these early permits also limited the permitted violation of Sabbath law by restricting the way that these deeds could be performed. As will be seen in the following chapters of this book, these features of directives that allow acts of healing and/or saving life recur in different ways in different written directives on acts of healing and/or saving life that were probably composed before the second century CE.

The early history of the Jewish debate on healing and/or saving life must now leave the sparse Jewish sources from before the first century CE, and turn to the gospels of the New Testament, which provide invaluable and otherwise irretrievable evidence of the Jewish debate in the first century CE.

---

22. Shemaiah and Abtalion may also be added to this list; see in Chapter 11 on b. Yom 35b.

Chapter 2

AN OVERVIEW OF THE SABBATH EVENTS IN THE GOSPELS

I. *General Background*

As is well known, the gospels of the New Testament describe the life and work of Jesus of Nazareth, a Jewish inhabitant of Galilee in the first century CE, whose actions and fate were intimately bound up with the practice and problems of the Jewish people of his time. The chapter above has described one of these problems, namely, the challenge to Jewish law caused by acts of healing and/or saving life. As was noted in this discussion, this problem is especially important on the Sabbath, because actions of healing and/or saving life are considered in Jewish law as 'work' and thus cannot be performed on the Sabbath day when all 'work' is banned. It is therefore no surprise that since Jesus was a healer who healed on the Sabbath day, this problem features prominently in the gospel texts. The gospels, all products of authors who lived in the first century, have thus preserved material relating to the Jewish debate on acts of Sabbath healing and/or saving life which relates almost entirely to the first century CE. (In contrast, the relevant Jewish material preserved in the earliest rabbinic texts is a mixture of sources from late post-biblical times till around the end of the second century CE.) The events when Jesus healed on the Sabbath day must therefore be considered in relation to the first-century history of the Jewish debate.

II. *A List of Gospel Healing Events Dated*
in Relation to the Sabbath

The gospels describe eleven events which are dated in relation to the Sabbath day, ten in which Jesus heals and/or saves life on the Sabbath itself, and one in which people wait until after the Sabbath in order to be healed. These basic facts cannot be in doubt especially in the gospels of

Mark and Luke because the latter were composed at a time when it can be expected that memories of these events were relatively fresh. To claim incorrectly that Jesus sometimes healed on the Sabbath or that healing was postponed until after the Sabbath, would therefore have harmed the historicity of these tales.

Listed below, and subsequently discussed in Chapter 3, are the ten accounts of events when Jesus healed on the Sabbath, and one account when healing was postponed until after the Sabbath day:

I.   Sabbath cures in which Jesus justifies his violation of Sabbath law with a *halachic* rabbinic argument *kal va-chomer* in at least one of the parallel accounts:
   1. Mark 2:23-28; Luke 6:1-5; Matt 12:1-8: Jesus 'cured' the starvation of his disciples and thus saved their lives.
   2. Luke 14:1-6: the cure of a man with dropsy.
   3. Luke 13:10-17: the cure of a woman with a bent back.
   4. Mark 3:1-6; Luke 6:6-11; Matt 12:9-14: the cure of a man with a withered hand. An argument *kal va-chomer* is found only in Matthew's account.
   5. John 7:14-25: an unidentified cure.

II. Sabbath cures in which Jesus does not justify his violation of Sabbath law:
   6. Mark 6:1-6; Luke 4:16-30; Matt 13:54-58: unidentified Galilean cures.
   7. Mark 1:29-31; Luke 4:38-39; Matt 8:14-15: the cure of the mother-in-law of Simon (or, the mother-in-law of Peter, according to Matthew).
   8. Mark 1:21-28; Luke 4:31-37: the removal of an evil spirit from a man.
   9. John 5:2-18: the cure of a crippled man.
   10. John 9:1-17: the cure of a man blind from birth.

III. A post-Sabbath cure:
   11. Mark 1:21, 32-34; Luke 4:31, 40-41; Matt 8:16: the cure of many people.

III. *Characteristics of Rabbinic*[1] *Halachic Arguments kal va-chomer in the Gospels*

In the first five of the events listed above Jesus justifies his violation of Sabbath law with a popular form of rhetoric used by the rabbinic sages called an argument *kal va-chomer*. This kind of argument has been much

---

1. Evidence from Jewish texts suggests that the title 'rabbi' was only used as an honorific title *after* 70 CE; see H. Shanks, 'Origins of the Title "Rabbi"', *JQR* NS 59 (1968) 152-7; S. Zeitlin, 'The Title Rabbi in the Gospels Is Anachronistic', *JQR* 59 (1968) 158-60; J. Donaldson, 'The Title Rabbi in the Gospels: Some Reflections on the Evidence of the Synoptics', *JQR* (1972–73) 287-91. The term 'rabbinic' is, however, used here for all arguments *kal va-chomer*, including those that were composed before 70 CE.

discussed, especially in relation to the logic that they use.[2] The following paragraphs will therefore provide only a brief, non-technical description of the features of the argument that are directly relevant for the discussion in this book.

All arguments *kal va-chomer* depend on the relationship between two chosen subjects or statements, one which is relatively 'light' or 'less restrictive' or 'less rigorous'—in Hebrew קל (*kal*)—in relation to the second which is relatively 'heavy' or 'serious' or 'more restrictive' or 'more rigorous'—in Hebrew חומר (*chomer*). These subjects can be related in various ways and a logical inference can then be made.

The two basic subjects or statements are often linked by the premise that if a permit is allowed for subject A which is 'heavier' or 'more serious' (חומר, *chomer*) in relation to subject B, it can then be assumed— and can therefore be concluded—that the same permit must be allowed for subject B, which is relatively 'lighter' or 'less serious' in relation to subject A (that is, subject B is relatively קל, *kal*). These kinds of argument are often used for *halachic* arguments *kal va-chomer*, that is, they are used for arguments concerned with an aspect of Jewish law, rather than for subjects with a moral or ethical intent (which are called *aggadic* arguments *kal va-chomer*). For example, a *halachic* argument *kal va-chomer* is used by the rabbinic sages in order to prove that the biblical law of an 'eye for an eye' (Exod 21:24) should *not* be invoked literally, but that the harm inflicted on the injured person should be evaluated in monetary terms, and the appropriate sum then be paid to the injured individual by the offender. This argument is based on the text of Exod 21:28-29, which states that the owner of an ox should be sentenced to death if his ox has killed a human being more than once. However, according to Exod 21:30, this capital sentence may be commuted to a fine:

2.   For detailed discussions of the technical aspects of rabbinic arguments *kal va-chomer*, see, e.g., M. Mielziner, *Introduction to the Talmud* (5th edn; New York: Bloch, 1968) 130-41, a minimally technical account; Jacobs, 'Hermeneutics', *Encyclopaedia Judaica*, vol. 8 (Jerusalem: Keter, 1971) 366-71; Sibley Towner, 'Hermeneutical Systems of Hillel and the Tannaim', 101-35; H. Maccoby, *The Myth-maker: Paul and the Invention of Christianity* (San Francisco: Harper & Row, 1986) 64-7; M. Elon, *Jewish Law, History, Sources, Principles*, vol. 1 (Philadelphia: JPS, 1994) 350; M. P. Fernandez, *An Introductory Grammar of Rabbinic Hebrew* (Leiden: Brill, 1997) 201; A. Sion, *Judaic Logic* (Geneva: Slatkine, 1997) 41-106, a very technical analysis.

Exodus 21:28-30

If an ox gores a man or a woman, so that they die, then the ox shall be surely stoned…but the owner of the ox shall be acquitted [of any crime]. But if the ox has gored [someone to death] with its horn in times past, and its owner had been warned, and he has not kept it in, but [the ox] has [again] killed a man or a woman, [then] the ox shall be stoned, and its owner also shall be put to death.

If there be laid on him a sum of money, then he shall give for the ransom of his life whatsoever is laid upon him.

It is obvious that capital punishment which damages *the whole body* is a relatively serious or 'heavy' (*chomer*) punishment in comparison with the punishment of a fine, which is relatively 'light' (*kal*) and therefore— it can be argued—damages only a *part of the body* of a person. If, then, capital punishment can be replaced with a fine (as stated at Exod 21:30), is it not reasonable to assume that the physical mutilation of the offender (for example, an 'eye for an eye'), which is relatively serious (or *chomer*) in relation to a fine (which is relatively *light*), may also be replaced by a less serious ('lighter') fine. This argument is expressed in the following way:

מילתא דרבי ישמעאל משפטים - מס' דנזיקין פרשה ח ד"ה עין תחת
מה במקום שענש הכתוב מיתה לא ענש אלא ממון, כאן שלא ענש מיתה
דין הוא שלא יענש אלא ממון.

Mekilta de-Rabbi Ishmael Nezikin 8

If [in the case of the owner of an ox who had killed more than one individual, noted at Exod 21:30], the [Pentateuchal] Law allows financial compensation instead of capital punishment, is it not logical that [a punishment of] financial compensation should also be allowed here [as in the case of Exod 21:24, which does not involve capital punishment]!

As will be seen, the only *halachic* argument used in the gospels to justify the violation of Sabbath law by an act of healing and/or saving life which argues in this way—that is, an argument that argues from a subject which is relatively 'heavy' (חומר, *chomer*) in relation to a subject which is relatively 'light' (קל, *kal*)—is the argument used to justify the behaviour of the disciples of Jesus when he met the Pharisees on the Sabbath in the Galilean fields (see on Mark 2:25-26, 28; Luke 6:3-5; along with Matt 12:3-5, 8), which is discussed in Chapter 3.

In contrast with the arguments described above (whose logical order proceeds from a subject that is *chomer* to a subject that is *kal*), the logical sequence of an argument *kal va-chomer* may also proceed in the order suggested by the name of this argument, that is, the argument proceeds from a subject which is relatively 'light', to a subject which is relatively 'heavy'—*kal* to *chomer*. For example, the following tannaitic argument justifies the fact that the Jewish God has the same generous attitude towards the wicked and the righteous, the wicked who in the context of the argument are relatively 'light' while the righteous are relatively 'heavy':

משנה מסכת סנהדרין פרק ו משנה ה

אם כן המקום מצטער על דמם של רשעים שנשפך קל וחומר על דמם של צדיקים.

Mishnah Sanhedrin 6.5
If God is sore troubled at the blood of the wicked that is shed, is it not reasonable to assume (קל וחומר) [He is troubled by] the blood of the righteous [that is shed]![3]

This kind of argument in Jewish sources is usually *aggadic*, that is, it is concerned with ethical and moral truths, rather than with an aspect of Jewish law.[4] The gospels, however, have preserved four *halachic* arguments of this type, that is, arguments *kal va-chomer* which establish an aspect of Jewish law; in this case they justify the violation of Sabbath law by an act of healing and/or saving life. These arguments occur at (1) Luke 13:15b-16, which justifies the Sabbath cure of a bent back; (2) Luke 14:5, which justifies the Sabbath cure of dropsy; (3) Matt 12:11-12, which justifies the Sabbath cure of a withered hand; and (4) John 7:24, which refers to an earlier unidentified cure of Jesus. These arguments will be discussed in Chapter 3.

The function of the opening and closing statements of arguments *kal va-chomer* is reflected in the technical names which were given to these parts of the argument by the *geonic* Jewish sages. According to their terminology, the opening statement of the argument was called הנדון, *ha-nadon*, 'the thing that is judged', whereas the conclusion of the argument was called הבא מן הדין, *ha-ba min ha-din*, 'the [conclusion which] comes from the thing judged'. These names thus express the thought that the conclusion of the argument is based on the opening claim. This fact is of special interest in the *halachic* arguments in the gospels, which are

---

3. Similarly, t. Ber 4.16 and 4.17. A simple argument in English on this pattern could be expressed: If you are prepared to risk your life by crossing a busy road to rescue a lost handkerchief, surely—*kal va-chomer*—you would be prepared to risk your life to cross a busy road to rescue a child!

4. The argument *kal va-chomer* of R. Eleazar b. Azariah which is based on circumcision, and which justifies healing on the Sabbath (recorded at t. Shab 15.16, and also attributed to Jesus at John 7.24), provides an example of a *halachic* argument *kal va-chomer* which argues from a subject that is 'light' to a subject that is 'heavy'.

based on the claim in the opening statement of the argument (*ha-nadon*) that it was permitted to save the life of an animal on the Sabbath day (see Luke 13:15b-16; 14:5; Matt 12:11-12). Since the conclusion of these arguments is based on this claim, it must be assumed that the basic principle of these statements was correct for the audience to whom these statements were addressed. Accordingly, even if the *halachah* (that is, the specific Jewish law) does not exist in the Jewish sources, these opening statements must be accepted as true for the people to whom the argument was expressed. In other words, the authenticity of the *halachic* arguments *kal va-chomer* in Matthew and Luke which are based on a practice of animal husbandry that allowed an animal to be healed and/or saved on the Sabbath day cannot be denied or their existence questioned merely because there may be little or no evidence for this particular *halachah* in any of the rabbinic texts.

A further aspect of rabbinic arguments *kal va-chomer* which is relevant for the arguments in the gospel texts is the fact that when these arguments are presented in a formal way the two statements (*ha-nadon* and *ha-ba min ha-din*) are often linked, in effect *bridged*, with one of several phrases. The most common of these links for arguments that deal with Jewish law in the tannaitic texts is the phrase קל וחומר, *kal va-chomer*, the phrase from which the name of these arguments is apparently derived. This name is even used when different bridge phrases appear in the argument itself, and even for arguments in which no bridge phrase appears.[5] As far as the gospel arguments are concerned, only one of these arguments includes a term which is equivalent to a bridge phrase, namely, the argument expressed in Mark's version of the story of Jesus and his disciples in the Galilean fields, in which the term ὥστε (Mark 2:28) serves to bridge the two main statements of the argument itself.[6] Otherwise, the absence of such a phrase in the arguments voiced

---

5. For example, the argument at t. Pes 4.14 is called an argument *kal va-chomer*, but has the bridge phrase אינו דין. Similarly, the argument preserved at *Mekilta de-Rabbi Ishmael* Nezikin 8, cited in the main text above, uses the bridge phrase דין הוא ש. Phrases in Hebrew (those in Aramaic are adaptations of corresponding Hebrew phrases—see the list in A. Sion, *Judaic Logic* [Editions Slatkine: Geneva, 1997] 89), which function to bridge the two sections of a rabbinic argument *kal va-chomer*, include: (1) על אחת כמה וכמה..., said to be used mostly for *aggadic* arguments, (2) כל שכן, (3) אינו דין ש, and (4) צורך לומר/אין צריך.

6. The formal Greek bridge phrases used by Matthew and Paul in *aggadic* arguments *kal va-chomer* include: most commonly, πολλῷ μᾶλλον, Rom 5:10, 15, 17; 2 Cor 3:9, 11; Phil 2:12, and the variant πολλῷ οὖν μᾶλλον at Rom 5:9—Matt 6:30 has οὐ πολλῷ μᾶλλον; 2 Cor 3:8 has πῶς οὐχὶ μᾶλλον; Matt 7:11; 10:25 and Rom 11:12, 24 have πόσῳ μᾶλλον; Phlm 16 has πόσῳ δὲ μᾶλλον. The adaptation

by Jesus to justify his Sabbath cures may reflect a deliberate attempt to reproduce the simplicity of the language in which Jesus spoke.[7] The absence of a bridge phrase does not however mean that an argument *kal va-chomer* has not been used.

It must also be noted that arguments *kal va-chomer* may not have been spontaneously expressed at the time or the place of the event in which they are now found, but, like the rhetoric composed as academic exercises in the Hellenistic and Roman schools, may have been composed at some other time and subsequently added to an appropriate event. Thus for example, it is most unlikely that the three arguments *kal va-chomer* in the Mishnah concerning the ritual of the Passover sacrifice on the Sabbath actually took place between three Jewish sages who came from two different generations (two from the second generation, R. Eleazar b. Hurcanus and R. Joshua b. Hananiah, and the third-generation sage R. Akiva, see m. Pes 6.2). It is also unlikely that this discussion took place on a day when the Passover sacrifice fell on the Sabbath, although both the time and place of the sacrifice are the subjects of their debate. Similarly, it is difficult to believe that Rabban Gamaliel was standing in a field with a 'forgotten' sheaf when he used an argument *kal va-chomer* to justify his opinion concerning the size of the sheaf (see m. Peah 6.6),

---

by Paul of the phrase על אחת כמה וכמה, which is used in the rabbinic argument *kal va-chomer* at m. Makk 3.15 (the latter serving as the basis for Rom 5:9, 10, 16, and 17), suggests that Paul was exposed to the terminology of both (a) Hebrew rabbinic arguments *kal va-chomer* and (b) Greek arguments *a fortiori*, but was not aware of the significant difference between the two; see N. L. Collins, 'The Jewish Source of Rom 5:17, 16, 10, 9: The Verses of Paul in Relation to a Comment in the Mishnah at m. Macc 3:15', *Revue Biblique* 112.1 (2005) 27-45. No bridge phrases appear in the arguments *kal va-chomer* expressed by Jesus in Luke (see Luke 13:15b-16; 14:5; 23:28-31), nor do they feature in the *halachic* argument *kal va-chomer* at Matt 12:11-12, when Jesus heals on the Sabbath.

7.   For a *halachic* rabbinic argument *kal va-chomer* with no formal bridge phrase, see, e.g., m. Neg 13.6: אמר רבי אלעזר מה אם אבן אחת ממנו מטמא בביאה הוא עצמו לא יטמא בביאה, R. Eleazar [b. Azariah] said, 'If one stone of the house can convey uncleanness by entering in, shall not [the house] itself convey uncleanness by entering in! Similarly, m. Ker 3.1, in which the terms קל and חומר are woven verbally into each section of the argument. Arguments *kal va-chomer* in the Hebrew Bible do not use technical expressions such as *kal va-chomer*, but whenever bridge phrases are used they are based on simple non-technical terms such as חן, וחן, והלא, הלא, איך, ואיך, אף, אף כי, ואף כי; see L. Jacobs, 'The *qal va-homer* Argument in the Old Testament', *BSOAS* 35.2 (1972) 221-7, and Sion, *Judaic Logic* (Geneva: Editions Slatkine, 1997) 84-5. For example, Jer 12:51: כי את רגלים רצתה וילאוך ואיך תתחרה את הסוסים, *If you have run with footmen and they have wearied you, then how can you contend with horses!*

or that R. Shimon bar Yohai was standing before an Egyptian or Edomite (or Idumaean) woman when he used an argument *kal va-chomer* to justify her acceptance as a Jewish wife (see m. Yeb 8.3). Although such arguments may have been inspired by particular situations, many are almost certainly the products of later thought, perhaps conceived during the debate of the Jewish sages in the *beit midrash* ('House of Study'), a place to which there are many references in the tannaitic texts.[8] For example, the following passage from the Mishnah records that the first-century Jewish sage, R. Tarfon (the text of y. Yom 3.7 refers to his service in the Temple), was called to the *beit midrash* in order to discuss the law relating to the transport of an animal that had died on the Sabbath and also to discuss the subject of an offering of dough that had become ritually unclean.

משנה מסכת ביצה פרק ג משנה ה

[ה]בהמה שמתה לא יזיזנה ממקומה. ומעשה: ושאלו את רבי טרפון עליה ועל [
החלה שנטמאה ונכנס לבית המדרש ושאל ואמרו לו לא יזיזם ממקומם.

<u>Mishnah Betzah 3.5</u>
If a [domesticated] animal died, it may not be moved [on the Sabbath] from its place. Once R. Tarfon was asked about this and about Dough offering that had become [ritually] unclean and he went to the House of Study (לבית המדרש) and enquired, and they [= the Jewish sages] said to him, 'We do not move them from their places [on the Sabbath]'.

It is clear from this text that neither of the incidents which inspired the later discussion took place in the *beit midrash*, and neither is it likely that R. Tarfon was present at either of the locations when either problem arose. Instead, specific incidents were discussed in retrospect in a different place by those who were not originally involved. As far as the gospel texts are concerned, this means that it cannot routinely be assumed that any rabbinic argument *kal va-chomer* cited during an account of an event was composed or spoken at the time of the event, especially when there is evidence to show that the contrary was the case.

Also of importance, especially in relation to the gospel texts, is the fact that *halachic* arguments *kal va-chomer* recorded in the tannaitic rabbinic texts are always expressed in Hebrew, rather than Aramaic.[9]

---

8.   In the Mishnah: m. Ber 4.2; m. Dem 2.3; 7.5; m. Shab 16.1; 18.1; m. Betz 3.5; m. Avot 5.14; m. Men 10.9; m. Yad 4.3. There are also twenty-two references in the Tosefta.

9.   One *aggadic* exception is recorded in an amoraic (rather than a tannaitic) source and is attributed to R. Shimon b. Yohai, who was active between the years 135 and 170 CE; see y. Shiv 9.1, and below.

This conforms with the fact that, as noted above, the bridge phrases used in these arguments in the tannaitic texts (whenever they appear) are *always* expressed in Hebrew, rather than Aramaic. While of course *halachic* arguments *kal va-chomer* are also expressed in Aramaic in amoraic (talmudic) texts, and bridge phrases may also be expressed in Aramaic, the non-use of this language in arguments *kal va-chomer* preserved in the tannaitic texts suggests that Hebrew was the language in which these arguments were originally and officially expressed. Thus the arguments *kal va-chomer* expressed by the young Hillel, who came from Babylon and who was therefore—it can be assumed—fluent in Aramaic, are recorded in Hebrew when he explained a *halachic* problem in Jewish law to the Bney Bathyra, the religious leaders in Jerusalem in the later first century BCE.[10] Anyone using an argument *kal va-chomer* to establish *halachah* in tannaitic times—such as a justification for the violation of Jewish law by an act of healing and/or saving life—is therefore likely to have expressed such an argument in Hebrew, especially when speaking to Pharisees, a tannaitic group who invariably composed such arguments in Hebrew themselves. The use of Hebrew for such arguments rather than Aramaic would therefore have given greater authority to the validity of the argument than would otherwise be the case. If, however, Jesus expressed *halachic* arguments in Aramaic, he would then be the only Jewish person recorded in tannaitic times who used Aramaic in this way in order to establish Jewish law. This observation is especially relevant to the argument expressed at Luke 13:15b-16, which is discussed in Chapter 3.

Finally, it is important to note that as for all *halachic* arguments, the logic of the argument cannot depend on the identity of the person by whom the argument is expressed, but must make complete sense within the argument itself. This simple fact has been disregarded in relation to the basic argument expressed by Jesus at Mark 2:23-28 (and the parallel texts), which has resulted in a serious misunderstanding of this gospel text, as is discussed in Chapter 3.

Let us now examine the ten events in which Jesus healed on the Sabbath, and one in which healing was postponed until after the Sabbath day. These will be discussed with the following questions in mind:

10. t. Pes 4.13-14. Hillel is credited with the original use of arguments *kal va-chomer* (see Sifra, Introd. 1-7; ARN A 37; t. San 7.11), but his use of this argument at t. Pes 4.13-14, without any further explanation, suggests that the Bney Bathyra were already familiar with these arguments. This may also be implied by the *aggadic* argument in m. Avot 1.5 attributed to Yose b. Yohanan, a leader of the Sanhedrin in the second century BCE.

(1) What—if any—is the connection between the argument *kal va-chomer* used to justify a particular cure and the cure that is performed? (2) What is the significance of any other *halachic* material in these events? (3) Who was present and who was *not* present at the *original* historical scene of a Sabbath cure?[11] (4) Was Jesus praised or criticised for a particular cure? (5) By whom was any praise or any criticism expressed?

---

11. The importance of the role of spectators in stories of Jesus' cures is rarely noted. Rare exceptions include L. T. Witkamp, 'The Use of the Traditions in John 5.1-18', *JSNT* 25 (1985) 9-47 (27, 29), and R. Bultmann, *The History of the Synoptic Tradition* (trans. J. Marsh; Oxford: Blackwell, 1963) 225-6, 423.

Chapter 3

THE SABBATH AND POST-SABBATH HEALING EVENTS IN THE GOSPELS

I. *Saving Life from Starvation: Mark 2:23-28; Luke 6:1-5; and Matthew 12:1-8*

A parallel translation of the three versions of this story is set out below. As will be the practice throughout this book, terms in Greek which are important in the discussion are indicated in parentheses after the relevant text:

Mark 2:23-28	Luke 6:1-5	Matthew 12:1-8
2^{:23} One Sabbath Jesus was going through the fields of growing wheat. And as they made a way,	6^{:1} On a Sabbath while he was going through the fields of growing wheat.	12^{:1} At that time Jesus on the Sabbath, went through the fields of growing wheat,
		his disciples were hungry
his disciples began plucking (τίλλοντες) the grain.	And his disciples plucked (ἔτιλλον)	and they began to pluck (τίλλειν) the grain
	and ate some heads of grain,	to eat.
	rubbing (ψώχοντες) them in their hands.	
²⁴ And the Pharisees said to him,	² But some of the Pharisees said,	² But when the Pharisees saw it, they said to him,
'Look! Why are they doing	'Why are you (plural) doing	'Look! Your disciples are doing
what is not lawful on the Sabbath?'	what is not lawful on the Sabbath?'	what is not lawful on the Sabbath!'

27

[25] And he said to them, 'Have you never read what David did,	[3] And Jesus answered, 'Have you not read what David did,	[3] He said to them, 'Have you not read what David did,
when he was in need		
and was hungry, he	when he was hungry, he	when he was hungry,
and those who were with him;	and those who were with him;	and those who were with him;
how he entered the house of God (τὸν οἶκον τοῦ θεοῦ) when Abiathar was High Priest,	how he entered the house of God (τὸν οἶκον τοῦ θεοῦ)	how he entered the house of God (τὸν οἶκον τοῦ θεοῦ)
and ate the sacred bread, which is not lawful for any but the priests to eat,	and ate the sacred bread, which is not lawful for any but the priests to eat,	and ate the sacred bread, which was not lawful for him to eat, but only for the priests
and also gave it to those that were with him?'	and also gave it to those with him?'	nor for those who were with him?[1]
		[5] Or have you not read in the law how on the Sabbath, the priests in the Temple violate the Sabbath, and are guiltless?
[27a] And he said to them,	[5] And he said to them,	[6] I tell you something greater than the Temple is here.
[27b] 'The Sabbath was made for man but not man for the Sabbath.		
		[7] And if you had known what this means, *I desire mercy, and not sacrifice*, you would not have condemned the guiltless.
[28] so that (ὥστε) the son of man is lord even of the Sabbath'.	'The son of man is lord of the Sabbath'.	[8] For the son of man is lord of the Sabbath'.

1. In order to show the parallelism of the versions, the last two clauses in Matt 12:4 are reversed.

A. *A Brief Summary of the Story and Some Problems in This Tale*
According to these accounts, Jesus was walking with his disciples on the
Sabbath in fields of growing grain which his disciples were plucking,
because they were hungry and needed to eat. This reason for their action
is stated by Matthew, and must also be implied for the versions of Mark
and Luke, for otherwise there is no reason for the grain to be plucked.
Similarly, although only Luke and Matthew state that the disciples of
Jesus ate the grain they had plucked, this must also be assumed for the
version of Mark because—once again—there is no other reason for the
grain to be plucked. The gospels then note that some Pharisees who were
present remarked to Jesus that his disciples were violating Sabbath law.
The Pharisees in Luke also involve Jesus himself in this act by addressing him with a plural 'you', thus: *Why are you* (ποιεῖτε) *doing what is not
lawful on the Sabbath?* (Luke 6:2). Jesus then justifies the action of his
disciples (and perhaps also his own, according to Luke) with a rhetorical
argument based on the biblical story of David at Nob (1 Sam 21:1-6).
The reply of Jesus in the gospel of Mark is interrupted with the declaration that *the Sabbath was made for man, rather than man for the Sabbath*
(Mark 2:27b). The final words of Jesus in all three versions of this tale,
which also mark the end of this story, seem to suggest that Jesus is the
ultimate authority for Sabbath law.[2]

This story raises questions relevant to the discussion in this book.
Why, for example, are the disciples so hungry that they were eating raw
grain, food which is normally only animal fodder? Why are the Pharisees
wandering in the fields on the Sabbath day rather than occupied in a
religious way? How does Jesus respond to the Pharisees' remark? Why
do Luke's Pharisees include Jesus in the actions of his men (Luke 6:2),
whereas Mark and Matthew clearly do not? Why does Jesus in Mark
refer to Abiathar the High Priest (Mark 2:26), and why do Matthew and
Luke not even mention a priest? What is the meaning of Mark 2:27b, and
why is this verse found only in Mark? If it refers to the creation of the
Sabbath, as some scholars suggest, how is this relevant in the context of
the tale? And how does the declaration that Jesus is 'Lord of the
Sabbath' fit into the account of the event as a whole?

These problems will be discussed in the analysis below. Meanwhile,
however, we must start with a problem that is not a problem of the story
but is a result of the belief of many commentators that the Pharisees
repeatedly and unjustly criticised Jesus for performing Sabbath cures.

---

2. E.g. R. A. Guelich, *Mark 1–8:26* (WBC 34A; Dallas: Word, 1989) 122:
'[Mark 2:28 is] a christological statement, [which] declares the son of man's
authority over the Sabbath'.

These commentators thus cannot believe that the comment of the Pharisees to Jesus in this tale was fully justified by the behaviour of the disciples (and possibly also of Jesus, according to Luke), and thus assert that although they were justified in making this remark, it was the Pharisees themselves who were somehow at fault. Can this be correct? One further question is the interpretation of the phrase 'making a path', ὁδὸν ποιεῖν (Mark 2:23), which has been queried by scholars on grammatical grounds. As will be seen, a proper understanding of the latter phrase and the words of the Pharisees sets the scene for the proper understanding of the story itself.

B. *The Comment of the Pharisees on the Actions of the Disciples*
Let us first consider the nature of the comment of the Pharisees on the behaviour of the disciples. Is their remark justified or could they themselves be somehow at fault? According to all three of the gospel accounts, the Pharisees commented that the disciples were violating Sabbath law (see Mark 2:24 and the parallel texts). This can only be related to the fact that in all three versions of this tale, the disciples of Jesus were violating Sabbath law by performing an action described with the verb τίλλω, which in the context of the disciples in the fields of growing grain can only refer to their action of 'plucking' this growing grain. The verb τίλλω in Hellenistic Greek most commonly refers to the plucking of hair or feathers.[3] The first-century BCE historian Diodorus Siculus has, however, preserved an example of this term used in the sense indicated in the gospels in a passage which is cited and translated below:

Diodorus Siculus 5 21 5
Τὴν δὲ συναγωγὴν τῶν σιτικῶν καίπῶν ποιοῦνται τοὺς στάχυς αὐτοὺς ἀποτέμνοντες καὶ θησαυρίζοντες εἰς τὰς καταστέγους οἰκήσεις· ἐκ δὲ τούτων τοὺς παλαιοὺς στάχυς καθ' ἡμέραν τίλλειν, καὶ κατεργαζομένους ἔχειν τὴν τροφήν.

The method they employ of gathering their grain crops is to cut off no more than the heads and store them away in roofed granges, and then each day *they pick out the ripened heads* (τοὺς παλαιοὺς στάχυς...τίλλειν) and grind them, thus obtaining their food.[4]

---

3. H. G. Liddell, R. Scott and H. S. Jones, *A Greek–English Lexicon* (Oxford: Clarendon, 1968), and H. G. Liddell, R. Scott, P. G. W. Glare and A. A. Thompson, *Greek–English Lexicon Revised Supplement* (Oxford: Clarendon, 1996) s.v. τίλλω.
4. Cited by W. F. Arndt and F. W. Gingrich, *A Greek–English Lexicon of the New Testament and Other Early Christian Literature* (2nd edn; Chicago: University of Chicago Press, 1958) s.v. τίλλω. This meaning of τίλλειν is not recorded in

Although the grain described by Diodorus has already been reaped, it seems reasonable to assume that when the ancient Britons 'picked out the ripened heads', their action was similar to the disciples of Jesus who 'plucked' the growing grain. Diodorus thus confirms—albeit inadvertently—that the term τίλλω in the gospels refers to an act of harvesting the grain, although with a method that was less aggressive or efficient than if a sickle or similar instrument was used.[5] This being the case, it is clear that the disciples of Jesus were violating Sabbath law. In effect, they were harvesting grain, which is one of the thirty-nine main actions prohibited on the Sabbath day (see m. Shab 7.2, cited in Chapter 1). There is thus little doubt that the Pharisees were correct when they noted that the disciples were violating Sabbath law.

Although scholars generally agree with this conclusion they also assert that this comment of the Pharisees is unreasonable and even wrong. If this is the case, the reply of Jesus to the Pharisees becomes a reproof of the Pharisees for making this remark, rather than a reply to their comment in relation to the violation by the disciples of Sabbath law. This understanding significantly affects how the story is understood. Before a proper investigation of this text can begin, it is therefore important to examine whether or not the Pharisees were more at fault than the disciples in this tale. This has been argued in the following three ways:

(1) *An Argument Based on Deuteronomy 23:26.* The claim most frequently used to excuse the behaviour of the disciples and therefore to accuse the Pharisees of committing some wrong is based on the text of Deut 23:26, *When you go into your neighbour's standing grain you may pluck the ears with your hand…* This seems to suggest that anyone was permitted 'to gather' or 'to harvest' the produce of a field although it belonged to another (expressed as 'your neighbour', רעֶךָ), as long as this was done only with hands. Some scholars thus suggest that Deut 23:26

Liddell, Scott and Jones, *A Greek–English Lexicon*, nor even in the Supplement, in which τίλλω in Matt 12:1 is cited with the meaning 'to pull out hair', which does not make sense in the context of the gospel story and may be derived from the usage of this verb in the Septuagint, which does not provide any meaningful parallels to the gospel texts.

5. For harvesting in ancient Egypt with instruments and threshing (here called 'de-husking', that is, the separating the grain spikelets from the cereal straw), which can also be assumed for the methods used in Galilee in the first century, see P. T. Nicholson and I. Shaw, *Ancient Egyptian Materials and Technology* (Cambridge: Cambridge University Press, 1999) 520-5, 562.

accounts for the behaviour of the disciples because they were legally harvesting the standing grain using only their hands.[6]

It is, however, most unlikely that Deut 23:26 should be understood literally. If this were the case, the society described would have tolerated a practice in which any casual passer-by could freely take produce from any farmer's field. Even if such a custom existed in the late first millennium BCE (when the text of Deuteronomy was probably originally composed), it is surely unlikely that so controversial a ruling was still in force some thousand years later, especially when evidence exists that the opposite is true. Directives in the Mishnah relating to Deut 23:26, which are expanded and confirmed in the amoraic texts, thus repeatedly stress that apart from those who could claim legal rights (which cannot be assumed for the disciples of Jesus), only labourers who had worked in a field—not mere passers-by, such as must be assumed for disciples of Jesus—were allowed to remove produce that was grown in a field. This licence, moreover, was allowed only if certain conditions were fulfilled. For example, if a man worked with grapes, he was allowed to eat only grapes, and only at fixed times, either during or after the harvest of the crop, as can be seen from the text below:

Mishnah Baba Metzia 7.2-5
These [men] may eat [of the produce on which they labour] by virtue of what is enjoined by the Law: [namely] he that labours on what is still growing *after the work is finished* [that is, after harvesting the crop], and he that labours on what is already gathered *before the work is finished...* If he worked among figs he may not eat grapes, and if [he worked] among grapes he may not eat figs... These are they that may not eat: he that labours on what is still growing while the work is still unfinished, and he that labours on what is already gathered after the work is finished... In no case have they [= the Jewish sages] said [that he may eat] save during the time of his labour, but, on the principle of restoring lost property to its owner, they have said, 'Labourers may eat as they go from one furrow to another or as they return from the winepress...' R. Eleazar b. Hisma says, 'A labourer may not eat more than the value of his hire'.[7]

6. Thus E. B. Cranfield, *The Gospel According to Mark* (Cambridge: Cambridge University Press, 1959) 114; W. D. Davies and D. C. Allison, *A Critical and Exegetical Commentary on the Gospel According to Saint Matthew*, vol. 2 (Edinburgh: T. & T. Clark, 1991) 307.

7. Similar comments are recorded in the Targums Neofiti and Onkelos on Deut 23:26 and a hint of the same attitude can be seen in the phrase 'labourer and his hire' at *Sifre Devarim* 266 on Deut 23:25. See also t. BM 8.6-9 and b. BM 87b on m. BM 7.2.

A story about R. Tarfon, a tannaitic sage who was active from before 70 CE,[8] illustrates the predictable attitude of those who lived in the first century CE towards those who helped themselves freely to the produce in a field. According to this tale, R. Tarfon was collecting produce from his own land when he was arrested by one of his tenants who did not recognise his master. He thought, therefore, that his master was a thief and proceeded to beat him severely:

> Kallah Rabbati 52b
> R. Tarfon...was eating figs from his garden when his tenant found him and [not recognising him] gave him a severe beating, but [R. Tarfon] said nothing. When he felt that he was [almost] dying R. Tarfon exclaimed, 'Woe to thee R. Tarfon!' Whereupon the tenant asked him, 'Are you R. Tarfon?' He replied, 'Yes'. [The tenant] arose, tore his hair and wept.[9]

As this story shows, and as might be expected, in the time of R. Tarfon (the first century CE) the removal of produce from a field by a non-authorised person who had no legal right to collect the crop (or, in the case of R. Tarfon, was *thought* to have no right) was obviously and rightly condemned as theft. In any case, even if the disciples possessed such a statutory right, it could not have been exercised on the Sabbath day because harvesting was (and is) forbidden on this day, as was noted above. For these reasons, therefore, it is most unlikely that there is any link between Deut 23:26 and the story of Jesus in the Galilean fields.

(2) *The Claim That the Disciples Were Collecting Their Rightful Dues.* A second vindication of the behaviour of the disciples—and the consequent condemnation of the Pharisees—is that the disciples were exercising a traditional right of the poor to gather grain which was set aside from the main harvest of a crop. These gleanings were called *leket* or *peah*. However, as the gospel story now stands, the conditions imposed on the collection of these offerings could not have been fulfilled. According to the statements in the tannaitic texts, the gift of *leket* was collected *at the time of harvesting the crop*, which means that *leket* could *not* be collected while the grain was still growing, that is, before harvesting had taken place. No harvesting is, however, indicated in the gospel

---

8. y. Yom 3.7: 'Said R. Tarfon, "I would stand in line among my brethren, the priests, and I inclined my ear to the high priest, and I heard him swallow up [the Divine Name] in the singing of the priests"'.

9. Based on the translation of J. Rabbinowitz, 'Kallah Rabbati', in *The Minor Tractates of the Talmud*, vol. 2 (London: Soncino, 1965) 438. The same story is found at y. Shevi 4.2.

event when the grain was still 'growing', because otherwise the grain could not have been 'plucked':

משנה מסכת פאה פרק ד משנה י / תוספתא מסכת פאה פרק ב הלכה יד
איזהו לקט? הנושר בשעת הקציר ובשעת התלישה...

Mishnah Peah 2.10 / Tosefta Peah 2.14
What counts as gleanings? Whatever drops down *at the time of harvesting and at the time of plucking...*

No harvesting is however indicated in the gospel event, when the grain was still 'growing', because otherwise the grain could not have been 'plucked'.

Similarly for *peah*—this concession to the poor could only be gathered *after* the harvest had taken place, and only with the permission of the owner of the crop (see t. Peah 2.6). *Peah* was thus collected *after* the harvest, when the 'corners' of the field were left for the poor, according to the directive of Lev 19:9, *When you reap the harvest of your land, you shall not reap your field to its border...*[10] It is, however, clear that the disciples of Jesus were wandering in the fields *before* the harvest had begun and there is no indication that they had been permitted to take any of the crop.[11] In any case, the basic problem still remains that the meeting of Jesus and his disciples with the Pharisees took place on the Sabbath, so that *even if* the disciples were entitled to gather either *peah* or *leket*, neither could have been gathered on the Sabbath day because, according to Jewish law, harvesting was forbidden on the Sabbath day. This theory must therefore also be dismissed.

---

10.   *Sifra*, Kedoshim 1.1, Chapter 6, on Lev 19:9 '*When you reap the harvest of your field...*' with the words, אין לי אלא קוצר, 'I learn only [that the obligation to set aside *peah* applies to produce] that one reaps'. Similarly the comment in later Jewish commentaries, אין פאה אלא מחמת כילוי, literally, 'There is no *peah* except as the consequence of finishing [the harvest]' (*Yalkut Shimoni Torah* 604 and *Pesikta Zutratah* [Lekah Tov] on Lev, Kedoshim 53.1).
11.   Mark 2:23; Luke 6:1; Matt 12:1. The claim of P. M. Casey, *Aramaic Sources of Mark's Gospel* (Cambridge: Cambridge University Press, 1998) 138-44, repeated in *The Solution to the 'Son of Man' Problem* (London: T&T Clark International, 2007) 121, that the disciples were collecting *peah*, is not based on evidence and is negated by the relevant Jewish sources; see, e.g., the mistaken claim on p. 143 of Casey's earlier book that 'halakhah probably allowed [the disciples] to go along a path plucking the grains of corn if they were only temporarily in need'. The same error is made by H. W. Basser, *The Mind Behind the Gospels: A Commentary to Matthew 1–14* (Boston: Academic Studies, 2009) 284.

(3) *An Argument Based on the Assumed Equivalence of τίλλω and* מלל.
A third argument claiming to vindicate the actions of the disciples
accepts that harvesting was prohibited on the Sabbath, but claims that
this applied only when harvesting is expressed with the verb θερίζω, the
Greek equivalent of the Hebrew קצר, one of the thirty-nine main
prohibited activities on the Sabbath day (see m. Shab 7.2). In other
words, whereas the action described with the verb θερίζω would be
forbidden, the action described by τίλλω was allowed. This seems to
assume that the term τίλλω has a significance which is not possessed by
the term θερίζω, which allows its performance on the Sabbath day.[12] This
theory thus accounts for the gospel use of the comparatively rare verb
τίλλω, rather than the verb θερίζω, the usual Greek term for harvesting,
which is the action that the disciples effectively perform.

This argument is based on an assumed semantic equivalence between
the verbs τίλλω and מלל in a passage in the Babylonian Talmud, translated below:

> Babylonian Talmud Shabbat 128a
> 'As for bundles of *si'ah*, *hyssop* and *koranith*[13] if they were brought in for
> fuel, one must not draw on them [for food] on the Sabbath; [if brought in]
> as animal fodder, he may draw on them on the Sabbath; and he may break
> [it] with his hand and eat [thereof], provided that he does not break it with
> a utensil. And he may crush (ומולל) it and eat, provided that he does not
> crush (מולל) a large quantity with a utensil'. [These are] the words of R.
> Judah. But the Sages say, 'He may crush (ומולל) [it] with the tips of his
> fingers and eat, provided, however, that he does not crush a large quantity
> with his hands in the [same] way as he does on weekdays. The same
> applies to *ammitha*, the same applies to *higgam*, and the same applies to
> other kinds of spices…'

As can be seen, this text deals only with the treatment on the Sabbath
of certain spices, rather than grain, and thus is not comparable with the
action of the disciples in the Galilean fields. It is unlikely, therefore, that
verb מלל, 'to crush' or 'to squeeze', served as a translation equivalent for
the verb τίλλω among first-century Jews.

---

12. Thus U. Luz, *Matthew 8–20: A Commentary* (trans. J. E. Crouch;
Minneapolis: Augsburg Fortress, 2001) 181 n. 28, claims that the activity of the
disciples was legal according to Jewish law; similarly, Basser, *The Mind Behind the
Gospels*, 311 n. 9, citing t. Shab 14.11. The significance of τίλλω rather than, for
example, θερίζω, will be discussed at the end of Chapter 4.

13. M. Jastrow, *A Dictionary of the Targumim, the Talmud Babli* (Israel: n.p.,
1972) ad loc. translates *si'ah* as a type of hyssop, *koranith* as thyme or origanum,
and (at the end of the paragraph) *ammitha* as Bishop's weed and *higgam* as rue.

This raises a question: Which verb in Hebrew (or Aramaic) served as a translation equivalent for τίλλω, as this verb is used in the gospel tale? The active verb τίλλω in the Septuagint corresponds with the Hebrew verb מרט, and refers to an act of plucking, especially to remove hair, either from human beings or from animals, while the passive form means 'polished' or 'smoothed', and is used with reference to skin, presumably (or at least originally) skin from which all the hairs have been removed.[14] These meanings can also be seen in the directives of the tannaitic and amoraic sages, in which the verb מרט frequently refers to the accidental or illegal removal of the wing or feather of a bird while preparing an animal for food according to Jewish law. Alternatively, it is used to describe an action that could be described as 'smoothing', for example, the removal of the hair from an animal, such as a goat, or the removal of the hair of a Nazirite. It is, however, self-evident that the action of the disciples of Jesus could not be described in any of these ways.

If, however, the Hebrew (or Aramaic) verb which served as a translation equivalent of τίλλω encompasses this meaning, this suggests that the term τίλλω as used by Greek-speaking Jews in the first century CE (among whom we can assume were Jewish readers of the gospels) possessed a wider semantic field than the verb מרט. In other words, it is reasonable to assume that the first-century Hebrew (or Aramaic) equivalent of the verb τίλλω included not only the meanings of the verb מרט described above, but in addition included a further meaning that described the action of the disciples in the fields of grain. Such a verb exists. Both these meanings are contained within the verb תלש, a term which appears both in Hebrew and Aramaic, although it is not used in the biblical texts, which accounts for the fact that there is no equivalent in the Septuagint. This verb, moreover, has a close, semantic equivalence with the verb מרט—and therefore also with τίλλω—as can be seen from

---

14. Isa 18:7, ἐκ λαοῦ τεθλιμμένου καὶ τετιλμένου...=...עַם מְמֻשָּׁךְ וּמוֹרָט, meaning, *a people tall and of glossy skin* (trans. *The Holy Scriptures* [Philadelphia: Jewish Publication Society of America, 1954]), or else meaning *smooth* (e.g. the trans. of J. N. Oswalt, *The Book of Isaiah: Chapters 1–39* [Grand Rapids: Eerdmans, 1986] 358). Similarly LXX Dan 7:4, ἐτίλη τὰ πτερὰ αὐτῆς... = ...הֲוֵיתִי עַד דִּי־מְרִיטוּ גַפַּיהּ means 'I observed it [the beast] until its wings *were plucked*...'; 2 Esd 9:3, καὶ ἔτιλλον ἀπὸ τῶν τριχῶν τῆς κεφαλῆς μου... = ...וָאֶמְרְטָה מִשְּׂעַר רֹאשִׁי means 'and I *tore out* the hairs from my head...', which was spoken in grief in response to the fact that the priests and Levites had married non-Jewish wives. 2 Esd 23:25 (= Neh 13.25) has μαδαράω, meaning 'to pull out hair' and thus 'to make bald', for the Hebrew מרט (וָאֶמְרְטֵם). Philo also uses τίλλειν when he describes how Joseph pulled out his hair in despair, and when the people in grief 'plucked the hair from their beards and their heads', see Ios 16 and Legat ad Gaius 223.

the following Aramaic paraphrase of Neh 13:25, in which the biblical compound אֶמְרְטֵם, 'and I plucked out their hair', is translated with the verb תלש in the phrase תלשינן שיער, literally, 'we may pluck out his hair'. This can be seen from the following text, in which the Hebrew terms are placed after the relevant terms:

Babylonian Talmud Moed Katan 16a
From which [holy text] do we derive that we may quarrel [with an offender], curse him, smite him, *pluck his hair* (ותלשינן שיער) and put on him an oath [so that he desists from his malpractices]? [This can be seen] from the [biblical] verse: And I contended with them, and cursed them, and smote certain of them and *plucked off their hair* (אֶמְרְטֵם) and made them swear by God (Neh 13:25).

As far as the tannaitic sources are concerned, the example cited below is one of many which shows the close semantic equivalence of the verbs תלש and מרט:

תוספתא מסכת שבת פרק ט הלכה כ
התולש כנף מן העוף הקוטמו והמורטו חייב שלש חטאות.

Tosefta Shabbat 9.20
He who pulls (התולש) a wing from the bird, who trims it, and who plucks it (והמורטו) is liable for three sin offerings.[15]

---

15. Similarly, the verb תלש is used at m. Yom 6.4 for plucking or pulling hair from an animal, for instance, from the hair of the scapegoat on the Day of Atonement: כבש עשו לו מפני הבבליים שהיו מתלשים בשערו ואומרים לו, טול וצא טול וצא..., 'And they made a causeway for it [= the scapegoat] because of the Babylonians, *who used to pull* שהיו מתלשים its hair, crying to it, "Bear [our sins] and be gone! Bear [our sins] and be gone!"...'
The following example shows תלש used for the wrongful removal (or, 'plucking out') of human hair, for which the wrongdoer was obliged to compensate the person he had wronged: 'If a man cuffed his fellow he must pay him a *sela*. R. Judah says in the name of R. Yose the Galilean: One hundred *zuz*. If he slapped him he must pay him two hundred *zuz*. If [he struck him] with the back of his hand he must pay him four hundred *zuz*. If he tore off his ear, *plucked out his hair* (תלש בשערו), spat and his spit touched him, or pulled his cloak from off him or loosened a woman's hair in the street, he must pay four hundred *zuz*. This is the general rule: all is in accord with a person's honour' (m. BK 8.6).
Other tannaitic examples of תלש used with reference to hair include: (1) t. BK 9.31: R. Simeon b. Eleazar says in the name of R. Hilpai b. Agra which he said in the name of R. Yohanan b. Nuri, 'If a person pulled out his own hair (מתלש בשערו), tore his clothing, broke his utensils, scattered his coins, in a fit of anger, he should be in your eyes as if he did an act of service for an idol; (2) t. Makk 5.5: There is he who plucks (תולש) two hairs and becomes liable on four counts, because of being a Nazirite, because of being a leper, because of [doing so] on a festival day, and

A further relevant feature of the verb תלש is the fact that it is considered as a sub-category (in Hebrew, תולדה, literally 'a descendant') of the thirty-nine *main* categories of work (אבות מלאות, 'fathers of work'), in this case a sub-category of the verb גזז, 'to cut', which, along with קצר, 'to harvest', is one of the thirty-nine *main* actions that are forbidden on the Sabbath day (see m. Shab 7.2, cited in Chapter 1). This is hinted at in the following text, in which the tannaitic sage R. Yose Hammeshulam explains that the act of 'plucking', for which he uses the general verb סיפר, 'to cut', must be considered as a sub-category of the verb גזז, literally, 'to cut':

תוספתא מסכת פרה (צוקרמאנדל) פרק ב הלכה ז

היו בה שתי שערות שחורות או לבנות בתוך גומא אחת פסולה בתוך שתי גומות כשרה. ר' יהודה אומר אפילו בתוך שתי גומות והן מוכיחות זו את זו פסולה. ... ר' יוסי בן המשולם אומר מספר את העליון ואינו חושש משום גוזז.

Tosefta Parah 2.7

If there were on [the red heifer] two black hairs or white ones in one follicle, it is unfit [to be used for the religious ceremony]. R. Judah says, 'Even in two follicles, and they are opposite each other, it is unfit...' R. Yose Hammeshulam says, 'One shaves (מספר) the top and does not reckon with the possibility that he is liable [for a punishment because of the violation of Jewish law] on account of shearing (גוזז)'.

The similar semantic fields of the verbs תלש and ספר, when the latter refers to 'cutting' or 'shearing', can again be seen in the following text:

ספרי במדבר פרשת נשא פיסקא כה

תער לא יעבור על ראשו, אין לי אלא תער תלש סיפסף וסיפר.

Sifre baMidbar 25

...*no razor shall come on his head* (Num 6:5)—I only know that the matter [in Num 6:5] concerns a razor—[How do I know that the prohibition does not also include] plucking, trimming or shearing it?

because of making a bald spot; (3) *Mekilta de-Rabbi Ishmael* Beshallah 1: As soon as the horn began to blow for the return, those of little faith among the Israelites began *plucking out their hair* (תולשין שעריהן) and tearing their garments until Moses said to them: It has been told to me by the word of God that you are free men. Therefore it says [at Exod 14:2] "That they turn back and encamp"' (for text and translation see J. Z. Lauterbach, *Mekilta de-Rabbi Ishmael*, vol. 1 [Philadelphia: The Jewish Publication Society of America 1976] 190; similarly, D. W. Nelson, *Mekhilta de-Rabbi Shimon Bar Yoḥai* [Philadelphia: Jewish Publication Society of America, 2006] 21.1).

The classification of the verb תלש as a *sub*category of the verb גזז is noted specifically in the following citation of the words of R. Simon b. Lakish, an early third-century amora, who again differentiates between תלש and מרט. In view, however, of the close overlapping semantic fields of these verbs which is repeatedly shown in the tannaitic texts, it is possible that the claim in this text that they are subcategories of two different main activities (תלש is a subcategory of one of the *main* prohibitions גזז, while מרט is a subcategory one of the thirty-nine *main* prohibitions, namely, מחק) may be motivated by an attempt of the Jewish sages to differentiate their meaning, although very little difference in their meanings exists:

תלמוד בבלי מסכת שבת דף עד עמוד ב

רבי שמעון בן לקיש: תולש חייב משום גזזז, קוטם חייב משום מחתך, ממרט
חייב משום ממחק.

Babylonian Talmud Shabbat 74b
Said R. Simon b. Lakish, 'For plucking (תולש) one is liable [for causing a violation of Jewish law] on account of the [main activity of] shearing (גזז), for trimming [the feather] he is liable on the score of [the main activity of] cutting, and for plucking (ממרט) he is liable under the head [that is, the main activity] of smoothing (ממחק)'.

Also significant for the discussion here is the fact that the verb תלש is used in the tannaitic texts for the removal, uprooting or harvesting of plants. This can be seen in the passage below in which תלש (expressed here as a *Niphal* infinitive) refers to the removal of a plant and its roots from the soil:

Mishnah Sheviit 6.3
It is forbidden to eat onions [that remain in the field until the Seventh Year] on which rain has fallen and which have sprouted, if their leaves are dark coloured. But if they are green they are permitted. Hananiah b. Antigonus says: If they can *be pulled up* (להיתלש) by their leaves they are forbidden, whereas in the year following the Seventh Year the like of these are permitted.[16]

Moreover, as can be seen from the following directive—one of many in the tannaitic texts—the action which is described by the verb תלש is also forbidden on the Sabbath day:

16. Similarly t. Shab 9.14: 'He who uproots (התולש) [a plant] either with his right hand or his left, behold, this person is liable [to make a sin offering for this violation of the Sabbath]…'

תוספתא מסכת שבת פרק ט הלכה יז

החופר והחורש והחורץ מלאכה אחת. הדש והכותש והנופט מלאכה אחת
התולש והקוצר והבוצר והמוסק והגודר והעודר מלאכה אחת הן.

Tosefta Shabbat 9.17

He who digs, ploughs, or cuts a trench, these are considered a single type of forbidden work [on the Sabbath]. He who threshes, beats flax or gins cotton, these are considered a single type of forbidden work [on the Sabbath]. He who *uproots* (תולש), reaps, cuts grapes, harvests olives, cuts dates or hoes—these are considered as a single type of forbidden labour [on the Sabbath].[17]

The same prohibition is expressed in the Mishnah using the symbol of a plant pot with a hole as the basis for defining whether or not a plant is attached (מחובר) to the ground. This is significant in Jewish law, because it is forbidden on the Sabbath to uproot a plant which is attached to the ground:

17. In a further example from many, the same prohibition is expressed in relation to the preparation of a quill pen: 'He who pulls (התולש) a wing from a bird, trims it, and plucks its down, is liable for three sin offerings [because he has violated the Sabbath in three different ways]' (t. Shab 9.20). The text of b. Shab 73b comments on t. Shab 9.20 as follows: 'A Tanna taught: Reaping, vintaging, gathering [dates], collecting [olives], and gathering [figs] are all one [form of] labour. R. Papa said, "He who throws a clod of earth at a palm tree and dislodges dates is liable to two [penalties], one on account of detaching (תולש) and one on account of stripping"'.

More complex arguments concerning 'uprooting' or 'detaching' are also expressed in the Babylonian Talmud; note, for example, 'If one intended to lift up something detached (התלוש), but cut off something attached [to the soil], he is not culpable [i.e. he has not violated the Sabbath]. [If he intended] to cut something detached (התלוש) [from the ground] but cut something attached [to the ground instead], Raba ruled, "He is not culpable". Abaye maintained, "He is culpable". Raba ruled, "He is not culpable, since he had no intention of a prohibited cutting". Abaye maintained, "He is culpable, since he had the intention of cutting in general"' (b. Shab 72b). Similarly, m. Bekh 3.3 gives instructions in relation to the pulling the hair of a sacrificial beast: 'R. Yose b. Meshullam says, "When a man slaughters a firstling he may prepare a place for the hatchet on either side and pluck out the hair (ותולש השער), provided that he does not removed it [to make use of it] so too, when a man plucks out hair (תולש השער) to inspect a place of blemish"' (m. Bekh 3.3; similarly, t. Bekh 2.18-19). Other examples of תלש, used in relation to the removal of hair include: m. Meil 5.3 (similarly, t. Eduy 2.9) and m. Par 2.5.

משנה מסכת שבת פרק י משנה ו

...התולש מעציץ נקוב חייב. ושאינו נקוב פטור...

Mishnah Shabbat 10.6

...If a man *plucks* (התולש) anything from a plant pot with a hole [which is underneath the pot, through which the root of the plant may grow] he is liable [that is, he has violated Sabbath law]. But if he [obtained the plant] from an *un*-holed plant pot he is not culpable [that is, he has *not* violated Sabbath law]...[18] [

The verb תלש is also frequently used in the early rabbinic texts with the general meaning 'to harvest' a crop, especially a crop that is 'detached or harvested from the ground', תלוש מן הקרקע. For example, concerning the identity of those who were allowed to eat the produce of a field, the Mishnah decrees:

משנה מסכת בבא מציעא פרק ז משנה ב

ואלו אוכלין מן התורה: העושה במחובר לקרקע בשעת גמר מלאכה, ובתלוש מן הקרקע עד שלא נגמרה מלאכתו בדבר שגדולו מן הארץ. ואלו שאין אוכלין העושה במחובר לקרקע בשעה שאין גמר מלאכה ובתלוש מן הקרקע מאחר שנגמרה מלאכתו ובדבר שאין גדולו מן הארץ.

Mishnah Baba Metziah 7.2

These [men] may eat [the produce on which they labour] by virtue of what is permitted by the Law: [namely] he that labours on what is still growing after the work is finished [at the time of harvesting the crops], and he that labours *on what is [already] harvested from the ground* (ובתלוש מן הקרקע) before the work is finished. [This applies only] to what grows from the soil. These are they that may not eat: he that labours on what is still growing while the work is still unfinished, and he that labours on what is [already] *harvested from the ground* (ובתלוש מן הקרקע) after the work is finished, and [he may not eat] of what does not grow from the soil.[19]

There is thus much evidence to show that although the basic meaning 'to harvest' is more common for the Hebrew (or Aramaic) verb תלש than for the Greek τίλλω, which more frequently refers to the plucking out of hair, nevertheless their overlapping semantic fields suggest that these verbs could be used as translation equivalents by Greek-speaking Jews in

---

18. This text is discussed by Rashi, b. Shab 95a.

19. Similarly, in relation to the laws of inheritance, an edict in the Mishnah (m. BB 8.7) states that any produce which is not harvested (תלוש) belongs to the heirs of the original owner of the land and if he left anything already harvested (תלוש), it belongs to his heirs. Similarly, in the Mishnah at m. Peah 4.10, the verb תלש refers specifically to the harvesting of grain. See also m. Shevi 6.2, t. Peah 2.14 etc.

Galilee and Judah in the first century CE. The use of the same verb to refer both to 'uprooting' and 'harvesting' may seem strange to English ears, but can be justified on the grounds that the term 'to harvest' may refer to the gathering of all kinds of crops, including those which could be uprooted (just as hair could be 'uprooted'), for example, root crops (see m. Shev 6.3, cited above), or crops that are gathered by cutting their stems (that is, gathered by reaping), such as wheat or barley. The frequent references in early Jewish texts to sheaves (עומר, אלומה), including 'the forgotten sheaf' (שכחה), and to instruments used for reaping such as a scythe (מגל or more rarely חרמש), in connection with these crops shows that their method of collection used instruments of these kinds.

It is thus reasonable to conclude that the Hebrew (or Aramaic) equivalent of the verb τίλλω in the first century CE was probably the verb תלש, rather than the verb מלל.[20] It is unlikely, therefore, that the action of the disciples in the Galilean fields can be understood by the action described with the verb מלל, so that this theory too must be dismissed. In any case, once again, we must return to the fact that the disciples of Jesus were violating Sabbath law by harvesting grain on the Sabbath day.

In summary therefore it can be assumed that the claim made by some scholars that the disciples of Jesus were in some way legally entitled to harvest grain on the Sabbath, and the claim that the Pharisees were at fault for commenting on their behaviour, must be firmly dismissed. Such claims should be regarded as part of the lengthy and sad history of the misinterpretation of this story in the gospel texts. Whether or not the disciples were legally entitled to harvest the grain may be interesting to debate, but it is totally irrelevant in the context of this tale, in which the comment of the Pharisees refers simply to the fact that the disciples of

20.   The verb τίλλω at Mark 2:26 (and parallel texts) is translated with the verb קטף by Delitzsch (1960) and Salkinson (1993) in their Hebrew versions of the New Testament. Although the meaning of קטף may overlap with תלש (see, e.g., t. Uktz 1.3: ...המקטף מלילות להכניסן בתוך ביתו, 'He who plucks ripe ears [of grain] to bring them into his house...'), the verb קטף means basically 'to cut off', rather than 'to pluck' (see e.g., t. BK 6.21, ...בזמן שאכלה יחורי תאנים או שקטפה לולבי גפנים, 'In a case which [the flock] ate the stems of figs or chops off the branches of vines...'). Moreover, the semantic range of the term קטף does not include the meaning of מרט (the Septuagint's translation of τίλλω). This justifies the title of the article תלישה בשבת והפולמוס הנוצרי־יהודי by Kister, which is translated in English 'Plucking of Grain on the Sabbath and the Christian Jewish Debate', in *Jerusalem Studies in Jewish Thought*, vol. 3 (Jerusalem: Magnes, 1983–84) 349-66 (in Hebrew, English summary vii–ix), and as 'Plucking on the Sabbath and the Christian–Jewish Polemic', *Immanuel* 24/25 (1990) 35-51, although this detail is lost in the English translation.

Jesus were violating Sabbath law. The Pharisees had every right to comment on this fact, which they do in a polite, factual and non-contentious way.

C. *What Is the Meaning of ὁδὸν ποιεῖν, Mark 2:23?*

As noted above, a further cause of difficulty in the gospel of Mark is the phrase ὁδὸν ποιεῖν. This is usually understood in the sense that the disciples of Jesus were 'making a way', which is a literal understanding of the phrase that seems to make sense in the context of the tale. If so, however, as many scholars observe, the phrase in Greek would probably be rendered ὁδὸν ποιεῖσθαι rather than ὁδὸν ποιεῖν.[21] In fact, the true meaning of the phrase ὁδὸν ποιεῖν in this context is explained by the verb τίλλω, and indicates a similar act. Grain in the ancient biblical world—either wheat or barley—was usually harvested with a sickle. More rarely it was harvested by hand, either by uprooting the whole plant or by harvesting the ears apart from the stalk.[22] The disciples of Mark were obviously not harvesting with a sickle, but 'had begun to make a way' (ἤρξαντο ὁδὸν ποιεῖν), by 'plucking the ears' (τίλλοντες τοὺς στάχυας). The action of 'making a way' in this manner and for this purpose is noted in the following tannaitic text which forbids the 'making of a way', in this case making a short cut (עושין קפנדריא) by plucking up the plants which were growing in a path:

> Mishnah Megilla 3.3
> Moreover R. Judah said: [Even] if a synagogue was in ruins, lamentation for the dead may not be made therein, nor may they twist ropes therein or stretch out nets therein, or spread out produce [to dry] on its roof, *nor making it a shortcut* (ואין עושין אותו קפנדריא), for it is written, *And I will bring your sanctuaries into desolation* (Lev 26:31)—[which means that] their sanctity [endures] although they lie desolate. If grasses spring up therein they may *not be plucked up* (לא יתלוש), because of grief of soul.

As can be seen, the action of 'making a short cut', in effect making a way (עשה...קפנדריא/דרך), is explained in the above text with the verb תלש, here meaning 'to pluck'. This, therefore, once again suggests that the verb τίλλω, a probable equivalent of the term תלש, refers both to plucking ears of grain (see the discussion above) and also to the uprooting of plants. The sequence ἤρξαντο ὁδὸν ποιεῖν and τίλλοντες in Mark's account thus shows that Mark has used the verb τίλλω after the phrase

---

21. E.g. R. H. Gundry, *A Commentary on His Apology for the Cross* (Grand Rapids: Eerdmans, 1993) 139-40.

22. For methods of harvesting in the ancient world, see Nicholson and Shaw, *Ancient Egyptian Materials and Technology*, 521-2.

ὁδὸν ποιεῖν, to refer to the sequence of the actions of the disciples in harvesting the grain, *and the disciples began to make a way [by] plucking the growing grain.* The suggestion of some scholars that the phrase ὁδὸν ποιεῖν should be replaced with the phrase ὁδὸν ποιεῖσθαι, meaning 'to walk along the path', in the sense 'to wend one's way', is therefore unnecessary and can be dismissed.[23] Not only is there no evidence for such a text (as many scholars note), but also—as one might imagine—there is no directive in Jewish law which prohibits simple walking from place to place on the Sabbath, unless perhaps by exceeding the Sabbath limit (the *eruv*) or by walking in a place which caused ritual impurity, neither of which actions is relevant here. As Mark's story now stands, the disciples of Jesus were violating Sabbath law both by 'making a path' (by uprooting plants) and by plucking grain, as the parallel phrases in Mark's text suggests. Both these actions violate Sabbath law because both in this context effectively harvest the grain, which is a forbidden activity on the Sabbath day.

It is clear therefore that for both these reasons in Mark, although only for the 'plucking' in the versions of Matthew and Luke, the Pharisees were justified in commenting on the public violation of Jewish law by the disciples of Jesus. Once again, we must conclude that the Pharisees cannot be faulted for their comment on this fact.

D. *Basic Details in the Reply of Jesus to the Pharisees*
How, then, does Jesus reply to the comment of the Pharisees regarding the public violation by his disciples of Sabbath law? As will be seen, his reply takes the form of a *halachic* rabbinic argument *kal va-chomer.* This depends for its understanding on (1) an acceptance of the midrashic changes made to the biblical story of David and the sacred bread which is used by Jesus in his reply, and (2) an understanding of the strange relationship between Sabbath and Temple law, especially as this was expressed by the early Jewish sages. These aspects of the argument will now be discussed.

(1) *The Midrashic Changes Made to the Biblical Story of David.* According to the biblical story of David to which Jesus refers in the first part of his argument (*ha-nadon*), the future King David was fleeing from King Saul when he arrived starving at the shrine of Nob.[24] He asked the

---

23. E.g. Guelich, *Mark 1–8:26*, 119, citing Latin *iter facere*, as in LXX Judg 17:8. Matt 12:1, ἐπορεύθη, and Luke 6:1, ἐγένετο ... διαπορεύεσθαι, attempt to smooth out the difficulty.

24. The term 'midrash' (from the Hebrew דרש, *drsh*, 'to investigate', 'to study'), is a Jewish homiletic method of exegesis, frequently based on a biblical text. For an

priest by whom he was met at the shrine for food and was told that the only food available was the sacred Temple bread. The priest, however, notes that the bread could be eaten by non-priests if the latter were in a state of sexual purity. David convinced the priest that this was the case for himself and his men. The priest then gave David the sacred bread, which—we assume—he shared with his men, thereby 'curing' their starvation and saving their lives. The biblical account, in 1 Sam. 21:1-6, is translated below:

> [1] Then came David to Nob, to Ahimelech, the priest. And Ahimelech came to meet David trembling, and said to him, 'Why are you alone and no one with you?' [2] And David said to Ahimelech the priest, 'The King has charged me with a matter and said to me, "Let no one know anything of the matter about which I send you, and with which I have charged you". I have made an appointment with the young men for such and such a place. [3] Now then, what have you at hand? Give me five loaves of bread or whatever is here.' [4] And the priest answered David, 'There is no common bread at hand, but there is holy bread; if only the young men have kept themselves from women'. [5] And David answered the priest, and said to him, 'Truly, women have been kept away from us as always when I go out, and [if] the "utensil" of [each of] the young men is holy [even when] it is an ordinary journey (דרך חל)—how much more (= it is therefore reasonable to assume also for) today, it will be holy in the "utensil" [of each man]!' [6] So the priest gave him the holy bread, for there was no bread there but the bread of the Presence, which is removed from before the Lord, to be replaced by hot bread on the day it is taken away.

The story cited by Jesus has, however, made the following significant changes to the biblical tale:

1. The biblical David came to a sanctuary at Nob (1 Sam 21:1), whereas David in the gospels arrived at 'the house of God' (see Mark 2:26; Luke 6:4; Matt 12:3).

2. The biblical tale notes that it was legal for a non-priest to eat the sacred bread, *if he was in a state of sexual purity* (1 Sam 21:4). David affirms this condition for himself and his men (1 Sam 21:6). The biblical David and his companions are thus *legally* entitled to eat the sacred bread. It is, however, stated specifically that the midrashic David and his companions were *not* legally entitled to eat the sacred bread (Mark 2:26; Luke 6:4; Matt 12:4), which means that in contrast with the biblical David, the

overview of rabbinic midrash, see, e.g., G. P. Porton, *Understanding Rabbinic Midrash: Text and Commentary* (Jersey City: Ktav, 1985) 1-18. The subject is further explored in the main text below.

midrashic David and his men violated the law of 'the house of God' by eating the sacred bread.

3. The priest at Nob gave David the sacred bread and was thus ultimately responsible for the biblical David's consumption of this food (1 Sam 21:6). In contrast, however, it was the midrashic David who was responsible for taking and eating the sacred bread. Mark only mentions a priest in passing (see Mark 2:26), while no priest is mentioned by Matthew or Luke.

4. The biblical David arrived alone at the sanctuary (1 Sam 21:1) and only refers to his companions, who do not appear (1 Sam 21:4-5). We can therefore only assume that if David was hungry, so also were his men, so that they also *legally* partook of the sacred bread. In contrast, we are told that the midrashic David was accompanied by his men when he arrived at 'the house of God' and that they were all hungry and they all illegally ate the sacred bread (Mark 2:26 and Luke 6:4; Matt 12:3 notes that the midrashic David arrived with his men, but because he has changed the structure of the argument *kal va-chomer* to a sorite—on which, see below—he leaves it to be assumed that the midrashic David and his men ate the sacred bread). The audience of the gospels thus knows for certain that both the midrashic David and his men illegally ate the sacred bread.

The midrashic changes made in the gospels to the biblical story of David have often been noted, but their significance has been overlooked. In fact, as will be shown in the paragraphs below, they are essential for the logic of the argument used by Jesus when he replies to the Pharisees, and without these changes, the argument of Jesus could not have been made.

The most important of the midrashic changes made to the biblical story in the reply of Jesus to the Pharisees are undoubtedly the change of name and the illegality of the act of the midrashic David in eating the sacred bread. As far as the change of name is concerned, it seems at first entirely innocuous that the shrine to which the midrashic David arrived was called 'the house of God', ὁ οἶκος τοῦ θεοῦ, because biblical sanctuaries are frequently called '(the) house of God'. Thus the sanctuaries at Gen 28:17, 22 and Judg 17:5 are known in the Septuagint as οἶκος θεοῦ, and similarly also the shrine at Shilo (probably the historical precursor of the shrine at Nob, Judg 18:31) and David's pre-Temple shrine in Jerusalem (2 Kgs 12:20). This name is also even used for some pagan shrines (Judg 9:27; 2 Chron 32:21). There is thus little doubt that this name *could* have been understood as a reference to the biblical shrine at Nob.

The name 'house of God' is, however, also the most common name in the Septuagint for the Temple in Jerusalem, and the works of Josephus confirm its use and popularity for the Jerusalem shrine in the first century CE.[25] Although therefore, as noted above, the shrine at Nob could also have been called '(the) house of God', it is more likely that, just as is assumed by many commentators of this text, the name 'the house of God' would be associated with the Temple in Jerusalem rather than with Nob or any other holy place.[26] The identity of this location in Jerusalem is strengthened by Mark's reference to Abiathar as a High Priest (Mark 2:26), since the role of the High Priest was strongly associated with the Temple in Jerusalem, whereas there was only a simple priest at Nob.[27]

As will be seen, it was, however, essential for the logic of the argument used by Jesus that the audience of this text would associate the words 'house of God' with the Temple in Jerusalem, rather than with the shrine at Nob. This is because of the different laws in these locations regarding those who were allowed to eat the sacred bread.[28] According to

25. (ὁ) οἶκος τοῦ θεοῦ is used for the First Temple at Isa 2:2 and Mic 4:2, and for the Second Temple at Eccl 4:17; 1 Chron 23:28; 2 Chron 3:3; 4:11; 5:14; 7:5; 22:12; 23:3, 9; 24:7; 34:9; 1 Esd 5:56; 2 Esd 3:9; 5:7; 6:5 (×2); 7:16, 23; 8:17, 30, 33, 36; 9:9; 20:35, 37, 39, 40. Other recurring names for the Temple in Jerusalem include (1) the plain, almost colloquial term 'the House', ὁ οἶκος, e.g., 3 Kgdms 6:36; 2 Esd 5:11; (2) the 'house of the Lord', οἶκος χυρίου, e.g., 3 Kgdms 7:26; Jer 42:4; Zech 6:15; 2 Esd 2:68; 1 Chron 22:1; 23:28; and (3) the slightly more common expression 'the house of the Lord God', (ὁ) οἶκος χυρίου τοῦ θεοῦ, e.g., Exod 23:19; 34:26; Deut 23:19; Isa 38:22; Zeph 1:9; 2 Chron 29:5; 34:8; 2 Esd 2:68. The terms ὁ οἶκος του Θεοῦ and ὁ οἶκος χυρίου seem to be interchangeable, see Josephus, War IV.281.

26. See, e.g., Gundry, *Apology for the Cross*, 142.

27. For Abiathar in the Hebrew Bible, see 1 Sam 21:1, 4, 5, 6. For Mark's reference to Abiathar, see below in the main text. The Hebrew Bible does not state that either Ahimelech or Abiathar were High Priests, but this might be assumed by a first-century individual who was aware of the position of High Priest in the Temple in Jerusalem, especially as Ahimelech is described in the Bible as spokesman for *the eighty five persons [i.e., priests] who wore the linen ephod* (1 Sam 22:12-15, 18) and the Bible relates that Solomon *made Zadok the priest instead of Abiathar* (1 Kgs 2:35; LXX 3 Kgs 2:35 refers to Zadok as 'the first priest'). In fact, Ahimelech could never have been High Priest in the Temple at Jerusalem, because he was murdered by Saul before the Temple was built (1 Sam 22:16-19). Josephus, however, states that Ahimelech and Abiathar were High Priests in Jerusalem (not Nob), see Ant VI.242, VII.110.

28. Some scholars note the change but overlook its significance. E.g. V. Taylor, *The Gospel According to Mark: The Greek Text with Introduction, Notes and*

the words of the biblical priest of Nob, non-priests were allowed to eat the sacred bread if they were sexually 'pure' (1 Sam 21:4). The biblical David claimed that this was the case for himself and his men because they had had no sexual encounters since their expedition began (1 Sam 21:5). His declaration was believed, with the result that the priest at Nob gave David the sacred bread which (we assume) he and his men subsequently ate. The right of an individual in a state of sexual purity to eat the sacred bread at Nob is stressed in the Septuagint which, in comparison with the biblical text, gives additional words to the priest. This are indicated *in italics* in the following translation, which corresponds with the Masoretic text of 1 Sam 21:4, 'And the priest answered David and said, "There are no permitted loaves in my hand for there are only consecrated loaves; if the lads have kept themselves from women, *then you will eat it*"'.[29] A similar addition occurs in the Greek text of 4QSam[b] and other fragments of the Septuagint, which again also note that 'if the young men have kept themselves from women, *[then] they may eat*'.[30] These Greek texts thus confirm that the condition of sexual purity demanded by the priest at Nob was believed and accepted as a genuine requirement for eating the sacred bread, and that this condition was fulfilled by David and his men. This means that the condition of sexual purity demanded by the priest and the assurance of the biblical David that this was the case for himself and his men was not a cynical ploy to deceive the priest, or perhaps to provide the priest with some kind of excuse for parting with the sacred bread, perhaps because the priest

Indexes (2nd edn; Grand Rapids: Baker Book House, 1981) 217, notes merely 'a free expansion of the original narrative'; D. Harrington, *The Gospel of Matthew* (Collegeville: Liturgical, 1991) 172 n. 4, notes that 'The expression [house of God] could suggest that it was the Jerusalem Temple. Of course, the Temple had not yet been built. The "house of God" is the shrine of the ark of the covenant at Nob...' Gundry, *A Commentary on His Apology*, 141, does not comment on the change, but claims that the differences 'strengthen' the argument of Jesus. In fact, without this and other changes, the argument could not be made. J. R. Donahue and D. Harrington, *Sacra Pagina the Gospel of Mark* (Collegeville: Liturgical, 2002) 111, note some differences, but do not comment on the essential fact that the consumption of the sacred bread by the biblical David is legal, but illegal in the gospels. Meier, *A Marginal Jew*, 4:275-6, implies without further explanation that Jesus deliberately 'mangles' the biblical tale.

   29. LXX 1 Kgs 21:5, καὶ φάγεται.

   30. P. F. Abegg, P. Flint and E. Ulrich, *The Dead Sea Scrolls Bible: Translated and with Commentary* (Edinburgh: T. & T. Clark, 1999) 231. Similarly A. Pietersma and B. G. Wright, eds., *A New English Translation of the Septuagint* (New York: Oxford University Press, 2007) 263.

supported David against Saul, as some commentators suggest.[31] On the contrary, the sexual purity of David and his men meant that the action of the *biblical* David in receiving and (we can presume) also eating and sharing the sacred bread was *entirely legal* according to the religious law at Nob.

No similar permit, however, existed in the Temple in Jerusalem, where the sacred bread was consumed only by the Temple priests (the 'sons of Aaron') and only within the Temple precincts. Only when a priest was *not* in a state of purity (such as sexual or corpse impurity), was he forbidden to enter the Temple precincts and thus forbidden to eat the sacred bread (because the latter could only be eaten within the Temple precincts, as noted above; of course his state of sexual impurity could be reversed by the ritual of purification). Leviticus 24:9 thus decrees *and [the twelve loaves of bread which was set before the Lord, shall be for Aaron and his sons, and they shall eat it in the holy place, a perpetual due.*[32] The exclusive privilege of the priests to eat the sacred bread is confirmed for Second Temple times by Nehemiah, who states that those who could not prove their priestly credentials *were disqualified for the priesthood as unclean, and the governor forbade them to partake of the most sacred food until there should be a priest able to consult the Urim and the Thummim* (Neh 7:65). The post-biblical Temple priests thus claimed that *the Omer and the Two Loaves [of Pentecost] and the sacred Temple bread are ours [that is, they are the property of the priests]* (m. Shek 1.4). R. Yose, probably the second-century R. Yose ben Halafta, similarly notes that *the loaves [of the sacred Temple bread] were shared out [only] among the priests* (m. Men 11.7).

The words of Jesus to the Pharisees thus specifically state that it was *not lawful for any but the priests to eat* the sacred bread (Mark 2:26;

---

31. E.g. Gundry, *A Commentary on His Apology*, 147, suggests—with no proof—that David lied to the priest. This opinion is, however, ancient—the second-century R. Shimon b. Yochai indicates an underlying, rabbinic debate on the legality of David's consumption of the sacred bread when he states that David was legally given the sacred bread, but even if he was not legally given this food, this act would have been excused because David was in danger of his life (b. Men 95b-96a). R. Shimon's comment is based wholly on the biblical text—he cites the Hebrew phrase דרך חל (1 Sam 21.5) and he implies that David was given the sacred bread by the priests (!) at Nob, rather than assuming that David took it for himself. As will be seen, the belief that David took the bread himself is essential for the midrashic tale used in the argument in the gospel texts.

32. For cleansing from sexual impurity, see Lev 15:18, 31. For purity in relation to the Temple, see E. P. Sanders, *Judaism, Practice and Belief 63BCE–66CE* (London: SCM, 1992) 70-2, 217-22.

Luke 6:4; Matt 12:4). The change of location from Nob to Jerusalem therefore means that David and his men committed an *il*legal act when they ate the sacred bread, which would *not* have happened at the shrine of Nob.

But why was it necessary for the midrashic David and his men to perform an illegal act and thereby to violate Temple law? This was because David and his men were in an extreme state of starvation, and thus violated Temple law in order to save their lives, as the gospel texts stress (Mark 2:26; Luke 6:4; Matt 12:4). In Nob, however, it was *not* necessary to act illegally to achieve the same end. The midrashic David was therefore placed in Jerusalem, rather than Nob.

The significance of the other midrashic changes made to the biblical story of David at Nob—the omission, in fact the suppression, of the role of the priest and the inclusion of David's men—will be discussed below.

(2) *The Relationship Between Sabbath and Temple Law.* As was noted above, in addition to an acceptance of the midrashic changes made to the biblical story of David at Nob, the reply of Jesus to the Pharisees depends on an understanding of the strange relationship between Temple and Sabbath law, in which the Sabbath ritual of the Temple in Jerusalem included many mandatory procedures which were totally forbidden outside the Temple on the Sabbath day. For example, ordinary worshippers were strictly forbidden to offer a sacrifice on the Sabbath (except when the day of the Passover sacrifice fell on a Sabbath, when it was required to sacrifice a goat or a lamb, t. Pes 4.13). On the other hand, within the Temple itself it was obligatory for the priests to sacrifice a lamb every morning and evening, including the Sabbath day (m. Pes 5.1). Similarly, it was forbidden for those outside the Temple to light a fire on the Sabbath, although this was mandatory on the Sabbath in the Temple where the priests were obliged to light the Temple lamps.[33]

There is little doubt that this religious anomaly was well known to all. The apparent conflict between Temple and Sabbath ritual is frequently noted in the rabbinic texts. For example, the Mishnah lists the actions of 'slaughtering' and related acts (such as 'flaying' and 'cutting up') among the thirty-nine main classes of work that are totally prohibited on the Sabbath day (see m. Shab 7.2, cited in Chapter 1). Yet it also provides detailed instructions for the slaughter of the two lambs that were offered in the Temple every day of the week.[34] Similarly, the

33. For a brief outline of the obligatory Temple ritual on the Sabbath, see *Encyclopaedia Judaica*, 15:997.
34. Compare m. Shab 7.2 with m. Tam 3.4.

tannaitic commentary on the book of Numbers notes that the Penta-teuchal command for the morning and evening daily sacrifice of a lamb within the Temple precincts (see Num 28:8-9) took precedence over (דוחה, meaning literally 'overrides') the mishnaic command that sacrifice was forbidden on the Sabbath day.[35]

The centrality of the Temple in Jewish life means that this clash of ritual was also known to ordinary people at large.[36] Practical proof of this fact can be seen from the ritual known and adopted by ordinary people whenever the day of the Passover sacrifice fell on a Sabbath which circumvented a violation of Sabbath law that forbade the transfer of objects on the Sabbath between different domains[37] by placing the sacrificial knives in the wool of the lamb, or if offering a goat, by tying the knife to the animal's horns.[38] There is thus little doubt that not only the Jewish sages but also ordinary Jewish people were aware of the

35. Sifre BaMidbar 144 (Sifre on Numbers). For the Hebrew text, see H. S. Horovitz, *Siphre d'BeRab* (Jerusalem: Wahrmann, 1966) § 65, pp. 61-2, trans. J. Neusner, *Siphré to Numbers* (2 vols.; Providence: Brown University Press, 1986) 2:21. Other references to the conflicting rules of the Temple and Sabbath law include: (1) the twice-voiced remark of the mid-second-century Jewish sage R. Josiah, in *Sifre*, see Horovitz, *Siphre d'BeRab*, § 65, pp. 61-2 (Hebrew; for translation see Neusner, *Siphré to Numbers*, 2:21), also § 142, pp. 188-9 (Hebrew, no published English translation); (2) the contradiction is mentioned among the five pairs of conflicting biblical statements which, according to the Jewish sages, were spoken *with one utterance*, a phrase which expresses the belief that the whole of the Torah was given by God, and that any apparent inconsistencies should be exposed and, if possible, reconciled by Jewish oral law, e.g., *Everyone that violates it shall surely be put to death* (Exod 31:14) and *And on the Sabbath day two he-lambs [must be sacrificed]* (Num 28:9) were both spoken with one utterance (these remarks appear in: *Mekilta de-Rabbi Ishmael*, Bahodesh 7; see Lauterbach, *Mekilta* 2:252); (3) *Sifre Deuteronomy* 233 (see the translation of R. Hammer, *Sifre: A Tannaitic Commentary on the Book of Deuteronomy* [New Haven: Yale University Press, 1986] 242); (4) Exodus Rabbah XVIII:4; (5) the contradiction is also mentioned twice in the Jerusalem Talmud at y. Ned 3.2 (see the translation by Neusner, *The Talmud of the Land of Israel: Nedarim*, vol. 23 [Chicago: University of Chicago Press, 1985] 53-4) and y. Shevu 3.8 (see the translation of Neusner, *The Talmud of the Land of Israel: Shevuot*, vol. 32 [Chicago: University of Chicago Press, 1983] 102); (6) *Yalkut Shimoni Torah* 196.

36. The centrality of the Temple in Jewish life in the first century CE is often noted by scholars, e.g., Sanders, *Judaism, Practice and Belief 63BCE–66CE*, 47-76.

37. For the prohibition of carrying on the Sabbath, see Exod 16:29, Jer 17:21-22 and m. Shab 7.2 (cited in Chapter 1).

38. t. Pes 4.14; y. Pes 6.1; b. Pes 66a. Presumably the knife was tied before the Sabbath began, as the act of tying was also forbidden on the Sabbath outside the Temple, see m. Shab 7.2.

strange, recurring conflict between Sabbath and Temple law and would thus have understood the allusion in the argument used by Jesus when he responded to the Pharisees in Mark's tale. This clash of mutually conflicting religious law was neatly described by the Jewish sages with the words, 'Temple law overrides Sabbath law', in Hebrew, עבודת מקדש דוחה את השבת.[39] Temple law was thus designated as relatively 'heavy' (*chomer*, חומר, or, using the derived verb, החמירה) in comparison (it is implied) with the relatively 'light' (*kal*, קל, or the derived verb הקל) Sabbath law.[40] In the Temple area, therefore, the only place where Temple law was in force, and thus the only place where Temple law and Sabbath law could both be in force at the same time, the conflicting demands of Temple and Sabbath law always resulted in the overriding of Sabbath law.

E. *The Argument of Jesus in Mark and Luke*

We now have sufficient understanding of the main themes of the argument used by Jesus to the Pharisees to understand the logic of its words.

As noted above, the first part of the argument (*ha-nadon*) is based on the *midrashic* account of the biblical story of David and the sacred bread, in which the starving David and his starving men arrived at the Temple in Jerusalem where they *il*legally took and ate the Temple bread in order to save their lives from starvation. It could thus be said in rabbinic style that David and his companions overrode Temple law, because of their hunger which was a threat to their lives.

The second part of Jesus' argument (*ha-ba min ha-din*) is based on the relationship between Sabbath and Temple law, namely, the fact that within the Temple area itself, Temple law took precedence over Sabbath law. Or, as this relationship is described by the Jewish sages (for example, at t. Shab 15.16), Temple law is 'heavier' or 'more serious' (*chomer*, חומר) in relation to the relatively 'light' (*kal*, קל) Sabbath law.

If, then, a particular permit is allowed in relation to Temple law, which is 'stricter' or 'more heavy' (*chomer*, חומר) in relation to the 'lighter' (*kal*, קל) Sabbath law, it can therefore be concluded that the same particular permit is allowed for the relatively 'light' (*kal*, קל) or 'less serious' Sabbath law.

The rabbinic argument *kal va-chomer* used by Jesus to the Pharisees in the Galilean fields combines these thoughts in the following way:

If David and his companions can override 'severe' Temple law, because they are starving and in danger of death, it is surely reasonable

---

39. Sifre BaMidbar 144. For further discussion on the term דחה see Chapter 5.
40. t. Shab 15.16.

to assume (קל וחומר) that David and his companions can also override the relatively 'lighter' Sabbath law because they are starving and in danger of their lives (*because whatever freedom is allowed for the stricter Temple law must surely also be allowed for the relatively 'light' Sabbath law*)![41]

This argument thus justifies the overriding of Sabbath law by David in order to 'cure' the starvation that was a threat to his life. If we also assume that the companions of David were ordinary men, this argument then justifies the violation of Sabbath law not only by the great King David, but also by ordinary people whenever starvation is perceived as a threat to their lives. The inclusion of David's men in the argument thus justifies the violation of Sabbath law by ordinary people in a situation of starvation that threatened their lives.[42] This shows the importance of the

---

41.   An argument *kal va-chomer* has often been suggested for Matt 12:3-8, but is generally not considered for Mark 2:25-28, for which other kinds of rabbinic rhetoric have been suggested. Thus S. H. Cohon, 'The Place of Jesus in the Religious Life of His Day', *JBL* 48 (1929) 97, suggests that the reply of Jesus is a rabbinic analogy (*gezerah shavah*) and also claims that Matthew adds another analogy with the words of Matt 12:6, concluding with a *kal va-chomer*. See also J. W. Doeve, 'Jewish Hermeneutics in the Synoptic Gospels and Acts', in *Jewish Hermeneutics in the Synoptic Gospels and Acts* (trans. G. E. Van Baaren-Pape; Assen: Van Gorcum, 1954) 106-7. D. Daube, 'Rabbinic Methods of Interpretation and Hellenistic Rhetoric', *HUCA* 22 (1949) 239-64 (255), identifies a *kal va-chomer* only at Matt 12:10-13. P. Sigal, *The Halakah of Jesus of Nazereth According to the Gospel of Matthew* (Lanham: University Press of America, 1986) 131-2, suggests that Matthew combines the rabbinic arguments *hekesh* and *kal va-chomer* with a *halachic* principle. D. Cohn-Sherbok, *Rabbinic Perspectives on the New Testament* (Studies in the Bible and Early Christianity, 28; Lampeter: Mellen, 1990) 35, suggests that Mark uses a *hekesh* (an analogy based on the fact that both David and the disciples are hungry) and that Matthew uses a *kal va-chomer*, pp. 38-9. For Matt 12:1-8, see, e.g., Luz, *Matthew 8–20*, 181-2, on Matt 12:5-6, who refers to 'a kind of *qal vahomer* conclusion', and the remarks of Davies and Allison, *The Gospel According to Saint Matthew*, 2:319. Kister, 'Plucking of Grain on the Sabbath and the Christian Jewish Debate' (in Hebrew) identifies an argument *a minor ad majus* for Matthew but not for Mark. As will be shown, none of these identifications are correct, because the basic form of the argument of Jesus has not been understood.

42.   Reasons proposed for the inclusion of the disciples of Jesus include the claim that the Pharisees must accuse the disciples of Jesus of violating the Sabbath, rather than Jesus himself, because 'the material in Mark 2:23-24 has been composed by a Christian community which was under criticism from Pharisaic opponents'; see A. J. Hultgren, 'The Formation of the Sabbath Pericope in Mark 2:23-28', *JBL* 91 (1972) 42. But such claims do not take account of the underlying, rhetorical structure of the text.

omission of any reference to the role of the priest at Nob, because the latter was responsible for giving the biblical David the sacred bread, whereas the argument of Jesus requires that only the midrashic David is responsible for this act. Otherwise, the midrashic David (and his men) would not have overridden sacred Temple law.

The *basic underlying thought* of the argument used by Jesus may thus be expressed as in the argument below, using rabbinic-type rhetoric and rabbinic-type ideas. This clearly shows that without the midrashic-type changes made to the biblical story of David (discussed above), especially the change of location from the shrine at Nob to the Temple in Jerusalem so that David committed an *il*legal act, it would not have been possible for this argument to be made:

A Rephrasing of the Argument of Jesus
If a person whose life is in danger because he is starving to death may override the relatively 'heavier' Temple law,
it can be inferred that (קל וחומר)
a person whose life is in danger because he is (also) starving to death may (also) override the relatively 'lighter' Sabbath law!

The final verse of the argument at Mark 2:28 is prefaced by the Greek term ὥστε, meaning 'so that'.[43] As was briefly discussed in Chapter 2, this term functions as a bridge between the two main statements of the argument *kal va-chomer*, thereby providing a simple, non-formal equivalent in Greek for one of the technical Hebrew phrases used in these types of argument, in this case probably the phrase *kal va-chomer*. The term ὥστε in Mark thus links (or 'bridges') the first statement of the argument (*ha-nadon*) with the second (*ha-ba min ha-din*), the latter providing the solution for the problem that the argument attempts to solve. No bridge phrase appears in the probably later version of the argument by Luke, an absence which is not unusual in rabbinic arguments *kal va-chomer* in the tannaitic texts (see Chapter 2). This does not mean, however, that the reply of Jesus to the Pharisees in Luke is not also an argument *kal va-chomer*. The omission of Luke may reflect an attempt to imitate the simple style of the language which Jesus used.[44]

43. Mark 1:27, 45; 2:2, 12; 3:10, 20; 4:1, 32, 37; 9:26; 10:8; 15:5. The basic meanings of this term, 'for this reason' or 'therefore', are confirmed by Arndt and Gingrich, *A Greek–English Lexicon of the New Testament*, s.v. ὥστε.

44. See also in the main text below in the story of Vespasian, cited at *The Fathers of Rabbi Nathan* A 6. As will be seen, the argument at Matt 12:3-5, 8 also does not include a bridge, but this is because the argument is expressed as a sorite, for which no bridge term is required. It is interesting that the biblical tale of David at

F. *The Final Section of Jesus' Argument—'The Son of Man Is Lord of the Sabbath'*

The last section of the argument of Jesus rephrased above concludes that just like David and his companions who overrode Temple law because they were starving and in danger of their lives, so also a person whose life is in danger because he is starving to death may override Temple law. But how, it will be asked, does this thought correspond with a literal understanding of the final section of the argument in the gospels themselves, *the son of man is lord of the Sabbath!*—κύριός ἐστιν ὁ υἱὸς τοῦ ἀνθρώπου καὶ τοῦ σαββάτου! (Mark 2:28; Luke 6:5; Matt 13:8)? The answer to this question displays the ingenuity of Mark (assuming he was responsible for the Greek version of this text) and also accounts for the fact that the reply of Jesus to the Pharisees has not been recognised as a rabbinic argument *kal va-chomer*, which undoubtedly it is.

Two important adjustments have been made by the translator of the final statement of the original, probably Hebrew argument that almost certainly underlies the gospel text.

First, the basic phrase 'to override the Sabbath' in the (assumed) underlying Hebrew argument has been replaced with the words, 'lord of the Sabbath' (κύριός...τοῦ σαββάτου), it being self-evident that the 'lord of the Sabbath' (whoever he might be) must, by virtue of his lordship, override Sabbath law. In other words, assuming that the original argument used by Jesus was expressed in Hebrew (as are all *halachic* arguments *kal va-chomer* in the tannaitic texts), the phrase κύριός...τοῦ σαββάτου, 'lord of the Sabbath', corresponds to the assumed underlying phrase in Hebrew דוחה את השבת, 'overrides Sabbath law', a phrase which is frequently used by the tannaitic Jewish sages to justify an act of healing and/or saving life that violates Jewish law.[45]

For the second of the changes made in the Greek translation to the underlying Hebrew text, the term 'David' or perhaps a general reference to 'any person', has been translated into Greek with the phrase ὁ υἱὸς τοῦ ἀνθρώπου, 'the son of man'. As a result, there are now in theory *two*

Nob itself also contains a biblical *kal va-chomer*; see 1 Sam 21:6: ויען דוד את הכהן ויאמר לו כי אם אשה עצרה לנו כתמול שלשם בצאתי ויהיו כלי הנערים קדש והוא דרך חל ואף כי היום יקדש בכלי, *And David answered the priest, and said to him, 'Of a truth women have been kept from us as always when I am on a journey, and [if] the "utensils" [= organs] of the young men are holy, even when it is a common journey how much more [we can assume they are holy] today when there will be holy bread in their "utensils" [= organs]!'*

45. See Chapter 5 for further discussion on the phrase דחה את השבת and Chapter 11 for the symbolic use of the term 'Sabbath' for all Jewish law.

possible meanings of this phrase, one less likely than the other, but both reflecting the two recognised uses of this idiom in Jewish Palestinian Aramaic, from which this expression is probably originally derived.[46]

Paradoxically, the less likely meaning has always been acknowledged by commentators of the text. Thus, just as in other examples of this phrase in the gospel texts, this phrase in the context of the reply of Jesus to the Pharisees refers reflexively to the speaker, in this case of course to Jesus himself. This meaning has been well explored by commentators, and only one example from the many which occur is cited below. This records the words in which R. Judah ha-Nasi, the probable editor of the Mishnah who was active towards the end of the second century, anticipates his future burial and resurrection after death:

תלמוד ירושלמי מסכת כתובות פרק יב הלכה ג

מילתא אמרה בסדין אחד הוא נקבר רבי. דרבי אמר כמה דבר נשא אזיל הוא אתי.

Jerusalem Talmud Ketuboth 12.3

It is said that Rabbi [Judah ha-Nasi] was buried wrapped in a single shroud [that is, very modestly]. He said, 'It is not as the son of man (בר נשא) goes that he will come again'.

R. Judah ha-Nasi refers here to the custom in Judaism of burying the dead as simply as possible, with no coffin or accoutrements, but wrapped only in a shroud. He, however, declares that this traditional lack of splendour that he expects at his burial will be replaced by his final glory when he 'comes again' at his future resurrection (after the coming of the Messiah, according to traditional Jewish belief). His statement that 'It is not as *the son of man* goes that he will come again', therefore uses the phrase 'the son of man' as a retrospective, circumlocutory third-person reference to himself. In other words, according to R. Judah, 'Although I [בר נפש, 'the son of man', namely R. Judah ha-Nasi], a mere individual, go to my burial wholly unadorned, it is not in this way [so modestly] that I will finally resurrect'.[47]

46. For a discussion of the Hebrew phrase '(the) son of man', see G. Vermes, *Jesus in His Jewish Context* (Minneapolis: Fortress, 2003) 80, 170, especially the summary on pp. 81-90.

47. Other examples include: (1) y. Ber 2.8, 'When R. Hiyya b. Adda (the son of the sister of Bar Kappara) died'; (2) when the biblical Cain declares to God, *Behold, Thou hast driven me out this day from the face of the ground, and from Thy face shall I be hid* (Gen 4:14), which is translated in the Geniza fragment of the Neofiti version of the Palestinian Targum as, *Behold, Thou hast banished me from the face of the earth this day, but a son of man* (בר נש) *is unable, O Lord, to hide from thee*. Cain thus refers to himself as a 'son of man'; (3) y. Shevi 9.1, which is discussed below.

The self-referential nature of the phrase 'son of man' used by Jesus in his reply to the Pharisees is stressed by the gospel authors by their insertion of a prefacing remark that interrupts the argument voiced by Jesus in order to announce that Jesus himself speaks. Mark and Luke thus insert the phrase *And he said to them* (Mark 2:27a and Luke 6:5). Similarly, but even more emphatically, Matthew provides Jesus with a first person claim, when Jesus states *I [Jesus] tell you...* (Matt 12:6), with the result that the audience of this text is left with no doubt that it is Jesus who speaks and thus refers to himself. This emphasis on the identity of the speaker and thus on the speaker's identity as 'the son of man' accounts for the close position of these introductory words to the phrase 'son of man'. This accounts for the presence of these otherwise unnecessary introductory comments within the argument which Jesus himself speaks.[48]

But why was it necessary to remind the audience of this text that Jesus was speaking and thereby to ensure a link between Jesus and the phrase 'son of man', especially when, apart from the Pharisees, Jesus is the only other person in this story who speaks and thus no one is likely to assume anything else?

The answer to these questions brings us to the second basic meaning of the Jewish Aramaic expression 'the son of man', which in fact is the true meaning of the phrase in the context of the argument which Jesus makes. This second meaning exploits the impersonal sense of the phrase '(the) son of man' in order to generalise the personal experience of the speaker, and thus also to generalise philosophically on the nature of the human state. In many texts, this meaning may be indicated at the same time as the self-referential use of the phrase discussed above.[49] For example, in the following passage, the phrase is used by R. Shimon b. Yochai

---

48. The function of the introductory words before the final section of the argument voiced by Jesus have been much debated, because, as is rightly claimed, they break into his speech, so that there is apparently no need to reiterate this fact. Neither do they lead to any kind of new material which would justify their presence in the text. For some of the many reasons suggested for the presence of these phrases, see Gundry, *A Commentary on His Apology*, 142-3. There is, moreover, little doubt that these introductory words in Mark were originally next to the final statement of the argument, but have been displaced by the interpolated statement of Mark 2:27b, as will be discussed in the main text below.

49. B. Chilton and C. A. Evans, eds., *Authenticating the Words of Jesus* (Boston: Brill, 2002) 260, claims that the phrase 'the son of man' in this quotation is merely a general term. If, however, *both* general *and* self-referential, the latter is related to the personal experience of R. Shimon b. Yochai.

in an argument *kal va-chomer* both to describe his own (self-referential) experience when he left the cave where he had hidden from the Romans for thirteen years and also to describe the general condition of humankind:

תלמוד ירושלמי מסכת שביעית פרק ט הלכה א

רבי שמעון בן יוחי עבד טמיר במערתא תלת עשר שנין. במערת חרובין. דתרומה
עד שהעלה גופו חלודה. לסוף תלת עשר שנין אמ', לינה נפק חמי מה קלא
עלמא? נפק ויתיב ליה על פומא דמערתא. חמא חד צייד צייד ציפרי' פרס
מצודתיה שמע ברת קלא, אמרה דימוס ואישתיזבת. אמר, ציפור מבלעדי שמיא
לא יבדא כל שכן בר נשא.

Jerusalem Talmud Sheviit 9.1

For thirteen years R. Shimon b. Yochai lived hidden in a cave. The cave was next to a carob tree. [He stayed there] until his body became afflicted with [a skin disease that resembled] rust. After thirteen years he said, 'Shouldn't I go out to see what has happened in the world?' He went out and sat at the mouth of the cave. He saw a certain hunter trapping birds. When Shimon heard a heavenly voice say 'Pardoned', the bird escaped. But if the heavenly voice said, 'Death', the bird was trapped. He said, '[If] without [the intervention of] heaven, [even] a bird does not perish, is it not logical to assume that [this is the same for] the son of man (בר נשא)!'

With regard to both the self-referential and the general use of the phrase '(the) son of man' in the text above, one scholar notes:

> [The argument *kal va-chomer* used by Shimon b. Yochai] cannot function unless both 'bird' and '(the) son of (the) man' are understood as classes of being, not particular entities. The point is that the divine care for animals demonstrates by analogy that human beings are not left hopeless, and Simeon goes on to leave the cave. The genre of being which is described by '(the) son of (the) man' obviously includes Simeon, since otherwise he could not reach the conclusion and undertake the action which he does. But the genre is no mere circumlocution for Simeon, since otherwise the class could not be compared to that of which the bird in the narrative is an instance of the entire set.[50]

In any case, it is obvious that within its own context the basic meaning or truth of any argument or statement—here a *halachic* argument, as will become clear in the discussion below—cannot depend in any way on the identity of the speaker, but has the same meaning or truth by whomsoever it is expressed. Similarly, for example, the statement in science

---

50. B. Chilton et al., *A Comparative Handbook to the Gospel of Mark* (Leiden: Brill, 2010) 533-4.

which claims that any two objects in the universe exert a mutual gravitational force has exactly the same meaning whether it was voiced by Isaac Newton or Marilyn Monroe (although of course the level of authority granted to each speaker would not be the same). Similarly, as far as the argument of Jesus is concerned, the fact that the identity of the speaker who voices the last section of the argument is so heavily laboured in the synoptic texts, is irrelevant to the overall meaning of the argument itself, which objectively justifies the violation of Sabbath law in order to prevent people from starving to death. In other words, in the context of the gospel argument itself, the phrase 'the son of man' must make sense within the argument itself, *irrespective and regardless of the identity of the person by whom it is expressed.* If this were not the case, the claim that the phrase 'the son of man' refers only to Jesus would mean that this section of the argument—*ha-ba min ha-din*—which serves as its conclusion, would be detached from the first section of the argument—*ha-nadon*—so that the argument itself would have no conclusion at all. But the lack of recognition of the rhetorical structure of the argument of Jesus as an argument *kal va-chomer*, which results in the detachment of the final part of the argument, combined with the strong semantic link between Jesus and the phrase 'son of man', means that this separation has been assumed, so that most commentaries claim that Mark 2:28 (and the parallel texts) is an independent statement about Jesus, rather than the climax of an argument *kal va-chomer* which justifies a specific violation of Sabbath law, which in fact is the case

It is clear therefore that *within the argument itself,* the phrase 'son of man' cannot refer to Jesus himself, even though Jesus is made to articulate these words. The question thus arises—to what or to whom does this phrase then refer? As for all conclusions of arguments *kal va-chomer,* the subject of the conclusion (*ha ba-min-ha-din*) must connect in some way to the first part of the argument (*ha-nadon*). The only subject in the first part of the argument that corresponds in some way with the phrase 'son of man' is the subject of 'David and his men'. In other words, the phrase 'son of man' must refer retrospectively to David and his men who are thus, in effect, the symbols for a universal and symbolic 'son of man'. This means that in the Greek version of the argument voiced by Jesus, David and his men (in the first part of the argument) have effectively been generalised by the phrase 'son of man' (in the last section of the argument). As a result, the experience of David and his men in acting illegally and thus violating Temple law in order to save life from starvation serves as the basis for a general permit for any man (or woman) to violate Sabbath law in order to save life from starvation. The primary and in fact the only true function of the phrase 'the son of man' in the argument used by Jesus is therefore *not* self-referential, as is commonly thought (and was intended by the Greek translator of this text), but refers generically to any Jewish person who, like David and his men, is in a situation when he (or she) must violate Sabbath law in order to prevent one or more individuals from starving to death.

In summary, therefore, it is clear that the translator of the underlying (probably) Hebrew sentence into Greek has attempted to exploit both meanings of the phrase 'son of man'. Because Jesus is speaking, as the Synoptists all stress, the phrase seems to refer back to Jesus himself. This, however, is an illusion. As noted above, the main function of this phrase in the final section of an argument *kal va-chomer* is to refer to David and his men, who are the subjects of the opening section of the argument (*ha-nadon*). *Within the argument itself*, the violators of both Temple and Sabbath law are thus symbolically the same.

Is it possible that the Greek phrase ὁ υἱὸς τοῦ ἀνθρώπου, 'son of man', was present in the underlying Semitic (probably Hebrew) text, the language in which the argument of Jesus was probably originally expressed? This is unlikely. No arguments *kal va-chomer* in the rabbinic texts use the phrase בן אדם, the literal Hebrew equivalent of the Greek phrase ὁ υἱὸς τοῦ ἀνθρώπου ('the son of man'). Instead, impersonal references to 'any man' in these arguments are made by prefacing the relevant masculine singular verbal participle with the definite article, for example הלומד,[51] literally, 'the one who learns', העובר, 'the one who sins', העושה, 'the one who performs',[52] and as appears in the thirty-nine main prohibitions in m. Shab 7.2 (see Chapter 1). It is thus doubtful that a Hebrew equivalent of the Greek phrase ὁ υἱὸς τοῦ ἀνθρώπου ever appeared in the argument of the underlying (probably) Hebrew text. In any case, it is also unlikely that Jesus, a religious Jew, would ever have claimed that he had authority over Sabbath law, which seems to be the present message of the final words of his argument, as most scholars note. This would suggest that Jesus was an equal of God, the Creator of the Sabbath, who according to orthodox Jewish belief (at least from rabbinic to modern times) is the ultimate source of all Sabbath law. The idea that any human being has authority over the Sabbath is thus wholly alien to traditional Jewish thought.

It must, however, be assumed that the person who translated the original argument into Greek was aware that the subject of the last section of the argument—in fact, grammatically a double subject, 'the

51. m. Avot 6.3.
52. Both examples from m. Makk 3.15.

son of man' and 'lord of the Sabbath'—functions logically as a parallel subject to the subject of the first part of the argument because this would have been clear from the structure and logic of the underlying argument in its (probably) original Hebrew form. The translator would therefore have been aware that neither the phrase 'lord of the Sabbath' nor the phrase 'son of man' are true parallels for the genre suggested by the subject of 'David and his men'. This anomaly, however, merely reflects the fact that the translator of this text decided to translate the last section of the argument in a way which glorified Jesus, although it shows little connection between the subjects of the first and the last sections of the argument as a whole. This lack of connection therefore cannot be used to deny that a rabbinic argument *kal va-chomer* underlies the present Greek text. The anomaly is merely the verbal price that must be paid for the way that the (probably) original Hebrew text has been translated into Greek. It can, however, be assumed that as far as the translator of this text was concerned, a far greater truth from the argument has emerged. Thus, instead of a relatively simple rhetorical rabbinic argument that justifies the violation of Sabbath law when saving life from starvation, the reader now learns that Jesus himself is the arbiter of Sabbath law, which is the commonly accepted meaning of Mark 2:28. It was clearly not important for the translator of this text that this message now distorts the argument a whole. This means, therefore, that the phrase 'And he said to them...' at Mark 2:28 (repeated at Luke 6:5 and Matt 12:8) is not a later addition to Mark's original text, but was used in order to emphasise a message which the translator of the original Hebrew text probably believed was far more significant than justifying a particular violation of Sabbath law, which was the original conclusion of the argument itself.

Assuming that the phrases 'son of man' and 'lord of the Sabbath' refer to Jesus (as the translator of the underlying Hebrew text almost certainly intended his readers to understand), a further, although accidental aspect of the translation into Greek of Mark 2:28 is the fact that Jesus is now retrospectively linked directly with David. As is well known, Mark claims this link when he notes that both David and Jesus (in his designation as Christ) are identified with the 'Lord' who sits on the right hand of God,[53] an echo perhaps of the Septuagint version of Ps 110:1, which uses the term κύριος for both 'Lord' and 'God'. The link is again made at Mark 11:10, when the crowd cry to Jesus, *Blessed is the kingdom of our father David that is coming*, and similarly at Mark 10:47, where the blind

---

53. Ps 110:1, cited at Mark 12:36.

Bartimaeus addresses *Jesus, Son of David*.[54] Although, therefore, the connection between Jesus and David within the argument voiced by Jesus is only fortuitous—a happy result of the coincidence of the reference to David in the original Hebrew argument and an ingenious Greek translation of the conclusion of the Jewish argument which justifies a particular violation of Sabbath law—the fact that it now connects David and Jesus would almost certainly have pleased Mark, by whom it was probably first made. The message of the final section of the Greek argument may even account for the inclusion of the story of Jesus and the Pharisees in Mark's original text, which is not especially impressive. Unlike other healing events in which Jesus is involved, this particular tale does not end in a description of any miraculous cure, but the disciples are merely justified in their acquisition of food (which will be further discussed below). Moreover, allowing one's followers to eat, especially on the Sabbath when eating is obligatory (so that the Sabbath is a 'delight', Isa 58:13), can hardly be considered as a memorable deed, even if it involved a violation of Sabbath law. The ingenious Greek translation of the final section of the underlying Hebrew text on which—we can assume—the final words of Jesus are based, however, transforms the argument used by Jesus by delivering a message that was surely significant and would resonate especially with his early followers, namely, the message of his supremacy over Sabbath law. This message thus provides a motive for a story to be built around the argument in which this message is contained. Jesus was then given this argument to express, so that the final message could refer back to himself. The ingenious translation of the last part of the argument may thus have inspired the composition of the story which now exists.

G. *A Summary of the Above Discussion on the Argument of Jesus*

The table below summarises the basic thought of the Jewish, probably Hebrew text on which the argument of Jesus to the Pharisees is based. The sections of the Jewish argument are written in parallel with the argument in Mark, which—apart from Mark 2:27, which is probably a later addition to Mark, as will be discussed—is probably the earliest version of this argument in the synoptic texts.

---

54. For other links between Jesus and David in the *New Testament*, see E. Lohse, 'Huiós David', in *Theological Dictionary of the New Testament* (ed. G. Kittel and G. Friedrich; trans. G. W. Bromiley; Grand Rapids: Eerdmans, 1985) 1224-5.

Mark 2:25-28	The Basic Thought in the Underlying Rabbinic Argument Kal va-Chomer
[25] [And he said to them],	
'Have you not read what David did when he was in need and was hungry, he and those who were with him?	
[26] How he entered the house of God when Abiathar was High Priest, and ate the sacred bread, which is not lawful for any but the priests to eat and also gave it to those who were with him.'	If a person whose life is in danger through starvation may override the relatively strict ('heavier') Temple law,
[27a] And he said to them, [[27b] 'The Sabbath was made for man, but not man for the Sabbath]	[No corresponding section in the rabbinic argument].
[28] so that (ὥστε)	we may infer that (= *kal va-chomer*, קל וחומר)
the son of man is lord of the Sabbath!'	a person whose life is in danger through starvation may override [the relatively less strict ('lighter')] Sabbath law!

The discussion above has shown that Jesus replied to the comment of the Pharisees with a rabbinic argument *kal va-chomer* based on a suitably adjusted, midrashic version of the biblical story of David and the sacred bread (1 Sam 21:1-6). This midrashic story recounts that the starving David and his men *i*llegally consumed the sacred bread, thus overriding sacred Temple law in order to save their lives. From this it can be assumed that the disciples of Jesus may also save their lives from starvation by overriding Sabbath law, because a permit which is allowed for the 'stricter' Temple law should surely also be allowed for the relatively less strict (or 'lighter') Sabbath law, in this case the law that prohibits harvesting on the Sabbath day.

The final section of the argument is interrupted with an announcement that Jesus is speaking, *And he said to them* (Mark 2:27a). This phrase prepares the audience of this text for two significant phrases in the second, final part of the argument, 'the son of man' and 'lord of the Sabbath', which seem to refer to Jesus himself. The logic of the argument itself, however, demands that the final section of the argument, in effect its conclusion, refers retrospectively to David and his men. The noun 'lord' in the phrase *lord of the Sabbath* in the last section of the argument thus serves as an ingenious translation equivalent for the phrase in the underlying Semitic text—probably the phrase דוחה את השבת,

'overrides the Sabbath'—which is implied in the last section of the underlying, probably Hebrew rhetorical rabbinic argument on which the argument of Jesus is probably based. The present Greek text of the last section of the argument has thus been ingeniously worded in a way that obscures the original conclusion of the argument. As a result, the final part of a Jewish argument *kal va-chomer* which justified the 'cure' of starvation by an act which caused a violation of Sabbath law has been effectively subordinated to a declaration of the authority of Jesus as the Lord and arbiter of Sabbath law. This triumphal declaration may have motivated the construction of this otherwise unremarkable story of a 'cure', which was then included among Mark's gospel tales.

This understanding of the gospel text thus shows that the three verses of Mark 2:25, 26 and 28 are essential parts of the argument which is voiced by Jesus, and must therefore have existed in Mark's original text.[55]

H. *Are the Disciples of Jesus Starving to Death?*
As noted above, the midrashic story of David which is told by Jesus in his argument claims that David and his companions violated (or 'over-rode') Temple law because they were in a state of starvation which endangered their lives. This story is then used to justify the behaviour of the disciples of Jesus when they violated Sabbath law. In the context of the story in which this argument appears, the use by Jesus of the midrashic tale of the starving David and his companions to justify the behaviour of the disciples must therefore mean that just as David and his companions were starving to death, so also the disciples of Jesus were starving to death. Were this not the case, the midrashic story of David could not have been used to justify the action of the disciples in harvesting grain on the Sabbath day.

It is, however, clear that the details of the Galilean story itself do not confirm the logic of the argument that the disciples of Jesus were starving to death. For a convincing portrayal of starving people in the first century who were forced to eat raw grain, we must turn instead to the description by Josephus of the emaciated people who were still alive at the end of the three-year siege of Jerusalem by the Romans. The scarcity of food meant that these people were forced to eat raw grain. In War V.426-27, Josephus writes:

> …The personal appearance of the wretches [who still survived the Roman siege] was an index whether they had it [= food] or not; those still in good condition were presumed to be well off for food, while those already

---

55. Some scholars claim that Mark 2:28 is a later gloss; see, e.g., Taylor, *The Gospel According to Mark*, 220.

emaciated were passed over, as it seemed senseless to kill persons so soon to die of starvation... Many [of those besieged in Jerusalem] clandestinely bartered their possessions for a single measure of wheat, if they were rich, or barley if they were poor; then shutting themselves up in the most remote recesses of their houses, some in the extremity of hunger devoured the raw grain,[56] others so baked it as fear and necessity dictated.

There is little doubt that Josephus refers here to a most unusual situation in which starving individuals were deprived of any food normally eaten by humans, and were thus forced to eat raw grain as a last resort to remain alive.[57] We would therefore expect that if the story of

56. Josephus, *The Jewish War, Books IV–VII* (trans. H. St. J. Thackeray and R. Marcus; Cambridge: Heinemann, 1961) 334, in which ἀνέργαστον is translated as 'unground'; compare Liddell, Scott and Jones, *A Greek–English Lexicon*, which translates σῖτος ἀνέργαστος as 'raw grain'.

57. According to the translation of 2 Kgs 4:42 in the RSV, Elishah the prophet was given 'fresh ears of grain', which Elishah ordered his men to eat. The phrase 'fresh ears of grain' (in Hebrew כרמל) is, however, translated in the Septuagint as παλάθας, literally 'fruit cakes'. The translator(s) into Greek of this text clearly did not consider that Elishah was so hungry that he ate raw grain. The Septuagint translates the term כרמל at Lev 2:14 as χίδρα νέα, 'unripe wheaten-groats', but this is a holy offering, and may not be relevant for human food. Similarly, on the basis of t. Ter 3.17, A. J. Peck, *The Priestly Gift in the Mishnah: A Study of Tractate Terumot* (Chicago: Scholars Press, 1981) 79, states: 'Even unparched, the kernels [of grain] are ready to be eaten', i.e., it was *normal* practice to eat kernels of raw grain. But this claim appears to be made on the basis of t. Ter 10.1, which states, *Heave-offering may not be given from produce whose preparation is unfinished instead of from produce whose preparation is finished...*, that is, with regard to grain, it is not allowed to give Heave-offering from raw grain because this is not offered in its final edible form. Peck seems to conclude that if indeed Heave-offering was given from raw grain (as t. Ter. 3.17 seems to suggest), the raw grain was therefore edible, although m. Ter 10.1 also states, 'But if this is done, the Heave-offering is valid', i.e., even if (in this case) raw grain is given for a Heave-offering, the latter is still valid. This suggests that it was *not* the usual practice to offer raw grain, which in any case was a holy offering, which—as noted above—should probably not be considered in the same category as human food. Apart from the event described by Josephus, there seem to be no other instances in Jewish sources when human beings consumed raw grain. There is, however, one example of a situation when raw grain was avoided, when the biblical Ruth and her companions chose to eat parched grain (קלוי) they had brought to the fields, that is, grain which had been roasted, which breaks down the starches and softens the hard kernels, and then becomes edible for human beings to eat, although they—like the disciples in Luke—had removed the chaff from their gleanings of raw grain (Ruth 2:17). Josephus thus describes Ruth's food as 'barley-meal' (ἄλφιτα), that is, barley that has been cooked. Similarly when Philo refers to basic food and drink, he refers to 'water from the spring' and 'barley-cake' (μᾶζα), rather than plain barley grain (Philo, De Som II 48).

Jesus in the Galilean fields described an historical event, the disciples of Jesus were in a similar situation and would be similarly described. But is this the case?

The answer to this question must definitely be *No*. The history of biblical lands does not indicate that there was a famine in the first half of the first century CE. As far as the gospel story is concerned, the impression that is conveyed on reading this text is that the disciples of Jesus were walking freely in the Galilean fields, with no signs of emaciation or physical weakness that starvation might bring. There is also no reason to doubt that they could easily have reached the nearby synagogue which was apparently subsequently visited by Jesus, where—we can assume—they would quickly have accessed more suitable food (see Mark 3:1 and Matt 12:9). This is inadvertently emphasised by the Pharisees, whose presence in the fields on the Sabbath means that the disciples were within the Sabbath limit (the Sabbath *eruv*) and thus could easily have walked to a location where proper food could be obtained, rather than wasting their energy plucking and attempting to eat indigestible raw wheat. Moreover, if indeed his disciples were starving to death, why did Jesus not tell the Pharisees and perhaps ask for their help, rather than engaging in a rhetorical debate? And why, if his disciples were starving to death to such an extent that they were forced to eat unsuitable food, did Jesus not ask for help from the local synagogue that he subsequently visited (according to Mark and Matthew), rather than embarking on the cure of a man with a withered hand, whose illness is not described as urgent in any way and who could therefore probably have waited a few hours until the Sabbath ended (at sunset) in order to be cured? In any case, why did the disciples not provide themselves with food for the Sabbath on the previous day, as was—and is—customary, according to the directions at Exod 16:22-23. And why, if the disciples were truly starving to death, does it appear that Jesus himself was also not starving, at least in the accounts of Mark and Matthew, although the plural Τί ποιεῖτε in Luke's question of the Pharisees to Jesus (Luke 6:2) may also implicate Jesus in the assumed starvation of his men? Did Jesus in the accounts of Mark and Matthew have food that he did not share with his men?

The lack of such details in the gospel tale combined with the relaxed, almost sunny atmosphere in the story itself provides ample material for commentators to deny that the disciples of Jesus were starving to death. But as was noted in detail above, the starvation of the disciples is an essential fact of the story because it is implied by the logic of the argument used by Jesus to justify the violation by his disciples of Sabbath law.[58] For just as the life of David and his companions was threatened by their starvation, which they rightly 'cured' by violating Jewish law (in this case, Temple law), so also the lives of the disciples were threatened by starvation, which they also rightly 'cured' by violating Jewish law, in this case Sabbath law. The starvation of the disciples of Jesus may therefore be denied because it is not specifically described. On the other hand, commentators cannot deny the logic of Jesus' argument to justify the behaviour of his disciples when they violated Sabbath law, which relies on the analogy with the story of David and his men, who like the disciples were starving to death, and violated Temple law. The individuals chosen by the author of the story to violate the Sabbath in this context were the disciples of Jesus, and the specific Sabbath violation chosen was that of harvesting grain, so that food would be obtained for their starvation to be 'cured'.

The facts of the story and the atmosphere generated in the story as a whole therefore do not confirm that the disciples of Jesus were starving to death and therefore forced to eat food which is otherwise only eaten by humans when they are in a desperately starving state. It is therefore not surprising that the gospel authors do not draw attention to this fact, which would have highlighted the awkward discrepancy in their story between logic of the argument and the situation in the tale. As a result, commentators may therefore vigorously deny the starvation of the disciples because, *as they rightly observe*, there is no verbal evidence of starvation within the story itself. Mark does not even mention that the disciples of Jesus were hungry and ate raw grain, leaving these vital facts to be assumed—for why otherwise would the disciples have violated the Sabbath by harvesting grain on the Sabbath day? He, however, attempts some realism with his claim that the grain plucked by the disciples was wheat, the main cereal crop in biblical lands in the first century CE. An alternative crop that the disciples could have plucked was barley, the second most common crop in biblical lands in the first century CE.

---

58. Some scholars have noted the link between the starvation of David and his men and that of the disciples. Thus H. B. Swete, *The Gospel According to St Mark* (3rd edn; London: Macmillan, 1909) 48, notes that 'David and his men find their counterpart in the Son of David and His disciples'. Similarly, Meier, *A Marginal Jew*, 4:271, comments that '[There is] a pattern of distinction-yet-connection between the leader and his followers (Jesus and his disciples) that is taken up in the scriptural narrative (David and those with him)'. Others, however, disagree, probably because they have not understood the argument used by Jesus; see, e.g., Gundry, *A Commentary on His Apology*, 141, who claims that '...*the need, hunger and action of David and his companions correspond to the disciples plucking ears of grain, not to any need, hunger and action of Jesus*'.

Barley as food for humans was, however, considered to be inferior to wheat.[59] It would thus be easier for Mark's audience to believe (even if only subconsciously) that the disciples ate raw grains of wheat rather than raw grains of barely, which thus accounts for the fact that the disciples plucked wheat.[60] It seems, however, that this was not sufficient to satisfy the questions that arose from the audience of Mark's text, so that Matthew and Luke, who were almost certainly responding to queries about the strange food of the disciples implied by Mark, provided further information, although only of the most minimal kind, because they too (like Mark) must have been aware of this serious flaw in the reality of the tale. Luke therefore notes briefly that the disciples ate the grain which they had first de-husked, presumably to imply that de-husked grain was acceptable for humans to eat (Luke 6:1). Matthew goes further and actually states that the disciples were hungry (Matt 12:1), thus *almost* conceding that they were starving to death.

The lack of specific evidence of the starvation of the disciples, even in Matthew, cannot however be used by commentators to deny the necessity for the starvation of the disciples. As noted above, the starvation of the disciples must be assumed by the audience of this tale, *despite the total lack of evidence that this was the case.*

I. *Implications of the Midrashic-type Nature of the Galilean Tale*
The unbridgeable discrepancy between (a) the logic of the story which requires that the disciples of Jesus were starving to death and (b) the lack of evidence for such a situation in the story, points to the conclusion that the story of Jesus and the Pharisees does not record an historical event. It is instead a fictional composition, composed in the tradition of Jewish midrashic tales. 'Midrash' is a general term for ancient Jewish exegesis, often linked loosely with a Jewish holy text, which aims to portray a truth of some kind which accords with the principles of Jewish thought.[61] This genre is best understood by some familiarity with examples from

59.   Barley was considered inferior to wheat because it has a lower gluten content and therefore does not rise well, its meal tastes bad and it is difficult to digest; see M. Broshi, *Bread, Wine, Walls and Scrolls* (Sheffield: Sheffield Academic, 2001) 124-5.

60.   It is often claimed that the reference to wheat at Mark 2:21 indicates that the event took place when the grains of wheat were almost ripe, before the wheat harvest took place; for instance, Gundry, *A Commentary on His Apology*, 145, claims that because the disciples plucked wheat, the event took place 'around May or June'. This of course may be the case, but only in a midrashic, non-historical sense.

61.   For an overview of the subject of rabbinic midrash, see n. 24.

the Jewish texts. The midrashic version of the biblical story of David at Nob has been discussed above, and two other examples follow below. Both are taken from *Avot de-Rabbi Nathan* (*The Fathers of Rabbi Nathan*), a commentary on the tractate in the Mishnah *Pirkei Avot* ('Ethics of the Fathers'), which includes material that dates back to the first century CE.[62] Like the story of Jesus in the Galilean fields, both of these stories are based on historical characters from the first century CE and each also ends with an argument *kal va-chomer*, which summarises the significance of the story as a whole. The first of these tales recounts how R. Akiva was inspired to begin a study of Judaism when he was forty years old:

The Fathers of Rabbi Nathan A 6
What were the beginnings of R. Akiva?
It is said: When he was forty years of age he had not yet studied a thing. One time he stood by the mouth of a well. 'Who hollowed out this stone?' he wondered.
    He was told: It is the water which falls upon it every day, continually. It was said to him, 'Akiva, has thou not heard, *The waters wear away these stones* (Job 14:19).
    Thereupon R. Akiva drew the inference with regard to himself:
    If what is soft wears down the hard,
    it can surely be inferred that
    the words of the Torah, which are as hard as iron, shall hollow out my heart, which is flesh and blood!

The second of these midrashic stories features the Roman general Vespasian, who destroyed the Temple and conquered Jerusalem in 70 CE:

The Fathers of Rabbi Nathan A 6
The men of Jerusalem did yet another thing [to try to defeat Vespasian]. [During Vespasian's siege of Jerusalem] they boiled straw [a substance with no nutrient value, but which left traces in a man's body-waste], which they ate. And every one in Israel stationed at the walls of Jerusalem would exclaim, 'Someone give me [even a small amount of proper food, such as] five dates [which leaves no evidence in a man's body-waste] and I will go down and capture [= behead] five [Roman] heads!' After he was given five dates, he would go down and capture five heads of Vespasian's men.
    When Vespasian looked at their body-waste and saw that it did not show any sign of wheat, he said to his troops,

62. Goldin, *The Fathers According to Rabbi Nathan* (New Haven: Yale University Press, 1955) xxi.

'If these men who eat nothing but straw kill a number of you in this
fashion,
    how [is it] [= is it not reasonable to assume that]
    they would kill you if they ate everything you [Romans] eat and
drink!'[63]

Similarly, it can be assumed that not only the story of David in the
argument of Jesus, but also the whole story of Jesus in the Galilean
fields, is a midrashic-type tale, which, as noted above, was probably constructed around an argument *kal va-chomer* which had been ingeniously
translated into Greek (probably from Hebrew) in a way that, *providing it
was spoken by Jesus*, declared the authority of Jesus over Sabbath law.
The argument (as distinct from the story itself) was also based on a
midrashic interpretation of the biblical story of David at Nob, in which
the future king and his companions were starving to death and thus
illegally violated Temple law by eating the sacred Temple bread in order
to save their lives. The author of the story in the gospels thus attempted
to depict an analogous situation in which people were similarly starving
to death, and were also forced to violate Jewish law, in this case Sabbath
law, so that—as is stated in the argument given to Jesus—it could be
claimed that these people were allowed to violate Sabbath law to 'cure'
starvation, because what was allowed for relatively strict Temple law
must surely also be allowed for the relatively lighter Sabbath law. As
noted above, the people chosen to violate Sabbath law were the disciples
of Jesus, and the religiously illegal action chosen for them to perform
was harvesting wheat on the Sabbath day. Finally, it was decided by the
author of the story that Jesus would not explain to his own disciples why
he allowed them to violate Sabbath law, as would be expected of a
tannaitic sage who—it can be assumed—would explain to his followers
the relevant Jewish law for any leniency that he allowed. Instead, Jesus
was made to justify this behaviour to Pharisees (a reason for this specific
audience will be discussed in Chapter 4). This meant that it was necessary for Pharisees to be present in the fields of grain on the Sabbath day,
although such a location was inappropriate for Pharisees on the Sabbath,
since they would more likely be found in the synagogue on the Sabbath
or in the *beit midrash*. As a result, the inappropriately placed Pharisees
were able to witness the behaviour of the disciples so that they could
then be addressed by Jesus with a rabbinic argument *kal va-chomer* that
was originally written in Hebrew and originally justified the violation of
Sabbath law to 'cure' hunger, but was now worded in Greek in a way
that proclaimed Jesus as the Lord and arbiter of Sabbath law. Jesus was

63. Based on Goldin, *The Fathers According to Rabbi Nathan*, 41, 47.

thus provided with a suitable audience to which he could address an argument *kal va-chomer*, which was one of the several types of rhetorical argument that the Pharisees themselves composed and used. In this way, with all its anomalies and resulting problems, was constructed this famous midrashic-type tale—'midrashic-type' rather than 'midrashic' because although it concludes with a Jewish truth, namely, that Sabbath law may be violated in order to save life from starvation, the ingenious Greek translation of the original (probably) Hebrew argument now also expresses the non-Jewish thought that Jesus was the arbiter of Sabbath law, which now appears to be the main message of the tale.

This conclusion cannot be challenged merely on the grounds that other details in the story are probably historically correct. It can be assumed that the author of this gospel tale would endow his narrative with facts that were already known, and thereby make the story as authentic as possible. It is therefore no surprise that Jesus in this tale is surrounded by his disciples in an open place, because this is how Jesus and his disciples often appeared. Similarly, Jesus spoke with the Pharisees, as was the case in other gospel events. Additionally, the phrase 'son of man' (see Mark 2:28 and the parallel texts) which is apparently used by Jesus in this story is also associated with Jesus in other events. All stories, including midrash, are based on a reality of some kind, and the fact that the story of Jesus and the Pharisees in the Galilean fields repeats details which also appear in other incidents in the gospels shows only that the author of the story was familiar with details in other incidents which are also recorded in other gospel tales.

J. Further Implications of the Midrashic-type Nature of the Galilean Tale
The midrashic-type nature of the story of Jesus in the Galilean fields means that this text cannot safely provide any proof that the historical Jesus ever engaged in a discussion with the Pharisees on the problem in Jewish law caused by healing on the Sabbath day, even if such discussions took place at other times. Neither can it be used to show that there was any hostility between Jesus and the Pharisees regarding healing on the Sabbath day. This latter is especially obvious when we consider that the author of any fictional-type tale, including of course midrashic-type tales, was free to focus on whatever aspects of the story he chose. He therefore could have shown true hostility between Jesus and the Pharisees, had he so wished. The sole basis for the claim of many commentators that the Pharisees were hostile to Jesus in the gospel tale is, however, the single statement of the Pharisees when they note that the disciples of Jesus were violating Sabbath law. This comment in all three

versions of the story is however more a polite observation than an accusation or an aggressive complaint. Mark's version of the tale merely notes that the Pharisees asked Jesus why his disciples *are doing what is not lawful on the Sabbath,* which can hardly be considered as hostile in any way. Luke's version of their question is equally bland, although he includes Jesus in the wrongful action of the disciples by asking *Why are you (plural) doing what is not lawful to do on the Sabbath?* This change of person (from third person plural ποιοῦσιν in Mark 2:24, to second person plural ποιεῖτε in Luke 6:2) may only reflect the fact that Jesus was considered as the leader of his men and was therefore ultimately responsible for their violation of Sabbath law, even if he was not directly involved, as Luke implies when he states at the beginning of his account that '(only) the disciples were plucking the grain'.[64] But in whatever way the change of person is explained, it is difficult to claim that Luke's Pharisees are aggressive to Jesus himself. The same lack of hostility in the Pharisees can also be observed in Matthew's version of their remark, which adds only an exclamation to Mark's version of the text, namely, Ἰδού!, '*Look!*', a term which can more accurately be described as an attempt at realism, rather than an accusation or reproach. In short, even according to Matthew's version of the tale (which some scholars claim is the most hostile to Jesus), the single remark of the Pharisees hardly turns the story into a 'controversy', or even a 'dispute'.[65] The mild, polite nature of the Pharisees remark to Jesus can be clearly appreciated and brought into perspective when it is compared with the following truly bitter confrontation between the Pharisees and Sadducees when they dispute each other's laws:

64. Luke 6:1. For the responsibility of a teacher for the behaviour of his disciples, see D. Daube, 'Responsibilities of Master and Disciples in the Gospels', *NTS* 19 (1972–73) 1-15.

65. See Matt 12:2. Increased Pharisaic animosity in Matthew's account is alleged, for example, by W. D. Davies and D. C. Allison, *A Critical and Exegetical Commentary on the Gospel According to Saint Matthew*, vol. 3 (Edinburgh: T. & T. Clark, 1997) 306. Similarly, Luz, *Matthew 8–20*, 180 n. 28 notes that the accusation of the Pharisees against the disciples 'is emphasized by Matthew'. This claim may be based on true examples of increased hostility to Jesus shown by Matthew in other events, for instance, the incident in the Temple in Jesus' last week (Matt 21:12-14) and his placement of the verse, 'For they no longer dared to ask him another question' (Matt 22:46), in comparison with Luke 22:46, which supplies the mildest account, and Mark 12:34, which is more polemic than that of Luke; see D. Bivin, 'Evidence of an Editor's Hand in Two Instances of Mark's Account of Jesus' Last Week?', in *Jesus' Last Week* (ed. R. S. Notley, M. Turnage and B. Becker; Leiden: Brill, 2006) 219, 221-4.

Mishnah Yadaim 4.7-8

The Sadducees say, 'We rail against you, O you Pharisees (קובלין אנו עליכם פרושים), for you declare ritually clean an unbroken stream of liquid'.

The Pharisees say, 'We rail against you, O you Sadducees (קובלין אנו עליכם צדוקים), for you declare clean a channel of water that flows from a burial ground'.

The Sadducees say, 'We rail against you, O you Pharisees (קובלין אנו עליכם צדוקים) for you say, "If my ox or my ass has done an injury they are culpable, but if my bondman or my bondwoman have done an injury they are not culpable..."'

They said to them, 'No! As you argue concerning my ox or my ass, which have no understanding, would you likewise argue concerning my bondman or my bondwoman, which have understanding!'

A Galilean Sadducee said, 'I rail against you, O you Pharisees (קובל אני עליכם פרושים), for you write in a bill of divorce the name of the ruler together with the name of Moses'.

The Pharisees said, 'We rail against you, O you Galilean Sadducee (קובלין אנו עליך צדוקי גלילי), for you write the name of the ruler together with the Name [of God] on the [same] page'.

It can, however, hardly be said that in the story of the meeting of Jesus and the Pharisees in the Galilean fields, the Pharisees 'rail against Jesus' (קובלים על ישו). Instead, they merely note that the disciples of Jesus were violating Sabbath law—a comment that they, as religious observers, were perfectly entitled to make.

An appreciation of the fictitious nature of the Galilean story also accounts for other anomalies that have been noted in this tale. For example, it explains why the Pharisees were wandering in the fields on the Sabbath day, when they might more appropriately be found in a synagogue or *beit midrash*, which thus vindicates the words of one modern scholar, E. P. Sanders, who is often cited in modern commentaries on this text: 'Pharisees did not organize themselves into groups to spend their Sabbaths in Galilean cornfields in the hope of catching someone transgressing'.[66] The fictional nature of this story also explains why the disciples were eating food that was more suitable for animals

66. E. P. Sanders, *Jesus and Judaism* (London: SCM, 1985) 265, repeated in Sanders, *Jewish Law from Jesus to the Mishnah* (London: SCM, 1990) 20, and cited, e.g., by Davies and Allison, *The Gospel According to Saint Matthew*, 2:304. Doubts concerning the historical presence of the Pharisees in this event are also expressed by F. W. Beare, 'The Sabbath Was Made for Man?', *JBL* 79 (1960) 272: 'Are we to imagine [the Pharisees] as out for a sabbath stroll in the country, where they happen to spot the disciples just as they are plucking a few heads of grain?' Similarly, Hultgren, 'The Formation of the Sabbath Pericope in Mark 2:23-28', 41.

than for humans, since the demands of the story mean that it was necessary to show them violating Sabbath law, and the way in which the
author of the story chose to show this violation was by harvesting grain,
which they were then obliged to eat in order to 'cure' the starvation that
was a threat to their lives, and which had caused them initially to violate
Sabbath law. Also explained is why Jesus did not ask the Pharisees for
help for his starving disciples, but instead indulged in a *halachic* debate,
and also why he apparently abandoned the starving disciples in the fields.
In short, there is little doubt that the story is not historical and thus never
took place.

K. *Jesus Could Not Have Composed or Voiced the Argument in the Galilean Tale*

The midrashic nature of the story also suggests that it is unlikely that
Jesus ever composed or voiced his argument to the Pharisees, because
otherwise an historical incident would have been reported in which this
argument was expressed. In fact, as any reader of the gospel will know,
there are no other appropriate events in the gospels when this argument
could have been expressed—the logic of the argument used by Jesus
demands the extreme starvation of one or more of the individuals in the
story which would surely have been a memorable event. There is thus
little point in suggesting that Jesus perhaps voiced this argument at
another time—the argument of Jesus is *not* appropriate for any other
occasion described in the gospels, which points to the conclusion that it
could not have been an argument that the historical Jesus ever composed
or voiced. This being the case, the historical Jesus cannot be associated
with last section of the argument which now implies that he is the arbiter
of Sabbath law.

The fact that the historical Jesus could not have voiced this argument
is also indicated by the Hebrew phrase that is indicated in the underlying
text of the last part of the present argument in Greek, namely, the
rabbinic thought that the act of saving life overrides Sabbath law. This is
the phrase שבת(ה) (את) דוחה, 'overrides the Sabbath law' (*docheh [eth]
[ha-]Shabbat*) which is indicated in the Greek version of this argument
by the phrase κύριός...τοῦ σαββάτου). As will be noted in Chapter 5 (the
detailed discussion would be disruptive here), it seems that the earliest
Jewish sage who used this phrase to refer to the fact that the *secular* act
of healing and/or saving life may override Sabbath law was either
R. Eleazar b. Azariah or R. Akiva, both of whom were active well into
the second half of the first century CE. This means, therefore, that the
argument used by Jesus to justify the violation by his disciples of

Sabbath law could not have been composed in the first half of the first century, when Jesus was alive, but was composed at least thirty to forty years after Jesus had died.

L. *Did Mark Compose the Argument Voiced By Jesus?*

Before answering this question, it is important to appreciate that the author of the midrashic *story* of the meeting between Jesus and the Pharisees need not be the same author who composed the argument *kal va-chomer* voiced by Jesus in his response to the Pharisees, which (as discussed above) was probably neither composed nor voiced by Jesus himself. Who, then, composed this argument? Was it Mark, who—in the absence of any other information—must be presumed to be the original author of the Galilean story (the cumulative evidence for this statement will be discussed below), or does it come from another source?

As has been noted in detail above, the argument *kal va-chomer* voiced by Jesus is based on a midrashic version of the biblical story of David and the sacred bread (1 Sam 21:1-6) and it is the midrashic changes made to the biblical story that enable the argument of Jesus to be made. Thus if the location of the event had not been changed from Nob to Jerusalem it would not have been possible to claim that David *il*legally ate the sacred bread, and without the removal of the role of the biblical priest of Nob (the priest in Mark takes no part in the event) it would not have been possible to claim that it was David who overrode Temple law. Similarly, if the companions of David had not been brought into the midrashic event, in contrast with his biblical companions who are only mentioned in the background, it would be less easy to claim that any individual could override Sabbath law in a case of starvation which threatened his (or her) life. In short, the midrashic changes made to the biblical story are essential for the logic of the argument with which Jesus justifies the behaviour of his men.

It is therefore unlikely that the midrashic story of David *originally* existed as a free-standing tale. If this were the case, it would be necessary to assume that a free-standing story was composed which contained the exact changes that were needed for its use as the basis for the argument *kal va-chomer* that now appears in the gospel texts. For what purpose could such a story be composed other than for use in the argument it which it is now preserved? Although there is evidence that a midrashic story of David *subsequently* became detached from the argument in which it now appears and thus subsequently became a free-standing tale (see the discussion on *Yalkut Shimoni Neviim, Remez* 130 in Chapter 11), it is clear from the history that is traced in this book that this happened well after the problem caused by acts of healing in Jewish law had been solved. It is thus safe to assume that the midrashic story of David was *originally* created for the purpose of its use in the argument *kal va-chomer* in which it now appears.

It can also be assumed that the midrashic changes made to the biblical tale could only have been made if the author of the midrash was familiar with the details in the biblical tale and that he originally composed the argument for an audience who were similarly acquainted with this tale. For example, the name of the place where the midrashic David violated Temple law—'the House of God'—is mentioned in the midrash because the author of the midrash knew that the biblical name of the shrine was Nob and wanted his audience to accept a different name. Similarly, the statement in the midrash that David *il*legally overrode Temple law by eating the sacred bread is mentioned only because it was known to the author of the midrash and to his audience that David's action was legal in the biblical tale. This can also be said about the presence of David's men, and the absence of the priest in the midrashic tale. In order to know if Mark—the assumed author of the Galilean story—was also the author of the argument voiced by Jesus in the Galilean tale, it is thus necessary to know if Mark was familiar with the details of the biblical story of David at Nob.

The answer to this question is clearly *No*. This is evident from Mark 2:23, in which Jesus asks the Pharisees whether they had *read* the midrashic tale of David and the sacred bread: *Have you read* (ἀνέγνωτε) *what David did, when he was in need and was hungry, he and those who were with him, how he entered the house of God when Abiathar was high priest and ate the sacred bread which was not lawful for any but the priests to eat, and also gave it to those who were with him?* (Mark 2:25). In which text could the Pharisees have read this midrashic tale? We can safely assume that rabbinic oral law—which includes midrash—was not officially written down until late in the second century CE. But the author of the story of Jesus and his disciples in the Galilean fields suggests that it was possible to read the midrashic story of David at Nob in the biblical text. This can only mean that the author of the Galilean tale assumed that the *biblical* account of David at Nob replicated the details of the *midrashic* tale. But as was noted in detail above, important features of the midrash are significantly different from the biblical account. By asking the Pharisees whether they had read the midrashic story of David in the biblical text, Mark (the presumed author of the Galilean story) therefore shows that he could *not* have been familiar with the biblical story of David at Nob. Mark's lack of biblical knowledge has in fact been noted by commentators with regard to his reference to Abiathar who—according to Mark—was the priest at the time that David arrived at the shrine (Mark 2:26). In fact it was Ahimelech, the father of Abiathar, who was the priest at that time, as is mentioned three times in the biblical account (1 Sam 21:1, 2, 8). It is also relevant to note that the presence of the midrashic Abiathar is superfluous to the argument voiced by Jesus in the story (as is proven by his absence from the versions of Luke and Matthew which make perfect sense), and thus could only have been mentioned if Mark was of the opinion that Abiathar met David at the shrine. But his reference to Abiathar is clearly a mistake, and shows, as one scholar notes, 'an egregious ignorance' of the biblical text.[67] This ignorance is also shown by his assumption that the details of the midrashic story of David are reproduced in the biblical text, especially his assumption that David committed an illegal act, which was wholly legal in the biblical tale. Even if this could reasonably be assumed from the biblical account (as noted above in the discussion on 1 Sam 21:1-6, the idea that the priest at Nob illegally gave David the sacred bread began in ancient times and has continued till today), still to be explained would be the change of name from 'Nob' to 'the House of God', the latter for a Jewish person living in the first century CE surely associated with the Temple in Jerusalem rather than Nob. The author of the Galilean story also assumes that David was responsible for taking the sacred bread, whereas this was wholly the responsibility of the priest in the biblical tale, as the latter states, *So the priest gave him [David] the holy bread* (1 Sam 21:6). There is also the problem of the companions of David, who arrived with the future king in the midrashic story, but are mentioned only in the background of the biblical tale. All in all it is therefore difficult to believe that the author of the story of the meeting between Jesus and the Pharisees in the Galilean fields could have been familiar with the story of David in the biblical text. The author of the Galilean story was therefore familiar *only* with the midrashic story of David within the argument used by Jesus and *believed* that this story replicated the details of the biblical tale. This being the case, the author of the Galilean story could *not* have been the author of the midrash used in the argument voiced by Jesus, and—as the author of the midrash was also probably the author of the argument—the author of the Galilean tale could not have been the author of the argument voiced by Jesus in this tale.

67. Meier, *A Marginal Jew*, 4:227, and n. 135 on p. 32, provides an analysis of some of the most 'contorted' claims that Mark's reference to Abiathar is essentially correct.

From whom therefore was this argument derived? There is no doubt that it was originally composed in order to solve the problem caused by an act of healing and/or saving life that violated Sabbath law, which, because it was based on the story of David and the sacred bread, was concerned with the specific 'cure' of starvation on the Sabbath day. It is, moreover, reasonable to assume that this religious problem was only a problem of Jewish concern. This can only mean that the argument was originally composed in a Jewish milieu. The rhetorical form of this argument—an argument *kal va-chomer*—further suggests that it was composed by an educated Jewish person, who was familiar with the composition of this rhetorical form. Moreover, as was noted briefly above and will be further discussed in Chapter 5, there is evidence to suggest that the original Hebrew argument was composed either by R. Eleazar b. Azariah, who is known both as an *aggadist* (and thus the possible author of the midrash of David used in the argument of Jesus) and a *halachist* (and thus the possible author of the argument itself, which justifies the violation of Jewish law), or by R. Akiva. Either of these sages can be attributed with the earliest, innovative use of the verb דחה (*dachah*), 'to override', in order to refer to a secular act of healing and/or saving life that overrides a religious Jewish law, which used in the phrase דוחה (את) (ה)שבת 'overrides the Sabbath (law)', which is suggested by a retroversion of the key phrase in the original Hebrew argument apparently voiced by Jesus in its original Hebrew text.

All of this suggests that either the author of the story—probably Mark—was present and heard the argument when it was voiced by a Jewish sage in the course of a (probably) theoretical discussion on acts of healing and/or saving life on the Sabbath day, or else this argument was conveyed to Mark, probably orally, by a person who was present at such an event. The argument was subsequently translated into Greek and Mark composed a story around this translation, perhaps in the way described above, which he then included in his gospel text.

A further, separate point of contact of Mark with either of these Jewish sources is also suggested by his reference to Abiathar (see Mark 2:26). As noted above, the priest who welcomed David in the biblical tale was *not* Abiathar (as Mark 2:26 claims), but Ahimelech, the biblical father of Abiathar.[68] It is, however, unlikely that the name of any priest was mentioned when Mark heard the argument *kal va-chomer* that he subsequently used in his Galilean tale. This is because—as noted above—the biblical priest who met David at Nob was ultimately responsible for

68. For the historical Abiathar, see 1 Sam 22:20; 2 Sam 8:17.

the *biblical* David's possession of the sacred bread, whereas the responsibility for taking the holy bread in the *midrashic* story can only be that of David alone. This is not only because the priest at Nob was entitled to eat the sacred bread (because he was a priest) and thus could not have committed an illegal act, but because the priest was not starving and in danger of his life, and therefore had no reason to violate Temple law. A reference to a priest in the argument *kal va-chomer* voiced by Jesus would therefore be pointless and could potentially invalidate the claim that it was David (and his companions) who overrode Temple law (which, according to the argument used by Jesus, ultimately gave anyone the right, in a case of starvation, to override Sabbath law). For these reasons, therefore, it is not likely that the name of any priest was mentioned during the discussions of the Jewish sages on the argument *kal va-chomer* which was subsequently heard or relayed to Mark. It is possible therefore that Mark had more than one contact with educated Jews, one when he learnt of the argument which he subsequently translated into Greek and gave to Jesus to express, and a second when the priest Abiathar was discussed.

The lack of necessity to include Abiathar in the argument further suggests that Mark genuinely assumed that a Temple existed in Jerusalem when David was alive, where a man called Abiathar acted as high priest, and where David and his companions *il*legally consumed the sacred bread. What is more, Mark seems to assume that these details were recorded in the biblical text. If so, it is unlikely that Mark referred to the name of Abiathar in order to reinforce the midrashic impression that David visited the Temple at Jerusalem rather than Nob.

It seems, moreover, that the absence of the priest in the versions of Luke or Matthew has nothing to do with their knowledge that Abiathar was not the name of the priest who met David at Nob. More likely they omitted any reference to a priest because—as noted above—the priest is superfluous to the midrashic tale. In fact, as noted above, he should not be included because it is the midrashic David, not the priest, who is responsible for the violation of Temple law, although this would not have been known to those who were not familiar with the biblical tale. This lack of knowledge can be assumed for Matthew and Luke from the fact that just as in the version of the story by Mark, these two authors also suggest that the Pharisees could read the midrashic story of David in the biblical text (see Luke 6:3 and Matt 12:3). If, however, Luke and Matthew had realised that Mark's reference to Abiathar was incorrect, it can also be assumed that they would also have realised that the Pharisees could not have read the midrashic story of David in the biblical text, and would therefore not have repeated Mark's suggestion in their own versions of the tale. In fact, they repeat the mistake of Mark.

To summarise: there is little doubt that Mark did not compose either the midrashic version of the story of David at Nob used in the argument that he gave to Jesus to voice in his Galilean tale, and neither did he compose the argument itself in which this midrashic story has been preserved. It is likely that this argument was ultimately derived from educated Jews, probably from a Pharisaic or rabbinic source. It seems that the argument given to Jesus by Mark existed in Jewish circles before it was used by Mark. If Mark's gospel was published in the late 60s or early 70s CE, as most scholars suggest, it can thus be assumed that the argument existed in Jewish circles at this time. The suggestion of Mark that the Pharisees were able to read the midrashic version of the story of David (Mark 2:25) used in the argument further suggests that Mark had not read or heard the biblical text of the story of David at Nob, a fact that is confirmed by his reference to Abiathar, rather than Achimelech, whom Mark claims was the priest at the shrine when David arrived. Mark's use of an argument which was probably originally composed in a Pharisaic setting, as well as his mistaken reference to Abiathar, further suggest that Mark had at least two separate contacts with educated Jews.

The repetition of Mark's claim by Luke and Matthew that the Pharisees could have read the midrashic story of David in the biblical text further suggests that Luke and Matthew, like Mark, were also unfamiliar with details of the biblical text of the story of David at Nob. Assuming that their accounts of the Galilean tale are ultimately dependent on Mark, the omission of these authors to any reference to Abiathar in the argument voiced by Jesus can then be explained by the simple fact that he is superfluous to the argument and thus need not be mentioned in their versions of the tale.

M. *Mark 2:27 Is an Interpolated Verse*

Mark's version of the argument voiced by Jesus to the Pharisees includes the following famous chiastic remark which is cited and translated *literally* below:

Mark 2:27:

τὸ σάββατον διὰ τὸν ἄνθρωπον ἐγένετο καὶ οὐκ ὁ ἄνθρωπος διὰ τόν σάββατον.

The Sabbath became for the sake of man and not man for the sake of the Sabbath.

It is, however, clear that the above *literal* translation does not make sense. This has given rise to more interpretive translations, such as that of the King James Version, which reads:

> The Sabbath was made for man, and not man for the Sabbath.

This declaration has aroused much debate. Why must it be translated in an approximate way in order to make sense, as can be seen in the translations above? Why is it found only in Mark, when Mark's text was almost certainly used as a source for the gospels of Matthew and Luke, who would surely have repeated such a memorable remark attributed to Jesus if it had been present in Mark's earlier text? Could it have been added to Mark after the compositions of Matthew and Luke? How is it relevant to the argument of Jesus, in which it is contained? If ἐγένετο refers to the creation of the Sabbath, as many scholars and translations apparently imply (see, e.g., the translation from the King James Version cited above) how is this relevant to the reply of Jesus to the Pharisees when he justifies the behaviour of his disciples on the Sabbath day?

Answers to these questions depend ultimately on the correct recognition of the basic structure of Jesus' response. As was discussed in detail above, Jesus replies to the Pharisees with a complete rabbinic argument *kal va-chomer*. But as can be seen in the translation below, the words of Mark 2:27 interrupt the basic logic of this argument, effectively detaching the last section of the argument (*ha-ba min ha-din*), especially when the latter is expressed in the way that corresponds more closely with the probable underlying original Hebrew text:

Mark 2:25-26:
> If David and his companions can override the relatively 'heavy' Temple law, because they are starving and in danger of death,

Mark 2:27:
> The Sabbath became/was created for the sake of man, and not man for the sake of the Sabbath.

Mark 2:28a:
> is it not then reasonable to assume that (ὥστε = *kal va-chomer*)

Mark 2:28b:
> David and his companions can also override the relatively 'lighter' Sabbath law because they are starving and in danger of death (because what is allowed for the stricter Temple law must surely also be allowed for the relatively 'light' Sabbath law)!

As can be seen, although Mark 2:27 lies within a rabbinic argument *kal va-chomer*, it disrupts its structure and sense.[69] However it is translated, the thought of this verse does not follow logically from what precedes, nor does it lead logically to the succeeding text. Instead, it disrupts the meaning of the argument and effectively detaches the first section of the argument (*ha-nadon*) from the second (*ha-ba min ha-din*). Its presence cannot be explained on the basis of the claim that it is a comment or decorative expansion of an aspect of the argument itself.[70] It is thus difficult to avoid the conclusion that *on this evidence alone*, Mark 2:27 is an interpolated text. Thus, assuming with a majority of scholars today that Matthew and Luke derived much of their material from the text of Mark, and that they would almost certainly have repeated this memorable statement, apparently made by none other than Jesus, had they found it in Mark's text, we can conclude that Mark 2:27 was interpolated into Mark after the completion of the gospels of Matthew and Luke.

Could this interpolation be identified as an isolated saying of Jesus that was later added to the text of Mark? This is unlikely. Not only is there no textual evidence for such a claim, but an existing and convincing source of this remark lies close at hand. In addition to the singular use of the term for 'Sabbath' in this verse, which is typical of texts derived from a Jewish source, many scholars have noted that the content of Mark 2:27 closely resembles a comment attributed to the late second-century Jewish sage R. Simon b. Menasia, which is preserved in Hebrew, in a tannaitic commentary on Exodus, the *Mekilta de-Rabbi Ishmael*. This source for the comment at Mark 2:27 has, however, generally been dismissed, almost certainly because the Hebrew text has not been examined in its original language and context.[71] The problems associated with

---

69. Gundry, *A Commentary on His Apology*, 148, summarises attempts to group these verses in a logical way.

70. An example of such an expansion in an argument *kal va-chomer* occurs at m. Makk 3.15, translated below, in which the extra, underlined comments in the argument could be omitted without affecting the sense of the argument: '[Lev 18:5 suggests that] if a man keeps himself apart from blood, which a man's soul abhors, he receives reward, [then], if he keeps himself apart from robbery and incest which a man's soul longs after and covets shall he gain merit for himself and his generation and the generations of this generation to the end of all generations, how much more so!'

71. R. Menasia's comment has usually been read only in translation and out of context, probably because of dependence on the collection of rabbinic sources of the New Testament of Strack and Billerbeck, *Kommentar zum Neuen Testament aus Talmud und Midrasch. Bd.2, Das Evangelium Nach Markus, Lukas und Johannes*

Mark 2:27 outlined above can, however, be resolved by an understanding of the comment of R. Menasia, within the context and the language in which this comment is preserved, which follows below:

מכילתא דרבי ישמעאל כי תשא - מס' דשבתא פרשה א

נשאלה שאלה זו בפניהם, מנין לפיקוח נפש שדוחה את השבת?...

(1) רבי יוסי הגלילי אומר, כשהוא אומר, 'אך את שבתותי תשמורו', אך חלק, ויש שבתות שאתה דוחה, ויש שבתות שאתה שובת.

(2) רבי שמעון בן מנסיא אומר, הרי הוא אומר, ושמרתם את השבת כי קדש היא לכם, לכם שבת מסורה, ואי אתם מסורין לשבת.

(3) רבי נתן אומר, הרי הוא אומר, ושמרו בני ישראל את השבת לעשות את השבת לדורותם, חלל עליו שבת אחת, כדי שישמור שבתות הרבה.

Mekilta de-Rabbi Ishmael Shabbatta 1
This question was asked before [the Jewish sages], From where [in Scripture] do we know that acts of healing and the saving of life override Sabbath law?...
(1) R. Yose the Galilean says, 'When it says: *But* (אך) *My Sabbaths you shall keep* (Exod 31:13), the [apparently superfluous] term *ach* (אך) [implies] a distinction [between one Sabbath and another]. [In other words, some] Sabbaths you must override [to perform acts of healing and/or saving life] and there are [other] Sabbaths on which you must rest'.
(2) R. Simon b. Menasia says, 'Behold [Scripture] says *And you shall keep* (ושמרתם) *the Sabbath, for it is holy to you* (לכם, Exod 31:14). [The second reference] to "you" (לכם), [means that] it (= the Sabbath) is passed down (מסורה) to you, and you are not passed down to the Sabbath (ואי אתם מסורין לשבת)'...*And you shall keep the Sabbath for it is holy to you*... This is the verse which R. Simon b. Menasia interpreted as saying, 'The Sabbath is passed down to you but you are not passed down to the Sabbath'.[72]

---

und die Apostelgeschichte, vol. 2.5 (Munich: Beck'sche, 1926–28). An exception is Casey, 'Culture and Historicity: The Plucking of the Grain (Mark 2:23-8)', *NTS* 34 (1988) 15, but there are also problems here; see Collins, 'Review: Aramaic Sources of Mark's Gospel (Cambridge, 1998)', *NT* 42/3 (2000) 286-91. The new edition of Mark's sources by Chilton et al., *A Comparative Handbook to the Gospel of Mark*, may help to clarify Mark's sources, although it is strange that the Hebrew and Aramaic sources are only transliterated. Surely scholars of the text of the New Testament should be expected to be familiar with the languages of Galilee and Judea in the first century CE?

72.   Another tannaitic chiasm is the unattributed remark at Sifre BaMidbar (Sifre to Numbers) 25: כל ימי נדר נזרו: כל ימי נדר נזרו, נדרו תלוי בנזירותו ולא נזירותו תלויה בנדרו, *All the days of the vow of his Naziriteship* (Num 6:5) [means that] the vow depends on his Naziriteship, and his Naziriteship does not depend on his vow.

(3) R. Nathan says, 'Behold it says, *Wherefore the children of Israel shall keep the Sabbath to observe the Sabbath throughout their generations* (לדרתם ברית עולם, Exod 31:16). This [otherwise superfluous phrase] implies that we should violate one Sabbath [by an act of healing and/or saving life] so that the person [who is healed or his life saved] will [be able] to observe many [other future] Sabbaths'.[73]

The *Mekilta*, a tannaitic text compiled in the late second century CE, begins with the question *From where [in Scripture] do we know that acts of healing and the saving of life override Sabbath law?* This is answered by three second-century tannaitic sages, who each offer a proof text from the Pentateuch—all from Exodus—which justifies acts of healing and/or saving life that violate Sabbath law. Their interpretations are based on a basic principle of orthodox Jewish belief that because the text of the Pentateuch was composed by God, and that because God is perfect (for otherwise He would not be God), so the text of the Pentateuch can have no flaws. The Pentateuch thus contains, for example, no superfluous words—for if God is perfect, as must be assumed, why should He repeat what He has already said? Any apparent repetition must therefore possess a significance that goes beyond the simple meaning of the text, and this significance is the duty of the Jewish sages to reveal.[74] In any case, it is always necessary to seek out the deeper, underlying meanings of this God-given text. As briefly discussed in Chapter 1, the discussions of the Jewish sages, which are usually based around the holy written texts, are known as 'the oral law'. In the passage above, R. Yose the Galilean claims that the apparently superfluous term אך ('but') in Exod 31:13 implies that some Sabbaths should be violated by the 'work' of healing and/or saving life, while others should be considered as normal Sabbath days, when no 'work' is performed. Similarly, R. Nathan claims the same meaning for the phrase 'throughout their generations' in Exod 31:16, which repeats the essence of the phrase 'the children of Israel' and means that the children of Israel—referring to the Jewish people—must perform acts of healing and/or saving life on one Sabbath in order that they will be alive to keep subsequent Sabbath days.

73. For text and translation, see Lauterbach, *Mekilta*, 3:197-8, Shab 1.
74. This hermeneutic may have originated from Nahum of Gizmo, the teacher of R. Akiva, to whom it is attributed at b. BB 138b; see Mielziner, *Introduction to the Talmud*, 125-6. For an analysis of the argument, see Yadin, *Scripture as Logos* (Philadelphia: University of Pennsylvania Press, 2004) 52-3, on Sifre Numbers 143, which interprets the reason given by the Jewish sages for the repetition of 'the second lamb' in Num 28:3-8.

The comment of R. Menasia is based on the two references to 'you' in Exod 31:14. The first of these is the subject of the verb ושמרתם, '*You shall keep*', in which the plural term 'you' is indicated by the ending of the Hebrew verb (תם-). The second reference to 'you' appears in the suffix of the inflected Hebrew preposition ל-כם meaning 'to-you'. This raises the (unspoken) rabbinic question, 'Why does the text of Exod 31:14 state that *YOU will keep the Sabbath* and then, apparently pleonastically, state that *the Sabbath is holy "to YOU"*, since—it could be argued—if *YOU*—the Jewish people—keep the Sabbath, it surely follows that it is holy to-*YOU!*' R. Menasia claims that the first 'you' is addressed to the Jewish people who keep the laws of the Sabbath, because the Sabbath has been 'transmitted' (מסורה, literally, 'it is transmitted') to the Jewish people. The second reference to 'you' refers to the fact that 'you'—again referring to the Jewish people—have not been 'transmitted' (אין מסורין) to the Sabbath. In other words, the Jewish people are in charge of the Sabbath, rather than the reverse, which means—R. Menasia implies—that the Jewish people may decide to allow acts of healing and/or saving life to take place on the Sabbath, despite the unavoidable violation of Sabbath law. It is clear that the comment of R. Menasia is not a simple free-standing remark, but one based on his interpretation of Exod 31:14, which thus gives his comment a reason to exist. In other words, his comment can only be appreciated if it is understood as an interpretation of Exod 31:14. This, however, is far from the case when the interpretation is presented in a completely new context and as a free-standing remark, as it now appears in Mark's text, which accounts for the fact that the sentence in Mark is not related to its surrounding text.

Final proof of the Hebrew origin of Mark 2:27 is the Greek translation of the verb מסר in the comment of R. Menasia. Within the comment of R. Menasia, this verb refers to the orthodox Jewish belief concerning the historical transmission of the Jewish oral law, including of course Sabbath law, from one generation to another, as is stated in rabbinic fashion using this verb:

Mishnah Avot 1.1
Moses received the [oral] Law from Sinai *and passed it down* (ומסרה) to Joshua and Joshua to the Elders, and the Elders to the prophets and the prophets *passed it down* (ומסרוה) to the men of the Great Assembly…[75]

The action of a transmission of any kind, corresponding with the verb מסר (perhaps with the verb παραδιδόναι, 'to pass over to another'), would

---

75. For a definition of מסר, see Jastrow, *Dictionary of the Targumim*, ad loc.

not however be appropriate in the context of Mark's text. On the other hand, a verb such as 'he created' (e.g. ἐποίησεν, Gen 1:1), although it makes sense when Mark 2:27 is isolated from its context (see the above non-literal translation of Mark 2:27 in the opening section of this discussion), is not suitable within the context of Mark 2:26-28. This is because it gives the impression that the text relates to the creation of the Sabbath, which is irrelevant to the content of the reply of Jesus to the Pharisees, in which Jesus justifies the Sabbath actions of his men. This fact has not however prevented some scholars from making this claim.[76] Accordingly, with such alternatives dismissed, the translator into Greek of R. Menasia's remark opted for a simple, apparently neutral term to translate the verb מסר, namely, the verb γίνομαι, in the form ἐγένετο, which thus accounts for the presence of this term in Mark's text. But as a result, this verb in this context cannot be translated with the usual meaning 'to become' or 'to be'—a meaning it takes elsewhere over fifty times in Mark—but must instead be rendered in a way that suggests 'was made' or 'was created', or even 'was given', terms whose literal semantic equivalent in Greek were rejected by the translator into Greek of the original Hebrew text.[77] The verb γίνομαι, in the form ἐγένετο, thus reflects an attempt to find a suitable translation for the verb מסר in the comment of R. Menasia which would enable his interpretation of Exod 31:14 to exist as a free-standing comment in Greek and could be inserted into Mark's text. The verb γίνομαι is thus a commendable, though misleading, translation for the Hebrew verb מסר. The difficult use of the verb ἐγένετο at Mark 2:27 is therefore evidence in itself that Mark 2:27 is a translation, and the existence of the interpretation of

76. See, e.g., C. S. Mann, *Mark: A New Translation Introduction and Commentary* (AB 27; Garden City: Doubleday, 1986) 239; Guelich, *Mark 1–8:26*, 124, who gives a brief history of the interpretation of this verse on p. 123; Gundry, *A Commentary on His Apology*, 148.

77. Commentators who have not taken account of the underlying Hebrew text include Guelich, *Mark 1–8:26*, 123-5, who suggests that ἐγένετο highlights that 'the sabbath was created for the benefit of the human creator, and as God's created gift stands at the service of humanity', although he then notes that this understanding 'begs the question of the disciples conduct, if indeed one is to take the sabbath seriously'. Similarly, Gundry, *A Commentary on His Apology*, 142, translates Mark 2:27, 'The Bible came into being for the sake of human beings [literally, "on account of man"] and not human beings on account of the Sabbath'. J. Marcus, *Mark 1–8: A New Translation with Introduction and Commentary* (AB 27; New York: Doubleday, 2000) 245, claims that the reference of Jesus to the creation 'appeals to God's intention in creation in order to qualify a Mosaic ordinance', a comment which does not relate to the surrounding context of this text.

R. Menasia, in which the corresponding instances of the verb מסר makes complete sense, clearly confirms this Hebrew source. The careful but compromised translation, moreover, suggests that the Greek translation of the remark of R. Menasia was not merely written as a note in the margin of Mark's text which was incorporated, perhaps accidentally, into the text itself, but that Mark 2:27 was deliberately and carefully translated from Hebrew into Greek in order to make it as suitable as was possible for its placement in Mark's text.

The position of the interpolation—between the present Mark 2:26 and 2:28—which interrupts the logic of the argument *kal va-chomer* voiced by Jesus, moreover suggests that like the many commentators of this text, the interpolator of 2:27 was not aware of the rhetorical form of the argument voiced by Jesus, probably because of the ingenious wording of the last section of this text. Were this not the case, we could assume that his interpolation would probably *not* have been placed within the argument itself, but might have been inserted either before the argument began at 2:25, or perhaps after its conclusion at 2:28. The fact of the interpolation would then have been more difficult to detect, because it would not have disrupted the logic of the argument *kal va-chomer* voiced by Jesus, and it would then have been necessary to rely for proof of the interpolation entirely on the compromised translation of the verb מסר, although this alone is probably evidence enough.

Since Hebrew was largely unknown outside Jewish circles in the first century CE, this suggests that the translation of R. Menasia's Hebrew interpretation and its subsequent interpolation was done by an educated, Jewish-born scribe. Moreover, since Jews were discouraged from even reading Christian texts, we can assume that they were equally discouraged from copying them out and definitely not encouraged to add Jewish texts to a Christian script. This being the case, it is reasonable to assume that this Jewish-born scribe had adopted Christian beliefs and that his conversion took place at a stage in his life after he had learnt to read and understand a rabbinic text. Alternatively, he could have heard the interpretation of R. Menasia in the *beit midrash*. The translation by this scribe of the verb מסר, although not wholly successful, also suggests that he was well versed in Greek. It can as well be assumed that this scribe did not copy the gospels of Matthew or Luke, since no manuscripts of these works include a similar remark.

When was Mark 2:27 added to Mark's text? As far as is known, this verse first appears in the gospel in the fourth-century manuscript of the Codex Sinaiticus. We can therefore assume that the scribe responsible for the interpolation lived sometime between the end of the second century, when R. Menasia was active, and the fourth century CE.[78] This further suggests that texts of Mark that do not include the present Mark 2:27 (namely, the 'western' texts of Mark, including Codex Bezae [D] and some Old Latin versions, a, c, e, ff) are ultimately derived from copies of Mark that date, at the earliest, from the late second century CE.

There is thus considerable evidence to show that Mark 2:27 is not an original part of Mark's gospel, but is a Greek translation of the Hebrew interpretation of Exod 31:14 by the late second-century Jewish sage, R. Simon b. Menasia, which could not have been added before R. Menasia was active in the late second century CE. Mark 2:27 was therefore added to Mark's gospel at least a century or so after its publication, which is well after the time that Jesus died. Unless therefore it is accompanied by a caveat in which its late interpolation is made clear, Mark 2:27 should not be included in any editions or translations of Mark's gospel text. Mark 2:27 could never have been spoken by the historical Jesus, although the present text of Mark implies that this is the case. Further evidence to support this conclusion will be discussed in Chapter 7.

N. *Matthew's Version of the Argument Used By Jesus, Matthew 12:3-5, 8*
Matthew's version of Jesus' reply to the Pharisees, in Matt 12:3-5, 8, like the argument used by Jesus in Mark, also includes additional material. The argument of Matthew, without the additions (which will be discussed separately), is translated below:

> [3] Have you not read what David did when he was hungry, and those who were with him;
> [4] How he entered the house of God and ate the sacred bread, which was not lawful for him to eat, nor for those who were with him, but only for the priests.
> [5] Or have you not read in the law how on the Sabbath, the priests in the Temple violate the Sabbath, and are guiltless? [6-7]...
> [8] For the son of man is Lord of the Sabbath.

Just as the argument of Jesus in Mark and Luke, the first section of Matthew's argument also refers to the illegal act of David in eating the sacred bread, and can thus be expressed in rabbinic style: *Action to save life from starvation is permitted to override Temple law.*

Matthew then refers to the mandatory, twice-daily sacrifice in the Temple of a one-year-old lamb (the daily *tamid*), which took place every day of the week, including the Sabbath.[79] Since sacrifice was otherwise forbidden for ordinary people on the Sabbath (apart from the time when the date of the Passover sacrifice fell on the Sabbath, see t. Pes 4.13), the daily sacrifice of the priests could be considered as a violation of Sabbath law. Matthew, however, states that the Temple priests were innocent, meaning that they were innocent of violating the Sabbath law, because they were merely obeying Temple law. The relationship between Temple and Sabbath law implied by Matthew could therefore be expressed in the style of the Jewish sages—*Temple law overrides Sabbath law*—as has been discussed above.

Finally, Matthew repeats the wording of the conclusion of the argument *kal va-chomer* in the text of Mark, which (as discussed in detail above) is almost certainly based on a Hebrew text which stated words to the effect that *the saving of life, in this case from starvation, overrides Sabbath law.*

The argument of Matthew, which uses terminology akin to that used in rabbinic argumentation, is set out below. The additions to Matthew's argument that are irrelevant for its logic are printed in italics:

Matthew 12:3-5, 8	The Rabbinic Argument Behind Matthew's Text
[3] …Have you not read what David did when he was hungry, and those who were with him; [4] How he entered the house of God and ate the sacred bread, which was not lawful for him to eat, nor for those who were with him, but only for the priests.	Just as David and his men override Temple law [when they unlawfully ate the sacred bread in order to save their lives from starvation],
[5] Or have you not read in the law how on the Sabbath, the priests in the Temple violate the Sabbath, and are guiltless?'	and just as Temple law overrides Sabbath law
[6] *I tell you, something greater than the Temple is here.* [7] *And if you had known what this means, 'I desire mercy and not sacrifice', you would not have condemned the guiltless.*	*Matthew's additions to the underlying Jewish argument.*
[8] For the son of man is Lord of the Sabbath.	So David/men may override (that is, become the Lord of) Sabbath law.

79. For the time of sacrifice of the first lamb, see m. Tam 1.2 and 3.7; for the sacrifice of the second lamb, see m. Tam 4.1.

As can be seen, the argument of Matthew is stated in the following three progressive steps:

Step 1:   If (A) David and his men override (B) Temple law (to save their lives from starvation)

Step 2:   and if (B) Temple law overrides (C) Sabbath [law], [we can therefore conclude that]

Step 3:   (A) David and his men are permitted to override (C) Sabbath [law] (to save their lives from starvation).

This argument may be symbolically expressed:

If A overrides B, and if B overrides C, it then follows that A overrides C.

This type of rhetorical argument is called a 'sorite'. Sorites are first associated with Eubulides, a Greek philosopher from the fourth century BCE, and became popular in the Greco-Roman world from around 50 BCE to 200 CE. The term 'sorite' is derived from the Greek noun σωρίτης (or σωρείτης), meaning 'heaped up', a term which reflects the structure of an argument that consists of a series (or a 'heap') of propositions linked by the fact that the conclusion of each proposition provides the subject for the next.[80] Matthew's sorite is circular—that is, the subject of the final statement repeats the subject of the initial statement. Other sorites begin with one subject and lead in a logical fashion to a different subject at their end. This type of sorite is particularly useful for 'proving' a relationship between different objects or concepts or facts, which may otherwise be difficult to link, especially sorites which begin with a negative entity and finally climax in an entity that is positive in some way. These can be regarded as a kind of game of word associations that has an ethical or moral intent. This type of sorite was a favourite of Paul, and three of them appear in his letter to the Romans, which was probably one of his earliest works. The following sorite connects suffering with hope:

---

80. Latin names for a sorite include 'gradiato', 'ascensio' and 'catena'. Greek names include *klimax* ('ladder' or 'escalation'), *epiplok* ('a plaiting together' or 'interlacing'), and *epoidokomesis* (with Aristotle, 'a building up'). A modern name is 'multi-premise syllogism', in which each proposition is a 'prosyllogism', except the last, which is the climax of all the preceding, logically interdependent prosyllogisms. For a description and partial collection of literary sorites in Jewish and Christian sources in tannaitic times, including references to the technical treatment of this subject, see H. A. Fischel, 'The Uses of Sorites *(Climax, Gradatio)* in the Tannaitic Period', *HUCA* 44 (1973) 119-51.

Romans 5:3-4

...ἡ θλῖψις ὑπομονὴν κατεργάζεται, ἡ δὲ ὑπομονὴ δοκιμήν, ἡ δὲ δοκιμὴ ἐλπίδα· ἡ δὲ ἐλπὶς οὐ καταισχύνει...

[3] ...(A) suffering makes for (B) endurance, [4] (B) endurance makes for (C) character, (C) character for (D) hope and (D) hope does not disappoint...

A second Pauline sorite connects those whom God knew in the past with those whom He glorified:

Romans 8:29-30

ὅτι οὓς προέγνω, καὶ προώρισεν συμμόρφους τῆς εἰκόνος τοῦ υἱοῦ αὐτοῦ, εἰς τὸ εἶναι αὐτὸν πρωτότοκον ἐν πολλοῖς ἀδελφοῖς· οὓς δὲ προώρισεν, τούτους καὶ ἐκάλεσεν· καὶ οὓς ἐκάλεσεν, τούτους καὶ ἐδικαίωσεν· οὓς δὲ ἐδικαίωσεν, τούτους καὶ ἐδόξασεν...

[29] For those whom He [God] (A) foreknew he also (B) predestined to be conformed with the image of His son in order that he might be the first-born among many brethren. [30] And those whom he (B) predestined He also (C) called and those whom He (C) called he also (D) justified and those whom He (D) justified He also (E) glorified...

A third example of this style connects the invocation of a preacher in whom people do *not* believe with a preacher who is believed:

Romans 10:14-15:

Πῶς οὖν ἐπικαλέσωνται εἰς ὃν οὐκ ἐπίστευσαν; πῶς δὲ πιστεύσωσιν οὗ οὐκ ἤκουσαν; πῶς δὲ ἀκούσωσιν χωρὶς κηρύσσοντος; πῶς δὲ κηρύξωσιν ἐὰν μὴ ἀποσταλῶσιν; καθὼς γέγραπται, Ὡς ὡραῖοι οἱ πόδες τῶν εὐαγγελιζομένων [τὰ] ἀγαθά.

[14] How then would they (A) invoke someone whom they do not (B) believe? And how are they to (B) believe in him of whom they have never (C) heard? And how are they to (C) hear without (D) a preacher? [15] And how can (E) a preacher preach unless he is sent? Even as it is written, *How beautiful are the feet of them that bring glad tidings of good things!*

In addition to the circular sorite at Matt 12:3-5, 8, Matthew can also be attributed with an historical sorite at Matt 1:2-16 (although it is rarely labelled with this name), which records the generations from Abraham to the final climax of the birth of Christ. The first and last part of this sorite is translated below:

[2] Abraham was the father of Isaac, and Isaac the father of Jacob, and Jacob the father of Judah...
[16] ...and Jacob the father of Joseph the husband of Mary of whom Jesus was born, who is called Christ.[81]

81. For the first-century influences on this sorite of Matthew, see Fischel, 'The Uses of Sorites', 128.

A final example of a sorite which helps to confirm the form's popularity in Jewish circles in the first century CE is translated below. Like the sorite of Matthew at Matt 12:3-5, 8, this too is circular. In this case, however, it consists of five interdependent statements, which finally connect the negative entity of the lack of proper conduct with the positive entity of the knowledge of Torah. This is attributed to the first-century sage R. Eleazar b. Azariah, who was active in the Temple before it was destroyed in 70 CE:

> R. Eleazar b. Azariah said:
> Where there is no proper conduct there is no Torah.
> Where there is no Torah, there is no wisdom.
> Where there is no wisdom, there is no reverence.
> Where there is no reverence, there is no understanding.
> Where there is no understanding, there is no knowledge.
> [*This proves that*]
> Where there is no knowledge there is no Torah.[82]

Other Jewish circular sorites composed by R. Akiva and his school, also probably in the first century CE, will be discussed in Chapter 6. For the moment, however, let us continue with discussion on the sorite of Matthew voiced by Jesus to the Pharisees in the Galilean fields. It is clear that this argument is based on the same midrashic understanding of the biblical story of David at Nob used by Mark and Luke, and that both the sorite and the argument *kal va-chomer* end in the same way. Why, then, did Matthew change the format of the probably earlier version of this argument in the gospels of Mark and Luke? A possible explanation lies in the fact that the sorite of Matthew is easier to understand because it states all the information which must be assumed for the argument of Mark and Luke, namely, that Temple law is relatively 'heavier' than the 'light' Sabbath law, because Temple law overrides Sabbath law within the precincts of the Temple, the only location where both Temple and Sabbath law were both in force. In contrast with the arguments of Mark and Luke, the sorite of Matthew states this fact by providing the example of the Temple priests who are 'guiltless' of a violation of Sabbath law when they perform the daily sacrifices in the Temple on the Sabbath (Matt 12:5), which is otherwise forbidden by Sabbath law.

Did Matthew himself initiate the improved presentation of the earlier argument preserved by Mark and Luke, or was he influenced by an outside source? This will be discussed in Chapter 6.

---

82. A. I. Katsh, 'Unpublished Geniza Fragments of *Pirke Avot* in the Antonin Geniza Collection in Leningrad', *JQR* 61 (1970–71) 11. See m. Avot 3.18 for a second version of this sorite, also attributed to R. Eleazar b. Azariah.

O. *Matthew's Two Additions to the Argument of Jesus*
Matthew makes two additions to the argument of Jesus:

> Matthew 12:6:
> But I tell you that in this place is one greater than the temple.

> Matthew 12:7:
> But if you had known what this means, *I will have mercy, and not
> sacrifice*, you would not have condemned the guiltless.

The first of these additions has no obvious source and thus seems to have
been composed by Matthew. Stated in rabbinic language, it suggests that
I, Jesus, override Temple law. This statement is then used in the following sorite, which ends with a re-use of Mark 2:28 (or Luke 6:5):

> Just as (A) Jesus overrides (or, just as 'this man is greater than', μεῖζόν
> ἐστιν ὧδε) (B) Temple law (τοῦ ἱεροῦ) (Matt 12:6)

> And just as (B) Temple law overrides (C) Sabbath law (according to
> Matt 12:5)

> So (A) Jesus (or, 'the son of man') overrides (or, 'is lord of') (C) Sabbath
> law! (Matt 12:8)

In the second of his additions, Matthew cites Hos 6:6, which he
interprets christologically, implying that 'loving kindness' is a symbol
for Jesus which overrides sacrifice, the latter a symbol for Temple law.
This thought can be expressed in rabbinic style *the person of Jesus
overrides Temple law.*[83] Jesus thus becomes the subject of the opening
premise of a new sorite which stresses the christological meaning of
Matt 12:8, namely, that Jesus overrides, or is the lord of, Sabbath law:

> Since (A) Loving kindness/Mercy/Jesus overrides (B) Temple law
> (according to Hos 6:6, cited at Matt 12:7),

> And since (B) Temple law overrides (C) Sabbath law (Matt 12:5),

> It can be concluded that (A) Loving kindness/Mercy/the son of man/Jesus
> overrides (C) Sabbath law!

The two additions to Matthew's version of the argument voiced by
Jesus thus create two internal sorites within the main sorite. The inver-
sion of the logical order of the statements of the sorite (in this case,
Matt 12:7 must be considered logically before Matt 12:5) can also be
observed in the tannaitic sorites which will be discussed in Chapter 6.

---

83. Other possible meanings of μεῖζον, 'greater', which are unlikely, are discussed and rejected by Davies and Allison, *The Gospel According to Saint Matthew*,
2:314.

And should the subject of the conclusion of Matthew's new sorites remain unclear, the final addition probably composed by Matthew, *you would not have condemned the guiltless* (Matt 12:6b), provides an allusion to the apparent lack of mercy shown towards Jesus at his crucifixion, thus emphasising that the subject of the new sorite is Jesus himself, rather than David and his men who are the true subjects of the argument as a whole. It seems that Matthew understood that the final section of the original argument *kal va-chomer* referred to the midrashic David and his men, rather than to Jesus, and thus, in a situation of danger to life caused by starvation, justified the violation of Sabbath law. He, however, distracts from this basic logic of the argument by his additions which suggest that Jesus is the true subject of the first section of the argument (*ha-nadon*), rather than David and his men, and thereby he adds to the Christology of his text.

The two additions furthermore suggest that Matthew had searched through the written Jewish holy texts to find a passage which could be interpreted to show that Temple law was overridden by an entity that could be considered as a symbol for Jesus. The argument voiced by Jesus could then both anticipate and emphasise the fact that Jesus should be regarded as the subject of the final section of the sorite, *For the son of man is lord of the Sabbath* (Matt 12:8), although the true subject of this section is David and his men (see above on Mark 2:28). He was not, however, entirely successful in his search, and could only find one biblical quotation which fulfilled this task.

P. *A Relative Chronology for the Three Versions of the Tale*

As will be seen in Chapter 4, the relative chronology of the composition of the gospels is important for helping to determine aspects of the first-century history of the Jewish debate on acts of healing and/or saving life. As far as concerns the dating of the publication of the gospels, most scholars today consider that the gospel of Mark appeared first, which was followed by the gospels of Luke, then Matthew and, finally, John. This order of publication of the synoptic texts can be confirmed by comparison of the different versions of the story of Jesus in the Galilean fields. A convenient starting point for this purpose is the fact that the accounts of Luke and Matthew do not include, and therefore, have removed, the unnecessary material in the version of Mark. Luke and Matthew thus omit the fact that the disciples of Jesus were 'making a way' (Mark 2:23) which, in effect, only repeats the earlier-stated fact that the disciples of Jesus were violating Sabbath law by harvesting grain on the Sabbath (see the above discussion on the phrase ὁδὸν ποιεῖν).

Although this omission loses the emphasis of Mark by not repeating the second of his references to the disciples' violation of Sabbath law, Luke and Matthew gain clarity by the removal of a phrase that is basically superfluous and whose true significance might not be understood because it is a literal translation of a Hebrew idiom that refers to the removal of plants. Luke and Matthew also omit any reference to Abiathar, whom Mark implies was the name of the priest who received David at Nob. As was discussed in detail above, this omission is unlikely to be due to their knowledge of the fact that Abiathar does not appear in the biblical tale of David and the sacred bread (as is often conjectured in commentaries on these texts), but probably because the priest is irrelevant in the story as a whole. The omission by Luke and Matthew of a reference to Abiathar, like their omission of the phrase ὁδὸν ποιεῖν, both therefore indicate the priority of Mark, as it is difficult to believe that later writers would introduce extraneous and distracting material into their narratives, especially material which did not add to the message of the tale.

A further indication of the priority of Mark is the fact that the versions of Luke and Matthew include details which answer two of the questions that could reasonably have been raised by the readers of Mark: (1) Did the disciples eat the raw grain that they plucked, as Mark seems to imply, although raw grain is usually only eaten by animals? (2) Were the disciples starving, as the analogy with the situation of David might suggest but which does not seem to be apparent in the story itself? Luke answers the first of these question with the information that the disciples dehusked the grain they had plucked, thus implying that it was now suitable for human beings to eat—and was indeed eaten—if the outer husks of the grain were removed (Luke 6:1). It is, however, significant that Luke does not state specifically either that the disciples were hungry or that they ate the raw grain. Luke therefore does not draw attention to facts which suggest the midrashic, non-historical nature of the Galilean tale. Similarly with Matthew, although he concedes that the disciples were hungry and that they ate the raw grains (Matt 12:1)—facts which can only be assumed with difficulty by the audience of Mark but which are essential for the logic of the story and, as has been discussed in detail above, should in theory be stated clearly in the three versions of the tale. The reason that they are not mentioned by Matthew is because these essential details are also its main anomalies, which reveal that the story of Jesus in the Galilean fields does not record an historical event. It can therefore be assumed that none of the synoptic authors wished to draw attention to these details, so that the version of the story in which these facts are least clear is likely to be the earliest, while the mounting pressure of the questions of the audience of the story arising from its earliest version suggests that the story in which these facts are clearest is likely to be the latest of the three accounts. In view of the proven inter-dependency of the synoptic authors, the questions that arise from the account of Mark and the partial but the most complete of the answers given by Matthew thus suggest that Mark provides the earliest version of this tale, while Matthew's is the latest version, and the version of Luke lies between them both.

But perhaps the most convincing evidence of the relative lateness of Matthew is the latter's use of a sorite (Matt 12:3-5, 8), which makes the argument of Jesus easier to understand in comparison with the argument *kal va-chomer* found in Mark and Luke (Mark 2:25-26, 28; Luke 6:3-5). As has been discussed in detail above, this is because the argument in the versions of Mark and Luke need their readers to supply the fact that because Temple law overrode Sabbath law, what is allowed for the stricter (or, 'heavier') Temple law should also be allowed for the com-paratively less strict (or 'lighter') Sabbath law. In contrast, the argument of Matthew is based on a simple series of interdependent statements, so that no further information from the audience need be supplied. On the reasonable assumption that an argument that is easier to understand was probably composed at a later time than the same argument which is more difficult to understand, especially if the author of the easier version was probably familiar with the more difficult versions of the tale, this again suggests that Matthew's version of the argument of Jesus, and thus also his version of the story in which this argument appears, is probably the latest of the three versions of the tale. The differences in the three versions of the story of Jesus in the Galilean fields is thus in accord with the generally accepted relative dates of the composition of the synoptic gospels themselves.

Q. Why Did the Disciples 'Pluck' Rather Than 'Harvest' the Grain? And Why Did They 'De-husk the Grain with Their Hands' Rather Than (Simply) 'De-husking' the Grain?

As has been repeatedly noted above, acts of healing and/or saving life performed on the Sabbath inevitably cause a violation of Sabbath law. It can therefore be expected that those by whom acts of healing and/or saving life were permitted would attempt to minimise their permitted violations of Jewish law. This can be seen in the first recorded permit of this kind, namely, the edict of Mattathias published in 167 BCE, which allowed fighting on the Sabbath, but limited this fighting to self-defence (see Chapter 1).

The principle itself is usually taken for granted and thus not openly stated in the rabbinic texts. A rare statement of this intention is, however, preserved in the following directive from the Tosefta in which this principle is expressed with the phrase הקל הקל, literally, 'the lightest [of] the lightest [violation of Jewish law]'. This phrase is used in the introduction to a sorite which provides an example of such a consideration by grading four forbidden foods in descending order of the degree of violation that they cause in Jewish law, thus showing how to limit the offence caused in Jewish law if the 'cure' of starvation is limited to these four forbidden foods:

תוספתא מסכת יומא (כפורים) פרק ד הלכה ד
מי שאחזו בולמוס מאכילין אותו הקל הקל.
כיצד? היו לפניו טבל ושביעית מאכילין אותו שביעית.
טבל ונבלה מאכילין אותו נבלה.
נבלה ותרומה מאכילי' אותו תרומה.
תרומה ושביעית מאכילין אותו שביעית.
עד שיאורו עיניו. ...

Tosefta Yoma 4.4
If ravenous hunger seized a person, they may feed [this] person that which [causes] the lightest of the lightest [violation of Jewish law] (הקל הקל).

How so? If there was before [this] person untithed produce and [the prohibited produce] of the Seventh year, they feed [this] person [the prohibited] produce of the Seventh year.

[If there is a choice between] untithed produce and carrion [they feed] carrion.[84]

[If there is a choice between] carrion and heave offering [they feed] heave-offering.

[If there is a choice between] heave-offering and [produce] of the Seventh year, [they feed] produce of the Seventh year, until his eyes are enlightened…

According to this sorite, of the four otherwise forbidden foods listed above which may be available for the 'cure' starvation: the greatest violation of Jewish law is caused by consumption of food that is untithed, with less violation being caused by the consumption of carrion, and even less violation being caused by the consumption of heave-offering. The least amount of violation is caused by the consumption of produce from the seventh year.

---

84. Eating untithed food may incur punishment of death by God (b. San 83a), whereas the eating of carrion involves the relatively lenient punishment of lashing (b. Yom 36b).

Although the principle of limited violation of Jewish law is rarely openly declared, the principle itself is implied in various ways. Thus the following directive from the Babylonian Talmud allows three gradually greater violations for the cure of a pregnant woman who craves 'holy flesh' (*terumah*, see on t. Yom 4.4 in Chapter 9) or even craves pork, the former presumably on a day when fasting is decreed, the latter a violation at any time. The permit begins with the cure that causes the least offence, when the woman is permitted to suck the juice of the meat through a straw. If no cure results, the woman is allowed to drink the juice of the meat, clearly a greater offence in Jewish law. If even this leniency brings no cure, the woman is allowed to eat the meat itself, which causes the greatest offence of all:

תלמוד בבלי מסכת יומא דף פב עמוד א

תנו רבנן: עוברה שהריחה בשר קודש או בשר חזיר—תוחבין לה כוש ברוטב,
ומניחין לה על פיה. אם נתיישבה דעתה—מוטב, ואם לאו—מאכילין אותה
רוטב עצמה, ואם נתיישבה דעתה—מוטב, ואם לאו—מאכילין אותה שומן
עצמו, שאין לך דבר שעומד בפני פקוח נפש חוץ מעבודה זרה וגילוי עריות
ושפיכות דמים.

Babylonian Talmud Yoma 82a
Our Rabbis taught: If a woman with child smelt holy flesh, or pork, we put for her a reed into the juice (רוטב) and place it upon her mouth. If thereupon she feels that her craving has been satisfied, it is well. If not, one feeds her with the juice itself. If thereupon her craving is satisfied, it is well; if not one feeds her with the fat meat itself, for there is nothing that prevents [the duty of] saving life, apart from of idolatry, incest and bloodshed [which are prohibited in any situation].[85]

The same principle can be seen in directives which allow an act of healing and/or saving life, but which limit the way that the permit may be performed. This aspect of these directives will be discussed in Chapter 10. In the meantime, however, we may note the two directives from Qumran which permit the life of a person who has fallen into a pit (or water) to be saved on the Sabbath, one of which allows the rescue to be performed only with a garment (which presumably was removed from the wearer and used as a rope), while the other specifically forbids the use of a ladder or a rope. Both these directives also forbid the use of an 'instrument'.[86] These restrictions thus limit the violation of Sabbath law

---

85. The Jerusalem Talmud, y. Yom 8.4, omits the intermediate cure: 'At the beginning [of her craving] they roast something for her on a spit [so she can suck it]. If she feels better, [then] good. If not, they give her the actual, prohibited food [that she craves].'

86. See on 4Q265 Frag 7, CD 11:16-17 in Chapter 1.

by preventing the carrying of equipment to the site of the rescue, since the act of carrying outside an earlier-defined area is forbidden on the Sabbath day (see m. Shab 7.2).

A directive might also limit the violation of Sabbath law by ensuring that no action continued after the permitted action has taken place. This can be seen in the following text, which allows the violation of Sabbath law by the removal of debris to rescue a person who is buried under-neath, but further decrees that if the individual is found dead, the Sabbath must not be additionally violated by taking the body away (presumably to prepare it for burial), in order to prevent an additional violation of Sabbath law:

משנה מסכת יומא פרק ח משנה ז

מי שנפלה עליו מפולת ... מפקחין עליו את הגל. מצאוהו חי מפקחין עליו ואם מת יניחוהו.

Mishnah Yoma 8.7
If a building fell down upon a person…they may clear away the ruin from above him [on the Sabbath]. But if the person is dead, they leave him.

Similar examples of attempts to limit the violation of Sabbath law can also be seen in the gospels when Jesus heals on the Sabbath day. For example, Jesus performed a Sabbath cure for a woman with a bent back merely by talking and touching her with his hands (Luke 13:12-13). Likewise, Jesus cured the mother-in-law of Simon simply by taking her hand (Matt 8:14), or by taking her hand and lifting her up (Mark 2:31), or else she was she was cured only with words, after the fever was rebuked (ἐπετίμησεν, Luke 4:39). Similarly, Jesus cured a man with dropsy only by 'taking' him (ἐπιλαβόμενος, Luke 14:4), presumably by the hand, just as he cured many others on the Sabbath apparently only with his hands (Mark 6:5), including the cure of a man with a withered hand, whom Jesus asked merely to stretch out his hand (Mark 3:3; Luke 6:10; Matt 12:13). In a similarly minimal fashion, Jesus removed an evil spirit from a man (see Mark 1:25 and Luke 4:35) by ordering the spirit to be silent, and to go away from the man—the simple verb λέγω is used in these texts.

It can, of course, be observed that Jesus usually also used the same minimal methods for healing on non-Sabbath days. He thus restored the sight of two blind men merely with a touch (Matt 20:34), followed by a few words (see Mark 1:41; 5:41; Luke 5:13; Matt 8:3; 9:29). At Matt 8:32 he removed demoniacs with the single word 'Go!'. Even more mini-mally, it is claimed that he raised the young man of Nain from the dead by merely touching his bier (rather than his body) and then pronouncing the words, 'Young man, I say to you—Arise!' (Luke 7:14). Jesus also effected a cure when his own body was touched by others (Mark 3:10; Luke 6:19) and even when only the fringes of his garment were touched (Mark 6:56; Matt 9:20; 14:36). Jesus also cured at a distance according to Matt 8:13 and Luke 7:10 (and also John 4:46-53, assuming that John records a different event). The only exceptions to these minimal cures occur when Jesus used a medicament to effect a cure—either his own saliva, or his own saliva mixed with clay.[87]

These minimal methods used by Jesus to heal on both Sabbath and non-Sabbath days are of course often understood as evidence of his divine skill. When used on the Sabbath, however, they have the added significance that they cause a minimal violation of Sabbath law, and thus provide further evidence of the respect and adherence of Jesus to Jewish law.

The method used by the Jewish sages to indicate an assumed minimal violation of Sabbath law that is relevant for the gospels is by means of the terminology that was used to identify the action that was allowed. This is probably based on the list of thirty-nine *main* acts—expressed in Hebrew as אבות מלאכות, 'fathers of works'—which are prohibited on the Sabbath day in the list preserved at m. Shab 7.2 (cited in Chapter 1). The fact that only the *main* acts are listed in this directive implies the existence of sub-categories of these acts—in Hebrew תולדות, 'descendants'—which, by definition and in comparison with these thirty-nine *main* defined acts, must therefore cause a lesser violation of Sabbath law. Accordingly, instead of permitting an action described by one of the main thirty-nine *main* categories of prohibited acts, the Jewish sages frequently permitted such an action with a sub-category instead, thus indicating—even if only euphemistically—a lesser permitted violation of Sabbath law. For example, Rabban Gamaliel the Elder, from the early first century CE, avoided the use of the verb כבה, 'to extinguish a fire',

---

87. Jesus cured with saliva alone, or with saliva plus clay when (1) he cured a blind, speech-impaired man on a non-Sabbath day by inserting his fingers into the man's ears, spitting and touching his tongue, looking up to heaven, sighing and expressing one word 'Ephphatha!' (Mark 7:33); (2) when he cured a blind man, again on a non-Sabbath day, by leading him by the hand, then anointing his eyes with his (Jesus') saliva, and then touching the man's eyes (Mark 8:23); and (3) when he applied a mixture of his saliva and clay to the eyes of a blind man, whom he then ordered to bathe in the Siloam pool, which John alleges took place on the Sabbath (John 9:6)—this event is discussed below in the main text. For other ancient references to the cure of eye problems with saliva, see Daniel Sperber, *Sidrah* (סידרא) 25-27, Minora (זוטא), 473-84 (475-78), and *JSIJ* (2012) 1-18 (18) (in Hebrew), http://www.biu.ac.il/JS/JSIJ/11-2012/Sperber.pdf.

which is the thirty-sixth of the thirty-nine *main* prohibited activities on the Sabbath, by referring to this activity with the phrase הבא להציל מן הדליקה, 'the one who comes to save from a fire' (see on m. RH 2.5 in Chapter 8). Similarly, a directive in the Tosefta which allows the demolishing of stone doors to save a child locked in a house, uses the verb שבר, 'to break', rather than the term סתר, 'to tear down', the latter being the thirty-fifth of the thirty-nine *main* prohibited activities on the Sabbath day (see on t. Shab 15.13, in Chapter 11). It is also possible that an allusion to the verb סתר may have been avoided with the term פיקוח, a *Piel* noun derived from the verb פקח, 'to clear away', which is used in the famous phrase פיקוח נפש which is associated with R. Ishmael (which is discussed in Chapter 5). Another example of such verbal avoidance may be provided by the second-century Jewish sage R. Yose b. Halafta, who uses the *Kal* (*Paal*) conjugation of the verb חתך, in the mishnaic directive of m. Shab 18.3 (which deals with circumcision on the Sabbath) rather than the *Piel* conjugation of this verb used in the thirty-first of the thirty-nine main prohibited actions at m. Shab 7.2. One more example may be provided by the use of the verb חמם, 'to warm', in the phrase מחמין חמין, 'one who warms water', or even simply a reference to 'warm water'—חמין—which avoids the use of the verb הבעיר, literally, 'to cause to burn', the thirty-seventh of the thirty-nine *main* acts which are prohibited on the Sabbath day and the same verb used for this strict prohibition at Exod 35:3 (see on t. Shab 15.15 and t. Shab 15.4, in Chapter 11).[88] It seems that even expressions that were considered synonymous with one of the thirty-nine *main* prohibitions were avoided in permits that allow an act of healing and/or saving life. Thus the phrase לעשות פה, 'to make a mouth', used by Jewish healers in tannaitic times to describe the lancing of an abscess, was considered by these sages to suggest an act of building, the thirty-fourth of the thirty-nine *main* prohibited actions forbidden in m. Shab 7.2. As a result, the lancing of an abscess on the Sabbath was allowed only if the action was described with the phrase להוציא לחה, 'to let out pus'.[89] As was noted briefly above, it is clear that such alternative terminology was often merely euphemistic— for example, there can be little or no practical difference between 'a person who comes to save from a fire', as described by Rabban Gamaliel

88. The same avoidance of terminology from the list at m. Shab 7.2 can be seen in the story of the Sabbath revival of Hillel the Elder, who, when he was young, was 'placed before a fire' (הושיבוהוא כנגד המדורה), b. Yom 35b; see Chapter 11).

89. See on m. Eduy 2.5 and t. Eduy 1.8, which is discussed in Chapter 11. Rashi on b. Shab 107a defines לעשות פה as בונה פתח, 'to build an opening'. See also Maimonides' Mishnah Torah, Shab 10.14.

at m. RH 2.5, and a person who extinguishes a fire, המכבה, as described in the thirty-sixth of the main prohibited actions at m. Shab 7.2. Nevertheless, it seems that such alternative terminology was acceptable, especially to pious Jews who would thereby have been reminded that whatever action of healing and/or saving life was permitted on the Sabbath, it should be deliberately performed with the least possible violation of Sabbath law.

It seems that the practice of avoiding a repetition or allusion to any of the thirty-nine *main* prohibited actions was known to Mark and probably also to Luke. This can be seen in verbs that they chose in order to describe the activity of the only other people in the gospels apart from Jesus who (midrashically) violated Sabbath law with an act of healing and/or saving life. According to Mark, this occurred when the disciples of Jesus in the Galilean fields 'plucked' the growing grain, an action described with the verb τίλλω (Mark 2:23, repeated at Luke 6:2 and Matt 12:2), which caused the Pharisees to remark that they were violating Sabbath law. As was discussed in detail above, the verb τίλλω is probably a translation equivalent of the Hebrew (or Aramaic) verb תלש, which is a sub-category (תולדה, 'a descendant') of the action described by the verb of גזז, 'to shear', the twelfth of the thirty-nine *main* categories of work which must *not* be performed on the Sabbath day (see m. Shab 7.2). The fact that the disciples were committing a s*ub*-category of a *main* offence thus suggests that they were minimising their violation of Sabbath law. It seems therefore that Mark—the assumed author of the Galilean tale—was aware that the action of 'plucking' the grains of wheat, which is the action performed by the disciples, would have been considered by the Jewish sages more akin to 'shearing' rather than to 'harvesting' (the latter of which is the third of the thirty-nine *main* prohibited actions at m. Shab 7.2), although it might be considered that 'harvesting' was the action that the disciples performed.

Terminology that also suggests a minimal violation of Sabbath law may also account for Luke's use in Luke 6:1 of the comparatively rare verb ψώχω, 'to de-husk', to describe the action of the starving disciples when they removed the chaff from the grain, presumably to make it more palatable to eat. The usual verb used in Hellenistic Greek for removing the husks from the grain is λικμάω. The action described by this verb is, however, potentially more violent than ψώχω, and thus may possess the potential to cause a greater violation of Sabbath law. This is evident from the more extreme meaning of this verb 'to grind into dust', which may be justified in relation to de-husking (or 'threshing') the grain because this action in ancient times was usually carried out with a large wooden pestle, or a heavy instrument of some kind.[90] Luke and Matthew both use this verb metaphorically and with this violent meaning at Luke 20:18 and Matt 21:44. The two verbs in Mishnaic Hebrew which describe the basic action of 'de-husking' are דש, 'to thresh', and זרה, 'to winnow', which are the fifth and sixth of the thirty-nine *main* actions that are prohibited on the Sabbath day. Either of these verbs may therefore be the Hebrew equivalents of the Greek verb λικμάω. The comparative rarity of the verb ψώχω thus suggests that this verb was the Hellenistic Greek equivalent of a Hebrew term which was considered as a sub-category of either of the verbs דש, 'to thresh', or זרה, 'to winnow', and which was considered to cause a lesser violation of Jewish law. Possible candidates for such equivalents of ψώχω are the verbs מלל or קלף, which are both used for de-husking, but are not listed among the thirty-nine *main* types of action that are forbidden on the Sabbath day. For example:

משנה מסכת מעשרות פרק ד משנה ה

המקלף שעורים מקלף אחת אחת ואוכל. ואם קלף ונתן לתוך ידו חייב. המולל
מלילות של חטים מנפה מיד ליד ואוכל.

Mishnah Maaseroth 4.5

One who de-husks barley removes the husks [from the kernels] one by one and eats [without tithing]. But if he de-husked [a few] kernels of wheat and placed them in his hand, he must [tithe]. One who rubs ripe ears of wheat may sift [the kernels] from one hand to the other and eat.

It is possible therefore that the verb ψώχω was used by Luke to show that his disciples attempted to minimise their violation of Sabbath law. In order to emphasise this important fact, Luke also notes that the grain was de-husked *by the disciples' own hands* (Luke 6:1).[91]

It could of course be claimed that the verbs τίλλω and ψώζω have no religious significance within Jewish law but are merely accurate descriptions of the actions of the disciples in the context of this event. After all, it is clear that the disciples did not use implements of any kind (such as sickles) to harvest the grain, so that the verb θερίζω may not be entirely appropriate for the action of the disciples when they plucked the grain, and neither did they use any utensils for de-husking the grain, so that the term λικμάω, 'to thresh', would also be incorrect. The discussion above has, however, shown that Mark at least had some contact with Jewish

90. For harvesting in ancient Egypt with instruments and threshing (here called 'de-husking', that is, the separating the grain spikelets from the cereal straw), which can be assumed to resemble the methods used in Galilee in the first century, see Nicholson and Shaw, *Ancient Egyptian Materials and Technology*, 520-5, 562.

91. The verb חבט may also describe threshing (see t. Ter 10.3), but more often means 'to press (olives)' or 'to beat'.

sages from whom he heard the *halachic* argument *kal va-chomer* which
he (or some other) subsequently translated into Greek and which he
subsequently used in his midrashic story of Jesus and the Pharisees in the
Galilean fields. Whether or not such contacts can also be proved for
Luke, an effort to suggest a minimal violation of Jewish law would
account for the use of the rare verb ψώζω, and also for the claim that the
de-husking was performed only 'with their hands'. It seems therefore
that both authors were aware of the principle of the minimal violation of
Jewish law, and this knowledge is reflected in the terminology they used
for the action of the disciples in the Galilean tale.

R. *Summary and Main Conclusions*
The main conclusions of the above discussion are briefly summarised
below:

(1) The synoptic gospels record a story in which the disciples of Jesus
were plucking, in effect 'shearing' (according to the *halachic* understanding of their action), the growing grain on the Sabbath, which is
prohibited by Jewish law on the Sabbath day. The Pharisees who were
present thus politely commented to Jesus that his disciples were violating
Sabbath law.

(2) Jesus defends, and thereby justifies the behaviour of his disciples
to the Pharisees with a *halachic* rabbinic argument *kal va-chomer*. This
argument is based on a midrashic version of the biblical story of David at
Nob (1 Sam 21:1-6), in which the midrashic David and his companions
*il*legally violate Temple law. Jesus then argues that if David and his companions can override, in effect, violate, the relatively strict (or 'heavy')
Temple law to save life from starvation, so then his disciples may also
override, in effect, violate the relatively less strict or 'lighter' Sabbath
law (in relation to the 'stricter' Temple law) to save their lives from
starvation. The argument of Jesus thus uses the alleged religiously *il*legal
behaviour of David and his men in relation to the relatively strict law of
the Temple in Jerusalem to justify the midrashically *il*legal behaviour of
the disciples of Jesus in relation to the relatively less strict Sabbath law.

(3) Luke repeats the argument *kal va-chomer* of Mark. Matthew,
however, rephrased the argument as a sorite, perhaps because a sorite is
easier to understand. (For further on this sorite, see Chapter 6.)

(4) The argument of Jesus expressed to the Pharisees was probably
originally composed in Hebrew, as are all rabbinic *halachic* arguments
kal va-chomer preserved in the tannaitic texts. The first part of the
argument (*ha-nadon*) has probably been translated into Greek in a literal
way. However, the conclusion (the second part of the argument, *ha-ba
min ha-din*), which in the original Hebrew argument expressed the idea

that an act of healing and/or saving life to cure starvation was permitted to override Sabbath law, has been translated in a non-literal and ingenious way that suggests that Jesus is the lord and arbiter of Sabbath law. This has been done by using the Greek phrase κύριός...τοῦ σαββάτου, 'lord of the Sabbath', as a translation equivalent probably for the underlying Hebrew phrase דוחה (את) (ה)שבת, meaning 'overrides the Sabbath'. The Greek phrase now implies that the 'lord of the Sabbath' (whoever this might be) must, by virtue of his lordship, override Sabbath law. In addition, the likely reference to David and his companions, who serve as symbols for any person, has been translated with the Greek phrase ὁ υἱὸς τοῦ ἀνθρώπου, 'the son of man'. As a result, rather than referring back to David and his men, the phrase 'son of man' now seems to refer back to Jesus, especially as the three gospel writers stress that it is Jesus who speaks. The original conclusion of the argument has thus been successfully obscured.

(5) The logic of the argument in the context of the story implies that just like David and his companions, the disciples of Jesus were starving to death and were consequently forced to eat raw grain, which is otherwise given only to animals to consume. Both contemporary history and the details of story, however, suggest that the disciples of Jesus were *not* starving to death and neither is it likely that they ever ate raw grain. The discrepancy between the implication of the logic of Jesus' argument and the details of the tale, which give little indication that the disciples were starving, even in Matthew's version of this story (the most informative of the three versions), indicates that the Galilean story is not an historical tale.

(6) The midrashic-type nature of the story means it is most unlikely that the historical Jesus could have voiced the argument in which he now declares his authority over Sabbath law. If this had been the case, an incident that could be accepted as historical—in this case, an incident which involved one or more starving individuals who were violating Sabbath law to 'cure' their starvation—would have been reported, and in which the argument now attributed to Jesus could have been voiced. This is also shown by a partial retroversion into Hebrew of the argument used by Jesus, in which the verb דחה (*dachah*) in the key phrase דחה (את) (ה)שבת (*dachah [et] [ha-]Shabbat*) is used in a way that cannot be traced before the second half of the first century CE, long after the active life of the historical Jesus must have ceased.

(7) The fictional, midrashic-type nature of this story also accounts for other anomalies in this Galilean tale—for example, the fact that the Pharisees were apparently roaming in the fields on the Sabbath day, rather than occupied in an activity associated with the Sabbath, such as

meeting for prayer or discussion in a synagogue or in the *beit midrash*. Similarly, it explains why Jesus himself was apparently not starving and did not ask for help for his starving men, either from the Pharisees whom he happened to meet, or from those whom he subsequently met in a nearby synagogue (according to Mark and Matthew), having apparently abandoned his men.

(8) The midrashic nature of the story also means that this account cannot be used as an example of Pharisaic enmity towards Jesus for performing Sabbath cures. In fact, quite the opposite—even though the author of this midrashic, fictional-type story was free to emphasise any criticism of Jesus, or even to invent such material had he so wished, as the story now stands, no enmity is shown to Jesus by the Pharisees who only comment politely on the disciples' violation of Sabbath law.

(9) We must assume that Mark was the author of the Galilean tale. He was *not* however the author of the argument voiced by Jesus within this tale. This is shown by the fact that the midrashic story of David used in the argument could only have been composed by someone who was familiar with the original story of David in the biblical text. However, Mark's lack of familiarity with the biblical text is shown, not only when he refers to Abiathar as the priest who welcomed David at Nob, but also when he assumes (through Jesus as his mouth-piece) that the Pharisees could read the midrashic story of David in the biblical text even although the midrashic story differs significantly from the biblical tale. It must therefore be assumed that Mark only heard the argument which he subsequently used in the story that he composed. It seems that Luke and Matthew were also unfamiliar with the biblical story of David because they repeat the suggestion of Jesus in Mark that it was possible for the Pharisees to read the *midrashic* story in the biblical text.

(10) The argument voiced by Jesus deals with the problem of the violation of Sabbath law caused by an act of healing and/or saving life, which is a problem that could only have been of any significance to Jews. It can thus be assumed that this argument was originally composed by an educated Jew, either a Pharisee or a first-century rabbinic sage, who was attempting to solve this difficult problem in Jewish law. The likely candidates for this role are R. Eleazar b. Azariah or R. Akiva. It seems that Mark heard this argument via his contact with the Jewish sages. The argument was subsequently translated into Greek and the ingenious translation of the last part of the argument (which suggests that Jesus was lord and arbiter of Sabbath law (see [4] above) may have inspired the story in which the argument now lies. There is thus evidence that Mark was in some way connected with Jewish circles, probably

Pharisees, if his gospel was published around 70 CE, when the Pharisees were still functioning as an active group.

(11) A comparison of the three accounts of the Galilean tale suggests that Mark's version was composed first, that Luke's came next, and that Matthew's text followed.

(12) The structure and logic of the argument *kal va-chomer* voiced by Jesus to the Pharisees at Mark 2:25-26 is now interrupted by the chiastic declaration of Mark 2:27. The interruption is proof in itself that Mark 2:27 was not included Mark's original text. This is confirmed by the strange meaning of the term ἐγένετο in this verse, which must be translated along the lines 'he created', rather than 'he became', which is the usual meaning of this term. This anomaly can be explained on the assumption that ἐγένετο is a compromise translation of the Hebrew verb מסר, 'to transmit', which occurs in a similar chiastic sentence composed in Hebrew by the late second-century sage R. Simon b. Menasia, in which R. Menasia interprets Exod 31:14 to justify acts of healing and/or saving life that violate Jewish law. It seems that this interpretation of R. Menasia was translated from Hebrew into Greek by an educated, probably originally Jewish scribe who had converted to Christianity, and who then inserted his translation as a free-standing sentence (that is, removed from a reference to Exod 31:14, the text originally interpreted by this remark) into the argument voiced by Jesus in Mark's text. As R. Menasia was active towards the end of the second century, the interpolation could not have been made before this time. The fact that it became part of Mark's text well after the publication of the gospels of Matthew and Luke thus explains why it is not present in either of these texts.

(13) Mark uses the verb τίλλω ('to pluck', Mark 2:23) to describe the action of the disciples, rather than a more common term, such as θερίζω ('to harvest'), which is the action that the disciples effectively perform. The verb τίλλω probably corresponds with the Hebrew (or Aramaic) term תלש which is a subcategory of one of the thirty-nine *main* actions that are prohibited on the Sabbath day. This suggests that Mark was aware that those who performed acts of healing and/or saving life on the Sabbath should attempt to minimise the inevitable resulting violation of Sabbath law. It is also possible that for the same underlying reason, Luke used the term ψώχω ('to de-husk', Luke 6:1) to describe the action of the disciples when they removed the chaff from the grain with their hands, rather than the more common term λικμάω, which is also used with the meaning 'to de-husk' in Hellenistic Greek, but implies the use of utensils, which, we can assume, would cause a greater violation of Jewish law.

II. *The Cure of a Man with Dropsy: Luke 14:1-6*

This Sabbath cure is recorded only by Luke. A translation of his account and the beginning of the next event (from v. 7 onwards) follows below:

> Luke 14:1-8, 12, 14
>
> 14^1 It happened when [Jesus] went to the house of one of the rulers of the Pharisees on the Sabbath to dine, that they were watching him in a menacing way (παρατηρούμενοι). ^{2} And behold, there was a man before him who had dropsy. ^{3} And replying (ἀποκριθεὶς) Jesus spoke to the lawyers and Pharisees, saying 'Is it lawful to heal on the Sabbath or not?' ^{4} But they were silent. Then he took him and healed him, and let him go (ἀπέλυσεν).
>
> ^{5} And he said to them, 'Which of you having an ass/son (ὄνος/υἱός)^{92} or an ox that has fallen into a well will not immediately pull him out on a Sabbath day?' ^{6} And they could not reply to this.
>
> ^{7} Now he told a parable to those who were invited while he was observing how they chose the places of honour, saying to them, ^{8} 'When you are invited by anyone to a marriage feast, do not sit down in a place of honour lest a more eminent man than you be invited by him...' ...^{12} He also said to the man who had invited him, 'When you give a dinner or a banquet, do not invite your friends or your brothers...but invite the poor... ^{14} and you will be blessed...you will be repaid at the resurrection'... [The rest of this section, Luke 14:15-24, is summarised below].

A. *The Story of the Cure and the Following Events*

Luke's story relates that Jesus was a guest at a Sabbath meal at the house of a 'ruler' of the Pharisees. It seems that from the time that he arrived, he was watched in a menacing way (παρατηρούμενοι, the same term used by Mark 3:2 and Luke 6:7 to express malicious intent) by the lawyers and Pharisees who—we must assume—were also invited to dine (Luke 14:1-2). A man with dropsy, presumably one of the guests, 'came before' Jesus. Then, apparently while observing (ἐπέχων) how the guests chose their seats, Jesus 'replied' (for no apparent reason) to those who were present, and asked a *halachic* question (a question concerned with Jewish law) regarding the legality of healing on the Sabbath day (Luke 14:3). Luke specifically notes that no one replied (14:4a). Jesus then 'took' the man with dropsy (presumably by the hand), healed him and sent him away (ἀπέλυσεν, 14:4). Jesus then justified this Sabbath cure with a tersely expressed rabbinic argument *kal va-chomer* (14:5) and Luke once again notes that no one replied (14:6). Jesus then delivered three moralising speeches, based on the metaphor of guests at a feast. First he

---

92. Mss. with alternative readings are listed in Nestle–Aland ad loc.

preached against excessive self-promotion, in this case by securing the best places at a marriage feast, since those who behave in this way are inevitably demoted when more worthier guests arrive (14:7-11). He then made a plea for the performance of good deeds, in this case by choosing guests from the poor, rather than the rich, because the rich will only repay hospitality in this life, whereas the poor will repay at the time of the resurrection of the just (14:12-14). Finally Jesus preached against the rejection of life-challenges, such as the rejection of invitations to dine (14:15-24).

B. *Some of the Problems in Luke's Tale*
(1) According to this story Jesus was invited to share a Sabbath meal at the house of one of the 'rulers of the Pharisees' where he performed a cure and then delivered three ethical-type speeches, all appropriately based on the metaphor of guests at a feast. Although this meal apparently took place on the Sabbath at the house of an important Pharisee, the Pharisee is not identified, and neither does the feast show any signs of a Sabbath meal. There are, for example, no prayers or blessings and the words of Jesus are not inspired by a Jewish religious text.[93] This event therefore is more typical of a Greek-style symposium with its banquet and formalised, often morally uplifting and entertaining, talk, which Pharisees could have attended on any day of the week, *except* on the Sabbath.[94] On the other hand, the evidence to be discussed below shows that, in accordance with Luke's claim, the cure took place on the Sabbath day. Luke therefore indicates a timing which is probably accurate for the cure but is most unlikely for the meal.

(2) It is also strange that probably even before the guests were seated (which is implied by the fact that Jesus first spoke to the people while he observed how they were choosing their seats, 14:7), Jesus suddenly 'replied' (ἀποκριθεὶς, 14:3) with a question concerning the legality of

---

93. J. M. Creed, *The Gospel According to St. Luke* (London: Macmillan, 1960), 188, therefore notes that 'the scene is a literary device to provide a setting for the sayings, all of which have in common the theme of a feast. The motive for including the healing of the dropsical man in the same setting is less obvious.' J. Nolland, *Luke 9:21–18:34* (WBC 35B; Dallas: Word, 1993), 747, notes that 'The sabbath setting is for the sake of vv. 1-6, but the meal setting is for the sake of the following units to v. 24'. The homilies in the *Pesikta de-Rav Kahana* (for this work see Strack and Stemberger, *Introduction to the Talmud and Midrash*, 321) date probably from the fifth or early sixth century, but undoubtedly represent an older tradition and represent the type of speech which Jesus could have made at a true Sabbath meal.
94. See the comments and references in Nolland, *Luke 9:21–18:34*, 745.

healing on the Sabbath day. Why did he ask a question at this inappropriate moment, while guests were arriving and were still finding their seats? To what remark did Jesus reply? And why is there no reply to the question Jesus asked (14:4b), either from the Pharisees or even rhetorically from Jesus himself? Did Pharisees and Jewish lawyers never respond to *halachic* questions and engage in debates? Can we assume that the subsequent cure and/or the justification for the cure provide an answer to this question, as some scholars suggest?[95] And what is the significance of the silence of the Pharisees and lawyers after Jesus justifies his cure (14:6)? Silence can be interpreted in many ways. Should this silence be understood as criticism of Jesus, as many scholars claim, or could it be explained in a way that relates to the content of the story as a whole?

(3) We are told that Jesus was a guest at the banquet of the Pharisees (14:1) which suggests that the man with dropsy was also a guest. Why then was this man dismissed by Jesus after he was cured (ἀπέλυσαν, 14:4b)? What gave one guest the right to dismiss another? Why was the man who had been cured, and thus now more able to enjoy a pleasant occasion, sent away, apparently even before the feast had begun? Even more strange is the fact that the man was dismissed by Jesus *before Jesus began to preach*. Do preachers ever dismiss a potential member of their audience, especially a person that the preacher had cured who would probably wish to stay and show gratitude for the cure he had received? Is the dismissal by Jesus of a man whom he healed the action of the same Jesus who firmly declared, 'He who has ears to hear, let him hear!'?[96]

(4) It is also very strange that the account of this cure does not end after Jesus has dismissed the person he has cured, but instead uniquely, and unlike any other gospel healing event, it continues *after* the dismissal by Jesus of the person he has cured.

C. *Evidence for a Sabbath Cure and Criticism of Jesus for Performing the Cure*

Did the cure take place on the Sabbath day? This day is indicated by the criticism of Jesus, which we can assume would not have occurred had the cure had taken place on a non-Sabbath day. This criticism is anticipated in the opening sentence of the story, which notes that the people at

---

95. Some possible solutions to this problem are offered by J. A. Fitzmyer, *The Gospel According to Luke X–XXIV* (AB 28A; New York: Doubleday, 1985) 1041.

96. Mark 4:23 (and in some mss 7:16); Luke 8:8; 14:35 (and some mss 12:21); 13:9; 21:4; Matt 11:15; 13:43; 25:29.

the event 'were watching him in a menacing way' (παρατηρούμενοι, 14:1). Subsequently, according to Luke's account, Jesus 'replied', although he had not yet been addressed (ἀποκριθείς, 14:3).[97] It is obvious, however, that if Jesus replied, he must have been addressed. Since no previous address to Jesus is noted in Luke's account, it must be assumed that the words to which Jesus replied have been omitted from Luke's tale. The reason for this exclusion can be explained on the reasonable assumption that the remark was not complimentary to Jesus, for otherwise it would not have been excluded from the text. In the context of the story of a Sabbath cure, and especially in view of the implied criticism of Jesus in the first sentence of this story (παρατηρούμενοι, 14:1), this suggests that Jesus was criticised for performing Sabbath cures by the ordinary Jewish people who were there at the time. It was thus this criticism to which Jesus replied. Even though the cure of the man with dropsy had not yet taken place, it seems that the observers of Jesus assumed it would occur. This helps to confirm the claim of Luke that the cure of the man with dropsy took place on the Sabbath since there is probably no other reason that such criticism would have been expressed.

D. *The Argument Used by Jesus to Justify His Cure*
The argument apparently used by Jesus to justify the cure of the man with dropsy does not make sense unless we assume that it is an elliptic version of an argument *kal va-chomer*, in which the first and second sections of the argument are expressed together. A fully expressed argument in English which accounts for the otherwise difficult references to a son and an ox is printed below:

> Luke 13:5 rephrased:
> If the life of a relatively lesser valued ('light', *kal*) animal, for example an ox, may be saved from drowning [in the water of a well or a pit] on the Sabbath,
>   is it not logical to conclude that (= *kal va-chomer*)
>   the life of a more relatively higher valued ('heavy', *chomer*) human being, for example a son, may also be saved from drowning [in his own body fluids] on the Sabbath!

The logic of this argument and its relationship to its context depends on an understanding of the nature of dropsy, the illness of the man whom Jesus cured. As medical dictionaries consistently note, dropsy is a

97. Liddell, Scott and Jones, *A Greek–English Lexicon*, s.v. ἀποκρίνω IV. Some ingenious suggestions have been made to explain this textual problem; see, e.g., I. H. Marshall, *The Gospel of Luke* (Exeter: Paternoster, 1976) 579, who claims that Jesus responds to an 'unspoken' rather than a verbal 'challenge'. This is not convincing.

symptom of a progressive and serious underlying disease which causes
an abnormal accumulation of fluid within the body, typically beneath
the skin, and especially (because of gravity) beneath the skin of the legs
and feet, which become swollen and enlarged.[98] These symptoms were
correctly described by the ancient Jewish sages, who believed that the
excess fluid in the tissues was water (the disease is also called 'hydropsy'),
as can be seen from the text below, which comments on the Job 28:25,
and He [that is, God] weigheth the waters by measure:

> Leviticus Rabbah XV.2
> Man is evenly balanced, half of him is water and the other half is blood.
> When he is deserving the water does not exceed the blood, nor does the
> blood exceed the water; but when he sins, it sometimes happens that the
> water gains over the blood and then he becomes a sufferer from dropsy
> (אידרופיקיאוס, *idrophikios*); at other times the blood gains over the water
> and he then becomes leprous.[99]

The names used by the Jewish sages for this potentially life-threatening symptom—either הדרוקן (*hydrokan*, which appears thirteen times in
the Babylonian Talmud) or אידרופיקיאוס (*idydrophikios*, see Lev Rab
XV.2 above), are clearly derived from the Greek term for water, ὕδωρ,
which is also the basis for the Greek name for dropsy, ὑδρώπικος.[100] A
person with dropsy could therefore be described as drowning in water, in
the container of his own skin.

Turning now to the logic of the argument used by Jesus to justify his
cure at Luke 14:5, it is clear that although the argument is tersely
expressed, this argument is basically a *halachic* rabbinic argument *kal
va-chomer* which is used to justify the specific cure of dropsy on the
Sabbath day. The argument is based on the assumption that it was the
usual practice of the Jewish people in the first century CE to heal and/or
save the life of an animal on the Sabbath although such an act caused a
violation of Sabbath law. The assumption that this procedure was official
oral Jewish law can be made simply from the fact that this is stated in

98. The early Jewish sages knew that dropsy could be fatal: 'Three [classes of
person] die [unexpectedly] even while they are conversing, namely, one who suffers
from bowel diseases, a woman in confinement, and one afflicted with dropsy'
(b. Eruv 41b). But 'dropsy' is progressive, and there is no indication that Luke's man
with dropsy was severely affected. See the discussion of Nolland, *Luke 9:21–18:34*,
747.
99. Trans. J. Israelstam, *Midrash Rabbah: Leviticus* (London: Soncino, 1939)
190.
100. For example, Marshall, *Luke*, 578; Nolland, *Luke 9:21–18:34*, 746. Other
references in ancient literature to dropsy are collected by H. Van der Loos, *The
Miracles of Jesus* (Leiden: Brill, 1965) 505-7.

Luke's argument, which means that this statement *must have been accepted in principle by the people to whom the argument was ultimately addressed,* because otherwise the final section of the argument (*ha-ba min ha-din*), would have no foundation on which to rest. Accordingly, since the argument is apparently addressed to the Jewish lawyers and Pharisees in the story, it can be assumed that the latter accepted the fact that it was permitted on the Sabbath to save the life of an animal that was drowning, although this principle is now only hinted at in the tannaitic texts.[101]

Assuming that υἱός, meaning 'son' (rather than ὄνος, meaning 'ass'), should be read at Luke 14:5—a reading which will be further discussed below—the relationship of the subject of the first part of the argument (*ha-nadon*) with the second part of the argument (*ha-ba min ha-din*) at Luke 14:5 then depends on the basic principle in Judaism that the life of a human being is valued more highly than the life of an animal. An obvious statement of this opinion can be seen in the declaration in the Pentateuch that man was permitted by God to rule over *the fish of the sea, and over the birds of the air, and over the cattle and over all the earth and over every creeping thing that creeps upon the earth* (Gen 1:26). This again is openly asserted in Ps 8:4-9:

> [4] What is man, that thou shouldst remember him, mortal man, that thou shouldst care for him? [5] Yet thou has made him little less than a god, crowning him with glory and honour. [6] Thou makest him master over all thy creatures; thou has put everything under his feet. [7] All sheep and oxen, all the wild beasts. [8] The birds in the air, and the fish in the sea, and all that moves along the paths of the ocean…[102]

101. The practice of healing and/or saving the life of an animal on the Sabbath is not directly stated in the rabbinic texts but is implied at m. Betz 3.4 (= t. Betz 3.3), which notes: 'If a firstling fell into a pit [on the Sabbath], R. Judah says, 'Let a skilled person go down and look at it. If it has incurred a blemish, let him bring it up and slaughter it [when required in the Temple]. Otherwise, it may not be slaughtered [in the Temple].' This directive thus takes for granted that an animal (in this case a firstling) should be removed on the Sabbath from a pit where it could die (by drowning or by lack of water and food etc.), and focuses on what should be done if this animal is saved but is no longer suitable for sacrifice in the Temple because it may now be imperfect in some way. This implies that an earlier probably *oral* tannaitic directive explicitly allowed the removal of an animal from a pit into which it had fallen on the Sabbath (as Luke 13:15b-16; 14:5 and Matt 12:11-12 also assume), without relating the incident to Temple ritual.

102. Trans. from *The New English Bible*. The theory of man's supremacy is challenged by the cynical Hellenistic third-century BCE writer Qohelet, who asserts that the spirits of both man and beast descend to the dust, thus deriding the common belief of the higher value of a human being compared with that of an animal, the

Since Judaism values the life of a human being above that of an animal, and since it was permitted to cure and/or save the life of an animal on the Sabbath, it can be argued with an argument *kal va-chomer* that what is permitted for a relatively less valued animal must surely be permitted for a relatively more highly valued man. The argument of Luke also adds the detail that both the animal and the man are drowning. This makes it specific for the situation of the cure, in this case, saving the life of an individual who could be described as drowning in some way.[103]

E. ὄνος or υἱός—'Son' or 'Ass'—at Luke 14:5?

The fact that Jesus uses an argument *kal va-chomer* to justify his Sabbath cure of a man with dropsy ends any doubt concerning the choice between the readings ὄνος or υἱός—'son' or 'ass'—which occur in different manuscripts of Luke 14:5. As was noted in in Chapter 2, rabbinic arguments *kal va-chomer* are based on the relative 'lightness' and 'heaviness' of two separate entities, which serve as the basis for the claim that what is applicable for a lighter, or lesser valued entity (קל, *kal*) is surely also applicable for a heavier, or more highly valued entity (חומר, *chomer*); or else, when appropriate, what is permitted for the 'heavier' entity is surely also permitted for the entity that is relatively 'light'. One section of the argument must therefore be presented as relatively 'light' in relation to the second section which is relatively heavy. If therefore one section of the argument at Luke 14:5 featured an animal, the second section of the argument could not (in general) refer to another animal, because the relative values of each section of the argument would then be the same. In the context of Luke 14:5, therefore, in order to achieve the conclusion that it is permissible to save the life of an individual with dropsy, the second part of the argument must feature a son, rather than any animal,

latter which claimed that the spirit of the former has an after-life 'upward', unlike the spirit of an animal which descends to the dust, see Eccl 3:19-21. The tannaitic sages also express belief in the superiority of man over animals, for example by their surprise that mishnaic law of m. San 7.4 commands the same punishment for an ox and a human for the sin of bestiality, thus implying the same culpability for both the man and the beast, 'He that has a connection with a male or with a beast and she that suffers connection with a beast, [their death is] by stoning. *[But] if it is the man who has sinned, how has the beast sinned?...*' (m. San 7.4).

103. The specificity of the argument at Luke 14:5, which justifies the Sabbath cure of dropsy, means that it cannot be a variant of the argument at Matt 12:11-12, which justifies the cure of the withered hand, as has been claimed, e.g., Marshall, *Luke*, 578. A withered hand shows the opposite symptom of the swelling typical of dropsy, so that the patient with a withered hand is not in danger of drowning, in any sense of this term.

while the first part of the argument must feature an animal, in this case an ox. This argument thus notes that as it is permitted on the Sabbath to save the life of a relatively lesser-valued animal, in this case an ox, it is then reasonable to assume that it is (also) acceptable to save the life on the Sabbath of a relatively high-value human being, here a son. In short, as many scholars agree, the noun υἱός meaning 'son', should be read in Luke's text, rather than the noun ὄνος, meaning 'ass'. It is possible that confusion between the two terms arose because of Luke's elliptical reporting of the argument, which reverses the natural order of the argument, referring to an ox in the opening section and a son in the concluding section. A possible result of the reversal meant that the argument was not recognised as a rabbinic argument *kal va-chomer*, so that the knowledge of the pattern of logic of this argument was not used to select the appropriate term in a manuscript. The problem was probably further exacerbated because of the obvious similarities and potential confusion between the written Greek words ὄνος and υἱός.

F. *Luke 14:1-6 Is a Composite Text*

When was the argument *kal va-chomer* in Luke's text originally composed? There are three possibilities: either before the cure, perhaps in order to anticipate the Sabbath healing of a common symptom of an illness, or else at the time of the cure, as is implied by Luke. Alternatively, it was composed retrospectively, inspired perhaps by a memory of a cure that Jesus or some other Jewish healer had earlier performed. The answer to this question will emerge from an appreciation of the composite nature of Luke's story, which will now be discussed.

As can be appreciated from the discussion above, some of the most puzzling problems of Luke's story of the cure centre around the dismissal by Jesus of the man he had cured. For example, it is strange that Jesus, who was apparently invited to the banquet, dismissed someone who was probably also invited (or, we can assume, had a right to be present), even before the banquet had begun. It is also strange that Jesus dismissed a person who, after his cure, could not only have better enjoyed the feast to which he had apparently been invited, but would also have been able to hear Jesus preach. It is safe to say that preachers do not usually dismiss a potential member of their audience, especially one who would (we can assume) have been grateful to the preacher for his cure and would have wanted to stay. The disquiet of commentators caused by the dismissal by Jesus of the man who was cured is often reflected in English translations by a misleading, apologetic translation for the verb ἀπέλυσεν (Luke 14:4) as 'he let him go', which hints that the man who was cured was anxious to leave, and that Jesus himself reluctantly agreed.[104] This resourceful translation does not however reflect the plain meaning of the text—the verb ἀπολύω indicates clearly that Jesus dismissed the man he had cured. It is thus significant that *in contrast with every other healing event in the gospels which end when Jesus parts from the person he has cured*, which is always specifically noted in these accounts, the cure of the man with dropsy is the *only* healing event in the synoptic gospels which apparently continues *after* Jesus has parted from the person he has cured.[105]

These problems can, however, be explained if we assume that *as in all other healing incidents when Jesus sends away the person he had cured*, the account of the cure of the man with dropsy originally ended when the man was dismissed. This being the case, the events that took place after the dismissal—the argument in which Jesus justifies his cure and his moralising speeches—are later additions to the story of the cure, and are

104. This translation is found, e.g., in RSV Luke 14:4 and J. A. Fitzmyer, *The Gospel According to Luke I–IX* (AB 28; Garden City: Doubleday, 1981) 1041.

105. There is only one possible exception, namely, the story of the cure of the cripple in John 5:2-18. Some scholars, however, consider with good reason that this story originally ended when the man Jesus cured walked away with his bed (John 5:9a), and that John has added further material to the tale (see n. 188, and the accompanying text). As far as the synoptic texts are concerned, only the event at Luke 14:1-6 apparently continues after Jesus has parted from the person he has cured. Thus: (1) At Mark 1:43, when, after the cure of a leper, '*[Jesus] sternly charged [the former leper] and forthwith sent him away*'. Jesus also dismissed lepers after their cure at Luke 5:14 and Matt 8:4. (2) At Mark 2:11, the incident ends when Jesus tells a paralytic '*Rise, take up your bed and go home*', thus sending him away. Similarly Jesus dismissed paralytics at Luke 5:24-25 and Matt 9:6-7, when the story ends. (3) At Mark 5:34, the scene ends when Jesus dismissed a haemorrhaging lady he had cured. Similarly at Luke 8:39, Jesus sent the man he has cured back to his house, *even though the latter begs to stay*. (4) At Matt 9:31, after Jesus cured two blind men, 'they went away' and this departure marks the end of the scene. (5) After healing a Syro-Phoenician girl, Jesus 'sent [the mother] away' to find her daughter at home, Mark 7:29-30, which must also be assumed for Matthew's account, see Matt 15:21-28, after which Jesus then departed (Mark 7:31; Matt 15:29). (6) At Mark 8:26, when Jesus healed a blind man and then sent him away (καὶ ἀπέστειλεν αὐτὸν), when the incident ends. (7) At Luke 17:19, when curing man with leprosy, Jesus says, *Arise, go thy way*, Ἀναστὰς πορεύου. (8) At Mark 10:52, after restoring the sight of Bartimaeus, Jesus tells him '*Go your—your faith has made thee whole*. And immediately he received his sight, and followed Jesus in the way'. The scene ends here and a new scene begins; similarly at Luke 18:43 and Matt 20:34. At John 9:7, Jesus parts from the blind man he has cured saying, '*Go! Wash in the pool of Siloam*'. (9) At John 5:8, after healing a paralytic, the scene ends when Jesus parted from the man saying, '*Rise, take up thy bed, and walk*'. (10) At John 11:44, after raising Lazarus, Jesus says to the onlookers, '*Loose him, and let him go!*'

not connected with the original event. If, then, no Pharisees or Jewish officials were present immediately after the cure, they cannot have been present before it began. This being the case, the cure did not take place 'in the house of a ruler who belonged to the Pharisees' but has been moved from its original (unknown) location and has been placed into the story of a feast where Pharisees were allegedly found. And since no 'lawyers and Pharisees' were present either before or after the event of the cure, neither were they present at the cure itself. No lawyers or Pharisees could therefore have criticised Jesus for the cure. This means that the man whom Jesus cured was not a guest at a feast and was not dismissed before the feast had begun. Neither did Jesus display the highly unusual and strange behaviour of a preacher who dismissed a person who would otherwise have heard him preach. This means that the cure did not take place at the 'house of one of the rulers of the Pharisees' (Luke 14:1), and that the historical location is unknown. Furthermore, the criticism of Jesus, which is anticipated by the term παρατηρούμενοι (Luke 14:1) and implied by the fact that Jesus 'replied' although he had not been addressed (ἀποκριθεὶς ὁ Ἰησοῦς, Luke 14:3, see the discussion above), which implies a negative comment from onlookers of the future cure, could *not* have come from Pharisees or Jewish lawyers (because none were there) and therefore must have come from the ordinary Jewish people who witnessed the cure.

Other anomalies that can now also be explained include the fact of the Sabbath timing, which is essential for the cure, but irrelevant for the banquet, which could probably have taken place any day of the week, *apart* from the Sabbath, because no Sabbath content is described at this event. This also accounts for the silence of the Pharisees or lawyers during the scene of the cure, since if no Pharisees or lawyers were present at the cure, nothing could be reported of the words they said. This also means that, like the midrashic-type story of the meeting of Jesus and the Pharisees in the Galilean fields, the Sabbath cure of the man with dropsy cannot be used as proof of friction between Jesus and Pharisees (or any other Jewish officials) for the performance by Jesus of a Sabbath cure.

G. *Did Jesus Voice the Halachic Argument to Justify His Cure, Luke 14:5?*

As the story now stands, this argument is voiced after the dismissal of the man Jesus cured. If indeed the story of the cure ended at the point when the cured man was dismissed, this means that the argument could not have been voiced at the event of the cure. In other words, the fact that the argument is not expressed *before* the dismissal of the man Jesus cured, means that it is probably not a part of the incident of the cure. Moreover, since the argument specifically justifies the cure of dropsy, and since there are no other occasions in the accounts of the life of Jesus when he cures a man with dropsy on the Sabbath when it would be appropriate for this argument to be expressed, it is thus most unlikely that this argument was composed or voiced on any other occasion by Jesus himself. The argument may therefore have been composed either in anticipation of the need to justify a Sabbath cure of dropsy on the Sabbath by a Jewish healer, or it was composed retrospectively, perhaps inspired by this Sabbath cure of Jesus, or some other Jewish healer who had treated a man with dropsy on the Sabbath day. Whatever the case, it can be assumed that the argument was added by Luke to his account of the cure.

H. *Do the Halachic Questions Belong to the Cures (Mark 3:4 [= Luke 6:9] and Luke 14:3)?*
Two *halachic* questions are posed by Jesus during the course of the gospel Sabbath cures, one preserved in Luke's account of the man with dropsy, *Is it lawful to heal on the Sabbath or not?* (Luke 14:3), and the other in the story of the cure of the man with a withered hand, *Is it lawful on the Sabbath to do good or do harm, to save life or to kill?* (Mark 3:4 which is repeated almost verbatim at Luke 6:9).[106] Were these questions asked by the historical Jesus, or were they derived from another source, thus making them later additions to the stories of the cures?

Long familiarity with the stories in which these questions are preserved—the cure of the man with dropsy (for Luke 13:4), and the cure of the man with a withered hand (for Mark 3:4 and Luke 6:9)—has led to their general acceptance within the narratives in which they occur. Objective evaluation, however, suggests that they are not originally a part of these gospel tales. They are voiced abruptly, without any apparent reason. They are also expressed at inappropriate times—the question at Luke 14:3 is apparently addressed to a crowd of people assembling for a banquet and even before they are seated (see Luke 14:7), and they are addressed to an audience which, as the above discussion has shown, was probably not even present at the time of the cure. Similarly, the question asked before the cure of the man with a withered hand is addressed to people who have come to the synagogue on the Sabbath, presumably to pray, rather than engage in *halachic* debate. Moreover, both questions

---

106. A further *halachic*-type question asked during the Sabbath cure of a man with a withered hand is to be found at Matt 21:10a. This is asked by onlookers, *not* by Jesus, and will be discussed below in the discussion on Matt 12:9-14.

are *halachic*, demanding a discussion on Jewish law, and yet those who regularly conducted such discussions, especially the Pharisees, were not present at either of these scenes—their absence at the cure of the man with dropsy has been discussed above, and their absence from the cure of the man with a withered hand will be discussed when this event is examined below. On the other hand, the ordinary people present at these cures were undoubtedly familiar with Jewish ritual procedures but are not generally associated with *halachic* debate.[107]

If then, as it appears, these *halachic* questions were not asked by the historical Jesus, from where were they derived? There can be only one general answer—since these questions are concerned with the problem of healing on the Sabbath, which was a subject of interest only to pious Jews, they could only have come from a Jewish source. The subject and context of these questions also suggests that they were originally posed in debates on the subject of the legality of Sabbath acts of healing and/or saving life which undoubtedly took place among the Jewish sages from Maccabean times (see on m. Shab 7.2, in Chapter 1).

This origin for the questions in the gospels is strengthened by the preservation of a similar *halachic* question, one dealing with the question of healing on the Sabbath, which is found in two tannaitic Jewish sources, the Tosefta and the *Mekilta de-Rabbi Ishmael*, compilations of Jewish oral law which were published soon after the end of the second century CE. However, in contrast with the first-century questions in the gospels which query the general religious legality of acts of healing and/or saving life on the Sabbath—should acts of healing and/or saving life be performed on the Sabbath, or should they not?—the question preserved in the tannaitic texts takes these actions for granted, asking instead how this principle is known. This suggests that the questions in these texts were asked *after* the problem of healing and/or saving life on the Sabbath had been solved, a fact confirmed by the answers they receive.

The question in the Tosefta is posed by R. Yose, probably R. Yose the Galilean, who was active in the mid-second century CE, who asks, *From where* (מנין) *[in the Jewish sources do we know that] for [an act of] healing and saving life, that it overrides the Sabbath [law]*?[108] Four

---

107. Ordinary Jewish people may be consulted on ritual, or show their knowledge of ritual, but not *halachah*. For example, (1) Nahum the scrivener informed the sages on an aspect of Peah (m. Peah 2.6); (2) the people know how to carry their sacrificial knives when the 14th of Nisan fell on the Sabbath (t. Pes 4.14); (3) the people objected to the method used during the ritual of the water libation at Succot (m. Sukk 4.9; Josephus, Ant XIII.372).

108. t. Shab 15.16-17: מנין לפיקוח נפש שדוחה את השבת?. For R. Yose identified as R. Yose the Galilean, see Chapter 5.

answers are provided: the first apparently by R. Yose himself, which is based on a midrashic interpretation of Exod 31:13 (discussed in Chapter 7); the second by R. Eleazar b. Azariah, a sage who was active around 70 CE, who offers an argument *kal va-chomer* based on the ritual of circumcision (which is discussed below in relation to John 7:23), the third is reported in the name of R. Akiva, whose public life began in the second half of the first century, who offers an argument *kal va-chomer* (which will be discussed in Chapter 5) and an argument based on Exod 22:1-2; and a final fifth 'proof' which is unattributed, but which was probably composed by the late second-century sage Samuel of Nehardea, and is based on a midrashic interpretation of Lev 18:5 (which will be discussed in Chapter 7). The editor of the Tosefta has thus used the question of R. Yose as a kind of heading under which he has col-lected the proofs of Jewish sages from different generations which prove the legality of Sabbath acts of healing and/or saving life.

The same question, although this time unattributed, is preserved in the *Mekilta de-Rabbi Ishmael*, and is answered similarly, although more extensively by six Jewish sages, again from a time both before and after R. Yose.[109] First is R. Ishmael, whose public life began in the late first century, who offers proof based on an argument *kal va-chomer* based on Exod 22:1-2 (discussed in Chapter 5), second is R. Eleazar b. Azariah, who provides the same argument *kal va-chomer* based on circumcision which is cited in the Tosefta (see later in this chapter), third is R. Akiva (a contemporary of R. Ishmael), who offers a sorite based on Exod 21:14 (which is discussed in Chapter 6); fourth is R. Yose the Galilean, who provides the same proof as in the Tosefta; fifth is R. Simon b. Menasia, a late second-century sage, with a proof based on a midrashic interpreta-tion of Exod 31:14 (which is discussed in earlier in this chapter and Chapter 7); and sixth is R. Nathan, a mid-second century sage, with a proof based on a midrashic interpretation of Exod 31:16 (which is discussed in Chapter 7). These passages in both the Tosefta and the *Mekilta* thus state in effect, *Yes—of course it is permitted to heal on the Sabbath (as suggested in Mark 3:4, Luke 6:9 and Luke 14:3) and thus not to kill (as suggested in Mark 3:4, Luke 6:9) and here are proofs based on Scripture that prove that such acts may be performed.*

These second-century tannaitic texts thus in effect provide positive answers to the questions which are asked in the first-century gospels. These answers thus show that there was now no further use for a question

---

109. *Mekilta de-Rabbi Ishmael* Shab 1, see Lauterbach, *Mekilta*, 3:197: מנין לפיקוח נפש שדוחה את השבת?. The sages and their replies to this question will be discussed in Chapters 5 and 7.

that served merely to open a discussion on the basic *halachic* legality of such acts, such as those preserved by Mark and Luke, because answers to such questions had now been found. It seems, therefore, that the first-century questions preserved in the gospels and the comparable second-century question preserved in the tannaitic texts come from opposite ends of the *halachic* search of the Jewish sages to confirm and find proof that acts of healing and/or saving life should take place on the Sabbath day. At the earlier, first-century stage of this debate are the questions preserved in the gospels which seem to query the basic legality of these acts, but which are posed in a way that expects a positive reply, while at the second-century stage of the Jewish debate is a question in which this positive reply is proven by the stated collection of acceptable proofs that had been exposed by the Jewish debate.

The intention to arrive at this positive end can in fact be seen in the earlier questions that are asked, thus strengthening the claim that these questions are linked. Although the questions in the gospels seem to leave room for both positive and negative replies, in reality it is clear that both of them expect a positive reply, since it can hardly be right to do wrong on the Sabbath which God had blessed and sanctified (Gen 2:3), as the alternative sections of these questions suggests. In other words, the Jewish sages who were active when these questions were asked were in favour of acts of healing and/or saving life on the Sabbath and searched for ways in which these actions could be proved. This suggests that the Pharisees and Jesus were in complete agreement regarding the need for acts of healing and/or saving life on the Sabbath day.

The questions in the gospels may thus be considered as earlier fore-runners of the later question in the tannaitic texts, in effect significant milestones along the historical path of the lengthy debate among the Jewish sages of the early first century and second century CE, to find ways to justify the performance of acts of healing and/or saving life that violated Jewish law.

This being the case, the questions in the gospels originally functioned in a similar way to those preserved in the tannaitic texts. That is, they are not rhetorical in the sense that they were asked so that the speaker could achieve an effect of some kind, which appears to be the case in the gospel accounts. Instead, the questions in the gospels originally served as subject-headings for discussions among the Jewish sages on the subject of acts of healing and/or saving life that violated Jewish law. The questions in the gospels have, however, been removed from this scholarly setting and placed in the context of events which record miraculous cures where they appear to be addressed to Pharisees (and lawyers and scribes, according to Luke) who were not even present at the historical cure. It is therefore no surprise that these questions sit awkwardly in their respective texts, and thereby provide convincing evidence that they have been added to an event to which they do not belong.

I. *Conclusions*
(1) There is no reason to doubt that in a location now unknown, the historical Jesus performed a cure on the Sabbath for a man with dropsy. This timing is indicated by the criticism of Jesus for performing Sabbath cures, which is hinted at, but not recorded, by Luke. There is also little doubt that the historical cure took place in front of ordinary Jewish people, who were therefore the people by whom Jesus was criticised.

(2) The historical story of the cure has been inserted within the story of an alleged Sabbath meal which took place in the house of a 'ruler' of the Pharisees, where Pharisees and Jewish lawyers had been invited to dine. In other words, the story of the cure does not belong within the story of the meal. This is indicated by the fact that, *unlike any other of Jesus' cures*, the story continues after the dismissal by Jesus of the person he cured. The material in the story after the dismissal is thus unlikely to be part of the original story of the cure. If, then, Pharisees and lawyers were not present after the dismissal of the man Jesus cured, they cannot have been present before the cure began. The original account of the story of cure thus began at Luke 14:1b (which describes the watching onlookers) and ended at Luke 14:4, when Jesus dismissed the man he had cured, and there is no evidence that any Pharisees or other Jewish officials were present at the scene of the cure.

(3) It is unlikely that either the *halachic* question (Luke 14:3) or the *halachic* argument *kal va-chomer* (14:5) were voiced by the historical Jesus. This can be assumed for the question at 14:5, because it is placed in Luke's text *after* the dismissal of the man Jesus cured, which probably marks the end of the incident, and thus is not part of the story of the cure. In contrast, although the *halachic* question has been placed within the story of the cure, it is intrusive within this context, not only because it is asked at an unsuitable moment in the story (but where else could it be placed?), but also because it is addressed to Pharisees and Jewish lawyers who almost certainly were not there. There is, moreover, evidence to suggest that such a question was asked by the Jewish sages in the early first-century stage of their search to find ways to justify acts of healing and/or saving life on the Sabbath day. This suggests that the question, like the argument, is derived from the contemporary debate of the Jewish sages and has been added by Luke to the story of the cure.

(4) As discussed in Chapter 2, the logic of any *halachic* argument *kal va-chomer* is based on the difference which is assumed for the relative values of two entities, one which is 'heavier' or of greater value, and the other which is 'lighter' and therefore of lesser value. A rabbinic argument *kal va-chomer* could therefore not be composed if the relative values of the two entities were the same. The argument of Jesus at Luke 14:5 must thus be based on the relative values of an animal and a man, rather than two animals, such as an ox and an ass. This means that in the context of Luke 14:5, the term υἱός (meaning 'son') should be read rather than ὄνος (meaning 'ass'). The *halachic* argument attributed to Jesus thus claims that because it is permitted by Jewish oral law to heal and/or save the life of an animal on the Sabbath, in this case an ox which can be saved from drowning in a well or a pit, it is reasonable to assume that the life of a human being may be healed and/or saved on the Sabbath, in this case a son who is suffering from an illness in which he is also drowning in water, that is, within the container of his own skin.

(5) The details in each section of the *halachic* argument *kal va-chomer* show that it is specific for its cure, that is, it could *not* be used to justify Sabbath cures in a general way.

(6) The only facts that can be known about the cure that the historical Jesus performed for a man with dropsy are: (a) it took place on the Sabbath; (b) a group of ordinary Jewish people included a man with dropsy—no Pharisees or any Jewish officials were present at the scene; (c) Jesus approached this group, and was watched by the people to see if he would perform a Sabbath cure; (d) Jesus performed the cure and was criticised by the people—though this criticism has been lost; (e) Jesus replied to this criticism, but his reply too has been lost (in Luke's account the reply of Jesus has been replaced with a *halachic* question); (e) finally, Jesus dismissed the man he had cured and the event ended at this point.

This order of events suggests that Jesus was criticised by the people after, rather than before, the cure, as Luke implies.

III. *The Cure of a Woman with a Bent Back: Luke 13:10-17*

Just as the story of the cure of the man with dropsy, this Sabbath cure is reported only by Luke. A translation of Luke 13:10-17 follows below:

13:10 Now he (=Jesus) was teaching in one of the synagogues on the Sabbath (ἐν τοῖς σάββασιν). [11] And there was a woman with a breath of infirmity (πνεῦμα...ἀσθενίας) for eighteen years, [which meant that] she was bent over and could not fully straighten herself. [12] And when Jesus saw her, he called her and said to her, 'Woman, you are freed from your infirmity (τῆς ἀσθενείας σου)'. [13] And he laid his hands upon her, and immediately she was made straight (ἀνωρθώθη), and she praised God. [14] And answering (ἀποκριθείς), the ruler of the synagogue, indignant that Jesus had healed on the Sabbath, said to the crowd (τῷ ὄχλῳ) that 'there are six days on which work should be done. Come (ἐρχόμενοι) on those days and be healed and not on the day of the Sabbath.' [15a] Then the Lord answered (ἀπεκρίθη) him (αὐτῷ) and said, 'Hypocrites! [15b] Does not each of you (ἕκαστος ὑμῶν) on the Sabbath untie (λύει) his ox or his ass from the manger, and lead it away to water it? [16] And ought not this woman, a daughter of Abraham whom Satan bound (ἔδησεν) for eighteen years, be untied (ἔδει λυθῆναι) from this bond (δεσμοῦ) on the Sabbath day?' [17] As he said this, all his adversaries (οἱ ἀντικείμενοι αὐτῷ) were put to shame (κατησχύνοντο); and all the crowd (πᾶς ὁ ὄχλος) rejoiced at all the glorious things that were done by him.

A. *An Overview of This Story and Some Problems That Arise*

According to Luke, the story began when Jesus was teaching (v. 10) a bustling crowd of people (v. 14) composed (mainly) of peasant-farmers (vv. 15b-16) who had deliberately come to a synagogue on the Sabbath (v. 10) in order to request cures (v. 14). Among the people in this crowd was a woman who had suffered for eighteen years (v. 11) with an illness called 'the spirit of infirmity', that is, her back was bent so that she could not fully stand up (v. 11). Jesus called to her and announced that she was 'freed from her infirmity' (v. 12). He then laid his hands on her body and she was 'made straight' (v. 13). The woman herself proceeded to praise God, and thus, in effect, thanked God (rather than Jesus) for effecting her cure (v. 13). The leader of the synagogue then replied (to whom is not stated) and angrily rebuked the crowd (although apparently not Jesus) for requesting Sabbath cures (although no one had requested a cure), because (he said) they knew that 'work' (by which he implied acts of healing and/or saving life) was forbidden on the Sabbath by Penta-teuchal law (v. 14). Jesus then 'replied' (although he had similarly not been addressed), apparently speaking to the leader of the synagogue (according to the term αὐτῷ, v. 15a), although the leader of the syna-gogue had not spoken to him. Jesus then uttered the pejorative plural term 'Hypocrites', apparently addressing the single leader of the syna-gogue (αὐτῷ, 'to him', v. 15a). Then he addressed the peasant-farmers, who presumably were a majority in the Sabbath crowd in the synagogue (v. 15b) with a *halachic* rabbinic argument *kal va-chomer* with which he justified his cure of the woman, although these peasant farmers had apparently never criticised the cure. Finally, although the incident Luke describes deals with only one deed, Jesus was praised by many people for his 'glorious deeds' and his (unidentified) enemies were put to shame (v. 17).

Some problems in Luke's story are discussed briefly below:

(1) The woman who was cured behaved completely in accordance with Jewish law. Evidence of her Jewish piety can be seen in the fact that after she was healed, she praised God, presumably attributing her cure to God rather than to Jesus, who, according to Jewish thought, had only in some way facilitated the cure, but was not ultimately responsible for producing a cure.[110] Moreover, although she had been ill for eighteen years (Luke 13:11), and contrary to the complaint of the leader of the synagogue who accused the people in the congregation for asking for Sabbath cures, neither the woman whom Jesus cured had asked for a cure, and neither had anyone else in the crowd. This accords with the fact that healing in Judaism is considered as 'work', which is forbidden on the Sabbath, so that asking a Jewish healer for a cure on the Sabbath would, in effect, ask the healer to sin.[111] This lack of requests not only casts serious doubts on the claim of the leader of the synagogue that the people in the crowd had come to the synagogue on the Sabbath to seek Sabbath cures (which is further discussed in [2] below), but the lack of verbal contact between Jesus and the woman or anyone else in the crowd also raises the question of how Jesus knew that she had been ill for eighteen years (Luke 13:16). Modern commentators often admire the lack of contact between Jesus and the woman, and claim that the unrequested cure shows his compassionate nature. But rarely—if ever—do they pause either to ask why the woman herself did not ask to be cured, or—in view of their complete lack of communication—ask how Jesus discovered how long she had been ill.[112]

(2) As noted above, the leader of the synagogue accused the crowd of seeking Sabbath cures (v. 14), although no one in the crowd had asked for a cure (13:10-13). Since no requests are made in the story itself, they

110. The Jewish belief that God alone is responsible for a cure, rather than a healer, will be further discussed in relation to John 9:1-14.

111. Therefore, with one exception for which there is a good reason (the cure of the mother-in-law of Simon, see below on Mark 1:29-31, Luke 4:38-39, with Matt 8:14-15), Jesus is *never* asked for a Sabbath cure.

112. This inconsistency is not noted in the following standard commentaries; see, e.g., A. Plummer, *A Critical and Exegetica Commentary on the Gospel According to S. Luke* (Edinburgh: T. & T. Clark, 1896) 341-3; Creed, *The Gospel According to St. Luke*, 183; Fitzmyer, *The Gospel According to Luke X–XXIV*, 1012-13; Marshall, *Luke*, 558-9; Nolland, *Luke 9:21–18:34*, 723-4; J. B. Green, *The Gospel of Luke* (Grand Rapids: Eerdmans, 1997), 521, 523-6.

can only be assumed on the basis of the future remark of the leader of the synagogue. The need for such an important retrospective assumption is jarring for the reader of the text, and suggests that some change has been made to the original tale. We are moreover told that the crowd who were present consisted mainly of peasant farmers (as is suggested at v. 15b), who—it is clear—were not working that Sabbath day. Their complete silence in relation to requests for Sabbath cures can thus be understood as an indication of their piety in relation to Sabbath law which forbade (and still forbids) 'work' of any kind on the Sabbath day. Their behaviour in this respect thus conforms with Jewish law. It is therefore no surprise that no one in the crowd asked Jesus to perform any cures, as this would, in effect, ask Jesus to sin. How then can we explain the fact that the leader of the synagogue accused the people of asking for Sabbath cures?

(3) The term ὄχλος is used by the leader of the synagogue to refer to the people in the synagogue whom he rebukes for seeking Sabbath cures (v. 14). Otherwise, ὄχλος in Hellenistic Greek is used for a 'moving crowd', a 'throng', a 'mob', or a 'multitude', for which there are over forty examples in the gospel of Luke and over twenty examples in Acts.[113] This term is thus used for a large group of people in an open public space, but most unsuitable for those who have come to a synagogue on the Sabbath, presumably—for the most part—in order to pray. The location of this event in a synagogue, which is stated by Luke at the beginning of the scene (v. 10), seems however to be confirmed by the presence of the leader of the synagogue (v. 14), whose presence in a synagogue can be expected on the Sabbath day. Elsewhere in his gospel Luke however refers to the people in a synagogue (rather than to the building itself) with the noun συναγωγή (e.g. Luke 4:20, πάντων οἱ ὀφθαλμοὶ ἐν τῇ συναγωγῇ ἦσαν ἀτενίζοντες αὐτῷ…, 'the eyes *of all in the congregation* were fixed on him…').[114] In any case, if 'a bustling, noisy

113. See Liddell, Scott and Jones, *A Greek–English Lex*icon, and Arndt and Gingrich, *A Greek–English Lexicon of the New Testament and Other Early Christian Literature*, s.v. ὄχλος. It could be argued that ὄχλος at Acts 24:12 refers to those in a synagogue, but the term here probably refers to people in the city. Problems with the term ὄχλος at Luke 13:14 are often 'solved' in English translations with the neutral term 'people'; see, for instance, the RSV. For the usage of a synagogue in the first century, see Emil Schürer: *The History of the Jewish People in the Age of Jesus Christ*, vol. 2 (ed. G. Vermes, F. Millar, M. Black and P. Vermes; Edinburgh: T. & T. Clark, 1979) 447-8. See, e.g., Philo, Mos. 2.214–216.

114. The term συναγωγή is also used by Luke to refer to a building, see Luke 4:28; 7:5; 11:43, and 20:46. The use of this term for both a building and a congregation (that is, a group of people who met for religious purposes) is confirmed by archaeological evidence which shows that buildings used for prayer in the first

crowd' wished to ask Jesus for Sabbath cures, why did they not go to a more suitable place, especially as the gospels repeatedly show that Jesus did not cure in fixed locations, but wherever he and the sick happened to meet?

(4) A further problem in this story (one of the few which is noted by commentators) is the plural noun 'Hypocrites' voiced by Jesus, which seems to refer to the *single* leader of the synagogue, because the term αὐτῷ, 'to him' (Luke 13:15a), follows directly after the words of the leader of the synagogue and before Jesus speaks, so that Jesus appears to speak 'to (a single) him'. The numerical disparity between this single person and the plural term 'Hypocrites' has been justified with the claim that Jesus speaks to 'you (the leader of the synagogue) *and to your kind*'.[115] This is ingenious but clearly incorrect. The true plurality of the term 'Hypocrites' is confirmed by the subsequent argument of Jesus which is addressed to 'each of you on the Sabbath [who] untie[s] his ox or his ass from the manger' (v. 15b), a detail which is generally not noted in commentaries on this text.

(5) The speech of the leader of the synagogue is introduced with the term ἀποκριθείς (v. 14), from the verb ἀποκρίνομαι, meaning 'to answer' or 'to reply'.[116] However, since the leader of the synagogue has not yet been addressed, how can Luke claim that this man 'replies'? It has been suggested that Luke uses this verb with its rare meaning in the Septuagint, 'to open a debate'.[117] But what debate does it open and why should Luke use a common term in an uncommon way? The words of Jesus which follow after the speech of the leader of the synagogue are also introduced with the same basic verb (ἀπεκρίθη, v. 15a), although, once again, no one has spoken to whom Jesus could reply.[118] Could this be explained by the term αὐτῷ (Luke 13:15b), which (as noted above) is usually translated 'to him' and which thus suggests that Jesus replied to

century CE were not always designated as synagogues so that the term συναγωγή might be used for either, see Dunn, *Jesus Remembered* (Grand Rapids: Eerdmans, 2003) 302–6.

115. E.g. Nolland, *Luke 9:21–18:34*, 723, 725.

116. Liddell, Scott and Jones, *A Greek–English Lexicon*, s.v. ἀποκρίνω IV.

117. F. Büchsel, '*krinō* [to judge]', in *Theological Dictionary of the New Testament Abridged in One Volume*, 474. Other possible examples of this use in the New Testament include: Mark 9:5; Luke 14:3; 17:17; 22:51; etc. For this use in the Septuagint, see 1 Kgs 9:17 (= MT 1 Sam 9:17); Judg 18:14; Num 11:28; 4 Kgdms 1:12 (= MT 2 Kgs 1:12).

118. The problem of translation is so acute, especially for Luke 13:14, that no translation may be offered; see, e.g., RSV and the Jerusalem Bible.

the leader of the synagogue? This is unlikely because the leader of the synagogue has not addressed Jesus, but has spoken only to the crowd whom (he says) came to the synagogue in search of Sabbath cures (which cannot be true, see [2] above). In any case, it was only Jesus who violated the Sabbath by performing a cure. Why, then, does the leader of the synagogue not upbraid Jesus? Does the term ἀπεκρίθη mean that Jesus began a second debate (as the rare meaning of ἀποκρίνομαι in the Septuagint might suggest)? If this is the case, it seems that two debates were opened by two different people at the same event within a short space of time, in a story in which no debate is found.

(6) Luke 13:17, the last section of the story, is generally acknowledged to be Luke's editorial addition, as will be noted briefly below.

Even in a story of extended length, and all the more so when the narrative is short (including v. 17, there are only one hundred and sixty Greek words), the number and complexity of problems suggest that the integrity of the original tale has somehow been compromised so that the story cannot be accepted just as it stands.[119]

---

119. In spite of the many problems, some of which have been described in the main text, the integrity of this story is often assumed; see, e.g., Fitzmyer, *The Gospel According to Luke X–XXIV*, 1010-11, who reviews a selection of standard commentaries, some of which do not even refer to any problems in the text; see, e.g., Goulder, *Luke: A New Paradigm* (Sheffield: Sheffield Academic, 1989) 565-6. This event is even frequently offered as an example of the cruel and stubborn attitude towards Jesus by thé Jews, exemplified by the (presumably) Jewish leader of the synagogue, who chastises his congregation merely for seeking cures (Luke 13:14). The leader of the synagogue is thus almost universally condemned. For example Vermes, *The Authentic Gospel of Jesus* (London: Allen Lane/Penguin, 2003) 48, calls him 'a small minded president whose criticism was directed at the weak and the sick, because he was too cowardly to criticise Jesus himself... The focus of the story falls therefore on the role of Jesus' healing in God's redemptive plan as the expression of his mission—in contradistinction to the Jewish institutions that threw up a dividing wall restricting access to God's mercy for this needy woman'. Similarly, Nolland, *Luke 9:21–18:34*, 725 notes his 'hidden hypocrisy' and Marshall, *Luke*, 556 comments on the simultaneous demonstration of 'the hypocritical attitude of the Jewish leaders which have already been castigated in 11:37-54', and 'the saving power of God in delivering his people from the power of Satan' which 'thus provides the kind of sign that should have been recognised by the Jews'. This Lucan event thus probably reveals more about the personal attitudes of such commentators towards Judaism, rather than a proper understanding of the text itself. Few commentators sympathise with the apparent predicament of the leader of the synagogue who seems to uphold an ancient Jewish tradition in which healing was postponed until after the Sabbath, unless perhaps when there was an immediate danger to life,

B. *The Original Language of the Story of the Cure, Luke 13:10-13*
According to Luke, the woman whom Jesus cured suffered from an illness called the 'breath of infirmity', πνεῦμα...ἀσθενείας (v. 11). This phrase does not otherwise exist in Greek. The Greek phrase, however, reflects a literal translation in the Aramaic idiom רוח שחלניא, literally, 'the spirit of weakness', an illness recorded in the Aramaic text of the *Genesis Apocryphon*, which suggests that the Greek phrase in Luke is a literal translation from Aramaic. The illness in the *Apocryphon* refers to a chronic disease which lasted for two years and which, just as in Luke's account of the cure of a woman with a bent back, was also cured by the laying on of hands.[120] Although the illness in the *Apocryphon* was shorter than the illness of the woman Jesus cured (two years as opposed to eighteen years), the resemblance is clear. In any case, Jesus himself confirms the Aramaic terminology when he uses a shortened form of the Aramaic-based Greek to tell the woman he cured that she was freed 'from her infirmity', referring to her illness as τῆς ἀσθενείας σου, literally, 'your weakness' (Luke 13:12). This terminology in the gospel tale thus compellingly suggests that (1) the cure took place among Aramaic-speaking Jews, (2) the story of this cure was originally told in Aramaic, and (3) this Aramaic story has been translated into Greek.[121] It can thus be assumed that the historical Jesus spoke to the woman in Aramaic,

which is surely unlikely for a woman who had already suffered from the same illness for eighteen years, and who never, it appears, even asked for a cure, but see, e.g., Green, *The Gospel of Luke*, 523.

120. *The Genesis Apocryphon* 20.20-21, 29. According to this text, after abducting Sarai (Abraham's wife) Pharaoh suffered with an illness which prevented him from approaching her for two years and was then cured by the laying on of hands. Although we do not know if the woman cured by Jesus suffered from the same illness as Pharaoh, the names given to these illnesses, their similarly protracted length and the method used for their cures suggests that the woman Jesus cured suffered from a similar disease. A contrary interpretation is suggested by Nolland, *Luke 9:21–18:34*, 723-4, who maintains that the term 'spirit of infirmity' means that the woman was 'possessed', that is, her illness was not physical. *The Genesis Apocryphon* was first published in 1956 and this Aramaic phrase in Luke is now noted by several scholars, including Marshall, *Luke*, 557, and Fitzmyer, *The Gospel According to Luke X–XXIV*, 1012. Nolland, *Luke 9:21–18:34*, 724, also tentatively mentions the link. Flusser, 'Healing Through the Laying-on of Hands in a Dead Sea Scroll', *Israel Exploration Journal* 7 (1957) 107-8, was the first to note that the illness of Pharaoh and the illness of the woman with a bent back were cured in the same way, and that *The Genesis Apocryphon* has the earliest reference in Jewish literature to a cure performed in this way.

121. Fitzmyer, *The Gospel According to Luke I–IX*, 82-5 suggests that the *whole* story of the cure, Luke 13:10-17, belongs to a Lucan source.

which most scholars consider was the usual language in which he spoke.[122] But was Aramaic the language in which Jesus then justified his cure?

C. *The Language of the Argument Used to Justify the Cure, Luke 13:15b-16*

In the final part of Luke's story Jesus justifies his cure with a rabbinic argument *kal va-chomer*. The argument is preceded by the term 'Hypocrites!' (v. 15a), which has no logical connection with the argument itself. The argument must therefore be considered without this term and is rendered below in a literal way:

> 13:[15b] Does not each of you on the Sabbath untie his ox or his ass from the manger, and lead it away to water it?
> [16] And ought not this woman, a daughter of Abraham whom Satan bound for eighteen years, be untied from this bond on the Sabbath day?'

Like the argument which justifies the cure of the man with dropsy (see above on Luke 14:5) this argument is also based on an accepted practice of animal husbandry on the Sabbath, which (we must accept) was allowed by Jewish oral law, and which permitted animals (although not humans) to be healed and/or saved on the Sabbath day. This argument thus assumes that the lives of animals are less valuable, and therefore (in rabbinic terminology) 'lighter' or 'less serious' (*kal*) in relation to human beings, which were (and are) considered more valuable and thus 'heavier' or 'more serious' (*chomer*) than the lives of animals. The first part of the argument at (13:15b, *ha-nadon*) is thus based on the fact that an animal deprived of water will probably die of thirst. The permitted prevention of its thirst, by loosening its bonds, is therefore an action that saves life. We must then assume (because this fact is not stated) that the 'bonds' of the woman which were causing her bent back (13:11 and 16) were a potential cause of her death, so that action performed to loosen these 'bonds' was an action performed in order to heal and/or save life. The permit that allows the restraints of a relatively less valuable (or 'lighter') animal on the Sabbath to be loosened, in order that it should be 'cured' by drinking (so that it does not die of thirst), is thus used to justify the act of 'loosening' on the Sabbath the bonds of a relatively higher valued ('heavier') human being, in this case, loosening the bonds of a woman with a bent back from the restraints of her illness, so that the

122. Vermes, Millar and Black, eds., *The History of the Jewish People*, 20; J. P. Meier, *A Marginal Jew*. Vol. 1, *Rethinking the Historical Jesus: The Roots of the Problem and the Person* (New York: Doubleday, 1987), 255-68; Casey, *Solution to the 'Son of Man' Problem*, 116-21.

illness is cured and her life thus saved. The details of the cure that Jesus has performed are thereby re-enacted in the argument with which Jesus justifies her cure. This argument is thus *specific* for the cure of the illness of a bent back and could not be used to justify any other cure.

The argument is now preserved in Greek but must have originally been expressed in Hebrew or possibly Aramaic. This is evident from the fact that in the environment of Galilee in the first century CE where—it is reasonable to assume—this argument was first composed, there are only two languages in which it could have been expressed with the play of words which cannot be realised in the present Greek text, but which must be assumed in the argument when it was first composed. This play of words depends on the terms in Hebrew (or Aramaic) for the verbs in English meaning 'it is permitted' and 'to untie'. Both meanings in Hebrew can be derived from the single root יתר, namely, להתיר (the *Hiphil* conjugation) meaning 'to untie', and מותר (the *Hophal* conjugation, which acts as the passive of the *Hiphil*) meaning 'it is allowed'. Both meanings in Aramaic can be derived from the *Kal* (*Paal*) conjugation of the root שרי.

This play of words in the argument of Jesus can be seen in the following English reconstruction of the basic argument when formally expressed. The relevant terms in Hebrew and Aramaic are indicated alongside the corresponding terms in English, which are underlined. The terms in square brackets help explain the argument, although such explanations are typically unvoiced in the sparsely worded style of the rabbinic texts:

A Formal Version of the Argument kal va-chomer at Luke 13:15b-16

A.   If it is allowed (שרי/מותר) to untie (לשרי/להתיר) [a lesser valued animal such as an] ox or ass [from its restraints, so that it may drink and thus not die (of thirst)] on the Sabbath,

       is it not logical to assume that (קל וחומר)

B.   it is [also] allowed (שרי/מותר) to untie (לשרי/להתיר) the bent back of [a more highly valued sick] woman on the Sabbath, [so that she also may not die]!

As can be seen, this argument includes a play of words involving two essential and opposing terms, which use the same verbal root, namely, (1) 'it is permitted' (שרי/מותר) and (2) 'to untie' (לשרי/להתיר).[123] These

---

123. Jesus' argument in the Peshitta is a simple translation of Luke 13:15b-16, and preserves the same colloquial, non-formal argument of the present Greek text.

terms are paired, and appear symmetrically in each of the two main sections of the argument (labelled above as sections A and B). It is safe to say that it would be impossible to reproduce even a similar play of words in a Greek version of this text. Many scholars in fact allege a play of words in the Greek version of the argument, based on the terms λύει and δέω. The term λύει first appears in Luke 13:15, where it refers to the loosening or untying of an animal. The same verb subsequently appears in the following verse in the form of the passive infinitive λυθῆναι, meaning 'to be untied', where it refers in the argument to the freeing of the woman who was cured from Satan's bond. The term δέω appears three times in Luke 13:16: first in the form ἔδησεν, meaning '(Satan) has bound'; subsequently in the impersonal form ἔδει, meaning 'it is binding' or 'it is necessary'; and finally as the noun δεσμός, which refers to a 'bond', that is, something used for binding.[124] But unlike the derivatives of שרי and מותר, the Greek terms are *not* symmetrically placed within the argument—only one occurs in the first part of the argument (namely δεω), while there are up to four related terms in the second part of the argument (namely λυθῆναι, ἔδησεν, ἔδει and δεσμοῦ). It is, moreover, possible that the term ἔδησεν is not part of the original, Semitic argument, but that the whole phrase ἣν ἔδησεν ὁ Σατανᾶς, 'whom Satan has bound' (Luke 13:16), is a later Greek addition to this argument, as will be discussed below. The number of Greek terms based on the verb δέω in the original argument is thus probably reduced to three, but this does nothing to improve their spatial distribution within the argument itself. The uneven and comparatively clumsy arrangement of these terms in Greek can be seen in the text below, in which Luke 13:15b-16 is divided into two parts, each corresponding with the two main sections of an argument *kal va-chomer*, when this argument is formally expressed. The relevant Greek terms are printed in bold text and underlined. The phrase ἣν ἔδησεν Σατανᾶς, which, as noted above, may have been added to the original Hebrew (or Aramaic) argument, is enclosed in square brackets:

---

124. This alleged play on words in Greek in relation to the verb λύειν, that is, just as an animal is loosed on the Sabbath, so also may be a woman, is noted, for example, by Lohse, 'σάββατον', in *Theological Dictionary of the New Testament*, vol. 7 (ed. Kittel and Friedrich; trans. Bromiley; Grand Rapids: Eerdmans, 1971) 25. Vermes, *The Religion of Jesus the Jew* (London: SCM, 1993) 23, does not note the semantic connection between 'permitting' and 'loosing', and claims that the healing of the woman with a bent back is 'portrayed in the language of magic as someone "bound" by the devil'. See also Green, 'Jesus and a Daughter of Abraham (Luke 13:10-17)', *CBQ* 51 (1989) 647.

A. ἕκαστος ὑμῶν τῷ σαββάτῳ οὐ <u>λύει</u> τὸν βοῦν αὐτοῦ ἢ τὸν ὄνον ἀπὸ τῆς φάτνης καὶ ἀπαγαγὼν ποτίζει;

B. ταύτην δὲ θυγατέρα Ἀβραὰμ οὖσαν, [ἣν <u>ἔδησεν</u> ὁ Σατανᾶς] ἰδοὺ δέκα καὶ ὀκτὼ ἔτη, οὐκ <u>ἔδει λυθῆναι</u> ἀπὸ τοῦ <u>δεσμοῦ</u> τούτου τῇ ἡμέρᾳ τοῦ σαββάτου;

A. Does not each of you on the Sabbath <u>untie</u> his ox or his ass from the manger and lead it to drink?

B. And this woman, a daughter of Abraham [whom Satan has <u>bound</u>] for eighteen years, <u>should</u> she not be <u>untied</u> from this <u>bond</u> on the Sabbath!?[125]

It is clear that the Greek version of the argument cannot reproduce the deliberate, symmetrical play of words that is indicated in the underlying text of the argument in Hebrew or Aramaic.

In which of these two languages was the argument composed? If in Aramaic, it would be the only *halachic* argument *kal va-chomer* originally expressed in Aramaic that is preserved in a text composed in tannaitic times. It is thus more likely that the argument was originally expressed in Hebrew, rather than Aramaic. This being the case, if it was spoken by the historical Jesus at the time of the cure, it would mean that Jesus spoke in Aramaic at the beginning of this event (see above on Luke 13:11 and 12) and then spoke in Hebrew to the peasant-farmers at the end of the same scene. Jesus would then have spoken in two languages to the same crowd of people within the same short space of time. This is surely unlikely. An underlying Hebrew version of the argument thus suggests that this argument is a later addition to the story of the cure. This being the case, it must be assumed that Luke 13:15b-16 was composed in Hebrew at a time *other than at the time of the cure that Jesus performed*, either before, in anticipation of such a cure, but more likely afterwards, perhaps inspired by this specific cure. It may also be assumed that the argument was composed by someone who knew that the cure had taken place before peasant-farmers (since it is addressed directly to them, Luke 13:15b). This person also knew that the woman Jesus cured had been ill for eighteen years, since this fact could not have been known to Jesus before he performed the cure. Subsequently, the formal Hebrew argument was translated into Greek, in a colloquial, informal style, probably in accordance with the way that the historical

---

125. Even a formal expression of the argument in Greek, based on the (assumed) Semitic original, would not rectify the asymmetrical arrangement of these related terms. Thus the phrase 'it is possible', would probably be rendered ἔξεστι, and a form of λύειν, 'to loosen', here 'to untie', would probably be used to translate the Hebrew root נתר (or the Aramaic root שרי). But these terms are not semantically related, and thus could not be used in Greek in a similar way as the implied Hebrew terms.

Jesus spoke, and was added to the story of the cure, which was also translated into Greek, although from Aramaic. The Aramaic and Hebrew parts of the resulting story and the Greek bridge between them (which is discussed below) were thus united in the language of Greek.

D. *From Where Was the Argument at Luke 13:15b-16 Derived?*

If the above analysis is correct, it is clear that the argument at Luke 13:15b-16, which justifies the cure that Jesus performed, was neither composed nor voiced by Jesus himself. Moreover, as was noted briefly above, since the gospel of Luke was composed in tannaitic times, and thus in this sense can be considered as a kind of tannaitic text, the probability that the argument of Jesus was originally composed in Aramaic and was therefore composed by Jesus at the time of the cure is further reduced by the fact that no *halachic* arguments *kal va-chomer* in Aramaic are preserved in the tannaitic texts. The additional fact that no arguments *kal va-chomer* based on permitted animal husbandry on the Sabbath appear in Mark's gospel, but first appear in the later gospel of Luke, further suggests that such arguments were first composed well after the time that Jesus had died. The likelihood that Jesus did not voice or compose this argument will become further evident from the summary of evidence in Chapter 4. This will show that if Luke 13:15b-16 can be attributed to Jesus, it was probably the only argument *kal va-chomer* that he ever composed.[126]

If, then, the argument cannot be attributed to Jesus, by whom was it composed? Since it justifies a deed of healing on the Sabbath, which was a subject of only Jewish concern, and since it shows knowledge of the structure of a rabbinic argument *kal va-chomer*, it is reasonable to assume that the argument was originally composed within an environment of educated Jews.[127] This may be confirmed by the combination of

126. Non-*halachic* (*aggadic*) arguments *kal va-chomer* are attributed to Jesus at Luke 23:28-31; Matt 6:28-30; 7:9-11; and 10:24-25.

127. The phrase 'daughter of Abraham' is assumed by some commentators to refer to a gentile, and thus is assumed to show Jesus widening his appeal to the non-Jewish world. This is based on the fact that Abraham is recognised as the father of the gentiles through Ketturah, his second official wife, while the Jewish people are regarded as the children of Jacob, the grandson of Abraham through Sarah, his first wife. The phrase 'daughter of Abraham' is, however, *never* used in Jewish texts to refer to a gentile. In fact, it occurs only once in the tannaitic texts (בת אברהם, Midrash Zuta 7.2) where it refers to Israel. It is not found in the Jerusalem Talmud but occurs in the Babylonian Talmud without a subsequent reference to Isaac and Jacob (which would identify it as a reference to a Jewish woman), in the form בת לאברהם or בתו של אברהם, e.g., b. Suk 49b; b. Hag 3a; b. Gitt 89a; b. Ket 72b;

animals used in the argument—an ox and an ass (Luke 13:15b)—which is used in the tannaitic texts as a symbol of all animals, as R. Akiva apparently explains along with R. Yose in the name of R. Ishmael, based on the text of Deut 5:14:

תוספתא מסכת בבא קמא פרק ו הלכה יח

...אחד שור וחמור ואחד בהמה חיה ועוף להרביע ולכלאים. ר' עקיבא אומ' כל .
אחד ואחד נתרבה במקומו ר' יוסה או' משם ר' ישמעאל בדברות הראשונות
הוא אומ' אתה ובנך ובתך ועבדך [ואמתך] ובהמתך. בדברות האחרונות הוא
אומ' אתה ובנך ובתך ושורך וחמורך וכל בהמתך שור וחמור בכלל היו. ולמה
יצאו להקיש עליהן מה שור וחמור האמורין לעניין שבת עשה בה שאר בהמה
חיה ועוף כשור וחמור אף שור וחמור האמורין לעניין כל דבר נעשה שאר בהמה
חיה ועוף כשור וחמור.

Tosefta Baba Kamma 6'18
...All the same are an ox, and ass and all other domesticated beasts, wild beasts and fowl, regarding bestiality and hybridisation. R. Akiva says, 'Each one is subject to an exegesis of inclusion in its appropriate location [in Scripture]'. R. Yose says in the name of R. Ishmael, 'The first version of the Ten Commandments states that *you and your son and your daughter and your man-servant and your maid-servant and your beast* (Exod 20:10). But the second version of the Ten Commandments says *You and your son and your daughter and your ox and your ass and every beast* (Deut 5.14). [This means that] and ox and an ass are covered in the

b. San 94b; and also in later rabbinic works, for example, *The Pesikta de-Rav Kahana* 5 and 15 and *Lamentations Rabba Prologue 1*, which both refer to the nation of Israel as 'the daughter of Abraham...the daughter of Isaac and the daughter of Jacob'. The phrase 'daughter of Abraham' also occurs in the post-tannaitic work 4 Macc 15:28 (composed between the first century BCE and first century CE), in which the mother of the seven sons is called a daughter of Abraham only because her bravery is compared with that of Abraham. The claim of some commentators that the phrase 'our father Abraham' is somehow equivalent to 'son of Abraham' is based on a misunderstanding of the term 'father', which in the contexts cited by these commentators can only mean 'forefather', although of course the meanings 'father' and 'forefather' may sometimes coalesce as in Luke 19:9, see e.g., Nolland, *Luke 9:21–18:34*, 724 on v. 16. Since therefore the phrase 'daughter of Abraham' is never used in Jewish texts to refer to a gentile, it is unlikely to have been recognised as such by the original audience of Luke. Moreover, in the argument in Luke's text it refers to the woman whom Jesus cured, who was almost certainly Jewish, as is indicated by the fact that she does not ask for a Sabbath cure (which, for a pious Jewish person, would be tantamount to asking Jesus to sin) and she thanks ('praises') God (rather than Jesus) for performing her cure, thus demonstrating the Jewish belief that it is God, rather than a human healer, who effects a cure. It is thus unlikely that the phrase 'daughter of Abraham' indicates a non-Jewish author of the argument, as is implied by commentators, for example Fitzmyer, *The Gospel According to Luke I–IX*, 191-2.

basic generalisation [in Exod 20:10]. Now just as when an ox and an ass are specified with reference to the Sabbath, the [oral Jewish] law has treated as equivalent to an ox and an ass other beasts, wild animals or fowl, so that when an ox and an ass are specified with respect to every other matter, the meaning is that all other [domesticated] animals, wild animals and fowl are to be treated as equivalent to an ox and an ass.[128]

There is thus little doubt that the argument attributed to Jesus by Luke, but which was probably never spoken by Jesus himself, originates from a Jewish source.

E. *The Bridge Between the Two Parts of the Story, Luke 13:14-15a*
The two parts of the story discussed above—the story of the cure and the argument used to justify the cure—are linked with a verse which contains all the material relevant to the leader of the synagogue, namely, Luke 13:14. According to Luke, the leader of the synagogue rebuked the people for seeking Sabbath cures. However, no one in Luke's story has asked for a cure, which suggests that Luke 13:14 is not part of the original story of the cure. Further evidence of this fact comes from Luke 13:15a, where Jesus replies (ἀπεκρίθη) apparently 'to him' (αὐτῷ). As noted above, this term in its context seems to refer to the leader of the synagogue, although Jesus himself has not been addressed, and despite the fact that his reply uses the plural term 'Hypocrites'. The plurality of this term is however confirmed in the subsequent argument of Jesus, which is addressed to peasant-farmers, expressed with the words, 'each of you (ἕκαστος ὑμῶν) on the Sabbath [who] untie[s] his ox or his ass from the manger' (Luke 13:15b). If then Jesus replied to many people, the term αὐτῷ cannot refer to singular 'him', in this case to the leader of the synagogue, although this is how the term is usually understood.

The key to the correct understanding of the term αὐτῷ is the plural term 'Hypocrites', which, along with his address to *many* peasant-farmers, means that Jesus addressed more than one person, that is, he addressed *a group*. The only *group* in this story is the crowd which is mentioned in the introduction to the words of the leader of the synagogue, *And answering the ruler of the synagogue indignant that Jesus had healed on the Sabbath, said to the crowd* (τῷ ὄχλῳ, Luke 13:14a). This suggests that the masculine singular term αὐτῷ at 13:15a refers to the masculine singular noun ὄχλος, and should therefore be understood as a reference to the crowd.

---

128. Similarly, m. BK 5.7.

Why did Jesus reply to a crowd? The likely answer to this question is indicated by the pejorative nature of the term 'Hypocrites!' used by Jesus to address the people in the crowd. In the context of the story, and especially in view of the argument in which Jesus apparently justifies his Sabbath cure and thus suggests that this cure was opposed by those by whom it was witnessed, the most likely explanation for this derogatory term is that Jesus was criticised by those who witnessed his Sabbath cure. According to the argument voiced by Jesus, which is addressed to 'each of you on the Sabbath who untie[s] his ox or his ass from the manger, and lead[s] it away to water', v. 15), the 'Hypocrites' who witnessed the cure consisted mainly of peasant-farmers who were the backbone of the first-century Galilean economy, and who thus were likely to be present at the scene of the cure.[129] It is also self-evident that these peasant-farmers were not 'working' in their fields on the day of the cure, which in this context must be due to the fact that it was the Sabbath day. These people were therefore behaving in accordance with Sabbath law, and in this sense were morally entitled to criticise Jesus for 'working' on the Sabbath by performing a Sabbath cure and violating Sabbath law. The argument voiced by Jesus, however, justifies his action of 'working' on the Sabbath with an argument *kal va-chomer* which is not only specific for the situation, but which is also especially appropriate for the people he addressed, since it is based on a situation of animal husbandry which would have resonated in their lives. The criticism of Jesus by these particular people thus rings true. It can, however, be assumed that the redactor of this text—probably Luke—did not wish to record that Jesus was criticised for Sabbath cures by ordinary Jewish people—in this case by peasant-farmers—and therefore omitted this criticism from the story of the cure.

This means that the verbal response of Jesus to the criticism of his Sabbath cure—that is, the term 'Hypocrites'—has been displaced in the narrative by the text of Luke 13:14, which now intervenes between the story of the cure and the retort of Jesus to his critics in the crowd. The material relating to the leader of the synagogue at Luke 13:14 has thus, in effect, replaced the criticism of Jesus by the Jewish peasant-farmers who witnessed the Sabbath cure. This further means that the phrase Ἀπεκρίθη δὲ αὐτῷ (which now begins Luke 13:15a) originally introduced the response of Jesus to the crowd and means *He replied to it*, that is, *Jesus replied to the crowd*. The verb Ἀπεκρίθη can therefore be understood with its usual meaning, literally, 'he (Jesus) replied', although in

129. Z. Safrai, *The Economy of Roman Palestine* (London: Routledge, 1994) 104ff.

Luke's present text it seems as if the leader of the synagogue replied. Subsequently, perhaps wishing to keep close to the original terminology of his source, the author of Luke 13:14 (probably Luke) used the same verb (in the form ἀποκριθείς) to introduce the speech of the leader of the synagogue.

F. *The Final Editorial Comment, Luke 13:17*

As many scholars note, Luke 13:17 is based on the Septuagint version of Isa 45:16, *All that are opposed to him shall be ashamed and confounded, and shall walk in shame*, which could be said to anticipate the Lucan theme of the future acknowledgment by doubters of Jesus as God.[130] Luke thus refers to 'shame', expressed as κατῃσχύνοντο at Luke 13:17, and as καὶ πορεύσονται ἐν αἰσχύνῃ in the Septuagint. Luke also cites the phrase οἱ ἀντικείμενοι αὐτῷ, 'his adversaries', to which he probably added the adjective πάντες, 'all', one of his favourite, recurring terms.[131] A further Lucan detail which helps confirm his authorship of this verse is the phrase 'all the crowd', πᾶς ὁ ὄχλος, which also occurs at Luke 6:19 and Acts 21:27. As many scholars conclude, it is likely that v. 17 is Luke's editorial addition to the story of the cure. Perhaps Luke attempted to account for the plurality of the term 'Hypocrites' by equating the latter with those who are 'ashamed and confounded'.

G. *The Non-Pharisaic, Perhaps Sadducean Identity of the Leader of the Synagogue*

The only Jewish official who is mentioned in this event is the leader of the synagogue. As he was probably a later addition to the tale (see above) and as—in any case—he is not identified as a Pharisee, and as no other Pharisees are mentioned in the account, we can presume that no Pharisees were present at the original historical event. It is unlikely therefore that the leader of the synagogue was a Pharisee, as this would surely have been mentioned by Luke. What then was his religious identity? Is there any hint of the type of person to whom Luke refers?

According to Luke, the leader of the synagogue justified his rebuke of the crowd for seeking Sabbath cures by referring to the written Pentateuchal law of Exod 20:9-10 (or Deut 5:13-14), *Six days you shall labour and do all your work. But the seventh day is a Sabbath to the Lord your God. In it you shall not do any work* (Luke 13:14). These words suggest the religious group to which the speaker belonged. As was briefly noted

130. For comment on this and other Lucan motifs, see e.g., Marshall, *Luke*, 599.
131. See Fitzmyer, *The Gospel According to Luke X–XXIV*, 1014, with reference to Luke 3:16; 4:15; and 9:1.

in Chapter 1, the earliest official religious reaction to the fact that the Pentateuchal text contains no indication that any of its laws may be violated, even for acts of healing and/or saving life, is the edict of Mattathias the Maccabean, probably issued in 167 BCE, which allowed fighting in self-defence on the Sabbath day. This, however, offered only a pragmatic justification for the religious leniency it allowed. The lack of religious justification can only be due to the fact that the Jewish sages of the time, probably the Pharisees, were aware that the Jewish holy sources did not include any mitigating exceptions to Jewish written law which would allow acts of healing and/or saving life on the Sabbath, and neither were there any incidents in these texts whose simple interpretation showed that such acts were approved. From around 167 BCE, therefore, it can be assumed that the Pharisees were aware that the only way in which acts of healing and/or saving life could be justified within Jewish law was through a further revelation of Jewish oral law, which they, the Pharisees, had a duty to disclose. This accounts for the 'revelation' of the *halachic* arguments *kal va-chomer* that are preserved in the gospel texts (it seems that this type of argument was a popular way in which the first-century Jewish sages justified acts of healing and saving life).[132] However, as will be seen especially in Chapter 11, whenever acts of healing and/or saving life could not be justified in this way, the Jewish sages issued permits without any justification or further argument (see, e.g., the directive of the [probably] Pharisaic leader of the Sanhedrin, Rabban Gamaliel the Elder at m. RH 2.5—cited in Chapter 9). It is therefore most unlikely that a Pharisee, especially in the first century, would cite Pentateuchal law to deny the possibility of acts of healing and/or saving life on the Sabbath day because he would have known that acts of healing and/or saving life on the Sabbath could only be allowed through a further revelation of Jewish oral law. This approach to the problem of healing and/or saving life is, however, effectively rejected when the leader of the synagogue cites written Pentateuchal law, and thus implic- itly denies that there is any solution at all. This suggests that the leader of the synagogue should be linked with the Sadducees, who, according to Josephus, followed Pentateuchal law and rejected 'the [oral] tradition of our forefathers'; that is, they rejected the tradition and further revelation of Jewish oral law:

132. The evidence for this statement is discussed in Chapters 4, 5 and 7. One first-century exception is noted in the tannaitic texts, namely, the edict of Shammai, which allowed a siege to be continued on the Sabbath, see Chapter 1.

Jewish Antiquities XIII.297-98
...the Pharisees had passed on to the people certain regulations handed down by former generations and not recorded in the laws of Moses, *for which reason they are rejected by the Sadducean group*, who hold that only those regulations should be considered valid which were written down (in Scripture) and that *those which had been handed down by former generations need not be observed.*

It is significant that Luke does not identify the leader of the synagogue as a Pharisee, although the ease with which such a claim might have been made is implied by the probability that the material which relates to this individual (Luke 13:14) was probably added to the scene by Luke himself, who was thus free to add any details that he wished. It seems, therefore, that this individual was intended by Luke to represent a Sadducean official who opposed the use of Jewish oral law to enable the performance of acts of healing and/or saving life which violated this law. He thus justified his opposition to deeds of healing and/or saving life by citing Jewish written law.

H. *Summary of the Proposed History of the Redaction of Luke 13:10-17*
It seems that the original account of this cure recorded a Sabbath event, when Jesus was among a crowd of Aramaic-speaking Jewish people composed mostly of pious Jewish peasant-farmers who, in accordance with Sabbath law, were not working on this day (Luke 13:15b). Among this crowd was a woman with a bent back. Although we can assume that Jesus was known as a successful healer, neither this woman nor anyone else in the crowd asked Jesus for a cure. This can be attributed to the fact that the people in the crowd were Sabbath observers (which is shown by their absence from their fields) and were aware that healing on the Sabbath caused a violation of Sabbath law. It can therefore be assumed that they would not have asked the Jewish Jesus to violate Sabbath law.[133] Jesus however had noticed a woman with a bent back among the crowd (Luke 13:12a). Without waiting for any kind of introduction, Jesus told this woman in Aramaic that she was now cured (13:12b). He then touched her with his hands (Luke 13:13—it remains unexplained why the cure was announced before it took place). The woman who was cured then praised God, in effect thanking God (rather than Jesus) for

133. There was, however, no problem in asking a non-Jewish healer for a Sabbath cure, as the following story suggests: 'R. Yohanan had [scurvy], and was receiving treatment from the daughter of [the Emperor] Domitian in Tiberias. On Friday he went to her. He said to her, "Do I need to be treated tomorrow [on the Sabbath]?"' (y. Shab 14.4 and y. AZ 2.2).

effecting her cure. Even though she was probably not in a synagogue at that moment on the Sabbath, this act of gratitude helps to confirm her Jewish identity, since Judaism considers that God (rather than a human healer) is ultimately responsible for any cure. The crowd then rebuked Jesus for performing a cure on the Sabbath (because Jesus had thereby been guilty of 'work'), although this criticism of Jesus is now missing from Luke's text. Jesus responded to their criticism with the retort 'Hypocrites' (Ὑποκριταί, Luke 13:15a), probably using the Aramaic term צבועין, and thus addressing the crowd with the same language he had used earlier to the woman he had cured. The original account of this incident probably ended here.

A memory of this cure subsequently inspired an unknown educated Jewish person to compose a rabbinic argument *kal va-chomer* which justified this cure. This argument was particularly appropriate for the peasant-farmers to whom it was addressed, because it is based on a leniency in agricultural Jewish oral law which permitted healing and/or saving the lives of animals on the Sabbath day (although no simple record of this permit now exists in the rabbinic texts). This would have resonated with the peasant-farmers to whom it was apparently addressed (Luke 13:15b-16). The Semitic origin of the original version of this argu-ment—which was probably composed in Hebrew (rather than Aramaic), as are all *halachic* arguments *kal va-chomer* preserved in the tannaitic texts—is indicated by a retroversion of a formal version of the present Greek argument into Hebrew (or Aramaic), which shows a play on words that is impossible to reproduce in Greek, and almost certainly featured in the original text. Subsequently, this argument was rendered into Greek, in an informal style, perhaps in order to imitate the simple, non-technical language used by Jesus himself. As a result, both the Greek translation of the semitic argument and the Greek translation of the Aramaic story of the cure, were now smoothly united in the language of Greek.

The fact that the historical Jesus almost certainly conducted the cure in Aramaic, although the argument which justifies the cure was almost certainly originally composed in Hebrew, suggests that it is most unlikely that the historical Jesus voiced the argument that now justifies his cure. This is further confirmed when we realise that *halachic* arguments *kal va-chomer* are typical of the rhetorical language used by the Jewish sages, and are therefore unlikely to have been addressed to the relatively uneducated peasant-farmers who—according to the words of the argu-ment itself—were witnesses of the cure (Luke 13:15). Neither could the historical Jesus have expressed the argument to the Pharisees, as is apparently the case in all other of the *halachic* arguments used by Jesus to justify his cures, because no Pharisaic witnesses are noted for this cure. Additionally, the argument voiced by Jesus contains information that Jesus could not have known, namely, the eighteen-year duration of the illness of the woman whom Jesus cured. Luke's reference to this fact in his introduction to the scene (Luke 13:11) could thus have been learnt by Luke from the argument *kal va-chomer* that was added to the story of the cure (13:15b-16), because apart from his announcement of the cure he had performed (13:12) Jesus only spoke to the woman to tell her she had been cured. (Her illness, a bent back, would have been visible and the historical Jesus would have had no need to be told the nature of her illness or that she needed a cure.) The probability that Jesus did not express this argument is also indicated by the fact that although rabbinic arguments *kal va-chomer* based on animal husbandry could be composed to justify action in *any* situation of healing and/or saving life (because the animal to be saved could be put into the same kind of situation as the man or woman to be saved), no similar arguments appear in the gospel of Mark. It is possible, therefore, that such easily composed arguments first appeared after the publication of Mark's gospel, which is well after the time that Jesus died. In any case, as will be seen from the cumulative evidence summarised in Chapter 4, if indeed Jesus voiced the argument now preserved at Luke 13:15b-16, it would probably be the only *halachic* argument *kal va-chomer* that Jesus ever expressed.

There is, however, no reason to doubt that the historical Jesus performed a cure on the Sabbath for a woman with a bent back. The Sabbath timing is confirmed by the fact that no one in the crowd asked to be cured, including the woman with a bent back, although she had been ill for eighteen years. This timing also accounts for the fact that the pious Jewish peasant-farmers who witnessed the cure (Luke 13:15) were not working, so that they were in a location where they were able to witness the cure. They were therefore the kind of people who, we can expect, would criticise a Sabbath cure, which in turn helps confirm that they criticised Jesus. Although this criticism has been removed from the tale, the probability that it happened further confirms that the cure took place on the Sabbath day, since no criticism can be expected if the cure had taken place on a non-Sabbath day.

The gap left by the removal of the criticism of Jesus was replaced with material which alleges the presence of a leader of a synagogue, perhaps a Sadducee (see the discussion above), who apparently witnessed the cure and rebuked the crowd of Jewish people who (he claimed) had asked for Sabbath cures. His rebuke took the form of a quotation from the Pentateuch (Exod 20:9, or Deut 5:12-15) which forbade any 'work'—in this case an act of healing and/or saving life—on the Sabbath day (Luke 13:14). This insertion accounts for the meaning of the otherwise problematic phrase ἀπεκρίθη δὲ αὐτῷ (Luke 13:15b). This phrase now appears to mean that Jesus addressed the leader of the synagogue, whom he insulted with the *plural* term 'Hypocrites'. In fact, before it was displaced (by Luke 13:14), the phrase ἀπεκρίθη δὲ αὐτῷ probably introduced the reply of Jesus to the people in the crowd who criticised the cure. It seems, moreover, that Luke, perhaps attempting to stay as close as possible to the terminology of the original story of the tale, introduced the material relating to the leader of the synagogue with the same verb ἀποκρίνομαι, here in the form ἀποκριθεὶς (Luke 13:14a). This accounts for the two uses of this verb, which implies that both Jesus and the leader of the synagogue replied to something that was said, although neither has been addressed in the present text.

Other more minor additions probably attributable to Luke include the title ὁ κύριος, 'the Lord', which functions as the stated subject of the verb Ἀπεκρίθη (Luke 13:15a) and serves to ensure that the audience of the text recognised that Jesus spoke the words reported in Luke 13:15-16. This fact was no longer clear because the original response of Jesus to the crowd (beginning with *Hypocrites*, Luke 13:15a) is now interrupted by Luke 13:14 (the material relating to the leader of the synagogue). This title for Jesus was used by the early Jewish Christians around the time of Luke, which means that this addition could date back to Luke.[134] The phrase 'whom Satan has bound' (Luke 13:16) may also be attributed to the activity of Luke. This can be assumed from the fact that the idea that it implies is alien to Jewish thought.[135] There are very few references to Satan in the tannaitic texts, which suggests that this reference would not have been used by the original author of the argument whose Jewish identity is suggested by his ability to construct a rabbinic argument *kal va-chomer* and his knowledge of Hebrew (or perhaps Aramaic).

Luke was also probably responsible for the claim placed at the beginning of this narrative (Luke 13:10) that the cure took place in a synagogue, which helps prepare the audience of the story for the presence of the leader of a synagogue, as it is of course likely that a leader of a synagogue would be found in a synagogue, especially on the Sabbath.

---

134. Fitzmyer, *The Gospel According to Luke I–IX*, 202-3.

135. For more on Satan in Luke, see Fitzmyer, *The Gospel According to Luke X–XXIV*, 1013 n. 16. There seem to be only two references to Satan in tannaitic texts: (1) t. AZ 1.18 (where a further reference is based on Ps 109:60) and (2) *The Fathers of Rabbi Nathan* A.9, probably compiled between 700 and 900 CE, in which the term occurs twice.

The synagogue, moreover, was a location in which Jesus had performed other Sabbath cures, as Luke could have learnt from the gospel of Mark.[136] It is interesting to note that Luke again uses this anticipatory technique to suggest that the cure of the man with dropsy took place within a feast of the Pharisees, when he prefaces his account with a sentence that refers to 'the house of a ruler who belonged to the Pharisees' (Luke 14:1) and thus prepares his audience for the presence of Pharisees, although it is unlikely that historical Pharisees were present at the cure (see the above discussion on Luke 14:1-6). The non-Jewish authorship of Luke for the introduction of the event (at Luke 13:10) may also be confirmed by the plural use of the term σάββατον to indicate a single Sabbath day (ἐν τοῖς σάββασιν) which is commonly associated with a non-Jewish source. The same can be said for the phrase ἐν μιᾷ τῶν συναγωγῶν, 'in one of the synagogues', since the term εἷς, 'one', used indefinitely as a partitive genitive, is typical of the style of Luke.[137] The placement of the cure within a synagogue, where it almost certainly did *not* take place, also accounts for the fact that Luke's synagogue is not identified in any way. This location is in fact disproved by the description of the people present in the synagogue as a 'bustling crowd' (ὄχλος, Luke 13:14). This term is therefore *lectio difficilior* in relation to a synagogue, where noisy bustling crowds are not usually found. The retention by Luke of the term ὄχλος therefore suggests that this detail of the story was strongly linked with the original event, and was consequently a term which Luke could not discard.

There is thus little doubt that the original story of the cure on the Sabbath of a woman with a bent back, now preserved by Luke, has been extensively modified and that no authentic version of the event now exists. Whether or not the above account of its redaction is wholly correct, it is clear that the story related by Luke cannot be accepted as it stands.

136. Mark 1:39, where Jesus 'cast out demons'; Mark 6:2, where he cured a man with a withered hand.
137. Similarly, Luke 5:17; 8:22; 13:10; 20:1, see Fitzmyer, *The Gospel According to Luke I–IX*, 121-2. M. Black, *An Aramaic Approach to the Gospels and Acts* (3rd edn; Oxford: Clarendon, 1966) 105, suggests that the partitive construction hints at a Semitic origin for this part of the event, since the term for 'one' in both Hebrew and Aramaic often functions as a full pronoun which is followed by a term indicating 'from', often appearing in Greek as a genitive noun, preceded by the partitive preposition ἐκ.

IV. *The Cure of a Withered Hand: Mark 3:1-6, Luke 6:6-11 and Matthew 12:9-14*

The three synoptic accounts of the cure by Jesus of a man with a withered hand are translated below. Each is preceded by the story of Jesus in the Galilean fields (printed in italics) because the juxtaposition of the two stories often serves as the basis for a claim that the Pharisees were present at both these events:

Mark 2:23–3:6	Luke 6:1-11	Matthew 12:1-14
2²³ *One Sabbath he was going through the grain fields: and as they made their way, his disciples began to pluck the heads of grain.* ²⁴ *And the Pharisees said to him, 'Look, why are they doing what is not lawful on the Sabbath?'* ²⁵ *And he said to them, 'Have you not heard what David did, when he was in need and was hungry, he and those who were with him.* ²⁶ *How he entered the house of God, when Abiathar was high priest, and ate the sacred bread, which it is not lawful for any but the priests to eat, and also gave it to those who were with him?'* ²⁷ *And he said to them, 'The Sabbath was made for man, not man for the Sabbath.* ²⁸ *So the son of man is Lord even of the Sabbath.'*	6¹ *On a Sabbath, while he was going through the grain fields, his disciples plucked and ate some heads of grain, rubbing them in their hands.* ² *But some of the Pharisees said, 'Why are you doing what is not lawful to do on the Sabbath?'* ³ *And Jesus answered and said, 'Have you not read what David did, when he was hungry, he and those who were with him?* ⁴ *How he entered the house of God and took and ate the sacred bread which is not lawful for any but the priests to eat, and also gave it to those who were with him?'* ⁵ *And he said to them, 'The son of man is lord of the Sabbath'.*	12¹ *At the time Jesus went through the grain fields on the Sabbath. His disciples were hungry and they began to pluck the heads of grain to eat.* ² *But when the Pharisees saw it, they said to him, 'Look, your disciples are doing what is not lawful to do on the Sabbath'.* ³ *He said to them, 'Have you not read what David did, when he was hungry and those who were with him,* ⁴ *how he entered the house of God and ate the sacred bread, which it was not lawful for him to eat, nor for those who were with him, but only for the priests?* ⁵ *Or have you not read in the law how on the Sabbath, the priests in the Temple violate the Sabbath and are guiltless?* ⁶ *I tell you, something greater than the temple is here.* ⁷ *And if you had known what this means, "I desire mercy and sacrifice", you would not have condemned the guiltless.* ⁸ *For the son of man is Lord of the Sabbath.'*

3:1 And again he entered the synagogue	6:6 On another Sabbath, when he entered the synagogue and taught,	12:9 And he went on from there and entered their synagogue.
and a man was there who had a withered (ἐξηραμμένην) hand.	a man was there whose right hand was shrunken (ξηρά).	10 And behold there was a man with a shrunken (ξηράν) hand
2 And they watched (παρετήρουν) him to see whether he would heal him on the Sabbath, so that they might accuse (κατηγορήσωσιν) him.	7 And the scribes and the Pharisees watched (παρετηροῦντο) him, to see whether he would heal on the Sabbath, so that they might find an accusation (εὕρωσιν κατηγορεῖν) against him.	
3 And he said to the man who had the shrunken hand, 'Come into the middle [of the synagogue]!'	8 But he knew their thoughts, and he said to the man who had the withered hand, 'Come into the middle [of the synagogue]!'	
4 And he said, 'Is it lawful on the Sabbath to do good (ἀγαθὸν ποιῆσαι/ἀγαθοποιῆσαι) or to do harm, to save life or to kill (ἀποκτεῖναι)?' But they were silent.	9 And Jesus said to them, 'I ask you, is it lawful on the Sabbath to do good (ἀγαθοποιῆσαι) or to do harm, to save life or to destroy it (ἀπολέσαι)?'	And they asked him, 'Is it lawful on the Sabbath to heal?' in order that they might accuse (κατηγορήσωσιν) him.
		11 He said to them, 'What man of you, if he has one sheep and it falls into a pit on the Sabbath, will not lay hold of it and lift it out? 12 Of how much more value is a man than a sheep! So it is lawful on the Sabbath to do good (καλῶς ποιεῖν)'

[5] And he looked round at them with anger, grieved at their hardness of heart, and he said to the man, 'Stretch out your hand'. He stretched it out, and his hand was restored.	[10] And he looked round on them all, and said to him, 'Stretch out your hand'. And he did so, and his hand was restored.	[13] Then he said to the man, 'Stretch out your hand'. And the man stretched it out, and it was restored, like the other.
[6] The Pharisees went out (ἐξελθόντες) and immediately (εὐθὺς) held counsel (συμβούλιον ἐδίδουν) with the Herodians against him, how they might destroy (ὅπως αὐτὸν ἀπολέσωσιν) him.	[11] But they were full of fury, and discussed together what they might do (ποιήσαειν) with Jesus.	[14] But the Pharisees went out (ἐξελθόντες) and took counsel (συμβούλιον ἔλαβον) against him how they might destroy (ὅπως αὐτὸν ἀπολέσωσιν) him.

The story begins after the meeting of Jesus and the Pharisees in the Galilean fields (according to Mark and Matthew), although on a different Sabbath (according to Luke). The versions of Mark and Luke subsequently continue along similar lines. The two gospels recount how Jesus entered a synagogue in which there was a man with a withered (or, shrunken) hand. The people in the synagogue watched Jesus in a menacing way because they wanted to see if Jesus would heal the man. Jesus then called the man over, and asked a *halachic* question (that is, a question concerning Jewish law) regarding the legality of performing Sabbath cures. The question ellicited no response. Jesus was angry, perhaps because of the opposition of his audience to Sabbath cures, although this is not stated. Jesus asked the man to stretch out his hand, which he then cured. The Pharisees, who are now mentioned for the first time, then left the scene with other Jewish officials and plotted that Jesus should be killed.

In contrast with the gospels of Mark and Luke, the version of Matthew states that after Jesus arrived at the synagogue, where there was a man with a withered hand, the onlookers (rather than Jesus in the accounts of Mark and Luke) asked a *halachic*-type question which, according to Matthew's subsequent remark, showed their negative attitude to Sabbath cures. Jesus then uttered a rabbinic argument *kal va-chomer* which justified his impending cure of the man with the withered hand. Jesus then asked the man to stretch out his hand, which he cured. Subsequently, now repeating the essence of Mark and Luke, Matthew states also that Pharisees then left the scene and plotted that Jesus should be killed.

Listed below are the differences in the versions of this story that are significant for the discussion here:

(1) *The timing of the event.* According to Mark and Matthew, the event took place on the Sabbath, immediately after the meeting between Jesus and the Pharisees in the Galilean fields (Mark 3:1; Matt 12:9). Luke places the event on a different Sabbath day (Luke 6:6).

(2) *The presence of Pharisees during the scene.* The presence of Pharisees (along with Jewish scribes) is specifically noted by Luke (Luke 6:7). However, neither Mark nor Matthew note their presence during the event. Apart from the Pharisees who are mentioned in the previous event, when they met Jesus in the Galilean fields, Mark and Matthew refer to their presence only after the cure of the man with the withered hand, when they apparently withdrew from the scene (Mark 3:6 and Matt 12:14). They are identified as Herodians, according to Mark.

(3) *The identity of the questioner(s).* According to Mark and Luke, it was Jesus who asked a *halachic* question at the beginning of this scene (Mark 3:4; Luke 6:9). According to Matthew, a *halachic* question was asked by the onlookers of the imminent cure (Matt 12:10).

(4) *The expectations of the questions.* The question of Jesus in Mark and Luke (Mark 3:4, and the almost verbatim repetition at Luke 12:9) seems to allow for two contrasting replies, in effect, 'Yes, doing "good" on the Sabbath (which in this context undoubtedly refers to acts of healing and saving life) is permitted', or, 'No, acts of healing and saving life are *not* permitted on the Sabbath', this negative act described as 'doing harm'. In contrast, the question of the onlookers in Matthew (Matt 12:10a) expects only a single reply, either Yes or No. This possible ambiguity is, however, removed by Matthew's following remark 'so that they might accuse him' (Matt 12:10b). That is, the onlookers in Matthew did *not* allow acts of healing and/or saving life on the Sabbath.

(5) *The thoughts of Jesus.* Mark and Luke claim that Jesus knew and criticised the thoughts of the onlookers of the cure (Mark 3:5 and Luke 6:8). Matthew is silent on this account.

(6) *The argument of Jesus to justify Sabbath healing.* Only Matthew records that Jesus justified his Sabbath cure (Matt 12:11-12).

Assuming this cure records an historical event, the following questions are relevant here:

1. Who were the historical witnesses of the cure?
2. Who criticised Jesus either before (by implication) or after the cure was performed?
3. Who composed the *halachic* questions asked in Matthew's account—the historical Jesus, Matthew, or some other—and what is its function within the story of the cure?
4. How does the *halachic* argument *kal va-chomer* in Matthew's version of the story (Matt 12:11-12) prove its case?

A. *Who Anticipated, Watched and Criticised Jesus for Performing the Cure?*

There is little doubt that the three synoptic authors wanted their audience to believe that Pharisees (and also Jewish scribes, according to Luke) waited and watched Jesus in an unfriendly way, both before and after he performed this cure. This *may* be seen in the versions of Matthew and Mark by the placement of this event immediately after the scene in the Galilean fields, which has led many scholars to claim that the Pharisees in the Galilean fields were also present at the cure of the man with the withered hand, and would thus account for the juxtaposition of these two scenes.[138] In the accounts themselves, Mark and Matthew suggest the presence of the Pharisees with the claim that Pharisees left the scene of the cure (ἐξελθόντες, Mark 3:6, which is repeated at Matt 12:14), which clearly implies that they were originally there.

Yet neither of these literary devices proves the presence of Pharisees at the event of the cure. The discussion above on the previous scene of Jesus and his men in the Galilean fields has shown that this story is almost certainly midrashic, so that the event itself is non-historical and probably never took place, and means that the midrashic Pharisees in the Galilean fields cannot turn into historical Pharisees in the following event. In any case, even if the historical Jesus met historical Pharisees in the Galilean fields, the possibility that *the same Pharisees* were also

---

138. Commentators thus claim the presence of Pharisees by assuming non-existent evidence. For instance, Gundry, *A Commentary on His Apology*, 149-52, esp. 149, states that the juxtaposition of the two incidents proves their chronological continuity because 'the two stories go together': '[Jesus] ignores the warning in the preceding story against violating the Sabbath' (what warning?, one might ask) and that Jesus addresses the Pharisees at Mark 3:5 (p. 151); similarly, Donahue and Harrington, *Sacra Pagina*, 115. In contrast, Marshall, *Luke*, 234, however, considers that Mark does not imply that the two events took place on the same day.

present at the cure of the man with a withered hand is difficult to accept. It would mean, for example, that after their meeting with Jesus in the Galilean fields, the Pharisees correctly anticipated that Jesus was going to a local synagogue, and then rushed on ahead and waited patiently in this synagogue until Jesus arrived, expecting him to cure a man with a withered hand who happened to be there. Even more unlikely is the assumption that Jesus would leave his starving disciples in the Galilean fields in order to visit a nearby synagogue, rather than to procure help for his men. In any case, even if the presence of historical Pharisees can be assumed from their earlier meeting with an historical Jesus in the Galilean fields, it is odd that they are not identified again at the beginning of the next scene, especially as the logic and style of the accounts of Mark and Matthew suggest that a reference to 'Pharisees' could easily have been inserted without causing a disruption of any kind to the text, perhaps at Mark 3:2 and Matt 12:10. The presence of the Pharisees would then be established, and no assumptions would need to be made. A simple reference to the presence of Pharisees could even have been placed within the accounts, as can be seen from the version of Luke (Luke 6:7). Instead, however, in the versions of Mark and Matthew the Pharisees who apparently met Jesus in the Galilean fields are mentioned six verses before the beginning of the following scene, according to Mark 2:24, and nine verses earlier, according to Matt 12:2. Even without the need for a modern standard of proof, and even if the story in the Galilean fields is historical (which is most unlikely), the contiguity of these events does not show that the same Galilean Pharisees were present at each. It is, however, possible that the scene of the cure of the man with a withered hand was deliberately placed after the meeting of Jesus and the Pharisees in the Galilean fields (probably first by Mark) in order to imply, without actually stating, their presence as a fact.

Alternatively, the presence of Pharisees at the cure of a man with a withered hand is implied by Mark 3:6 and Matt 12:14 (which repeats the essence of Mark 3:6). These verses state that Pharisees withdrew after the man had been cured, which naturally implies that they were originally there. This possibility is, however, considerably weakened by the fact that the reference is retrospective, which is odd (even if graced with the scholarly term of 'foreshadowing') because it requires a re-assessment of the main event *after* it has occurred and thus interrupts the logical sequence of the narrative of the tale. In any case, as can be seen by the reference to their presence at Luke 6:7, the presence of the Pharisees could easily have been mentioned during the event itself.

Moreover, the historical reliability of Mark 3:6 (and therefore also of Matt 12:14, which repeats the essence of Mark 3:6, and also Luke 6:11), is severely undermined by a detailed examination of the verse itself. Although it includes Markan vocabulary—the adverb εὐθύς and the verb ἐξέρχομαι—which give an impression of the authorship of Mark, other significant terms in this verse suggest that the opposite is the case. In any case, vocabulary which echoes the vocabulary used by the author of a text is not proof in itself of the integrity of a text.[139] More relevant here are the several terms which cannot be associated with Mark himself. These include: (1) the expression συμβούλιον ἐδίδουν, 'to form a plan', which is unexpected in view of the more common συμβούλιον ποιεῖν (corresponding with the Latin phrase *consilium facere*), which occurs at Mark 15:1;[140] (2) the absence of the verb ζητέω, which is odd in view of Mark's use of this term in other contexts which describe plots against the life of Jesus, for example, Mark 11:18; 12:12; 14:1, 11, 55; (3) the use of ὅπως in the phrase ὅπως αὐτὸν ἀπολέσωσιν, which is unexpected in view of the use by Mark of the more simple πῶς, as can be seen at Mark 11:18, and the similar terminology at Mark 14:1 and 15:1; (4) the inconsistency of terminology—the verb ἀποκτεῖναι, 'to kill', is used at Mark 3:4, but a different, although synonymous verb ἀπολέσωσιν is used at Mark 3:6. These examples of non-Markan vocabulary and non-Markan style within a verse of only fifteen Greek words strongly suggest that Mark 3:6 was not composed by Mark.

This in itself does not of course negate the historicity of the facts it reports. The historicity of these facts is, however, seriously challenged by the following discrepancies. First, as many scholars have noted, although this verse claims that Pharisees plotted to kill Jesus (which is echoed at Matt 12:14), no Pharisees are linked with events around his death. This inconsistency may account for the silence of Luke on this detail in the verse, although Luke 6:11 otherwise repeats the essence of Mark's text. The accusation of Mark 3:6 that Herodians plotted to kill Jesus is similarly uncorroborated, and neither is it confirmed by Matthew or Luke. Mark refers to Herodians only one other time, when they came to 'entrap' Jesus (Mark 12:13) in a passage which again has aroused suspicion that it is also an addition to Mark's text.[141] Moreover, whereas

---

139. The term εὐθύς appears in Mark forty-three times, eight times in Matthew, and three times each in Luke and John. For the uses of εὐθύς, ἐξέρχομαι and the redactional nature of Mark 3:6, see E. J. Pryke, *Redactional Style in the Marcan Gospel* (Cambridge: Cambridge University Press, 1978) 87-9.

140. Guelich, *Mark 1–8:26*, 138; Gundry, *A Commentary on His Apology*, 156.

141. For suggestions for the identity of Mark's Herodians, see Guelich, *Mark 1–8:26*, 138, and 177 for the redactional nature of Mark 12:13.

the cure of the man with a withered hand took place in Galilee, Matthew links Herodians with the Pharisees only in Jerusalem (Matt 22:16).

A further problem in Mark's text is the fact that although the violation of Sabbath law was (and still is) considered in Judaism as a sin, it is considered in Judaism as a sin against God, *not* a sin against man. This means in practice that it is punishable *only* by God, and *only* if God wishes to punish this sin. R. Yohanan b. Zakkai, a first-century Jewish sage, therefore only hesitantly (חוששני, 'I am doubtful', m. Shab 16.7) advised that an individual who covered a scorpion on the Sabbath, presumably to prevent it from stinging and thus causing death (considered by the amoraic commentators as 'hunting', which is the twenty-fifth of the thirty-nine *main* actions which are prohibited on the Sabbath) should make atonement for the violation of the Sabbath merely with a sin-offering, a punishment used for an accidental violation of Jewish law.[142] In general, however, the rabbinic sages were of the opinion that the punishment for violating Sabbath law was the penalty of *karet*, literally 'a cutting off', or 'extirpation', which is the biblical penalty for certain deliberate sins for which the sinner's life (or, 'soul') might be 'utterly cut off'. This was interpreted by the later Jewish sages as a premature, sudden death which *only ever* occurs through *the will of God*.[143] Thus when the late first-century sage R. Tarfon was approached by a pregnant lady who asked him if she could eat on the Day of Atonement, a day of total abstinence from food and drink, whose laws are considered similar in their severity to Sabbath law, R. Tarfon denied this request but cited Ps 58:3, and thus prophesied a dire fate for the mother and possibly also the child, should this sin be performed, *The wicked are estranged from the womb. Speakers of lies go astray as soon as they are born.*[144] No

---

142. m. Shab 16.7, which is the subject of commentary at y. Shab 14.1 and b. Shab 121b.

143. For sins meriting the punishment of *karet* see J. Milgrom, *Leviticus 1–16* (AB 3; New York: Doubleday, 1991) 457-60. The Mishnah at m. San 7.4 advocates death by stoning for the violation (מחלל) of the Sabbath, but m. San 7.8 modifies this punishment to *karet*. The Babylonian Talmud (b. San 46a) notes that a man from Greek times was stoned to death for riding a horse on the Sabbath, a forbidden Sabbath act (m. Beza 5.2). It is unlikely, however, that this punishment was imposed—the amoraic sages express surprise at the penalty ('*not because he was liable thereto*') because the prohibition against riding on the Sabbath is only a *shebuth*, namely, a rabbinic injunction which forbids a certain act because it resembles, or it could lead to, a prohibited act of work, and therefore does not deserve a penalty of death.

144. y. Yom 8.4.

human punishment was, however, threatened for this potential serious violation of Jewish law. In any case, the permitted violations listed in Chapter 11 of the present study will show that Jewish law was regularly violated in the first century CE in order to heal and/or to save life, with the full permission of the Jewish sages, and with no threat of punishment for the individuals involved. We must therefore conclude that it is highly improbable that Pharisees or any other Jewish official would ever have conspired that Jesus should be killed merely because he violated Sabbath law by curing a man with a withered hand.[145]

The serious historical and textual problems in Mark 3:6, a single Greek sentence of fifteen words, thus helps to confirm the suggestion of several scholars that Mark 3:6 was probably not composed by Mark, but is a later addition to his gospel text, which was added to Mark before the publication of Luke, who repeats its main facts. Neither this verse nor the repetition of its essence at Luke 6:11 and Matt 12:14 can therefore be used as evidence to claim that the Pharisees were present when Jesus cured a man with a withered hand.[146] It is possible, however, that this verse was originally added to Mark's text, in order to strengthen the otherwise unlikely claim that the juxtaposition of this story immediately after the story of the Pharisees in the Galilean fields means that Pharisees were indeed present at this Sabbath cure. This means that the presence of the Pharisees at the cure of a man with a withered hand is wholly dependent on the positioning of this event after the midrashic-type story of Jesus and the Pharisees in the Galilean fields, which, as discussed above, is not difficult to disprove.

How, then, should we consider the specific claim of Luke, who does not rely on hints or allusions, but simply declares the presence of 'scribes and Pharisees' within his account (Luke 6:7)? This claim, however, must also be dismissed. A close examination of Luke's text shows that just as for the story of Jesus in the Galilean fields, the account of Luke is based on Mark, whose text he also similarly tries to improve. Thus whereas Mark continues the story from the previous event, probably to

---

145. In spite of the complete lack of evidence, some modern scholars still insist that human punishments were imposed for the violation of the Sabbath; see, e.g., Donahue and Harrington, *Sacra Pagina*, 111, who claim that the violation of the Sabbath was 'fraught with penalties'. Davies and Allison, *The Gospel According to Saint Matthew*, 2:316, correctly note, however, that 'There is no evidence that the primitive community was taken to task for healing on the Sabbath'.

146. Thus, Bultmann, *The History of the Synoptic Tradition*, 63; Guelich, *Mark 1–8:26*, 138; other scholars are listed by Pryke, *Redactional Style in the Marcan Gospel*, 12.

imply the presence of the same Pharisees in the consecutive scenes, Luke avoids any problems caused by this sequence of events (such as the apparently thoughtless, even cruel, abandonment by Jesus of his starving disciples) with the claim that Jesus arrived at the synagogue 'on another Sabbath day' (Luke 6:6). Luke also states at the beginning of his narration that the event took place on the Sabbath (Luke 6:1), in contrast with Mark and Matthew who give this information only *after* the event has begun (when the onlookers watched to see if Jesus would heal on the Sabbath day, Mark 3:2 and Matt 12:10). Luke also helps his audience to understand the nature of the illness of the man whom Jesus cured by replacing the rare adjective ἐξηραμμένος used at Mark 3:1 with the more common term ξηρός (Luke 6.6), which was repeated by Matthew (Matt 12:10). In addition, Luke notes that it was the right hand of the man that needed to be cured, which, assuming he was right-handed and thus mainly dependent on the use of this hand, may suggest a greater necessity for his immediate cure.[147] Luke also modifies Mark's claim to know the detailed thoughts of Jesus (see Mark 3:5) by describing the reaction of Jesus to his onlookers in a more realistic way (see Luke 6:8). Significantly, more-over, for the discussion here, Luke also states specifically that Pharisees were present at this event (Luke 6:7), which he may have believed. These improvements, compared with the account of Mark, thus enhance the logic of Mark's story and ensure that it was no longer necessary merely to assume the presence of Pharisees as this is now stated in the story itself.[148] It is, however, unlikely that Luke provides an independent account, which means that his claim that 'scribes and Pharisees' (see Luke 6:7) were present at the cure can be safely dismissed.

The presence of Pharisees at the cure of the man with the withered hand has therefore little basis in any of the three versions of this tale, although this is probably what the authors of these texts (especially Luke) want their readers to believe. Assuming that this cure by Jesus records an historical event which took place on the Sabbath, we must therefore conclude that the only witnesses of this cure were ordinary Jews, probably Galileans, since Jesus was in Galilee at the time of the cure. It is thus clear that these Galileans did not approve of the deed

147. A further possible enhancement made by Luke to Mark's text is the change of Mark's ἀγαθὸν ποιῆσαι, 'to do good' (Mark 3:4) to the more sophisticated ἀγαθο-ποιῆσαι (Luke 6:9), thereby elevating the status of Jesus by upgrading the language he used to the Pharisees, the then Jewish elite.

148. Thus, for example, Marshall, *Luke*, 233: 'The alterations made by Luke to his source are insignificant, and contribute, as often, simply to the clarification and better styling of the narrative'.

Jesus performed, and even showed their disapproval before it was performed. This account for the description by Mark and Luke of the waiting onlookers with the verb παρατηρέω, which—as commentators note—refers to these onlookers' malicious intent (Mark 3:2 and Luke 6:9).[149] Similarly, the three synoptic authors note that the onlookers intended to accuse Jesus (κατηγορέω, Mark 3:2; Luke 6:9; Matt 12:10), no doubt for performing this Sabbath cure. The condemnatory attitude of these people is further stressed by the claim that Jesus was sorrowful at their 'hardness of heart' (Mark 3:5), which is also hinted by Luke (at Luke 6:8). The opposition to Jesus' Sabbath cures by ordinary people, most of them similarly identifiable as Galileans, has also been noted in the events recorded at Luke 13:10-17 and 14:1-6, and will be seen again at Mark 6:1-6.

B. *The Function and Origin of the Question in Matthew's Account, Matthew 12:10a*
At Matt 12:10a, the onlookers of the impending cure of a man with a withered hand ask Jesus, Ἐι ἔξεστιν τοῖς σάββασιν θεραπεῦσαι;—*Is it lawful to heal on the Sabbath?*

In contrast to the *halachic* questions of Jesus (Luke 14:3 and Mark 3:4, the latter repeated at Luke 6:9), which allow for the possibility of two replies (see the discussion above), the question of the onlookers at Matt 12:10a expects only one. The nature of this reply, whether negative or positive, is shown in Matthew's subsequent remark, which notes that the question was posed by the onlookers *in order that they might accuse him* (Matt 12:10b). This can only mean that Matthew's question expects a negative reply, along the lines, *No! It is not lawful to heal on the Sabbath [because healing on the Sabbath causes a violation of Sabbath law]!* It is clear that the onlookers who ask the question in Matthew's version of the story were opposed to acts of healing on the Sabbath day.[150]

Since therefore Matthew probably expects his audience to identify these onlookers as Pharisees (which, as discussed above, is implied by the continuity of this event with the previous Galilean story and by the

---

149. The verb παρετήρουν thus negates the concern of Gundry, *A Commentary on His Apology*, 155, that if Mark 3:6 'falls away' from the original version of the story, then all antagonism to Jesus disappears and 'the scrutinizing of Jesus to see whether he will heal on the Sabbath (v. 2a) either becomes innocent rather than antagonistic, or if still antagonistic, unoriginal and therefore subject to falling away with the other antagonistic additions'.

150. Thus Davies and Allison, *The Gospel According to Saint Matthew*, 2:319.

retrospective implication of Matt 12:14), then, in contrast with the attitude to acts of healing and/or saving life on the Sabbath shown by Jesus in this and other Sabbath healing events, the attitude of the alleged Pharisees was firmly opposed. Matthew has therefore replaced the references of Mark and Luke to the attitude of these alleged Pharisees, which is intimated in Mark by their failure to reply to the question of Jesus (Mark 3:4) and by Mark's reference to the 'anger' of Jesus and his grief at their 'hardness of heart' (Mark 3:5) and by the claim of Luke that the Pharisees 'watched Jesus in a menacing way' so that they might 'accuse' him (Luke 6:7) and that Jesus knew of their negative thoughts (Luke 6:8). In short, the question of Matthew ingeniously replaces the details in Mark and Luke which raises the question 'how could this be known?', so that the negative intentions of the alleged Pharisees are exposed in a simple and obvious way. This accounts for the fact that it is the onlookers who voice this question in Matthew (rather than Jesus in the versions of Mark and by Luke)—Matthew wishes to emphasise his belief in the opposition of Pharisees to Sabbath cures. This opposition is, however, a fallacy, as will be seen in Chapters 5 to 12 of this book, especially Chapter 11. It is therefore most unlikely that the question at Matt 12:10 was voiced by historical Pharisees, who—in any case—were probably not present at the scene of the cure.

This suggests that this question was composed either by the ordinary Jewish people who subsequently witnessed the cure of a man with a withered hand, or by Matthew, by whom it was added to his version of the event. The former is unlikely because the question is *halachic*, that is, it is concerned with an aspect of Jewish law. This is not the type of question that might be expected even from pious ordinary Jewish people, who—like Jesus—were concerned with the performance of Jewish ritual rather than a revelation of Jewish oral law. In any case, the question is not recorded in the earlier versions of this story by Mark and Luke, who were closer in time to the actual event and therefore more likely to record what took place. This leaves Matthew as the most likely author. His motives for adding this question to the story have been discussed above. Moreover, the similarity with his question and the question in Luke's earlier gospel at Luke 14:3, *Is it lawful to heal on the Sabbath or not?*, suggests that Matthew adapted the question in Luke merely by omitting the phrase 'or not', and then included this significantly shortened enquiry into his account. It is thus no surprise that this question does not appear in the earlier versions of this story by the publications of Mark and Luke.

C. *Did the Historical Jesus Voice the Argument at Matthew 12:11-12?*
The argument given to Jesus to voice at Matt 12:11-12 is expressed as a
rabbinic argument *kal va-chomer*. Just as in the arguments at Luke
13:15b-16 and 14:5, discussed above, this argument is also based on the
relatively higher value given in Judaism to the life of a human being, in
relation to the relatively lower value given to the life of an animal. Since,
therefore, Jewish law allows the violation of Sabbath law to save the life
of a relatively 'light' (קל), less valued animal (which happens in this case
to have fallen into a pit or a well on the Sabbath, a turn of events that
endangers its life), it follows that it should also be permitted to allow the
same violation of Sabbath law for a relatively 'heavy' (חומר), and therefore more highly valued, human being (in this case, a man with a
withered hand, for who can know whether his illness, if not healed,
would lead to his death?). However, unlike the arguments in Luke, each
of which is based on a situation in which the plight of the animal to be
cured and/or saved resembles in some significant way the plight of the
human being who must be cured and/or saved, and are therefore specific
for the cures that are performed, there are no significant similarities
between the situation of the animal and the situation of the human being
in the argument preserved at Matt 12:11-12. We must therefore assume
that just as a gazelle is used as the symbol for any animal that must not
be hunted on the Sabbath (see the twenty-fifth of the main prohibited
Sabbath activities at m. Shab 7.2, discussed in Chapter 1), so that this
prohibition extends for example to a scorpion (see on m. Shab 16.7 in
Chapters 9 and 11), the sheep that has fallen in a pit (or a well) in the
first part of Matthew's argument (*ha-nadon*) is also merely a symbol for
any animal that may be saved on the Sabbath day, according to Jewish
oral law. This argument in Matthew is thus used in a *general* way to
argue that if an animal—such as a sheep—may be healed and/or its life
may be saved on the Sabbath, so also may the life of a human being be
saved or he may be healed by any action in any situation on the Sabbath
day. Unlike the arguments in the earlier gospels of Mark and Luke which
justify only specific cures (Mark 2:25-26, 28 and the parallel texts justify
a cure for starvation; Luke 13:15b-16 justifies the cure of a bent back;
and Luke 14:5 justifies the cure of dropsy), this argument instead
answers the *general* question asked by the alleged Pharisaic onlookers at
Matt 12:11-12, and thereby provides a *general* argument to justify any
cure. As will be seen in the following chapters of this book, the change
from specific to general justifications in arguments that allow an act of
healing and/or saving life marks a significant change in Jewish oral law,
and the earliest manifestation of this change is the argument in Matthew

at Matt 12:11-13, and the arguments of R. Akiva and R. Ishmael, which will be examined in Chapter 5. As the latter were composed well after Jesus must have died, this again confirms the suggestion of scholars that Matthew added this argument to his version of the story, probably as a reply to the general *halachic* question addressed to Jesus by the onlookers at the opening of the scene.[151] Thus, as this opening *halachic* question is probably an invention of Matthew (see above), so then is the closing *halachic* reply that Matthew provides—it is unlikely that either was spoken by the historical Jesus himself.

D. *Conclusions*

(1) A close examination of the gospel accounts of the cure of a man with a withered hand suggests that although Mark and Matthew imply the presence of Pharisees, and although this is stated explicitly by Luke (who also refers to Jewish scribes), there is no evidence that Pharisees or any other Jewish officials witnessed the event, either before, during or after the incident itself,

(2) This can only mean that the criticism of Jesus which is implied in all three versions of this tale could not have come from Pharisees or any Jewish official, but from ordinary Jewish people, who were present in the Galilean synagogue where the event took place on that Sabbath day.

(3) The *halachic* question preserved at Mark 3:4 (which is repeated almost verbatim at Luke 6:9) probably originates from Pharisaic or rabbinic debate on the question of healing and/or saving life. It is unlikely to have been asked by the historical Jesus himself.

(4) The question asked by the onlookers at Matt 12:10 was probably composed by Matthew, based on the text of Luke 14:3. It functions to prove the opposition of the onlookers to Sabbath cures. Matthew implies that these onlookers were Pharisees.

(5) The *halachic* argument *kal va-chomer* at Matt 12:11-12 is based on a practice allowed in Jewish oral law that permitted curing and/or saving the life of an animal on the Sabbath. The argument claims that if it is permitted to cure and/or save the life of a relatively less valued animal, then it must also be allowed to cure and/or save the life of a more highly valued human being. In contrast with earlier arguments *kal va-chomer* which justify Sabbath cures in the synoptic texts that are specific for their cures, this argument is used in a *general* way to answer the question at Matt 12:10. If, as is likely, the argument was added by Matthew to the tale, then so also was the question to which the argument replies.

151. The opinion, for example, of Davies and Allison, *The Gospel According to Saint Matthew*, 2:319.

(6) If, then, the *halachic* argument *kal va-chomer* at Matt 12:11-13 was composed by Matthew, it could not have been voiced by the historical Jesus himself. In any case, as the discussion below will show, general arguments *kal va-chomer* which justify any action in any situation of healing and/or saving life were probably first composed in the second half of the first century CE.

V. *An Unidentified Sabbath Cure, John 7:14-25*

The gospel of John alleges that Jesus performed three Sabbath cures. One of these cures is identified as a 'deed' of healing, at which everyone marvelled. Jesus in John then uses an argument *kal va-chomer* to justify this deed. A reference to this cure occurs after a discussion on the nature of the teaching of Jesus. A translation of John's account follows below:

[7:[14-18] A discussion on the nature of the teaching of Jesus which continues...] [19] 'Did not Moses give you the law? Yet none of you keeps the law. Why do you seek to kill me?'
[20] The people answered, 'You have a demon! Who is seeking to kill you?'
[21] Jesus answered them and said, 'I did one deed and you all marvel (καὶ πάντες θαυμάζετε) because [of it].[152] [22] Moses gave you circumcision (not that it is from Moses, but from the fathers), and you circumcise a man upon the Sabbath. [23] If on the Sabbath a man receives circumcision, so that the Law of Moses may not be broken (εἰ περιτομὴν λαμβάνει ἄνθρωπος ἐν σαββάτῳ ἵνα μὴ λυθῇ ὁ νόμος Μωϋσέως), are you angry with me because on the Sabbath I made the whole [body of a] man well (ὅλον ἄνθρωπον ὑγιῆ)! [24] Do not judge by appearances, but judge with right judgment.' [25] Some of the people of Jerusalem therefore said, 'Is not this the man whom they seek to kill?'

A. *Did Jesus Voice the Argument That Retrospectively Justifies a Sabbath Cure?*

This argument is not found in any of the synoptic gospels, which were written closer in time to the life of the historical Jesus than the gospel of John and are therefore more likely to have recorded his words. This suggests that this argument was not composed or voiced by Jesus himself.

---

152. Here understanding διὰ τοῦτο as a retrospective reference to the 'one deed', with RSV, rather than, as usually understood, an introduction to the next sentence at John 7:22.

Confirmation for this conclusion comes from a close analysis of the argument itself, which is based on the necessity to perform the ceremony of circumcision on the Sabbath whenever a Jewish male child is born eight (inclusive) days earlier on the previous Sabbath day. The ceremony on this day thus avoids a violation of 'the law of Moses' (John 7:23), a reference to Jewish written law which includes the command that circumcision of a male Jewish child must take place on the eighth (inclusive) day after birth. The argument in John then continues with the claim that because circumcision is carried out on the Sabbath, this justifies 'making the whole body well' on the Sabbath—that is, the act of circumcision on the Sabbath justifies a deed of healing and/or saving life on the Sabbath day. As it would not be necessary to justify an act of healing and/or saving life on the Sabbath unless it caused a violation of Jewish law, it must be assumed that John's audience would recognise that the incident to which he refers was an act of healing and/or saving life that took place on the Sabbath.

John's version of the argument makes little sense. John gives the impression that the people wilfully violated Sabbath law by performing acts of circumcision on the Sabbath, whereas this was necessary if a male Jewish child was born eight (inclusive) days earlier, on the previous Sabbath day. However, even if this aspect of circumcision was clarified by John, the simple fact that the act of circumcision on the Sabbath violates Jewish law does not justify the violation of Sabbath law that results from a deed of healing and/or saving life. The audience of John must therefore be told what special aspect of circumcision allows this argument to be made. The lack of such an explanation in the text of John thus suggests that John was genuinely of the opinion that because circumcision was a 'law of Moses' that took place on the Sabbath and violated Sabbath law, so also acts of healing and/or saving life should take place on the Sabbath because they also violated Sabbath law. In other words, John seems to assume that merely because one ritual performed by the people caused a violation of Sabbath law, so also should acts of healing and/or saving life violate Sabbath law. This does not make sense.

In order to understand the argument in John it is therefore necessary to explain why the argument refers specifically to circumcision, rather than to any other ritual that overrides Sabbath law. For this it is necessary to refer to an argument *kal va-chomer* preserved in the Jewish tannaitic sources which also uses the act of circumcision to justify the violation of Sabbath law by an act of healing and/or saving life, and which may be connected with the argument in John. This is the argument attributed to the first-century sage R. Eleazar b. Azariah, who was active in the second half of the first century. His argument is preserved in the two following tannaitic reports:

תוספתא מסכת שבת פרק טו הלכה טז

ר' ליעזר או' מילה דוחין עליה את השבת מפני מה? מפני שחייבין עליה כרת לאחר זמן. והרי דברים קל וחומר—ומה על אבר אחד ממנו דוחה את השבת דין הוא שידחה שבת על כולו!

<u>Tosefta Shabbat 15.16</u>
R. Eleazar b. Azariah says, 'As to circumcision, on account of which one overrides Sabbath [law], why is this so? It is because on account of it one is liable to extirpation [if it is done] after [the right] time. Now the matter can be decided with an argument *kal va-chomer* (קל וחומר)—if on account of a single limb (על אבר אחד) of a person, one overrides Sabbath law (דוחה שבת), is it not logical that one should override Sabbath law (שידחה שבת) [in order to heal and/or save the life of] the whole of him (על כולו)!'

מכילתא דרבי ישמעאל כי תשא - מסכתא דשבתא פרשה א

נענה רבי אלעזר בן עזריה ואמר, מה מילה שאינה אלא אחד מאיבריו של אדם דוחה שבת, קל וחומר לשאר כל גופו!

<u>Mekilta de-Rabbi Ishmael Shabbatta 1</u>
R. Eleazar b. Azariah answered [the question on how it is known that acts of healing and/or saving life override Sabbath law] and said, 'If in performing the ceremony of circumcision which affects only one member of the body (אחד מאביריו של אדם), [this] overrides Sabbath law (שידחה שבת), does it not follow (קל וחומר) [that one also overrides Sabbath law] for the rest of his body (שאר כל הגוף) [when all the rest of the body needs healing or is in danger of its life]!'

The version of R. Eleazar's argument in the Tosefta first notes that if circumcision is not performed at the right time, that is, is not performed on the eighth inclusive day after a male birth, this may be punished (by God) with the punishment of 'cutting off'. R. Eleazar then argues that if circumcision is permitted to override Sabbath law for the sake of 'healing' one part of the human body (namely, 'healing' the male member of the body by means of the act of circumcision), it must then also be permitted on the Sabbath to heal and/or save all the parts of a person, that is, it must then be permitted to heal and/or save life. This conclusion in the Tosefta is expressed with a repetition of the phrase 'overrides the Sabbath', while the *Mekilta* more elliptically notes that what is permitted for the single limb of a person, must also be allowed for the person as a whole.

Assuming the knowledge of the audience that it is sometimes necessary to violate Sabbath law by the ritual of circumcision, which is made explicit only in the Tosefta (and therefore suggests that the version in the Tosefta may be the earliest version of this text), the argument of R. Eleazar thus transforms the act of circumcision into an act of healing and/or saving life. As a result, both sections of the argument composed by R. Eleazar now, in effect, compare different acts of 'healing': (a) the act of healing brought about by circumcision which overrides the Sabbath in order to 'heal' one part of a body, and (b) the act of healing and/or saving life that heals the whole of a human body. John, however, has failed to point out the alleged 'healing' aspect of circumcision on which the tannaitic argument depends, and without which it does not make sense. As noted above, John merely uses the act of circumcision to say that if this is allowed to violate the Sabbath, so ought an act of healing and/or saving life be allowed to violate Sabbath law. It is, however, hardly necessary to say that circumcision is not generally considered in any way as an act of healing and that this aspect of the ritual must be pointed out for the argument to be understood. If, then, it was necessary for R. Eleazar to make this unusual claim for the act of circumcision for the Jewish audience for whom he wrote, surely this was necessary also for John, whose gospel was certainly intended for a wider audience, many of whom would almost certainly not be aware that circumcision could be regarded as healing in any way, and thus not be aware how the argument made sense.

The omission of essential facts in the argument of John thus means almost certainly that John did not understand the logic of the argument he records, which is why commentators of John 7:23 are obliged to turn to the words of R. Eleazar to explain his text.[153] As it is unlikely that a version of an argument which does *not* make sense is earlier than a version of the same argument in which the sense is clear, it can be assumed that the argument expressed at John 17:23 was not composed by John, but was derived from the argument composed by R. Eleazar, (especially as the argument of R. Eleazar is not attributed to any other sage). R. Eleazar was probably active from around 70 CE until sometime

153. Commentators of John 7:23 who do *not* refer to the argument of R. Eleazar to explain this text therefore do not themselves always appear to understand the argument. For example, Lindars, *The Gospel of John* (London: Marshall, Morgan & Scott, 1972) 292, states that the argument is expressed as a *kal va-chomer*, although the argument of John is more like a *gezerah shevah*. Lindars further claims that the 'lighter' and 'heavier' aspect of the argument reflects that 'the work of salvation surpasses the laws which make way for salvation', which is not the primary meaning of John's text. The logic of the argument can only be explained with reference to the argument of R. Eleazar, *even if this is not acknowledged*, for example, by R. E. Brown, *The Gospel According to John (I–XII)* (Garden City: Doubleday, 1966) 313.

between 117 CE (the death of Trajan) and 131 CE (the outbreak of the Bar Kochba revolt), which means that he was active around thirty to forty years after the historical Jesus had died.[154] If then he was responsible for the composition of the argument, as appears to be the case, the argument in John's text could *never* have been expressed by the historical Jesus. The dates of the activity of R. Eleazar also suggest that he was a contemporary of John, which makes it possible for John's argument to be derived from this sage. We may surmise that the argument was subsequently translated from Hebrew into Greek and probably heard— rather than read—by John (reading the text of the argument would probably have allowed him to report the argument accurately), who subsequently inserted it into his text, giving it to Jesus to express.

A further indication that the argument could never have been expressed by the historical Jesus is its general nature. In other words, it could be used to justify any action in any situation of healing and/or saving life that violates Jewish law. As will be discussed in Chapters 4 and 5, it seems that such general arguments were composed only in the second half of the first century CE, well after the time that the historical Jesus must have died.

B. *To What Cure of Jesus Does John Refer?*
John's account of this cure gives no indication either of the nature of the cure, or the day on which it took place. As far as the nature of the cure is concerned, the fact that 'everyone marvelled' (John 7:21) when the deed was performed suggests that it was most impressive. This further suggests that it was probably recorded in the synoptic gospels, which were composed closer in time to the life of the historical Jesus, and therefore probably recorded the most striking of his cures. Nevertheless, this event is often linked by scholars with another of the earlier cures recorded by John, namely, the cure of a crippled man (John 5:2-9a), because John uses similar vocabulary when reporting this cure. In addition, he claims that the event was the cause of a threat to Jesus' life, as is also alleged at

---

154. R. Eleazar b. Azariah was a younger contemporary of the sages Gamaliel II, Eliezer b. Hurcanus and Joshua b. Hananiah, and he was a senior of Akiva (Sifre, Deut. 32; b. San 101a). His public life thus overlapped the second and third generations of tannaim, c. 80–135 CE. He is placed in the second generation of tannaitic sages by H. Danby, *The Mishnah: Translated from the Hebrew with Introduction and Brief Explanatory Notes* (Oxford: Oxford University Press, 1933) 799, and in the third generation by M. Margaliot, *Encyclopaedia for the Sages of the Talmud and the Geonim* (2 vols.; Tel Aviv: Yavneh, 2000) 1:52 (in Hebrew).

John 7:19.[155] These links are, however, unconvincing. It is unlikely that anyone plotted against Jesus after the (unidentified) cure mentioned at John 7:21, because according to the text of John himself, 'everyone marvelled' at the time of this cure. Moreover, verbal repetition when describing similar incidents does not mean that these incidents are the same. Weather forecasts are reported with great repetition of vocabulary, but this does not mean that they report the same event. In any case, the single stated feature of the cure to which John 7:21 refers—that everyone 'marvelled'—is not replicated in the cure of a crippled man.

What then can be deduced about John's unidentified cure? First, it can be assumed that it probably took place on the Sabbath, because it would not have been necessary to justify a cure—even many years after the cure was performed—if the latter had taken place on a non-Sabbath day. Secondly, the fact that John uses an argument to justify this cure suggests that the earlier cure was not justified in any way. John was thus provided with a reason to supply such an argument. This seems more reasonable than assuming that John changed the argument that Jesus had used at one of his Sabbath cures. In any case, Jesus only justified his Sabbath cures when he was criticised, which was not the case for the earlier cure, because according to John 'everyone marvelled' (John 7:21) at this earlier cure; Jesus would therefore have had no reason to justify his cure. From this we can conclude that no Pharisees or Jewish officials were present at the earlier cure, because according to the present gospel versions of Jesus' Sabbath cures, Jesus expresses *halachic* material (either a *halachic* question and/or a *halachic* argument *kal va-chomer* in order to justify a cure) *only* when at least one Jewish official is present or is implied to be present at the time of the cure. The earlier cure to which John refers may therefore be identified by the following features: (1) it probably took place on the Sabbath; (2) Jesus probably did not justify the cure; (3) it is unlikely that any Jewish officials were present or even implied to be present at the original scene of the cure; and (4) everyone marvelled at the time of the cure.

There is only one earlier event in which these features are all found, namely, the Sabbath cure by Jesus of a man with an evil spirit, described at Mark 1:21-28 and Luke 4:31-37 (discussed separately below). This event takes place on the Sabbath, with no Jewish officials either identified or implied. It is also not justified in any way, and is also greeted

155. John 5:18 notes that 'the Jews sought to kill him' (ἐζήτουν αὐτὸν οἱ Ἰουδαῖοι ἀποκτεῖναι), which echoes the question of Jesus at John 7:19, 'why do you seek to kill me?' (τί με ζητεῖτε ἀποκτεῖναι). Both John 5:9a and 7:23 use the adjective ὑγιής, 'healthy'.

with universal 'marvelling' at the time of the cure. For those readers of John who need evidence of verbal repetition from one text to another in order to verify such a link, the verb θαυμάζετε used at John 7:21, which describes the 'wonder' of the onlookers, is partially echoed in the accounts of the cure of a man with an evil spirit with the verb ἐθαμβήθησαν at Mark 1:27 and the noun θάμβος at Luke 4:36. Mark's verb, θαμβέομαι, is used only three times by Mark (Mark 1:27; 10:24, 32) and only once in Luke (Acts 9:6), and the related noun θάμβος is only used in the New Testament by Luke (Luke 4:36; 5:9; Acts 3:10). On the other hand, the verb θαυμάζω, used at John 7:21, is common in all the gospel texts. It seems, therefore, that John has used the common verb θαυμάζω in place of the comparatively rare terms θάμβος and θαμβέομαι used by Mark and Luke. The absence of an accurate repetition of terms by John thus suggests that he had not read a report of this event in the gospels of Mark and Luke, which might have led to the repetition of a relatively rare term, but had heard of the event which he reported himself in a vernacular way. Alternatively, we must assume that John deliberately simplified the vocabulary that he used. It seems also that John decided to rectify the fact that this cure was not justified and thus supplied an argument *kal va-chomer* which had not been used in the earlier event.

If, then, the incident reported at John 7:21 refers to the Sabbath incident when Jesus cured a man with an evil spirit, this report cannot be counted as a separate Sabbath cure. The possibility will, however, be taken into consideration in the summary of the relevant evidence from the gospel Sabbath healing events, in Chapter 4.

C. *Conclusions*

(1) There is good reason to believe that John 7:23 refers to a Sabbath healing event earlier described at Mark 1:21-28 and Luke 4:31-37, when Jesus cured a man with an evil spirit. If this is correct, the event described by John cannot be counted as a separate Sabbath cure.

(2) It is unlikely that the argument now attributed to Jesus at John 7:23 was originally expressed by Jesus. It was probably composed by the late first-century Jewish sage R. Eleazar b. Azariah, an older contemporary of John, and was subsequently translated from Hebrew into Greek. The argument in Greek was probably heard (rather than read) by John, who incorporated what he considered were its essential details into his text. John's version of the argument, however, shows that he did not understand its underlying logic, which helps to confirm that he did not compose this argument himself.

(3) A further indication that the argument was not composed or voiced by the historical Jesus is the fact that John 7:23 is a general argument that justifies *any* action in *any* situation that necessitates an act of healing and/or saving life. As will be discussed in Chapters 4, 5 and 7, general arguments for this purpose were composed only at the earliest from around 70 CE, many years after the historical Jesus must have died.

(4) In spite of the suggestion at John 7:19 and 25, which seems to link the Sabbath cure that Jesus performed with a plot against his life, this is unlikely. Jesus through John clearly states that he (Jesus) was universally praised when the cure was performed (John 7:21). In any case, as was shown in the discussion above on Mark 3:6, although an act of healing and/or saving life causes a violation of Sabbath law, it is unlikely that anyone was ever condemned to death by the Jewish sages for performing a Sabbath cure.

VI. *Galilean Sabbath Cures: Mark 6:1-6, Luke 4:16-30 and Matthew 13:54-58*

The three versions of this incident are translated below:

Mark 6:1-6

6^1 He went away from there and came to his own country (εἰς τὴν πατρίδα αὐτοῦ), and his disciples followed him. ²And on the Sabbath he began to teach in the synagogue. And many who heard him were aston-ished, saying, 'Where did this man get all this? What is the wisdom given to him? What mighty deeds (αἱ δυνάμεις) are wrought by his hands! ³ Is not this [man] the carpenter, the son of Mary and brother of James and Joses and Judas and Simon, and are not his sisters here with us?' And they took offence at him (καὶ ἐσκανδαλίζοντο ἐν αὐτῷ). ⁴ And Jesus said to them, 'A prophet is not without honour except in his own country, and among his own kin, and in his own house'. ⁵And he could do no mighty work (δύναμιν) there except that he laid his hands upon a few sick people and he healed them. ⁶And he marvelled because of their unbelief.

Luke 4:16, 20-30

4^{16} And he came to Nazareth, where he had been brought up: and, as his custom was, he went into the synagogue on the Sabbath, and stood up to read... [Jesus then read from the book of Isaiah]...²⁰ And he closed the book, and he gave it back to the attendant, and sat down. And the eyes of all them that were in the synagogue were fastened on him. ²¹ And he began to say unto them, 'This day is this scripture fulfilled in your ears'. ²² And all spoke well of him, and wondered at the gracious words which proceeded out of his mouth. And they said, 'Is not this Joseph's son?' ²³ And he said unto them, 'You will surely say unto me this proverb: Physician, heal thyself. Whatever we have heard done in Capernaum, do also here in thy country.' [24] And he said, 'Truly I say unto you, No prophet is accepted in his own country. [25] But I tell you in truth, many widows were in Israel in the days of Elijah, when the heaven was shut up three years and six months, when great famine was throughout all the land. [26] And Elijah was sent to none of them, but only to Zarephath, in the land of Sidon, to a woman who was a widow. [27] And many lepers were in Israel in the time of Elishah the prophet; and none of them was cleansed, but only Naaman the Syrian.' [28] When they heard these things, all in the synagogue were filled with wrath. [29] And they rose up, and thrust him out of the city, and led him to the brow of the hill on which their city was built, that they might throw him down headlong. [30] But he passing through the midst of them went away.

Matthew 13:54-58

13[54] And coming to his own country (εἰς τὴν πατρίδα αὐτοῦ), he taught them in their synagogue, so that they were astonished, and said, 'Where did this man get this wisdom, and these mighty deeds (αἱ δυνάμεις)? [55] Is not this the carpenter's son? Is not his mother called Mary? And are not his brothers James, and Joses, and Simon, and Judas? [56] And are not his sisters all with us? Where then did this man get all this?' [57] And they took offence at him (ἐσκανδαλίζοντο ἐν αὐτῷ). But Jesus said to them, 'A prophet is not without honour, save in his own country, and in his own house'. [58] And he did not do many mighty deeds (δυνάμεις) there because of their unbelief.

A. *Significant Facts in These Accounts*

Mark's gospel notes that when Jesus was *in his own country* (Mark 6:1) he was criticised ('and they took offence at him', Mark 6:3) for his 'mighty deeds' (Mark 6:2 and 5). These deeds are subsequently defined as healing the sick (Mark 6:5). This can only mean that Jesus when in Galilee was criticised for Sabbath cures. The reference to members of his immediate family (Mark 6:3) and the absence of any reference to Jewish officials, whose criticism of Jesus would surely have been noted if it had occurred, suggests that those who criticised Jesus (Mark 6:3-6) were drawn solely from an audience of ordinary Galilean Jews.

Luke 4:16-30 and Matt 13:54-58 both report a similar event which also took place in Galilee (Nazareth, according to Luke 4:16, and *in his own country*, according to Matt 13:54, who thus repeats Mark). The absence of any Jewish officials from their descriptions also suggests that the criticism of Jesus, which they both imply, came from ordinary people rather than from any Jewish officials. Matthew again echoes Mark with the claim that Jesus was criticised ('and they took offence at him') for his 'mighty deeds' (δυνάμεις, Matt 13:54, 58), thus once again repeating a term from Mark 6:2. This helps to confirm that although Matthew does not further define these 'deeds', and neither does he refer to the Sabbath, he also refers to the performance by Jesus of the same Galilean Sabbath cures. In any case, Jesus is (of course) only criticised for his cures when they take place on the Sabbath day (because this is the only way in which the cures of Jesus could have violated Jewish law).

Luke, however, uniquely suggests that Jesus was criticised not for his Sabbath cures but for his claim that he (Jesus) had cured more people than the prophets Elijah and Elisha (Luke 4:25-27). In the light of the evidence of Mark and Matthew, this can be explained as an attempt by Luke to avoid making public that Jesus was criticised for his Sabbath cures by the very people he had ostensibly come to save.

B. *Conclusions*

(1) Mark 6:1-6 describes a Sabbath healing event when Jesus was criticised by ordinary Jewish Galileans, including his own family. Matthew probably also describes this event but refers more obliquely to the criticism of Jesus. Luke prefers to relate the criticism of Jesus to his alleged claim that he had performed more cures than the prophets Elijah and Elisha. Luke thus deflects attention from the criticism of Jesus by ordinary people for his performance of Sabbath cures.

(2) There is no reference to any Jewish officials at this event. We must therefore assume that none were there.

(3) Although he was criticised for performing these cures, Jesus did not justify any of these cures. A review of the Sabbath healing events, however, suggests that this could be expected because Jesus of the gospels never justifies his Sabbath cures unless Pharisees and/or one or more Jewish officials (especially lawyers or scribes) are present or are implied to be present at the scene of the cure.

VII. *The Cure of the Mother-in-law of a Disciple of Jesus:*
Mark 1:29-31, Luke 4:38-39, with Matthew 8:14-15

The three versions of this story are translated below:

Mark 1:21, 29-32

1:21 ...And immediately (εὐθὺς) on the Sabbath he entered the synagogue and taught... 29 And urgently going out (εὐθὺς...ἐξελθόντες) from the synagogue they went to the house of Simon and Andrew, with James and John. 30 Now Simon's mother-in-law lay sick with a fever (πυρέσσουσα), and urgently (εὐθύς) they told him of her. 31 And he [= Jesus] came and took her by the hand and lifted her up, and the fever left her; and she served them. 32 That evening at sundown ('Οψίας δὲ γενομένης) they brought all who were sick or possessed with demons...

Luke 4:31, 38-40

4³¹ And [Jesus] went down to Capernaum, a city of Galilee, and he was teaching them on the Sabbath... ³⁸ And he [= Jesus] arose and left the synagogue, and entered Simon's house. Now Simon's mother-in-law was ill with a high fever (πυρετῷ μεγάλῳ), and they asked (ἠρώτησαν) him for her. ³⁹ And he stood over her and rebuked the fever, and it left her; and immediately she rose and served them. ⁴⁰ Now when the sun was setting (Δύνοντος δὲ τοῦ ἡλίου) all those who had any that were sick with various diseases brought them to him.

Matthew 8:14-16

8:¹⁴ And when Jesus entered Peter's house, he saw his mother-in-law lying sick with a fever (βεβλημένην καὶ πυρέσσουσαν). ¹⁵ He touched her hand and the fever (ὁ πυρετός) left her and she rose and served him. ¹⁶ That evening at sundown (Ὀψίας δὲ γενομένης) they brought to him many who were possessed with demons...

These three accounts relate that on one Sabbath day, Jesus and disciples hurried (εὐθὺς, Mark 1:21) to the house of the mother-in-law of one of his disciples, who was suffering from a 'great' fever (πυρετῷ μεγάλῳ, Luke 4:38, with Mark 1:30 and Matt 8:14), that is, in the eyes of onlookers, she was seriously ill. The disciples urgently (εὐθὺς, Mark 1:30) asked (ἠρώτησαν, Luke 4:38) Jesus to perform a cure which Jesus then performed (Mark 1:13; Luke 4:39; Matt 8:15) by merely touching her with his hand (according to Matt 8:14) or by rebuking the fever (according to Luke 4:39) or taking her by the hand and lifting her up (according to Mark 1:31). The cured lady then 'served Jesus and his disciples' (Mark 1:31; Luke 4:39; Matt 8:15). No criticism of Jesus is recorded for this cure. Subsequently, according to Mark and Luke, it was sunset, which marked the end of the Sabbath day (Mark 2:32; Luke 4:40).

A. *Does Matthew Report the Same Event?*

The main differences between Matthew's account and the accounts of Mark and Luke are Matthew's identification of the mother-in-law of Peter (rather than Simon) and his lack of a direct reference to the Sabbath, which both Mark and Luke state was the day when the cure took place. Matthew's omission of this timing can, however, be explained by the fact that he places the cure among the incidents in Capernaum, when Jesus travelled from place to place, which could not have happened on the Sabbath because Jesus would have exceeded the Sabbath *eruv*, a distance of two thousand cubits.[156] The difference in the identity of the woman

___

156. m. RH 2.5 and m. Eruv 4.3, 4, 7. Sabbath journeys were limited to 2000 cubits, about 1000 yards or 950 metres.

who was cured is not easy to explain. Nevertheless, in all three accounts she is the mother-in-law of one of the disciples of Jesus (Mark 1:29; Luke 4:38; Matt 8:14). The details which are common to the three stories, however, suggest that Matthew records the same event.

Thus all three gospels agree that the woman Jesus cured was very sick with a fever (Mark 1:30; Luke 4:38; Matt 8:14-15)—the term πυρέσσου-σαν at Matt 8:14-15 provides a verbal echo of the term πυρέσσουσα at Mark 1:30. According to all three versions, she was cured by Jesus in her house (Mark 1:29; Luke 4:38; Matt 8:14), either when Jesus took her by the hand (Mark 1:3; Matt 8:15) or when Jesus 'rebuked' the fever (Luke 4:39). Subsequently, according to all three versions, she 'served' Jesus and his disciples (Mark 1:31; Luke 4:39; and Matt 8:15). Finally, all three versions of the story note the sunset of the day on which the cure took place, which, assuming that the cure took place on the Sabbath, indicates the end of the Sabbath day. Although Matthew's version of this event could not have taken place on the Sabbath (because, as noted above, he has placed the event at the end of a day that Jesus spent travelling in Galilee, which could not have happened on the Sabbath), it seems that the account of Matthew is based mainly on that of Mark, so that all of the three synoptic accounts are based on a story in which the cure of the mother-in-law of one of the disciples of Jesus took place on the Sabbath day.[157]

B. *Why Was Jesus Not Criticised for Performing This Sabbath Cure?*
The lack of criticism of Jesus for this Sabbath cure can be explained by the perceived severity of the illness of the woman whom Jesus cured. This is indicated primarily in all three accounts, first by the fact that in contrast with every other Sabbath healing event, this is the *only* Sabbath healing event when Jesus is asked to perform a Sabbath cure. (Jesus is *always* otherwise asked for a cure—either directly with a request, or indirectly, when the sick person is presented to Jesus either by others or by himself—whenever he heals on *non*-Sabbath days.) The lack of requests to heal on the Sabbath in all the other Sabbath events is, however, wholly understandable in view of the fact that—as has been noted many times above—healing in Judaism is considered as 'work' which is prohibited on the Sabbath, so that a request to a Jewish healer to heal on the Sabbath is effectively a request for the healer to sin by causing a violation of Sabbath law. Luke thus notes that after arriving at the place where a woman was ill, the disciples asked (ἠρώτησαν, Luke 4:38)

---

157. See Gundry, *A Commentary on His Apology*, 86–92, for a lengthy discussion of this incident.

Jesus to perform a cure. Similarly, but with more tact, almost certainly to avoid a direct request to violate Sabbath law, Jesus and his disciples 'urgently leave the synagogue' to bring him quickly to the woman (εὐθύς...ἐξελθόντες, Mark 1:29) and 'urgently tell' (εὐθὺς λέγουσιν, Mark 1:30) him that the woman was ill. This indirect approach for a request for a Sabbath cure, *even from a gentile* (who, of course, has no obligation regarding Sabbath law), is clearly articulated in the following mishnaic text:

> Mishnah Shabbat 16.6
> If a gentile came to put out the fire [on the Sabbath] they may not say to him, 'Put it out' or [even] 'Do not put it out', since they are not answerable for his keeping the Sabbath [that is, the gentile cannot be directly requested to help, but must freely volunteer].

A further illustration of this euphemistic approach is illustrated in the amoraic sources by the story of R. Immi, who needed help to extinguish a fire that had begun on the Sabbath. Although such action was officially permitted in Jewish oral law even before 50 CE (see on m. RH 2.5, discussed in Chapter 9) R. Immi was anxious to avoid what he considered was a Sabbath violation, even by the non-Jewish Arameans whom he asked for help. He thus only hinted that help was needed to extinguish the fire by issuing a proclamation in the market place hinting at an unspecified reward.

> Jerusalem Talmud, Shabbat 16.7
> In the time of R. Immi, a fire broke out in the village. R. Immi issued a proclamation in the market place of the Arameans, saying, 'Whoever does [something] will not lose out!'[158]

Similarly, therefore, although Luke actually notes that the disciples 'asked' (ἠρώτησαν) Jesus to perform a cure, Mark more euphemistically notes only that it was 'urgent' for Jesus to attend. The tactful and restrained way in which both their requests were made does not, however, mean that in the eyes of the onlookers, the woman Jesus cured was not dangerously ill. Luke himself indicates the severity of her illness by referring to her fever with the term πυρετός, the same noun used to describe the life-threatening illness of the son of an official in Capernaum (John 5:46-53). Similarly, Matthew and Mark use the related participle πυρέσσουσα (Mark 1:30; Matt 8:14) and thus again stress the severity of

---

158. Similarly, b. Shab 121a. The same reluctance to make an urgent request that violates Jewish law is discussed at b. Shab 150a, which comments on m. Shab 23.3, in which the hire of labourers on the Sabbath is forbidden, even if hired through a third party.

the illness of the woman whom Jesus cured. Luke further emphasises her severe illness with the term μέγας, thus noting that the sick lady suffered with 'a severe fever', πυρετῷ μεγάλῳ (Luke 4:38), an adjective used by Galen to indicate a dangerous illness that could lead to death.[159] The extreme sickness of the woman is further confirmed by her recumbent position when Jesus arrived, a fact which is implied by Mark and Luke, who note that she was 'lifted' by Jesus after she was cured (Mark 1:31; Luke 4:39), and even more explicitly by Matthew, who notes that Jesus saw the woman 'lying sick with fever' (Matt 8:14). One scholar thus notes, 'Her lying down [when Jesus arrived with his disciples] instead of serving the men, especially the guests, shows how severe the fever is. We should not allow modern advances in medicine to lead us into underestimating the seriousness of fever in ancient times. The historical present tense λέγουσιν, "they speak", underlines the severe nature of her plight.'[160]

The lack of censure of Jesus for the performance of this cure has been attributed to the fact that the event took place in private, 'without anyone being present who is hostile to Jesus'.[161] This, however, implies that no other healer could have been censured for this cure, which cannot be correct. Criticism for this cure could have been directed at any Jewish healer by whom this act was performed because any Jewish healer would cause a violation of Sabbath law by healing on the Sabbath day.

Another explanation offered for the lack of criticism of Jesus is the fact that no Pharisees witnessed the cure, an assumption that presumes that Jewish officials, especially Pharisees, always condemned Jesus for performing Sabbath cures. Yet, as will be seen in Chapters 4, which summarises the discussions on the gospel events, and also in Chapter 11, which lists directives that allow acts of healing and/or saving life which can be dated to a time before 70 CE, this assertion too is unlikely to be correct—the Pharisees and Jesus were in complete agreement about the necessity for Sabbath cures. In any event, in perhaps the most obvious

159. Galen, Different. Febr. i 1 (vii 275), cited by W. K. Hobart, *The Medical Language of Luke* (Dublin: Hodges, Figgs & Co.; London: Longmans, Green & Co., 1882) 4. The term μέγας is also used by Hellenistic physicians in the phrase συνεχομένη πυρετῷ μεγάλῳ, 'afflicted with a serious fever', to describe a life-threatening disease. See Hobart, *The Medical Language of Luke*, 3-4 for extensive references to Hippocrates and Galen. For an illness that was relatively benign, the term μικρός, 'small', was used.

160. Gundry, *A Commentary on His Apology*, 86.

161. Bas M. F. van Iersel, *Mark: A Reader-Response Commentary* (trans. W. H. Bisscheroux; JSNTSup 164; Sheffield: Sheffield Academic, 1998) 139.

case when Jesus is criticised for performing Sabbath cures (see above on Mark 6:1-6 and Luke 4:16-30 with Matt 13:53-58) there is no record that Jewish officials were present at the event.

We are left with the explanation that Jesus was *not* criticised for this Sabbath cure because, in the perception of the onlookers—here, the disciples of Jesus—the woman he cured was seriously ill and would have almost certainly died had not Jesus intervened. The details of this event preserved especially by Luke therefore suggest that in spite of any general opposition to Sabbath cures by pious Jewish individuals (who will be further discussed in Chapter 4), especially when such requests were perceived to be non-urgent and thus could probably wait until sunset to be cured (the end of the Sabbath day), nevertheless acts of healing and/or saving of life by a Jewish healer on the Sabbath were tolerated, perhaps even indirectly encouraged, in the first century CE whenever it was felt that there was a serious threat to life.

C. *Conclusions*

(1) This is the only Sabbath gospel event at which Jesus is requested to perform a Sabbath cure. The lack of requests for other Sabbath cures can be explained by a reluctance of pious Jews to ask a Jewish healer to sin by healing the sick and thus violating Sabbath law, especially when the illness was thought to be non-urgent.

(2) The request in Luke's gospel made to Jesus for this particular cure is thus highly significant, and can be explained by the fact that in the perception of witnesses, the woman cured by Jesus was seriously ill and in danger of her life.

(3) The severity of the woman's illness is confirmed in all the three versions of this tale by references to her 'fever', which Luke calls 'severe', and by her recumbent position when she was ill.

(4) The indirect nature of the request for her cure, especially in the account of Mark, less so in Luke, cannot therefore be used by commentators to deny the severity of the illness of the woman Jesus cured. As was noted in (1), making a direct request to a Jewish healer to perform a Sabbath cure was a request to this healer to violate Sabbath law.

(5) The severity of the illness of the woman whom Jesus cured adequately explains why Jesus was not censured for performing this cure.

(6) The fact that no Jewish officials were present at the scene of this cure has nothing to do with the lack of criticism of Jesus for performing this cure.

VIII. *The Removal of an Evil Spirit: Mark 1:21-28*
and Luke 4:31-37

As Mark's account of this event is repeated almost verbatim in the account of Luke, only Mark's version is cited below:

> 1:21 And they went into Capernaum; and immediately on the Sabbath he entered the synagogue and taught. 22 And they were astonished at his teaching, for he taught them as one who had authority, and not as the scribes. 23 And immediately there was in their synagogue a man with an unclean spirit (ἐν πνεύματι ἀκαθάρτῳ). 24 And he cried out, 'What have you to do with us, Jesus of Nazareth? Have you come to destroy us? I know who you are, the Holy One of God.' 25 But Jesus rebuked him, saying, 'Be silent and come out of him!' 26 And the unclean spirit (τὸ πνεῦμα τὸ ἀκάθαρτον) convulsing him and crying with a loud voice, came out of him. 27 And they were all amazed (ἐθαμβήθησαν ἅπαντες; similarly, ἐγένετο θάμβος ἐπὶ πάντας, Luke 4:36). So that they questioned among themselves, saying, 'What is this? A new teaching! With authority he commands even the unclean spirits, and they obey him.' 28 And at once his fame spread everywhere throughout all the surrounding region of Galilee.

The following report of Matthew *may* describe the same event:

> 8:16 That evening they brought to him many who were possessed by demons; and he cast out the spirits with a word, and cured all who were sick. 17 This was to fulfil what had been spoken through the prophet Isaiah, 'He took our infirmities and bore our diseases'.

Matthew's account of the above event may have been inspired by the description of the incident recorded by Mark and Luke, but is much briefer and is significantly different. Unlike the accounts of Mark and Luke, it seems to be written to fit a prophecy in Isaiah (Isa 53:4). There is, moreover, no reference to the Sabbath and the event is not located in a synagogue. Matthew also notes that Jesus cast out many demons from many people, rather than the single demon cast out from one person, as in Mark and Luke. It is thus unclear whether Matthew describes a Sabbath healing event, so that discussion of his text is not relevant here.

A. *This Event Is a Sabbath Cure*
As the scholar Geza Vermes succinctly remarked, 'In the world of Jesus, the devil—to whom Mark refers in the above incident with the phrase, τὸ πνεῦμα τὸ ἀκάθαρτον, "the unclean spirit"—was believed to be at the basis of sickness and sin'.[162] An act of exorcism in order to remove

---

162. Vermes, *Jesus the Jew*, 58-63, esp. 61. A direct link between sickness and sin is stated explicitly in the New Testament at John 9:2 and Jas 5:13-16.

sin must therefore also be considered as a cure for an illness, and the incident described above must therefore be included among Jesus' Sabbath cures. This may be confirmed if indeed the cure noted at John 7:23 refers to the same event (see above on John 7:14-25).[163]

Although the above cure took place in public, in a synagogue on the Sabbath, it did not result in any criticism of Jesus, which would surely have been reported, if such criticism had been made.[164] Instead, according to Mark, Jesus was praised for this cure 'in the whole region surrounding Galilee' (Mark 1:28), and according to Luke, 'into every place of the country round about' (Luke 4:37). Both these reports show a widespread knowledge of the cure, so that the lack of criticism of Jesus for performing this cure cannot be related to ignorance of the fact that it ever took place. One scholar thus notes:

> [The term] 'all' [at Mark 1:27 and Luke 4:36] emphasizes the universality of their amazement [of the onlookers] and thereby the impressiveness of the exorcism. The very fact that the amazement prompts discussion among the onlookers further emphasizes the impact of the exorcism on them. The interrogative form of 'What is this?' demonstrates their amazement... The repetition of 'teaching' and 'authority' (Mark 1:22) completes the framing of the exorcism so as to make it support Jesus' authority as a teacher... which surpasses anything the audience have heard or seen before.[165]

It is clear from the versions of Mark and Luke that all those who were present considered that the disturbance in the synagogue caused by the man whom Jesus cured was sufficiently urgent as to require an immediate cure. This explains why Jesus was not criticised for this cure. The absence of even indirect requests for a cure, similar to those noted for the Sabbath cure of the mother-in-law of Simon (discussed above), can be

163. For some scholarly classifications of this event, which are essentially subdivisions of healing, see Collins, *Mark: A Commentary* (Minneapolis: Augsburg Fortress, 2007) 165-7 and n. 53.

164. Some scholars ingeniously excuse the lack of criticism of Jesus; for example, according to van Iersel, *Mark*, 135, the lack of criticism of Jesus results from the fact that the opponents of Jesus 'have not yet been introduced', which seems to imply that when the reader first meets the Pharisees, they are formally introduced. But this cannot be correct—at the first meeting with the Pharisees, at Mark 2:16 and 18, they are *not* formally introduced—we merely learn at v. 16 that 'the scribes of the Pharisees' saw that Jesus was eating with sinners, and at v. 18 that the disciples of John were fasting with the Pharisees. Similarly apologetic, Meier, *A Marginal Jew*, 4:252, suggests that Mark composed an 'ideal scene' in order to encapsulate 'the sort of thing' Jesus was known to have done on the Sabbath: teaching in the synagogues and performing healings or exorcisms.

165. Gundry, *A Commentary on His Apology*, 77.

explained by the sudden onset of the illness, which presumably was not manifest before the man who was cured arrived at the synagogue on that Sabbath day.

B. *Conclusions*

(1) While in a synagogue on the Sabbath, and in front of many witnesses, Jesus cured a man with an evil spirit which had caused him to scream.

(2) Jesus was universally praised for performing this urgent cure.

(3) The apparent sudden onset of the illness in the presence of Jesus accounts for the fact that, unlike for the serious illness of the mother-in-law of one of his disciples, Jesus was not asked to perform this Sabbath cure, but volunteered immediately to perform the cure.

(4) The lack of criticism for Jesus for performing this Sabbath cure can be explained by the severity of the illness, and the need to perform an immediate cure (see above on the cure of the mother-in-law of a disciple of Jesus, Mark 1:29-31, Luke 4:38-39, with Matt 8:14-15).

(5) Jesus did not justify the fact that he had violated the Sabbath when performing this cure.

(6) No Jewish officials are recorded in this scene.

IX. *The Cure of a Crippled Man, John 5:2-18*

The story of this cure occurs only in John. A translation of his account follows below:

> $5^{:2}$ Now there is in Jerusalem by the Sheep Gate a pool, in Hebrew called Bethesda, which has five porticos. ^{3} In these lay a multitude of invalids, blind, lame, paralysed. ^{4} ... ^{5} One man was there, who had been ill for thirty-eight years. ^{6} When Jesus saw him and knew that he had been lying (κατακείμενον) there a long time, he said to him, 'Do you want to be healed?' ^{7} The sick man answered him, 'Sir, I have no man to put me into the pool when the water is troubled, and while I am going another steps down before me'. ^{8} Jesus said to him, 'Rise, take up your pallet and walk'. ^{9a} And at once the man was healed and he took up his pallet (κράβαττον) and walked.
> ^{9b} Now the day was the Sabbath. ^{10} So the Jews said to the man who was cured, 'It is the Sabbath, it is not lawful for you to carry your pallet'. ^{11} But he answered them, 'The man who healed me said to me, "Take up your pallet and walk"!' ^{12} They asked him, 'Who is the man who said to you, "Take up your pallet and walk"?' ^{13} Now the man who had been healed did not know who it was, for Jesus had withdrawn, as there was a crowd in the place. ^{14} Afterward, Jesus found him in the Temple, and said to him, 'See you are well! Sin no more, that nothing worse befall you'. ^{15} The man went away and told the Jews that it was Jesus who had healed

him. [16] And this was why the Jews persecuted Jesus, because of these things that he did on the Sabbath. [17] But Jesus answered them, 'My father is working still and I am working'. [18] This was why the Jews sought all the more to kill him because he not only broke the Sabbath, but also called God his own father, making himself an equal with God.[166]

A. *A Summary of This Event and Problems Which Are Raised*
Although the cure of the sick man by Jesus took place before a 'multitude' of sick people, including the 'blind, lame and paralysed' (John 5:3), and probably also before others who accompanied some of the sick—interestingly, however, no Pharisees or any other Jewish officials who would surely have been noted if they had been there— Jesus was not criticised *at the time of* the cure.[167] After the cure Jesus asked the man to carry his bed (John 5:8) and the man obeyed. Assuming that his former condition made such a task difficult, or even impossible, this provides proof that the man was cured. It also indicates, as many scholars conclude, that the man Jesus cured was formerly lame.[168] After the cure, the reader of John's text is suddenly told that the event happened on the Sabbath (John 5:9b). This means that, in spite of the instruction from Jesus to carry his bed, this action should not have happened

166. An alternative translation of John 5:18 suggests that the participle ποιῶν, 'making', in the phrase 'making himself an equal with God', should be translated as a simple past tense, 'he made'. The fact that Jesus made himself an equal with God therefore does *not* depend on the fact that he called God *My Father*; see R. W. Funk, R. W. Hoover and the Jesus Seminar, *The Five Gospels: The Search for the Authentic Words of Jesus* (San Francisco: HarperSanFrancisco, 1993) 414. But no evidence exists for this reading.

167. How Jesus knew that the man had been ill for a long time (John 5:6) has caused much debate, but is not relevant to the discussion here.

168. The man Jesus cured is not described as 'lame'. This, however, is the opinion of most scholars, based on (1) the context, (2) the similarities with Mark 2:1-12 which may suggest a common source, and (3) specific vocabulary, e.g., κατακεῖσθαι, which is used for the severely ill mother-in-law of Simon whom Jesus cures (Mark 1:30, see John 5:6); see also R. Bultmann, *The Gospel of John: A Commentary* (trans. Beasley-Murray; Oxford: Blackwell, 1971) 241 n. 1. A former cripple similarly demonstrates his cure at Mark 2:12a. Demonstrations of health are often noted in stories of miraculous cures; see Martyn, *History and Theology in the Fourth Gospel* (New York: Harper & Row, 1968) 4. In fact, if the cripple had arrived at Bethesda alone, as he implies when he claims that no one helped him to enter the pool (John 5:7), it seems that he himself carried his bed to this place before he met Jesus. In other words, he carried his bed before and after his cure. This being the case, what kind of cure did Jesus perform?

because (as the former invalid is later told by 'the Jews') carrying on the Sabbath is prohibited by Jewish law. The man was thus criticised by 'the Jews' for his act of carrying, although (strangely) there is no criticism of Jesus, who issued the command (John 5:11).[169] 'The Jews' then asked the former cripple by whom he had been cured (John 5:12), and the man replied that he did not know (John 5:13). It seems that although he was suddenly cured after an illness that had lasted for thirty-eight years, he did not even trouble to ask his healer's name.

The scene of this story then moves to the Temple, where Jesus happened to meet the man he had cured and where he warned him against committing further sins. There is, however, no indication why this important advice was not issued by Jesus at the time of the cure. Moreover, as was noted in the paragraph above, there is also no indication that his former patient asked Jesus his name, or that Jesus himself imparted this fact (John 5:14). Nevertheless, it seems that the man subsequently went to 'the Jews' and told them Jesus' name.[170] Subsequently Jesus appeared before 'the Jews', although no details are given as to how this was arranged (John 5:15). Neither is there a record of what was said by 'the Jews'. John's report of this meeting between Jesus and 'the Jews' does not even refer to the cure of the cripple that Jesus had performed, although it was apparently the reason for the encounter to be arranged. Moreover, although 'the Jews' knew nothing about Jesus—apparently they had only just learnt his name—it seems that they wished to discuss other Sabbath cures that Jesus had performed (John 5:16). Jesus then justified his performance of (unidentified) Sabbath cures with the words *My father is working still and I am working* (John 5:17). John then claims that 'the Jews' sought to kill Jesus for this last remark, and also because he healed on the Sabbath, and because he addressed God as *My father*, which according to John was highly offensive to 'the Jews' (John 5:16, 18).

169. The conflict is noted by E. Haenchen, *John: A Commentary on the Gospel of John*. Vol. 1, *Chapters 1–6* (trans. R. W. Funk; Philadelphia: Fortress, 1984) 246-7.

170. Some commentators claim that the cured man gave the name of Jesus to 'the Jews' because he was 'vindictive'; see, e.g., Lindars, *The Gospel of John*, 210, and Brown, *John I–XII*, 209. Similarly, J. N. Sanders and B. A. Mastin, *The Gospel According to St John* (London: A. & C. Black, 1968) 162, claim that '[The cured man] is quite ready to co-operate with Jesus' enemies'. In fact, the cured man was only responding to a request. Moreover, since he did not even know Jesus' name, it is unlikely that he knew anything about Jesus, so there is no reason for labelling him as evil in any way.

Assuming that John's description of the cure records an historical event,[171] the following questions are relevant here: (1) Does John repeat a description of an earlier cure or is the cure not recorded in the synoptic texts? (2) Did the cure take place on the Sabbath? (3) Was Jesus criticised for performing this cure? (4) Could the phrase 'my father' used by Jesus about God have caused offence to 'the Jews'? (5) Could the historical Jesus have justified his Sabbath cures with the words reported at John 5:17? If not, who was responsible for making this claim?

B. *Does John Describe an Earlier Recorded Cure?*

Some scholars suggest that the story in John is a variant of the cure of the paralytic described at Mark 2:1-12.[172] But this is unlikely. There are indeed similarities—both stories relate how a paralysed man was healed by Jesus and that he subsequently walked while carrying his bed. Both texts also refer to his bed with the rare term κράβαττος, and both connect the illness of the man with former sin, although this connection is made by John well *after* the cure, at an accidental meeting of Jesus and the man he cured (see Mark 2:5 and John 5:14). Other details, however, negate any claim that John is describing the same event.[173] These include: (1) the location of the events—Mark 2:4 describes an event which occurred inside a house in Capernaum into which the sick man has been lowered to Jesus through the roof, while John 5:1 describes an event which took place outside, at the pool of Bethesda near the Sheep Gate in Jerusalem; (2) the sick man described at Mark 2:3 was a paralytic who was carried by four men, and there is no indication how long he had been ill, while John 5:5 describes a lone, apparently unaccompanied man, probably a cripple, who had been ill for thirty eight years; (3) Mark 2:3-4 notes that the cripple was brought to Jesus, which is an indirect request for healing (for otherwise, there is no reason for the cripple to be brought), while John 5:6 notes that the paralytic was approached by

171. The historicity of the cure of the cripple is accepted, e.g., by Meier, *A Marginal Jew*, 4:257.

172. For example, Lindars, *The Gospel of John*, 52, 209, 215, considers that John 5:1-18 is 'a fusion of 'a non-Synoptic Jerusalem tradition and the well-known Galilean story in Mark 2:1-12' (p. 52). Other scholars consider that John 5:2-18 records a different event, for example, J. P. Meier, *A Marginal Jew*. Vol. 2, *Rethinking the Historical Jesus: Mentor, Message and Miracles* (New York: Doubleday, 1994) 680-1. The possibility that John 5:2-18 is a kind of doublet of John 9:1-14 is also dismissed by C. S. Keener, *The Gospel of John: A Commentary*, vol. 1 (Peabody: Hendrickson, 2003) 639-40.

173. Thus Brown, *John I–XII*, 208-9, and Meier, *A Marginal Jew*, 2:680-1.

Jesus, who volunteered a cure; (4) Mark 2:2 notes that many people were familiar with Jesus as a healer, but John 5:7 implies that Jesus as a healer was unknown either to the cripple, who believed that he would be healed by the waters of the pool, or to 'the Jews'. These significant differences thus suggest that it is unlikely that John and Mark are describing the same event. It seems that John may have recorded a cure that is not described elsewhere.

C. *Did the Cure Take Place on the Sabbath?*

Although John could have stated at the beginning of his account that this cure took place on the Sabbath (as in all the synoptic accounts of Sabbath cures), this fact is not announced until after the cure (John 5:9b), when the next episode begins. As a result, especially if we assume that the audience of this text was familiar with the earlier gospels and was aware that healing on the Sabbath could be problematic for Jesus, then instead of admiring this miraculous cure, the audience must now revise their impression of the event and must anticipate that it could provide yet one more example of the criticism of Jesus for performing a Sabbath cure. Similarly, as the story unfolds, the act of carrying his bed by the former paralytic which had provided such apt proof that the cripple was now cured, must now be considered in a negative way, as a reason for a threat against Jesus' life, because it was Jesus who had commanded this violation of Sabbath law.[174] One scholar thus notes that the notice of the Sabbath is brought into the account 'almost as an afterthought', which is justified by the claim of 'peculiar Johannine technique', which can also be seen in the same late announcement of the Sabbath after the cure described at John 9:17.[175] This explanation, however, does not account for the problems caused by the late announcement of the Sabbath date, and does not even seem to consider that this announcement could be a late addition to both these events, neither of which happened on the Sabbath day.[176]

---

174. Martyn, *History and Theology in the Fourth Gospel*, 53. For others who have commented on this detail, see Witkamp, 'The Use of Traditions in John 5.1–18', 44 n. 96.

175. Brown, *John I–XII*, 210, echoed by M. H. Burer, *Divine Sabbath Work* (Winona Lake: Eisenbrauns, 2012), 24.

176. Meier, *A Marginal Jew*, 2:681, refers to the mention of the Sabbath at John 5:16 as a 'tack on' for the motifs of the Sabbath and sin discussed at John 5:13-45. The location of the Sabbath announcement is justified by Burer, *Divine Sabbath Worship*, 126, because it is positioned 'in a dramatic way...by introducing it after the healing narrative itself. Thus [John] formats this important aspect of the setting

In any case, it is unlikely that the Jewish Jesus would have told the former cripple to carry his bed if the cure had taken place on the Sabbath day. As noted in the directive at m. Shab 7.2, carrying on the Sabbath is forbidden unless within a predefined space (see m. Shab 7.2, cited in Chapter 1), of which there is no indication in John's account. The Jewish religious orthodoxy of Jesus may be inconvenient for those who reject the literal meaning of his declarations that he came not to change Jewish law by 'one jot or one tittle' (Matt 5:8) and that 'it is easier for heaven and earth to pass away than for one tittle of the law to drop' (Luke 16:17).[177] Yet the traditional Jewish piety of Jesus is difficult to deny, especially as unprejudiced research shows that Jesus behaved according to Jewish rabbinic custom and law.[178] Thus the synoptic gospels note that he frequently went to the synagogue on the Sabbath, where he taught and once read from the book of Isaiah and often visited a synagogue at other times.[179] He travelled to Jerusalem at the pilgrim festivals of Tabernacles and Passover.[180] He ate the Passover sacrifice at a ceremony within the city walls at the appropriate time.[181] He wore a garment with tassels[182] and fulfilled the duty of paying the Temple half-shekel.[183] He advised a leper to follow ritual law.[184] His Jewish orthodoxy was known also to his contemporaries, as can be seen from the fact that a haemorrhaging

by presenting the necessary information to understand the narrative in unusual order', which seems to mean that its location of the announcement is dramatic because it is unusual, although the fact it is 'unusual' does not mean that it is dramatic.

177. The Siloam pool was cut into the rock on the southern slope of the city of David, the original site of Jerusalem.

178. For example, Vermes, *The Religion of Jesus*, Chapter 2, esp. pp. 13, 18-21; A.-J. Levine, *The Misunderstood Jew: The Church and the Scandal of the Jewish Jesus* (New York: HarperOne, 2007) 17-52.

179. Three of Jesus' Sabbath cures apparently occurred in a synagogue: (1) Mark 3:1-6; Luke 6:6-11; Matt 12:9-14, the cure of a man with a withered hand; (2) Mark 1:21-28; Luke 4:31-37, the removal of an evil spirit from a man; and (3) Luke 13:10-17, the cure of a woman with a bent back. Even if these settings are not correct (see on Luke 13:10-17, above) the fact that Jesus is placed in a synagogue probably corresponds with a location where he was often found. For the frequent presence of Jesus in a synagogue at other times, see Mark 1:39; 6:2 (on the Sabbath); Luke 4:15, 17 (when Jesus read from the book of Isaiah), 44; Matt 4:23; 9:35; 13:54; John 6:59; 18:20.

180. John 7:14.

181. Matt 26:17-19; Mark 14:12-16; Luke 22:7-15.

182. Num 15:38-39 with Matt 9:20; 14:36; Mark 6:56; Luke 8:44.

183. Matt 17:24-27.

184. Lev 14:1-17, with Matt 8:68; Mark 1:44; Luke 5:14.

woman did not touch Jesus himself but touched only the tassels of his garment, thereby obeying a law of *niddah*, which requires the physical separation of men from women who are menstruating or discharging blood in any way.[185] Similarly, whereas Jesus is always requested in some way—either directly, or indirectly—to perform *non*-Sabbath cures, he is asked to perform a Sabbath cure *only* in the case of the very serious illness of the mother-in-law of one of his disciples (see above on Mark 1:29-31 and Luke 4:38-39). Matthew also seems to appreciate the Jewish orthodoxy of Jesus when he places the cure of this woman on a non-Sabbath day when—according to Matthew—Jesus travelled in Galilee, and thus did not violate the Sabbath *eruv* as would have been the case if the cure of the mother-in-law of Peter (according to Matthew) had taken place on the Sabbath day. As one scholar states: 'Nowhere in the Gospels is Jesus depicted as deliberately setting out to deny or substantially alter any commandment of the Torah in itself'.[186] This means that in John's account of the cure of the cripple, when Jesus tells his former patient that he must no longer sin (John 5:14), he does not refer to the fact that his former patient violated the Sabbath by carrying his bed, but instead alludes to the ancient belief that illness was the result of sin that had been committed earlier in life. In short, although he may have been marginalised historically by many Jews, the historical Jesus could never have been called a marginal Jew as far as his Jewish religious practice was concerned. It is thus most unlikely that Jesus would have asked the former cripple to violate Jewish law by carrying his bed if the cure had taken place on the Sabbath day.[187]

It is also clear that Jesus was *not* criticised for performing this cure, either during or immediately after the event, as might be expected if he had performed a Sabbath cure. Nor was he criticised for performing the cure when he later met with 'the Jews'—although John gives the impression that the meeting was arranged as a result of the offence caused

185. Luke 8:44; see Lev 15:24.

186. Vermes, *The Religion of Jesus*, Chapter 6, esp. p. 13 and pp. 18-21. On pp. 24-45, Vermes shows that the attitude of Jesus to the Jewish dietary and other Jewish practices and laws, including ethical laws, conforms to Jewish practice and belief. Vermes then suggests that the exceptions to this rule occur when there are 'conflicting laws, where one has to override the other [for example, healing on the Sabbath], or on the precise understanding of the full extent of a precept'.

187. For further on the unlikely possibility that the cure of the cripple took place on the Sabbath, see Eltester, *Judentum, Urchristentum, Kirche: Festschrift für Joachim Jeremias* (Beifte zur Zeitschrift für die neutestammentliche Wissenschaft und die Kunde der älteren Kirche 26; Berlin: Töpelmann, 1960) 79-80.

by the cure, the latter is not mentioned at the meeting itself. In any case, this meeting apparently only took place after an accidental encounter between Jesus and the cripple he had already cured, when Jesus advised the man no longer to sin (which itself is curious, not least because this advice should surely have been given at the time of the cure), which casts serious doubt that this event happened in the way John describes. Even if the meeting indeed took place, it is thus unlikely to have happened as a result of the cure, which means that there is no reliable evidence that Jesus was criticised for performing this cure. It is even possible that the story of the cure originally ended at John 5:9a, *before* the reference to the Sabbath, or perhaps with the addition of the advice of Jesus to the former cripple at John 9:14, when Jesus parted from the man he had cured, as some scholars suggest.[188]

Could John have been aware of the many problems caused by his claim that the cure of the cripple took place on the Sabbath day? If this is the case, why did he place the event on this day?[189] As some scholars note, although neither the Sabbath timing nor the location of this event in Jerusalem are necessary for the story of the cure, these details set the scene for the subsequent events, namely, the confrontation between Jesus and 'the Jews' in Jerusalem which leads to a discussion on healing on the Sabbath (John 5:17-18), and finally to a monologue of Jesus in which he describes his relationship with God (John 5:19-47). It seems, therefore, that the cure itself was placed on the Sabbath to provide a suitable background for the following events rather than for the sake of the cure itself.

Even if the cure of the cripple described by John records an historical event, it is therefore most unlikely that it took place on the Sabbath, and therefore cannot safely be counted among Jesus' Sabbath cures.

D. *Did the Historical Jesus Say 'My Father Is Working Still, and I Am Working', John 5:17?*
According to John 5:17, Jesus justified his Sabbath cures with the words, *My Father is working still, and I am working.* John then interprets this remark with the claim that 'the Jews' used this remark '*to kill him because he not only broke the Sabbath, but also called God his own*

188. Meier, *A Marginal Jew*, 4:257 with further refs on p. 315.
189. Some scholars suggest that Mark 2:1-12 and John 5:2-9a have a common source, or that the story in John is derived from that of Mark; see, e.g., Lindars, *The Gospel of John*, 52, 209, 215. For opposition to this opinion, see Meier, *A Marginal Jew*, 2:680-1.

father, making himself an equal with God (John 7:18). John thus suggests that 'the Jews' sought the death of Jesus because he violated Sabbath law, presumably—we must assume—by acts of healing on the Sabbath, and because he referred to God as his father and thereby—John asserts—claimed that he was an equal of God, which offended the Jews. Could either of these accusations be in any way correct?

Let us first consider the possible offence caused by the phrase *My Father*. As many commentators have observed, the Jewish God has been called 'Father' from biblical times. This term can be used either with or without a possessive adjective. For example, in Ps 68:6 (LXX 67:6), God is 'a father of the fatherless', or else God is addressed as '*my* Father' in Ps 89:27 (LXX 88:27), and as '*our* Father' in the fifth, sixth and nineteenth blessing of the *Amidah*, a Jewish prayer that goes back to tannaitic times. There are also many biblical names that begin 'my father', clearly referring to God, for example, the name Avi itself (אבי, 'my Father', 2 Kgs 18:2), Avidan (אבידן, 'My Father is a judge/has judged', Num 1:11), among many others. The address *My Father* to God was probably also used by the late first-century Galilean Jewish charismatic Hanina b. Dosa, who was apparently addressed by 'a heavenly voice' (a rabbinic euphemism for God) as 'my son', which suggests that Hanina addressed God as 'My Father', but does not imply that God and b. Dosa were equal in any way.[190] For the Jewish Jesus, the words 'My Father' or simply 'Father' (there is no difference in meaning in Jewish texts) are therefore merely polite and affectionate names for God based on the metaphor of the relationship between a father and his child, which suggests that there is a similar relationship between the Jewish people and God. Thus, just as a child is subordinate to his father, so the Jewish people are subordinate to God, and are subject to His rule. But this does not even hint at equality with God. It must also be noted that all five strata of tradition in the gospels (Mark, *logia* material, Matthean special material, Lucan special material, and material in John) are unanimous in affirming that Jesus frequently (on sixty-one other occasions) addressed God as 'my Father', none of which caused offence to any Jews.[191] We can only

190. For R. Hanina b. Dosa and 'my son', see b. Ber 17b; b. Taan 24b; b. Hull 86a; for the use of 'my father' by King Solomon, see b. Shab 14b.

191. Jeremias, '"Abba" as an Address to God', in *The Historical Jesus in Recent Research* (ed. J. D. G. Dunn and S. McKnight; Winona Lake: Eisenbrauns, 2005) 201-6, esp. p. 201. For a detailed textual analysis of the use by Jesus of this expression, see Burer, *Divine Sabbath Worship*, 131-2.

conclude that John's claim that the reference of Jesus to God as *My Father* was offensive to Jewish ears is wholly incorrect.[192]

Is it then possible that John's accusation that Jesus declared himself an equal of God relate to the words he is alleged to have said, namely, *My Father is working still and I am working* (John 5:17)? This indeed is possible, *providing that they were spoken by historical Jesus*. These words make sense against the backdrop of the search of the Jewish sages to find proof in the words of the Jewish God that He indeed intended acts of healing and/or saving life to be performed on the Sabbath day. In this context, therefore, the words attributed to Jesus can be traced back to the Hebrew or Aramaic versions of Gen 2:2, which are cited and translated below. Only one English translation is supplied because the Aramaic text is a simple literal translation of the Hebrew text:

Hebrew: ויכל אלהים ביום השביעי מלאכתו אשר עשה וישבת ביום השביעי
מכל מלאכתו אשר עשה:

Aramaic: ושיצי יי ביומא שביעאה עבידתיה דעבד ונח ביומא שביעאה מכל
עבידתיה דעבד:

And on the seventh day (ביום השביעי / ביומא שביעאה) God ended His work which He had done and He rested on the seventh day (ביום השביעי / ביומא שביעאה) from all His work which He had done.[193]

As can be seen, the above versions of Gen 2:2 both claim that God finished His work on the *seventh* (rather than on the *sixth*) day of the week and (also) that He rested on this same *seventh* day. In other words, according to the Hebrew and Aramaic versions of Gen 2:2, the Jewish God both worked and rested on the Sabbath day. Assuming that this 'work' of God on the Sabbath included acts of healing and/or the saving of life (although the 'work' of God is not further defined in either text), it could therefore be claimed that God 'worked' on the seventh, Sabbath

192. Scholars who have accepted John's claim regarding the offence caused by *My Father* include Bultmann, *The Gospel of John: A Commentary*, 244, who notes that 'The Jews rightly understand that Jesus makes himself equal to God in these words, and so for their ears it is an insane blasphemy'; Lindars, *The Gospel of John*, 219, claims that 'Nothing could be more provocative to Jews...'; C. K. Barrett, *The Gospel According to St John: An Introduction with Commentary and Notes on the Greek Text* (2nd edn; London: SPCK, 1978) 256; G. R. Beasley-Murray, *John* (WBC 36; Dallas: Word, 1991) 75, claims that Bultmann (above) is 'undoubtedly correct'. One wonders if these scholars have examined the evidence.

193. In contrast, the *Greek* Septuagint version of Gen 2:2 states that God finished His work on the *sixth* day of the week and rested on the *seventh* day. This makes complete sense in relation to the Jewish belief that God rested from the work of creation on the seventh day of the week.

day by performing acts of healing and/or saving life. The Pentateuch itself, however, strictly forbids 'work' on the Sabbath for the Jewish people themselves.[194] This means that as far as concerns 'work' on the Sabbath day, the actions of God are unique and cannot be imitated by man. If, therefore, Jesus claimed that he was allowed to 'work' on the Sabbath by performing acts of healing and/or saving life because, according to the Semitic versions of Gen 2:2, God also 'worked' on the Sabbath with acts of healing and/or saving life, this means that Jesus claimed that he could behave like God and thus, in some way, shared the divinity of God. This would undoubtedly have offended Jewish ears.

It is, however, most unlikely that the historical Jesus could ever have justified his acts of healing on the Sabbath in this particular way. If Jesus healed on the Sabbath day because he somehow shared the divinity of God, this would mean that only Jewish people who could make the same claim of shared divinity with God were permitted to heal on the Sabbath day. If, as we might expect, this claim was rare, Jesus would therefore effectively be claiming an exclusive right among the Jewish people to perform acts of healing and/or saving life on the Sabbath day. On the other hand, an unspoken assumption of all the Sabbath cures that Jesus performed is that they could be performed by all Jewish healers on the Sabbath day. Jesus was surely advocating the regular performance of Sabbath cures by all Jewish healers, not only by himself. He therefore did not prohibit his Jewish disciples from performing Sabbath cures when he showed them how to heal, and there is little doubt that they, like Jesus, also healed on the Sabbath, although no records of such events exist.[195] In any case, Jesus himself was surely aware of the many acts of healing and/or saving life that were regularly performed in his time by ordinary Jewish people on the Sabbath day. This topic will be discussed in detail in Chapter 11 of this book. Meanwhile, however, an example of such leniency can be seen in the edict of Rabban Gamaliel the Elder, which was issued before around 50 CE (when Rabban Gamaliel died) and refers to the permitted actions of five different groups of people (not merely individuals!) who would regularly have violated Sabbath law in order to heal and/or in order to save life. These included midwives, fire-fighters, those who fought in self-defence, those who saved people from

194. Exod 20:8-11; 31:12-17 (in which *karet* is the punishment for the violation of Sabbath law); Lev 16:29-31; 23:3; Deut 5:12; Isa 56:2; 58:13; Jer 17:22; Ezek 20:13, 20; 44:24; 45:17; 46:1-8.

195. Mark 6:7-13; 9:28; Luke 9:1-6; Matt 10:1-8 etc. For a discussion of the healing activities of the disciples (although none are recorded on the Sabbath), see Van der Loos, *The Miracles of Jesus*, 216-28.

a flood, and those who saved people from beneath fallen debris.[196] On this evidence alone—and more evidence will be presented in Chapter 11—it is clear that with the knowledge and consent of Rabban Gamaliel himself, who was probably a Pharisee and leader of the Sanhedrin and thus one of the most important of the Jewish leaders of his time, many Jewish people in the first half of the first century regularly performed acts of healing and/or saving life on the Sabbath and thus regularly violated Sabbath law. If, therefore, Jesus justified his acts of healing on the Sabbath on the basis that he was allowed to behave like God, the same divine permit must also be extended to these many others who also healed and/or saved life on the Sabbath day, which makes little sense, and thus strongly suggests that Jesus could not have justified his acts of Sabbath healing with the verse that is cited at John 5:17.

This is further confirmed when we note that if indeed the historical Jesus expressed the words of John 5:17, they must have been voiced at an historical event, in this case the meeting between Jesus and 'the Jews' described at John 5:16-17. The historicity of this meeting is, however, difficult to accept. In addition to the fact that it is not described in the earlier synoptic texts, which probably include the outstanding events in the last years of Jesus' life, the events that led to the meeting are so improbable that, even allowing for a lower standard of proof that is probably acceptable from ancient texts, they are difficult to accept as historical fact. These events began with an accidental encounter between Jesus and the man whom he had cured, when Jesus gave this man vital advice that he should surely have imparted when they first met. The man who was cured did not ask Jesus his name at their first meeting, and neither, it seems, did he ask it when they subsequently met. Nevertheless, he apparently communicated the name of Jesus to 'the Jews', the latter who apparently never heard about Jesus, but whom they then met. 'The Jews' then questioned Jesus about his Sabbath cures (how could they have known about them?), although the cure of the cripple that apparently led to this meeting is not even mentioned, and, in any case, probably did not happen on the Sabbath day. Perhaps all this can be explained on the basis of faith. But for those who demand even a little more realism when dealing with an ancient, religious text, especially when the latter purports to report historical truth, there is a distinct lack of any convincing evidence regarding the authenticity of these events, which throws doubt on their culmination, namely, the alleged meeting between Jesus and 'the Jews', when Jesus apparently uttered these famous words.

---

196. See on m. RH 2.5, which is discussed in detail in Chapter 9.

If indeed a meeting between Jesus and the Jews took place, surely a more credible background would have been described. As it is, however, the events before the meeting seem to have been contrived in order to suggest that Jesus met 'the Jews', which casts grave doubt that this meeting took place. On these grounds alone, it is thus doubtful that the historical Jesus expressed the words that are alleged at John 5:17. There is moreover no other appropriate event described in John (or in the synoptic gospels) that Jesus could ever have expressed such words.

The cumulative evidence thus suggests that historical Jesus probably never expressed the words which he now apparently utters at John 5:17, and therefore could not have offended 'the Jews' by uttering these words.

E. *From Whom Was John 5:17 Derived?*
As noted above, the alleged justification for his Sabbath cures voiced at John 5:17 is based on the Hebrew (or Aramaic) version of Gen 2:2. We can assume that John was familiar with the *Greek* version of Gen 2:2, which states, *And on the sixth day* (τῇ ἡμέρᾳ τῇ ἕκτῃ) *God ended his works which He had made...* There is, however, no evidence that John was even slightly familiar with Gen 2:2 in Hebrew or Aramaic, as these languages were largely unknown outside Jewish circles in biblical lands in the first century CE. This suggests that the alleged words of Jesus cited by John probably originated from early *Jewish* followers of Jesus, who believed that Jesus was allowed to behave like God, as is implied by John 5:17, which indeed would have offended the Jewish sages, as John claims. It is, however, unlikely that the argument would have originated from the Jewish sages themselves, who accepted that God might have 'worked' on the Sabbath day, as seems to be implied in the Hebrew and Aramaic versions of Gen 2:2, but would have vehemently denied that this would justify the same behaviour by any individuals among the Jewish people themselves.[197]

197. Midrash Gen Rab. X.9 preserves the explanations of the Jewish sages for the Hebrew version of Gen 2:2 who claim it describes the special actions of God. R. Ishmael (active around 90–135 CE) states that in Gen 2:2 the action of God 'is like a man striking a hammer on the anvil, raising it by day and bringing it down by night'. The second-century sage R. Shimon b. Yochai claimed that Gen 2:2 indicates the accurate time-keeping of God, which men cannot understand, but must accept by adding time to the duration of the Sabbath, in order to prevent encroaching on the time that God has set aside for the Sabbath day. A further suggestion is that God's Sabbath 'work' was the creation of the Sabbath itself. For other explanations, see Burer, *Divine Sabbath Healing*, Chapter 3, esp. 100-102.

F. *Conclusions*

(1) John's account of the cure by Jesus of the cripple at Bethesda (John 5:1-9a perhaps also including v. 14b) may record an historical cure which is not noted in any of the earlier gospel texts. It is, however, unlikely that this event took place on the Sabbath, although this is what John claims (John 5:9b).

(2) The tenuous connection between the cure of the cripple and the subsequent meeting between Jesus and 'the Jews' casts doubt on the historicity of the meeting itself. As criticism of the historical Jesus by 'the Jews' for performing this alleged Sabbath cure rests entirely on the historicity of this meeting, and even then, cannot be assumed for the cure of the cripple that Jesus performed, it is unlikely that Jesus was criticised for performing this cure.

(3) Although John claims that the reference by Jesus to God as 'My Father' was offensive to 'the Jews' (John 5:18), this cannot be correct.

(4) It is also most unlikely that the historical Jesus justified his acts of healing on the Sabbath on the basis that he was entitled to behave like God on the Sabbath day (John 5:17), which would have meant that only Jewish people who were allowed to behave like God were allowed to perform acts of healing and/or saving life that violated Jewish law. Jesus would have known in his time that the Jewish sages officially permitted many ordinary Jewish people to perform specific acts of healing and/or saving life on the Sabbath and thus officially allowed them to violate Jewish law. It is therefore unlikely Jesus uttered this remark (John 5:18), although this *could* have been the case if he had made this claim.

(5) The likelihood that Jesus spoke the words of John 5:17 is also lessened by the dubious historicity of the meeting between Jesus and 'the Jews', to whom Jesus is alleged to have spoken these words.

(6) The claim of John 5:17 that the Jewish Jesus was somehow equal to God may, however, have been made by Jewish followers of Jesus, who were familiar with the Hebrew or Aramaic version of Gen 2:2, and who nurtured a belief in the divinity of Jesus. These people would, however, have conveniently ignored the many specific acts of healing and/or saving life that were regularly performed with the permission of the Jewish sages by ordinary, non-divine, Jewish people on the Sabbath day in the first century CE (see Chapter 11).

X. *The Cure of a Man Blind from Birth, John 9:1-17*

As for the cure of a crippled man, this story is again found only in John. A translation of his account follows below:

> John 9:[1] As [Jesus] passed by, he saw a man blind from birth. [2] And his disciples asked him, 'Rabbi, who sinned, this man or his parents, that he was born blind?' [3] Jesus answered, 'It was not that this man sinned, or his parents, but that the works of God might be made manifest in him. [4] We must work the works of Him who sent me, while it is day; night comes when no one can work. [5] As long as I am in the world, I am the light of the world.' [6] As he said this, he spat on the ground and made a clay from the saliva and anointed the man's eyes with the clay, [7] saying to him, 'Go wash in the pool of Siloam' ([the name] means 'Sent'). So he went and washed and came back seeing. [8] The neighbours and those who had seen him before as a beggar, said, 'Is not this the man who used to sit and beg?' [10] Some said, 'It is he'. Others said, 'No, but he is like him'. He said, 'I am the man'. [11] They said to him, 'Then how were your eyes opened?' [12] He answered, 'The man called Jesus made clay and anointed my eyes and said to me, "Go to Siloam and wash". So I went and washed and received my sight.' They said to him, 'Where is he?' He said, 'I do not know'.
> [13] They brought the man who had formerly been blind to the Pharisees. [14] Now it was a Sabbath day when Jesus made the clay and opened his eyes. [15] The Pharisees again asked him how he had received his sight. And he said to them, 'He put clay on my eyes and I washed, and I see'. [16a] Some of the Pharisees said, 'This man is not from God, for he does not keep the Sabbath'. [16b] But others said, 'How can a man who is a sinner do such signs?' There was a division among them. [17] So they again said to the blind man, 'What do you say about him, since, he has opened your eyes?' He said, 'He is a prophet'. ['The Jews' then attempt to verify the facts of the cure and the story ends with a homily by Jesus which includes a reference to the metaphorical blindness of the Pharisees.]

This story has given rise to much debate of which the following aspects are relevant here. (1) Did those who learnt of the cure—called variously 'neighbours', 'those who knew the blind man before he was cured', 'others', 'Pharisees', and 'the Jews'—criticise Jesus for performing this cure? (2) Was Jesus criticised after the cure by Pharisees who met to discuss whether or not Jesus was a sinner (John 9:16)? (3) Did this cure, which appears to be unique, take place on the Sabbath?

A. *Was Jesus Criticised for Performing This Cure at the Time It Was Performed?*

The account of John gives no indication that Jesus was criticised at the time of the cure. The only reaction of 'neighbours and others'—but, significantly, no Pharisees or Jewish officials who would surely have been mentioned if they were there—was astonishment that Jesus had cured a man who was blind from birth. They were also curious to know how the cure was performed (John 9:8-12). Any criticism of Jesus for performing this cure could thus only have happened after the cure. We must therefore consider whether the subsequent events could ever have taken place.

B. *Was Jesus Criticised for Performing This Cure in Events After the Cure?*

According to John, after the cure the Pharisees discussed whether Jesus was a sinner. Following some debate, some Pharisees assume that anyone who violates the Sabbath cannot 'be from God'. Subsequently, after the apparently Pharisaic remark in which they ask how a man who is a sinner can do 'such signs', it seems that some of the Pharisees decided that a person who violates Sabbath law should not be able to perform successful cures (John 9:16a). Others, however, note that although Jesus violated Sabbath law (with acts of healing and/or saving life) and therefore, they imply, was a sinner, they also admit that he performs successful cures (John 9:16b).

It is, however, unlikely that this discussion took place and thus unlikely that Jesus was criticised for this specific cure which is not even discussed. As was noted in Chapter 1, any act of healing and/or saving life is considered in Judaism as an act of work, which according to Pentateuchal written Jewish law is totally prohibited on the Sabbath day. This means that any act of healing and/or saving life performed on the Sabbath by a Jewish healer *invariably and inevitably* causes a violation of Sabbath law. Any Jewish healer who heals and/or saves life on the Sabbath is therefore inevitably a sinner, whether or not his (or her) action results in a cure. It is clear that John has completely misunderstood how acts of healing and/or saving life on the Sabbath cause a problem in Jewish law and his basic claim that the Pharisees discussed the success or failure of a Sabbath cure in relation to the sin of the healer (John 9:16) must therefore be dismissed. It is thus unlikely that this Pharisaic debate ever took place.

The continuation of John's account of this event (this text is not cited above) again shows John's failure to understand some principles of Judaism, and therefore adds to the scepticism that surrounds his claim of a Pharisaic discussion after the cure. Thus he is again mistaken when he states that because Jesus was considered a sinner, the man who was cured should give thanks to God rather than to Jesus, although Jesus apparently effected his cure (John 9:24). According to ancient Jewish belief, it is *always* God who is responsible for healing and/or saving life, and therefore always God who should be thanked for a cure. This is based on an understanding of Exod 15:26, *If you will diligently listen to the voice of the Lord your God and will do that which is right in His eyes…I will put none of these diseases upon them which I have put upon Egypt, for I am the Lord who heals you.* The role of the healer in relation to a cure is thus a very grey area and difficult to define. This can be seen from the attempt made by the first-century Jewish healer R. Hanina b. Dosa, who stated that only if his prayer was accepted by God would a sick person be cured:

Mishnah Berachoth 5.5
They tell of R. Hanina b. Dosa that he used to pray over the sick and say, 'This one will live', or 'This one will die'. They said to him, 'How do you know?' He replied, 'If my prayer is fluent in my mouth I know that he is accepted. And if it is not I know that it is rejected.'[198]

Similarly, R. Akiva utterly condemned a man who whispered charms over a wound, and then muttered the words of Exod 15:26, because (according to R. Akiva) this might suggest that he, the healer, was the agent of the cure.[199] It is, of course, not entirely logical that although a Jewish healer is *not* considered responsible for a Sabbath cure, Judaism considers that he has violated Sabbath law by performing a Sabbath cure. Religion, however, is not an exact science, and in view of the ancient Jewish belief that God alone is responsible for any cures, it is understandable that 'the Jews' in John 9:24 objected to the fact that the former blind man thanked Jesus for his cure, and demanded instead that he give

198. The earliest discussion on the contribution of a healer towards effecting a cure which is not in the power of the healer but which is the gift of God, is carefully synthesised by the second-century BCE author Ben Sira, Eccl 1:15. For further on this subject, see Vermes, *Jesus the Jew*, 58-65.

199. m. San 10.1; also t. San 12.10. For לחש, 'to whisper charms', see H. Albeck, *The Mishna: Seder Nezikin* (Jerusalem: Dvir, 1988), and Danby, *The Mishnah* on m. San 10.1. Similarly, the *Mekilta de-Rabbi Ishmael* asks, 'Why does Scripture say, *For I am the Lord that healeth thee?*', and then provides the reply: 'God said to Moses, "Say to Israel: The words of the Torah which I have given you are life unto you, as it is said, *For they are life unto those that find them*" (Prov 4:22). [This means that] they are health unto you, as it is said, *It shall be health to thy navel, and marrow to thy bones* (Prov 3:8).' For the text and a translation, see Lauterbach, *Mekilta*, 2:96.

thanks to God. This request, however, has no connection with the question concerning the sin of Jesus by performing Sabbath cures. The same request to thank God rather than the Jewish healer would have been made if the cure had taken place without any violation of Jewish law, such as cures that were performed on non-Sabbath days (unless, of course, the specific method used violated some other Jewish law). It is once again clear that John does not understand the problem in Judaism caused by acts of healing and/or saving life on the Sabbath day.

Although therefore it may seem that a healer has somehow brought about a cure, only God must be thanked for effecting the cure. In any case, it is totally irrelevant whether or not a Jewish healer has sinned, which—as noted above—is inevitable when an act of healing is performed on the Sabbath day. Luke's lady with the bent back thus thanked God, rather than Jesus, after she was cured *on the Sabbath day*, after Jesus had 'sinned' (Luke 13:13). Similarly, the cripple thanked God after the apostle Peter had mediated a cure, although this did not take place on the Sabbath day (Acts 3:8).

Neither can 'the Jews' in John be censored for attempting to verify the cure of the blind man (vv. 18-23). What can be wrong in verifying a cure, especially if it is completely unexpected, as the cure of a man who was blind from birth? A similar attempt to verify a cure is recorded in the following story of first-century R. Hanina b. Dosa:

> Jerusalem Talmud Berachot 5.5 (= Babylonian Talmud Berachot 34b)
> Once Rabban Gamaliel's son fell ill and he sent two students to R. Haninah b. Dosa in his town [to find out from him if his son would be cured]. He [Haninah] said to them [the students], 'Wait for me while I go up to the attic [to pray]'. He went up to the attic, came down, and said to them, 'I am certain that Rabban Gamaliel's son has recovered from his illness'. [The students] made note [of the time of day that this happened]. [Later they confirmed that] at that very moment [when R. Hanina b. Dosa had finished his prayer, the son of R. Gamaliel was cured] and asked for food.

The fact that the boy was cured at the very moment that R. Hanina had finished his prayer was thus accepted as evidence of a miraculous cure which was mediated by R. Hanina, and which, in the opinion of the Jewish sages, without his aid, would not have occurred. Similarly, Josephus reports that the exorcist Eleazar provided proof that he had removed a spirit from a man by asking the spirit to spill a basin of water that was placed nearby.[200] The attempt of 'the Jews' to verify the cure of

---

200. Josephus, *Ant* VIII.48.

a man blind from birth is thus entirely credible and sensible, and cannot be considered as criticism of Jesus, as is assumed by some commentators of this event.

John's story of the cure leads directly to a short discussion which features two of his favourite themes: (1) the theme of 'Jesus sent by God', which—according to John—negates the earlier comment of the Pharisees who claim that because Jesus had violated the Sabbath, he was not 'from God' (John 9:16a), and (2) the theme of 'signs' (σημεῖα), which continues the comment that the success of the cure meant that Jesus was not a sinner (John 9:16b), thus, *'How can a man who is a sinner do such signs?'*[201] Once again, it must be noted that this section of the story provides no information on the possible criticism of Jesus for performing the cure of a man blind from birth.

C. *Did This Cure Take Place on the Sabbath?*

No reference to the Sabbath occurs at the beginning of John's account, and this timing is finally announced after the beginning of the second part of the tale (John 9:14), which is thirteen verses *after* the start of the story of the cure. Like John's account of the cure of the cripple (John 5:2-18, see above), this delayed announcement of the Sabbath is difficult to explain, especially when an earlier reference could easily have been made, or even a reference within the story itself. Moreover, rather than helping the narrative to flow, this late notice of the Sabbath causes similar difficulties because it demands a retroactive evaluation of the cure itself—should the latter be considered as another wonderful miracle of Jesus, as first appears, or is it yet one more example of conflict between Jesus and Jewish officials, as those who were familiar with similar Sabbath events in the earlier gospels may have thought? It must also be noted that although many people knew about the cure, none of them criticise Jesus for performing the cure. Additional evidence against a Sabbath cure comes from the method used by Jesus to perform this cure, in which he mixed his own saliva with clay (John 9:6) thus—as far as Jewish law is concerned—performing the act of kneading on the Sabbath day. 'Kneading', however, is one of the thirty-nine main activities (the tenth) which is forbidden on the Sabbath in a directive which probably dates from Maccabean times.[202] Even more specific for the action of Jesus is an anonymous directive in the Tosefta which notes specifically

201. For a summary of the topic of 'signs' in John, see Barrett, *The Gospel According to St John*, 75-8.

202. See in Chapter 1 on m. Shab 7.2, 'The main classes of work [to be avoided on the Sabbath] are forty save one: ...kneading...'

that a healing medicament may only be applied to the body, including specifically the eye, *before* the Sabbath begins (described as 'the eve of the Sabbath'), and thus prohibits the application of a medicament on the Sabbath itself:

תוספתא מסכת שבת פרק א הלכה כג

...נותנין קילור לעין ואספלנית למכה בערב שבת עם חשיכה והן מתרפין והולכין
כל השבת כולה...

Tosefta Shabbat 1.23

...They put an eye-salve on the eye and a poultice on a wound on the eve of the Sabbath, at dusk, and [= so that] they continue to undergo healing throughout the entire Sabbath...

The Mishnah similarly notes that '[he is culpable who] takes out...eye paint [on the Sabbath]'.[203]

A prohibition against mixing a medicament on the Sabbath which was in force in the first century CE is also implied in a story from the Tosefta, which reports that R. Meir (135–170) allowed his contemporaries to mix a medicament on the Sabbath, but would not allow the same treatment for himself because the procedure was not allowed by his colleagues. This can only mean that there existed an earlier directive that prohibited the mixing of ingredients to provide medicine for use on the Sabbath, which in fact is stated in the introduction to this tale:

תוספתא מסכת שבת פרק יב הלכה יב

... עושין אלונתית לחולה בשבת. אימתי? בזמן שטרפ' מערב שבת לא טרפה
מערב שבת אסורה שאין טורפין בתחלה בשבת אין טורפין יין ושמן לחולה
בשבת.

רבי שמעון בן אלעזר אומר משום רבי מאיר טורפין יין ושמן לחולה בשבת אמ'
ר' שמעון בן לעזר פעם אחת חלה ר' מאיר ובקשנו לעשות לו ולא הניחני אמ' לו
רבינו תבטל דבריך בחייך אמ' לנו אף על פי שאני אומ' כן לא מלאני לבי מימי
לעבור על דברי חבירי.

Tosefta Shabbat 12.12

...They prepare a wine-potion for an invalid on the Sabbath. When [does this happen]? [When] it was prepared on the eve of the Sabbath [that is, they prepare it on Friday afternoon before the Sabbath began]. But if it was not mixed on the eve of the Sabbath, it is prohibited to do so. For they do not begin to mix on the Sabbath [itself]. They do not mix wine and oil for a sick person on the Sabbath.

[But] R. Simeon b. Eleazar says in the name of R. Meir, 'They *do* mix wine and oil for a sick person on the Sabbath'. Said R. Simeon b. Eleazar, 'Once R. Meir fell ill [on the Sabbath], and we wanted to prepare it for

---

203. See m. Shab 8.3. See also m. Shab 10.6, which forbids a woman to paint her eyelids.

him, but he did not let me do so. [I said to him] "Our master, will you nullify your opinion during your own lifetime?" He said to us, "Even though
that happens to be my opinion, my heart has never been so puffed up in
my whole life as to let me violate the opinion of my colleagues (חביריי)".'

As will be shown in Chapters 9 and 10 of this book, an apparent leniency
in directives that permitted acts of healing and/or saving life can only be
detected in such directives after around 70 CE. It is unlikely, therefore,
that Jesus would have mixed a medicament for a sick person on the
Sabbath before 70 CE, especially when he was in Jerusalem, probably
near the Siloam pool, a public place which was situated close to the
Temple itself, and especially as Jesus used other methods for healing on
the Sabbath which would have caused a lesser violation of Sabbath law.
It may also be significant that neither of the two other events in which
Jesus applies a medicament to effect a cure—he applies saliva to the eyes
of a blind man (Mark 8:22-26) and to the tongue of a dumb man (Mark
7:32-37)—took place on the Sabbath day.[204]

Although, therefore, Jesus may have cured a man who was blind from
birth, the cumulative evidence suggests that the cure was not performed
on the Sabbath day.[205]

D. *Conclusions*

(1) There is no reason to doubt that the historical Jesus cured a man who
was blind by birth. There is, however, no evidence that he was criticised
for performing this cure, either by ordinary Jewish people at the time of
the cure, or subsequently by Pharisees or by John's 'the Jews'.

(2) The lack of criticism of Jesus is no surprise since the cure itself
probably did not take place on the Sabbath, and therefore could not have
caused a violation of Sabbath law. This accounts for the fact that Jesus
was not criticised for performing the cure, and neither did he voice an
argument to justify the cure.

(3) No Jewish official witnessed the cure.

(4) Although the Pharisees may have discussed the success of the cure
that Jesus had performed, it is unlikely that they discussed this cure or
any of the cures of Jesus in relation to the Sabbath, or in relation to their
success, in the way described at John 5:15-17. This casts doubt on the
historicity of the discussion itself.

204. For references to discussions on the source of the story of the cure, see
Ensor, *Jesus and His 'Works': The Johannine Sayings in Historical Perspective*
(Tübingen: J. C. B. Mohr, 1996) 101-3.

205. This is the opinion of Meier, *A Marginal Jew*, 2:695, who refers to the
addition of the Sabbath at John 9:14 as 'a springboard for the evolving controversy
that fills the rest of Chapter 10'.

XI. *Post-Sabbath Cures, Mark 1:21, 32-34 and Luke 4:31, 40-41, with Matthew 8:16*

The three accounts of these post-Sabbath cures are translated below:

Mark 1:21, 32-34

1[21] And they went into Capernaum and immediately on the Sabbath [Jesus] entered the synagogue and taught... [32] That evening, at sundown (Ὀψίας δὲ γενομένης, ὅτε ἔδυ ὁ ἥλιος), they brought to him all who were sick or possessed with demons. [33] And the whole city was gathered together about the door. [34] And he healed many who were sick with various diseases, and cast out many demons...

Luke 4:31, 40-41

4[31] And [Jesus] went down to Capernaum, a city of Galilee. And he was teaching them on the Sabbath... [40] Now when the sun was setting (Δύνοντος δὲ τοῦ ἡλίου), all those who had any that were sick with various diseases brought them to him; and he laid his hands on every one of them and healed them. [41] And many demons came out of many [people]...

Matthew 8:16

8[16] That evening (Ὀψίας δὲ γενομένης) they brought [to Jesus] many who were possessed with demons; and he cast out the spirits with a word, and healed all who were sick.

A. *The Significance of the Timing of This Healing Event*
The reports of Mark and Luke provide clear evidence that in the time of Jesus at least one group of ordinary Jewish Galileans followed a tradition in which healing was avoided on the Sabbath day. For there can be no other reason that according to their accounts, after Jesus had cured the mother-in-law of one of his disciples (see above on Mark 1:29-31 and Luke 4:38-39), a group of Galileans waited until after sunset (Mark 1:32 and Luke 4:40), the astronomical sign of the end of the Sabbath, in order to ask Jesus to heal their sick.[206] Why otherwise would they have waited till the evening to bring their sick to be healed? This timing is noted without any polemic, and there is no reason to doubt its accuracy or the intention to report a simple fact. The same timing is also indicated by Matthew (Matt 8:16), although he does not note that the previous incident took place on the Sabbath. This, however, is irrelevant; as the discussion above on his text has shown, his account of the previous

---

206. See, e.g., Gundry, *A Commentary on His Apology*, 87. For the temporal limits of the Sabbath, see, e.g., E. J. Weisenberg, 'Calendar', in *Encyclopaedia Judaica*, vol. 5 (Jerusalem: Keter, 1971) 43-4.

incident is probably based on the account of Mark, who notes that the cure of the mother-in-law of one of the disciples took place on the Sabbath day.

The fact that the three synoptic authors all agree that sick people waited until after the Sabbath in order to be cured thus helps confirm the accuracy of this timing of the event. As is well known, these authors often report the same event with different timings, even if they differ by only a few hours.[207] If, then, one of these three authors had considered that the people came to Jesus for healing at a different time (that is, other than *after* the Sabbath day), this detail would probably have been noted in their texts. It is also significant that no accounts of this event refer to Jewish officials of any kind, which suggests that it was the wish of the ordinary people of Galilee (rather than that of Jewish officials) to delay their requests for healing until *after* the Sabbath and thus avoided acts of healing on the Sabbath day. The synoptic gospels have thereby preserved evidence that a group of first-century ordinary Galilean Jews avoided requests for Sabbath cures, which, against the background of the problem in Judaism concerning acts of healing and/or saving life on the Sabbath, can only be explained on the assumption that they considered such acts as acts of 'work' which were therefore prohibited on the Sabbath day.

B. *Attempts to Avoid the Conclusion That Galilean Jews Avoided Cures on the Sabbath Day*
In spite however of the convincing evidence from the above texts that a group of Galilean Jews avoided requests for cures on the Sabbath day, this conclusion has been avoided and contested in various ways.

207. For a list of discrepancies in the gospels (including John) regarding the timing of events, see, e.g., Swete, *The Gospel According to St Mark*, lxix-lxxi, and Gundry, *A Commentary on His Apology*, 671-82. Among the synoptists, these include: (1) the healing of a leper, which Matthew places on the same day that Jesus heals the mother-in-law of a disciple, but which Mark places on the following day (Mark 1:29-31, 35, 40-45; Matt 8:2-4, 14-17, 24); (2) the day in Capernaum is a Sabbath for Mark 1:21, 29, but not for Matthew; (3) Matthew's Jesus displaces the dealers from the Temple on the day that he enters Jerusalem, whereas for Mark it occurs on the morning of the second working day (Matt 21:1, 12; Mark 11:1, 11, 15, 20); (4) for Mark, the fig tree withers on the morning of the third day after the entry of Jesus to Jerusalem, whereas for Matthew it withers on the morning of the second day (Matt 21:1, 17, 19; Mark 11:1, 11, 15, 22); (5) for Matthew, the first day of the Passover week was on day three of Jesus' entry to Jerusalem, but on the fourth working day for Mark (Matt 21:1, 17, 18; 26:6, 26; Mark 11:1, 11, 15, 22; 14:3, 12, 17); (6) Luke usually follows the timing of Matthew, but notes that the interrogation of Jesus by the Jewish officials took place after daybreak, whereas for Matthew and Mark it is placed before dawn (Luke 22:66; Matt 26:62; 27:1; Mark 14:55ff.; 15:1).

It has been suggested, for example, that the people waited until after the Sabbath because they did not wish to carry the sick to a healer to be healed, which might be necessary if the patient was crippled in some extreme way.[208] This claim is based on the last of the thirty-nine prohibited main actions on the Sabbath day (m. Shab 7.2, cited in Chapter 1) that unless carrying within a defined space ('a domain', in Hebrew, רשות), carrying was forbidden on the Sabbath day. An example of this law in action can be seen from the criticism by 'the Jews' of the man who carried his pallet on the Sabbath day (John 5:9b-10). It cannot, however, be assumed that all those who were sick needed to travel from different domains or even needed to be carried to Jesus to be cured. As is well known, many of the people whom Jesus cured did not need to be carried to the scenes of their cure.

A further, desperate effort to negate the implications of this tale admits the evidence for a deliberate post-Sabbath timing, but claims that this reflects 'an earlier stage in the tradition when such *fine points* [*sic*] regarding Jewish law were more pertinent than for Mark or his audience'.[209] But apart from the fact that there is no textual evidence of any kind to support this claim, which ignores the evidence of Matthew and Luke, it ironically confirms that it was indeed the custom of ordinary Jewish Galileans in the first half of the first century CE to avoid seeking cures on the Sabbath day.

It has also been argued that people delayed seeking cures on the Sabbath in order to avoid censure of the Jewish authorities.[210] But assuming that the Jewish authorities had the power to enforce traditional Jewish law, their assumed censure of the people for seeking Sabbath cures would again only confirm the Jewish law that forbade acts of healing on the Sabbath day.

C. *Conclusions*

(1) Mark and Luke both describe an incident when a group of ordinary Jewish Galileans wait until after the Sabbath to ask Jesus to perform cures. This timing is confirmed in Matthew's account.

---

208. For example, Marshall, *Luke*, 196, claims that this post-Sabbath healing arose in order to prevent carrying on the Sabbath; see also Gundry, *A Commentary on His Apology*, 87.

209. See Guelich, *Mark 1–8:26*, 65.

210. For example, Iersel, *Mark*, 139; S. T. Lachs, *A Rabbinic Commentary on the New Testament* (Hoboken: Ktav, 1987) 63.

(2) In the context of the problem in Judaism caused by healing on the Sabbath day, the timing of these requests can only be explained on the assumption that the ordinary Jewish Galileans described in this event wished to avoid asking a Jewish healer, here Jesus, for cures on the Sabbath, because healing on the Sabbath was considered as 'work', which was prohibited on the Sabbath day. Their requests to Jesus, or to any other Jewish healer, would therefore have been considered as requests to the healer to violate Jewish law.

(3) No convincing arguments have ever been produced which negate this understanding of the timing of this event.

This completes the review of the Sabbath and post-Sabbath healing events as they are recorded in the gospel texts. The following chapter will summarise the main conclusions that emerge. This will lead to an overall picture of significant trends in the Jewish debate on acts of healing and/or saving life, which cannot be detected from the separate incidents alone. For the details on which the following summaries are based, readers should of course refer back to the discussions above.

Chapter 4

SABBATH HEALING IN THE GOSPELS:
SUMMARY OF CONCLUSIONS OF CHAPTER 3

I. *On How Many Sabbaths Did the Historical Jesus Perform Cures?*

The discussions above suggest that although the gospels relate that Jesus performed cures on ten Sabbath days, probably only six of these can be regarded as historical cures. The four non-Sabbath cures include the two reported by John which may be historical but probably did not take place on the Sabbath, namely, the cure of a crippled man (John 5:2-18), and the cure of a man blind from birth (John 9:1-17). The cure reported at John 7:21 may well be a further reference to the Sabbath event when Jesus removed an evil spirit from a man (Mark 1:21-28 and Luke 4:31-37) so that the account of John cannot be counted as a separate cure; and finally, the 'cure' by Jesus of the starvation of his disciples, when Jesus met the Pharisees on the Sabbath in the Galilean fields, is probably a midrashic-type, fictional narrative, rather than one of the historical cures (Mark 2:23-28; Luke 6:1-5; Matt 12:1-8). The six, or perhaps seven historical cures (seven, if we assume that the cure reported at John 7:21 is not a second account of an earlier cure) are listed below:
1. Mark 1:21-28; Luke 4:31-37: the removal of an evil spirit from a man;
2. Mark 1:29-31; Luke 4:38-39: the cure of the mother-in-law of Simon, probably also reported at Matt 8:14-15;
3. Mark 3:1-6; Luke 6:6-11; Matt 12:9-14: the cure of a man with a withered hand;
4. Mark 6:1-6 with Luke 4:16-23 and Matt 13:58: unidentified cures for unidentified people;
5. Luke 13:10-17: the cure of a woman with a bent back;
6. Luke 14:1-6: the cure of a man with dropsy;
7. John 7:14-25: an unidentified cure, which may refer to the cure earlier described at Mark 1:21-28 and Luke 4:31-37.

II. *No Pharisees Witnessed or Criticised the Sabbath Cures*

The cumulative evidence from Chapter 3 suggests that *no Pharisees or any other Jewish official was ever present at any of these cures*, even when Jesus was criticised for performing a cure. No Jewish officials could therefore have criticised the historical Jesus for performing a cure at the time of each event. There is, moreover, also no reliable evidence that Jesus was ever criticised by any Jewish officials *after* these events. The evidence on which these statements are based has been discussed in detail in Chapter 3, and is briefly summarised below:

(1) With regard to the Sabbath cure of the man with a withered hand (Mark 3:1-6; Luke 6:6-11; Matt 12:9-14), neither Mark nor Matthew (whose report is based on Mark) note that any Pharisees or any other Jewish officials were present during this event. Their presence has therefore been claimed either on the assumption that these individuals can be carried over from the previous scene (when the Pharisees met Jesus in the Galilean fields, Mark 2:23-28; Luke 6:1-5; and Matt 12:1-8) and transferred into the scene of the cure of a man with a withered hand; or else it is claimed that their presence is indicated by the allegation that they withdrew from the scene (see Mark 3:6, whose essential information is repeated at Luke 6:11 and Matt 12:14). As far as the former of these claims is concerned, this is unlikely because—as was discussed in Chapter 3—the previous scene is probably midrashic and thus never took place. Even if the meeting in the Galilean fields records an historical event, it is difficult to believe that Jesus would abandon his starving disciples, or that the Pharisees would rush on ahead of Jesus, knowing where he was going, and then wait in anticipation for Jesus to arrive (see Mark 3:2, and less overtly Matt 12:10). As far as concerns the second of the suggestions for Pharisaic presence at the scene of the cure of the man with the withered hand, this is entirely dependent on the claim that they left the scene after the cure. But this claim is unreliable because there is evidence to suggest that Mark 3:6 is a later addition to Mark's original text. In fact, this verse may have been added for the very purpose of indicating the presence of Pharisees during the scene. Moreover, although Matthew places a rhetorical question on Jewish *halachah* into the mouths of the onlookers at the scene of the cure, which implies their Pharisaic identity, there is evidence to suggest that this question was composed by Matthew (based on Luke 14:3), by whom it was added to his version of the tale. Once again therefore this does not supply proof of the presence of Pharisees at this event. Luke's specific assertion that 'scribes and Pharisees' were present at the scene (Luke 6:7) is also unreliable because the account of Luke depends closely on Mark, and therefore cannot be

accepted as an independent source. Based on the gospel evidence alone, it is therefore unlikely that any Pharisees or other Jewish officials were present at the historical scene of this cure, which means that no Jewish official could have criticised the historical Jesus for performing this cure, either when it took place, or subsequently, at a later time.

(2) With regard to the Sabbath cure of the woman with a bent back (Luke 13:10-16), the only possible candidate for Pharisaic or Jewish official identity in this event is the leader of the synagogue, who is almost certainly a later addition to the story of the cure. No Pharisees or Jewish officials could therefore have criticised the historical Jesus for performing this cure.

(3) The complete absence of Jewish officials from the Sabbath event when the historical Jesus cured a man with dropsy, recounted at Luke 14:1-6, is based in part on the observation that *unlike any other of the synoptic accounts of healings by Jesus*, whether on the Sabbath or on non-Sabbath days, the story of the cure continues after Jesus has dismissed the person he has cured. With two dubious exceptions, the dismissal of the person he has cured *always* otherwise signals the end of the event. This suggests that the material *after* the dismissal of the cured man, the material which features Pharisees and lawyers, does not belong to the original story of the cure. If then no Pharisees or Jewish officials were present after the cure, none could have been present at the cure itself, which means that the setting of the story in the house of 'a ruler of the Pharisees' and the alleged presence of other Pharisees and lawyers has also been added, in this case, prefixed, to the original tale. This means, therefore, that no historical Pharisees or Jewish officials were present at the scene of the cure, so that none could have been criticised the historical Jesus for performing the cure.

(4) No Pharisees or Jewish officials of any kind are identified in the Galilean Sabbath cures described at Mark 6:1-6, nor are any present in the versions of this event described at Luke 4:16-30 and Matt 13:53-58. Once again, therefore, the historical Jesus could not have criticised by any Pharisees or Jewish officials for performing these cures.

(5) There is no evidence of the presence of any Jewish officials when Jesus removed an evil spirit from a man in a synagogue on the Sabbath (Mark 1:21-28; Luke 4:31-37). In any case, Jesus was universally praised for this cure.

(6) Only the ordinary Galilean disciples of Jesus were present at the scene of the Sabbath cure of the mother-in-law of one of Jesus' disciples (Mark 1:29-31; Luke 4:38-39, with Matt 8:14-15). No criticism of Jesus is reported for this cure.

(7) and (8) It is very doubtful that the reports by John of the cure of the crippled man (John 5:2-18) and man blind from birth (John 9:1-14) took place on the Sabbath. In any case, John does not record any criticism of Jesus for performing these cures, which were witnessed only by ordinary Jewish people. Jesus could therefore only have been criticised by Jewish officials *after* the event. Furthermore, the subsequent discussions between Jesus and 'the Jews' or between Jesus and the Pharisees reported by John (John 5:15-18; 9:13-17), do not refer to any earlier cures. These discussions, moreover, are so loosely connected with the preceding cures and contain such serious misconceptions regarding the problem in Judaism caused by acts of healing and/or saving life that it is difficult to believe that they ever took place. It is thus safe to conclude that Jesus was not criticised for either of these cures, either when they were performed or after the events. This of course would not be surprising if, as it seems, neither of these cures took place on the Sabbath day.

(9) The reference of Jesus to an earlier Sabbath cure at John 7:21 clearly states that everyone marvelled at the time of the cure, which suggests that no one originally criticised the cure. Nor is there any suggestion that Jesus was criticised at a later time. In any case, there is no reference in John's text to the presence of Pharisees or any other Jewish official who might have witnessed this cure.

(10) The only Sabbath story in the gospels which suggests that Jewish Pharisaic officials witnessed a Sabbath cure describes how Jesus apparently 'cured' his disciples from starvation by allowing them to harvest and eat grain (Mark 2:23-28; Luke 6:1-5; Matt 12:1-8). The consumption of this kind of food suggests that the disciples were in extremis, starving to death. This condition of the disciples is also indicated by the logic of the argument used by Jesus to the Pharisees to justify the Sabbath violation of his men. On the other hand, there is nothing in the story that suggests that either Jesus or his men were starving to death. The unbridgeable gap between the needs of the story and the story itself thus suggests that the tale of the cure is a midrashic-type tale, and thus does not provide proof that the Pharisees criticised the historical Jesus for this 'cure'. In any case, the Pharisees in this story do not criticise Jesus for 'curing' his disciples, but only enquire politely why the disciples were violating Sabbath law, a question which, as religious Jews apparently observing the violation of the Sabbath they surely were fully entitled to ask.

In summary, therefore, as was stated above, it is difficult to avoid the conclusion that no Pharisees or any other Jewish officials were present at any of the historical Sabbath cures performed by the historical Jesus, and therefore that no Jewish officials could ever have criticised the historical Jesus for performing a Sabbath cure. There is also no convincing evidence that Jesus was criticised by any other Jewish official after he had performed any of these cures.

III. *Who Criticised Jesus for Performing Sabbath Cures?*

The general air of menace in at least four of the historical Sabbath cures leaves little doubt that the historical Jesus was criticised for performing these cures. If, then, the criticism of Jesus did not come from Pharisees or from any other Jewish officials, neither at the historical time of the cures (because no Jewish officials were ever present), nor after they were performed, from whom, can we deduce, did this criticism come? A simple process of elimination suggests that in the absence of the Pharisees or any other Jewish official, this criticism of the historical Jesus could only have come from ordinary Jewish people who witnessed these cures. The evidence for this claim is briefly summarised below:

(1) An analysis of Luke's account of the cure of a woman with a bent back (Luke 13:10-17) shows that the people in the crowd were the only people in the story to whom the historical Jesus could have expressed the pejorative, plural term 'Hypocrites' (Luke 14:15a), which—there is evidence to suggest—was voiced in response to the criticism he received from these people for performing this Sabbath cure, although this criticism has been removed from the narrative of the tale. The people are identified in the argument apparently used by Jesus as 'those who untie their ox and their ass' (Luke 14:15), that is, they were Jewish peasant-farmers, probably from around Jerusalem (see Luke 9:51, 53, 56; 13:22) who were not 'working' in accordance with Sabbath law, and who were thus able to be present at the scene of the Sabbath cure and morally entitled—as Sabbath-keepers themselves—to criticise the historical Jesus for 'working' on the Sabbath day.

(2) It is unlikely that the cure of the man with dropsy took place before Pharisees and lawyers, as Luke suggests (see on Luke 14:1-6 in Chapter 3). Instead it seems that the historical event took place in an unknown location before ordinary pious Jewish people who perhaps lived around Jerusalem (see Luke 9:51, 53, 56; 13:22) and who criticised the historical Jesus for performing the cure. This is indicated by the fact that Jesus 'replied' (ἀποκριθεὶς, Luke 14:3), although in the present version of the story he has not been addressed. However, just as in Luke's story of the cure of the woman with a bent back (Luke 13:10-17), their criticism of Jesus has been removed from the tale.

(3) The account of the Galilean Sabbath cures at Mark 6:1-6 plainly states that ordinary Galilean Jews, including those from his own family, criticised the historical Jesus for performing Sabbath cures. Matthew also admits that Jesus was criticised by ordinary Galileans, but—for obvious reasons—tones down this criticism (see Matt 13:53-58). Luke 4:16-30 also agrees that Jesus was criticised by ordinary people but blames their disapproval on the alleged claim of Jesus that he had cured more people than the biblical prophets Elijah and Elisha. As this claim is not repeated elsewhere, it is possible that it was added by Luke in an attempt to suppress the fact that the historical Jesus was criticised by ordinary Jewish people for performing Sabbath cures.

(4) The probable absence of any Jewish officials on the Sabbath when the historical Jesus cured a man with a withered hand means that criticism could have come only from some of the ordinary, pious Jewish people from Galilee who waited 'to accuse' Jesus for performing this cure (Mark 3:2, 5; Luke 6:7; Matt 12:10) and whom Jesus allegedly admonished for their 'hardness of heart' (Mark 3:5; Luke 6:8). Their menacing anticipation also suggests that these people knew of, and had criticised the historical Jesus, for other earlier unrecorded Sabbath cures. These cannot include the probably earlier cures described at Mark 1:29-31 (with Luke 4:38-39) and Mark 1:21-28, as Jesus was not criticised at either of these events. But, as might be expected, it seems that other Sabbath cures for which Jesus was criticised by the same ordinary pious Jewish people have not been recorded in the gospel texts.

(5) The negative attitude of some ordinary pious Jews to Sabbath cures performed by the historical Jesus (and undoubtedly also by other Jewish healers) is indirectly confirmed by the incident described at Mark 1:21, 32-34 (and also probably at Luke 4:31, 40-41 with Matt 8:16), in which ordinary Jewish Galileans waited until after the Sabbath to bring their sick to Jesus to be cured.

(6) The criticism of the historical Jesus by ordinary Jewish people for performing Sabbath cures is also reflected in the fact that in contrast with the requests, both direct and indirect (the latter when sick people merely presented themselves to Jesus without a verbal request), which *always* precede the cures of Jesus on non-Sabbath days, *there is only one incident in the gospels when Jesus is asked to perform a Sabbath cure.* This occurs when the disciples of Jesus ask him to cure the mother-in-law of one of his disciples (Mark 1:29-31 and Luke 4:38-39 with Matt 8:14-15). This exceptional request can, however, be explained by the fact that in the perception of onlookers, the woman Jesus cured was dangerously ill and without the intervention of a healer would probably have died.

The criticism of a Jewish healer by ordinary Jews, rather than by any Jewish leaders, for healing on the Sabbath in recorded events (and also probably in other unrecorded events, see paragraph [3] above) is, however, no surprise. In the earliest recorded incident when there was a response of the religious leaders to the clash between Sabbath law and the need for acts of healing and/or saving life, namely, the event recorded at 1 Macc 2:29-41 (briefly discussed in Chapter 1), when pious Jews chose to die rather than violate Sabbath law, those who chose to die are not identified as Jewish leaders of any kind, which suggests that these people were ordinary pious Jews. In contrast, it is clear that Mattathias and his colleagues disagreed with their action and thus issued an edict which allowed them to fight on the Sabbath day, although only in self-defence. The evidence that ordinary pious Jews criticised the historical Jesus for performing Sabbath cures therefore suggests that the tradition of these pious Maccabeans to avoid acts of healing and/or saving life on the Sabbath day, in order to avoid a violation of Sabbath law was still alive in Galilee, and perhaps also in Judea, over two hundred years later, in the first century CE.[1] The fact that the second century R. Yose the Galilean was interested in the problem in Jewish law of acts of healing and/or saving life may even be a reaction to the strong Galilean opposition to acts of healing on the Sabbath day due to a rigid adherence to Pentateuchal law, an attitude which he attempted to change by providing religious proof that such actions were allowed.[2] All in all, therefore, it is not surprising to find evidence in the gospels that ordinary Jewish people living in Galilee and probably also in Judea in the early first century generally avoided asking for cures on the Sabbath day and thus criticised Jesus, a Jewish healer, when he performed these cures.

On the other hand, the cure of the mother-in-law of Simon (Mark 1:29-31; Luke 4:38-39, with Matt 8:14-15) and the removal of an evil spirit from a man (Mark 1:21-28; Luke 4:31-37) suggests that by the first century CE, the strict uncompromising attitude of these earlier Jews had been modified to the extent that there was now a conscious acknowledgment of the fact that acts of healing and/or saving of life must take place even on the Sabbath whenever there was a perception of immediate danger to life. This would account for the fact that Jesus was not criticised

1. 1 Macc 2:29 states that 'many *went down* (κατέβησαν) to dwell in the desert'. Since it is traditional to speak of 'going up' and 'going down' when approaching and leaving Jerusalem, it is possible that these pious Maccabeans from the second century BCE came from an agricultural area (they were accompanied by animals) in the north.
2. t. Shab 15.16; Mekilta de-Rabbi Ishmael, Shab 1, Lauterbach, *Mekilta*, 3:198.

when he removed an evil spirit on the Sabbath, and why the disciples
of Jesus asked him to perform a Sabbath cure. It is also possible that
the very public example and influence of Jesus, who must certainly be
counted as an ordinary Jewish person as far as his social status is
concerned, helped to moderate the strict, pious attitude of at least some
of the people in his own social class, and thereby to effect the eventual
general acceptance by ordinary Jews, especially those in Galilee, of the
basic principle of the necessity to heal and/or save life at any time and by
any means, as will be evident in the further chapters of this book.

IV. *Why Is It Implied That Jesus Addressed* Halachic *Material to Non-existent Pharisees?*

The above discussions have shown that with the possible exception of
Luke 13:15b-16, when Jesus of the gospels (as opposed to the historical Jesus) apparently addressed a *halachic* argument *kal va-chomer* to
peasant-farmers, the *halachic* material voiced by the Jesus of the gospels
(rather than the historical Jesus) in the Sabbath healing events is always
addressed to Jewish officials, who are usually Pharisees, and sometimes
also to Jewish lawyers and scribes (the latter according to Luke 6:7, 9
and Luke 14:1, 3, 5), as well as to those whom John calls 'the Jews', who
are generally assumed to be Jewish officials of some kind (John 5:16,
17). In fact, however, as the above discussion has shown, it is unlikely
that any of these Jewish officials were present at these events. These
Jewish officials are therefore non-historical. Why then are they addressed
by Jesus of the gospels in his historical and alleged Sabbath cures?

A traditional reply to this question is that the gospels wished to record
the historical antagonism of the Pharisees towards Jesus for performing
Sabbath cures which (it seems) led them to condemn him to death for
this violation of Sabbath law. This, however, cannot be correct. No,
Pharisees are implicated in the final events in Jesus' life, and, as has been
shown in the discussion above, it is most unlikely that any historical
Pharisees were present at these cures. Why, then, we must ask, is their
presence alleged at these events? Why is Jesus of the gospels shown
voicing *halachic* arguments and asking *halachic* questions at the historical Sabbath healing events, which he addressed to non-historical
Pharisees and also sometimes non-historical Jewish officials who were
also not there?

The answer to this question is almost certainly related to the social
status of the historical Jesus, who was not in any way noble or rich by
birth. He was probably trained by his father as an artisan of some kind,

but abandoned this work for the life of an itinerant healer and preacher. In fact, from the gospel evidence itself, it is clear that the historical Jesus was one of many such Jewish healers who wandered around Galilee in the early first century CE. Thus, according to Mark and Luke, Jesus sent his twelve disciples to preach and to heal (the latter expressed as 'casting out demons'),[3] and the fact that they actively engaged in such tasks is shown by their complaint to Jesus that they did not always succeed.[4] Luke also records that Jesus sent out up to seventy-two disciples to heal, who must have been active because they report successful cures.[5] The gospels also allude to others who healed,[6] including the activities of an exorcist (that is, another healer) who healed in Jesus' name.[7] The gospels note also that a woman with 'a flow of blood for twenty years' had been treated by 'many physicians' (ὑπὸ πολλῶν ἰατρῶν, Mark 5:26, similarly Luke 8:43) before she came to Jesus in order to be cured. In addition, after the death of Jesus, the disciples performed 'many wonders and signs' which must include cures (Acts 1:43). Peter himself healed a disabled beggar (Acts 3:1-8) and he apparently even cured with his shadow (Acts 5:15). Many other successful acts of healing are depicted in Acts.[8] It can thus be assumed that there were at least thirteen poor itinerant Jewish healers in Galilee while Jesus was alive, and probably many more, if Luke can be believed, and perhaps even more after Jesus had died. There is thus little doubt that the healing activity of Jesus was far from unique.[9]

3. Mark 3:15-19 and Matt 10:1-8 refer to twelve named disciples who were healers. Mark 6:7, 13 and Luke 9:1-2, 6 refer to twelve unnamed disciples who were healers.

4. Mark 9:17-18, 28; Luke 9:40; Matt 17:16, 19. Also Mark 16:17-18 (after the crucifixion).

5. Luke 10:1, 9, 17-20.

6. Luke 4:23 refers to an old adage based on the fact that physicians could not cure themselves.

7. Mark 9:38-41; Luke 9:49-50; Matt 10:42. The Tosefta reports that Yaakov of Kefar Sama came to heal R. Eleazar b. Damah in the name of Jesus son of Pantera (t. Hull 2.22; cf. y. Shab 14.4 and Kohelet Rabbah X.6).

8. Acts 5:16; 6:8; 8:7; 9:34, 40-41; 14:3 (the 'signs and wonders'—σημεῖα καὶ τέρατα—performed by the disciples in Iconium probably included acts of healing); 14:8-10; 16:16-18; 19:11-12; 20:9-12 (in which a dead man was revived); 28:8-9. For a review of healers in the Roman world, see J. Moles, 'Jesus the Healer in the Gospels, the Acts of the Apostles, and Early Christianity', *Histos* 5 (2011) 117-82.

9. Mark 7:8. Mark 5:26 notes that a haemorrhaging woman spent all her money on doctors before she was cured by Jesus.

There is, moreover, no indication that the historical Jesus was ever paid for his cures—Jesus even instructed his disciples that they should never accept money for performing cures or travel with food. These healers, however, expected charity, as is emphasised by Jesus, who commanded that his disciples must punish those who did not 'receive' them or who did not 'listen' to them, by 'shaking the dust' from their feet when they left.[10] It can be assumed, therefore, that Jesus and his disciples were wholly dependent on charity, which they expected and took for granted, for all aspects of their lives. It would not be surprising that in spite of their preaching and their ability to perform cures, they were considered as beggars by many contemporary Jews, and were therefore regarded among the lowest in the social scale.

The lowly status of Jesus could well have been confirmed in the eyes of the Jewish sages by the fact that although he *may* have been born in Judea, as Luke and Matthew claim, Jesus of the gospels is always known as 'Jesus of Nazareth', an inhabitant of Galilee, where there was little Jewish learning, as far as the Jerusalem sages were concerned, and from where no Messiah would ever come, according to the Pharisees and the people of Jerusalem (John 7:41-42, 52). Nicodemus, a Galilean 'ruler of the Jews' (ἄρχων, John 3:1), and thus, we can assume, a person of some eminence who was learned in Jewish law, was therefore denigrated by the Pharisees in Jerusalem because they claimed that his Galilean roots meant that he was ignorant of Jewish law (John 7:52). The negative opinion of the Jerusalem sages is echoed by the maidservant of the Jerusalem high priest, when she remarked disparagingly on the Galilean speech (λαλιά) of Peter, the Galilean disciple of Jesus (Matt 26:73). The same negative stereotyping of Galileans is also recorded in the rabbinic Jewish texts. Thus the general ignorance of Galileans concerning Jewish law seems to be implied by the sages in Jerusalem when they note that although the eminent R. Yohanan b. Zakkai, the designated heir of Hillel the Elder, lived in Galilee for eighteen years, he was consulted only twice on cases of Jewish law. R. Yohanan was therefore inspired to make the now famous lament, 'O Galilee, Galilee, you have hated the Torah. You will end up working for oppressors!', although no specific reason is given for this remark.[11] Similarly, like the maidservant of the high priest mentioned above, the sages of the Babylonian Talmud also ridiculed the pronunciation of Galileans, noting that it was not 'exact' (דייקני), and provided amusing examples of the mistakes that were made when similar

---

10. Mark 6:8-11; Luke 9:3-5; 10:4, 11, 35; Matt 10:8b-14.
11. y. Shab 16.8.

sounding words were mispronounced.[12] The use of a whole geographic region to differentiate the eminent second-century Jewish sage R. Yose *the Galilean* may even suggest a reasonable basis for this prejudice, as it implies the scarcity of Galilean sages in comparison with the many sages from Judea, for whom the epithet 'the Judean' would certainly not differentiate one sage from another. Although, therefore, R. Yose the Galilean established a reputation for piety and a deep knowledge of Jewish law, he also suffered from the general prejudice of Judeans. This can be seen in the story about Beruriah, who, if she is correctly identified as the learned and honoured wife of R. Meir, herself came from Sikhnin, a town in Galilee. Nevertheless, she apparently referred to R. Yose as a 'stupid Galilean', merely because he used more words than were strictly needed—he used four words instead of two as far as the written text is concerned—when he asked her the way to Lod. He thereby engaged in what was called by a Jerusalemite 'unnecessary speech with a woman', which was discouraged by Jewish oral law:[13]

תלמוד בבלי מסכת עירובין דף נג עמוד ב

רבי יוסי הגלילי הוה קא אזיל באורחא, אשכחה לברוריה, אמר לה, באיזו דרך
נלך ללוד? אמרה ליה, גלילי שוטה, לא כך אמרו חכמים אל תרבה שיחה עם
האשה. היה לך לומר, באיזה ללוד?

Babylonian Talmud Eruvin 53b

R. Yose the Galilean was once on a journey when he met Beruriah. 'By-what road' he asked her, 'do-we-go to-Lydda?' (דרך [2] באיזו [1] ללוד? [4] נלך [3]). 'Stupid Galilean', she replied, 'Did not the Sages say "Engage not in much talk with women"? You should have asked, "By-which [road] to-Lydda?"' (?ללוד [2] באיזה [1]).

Even if this story was composed before the reputation of R. Yose the Galilean was established, the fact that it was preserved helps to confirm the self-styled superiority of the sages of Jerusalem towards this most eminent of Jewish sages, merely because of his Galilean roots. How much more disdainful would they therefore have been regarding a poor itinerant healer such as Jesus, who had no formal training in Jewish law.[14]

12. b. Eruv 53b.

13. m. Avot 1.5: Jose b. Yohanan of Jerusalem said, '…and talk not much with a woman—אל תרבה שיחה אם האשה...'

14. John 7:15, 'The Jews marvelled at [the teaching of Jesus] saying, "How is it that this man [= Jesus] has learning when he never studied!"' Similarly Mark 1:22: 'And they were astonished at his learning for he [=Jesus] taught them as one who had authority and not as the scribes'. Similarly Mark 6:2, 'And on the Sabbath he [=Jesus] began to teach in the synagogue and many who heard him were astonished, saying "Where did this man get all this? What is the wisdom given to him?…"'

A similar deriding of the assumed lack of knowledge of Galileans can be seen in a story of 'a certain Galilean' who was travelling in Babylon and was asked to lecture in public on the text of the first chapter in the book of Ezekiel, which describes the heavenly chariot. This subject is regarded in Judaism as esoteric learning and is thus confined to a select educated few. Nevertheless, the Galilean announced that he would comply. He was then stung by a wasp on his forehead (presumably the seat of his ignorance) and promptly died, a fate which his potential Babylonian audience claimed that his (Galilean) stupidity fully deserved.[15]

For those with such a socially blighted background in the first century CE, a route to social elevation was provided by officially joining the Jewish sages, especially the Pharisees before 70 CE, who were undoubtedly the most respected of the Jewish religious leaders of their time.[16] Although we do not know what requirements were demanded from those wishing to join this religious group, the tradition of the rabbis who took over from the Pharisees after the Temple was destroyed suggests that the Pharisaic community was open to anyone—poor and rich alike, educated or not-educated—provided they were prepared to study to achieve a deep knowledge of Judaism, especially Jewish law, and showed a deep personal commitment to a Pharisaic way of life. The Mishnah thus states that 'a learned (Jewish) person born from an illegal sexual union (and therefore among those with the lowest social status) takes precedence over an ignorant high priest'.[17] Perhaps the most famous of those who raised their status in this way is R. Akiva, who seems to have been even more handicapped than Jesus as far as his lowly beginnings are concerned. He was born into poverty and began his working life as a shepherd, an occupation of low social status, often the work of the youngest son who had little prospect of inheriting land. Unlike Jesus, who could read, apparently even from the Torah scroll (Luke 4:17), and whose Jewish religious behaviour shows that he was knowledgeable in

---

15.   b. Shab 80b. See also b. Hag 11b, 13a and 14b.

16.   Josephus, Ant XVIII.15 states that '[the Pharisees were] extremely influential among town dwellers, and all rites of divine worship are performed according to their direction'. Josephus, Ant XVIII.17 states that the Pharisees were so much preferred by ordinary people that the latter forced the Sadducees to adopt their Pharisaic rituals 'since otherwise, the masses would not tolerate them [= the Sadducees]'. Similarly, Ant XIII.288, 'And so great is their [= the Pharisees'] influence with the masses that even when they speak against a king or high priest, they immediately gain credence'; see also Ant XIII.297-98, cited in the main text above.

17.   m. Hor 3.8, אם היה ממזר תלמיד חכם וכהן גדול עם הארץ, ממזר תלמיד חכם קודם לכהן גדול עם הארץ.

the ritual of Jewish law, the future R. Akiva began to study only when he was forty, before which time he was illiterate and ignorant in matters of Jewish concern. Yet none of these impediments prevent him from becoming one of the most revered of the Jewish sages both in his own time and today.[18] Poverty was similarly no bar to the elevation of the great Hillel the Elder, who was so poor when he was young that he had to help support his family and could not even pay for entry to the *beit midrash*.[19] Other sages, such as the first-century sage R. Eleazar b. Hurcanus came from wealthier backgrounds, but like R. Akiva, also began to study at a relatively late age and from a low level of religious knowledge.[20] The community of rabbis was even open to those whose early life was questionable from a moral point of view, such as the late second-century R. Simon b. Lakish, who was formerly a gladiator and bandit, occupations not usually associated with the rabbinic way of life, who even gained enough Jewish respectability to be allowed to marry the sister of the eminent R. Yohanan b. Nappatha, one of the editors of the Jerusalem Talmud.[21] Even if these details are partly legendary, their preservation confirms the general principle that entry to the community of the Jewish sages was open to anyone, including those who were poor and uneducated as far as Jewish matters were concerned. It is therefore unlikely that the poverty of Jesus and his probable low social status would have been a bar to his official acceptance by the Pharisees, had he so wished. But no proof exists that this ever occurred. Mark and John even note that Jesus had no formal Jewish education, a fact which could not have enhanced his status or given him any religious authority, especially as the future Messiah, among the pious Jews of his time, and was therefore not in the interests of these authors to record.[22] We must therefore assume that it is probably correct.

Accordingly, in order to differentiate Jesus from other poor Jewish healers, and to elevate his status from that of a lowly Galilean Jew, and, in the eyes of some people, from that of a mere beggar (in spite of the fact that he performed wonderful cures), Jesus of the gospels is therefore presented in the Sabbath healing events apparently in the company of the

18.   b. Ber 27b; ARN A 6; b. Pes 49b, in which R. Akiva describes himself as an *am ha-aretz*, that is, a person ignorant in matters of Jewish concern; b. Ned 50a; ARN A 6.

19.   b. Yom 35b.

20.   According to ARN A 6 and B 12, 13, Hurcanus began to study at the age of 21.

21.   b. Gitt 47a.

22.   See n. 14.

Pharisees, asking significant *halachic* questions and using the same kind of *halachic* rhetorical arguments that the Pharisees themselves used. Thus, although there is never any response to this material—neither to the *halachic* questions nor to the *halachic* arguments (which in itself should arouse suspicion concerning the historicity of these encounters, especially in view of the evidence in the tannaitic texts, in which such questions and answers are repeatedly part of a dialogue of some kind), Jesus is shown in effect debating with the Pharisees using the arguments and the language that they themselves used, and on the topic of healing on the Sabbath, a subject with which he, as a healer, was deeply involved and which was undoubtedly an issue of mutual concern. Jesus of the gospels is thus transformed into an equal of the Pharisees, having side-stepped the requirement for any formal Jewish study which he had never undergone. Thereby, in one midrashic-type picture, Jesus overcame his disadvantaged lowly status, his Galilean origins and any stigma concerning his impoverished way of life, with the result his prestige was now significantly enhanced, probably far beyond that of any of the many other Jewish healers of his time. Without any appreciation of the fact that these situations are illusory and wholly contrived, commentators of the gospels thus frequently note approvingly that Jesus debated with the Pharisees on their own terms.[23]

In fact, Jesus of the gospels was now presented to a first-century Jewish audience as an individual similar to the revered first-century healer R. Hanina b. Dosa, who was probably not known to Jesus, but who was almost certainly known to the authors of the gospels, since he was active around the time of the fall of the Temple in 70 CE. Like Jesus, he came from Galilee and was very poor and lived as a pious Jew. Like Jesus, he was not concerned with the development of Jewish law, so that—again like Jesus—no *halachot* (Jewish laws) are cited in his name. Like Jesus, he was *not* known for his scholarship, but for his saintliness and his ability to perform miracles—for example, he caused rain to fall and also cease to fall—and for his acts of healing—for example, he healed the sons of R. Yohanan b. Zakkai and Rabban Gamaliel II.[24] Like Jesus he was also known for his moralistic aphorisms, for example: *Whosoever's fear of sin precedes his learning, his learning will endure;*

23. For example, W. D. Davies and D. C. Allison, *A Critical and Exegetical Commentary on the Gospel According to Saint Matthew*, vol. 2 (Edinburgh: T. & T. Clark, 1991) 319, note in relation to Matt 12:11 that 'Matthew is intent on sharpening Jesus' *halachic* logic and making him a first-rate debater'.

24. y. Ber 5.5, b. Ber 34b. The Mishnah describes how R. Hanina b. Dosa knew if someone he had tried to heal would get well; see m. Ber 5.5, cited in the main text.

but where learning precedes fear of sin, learning will not endure. Similarly, *Where a man's works are greater than his learning, his learning will stand; but where his learning is greater than his works, his learning will not endure.*[25] And crucially, like Jesus, Hanina b. Dosa is described in the company of Jewish sages, although in this case they are named, for example R. Yohanan b. Zakkai (his teacher), Rabban Gamaliel II and R. Eleazer of Modi'im.[26] So renowned was he that the Mishnah even claims symbolically that after the death of Hanina, those who worked miracles ceased to exist.[27]

The alleged historical interaction between Jesus and the Pharisees in the Sabbath healing events thus significantly changes the standing of Jesus presented by the authors of the gospel texts, transforming him into a Hanina b. Dosa of earlier times.[28] But as noted above, this is a

25. See also m. Avot 3.10 and 3.11.

26. b. Ber 34b; Mekilta de-Rabbi Ishmael Amalek 4, Lauterbach, *Mekilta*, 2:183 describes R. Hanina ben Dosa as 'a man of truth'. The tannaitic texts provide only a few names of prominent Jewish sages from the first third of the first century. They include Rabban Gamaliel the Elder, a Pharisee according to Acts 5:34, Akabya b. Mahalaleel, famous for his knowledge and piety (m. Eduy 5.6), and R. Chanina, the deputy high priest (b. Yom 39a). None of these feature in the gospel healing incidents. The fact that no Pharisees are named in any of the gospel Sabbath healing events may add further evidence that none were ever there—if they had been there, why are they not named? The lack of a name is especially strange in the case of 'a ruler who belonged to the Pharisees' (Luke 14:1), as the names of Jewish 'rulers' are often known.

27. m. Sot 9.15. This mishnaic eulogy has been interpreted in several ways. A. Büchler, *Types of Jewish-Palestinian Piety: From 70 BCE to 70 CE* (London: Jews' College, 1922) 81-2, suggests that it refers to the fact that Hanina b. Dosa devoted his life to deeds of loving kindness.

28. The probable fact that the historical Jesus in the historical Sabbath healing incidents did not address historical Pharisees does not, of course, have relevance for the historicity of other recorded clashes of Jesus with Pharisees on other aspects of Jewish law. It seems that Jesus in general had no love for the Pharisees, and thus referred to them directly with the unforgettable terms 'vipers' (ἔχιδνα, which was also used by John the Baptist, Luke 3:7; Matt 3:7; 12:34; 23:33) and 'Hypocrites' (Mark 7:6; Luke 11:44; Matt 15:7; 22:18; 23:13, 14, 15, 23, 25, 27, 29). In fact, Pharisees are sometimes similarly unpopular in tannaitic texts (see, for example, m. Sot 3.4; t. Ber 9.5; t. Sot 5.5). According to the gospels, Jesus clashed with Pharisees on the rituals of hand washing and fasting, and his claim to forgive sins. At Mark 2:16; Luke 5:30; 15:2; Matt 9:11, Pharisees object to the fact that Jesus ate with publicans and sinners; at Mark 7:2 and Matt 15:2, Pharisees object to the lack of ritual washing before food; at Luke 5:33, they criticise the neglect of fasting; at Luke 5:21, they criticise Jesus for forgiving sins. The antagonism apparently shown by the Pharisees towards Jesus in these situations should not, however, be

misconception—the Jesus who apparently addressed Pharisees in the Sabbath healing events cannot be the historical Jesus, because no Pharisees were there. In fact, as is summarised in the following section, Jesus did not compose or voice any of the *halachic* material in the Sabbath healing events, which shows that this could not have been addressed to Pharisees, even if they were there.

V. *The Historical Jesus Did Not Compose or Voice the* Halachic *Material in His Sabbath Cures*

The examination of the individual Sabbath healing accounts in Chapter 3 has shown that the *historical* Jesus probably neither composed nor voiced any of the *halachic* material in the gospel accounts of his Sabbath cures. In fact, this is also evident from the absence of historical Pharisees or any other Jewish officials in these events, although it may seem from the way in which these events are related that it is to one or more of these people that the *halachic* material is addressed. It is obvious, however, that material which is addressed to people who were not there is not likely to be part of the historical event. The evidence for the claim that the historical Jesus did not state any of the *halachic* material in the Sabbath healing events can, however, be approached in a different way, as will be evident in the short summaries below.

According to the gospel accounts of the Sabbath healing events, Jesus voiced three types of *halachic* material:

(1) Five rhetorical arguments *kal va-chomer*, each of which justifies a different cure: (i) Mark 2:25-26, 28, repeated at Luke 6:3-5 and rephrased as a sorite at Matt 12:3-4, 8, which justifies the cure of the disciples from starvation; (ii) Matt 12:11-12, which justifies the cure of a man with a withered hand; (iii) Luke 13:15b-16, which justifies the cure of a woman with a bent back; (iv) Luke 14:5, which justifies the cure of a man with dropsy; (v) John 7:24, which justifies an unidentified cure, perhaps the cure of a man with an evil spirit described at Mark 1:21-28 and Luke 4:31-37.

---

automatically transferred to the Sabbath healing events, which has led to condemnation of the Pharisees also in these events *even when they are silent* (which must in fact be the case if they were not historically present) as in the cure of the man with dropsy (Luke 14:4, 6) and the cure of the man with a withered hand (see especially Mark 3:2, 4; Luke 6:7) and *even when no criticism of Jesus is expressed*, as in the story of Jesus and the Pharisees in the Galilean fields, when the Pharisees merely remark politely that the disciples of Jesus are violating Sabbath law.

(2) Two *halachic* questions: (i) a question Jesus asks before the cure of a man with a withered hand in Mark 3:4, which is repeated almost verbatim at Luke 6:9, and (ii) a question Jesus he asks before the cure of the man with dropsy in Luke 14:3. (A third *halachic*-type question is asked by onlookers at Matt 12:10, and therefore, on this evidence alone, cannot be attributed to Jesus.)

(3) A *halachic*-type argument based on an interpretation of the Hebrew (or Aramaic) text of Gen 2:2 (John 5:17).

A. *The Halachic Arguments kal va-chomer Which Justify Specific Sabbath Cures*
(1) *Mark 2:25-26, 28, Luke 6:3-5, an argument kal va-chomer which justifies the 'cure' of starvation, and which is rephrased as a sorite at Matthew 12:3-5, 8.* The story of the meeting between Jesus and the Pharisees in the Galilean fields is probably a midrashic-type fictional tale. This is revealed mainly by the fact that the logic of the argument *kal va-chomer* used by Jesus requires that the disciples of Jesus were starving to death, which is not the reality of the story itself. As there is no other suitable situation in the gospels when this argument could have been expressed, it is unlikely that it was ever expressed by the historical Jesus himself. There is, however, evidence that the argument existed in Hebrew in Jewish sources (see Chapter 6) and was perhaps originally composed by R. Eleazar b. Azariah, or by R. Akiva, both of whom were active in the second half of the first century, well after the time that Jesus died. We must conclude that Jesus himself could not have expressed the argument with which he is now linked in this Galilean tale.

(2) *Matthew 12:11-12, an argument kal va-chomer which apparently justifies the cure of a man with a withered hand.* This argument does not appear in the versions of this cure in the earlier gospels of Mark and Luke, which can be assumed to have preserved the most memorable of Jesus' words. Moreover, as will be seen in the discussion below on the specific and general arguments *kal va-chomer* preserved in the gospel texts, if this argument was composed in the time of Jesus, it is likely that it would justify this specific cure. In order for this to happen, the argument would therefore have replicated one or more or the significant features of the situation which required a cure, in the material of the opening section of the argument (*ha-nadon*), in this case a detail which replicates or evokes a detail of the cure of a man with a withered hand. But rather than specifically justifying the cure, this argument in Matthew functions to reply to the general *halachic*-type question asked by the onlookers at Matt 12:10. The argument in Matthew is thus used as a

general argument to supply a *general* answer to the *general* question asked by the onlookers at Matt 12:10. As will be discussed at the end of this chapter, it is probable that such general arguments were composed only in the second half of the first century, well after the time that Jesus had died.

(3) *Luke 14:5, an argument kal va-chomer which justifies the cure of the man with dropsy.* The account of the cure of the man with dropsy continues after Jesus has parted from the man he has cured, which is unique in the synoptic accounts of any of the cures that Jesus performed. This strongly suggests that the material which follows the dismissal of the man Jesus cured is not part of the original story of the cure, but is a later addition to the story, which, we can assume, was probably added by Luke. Accordingly, as the *halachic* argument now attributed to Jesus is part of the material *after* the dismissal, it is unlikely that it was voiced at the original event. Furthermore as this argument is specific for its cure and as there is no other appropriate event in the gospels for it to be expressed, it is unlikely that the argument was composed or voiced by the historical Jesus himself.

(4) *John 7:23, an argument kal va-chomer which justifies an unidentified cure.* This argument is not recorded in the earlier synoptic gospels, which can be expected to have preserved the most memorable words of Jesus, which suggests that it was never spoken by Jesus himself. This is especially the case if the incident refers to the removal of an evil spirit from a man, which is recorded at Mark 1:21-28 and Luke 4:31-37, in which no argument is expressed. In fact, this can be expected as Jesus is never given an argument *kal va-chomer* to express unless there is criticism of the cure he has performed which is not the case here. It seems, therefore, that John supplied an argument to justify this cure which he may have considered was missing from the synoptic account.

It is furthermore evident that the argument of Jesus recorded by John cannot be properly understood without reference to the argument attributed to R. Eleazar b. Azariah, which is based on the same details, and is also phrased as an argument *kal va-chomer*. Unlike the argument of John however, the argument of R. Eleazar includes all the details which are necessary for the argument to be understood. In particular, R. Eleazar suggests that the act of circumcision should be considered as an act of healing one part of the human body, so that if this act is allowed on the Sabbath, so also it should be allowed to heal the whole of a human body on the Sabbath day. John, however, omits this essential detail and seems to insist that the mere violation of Sabbath law by the act of circumcision justifies the violation of Sabbath law by an act of healing and/or saving life, which does not make sense. This suggests, therefore, that the argument of John is a misremembered recollection of the argument of R. Eleazar, who was probably an older contemporary of John and active in the second half of the first century CE, long after Jesus had died. This is confirmed by the fact that, as will be discussed further below and in the following chapters of this book, *general* arguments *kal va-chomer* to justify acts of healing and/or saving life, of the type composed by R. Eleazar based on circumcision, were probably not composed until the second half of the first century, well after the time that Jesus died. The cumulative evidence thus suggests that the argument in John could never have been voiced by the historical Jesus himself.

(5) *Luke 13:15b-16, an argument kal va-chomer that justifies the cure of a woman with a bent back.* There is little doubt that Jesus conducted the cure in Aramaic. On the other hand, an examination of the language of this argument suggests that it was almost certainly originally composed in Hebrew as are all other arguments *kal va-chomer* preserved in the tannaitic texts. This being the case, as it is unlikely that Jesus conducted the cure in Aramaic and then justified it in Hebrew, it is unlikely that the argument that justified the cure was voiced at the time of the cure, and thus unlikely it was voiced by the historical Jesus himself. The fact of its addition has, however, been obscured by the fact that both parts of Luke's story—the cure and the argument—have been unified in Greek.

Other indications that the historical Jesus could never have expressed this argument include the fact that the argument attributed to Jesus in this scene refers to the eighteen-year illness of the woman whom Jesus cured, although this could not have been known to the historical Jesus himself because—as many scholars note—apart from the announcement by Jesus of her cure, there is no verbal communication between Jesus and the woman, and neither between Jesus and any other person at the scene. It is thus unlikely that this detail of the woman's illness was known to Jesus, which casts doubt on the possibility that he voiced the argument in which this detail occurs. This is also suggested by the fact that although arguments *kal va-chomer* based on the leniency of Sabbath law relating to the care of animals on the Sabbath day are easy to compose (because the animal can be placed in any situation of danger to its life), no similar arguments appear in the (probably) earlier gospel of Mark. This suggests that such arguments were not composed until after the publication of Mark's gospel, which is well after the time that Jesus died. If, however, Jesus composed and/or voiced the argument that justifies the cure of the woman with a bent back, it is probably the only *halachic* argument *kal va-chomer* that Jesus ever composed and/or voiced.

Although this argument is probably the most problematic of the arguments as far as its origins are concerned, the balance of evidence thus suggests that it was probably neither composed nor spoken by the historical Jesus himself.

B. *The Halachic Questions Apparently Asked by Jesus*

The *halachic* questions preserved in the cure of the man with a withered hand in Mark 3:4 and Luke 6:9, and Luke's account of the man with dropsy (Luke 14:3), are expressed suddenly without any surrounding material that suggests a reasonable context for such questions to be asked. In fact, the questions are inappropriate for both the settings in which they are now placed, one within a Sabbath service, which is not a context for *halachic* debate, and the other at a time when people were apparently assembling before a formal feast, which in any case probably did not take place. These observations suggest that the *halachic* questions have been added to the original scene of the cure. Evidence preserved in the tannaitic texts, moreover, suggests that these questions in Mark and Luke are early forerunners of at least one of the later questions which were debated by the second century Jewish sages, before they had discovered acceptable 'proof' that the Jewish God indeed intended His people to heal and/or save life on the Sabbath day. This accords with the fact that the *halachic* questions asked by Jesus of the gospels expect a positive reply, which was the expectation of the Jewish sages, as will be discussed in the closing chapter of this book.

C. *The Halachic Argument at John 5:17*

The analysis of this text in Chapter 3 showed that *halachic*-type argument at John 5:17 is based on the Hebrew (or Aramaic) version of Gen 2:2. This semitic text seems to suggest that God himself both 'worked' and rested on the Sabbath day. (In contrast, this verse in the Septuagint suggests that God only rested on the Sabbath day.) Assuming that this 'work' of God in the Hebrew (or Aramaic) version of Gen 2:2 refers to acts of healing and/or saving life (although there is no indication of its nature in the biblical text, in which means that it could refer to any kind of 'work'), the argument used by Jesus thus apparently suggests that Jesus could behave like God in relation to acts of healing and/or saving life. This furthermore suggests that only those who claim that they can behave like God should perform such acts. Yet Jesus must have known that many ordinary Jewish people frequently engaged in acts of healing and/or saving life on the Sabbath day, including probably his own disciples whom he instructed how to heal (see especially on m. RH 2.5 in Chapter 9 and the directives that allowed acts of healing and/or saving life which were probably issued before 50 CE which are listed in Chapter 11). In any case, it can be assumed that the underlying message of all the Sabbath healings of Jesus, which were almost all performed in public, was that healing on the Sabbath was *not* an activity that was exclusively allowed for those who claimed that they might behave like God, but was an activity which any Jewish healer should freely perform. In short, Jesus was fighting for the regular practice of acts of healing *by any Jewish healer on the Sabbath day*. He would therefore have never justified his acts of Sabbath healing with reference to Gen 2:2.

Moreover, the fact that this argument is not recorded in the earlier synoptic texts which probably recorded the most memorable words of Jesus, again suggests that this argument was not voiced by the historical Jesus himself. This conclusion is further strengthened by the dubious historicity of the events leading to the meeting, and the meeting itself (John 5:10-47) when this argument was voiced.

In summary, whether from the probable fact that no historical Pharisees or Jewish officials were present at the scenes of the Sabbath cures, so that none could be addressed with any *halachic* material, or from an analysis of the texts themselves, the evidence discussed in detail in Chapter 3 which is summarised above suggests that none of the *halachic* material which Jesus now speaks in the Sabbath healing events was either composed and/or voiced by the historical Jesus himself. This conclusion will, however, come as no surprise to scholars who regard Jesus as an inspired charismatic leader, whose activity and gifts, like those of R. Hanina b. Dosa, lay in his ability to communicate, to arouse, to motivate, to inspire and to empower his followers to lead a pious Jewish life, rather than in the formulation of Jewish oral law, although he himself was committed to live according to this law.[29] This being the case, the rhetorical questions and arguments in the gospels in relation to healing and saving life have little or nothing to do with the birth or

29. For Jewish charismatics, see Vermes, *Jesus the Jew*, 58-82, esp. 80-2; G. Sarfatti, 'Pious Men, Men of Deeds and the Early Prophets', *Tarbiz* 26 (1956–57) 126-53 (Hebrew), II–IV English summary. For a recent survey of neo-Weberian researches on charismatic leadership in the fields of political and managerial sciences, which shows how charismatic leadership communicates vision and empowers followers, and thus has many points in common with the authority of Jesus, see P. Piovanelli, 'Jesus' Charismatic Authority: On the Historical Applicability of a Sociological Model', *Journal of the American Academy of Religion* 73.2 (2005) 395-427.

problems of the early Church, as some scholars suggest.[30] They have, however, been linked with these topics merely because the life of the historical Jesus who was a healer and the lives of those who authored the written accounts of his deeds coincided with the time of heightened Jewish debate which sought to justify Sabbath acts of healing and/or saving life within the framework of Jewish law.

VI. *By Whom Were the Halachic Questions and Arguments Originally Composed?*

If the historical Jesus did not compose and/or voice the *halachic* material in the Sabbath healing events, by whom can we assume this material was composed? Apart from the argument based on Gen 2:2, which probably originated among Jewish followers of Jesus (see the discussion in Chapter 3), there can only be one general answer—since this material is concerned with the *halachah* of acts of healing and/or saving life that violate Sabbath law, and since this subject could only have been of concern to the Jewish people of the time, the material that Jesus uses must have been derived from those in the Jewish community who were concerned with this problem of Jewish law. This does not necessarily mean that it was derived from those who were contemporary with Jesus. The discussion above has shown that at least some of this material, in particular the *halachic* arguments *kal va-chomer*, was probably derived from those who were contemporary with the authors of the gospels themselves. Thus, the implication of the underlying phrase דחה (את) (ה)שבת in the argument used in the Galilean fields suggests that it was composed by either by R. Eleazar b. Azariah or by Rabbi Akiva (this is discussed in detail in Chapter 5). On the other hand, the convenience and versatile universality of the arguments based on the practice of saving the life of an animal on the Sabbath which are new in Luke (Luke 13:15b-16; 14:5; and also Matt 12:11-12) suggests that they would also have been cited by Mark if they had been composed when his gospel was written. The fact that they do not appear in Mark thus suggests that they were not composed until the time of the publication of Luke; and the argument based on the ritual of circumcision (John 7:23) was almost certainly composed by R. Eleazar b. Azariah (as was discussed in Chapter 3). In short, the *halachic* arguments now attributed to Jesus of the gospels, but which the historical Jesus probably neither composed nor expressed, may have been derived from the Pharisees (if

---

30. E.g. Hultgren, 'The Formation of the Sabbath Pericope in Mark 2:23-28', 112-15, esp. on the versions of Mark 2:25-28.

perhaps R. Eleazar b. Azariah was a Pharisee) but more likely from their later rabbinic successors in the course of their discussions on acts of healing and/or saving life that violated Sabbath law. There is also little doubt that the *halachic* questions were also derived from one or other of these Jewish groups. These questions and arguments have, however, been removed from their original context of discussion within the *battay-midrash*, and have been added to stories of Jesus' Sabbath cures. Combined with the attempt to suggest the presence of Pharisees in up to six of the gospel Sabbath cures, the authors of the gospels thus give the impression that *halachic* material voiced by Jesus was addressed to Pharisees, although it is unlikely that any Pharisees were present at these events.[31] The contrived nature of this arrangement is perhaps most clearly illustrated in the story of the starving disciples in the Galilean fields, who are not taught by their master the relevant Jewish law, as would probably be described in a rabbinic text when a Jewish sage and his disciples are placed in a situation which demands a knowledge of Jewish law.[32] Instead, in this story the disciples are ignored, and Jesus teaches the Pharisees, the very people by whom his teaching may well have been composed.

The link between (a) the Pharisees and the rabbis and (b) the rhetorical *halachic* language in the Sabbath healing events in the gospels is, however, no surprise. This type of rhetoric in post-biblical times is first associated with the Jewish sage Hillel the Elder, who apparently used an argument *kal va-chomer* at the very beginning of his public career in the second half of the first century BCE.[33] The fact that this argument was understood by his audience of the Bney Bathyra, the Temple officials at the time, indicates that this kind of rhetoric was already familiar to the Jewish sages. Hillel is not named as a Pharisee in any rabbinic text (in

---

31. Other arguments *kal va-chomer* that are attributed to Jesus in the gospels are not *halachic* but *aggadic*, that is, they are moral, ethical arguments, rather than arguments concerned with Jewish law; see Luke 23:28-31; Matt 6:28-30; 7:9-11; and 10:24-25. There is therefore no need to address them to Jewish officials. The same is true for arguments *kal va-chomer* in the letters of Paul.

32. For example, t. Ber 4.16, in which Rabbi Tarfon, who was active before the destruction of the Temple in 70 CE (see y. Yom 3.7), explains to his disciples the relevant Jewish law, which he justified with three rabbinic arguments *kal va-chomer*, after he is brought water to drink. See also m. Ber 2.5, 6, 7, when Rabban Gamaliel the Elder briefly discusses with his disciples the subjects of prayer after marriage and rituals after death. Also, in m. Nid 8.3 Rabbi Akiva teaches his disciples a lenient attitude in the interpretation of one of the rules *of niddah*. See also t. Ber 3.30.

33. Hillel's argument *kal va-chomer* justified the precedence of the Passover sacrifice over Sabbath law, see t. Pes 4.14.

which no individual is labelled in this way), but his Pharisaic identity can be assumed from the fact that he was a pupil of Shemaiah and Abtalion, whom Josephus names as the Pharisees Pollion and Samias.[34] In any case, both Hillel and Shammai are named as Pharisees in Jerome's commentary on Isa 8:14, although this may be questioned because of its relatively late date of composition at the beginning of the fifth century CE.[35] The Mishnah and Tosefta and the later rabbinic texts record that arguments *kal va-chomer* were used by the Pharisees and it is clear that this rhetorical device continued to be used by their successors, the rabbinic sages.[36]

In conclusion, it is clear that in spite of the impression given in the gospels, which has resulted in a deeply negative opinion of Pharisees adopted by many readers of these texts, it is most improbable that Jesus himself *ever* debated or clashed personally with the Pharisees on the subject of Sabbath acts of healing and/or saving life. It seems, in fact, that Jesus is made to ask questions and to voice arguments to the Pharisees, some of which were composed by Pharisees themselves and the rest by the rabbinic sages who were the spiritual successors of the Pharisees around and after 70 CE. Contrary to the opinion usually voiced, the historical Jesus and the historical Pharisees were in complete agreement that acts of healing and/or saving life must be allowed to take place on the Sabbath day.

---

34. For commentary on Josephus, Ant XV.3, see Strack and Stemberger, *Introduction to the Talmud and Midrash*, 71.

35. R. Gryson and P.-A. Deproost, *Commentaires de Jérôme sur le prophète Isaïe* (Freiburg: Herder, 1993) 373, 'The Nazarenes interpret the two houses [of Isa 8:14] as the two families of Shammai and Hillel, from whom the scribes and the Pharisees originated...' Jerome's source of information may be oral, since no individuals are ever identified as Pharisees in the Jewish texts.

36. Two examples of Pharisaic arguments have been preserved (although the fact that no individuals in Jewish texts are ever identified as Pharisees means that there are probably more), namely m. Yad 4.7 and t. Yad 2.20. Rabban Gamaliel 1 ('the Elder') is identified as a Pharisee at Acts 5:34. Assuming that he is the Rabban Gamaliel at m. Peah 6.6 (as identified by Danby, *The Mishnah*, 822), and assuming that, like his grandfather, he too was a Pharisee, another Pharisaic argument *kal va-chomer* may be preserved m. Peah 6.6. The Sadducees may also have composed and used these arguments, although the only two preserved examples—m. Yad 7.7 and t. Yad 2.20—merely disprove Pharisaic *halachah*, rather than establish Sadducean law. It seems that the Sadducees had no problem in understanding the arguments *kal va-chomer* of the Pharisees here, and, assuming that the Bney Bathyra were Sadducees, also at t. Pes 4.14.

VII. *Development in Rhetorical Arguments to Justify*
Acts of Healing and/or Saving Life

Evidence from the gospels discussed above shows that five arguments *kal va-chomer* preserved in the gospels, which justify acts of healing on the Sabbath, were almost certainly composed by the Jewish sages and show a development in the way that they argue to justify acts of healing and or saving life.

As was also briefly mentioned above, these arguments are of two types, either specific or general. The term 'specific' used to describe an argument relates to the fact that these arguments justify, in effect permit, a specific cure, and could not be used to justify, or to permit, any other cure. This is achieved by the incorporation of one or more details in the first part of the argument (*ha-nadon*) which are significant in the situation of the person to be healed and/or saved. Thus, the fact that David and his men were starving in the first part of the argument at Mark 2:23-26, 28 mirrors the alleged starving disciples whose starvation must be 'cured'; the fact that the restraints of an animal need to be loosened to save its life mirrors the fact that there are restraints on the back of a woman with a bent back that need to be loosened to save her life at Luke 13:15b-16; and the fact that an ox has fallen into the water of a well mirrors the fact that a man is drowning in his own body fluids and needs to be cured at Luke 14:5. In other words, these arguments are *permits* for action to heal and/or save life in a specific situation, with the added bonus that whatever action is needed can be justified within Jewish law. The fact that they first appear or only appear in the two earliest gospels, and that no new specific arguments appear in the later gospels of Matthew and John, also suggests that specific arguments are probably the earliest type of rabbinic arguments *kal va-chomer* which were composed to justify a specific act of healing and/or saving life.

In contrast with the specific arguments in Mark and Luke, the later gospels of Matthew and John have preserved general arguments *kal va-chomer*—'general' in the sense that these arguments could be used to justify *any* action in *any* situation of healing and/or saving life. Unlike the specific arguments, therefore, the first section of each of these general arguments does not replicate any of the significant details in the situation of the individual who needs to be healed and/or saved, but is based on a subject which is then used to conclude a general rule that justifies any act in any situation of healing and/or saving life that violates Jewish law. The argument used by Matthew at Matt 12:11-12 is based on a version of the specific arguments in Luke, which themselves were based on the fact that it was permitted to heal and/or save the life of an animal on the

Sabbath day. Matthew in fact seems to refer to a specific situation when a sheep has fallen into a pit. However as this situation has nothing in common with the situation of the person who needed to be cured—namely, a man with a withered hand—the identity of the animal and its fall into the pit must be considered as symbols of the location and the person who must be cured. Matthew thus used this argument in a general way, in order to reply to the general *halachic*-type question asked by the onlookers at the beginning of the scene, *Is it lawful to heal on the Sabbath day?* (Matt 12:10), rather than as a specific justification of the cure itself.

The second of the general arguments *kal va-chomer* is preserved at John 7:23, and as the above discussion of this text suggests, is an attempt to repeat the general argument attributed to R. Eleazar b. Azariah, which is based on the claim that because circumcision on the Sabbath 'heals' part of a man (who is clearly a symbol for any human being), so then it must be permitted on the Sabbath to heal and/or save the life of the whole of any man (see the discussion in Chapter 3). This argument could thus be used to justify any action in any situation which necessitates an action of healing and/or saving life.

The change from specific to general arguments *kal va-chomer* which is evident from a comparison of the arguments *kal va-chomer* in the two earliest gospels of Mark and Luke compared with the two later gospels of Matthew and John thus suggests a change in the thinking of the Jewish sages in the first century CE which brought about a significant improvement in the arguments used to justify acts of healing and/or saving life. This began with a policy that only specific violations of Sabbath law in order to heal and/or save life should be allowed, and thus only specific justifications should be composed. Later however, apparently sometime between the publication of the gospels of Luke and Matthew, the policy of the Jewish sages changed to allow the composition of general arguments which could be used to permit any action in any situation of healing and/or saving life that violated Jewish law. These general arguments are clearly more useful than specific arguments because they obviate the need to issue specific directives or to compose specific justifications for different situations of healing and/or saving life. As a result, and, as will be seen in Chapters 5 and 7, further general arguments were composed by the Jewish sages in the late first century and second century CE which add to the relatively sparse evidence in the gospel texts.

Although the gospels have preserved only a total of five arguments *kal va-chomer* relating to acts of healing and/or saving life, the change from specific to general arguments is highly significant because it shows a progressive and logical improvement in the approach of the Jewish sages towards the problem in Jewish law caused by acts of healing and/or saving life, which anticipate the general arguments that were composed by the Jewish sages in the late first century and second century CE.

VIII. *The Fate of Arguments kal va-chomer Based on the Permit to Save Animals on the Sabbath*

It is not difficult to appreciate that arguments *kal va-chomer* based on the fact that it was permitted to heal and/or save the life of an animal on the Sabbath could be used as a simple template to justify the violation of Jewish law by *any* action in *any* specific situation of healing and or saving life. All that was needed was to construct an argument *kal va-chomer* in which the situation of the animal in the first part of the argument (*ha-nadon*) bore a significant resemblance to the situation of the person who needed to be healed and/or saved, as in the arguments at Luke 13:15b-16 and 14:5. For example, if it was necessary to save an individual from a fire, an argument *kal va-chomer* could be constructed based on the fact that if—as was the case—it was permitted on the Sabbath to save an animal from a fire, this would surely justify the healing and/or saving of the life of an individual from a fire. (This latter situation could even be used to justify the healing of an individual with a fever which could be described as burning like a fire.) Moreover, such arguments would be even more useful if the animal was placed in a symbolic situation which would then justify action in any situation of healing and/or saving life, as is the case for the argument of Matthew at Matt 12:11-12 (see the discussion above on this text). The ubiquitous convenience of these types of argument is thus very clear and it is therefore very likely that many more than the three examples preserved in the gospels, either specific (like Luke's) or general (like Matthew's), were composed in the first century CE.

These arguments in the gospels show a knowledge of the rhetorical form of an argument *kal va-chomer*, and at least one of the three was almost certainly originally composed in a Semitic language, probably Hebrew rather than Aramaic (see the discussion on Luke 13:15b-16 in Chapter 3), a language which was not generally known outside Jewish circles in Galilee and Judea in the first century CE. It is probable, therefore, that the arguments in the gospels were composed by educated Jews, perhaps by the Jewish sages themselves. This being the case, it is therefore surprising that no trace of these arguments now exists in any Jewish written source. Why is this so? A possible reason may be related to the fact that these arguments are not based on a holy text, but on an anomaly of Jewish oral law which allowed animals (although not humans) to be healed and/or saved on the Sabbath day. In the background of an economy in Galilee and Judea of which a small, but significant proportion was based on animals (especially around Jerusalem where animals were needed for Temple rites), this surely made sense.[37] On the other hand, the fact that this practice was not based on Pentateuchal law may have been sufficient reason for these arguments not to be preserved, especially when other arguments were 'revealed' by the late first-century and second-century Jewish sages which were firmly based on Pentateuchal texts, as will be seen in Chapters 5 and 7.

IX. *Jesus Was Not Linked with the Community in Qumran*

A further interesting aspect of the *halachic* arguments *kal va-chomer* based on the permit to heal and/or save the life of an animal on the Sabbath, which were apparently used by Jesus in the gospels of Matthew and Luke, relates to the suggestion of some scholars that Jesus was somehow linked through John the Baptist with the community in Qumran. This community, however, strictly forbade the saving of the lives of animals on the Sabbath day. This is stated clearly and then emphasised in the texts from Qumran by the term אדם, which refers to the saving of the life of a 'man' in the expression נפש אדם, 'the life of a man', and which thus exclude animals from acts of healing and/or saving life on the Sabbath day.[38] Thus even though the historical Jesus himself probably did not voice the *halachic* arguments based on animal husbandry on the Sabbath which are recorded in the gospel of Matthew and Luke, and even though the logic of these rhetorical arguments does not depend on the identity of the person by whom it is expressed, it is surely unlikely that Jesus would have been attributed with such arguments if he was part of a community in which this license was not allowed—in the agricultural economy of first-century Galilee and Judea, the ordinary people to whom the gospels were addressed would surely have recognised the different identities of those who saved their animals on the Sabbath and those who did not, so that they would have shown some disbelief if an argument *kal va-chomer* based on the practice of healing and/or saving the life of an animal on the Sabbath was uttered by someone by whom such a practice was not allowed. It is unlikely, therefore, that Jesus

37. For the importance of animals in the economy of Roman Palestine, see Z. Safrai, *The Economy of Roman Palestine* (London: Routledge, 1994) 165-82.
   38. On 4Q265 Frag 7 and CD 11:16-17, see Chapter 1.

would have been attributed with these arguments if healing and/or saving the life of animals on the Sabbath was not a principle of which he approved. This suggests that Jesus was not linked in any meaningful way with the community of Jews who lived in Qumran.

X. *Conclusions: The Continuation of the Jewish Debate*

(1) Evidence from the gospels of the New Testament discussed above suggests that the most popular way in which acts of healing and/or saving life which violated Jewish law could be justified in the first century CE was with *halachic* rabbinic arguments *kal va-chomer*. These, in effect, are simple permits to perform acts of healing and/or saving life on the Sabbath, which are then justified according to Jewish law.

(2) At first, specific arguments were composed which justified and thus permitted action in specific situations of healing and/or saving life. Subsequently, towards the end of the first century, it is clear that general arguments were composed which could be used to justify and thus permit any action in any situation of healing and/or saving life.

(3) Arguments *kal va-chomer* based on the fact that it was permissible to cure and/or save the life of animals on the Sabbath were probably composed by the Jewish sages from around the time of the publication of the gospel of Luke. But none have been preserved in the Jewish rabbinic texts. This may be due to the fact that these arguments were not based on Pentateuchal law.

(4) Although probably not composed or voiced by the historical Jesus, the use of arguments *kal va-chomer* based on the fact that it was permissible to cure and/or save the life of animals on the Sabbath (which are attributed to Jesus in the gospels of Luke and Mark) suggests that Jesus was not a member of the community in Qumran, for whom it was forbidden to heal and/or save animals on the Sabbath.

(5) The gospel evidence ceases towards the end of the first century, when the last of the gospels was finally composed. The history of the Jewish debate on acts of healing and/or saving life must therefore now return to the Jewish texts. As will be seen, the relevant facts preserved in these texts fortuitously begin by overlapping the time when the gospel history ends, with evidence that emerges from the second half of the first century CE.

Chapter 5

THE TERMS AND ARGUMENTS OF R. ELEAZAR B. AZARIAH, R. AKIVA AND R. ISHMAEL AND THEIR SCHOOLS

I. *Who Expanded the Use of* דחה—*R. Eleazar b. Azariah or R. Akiva?*

The analysis of the argument apparently used by Jesus in the story of his midrashic meeting with the Pharisees in the Galilean fields (see above in Chapter 3) suggests that the final section of this argument is based on an underlying Hebrew text in which the verb דחה (*dachah*) is used to describe the 'overriding' or 'suspension' of Sabbath law by a *secular* act of healing and/or saving life, in this case by the action of plucking grain, an action which 'cured' the starvation of the disciples of Jesus which was a threat to their lives. In biblical texts, the term דחה refers simply to the physical act of pushing away. However, in the earliest example of the use of this verb in the rabbinic texts of Jewish law, this term is used in a technical, legal sense and refers to the temporary 'pushing away' or 'overriding' or 'replacement' of one Pentateuchal law by another. In the earliest example of this use, the verb refers to the overriding of the law of the Passover sacrifice over Sabbath law whenever the 14th of Nisan (the date of the Passover sacrifice according to the Pentateuch, see Lev 23:5 and Num 28:16) fell on the Sabbath, when no sacrifices by ordinary people were otherwise allowed.[1] It seems, however, that the text of Mark 2:28 preserves the earliest example of the innovative verb דחה, in which this term does *not* refer to the overriding of one Jewish ritual by another—or, according to orthodox Jewish thought, the overriding of one God-given law by another God-given law—but instead refers to the overriding of Jewish law by an action which is *not* a prescribed Jewish ritual, namely, an act of healing and/or saving life.

---

1. t. Pes 4.13-14. See Jastrow, *Dictionary of the Targumim*, s.v. דחה. Lauterbach's preferred translation in the *Mekilta de-Rabbi Ishmael* is 'to set aside'.

It is, however, most unlikely that Mark composed the Hebrew argument in which this term probably originally appeared, but adapted it from its Jewish source (see the discussion in Chapter 3). A likely candidate for this Jewish source is R. Eleazar b. Azariah. Most scholars assume that this Jewish sage began his public activity after 70 CE. It is possible, however, that that R. Eleazar b. Azariah died between 117 and 131 CE (that is, after the death of Trajan and before the start of the Bar Kochba revolt), so that he was active before the Temple was destroyed (especially if the earlier date of his death is assumed), and therefore could have been a contemporary of both Mark and John.[2] R. Eleazar is, moreover, probably one of the earliest Jewish sages to be credited in Jewish texts with the use of the verb דחה in the innovative way that it was probably also used in the argument *kal va-chomer* preserved in the gospels, as can be seen in the text cited below:

תוספתא מסכת שבת פרק טו הלכה טז
ר' ליעזר או' מילה דוחין עליה את השבת מפני מה? מפני שחייבין עליה כרת
לאחר זמן. והרי דברים קל וחומר, ומה על אבר אחד ממנו דוחין את השבת דין
הוא שידחה שבת על כולו.

Tosefta Shabbat 15.16
R. Eleazar [b. Azariah] says, 'As to circumcision, why does it override the Sabbath? It is because one is liable to [the punishment of] *karet* if it is not done on time. We can thus argue logically: If on account of a single limb (that is, the male member of a person) they override (דוחין) the prohibitions of the Sabbath, is it not logical that they should override the prohibitions of the Sabbath (שבת שידחה) on account of [saving] the whole of him!'[3]

Authorship by R. Eleazar b. Azariah of the argument (now preserved in Greek by Mark and Luke) may be confirmed, at least in part, by the fact that R. Eleazar b. Azariah is known both as an *aggadist* and a *halachist*. Both of these skills are displayed in the argument in Mark—the argument itself is based on a midrash based on the biblical story of David at Nob (1 Sam 21:1-6) which was composed by an *aggadist*, while the argument which 'proves' that the violation of Sabbath law is

2. S. Safrai, 'Eleazar b. Azariah', in *Encyclopaedia Judaica*, vol. 6 (Jerusalem: Keter, 1971) 586, suggests that the reference to 'R. Eleazar' at b. Meg 26a, in which 'the synagogue of the Tarsians (= filigree craftsmen) in Jerusalem sold [their synagogue] to R. Eleazar and he used it for his own purposes', refers to the activity of R. Eleazar b. Azariah before the destruction of the Temple in 70 CE.
3. The argument is repeated and also attributed to R. Eleazar b. Azariah in the *Mekilta de-Rabbi Ishmael* Shab 1.

permitted to save life from starvation was composed by a *halachist*. It is also clear that R. Eleazar b. Azariah was interested in the problem of healing and/or saving life since two permits have been preserved in his name (the argument preserved in the gospels would make a third). Thus he is credited with the 'discovery' of a biblical verse to justify washing the wound of circumcision when the third day after this ritual fell on the Sabbath (m. Shab 19.3), and he was also the author of the composition of the argument *kal va-chomer* cited above. For these reasons, therefore, it is possible that R. Eleazar, rather than R. Akiva, was the original author of the argument *kal va-chomer* which was subsequently translated into Greek and re-used by Mark in his midrashic-type story of Jesus and the disciples in the Galilean fields.

It is however possible that it was R. Akiva, rather than R. Eleazar, who was the first of the Jewish sages to use דחה in the innovative way discussed above. The discussion at the end of Chapter 4, suggests that general arguments that justify acts of healing and/or saving life were only composed towards the end of the first century. This being the case, the generality of R. Eleazar's argument cited above, which could be used to justify *any* action in *any* situation of healing and/or saving life, suggests that it was composed towards the end of the first century CE, which would account for the fact that it only appears in the latest of the gospels (at John 7:23) but not in the earlier synoptic gospel texts. If, then, R. Eleazar's argument was composed late in the first century, it is possible that the very earliest use of the term דחה to suggest the over-riding of Sabbath law by a secular act of healing and/or saving life should be attributed to R. Akiva, a younger contemporary of R. Eleazar b. Azariah, by whom it is also used in this way in a text that may have been composed before the argument of R. Eleazar cited above, although it is also a general (rather than specific) argument that justifies acts of healing and saving life:

תוספתא מסכת שבת פרק טו הלכה טז

אמ' ר' עקיבא וכי במה החמירה תורה בעבודה או בשבת? החמירה בעבודה
יותר מבשבת. שעבודה דוחה את השבת ואין שבת דוחה אותה. והרי דברים קל
וחומר: ומה עבודה שדוחה את השבת ספק נפשות דוחה אותה שבת שעבודה
דוחה אותה אינו דין שספק נפשות דוחה אותה. הא למדת שספק נפשות דוחה
את השבת.

Tosefta Shabbat 15.16
Said R. Akiva, 'Now did the Torah impose a stricter rule, on Temple law or on Sabbath law? It is stricter on Temple law than on Sabbath law. This is because Temple service overrides (דוחה) Sabbath law, but Sabbath law does not override (דוחה) it [= Temple law]. This gives rise to an argument *kal va-chomer*: For if Temple law overrides (שדוחה) Sabbath law, [and]

an act of healing and/or saving life overrides (דוחה) it [= Temple law], [then], Sabbath law, that Temple law overrides it (שדוחה), may we not conclude that acts of healing and/or saving life overrides (דוחה) it [= Sabbath law]. Thus you have learnt that acts of healing and/or saving life overrides (דוחה) Sabbath law.'

This argument rephrases the essence of the specific argument apparently used by Jesus in the midrashic-type story of the Galilean fields, which justifies the violation of Sabbath law for the specific 'cure' for starvation. As the discussion at the end of Chapter 4 suggests, it is likely to have been composed earlier than the argument based on circumcision attributed to R. Eleazar b. Azariah at t. Shab 15.16. R. Akiva uses the term דחה in this innovative way in the statement that 'Any [act of] work that can be done just before the Sabbath does not override the Sabbath (אינו דוחה את השבת). But what cannot be done just before the Sabbath overrides the Sabbath (דוחה את השבת).'[4] The term again appears in a another argument *kal va-chomer* attributed to R. Akiva, recorded in the Tosefta at t. Shab 15.17 (which will be discussed below).

In any case, the fact that the term דחה used in this significantly innovative way is not used by any Jewish sages earlier than R. Eleazar b. Azariah and R. Akiva, who lived well after the time that Jesus must have died, provides further evidence—in addition to the midrashic nature of the story, see Chapter 3—that the argument apparently voiced by Jesus in the story of the starvation of his disciples in the Galilean fields could not have been composed or voiced by the historical Jesus himself. The frequent use of the verb דחה in relation to acts of healing and/or saving life by the younger contemporaries of R. Eleazar b. Azariah and by subsequent tannaitic sages, but not by sages from earlier times, also helps to confirm that the initial use of this term did not occur before the time of R. Eleazar, for otherwise we would expect it also to be used by earlier sages. For example, it is absent from the edict of Shammai (see t. Eruv 3.7, cited in Chapter 1), from the edict of Rabban Gamaliel (m. RH 2.5, cited in Chapter 9) and from the comment of R. Yohanan b. Zakkai (see m. Shab 16.7, also cited in Chapter 9)—all of which were composed well before 70 CE, and all of which might have used the term דחה to refer to an act of healing and/or saving life that overrode Jewish law, if this innovative use had been current in their time. On the other hand, this term is repeatedly used in this way by Jewish sages who were either contemporary with R. Akiva or who lived after his time. Thus it is used by R. Ishmael in the *Mekilta de-Rabbi Ishmael* Shab 1 (a text discussed below), by the second-century Jewish sages R. Mattithiah b.

---

4. m. Shab 19.1 (= m. Pes 6.2 and m. Men 11.3).

Heresh (at m. Yom 8.6), by R. Yose the Galilean (at t. Shab 15.16) and by R. Simon b. Menasia (in the *Mekilta de-Rabbi Ishmael* Nez 4), and occurs over two hundred times in the amoraic texts. This reflects the extreme usefulness of דחה when used in this way, which surely would have appeared earlier than the time of R. Eleazar and R. Akiva, if this extended semantic meaning had been developed in earlier times.

II. *The Special Terminology and Arguments of R. Akiva and His School*

Although we cannot be certain whether it was R. Eleazar b. Azariah or R. Akiva who was the first to use the term דחה to refer a secular act of healing and/or saving life that overrides a Pentateuchal law, there is little doubt that it was R. Akiva who composed and first used the two technical phrases which refer generally to *any* action in *any* situation of healing and/or saving life in which it is necessary to violate Jewish law, namely, (1) להחיות נפש בספק, literally, '[a situation in which it is neces- sary] to cause life [even when] in doubt', and (2) ספק נפשות, literally, '[a situation in which there is] doubt of lives'. Shortened versions of these phrases also occur in both attributed and unattributed statements in tannaitic sources which have long been linked with R. Akiva and his school. These phrases of R. Akiva will now be discussed.

A. *'To cause life when in doubt'*—להחיות נפש בספק, *lechayot nefesh be-safeq*
The phrase *lehachayot nefesh besafeq*, להחות נפש בספק, literally '[a situation in which it is necessary] to cause life [even when] in doubt', is preserved in an argument *kal va-chomer* in the Tosefta which is based on R. Akiva's midrashic interpretation of Exod 22:2, *If the thief is found breaking in and is struck so that he dies, there shall be no blood guilt for him.* The text and a translation of this argument are printed below. (The additions to the translation, printed in square brackets, expand the thought of the argument, but are not of course part of the original text.)

תוספתא מסכת שבת פרק טו הלכה יז

ר' אחא אמ' משם ר' עקיבא הרי הוא אומ', אם במחתרת ימצא הגנב והכה ומת אין לו דמים...

בעל הבית—מהו ודיי או ספק הוי או' ספק: אם הורגין נפש להחיות נפש בספק, דין הוא שידחו את השבת להחיות נפש בספק.

Tosefta Shabbat 15:17
R. Aha says in the name of R. Akiva, 'Behold, Scripture says, *If the thief* (הגנב) *is found breaking in and is struck so that he dies, there shall be no blood guilt for him* [that is, the person in the building who killed the thief is not guilty of the thief's murder] (Exod 22:2).

Now concerning the [safety of the life of the] occupant of the building—is this a matter of certainty or a matter of doubt? You must say that it is a matter of doubt [since Scripture refers only to a *thief* rather than to a *murderer*, רוצח, so that we do not know if this thief intended only to steal, as the term 'thief' (גנב) suggests, or came also to kill, as the term רוצח might suggest].

Now, if one kills [that is, violates Jewish law] one man [here, the intruding thief] in order to save life [here, the life of the occupant of the building who saves his own life] when there is doubt [whether the thief is merely a thief or is both a thief and a murder who intends both to steal and to kill],
 then, is it not logical to assume that
 one overrides [the laws of] the Sabbath, [in a situation] to save a life [which is] in doubt [because if the intruder is merely called a thief, there is doubt whether or not he also came to kill].'

Exodus 22:1 begins with the comment that a thief who intrudes uninvited into a building may be 'struck' so severely, presumably by the occupant of the building, so that he dies. The phrase 'no blood guilt' (אין לו דמים) indicates, however, that the person by whom the thief is killed is not guilty of murder, or as this is phrased in the biblical text, to the perpetrator of the killing 'there is not to-him blood-guilt'. This is understood by R. Akiva to imply that the person by whom the intruder was killed had *doubt* whether (a) the intruder came only to steal, which is a reasonable assumption because the biblical text refers only to a 'thief' (גנב) rather than a murderer (רוצח, a term that does not appear in the biblical text), or whether (b) the thief came both to steal and to kill. According to the argument of R. Akiva, the presence of doubt justifies the killing of the thief. This understanding of the verse is repeated in the version of his argument preserved in the *Mekilta de-Rabbi Ishmael*:

Mekilta de-Rabbi Ishmael Nezikin 13
If the thief is found breaking in... With what case does this law deal? With a case where there is doubt (ספק) whether the thief came merely to steal or to kill as well.[5]

The argument of R. Akiva can now be stated as follows: If there is doubt whether the biblical thief came (a) to steal or (b) to steal and to kill, then, since according to Exod 22:1 it is legitimate for the occupant

5. For a text with translation, see Lauterbach, *Mekilta*, 3:101.

of the building to kill a thief who comes to kill (rather than only to steal, an action that can be expected from someone who is called a 'thief'), it is on the basis of doubt that the thief must be killed in order to save life, in this case referring to the life of the person by whom the thief was killed. The existence of doubt is thus the critical factor in this argument which allows the occupant of the building legitimately to kill the intruding thief (even though the occupant of the building does not know whether the thief came also to kill) and thus save (his own) life. The concept of doubt thereby serves as the basis for an argument concerning the saving of life, even though this is at the expense of Jewish law, in this case the law prohibiting murder, which—as one might expect—is contrary to Jewish law.

The argument of R. Akiva may thus be simply expressed:

> If according to Exod 22:1, the existence of doubt allows the removal of life, which overrides Jewish law, in this case the law which prohibits murder, is it not logical that (דין הוא) the existence of doubt (also) allows the saving of life (להחיות נפש בספק) by overriding Jewish law, in this case by overriding Sabbath law![6]

As can be seen, this argument does not refer to the specific situation which necessitated an act of healing and/or saving life, such as the arguments first found or only found in the gospels of Mark and Luke (see on Mark 2:25-26, 28; Luke 13:15b-16; 14:5, in Chapter 3). Instead, the argument justifies *any* act of healing and/or saving life in *any* situation. The expression להחיות נפש בספק can thus be considered as a neutral expression referring both to the situation and the action that must be taken to heal and/or save life. This is also the case for the examples of the use of this Akivan terminology which are examined below.

B. *The Sorite of R. Yose the Galilean*
The argument of R. Akiva is replicated in a sorite which is not attributed to R. Akiva, but to R. Yose, probably R. Yose the Galilean, a pupil and subsequently a colleague of R. Akiva.[7] This sorite shortens the phrase of R. Akiva להחיות נפש בספק (*lehachayot nefesh be-safeq*) to the single term להחיות (*lehachayot*), 'to cause to save life'. The sorite of R. Yose is cited below:

---

6. Assuming that the phrase דין הוא, *din hu*, is synonymous with the expression קל חומר, *kal va-chomer*.
7. For further discussion on sorites, see above on Matt 12:3-5, 8 in Chapters 3 and 6.

מכילתא דרבי שמעון בר יוחאי פרק כא פסוק יד וכי

וכי יזד איש על רעהו להרגו בערמה מעם מזבחי תקחנו למות ... אמ' ר' יוסי קל

וחומר הן הדברים:

מה עבדה [שהיא דוחה] את השבת

דוחין אתו ממנו, להמית נפש מפני [נפש,

שבת] שעבדה דוחה את השבת

דין הוא

שידחו אות[ה בשביל להחיות]!

Mekhilta de-Rabbi Shimon bar Yochai 21.14

But if a man comes wilfully upon his neighbour, to slay him treacherously;
you shall take him from my altar, that he may die (Exod 21:14)... R. Yose
says, 'It is logical to deduce [literally, "it is a matter of an argument *kal
va-chomer*"] that:

If (B) Temple service, which [overrides] (C) the Sabbath [law],

you should delay/override him [i.e. the priest] from it [i.e., from Temple
service], in order to [save the life of a person who would otherwise] be
caused to die [with respect to his] life, because [he took] a life,

[then for the] (C) Sabbath, which Temple service overrides (C) [the
Sabbath]

is it not logical

that they would override (C) it [i.e. the Sabbath] to (A) keep alive
[someone who is accused of causing death]!'[8]

The biblical proof text on which this argument is based states that a
priest who has deliberately (בערמה, *be'ormah,* 'with guile') committed a
murder may be removed from the Temple, *even while he is serving at the
altar*, and then put to death.[9] On the other hand, the midrashic interpretation of Exod 21:14 in the above sorite suggests that although the priest
may be taken down from the altar *even while he is performing his priestly
duties*, this act is permitted so that the priest will act as a witness for the
defence of another person who is accused of murder (which implies—
contrary to the biblical text—that someone *other than the priest* is
charged with the crime of deliberate murder). It is then assumed that the
evidence of the priest is responsible for saving life, in this case the life of
the person on trial for murder, who might otherwise be sentenced to
death if the priest did not witness on behalf of his defence. The Babylonian Talmud attributes this midrashic interpretation of Exod 21:14 to
R. Akiva:

8. For another translation, see Nelson, *Mekhilta de-Rabbi Shimon Bar Yoḥai*
(Philadelphia: Jewish Publication Society, 2006) 280.

9. The literal understanding of Exod 21:14 is clearly stated in two tannaitic
commentaries, *Mekilta de-Rabbi Ishmael* Nezikin 4 (Lauterbach, *Mekilta,* 3:38) and
Mekhilta d'Rabbi Sim'on bar Jochai, Nezikin 21.14, see D. W. Nelson, *Mekhilta
de-Rabbi Shimon Bar Yoḥai* (Philadelphia: Jewish Publication Society, 2005) 279.

תלמוד בבלי מסכת יומא דף פה עמוד א-ב

נשאלה שאלה זו בפניהם: מניין לפקוח נפש שדוחה את השבת?...נענה רבי
עקיבא ואמר: +שמות כא+ וכי יזד איש על רעהו וגו' מעם מזבחי תקחנו למות.
מעם מזבחי—ולא מעל מזבחי. ואמר רבה בר בר חנה אמר רבי יוחנן, לא שנו
אלא להמית—אבל להחיות—אפילו מעל מזבחי.

Babylonian Talmud Yoma 85a-b

This question was asked: From where [do we know that] a situation of
healing and/or danger to life overrides Sabbath law?...
R. Akiva answered and said: *If a man comes presumptuously upon his
neighbour...you will take him from My altar that he may die* (Exod 21:14),
that is, only off the altar, but not down from the altar. And in this connection Rabbah b. Bar Hana said in the name of R. Yohanan, 'That was
taught only when one's life is to be forfeited—but to save life one may
take one down even from the altar!'[10]

R. Akiva's enigmatic midrashic interpretation of Exod 21:14 has
recently been explained by one scholar as follows:

> If one had been sentenced to death, there is ample provision for a revision,
> if even at the last moment someone claims to have found evidence of the
> accused's innocence. If a priest has such evidence, or is only believed to
> have it, he would be taken down from the altar even after he had com-
> menced, and before having completed, his service.[11]

But however the above midrash is explained, it is clear from the words
of R. Yose that according to the interpretation of Exod 21:14 by R. Akiva,
the life of a person accused of deliberate murder may be saved by the
violation of Temple law, which in this case is caused by interrupting the
service of a priest at the Temple altar, so that he may act as a witness for
the defence of the man who is accused of murder. This understanding of
the biblical verse may therefore be expressed in the style of the Jewish
sages (see Chapter 2), 'The saving of life overrides Temple law'.
     The sorite of R. Yose can thus be stated:

> Since (B) Temple law, which overrides (C) Sabbath law, is overridden
> by (A) the saving of life (namely, the life of someone who is accused of
> taking life),
> so that
> (A) the saving of life (of someone who is accused of taking life)
> overrides (C) Sabbath law!

10.   Trans. Jung, *Yoma*, 420-1. A similar argument is found in the *Mekhilta de-
Rabbi Shimon R. Yochai*, where this explanation is attributed to R. Yose the Galilean,
a pupil and later colleague of R. Akiva; see Nelson, *Mekhilta de-Rabbi Shimon Bar
Yoḥai*, 280, cited below. But as Nelson remarks in n. 117, '[This section] is
incomplete and somewhat incongruous with what precedes it'.
11.   Jung, *Yoma*, 420-1, 412 n. 2

The link between the above argument of R. Yose and R. Akiva is shown both by the use of the midrashic explanation of R. Akiva, and by the term להחיות, 'to cause to life', the final words of the sorite of R. Yose, which echo the expression first attributed to R. Akiva, להחיות נפש בספק, 'to cause life to be lived when in doubt'.

C. *'Doubt of lives'*—ספק נפשות, *safeq nefashot*

The Tosefta also attributes the similar phrase להחיות נפש בספק to R. Akiva, again within a sorite. This argument does not identify the specific biblical text on which it is based (a significant omission which will be discussed in Chapter 6). Nevertheless, it is clearly based on proof from a text which, like the midrashic interpretation of the biblical story of David and the sacred bread (1 Sam 21:1-6), leads to the conclusion that healing and/or the saving of life overrides Temple law. The sorite is one of the answers given in response to a *halachic* question which seeks proof that acts of healing and/or saving life are permitted to override Sabbath law. Both question and sorite are printed below:

תוספתא מסכת שבת פרק טו הלכה טז

אמ' ר' יוסה מנין לפיקוח נפש שדוחה את השבת?...

אמ' ר' עקיבא וכי במה החמירה תורה בעבודה או בשבת החמירה בעבודה יותר
מבשבת שעבודה דוחה את השבת ואין שבת דוחה אותה. והרי דברים קל
וחומר:

ומה עבודה שדוחה את השבת,

ספק נפשות דוחה אותה

שבת שעבודה דוחה אותה

אינו דין

שספק נפשות דוחה אותה.

הא למדת שספק נפשות דוחה את השבת

Tosefta Shabbat 15.16

Said R. Yose, 'From where do we know that the saving of life overrides Sabbath law?'...

Said R. Akiva,

Preamble to the argument:

'Now in what regard did the Torah impose a stricter rule? Was it for Temple service or for the Sabbath? It was more strict for Temple service than for the Sabbath.

For (B) Temple service overrides (c) [the laws of] the Sabbath, but the [laws of] Sabbath do not override it [= the Temple service].

From this it can be deduced:

The argument of R. Akiva:

If (B) Temple service overrides (C) [the laws of] the Sabbath

and (A) a [situation of] doubt of [the saving of] lives (ספק נפשות)

overrides (B) it [= Temple service],

then, if (C) [the laws of] the Sabbath, which (B) Temple service overrides,
is it not logical that
a [situation which involves] (A) the saving of life (נפשות ספק, literally
"doubt of lives") overrides (C) it [= the laws of the Sabbath]!
Summary of the argument:
Thus you have learned that (A) [a situation of] doubt of the saving of life
(ספק נפשות, literally, "doubt of lives") overrides (C) [the laws] of the
Sabbath!'[12]

The argument of R. Akiva may be expressed as follows:

The clash between Temple and Sabbath law that occurs within the
Temple precincts (which is stated both in the preamble to the argument
and within the argument itself) indicates that Temple service is more
'severe' (חומר) than Sabbath law, which is relatively 'light' (קל).
Moreover, since we also know that '[a situation of] doubt of lives',
meaning 'a situation of danger to life', overrides Temple service, it can
then be argued:
    Since (A) a situation of danger to life overrides (B) Temple service,
    And (B) Temple service overrides (C) [the laws of] the Sabbath.
    Thus since (B) Temple service overrides (C) [the laws of] the Sabbath
    is it not logical to conclude that
    (A) a situation of danger to life overrides (C) [the laws of] the
    Sabbath!
You can therefore conclude that the saving of life overrides Sabbath law.

As can be seen, the argument above replicates the argument of the
sorite of R. Yose in the *Mekhilta de-Rabbi Shimon bar Yochai* 21.14,
discussed above. Moreover, just as in the latter, this argument does not
refer to a specific situation, such as the arguments *kal va-chomer* first
found, or only found, in the gospels of Mark and Luke. Instead, the
neutral expression ספק נפשות, literally 'doubt of lives', effectively
anonymises the situation which is permitted, with the result that, once
again, the sorite justifies action in *any* situation of healing and/or saving
life, in which the necessary action causes a violation of Jewish law.

The phrase ספק נפשות also occurs in three other tannaitic texts, all
unattributed, but all found in compilations which are associated with the
school of R. Akiva. The text from the *Mekhilta de-Rabbi Shimon bar
Yochai* follows below:

12. For a translation, see J. Neusner, *The Tosefta: Translated from the Hebrew:
Second Division Moed* (New York: Ktav, 1981) 62.

מכילתא דרבי שמעון בר יוחאי פרק כב פסוק (ב) אם

(א) אם במחתרת ...

[...] (ב) אם זרחה השמש עליו וכי עליו] [בלבד חמה זורחת והלא על כל העולם
כולו היא זורחת. אלא מה] [זריחת השמ]ש? שהיא ב>ג<לוי כך כל דבר שהוא
בגלוי. מה [זריחת השמש]? [שהוא שלם לו] (שהוא שלום לו) [דם לו דמין לו בין
בחול ובין בשב[ת כך] [כל דבר ש]הוא שלם לו >דם לו דמים לו< בין בחול
(ו)בין בשבת וכן הוא אומ' כי כ[אשר יקום] איש על רעהו וגומ' (דב' כב כו) הרי
זה כזה מה זה ספק נפשות אף זה ספק נפשות.

Mekhilta de-Rabbi Shimon bar Yochai 22.2

If a thief is found breaking in and is struck so he dies, there shall be no
blood guilt for him (Exod 22:1). But if the sun has risen upon him, [there
shall be blood guilt for him] (Exod 22:2).
And does the sun shine upon him alone? Doesn't it shine on the entire
world? Rather [it says this to make the point that] just as the shining sun
is obvious, so too in any event where [the robber's intention not to cause
harm] is obvious. Just as when the sun, which is peaceful to him, shines
on him, there is bloodguilt, so on the Sabbath, so too any instance where
[it is obvious] that he is peaceful to him, there is bloodguilt whether on a
weekday or on the Sabbath.

And thus Scripture says that *when a man attacks his neighbour...*
(Deut 22:26). Behold both [texts of Exod 22:1 and Deut 22:6] are similar.
The former demonstrates a case of doubt [in a situation concerning the
duty of saving] lives (ספק נפשות) and the latter [similarly] demonstrates a
case of doubt [in a situation concerning the duty of saving] lives (ספק
נפשות).[13]

This text begins (confusingly) with R. Ishmael's interpretation of
Exod 22:2, which is one of the three verses in the Torah which, according to R. Ishmael, should *not* be literally understood so that the reference
to the sun in Exod 22:2 means that the intentions of the thief are obvious
and clear.[14] This means in this context that the biblical label for the
intruder as a 'thief' indicates truly that the intruder is a thief, rather than
a (potential) murderer, which means (according to R. Ishmael) that the
thief intruded into the building only to steal, rather than both to steal and
to kill. If then the thief is killed by the occupant of the building, this
means that the occupant is guilty of murder.

On the other hand, Exod 22:1 states that 'there is no blood guilt for
him' (אין לו דמים), which means that the occupant of the building is *not*
guilty of murder. Therefore, in view of the literal understanding of

---

13. For the text and translation with some commentary, see Nelson, *Mekhilta de-
Rabbi Shimon Bar Yoḥai*, 320.
14. *Mekilta de-Rabbi Ishmael*, Nezikin 6, Lauterbach, *Mekilta*, 3:53, which is
repeated at y. San 8.8.

Exod 22:2 (indicated in the paragraph above), this must mean that the intention of the thief could *not* have been clear. In other words, there is *doubt* that the thief came only to steal, so that, as stated in Exod 22:1 (which is in contrast with the meaning of Exod 22:2), the occupant of the building in Exod 22:1 who kills the intruder-thief is *not* guilty of murder. R. Ishmael thus arrives at the same conclusion as R. Akiva regarding the concept of 'doubt' implied in Exod 22:1 (discussed above) but reaches this conclusion in a more circuitous way, via an understanding of Exod 22:2. It seems that R. Ishmael has adapted the argument of R. Akiva, who was thus probably the first to interpret Exod 22:1 in this way.

In addition, presumably because Exod 22:1-2 does not state on which day of the week this event took place, this text now claims that the event could have *happened on any day of the week including the Sabbath.* If then the murder of the intruder took place on the Sabbath, it can be argued that life may be saved at the expense of Jewish law on the Sabbath, whenever there is a situation of 'doubt', or, as this idea is expressed in the text above, whenever there is a situation of 'doubt of lives' (ספק נפשות).

Although the argument in this text incorporates the argument of R. Ishmael, the phrase 'doubt of lives' (ספק נפשות) must be linked with R. Akiva, since it is used by R. Akiva in the Tosefta (t. Shab 15.17, see above), in a simple argument which unlike the above argument in the *Mekhilta de-Rabbi Shimon bar Yochai*, which is based on the argument of R. Ishmael, does not incorporate the work of any other sage. It seems that the version of the argument in the *Mekhilta de-Rabbi Shimon bar Yochai* is a later version of the relatively simpler argument of R. Akiva preserved in the Tosefta, which has been modified by the addition of the argument of R. Ishmael. A further link with R. Akiva is indicated by the fact that the eponymous author of the *Mekhilta de-Rabbi Shimon bar Yochai* in which this argument appears, was a pupil of R. Akiva for thirteen years.[15] His compilation is even known in medieval Jewish sources as the *Mekhilta de-Rabbi Akiva*, a name that is appropriate, because it is generally acknowledged that the *Mekhilta de-Rabbi Shimon bar Yochai* is a product of the school of R. Akiva.[16]

A further tannaitic example of the expression ספק נפשות occurs in the following directive in the Mishnah, a compilation of oral law which is also heavily dependent on the opinions of R. Akiva:[17]

---

15. b. Ket 62b; Lev Rab XXI.8.
16. Strack and Stemberger, *Introduction to the Talmud and Midrash*, 282.
17. Strack and Stemberger, *Introduction to the Talmud and Midrash*, 136.

משנה מסכת יומא פרק ח משנה ו
ועוד אמר רבי מתיא בן חרש החושש בגרונו מטילין לו סם בתוך פיו בשבת מפני
שהוא ספק נפשות וכל ספק נפשות דוחה את השבת:

<u>Mishnah Yoma 8.6</u>
Moreover R. Mattithiah b. Heresh said, 'If a man has pain in his throat
they may drop medicine into his mouth on the Sabbath, since there is [a
situation of] doubt of lives (ספק נפשות) and every time there is [a situation of] doubt of lives (ספק נפשות), this overrides the Sabbath [laws]'.

R. Mattithiah first refers to a specific situation in which it is permissible to violate Sabbath law. He then issues a general rule, using the phrase
ספק נפשות as a general term for *any* permitted action in *any* situation of
healing and/or saving life.

A third variant of the phrase ספק נפשות occurs in the Tosefta, in which
the plural noun נפשות ('lives'), in the expression ספק נפשות, is shortened
to the singular noun נפש (literally, 'life'), thus producing the modified
phrase ספק נפש, as is evident in the text and translation below:

תוספתא מסכת שבת פרק טו הלכה יא
מפקחין על ספק נפש בשבת והזריז הרי זה משובח ואין צריך ליטול רשות מבית
דין.

<u>Tosefta Shabbat 15.11</u>
They remove debris [in a situation of] doubt of life on the Sabbath, and
the one who acts quickly, behold he must be praised, and it is not
necessary to seek permission from the Jewish court.

Although this directive has no attribution, it can be linked with
R. Akiva by virtue of the fact that the term ספק ('doubt') used in relation
to acts of healing and/or saving life are connected with this sage in the
texts discussed above.

It is thus clear that there are two basic general expressions in the
tannaitic *halachic* texts which can be associated directly or indirectly
with R. Akiva, and which function as a label for *any* permitted action in
any situation of healing and/or danger to life, whenever this action
entails a violation of Jewish law. These are the phrases להחיות נפש בספק,
literally, 'to cause to live [when] life is in doubt', and the expression
ספק נפשות, literally, 'doubt of lives'.

D. *The Significance of* ספק, *'Doubt', in Relation to Acts of Healing
and/or Saving Life*
Both of the special expressions of R. Akiva discussed above include the
term 'doubt' (ספק), an antonym of the term ודיי, 'certainty', as can be
seen from the record of the argument of R. Akiva based on Exod 22:1
(t. Shab 15.16, cited above). In contexts of healing and/or saving life, the

term ספק both identifies and solves a problem which is integral to all situations of healing and/or saving life, and is especially important for Jewish law. First, there is *doubt* concerning the necessity to intervene, because whoever needs healing or is in danger of his life might be cured or saved without any intervention, and thereby would avoid a violation of Jewish law (even if the latter is permitted). This kind of 'doubt' is noted in t. Shab 15.15, which reads: *They heat water for a sick person on the Sabbath, whether to give it to him to drink or to heal him with it, and they do not say, 'Let us wait [to see what happens] to him, perhaps he will live [without it]'*. Secondly, there is doubt concerning the efficacy of intervention. In other words, will the act of healing and/or saving life be performed successfully and the sick person live? Or will it be performed in vain and the person in need of healing and/or saving will die, when, once again, there would be an unnecessary violation of Jewish law? This latter type of doubt is foreseen in a directive in the Mishnah, which notes that when the Sabbath is violated by attempting to free a person who is buried beneath rubble, the person who is buried may not be found alive (m. Yom 8.7).

The attributions in the texts above suggest that it was R. Akiva by whom the concept of doubt was first officially connected with situations of healing and/or saving life. This being the case, although a directive may have been composed at an earlier time, any references to 'doubt' in relation to acts of healing and/or saving life incorporated in a directive should probably be dated no earlier than his time. For example, references to 'doubt' can be found in the introduction to the list of directives at t. Shab 15.11-13 (which will be further discussed in Chapter 11), and in the remark of the Jewish sages in which they criticise the argument *kal va-chomer* attributed to R. Eleazar b. Azariah (see t. Shab 15.16 and the *Mekilta de-Rabbi Ishmael* Shab 1).

Let us now turn to the special terminology and the argument *kal va-chomer* associated with R. Ishmael and his school.

III. *The Terminology of R. Ishmael*—פיקוח נפש, *Pikkuach Nefesh*

As was noted in the discussion above, the argument of R. Akiva based on Exod 22:1 was probably adapted and used by R. Ishmael (see above on the *Mekhilta de-Rabbi Shimon bar Yochai* 22.2). In contrast, however, with the terminology associated with R. Akiva, the famous contemporary of R. Akiva, namely, R. Ishmael, is linked with the expression פיקוח נפש, *pikkuach nefesh*. This phrase is used in three tannaitic texts, the *Mekilta de-Rabbi Ishmael*, the Tosefta, and *Sifra*, a tannaitic commentary on Leviticus.

A. *Two Attempts to Define the Meaning of the Phrase* פיקוח נפש
What is the meaning of the phrase פיקוח נפש? A short answer is that it
means the same as the phrase of R. Akiva, ספק נפשות. This can be seen
in the following texts, which both ask the same question, each one using
a different phrase. The first of these texts is attributed to R. Yose,
probably R. Yose the Galilean, who uses the phrase פיקוח נפש:

תוספתא מסכת שבת פרק טו הלכה טז
אמ' ר' יוסה מנין לפיקוח נפש שדוחה את השבת?

Tosefta Shabbat 15.16
Said R. Yose [the Galilean], 'How do we know that a situation of danger
to life (פיקוח נפש) overrides Sabbath law?'

The second of these texts, in which the alternative phrase ספק נפשות is
used, is unattributed and preserved in the Jerusalem Talmud:

תלמוד ירושלמי מסכת יומא פרק ח הלכה ה
מניין שספק נפשות דוחה את השבת?

Jerusalem Talmud Yoma 8.5
From where [in the holy texts] do we know that the saving of life (ספק
נפשות) overrides Sabbath law?

As for the comparable expressions associated with R. Akiva, the term
נפש (*nefesh*) in the expression פיקוח נפש can only mean 'life', referring
to the life of a human being and also possibly to the life of an animal
(compare the more exclusive term אדם, 'man', in the expression נפש אדם
found at Qumran, which effectively limits Sabbath acts of healing and/or
saving life to human beings).[18] The term פיקוח (*pikkuach*) is, however,
less easy to define. It is often suggested that its meaning is related to the
Piel verb from which it appears to be derived, namely פקח, 'to open a
heap of debris', which may suggest that the combination פיקוח נפש
originally referred specifically to an 'attempt to save the life of a person
(or animal) buried in debris'.[19] The term פיקוח may thus be explained as a
Piel noun derived from the *Piel* verb פקח, which was chosen as a
*sub*category of the verb סתר, 'to demolish', the thirty-fifth of the thirty-
nine *main* prohibited activities on the Sabbath day (see m. Shab 7.2, in
Chapter 1).
But this literal definition of the term פיקוח gives no impression of its
wider, general meaning, which, like the phrase of R. Akiva, ספק נפשות,
can be understood to refer to *any* action which is taken in *any* situation of

---

18. 4Q265 Frag 7, col. 1. 6-9; CD 11:16-17.
19. Thus Jastrow, A *Dictionary of the Targumim*, s.v. פקח.

healing and/or danger to life, whenever that action involves a violation of Jewish law. This is demonstrated in the earliest attempt of the Jewish sages to define this phrase, which is preserved in the Tosefta, in an editorial summary which follows two directives which prohibit certain methods used for breastfeeding a child. The act of breastfeeding a child is an action which saves life (because this is the only kind a food a young child will take). There are however certain times and/or situations when breastfeeding is forbidden by Jewish oral law. Nevertheless, these forbidden methods must be used in order to save life. The Tosefta thus notes:

תוספתא מסכת שבת פרק ט הלכה כב

לא תקל אשה מדדיה ותחלוב לתוך הכוס או לתוך הקערה ותניק את בנה. אין
יונקין לא מן הנכרית ולא מבהמה טמאה. ואם היה דבר של סכנה אין כל דבר
עומד בפני פקוח נפש.

Tosefta Shabbat 9.22

A woman should not express milk from her breasts into a cup or a plate and thus feed her child. They do not suckle [a child] from a gentile woman or from a [ritually] unclean animal.

But if it was a matter of danger to life (סכנה, *sakanah*), nothing stands in the way of [action in a situation] of danger to life (פיקוח נפש).

It is evident from the above text that the phrase, פיקוח נפש, has nothing to do with either removing debris (the basic meaning of the verb פקח from which the noun פיקוח may be derived) or with feeding a young child. Moreover, if the last statement in the above quotation was a simple declaration of the principle that healing and/or saving life was permitted on the Sabbath, it can be assumed that the same term would appear in both sections of the sentence, thus, 'But if it was a matter of danger-to-life (סכנה, "danger"), nothing whatsoever stands in the way of danger-to-life (סכנה, "danger")'. The replacement of the second (theoretical) occurrence of the term סכנה with the expression פיקוח נפש thus means that the term סכנה now defines the phrase פיקוח נפש, which, it can be assumed, refers to the potential danger to life in *any* situation that requires an act of healing and/or saving life.

This definition, however, does not depend on the *tannaitic* usage of the term סכנה. As might be thought, the expressions ספק נפשות and פיקוח נפש always include the assumption that the action of healing and/or saving life to which each phrase refers involves a violation of Jewish law. In other words, neither the phrase ספק נפשות nor the phrase פיקוח נפש is *ever* used for a situation of healing and/or saving life that does *not* involve a violation of Jewish law. On the other hand, apart from its usage in t. Shab 9.22 cited above, the term סכנה in the tannaitic texts *always*

refers to a simple situation of danger without the extended implication that the action that must be taken to deal with this causes a violation
of Jewish law. In contrast, the term סכנה in the amoraic texts refers to
any situation of danger, *whether or not* the action involved to deal with
the danger causes a violation of Jewish law. The phrase פיקוח נפש, which
always includes the implication that the action sanctioned will cause a
violation of Jewish law, is therefore defined in the Tosefta, a tannaitic
work, by a term whose tannaitic usage *never* involves the implication of
a violation of Jewish law. It is also significant that the text from the
Tosefta cited above is the single example in the tannaitic texts in which
the term סכנה has the extended implication of a violation of Sabbath
law.[20] These anomalies can thus be explained on the assumption that
the use of the term סכנה to define the phrase פיקוח נפש in the text from
the Tosefta cited above (t. Shab 9.22) does *not* reflect the usage of the
Tosefta, the text in which this definition is found, but instead reflects
the usage of the amoraim. This suggests that the definition of the phrase
פיקוח נפש at t. Shab 9.22 is an amoraic addition to the Tosefta, perhaps
inserted by R. Oshaiah, a first-generation amora (220–250 CE), who
was probably one of the editors of the Tosefta (the other was his teacher
R. Hiyya), by whom the term סכנה is used in the Babylonian Talmud
with the extended meaning of an action that violates Sabbath law:

תלמוד בבלי מסכת שבת דף ל עמוד א

תנא נמי רישא פטור. והדתני רבי אושעיא אם בשביל החולה שיישן—לא יכבה,
ואם כבה—פטור אבל אסור—ההיא בחולה שאין בו סכנה, ורבי שמעון היא.

Babylonian Talmud Shabbat 30a
And as for what R. Oshaiah taught: If it is for the sake of a sick person,
that he should sleep, he must not extinguish it [the light]. But if he
extinguishes it, he is not liable, though it is forbidden—that refers to one
who is not in danger of this life (סכנה), and agrees with R. Simeon.

    A second ancient attempt to define the expression פיקוח נפש can be
found in a fragment of the *Mekilta de-Rabbi Ishmael* which was preserved in the Cairo Geniza, and in which the phrase קיום נפש, literally,

---

20. The simple meaning of the term סכנה can also be observed in the tannaitic
texts for the phrase סכנת נפשות, which is apparently never used by the tannaim in
contexts which involve a violation of Jewish law. For סכנת נפשות in the Mishnah,
see: Ter 8.6; Hul 3.5; Tosefta: Ber 5.8; Ter 7.16; Shab 6.14; 14.9; MK 1.7; Gitt 3.6;
AZ 6.6; Hul 3.19. The phrase סכנת נפש (note the singular use of סכנה) does not
appear in tannaitic or amoraic texts. The earliest example occurs in *Midrash
Tanchuma*, Lech Lecha 16.

'the preservation of life', replaces the phrase פיקוח נפש in a passage which is otherwise the same in the standard manuscript versions of this text. The passage from the Geniza follows below:

כבר היה ר' ישמאיל א'ומ' ר' אלעזר ור' עקי' מהלכין / בדרך ולוו הסרד
וישמעאל בנו שלרבי אלעזר בן עזר' / מהלכין אחריהן ונשאלה שאילה מיני
לקיום נפש / שידחה את השבת? היה רבי ישמעאל אום' אם במחתרת / ימצא
הגנב והוכה ומת וג' ספק שבא / להרג והרי הדב' קל וחומ': מה אם שפיכות
דמים שהיא/ מטמא את הארץ ומסלקת את השכינה הרי היא דוחה / את
השבת קול וחומ' לקיום נפש שידחה את השבת.[21]

Once R. Ishmael, R. Eleazar [b. Azariah] and R. Akiva were walking along the road and Lev[i] the net maker and Ishmael, the son of R. Eleazar b. Azariah, were following behind. And the [following] question was asked, 'From where [in Scripture do we know that] the preservation of life (לקיום נפש) overrides the Sabbath?' And R. Ishmael answered [and] said, 'If a thief is found breaking in and he is hit and dies…there is doubt that he came to steal [and] doubt if he came to kill. So things may be argued *kal va-chomer*: If the shedding of blood defiles the land and drives away the presence of God, and this overrides Sabbath law, is it not reasonable that the preservation of life (קיום נפש) will [also] override the Sabbath law!'

This raises the question—was the phrase קיום נפש used in tannaitic times as an alternative to the phrase פיקוח נפש, or is it an interpretation of medieval times? In fact, it is unlikely that the phrase קיום נפש appeared in the earliest (tannaitic) manuscript of the *Mekilta* where we now read פיקוח נפש, because it is not reproduced in any other of the texts of this source.[22] There is, moreover, little doubt that the scribe of the *Mekilta* was familiar with the phrase קיום נפש because the same phrase also occurs in what must be assumed to be the earliest editions of the *Mekilta*, in a section which deals with the maintenance of a wife by her husband, in the text and translation that follows below:

<u>מכילתא דרבי ישמעאל משפטים—מס' דנזיקין פרשה ג ד'ה אם אחרת</u>
אמרת ק'ו ומה דברים שאינן קיום נפש, אי אתה רשאי למנע ממנה, דברים שהם
קיום נפש, דין הוא שלא תהא רשאי למנוע הימנה.

21. Kahana, *The Genizah Fragments of the Halakhic Midrashim, Part I* (Jerusalem: Magnes, 2005) 150-1, lines 26-33 no. 153 (St Petersberg Antonin 239), compare H. S. Horovitz and I. A. Rabin, *Mechilta D'Rabbi Ismael* (Jerusalem: Wahrmann, 1970) 140, and Lauterbach, *Mekilta*, 3:197-8.

22. For the earliest manuscripts and printed editions of the *Mekilta de-Rabbi Ishmael*, see Lauterbach, *Mekilta*, 1:xxviii-xxxv.

Mekilta de-Rabbi Ishmael, Nezikin 3 (on Exod 21:7-11)
You reason by the method of *kal va-chomer*: If you cannot withhold from
her things which are *not* necessary for sustaining life (קיום נפש), is it not
logical to assume that you [also] cannot withhold from her things that are
necessary [for sustaining life].[23]

The phrase קיום נפש also occurs in the Jerusalem Talmud and some
later texts.[24] The fact that it is not used to define the expression פיקוח נפש
in any of the *tannaitic* texts, however, suggests that its presence in the
fragment of the Geniza may be a result of the initiative of the scribe of
this manuscript, who—as shown above—would have been familiar with
the phrase, and by whom it was substituted for the phrase פיקוח נפש,
which—it appears—the scribe wanted to define.

Let us now turn to a brief survey of the tannaitic texts in which the
expression פיקוח נפש is found.

IV. *Tannaitic Texts Which Include the Expression* פיקוח נפש

The phrase פיקוח נפש occurs in three tannaitic texts: (1) the *Mekilta de-
Rabbi Ishmael*, (2) the Tosefta and (3) *Sifra* to Leviticus. These will now
be discussed.

A. *The Phrase* פיקוח נפש *in the Mekilta de-Rabbi Ishmael*
This phrase appears ten times in the *Mekilta de-Rabbi Ishmael*, in five
different locations, which are each considered below. Unlike the Tosefta,
which contains the phrases of both R. Akiva and R. Ishmael, the *Mekilta
de-Rabbi Ishmael* contains *only* the phrase of R. Ishmael, although each
of the passages in which it appears presents the arguments of R. Akiva,
and one of these passages is even attributed directly to R. Akiva.

(1) *Mekilta de-Rabbi Ishmael, Shabatta 1*. The phrase פיקוח נפש occurs
twice in this text, first in the editorial question on the subject of saving
life within Jewish law (section A in the translation), and subsequently in
the first of the replies (section B):

מכילתא דרבי ישמעאל כי תשא—מס' דשבתא פרשה א ד'ה פרשת כי
כבר היה רבי ישמעאל ורבי אלעזר בן עזריה ורבי עקיבא מהלכין בדרך, ולוי
הסדר ורבי ישמעאל בנו של רבי אלעזר בן עזריה מהלכין בדרך אחריהם,
ונשאלה שאלה זו בפניהם, מנין לפיקוח נפש שדוחה את השבת?
נענה רבי ישמעאל ואמר, הרי הוא אומר, +שמות כב א+ אם במחתרת ימצא
הגנב,...

23. Lauterbach, *Mekilta*, 3:28.
24. *Mekilta de-Rabbi Ishmael*, Nez 3 (× 2); y. Ket 5.7 (× 2); *Pesikta Zutra,
Shemot* 21; *Yalkut Shimoni Torah Remez* 221 (× 2).

ומה זה הוא, ספק שבא לגנוב ספק שבא להרוג,
והרי דברים קל וחומר,
ומה שפיכות דמים, שמטמא את הארץ ומסלקת את השכינה, הרי היא דוחה
שבת,
קל וחומר
לפיקוח נפש, שדוחה את השבת.

<u>Mekilta de-Rabbi Ishmael Shabbatta 1</u>
(A) *Editorial Introduction*:
R. Ishmael, R. Akiva and R. Eleazar b. Azariah were once on a journey,
with Levi the net maker and Ishmael, the son of R. Eleazar b. Azariah,
following them. And this question was asked, 'From where do we know
that [action in a situation of] danger to life (פיקוח נפש) overrides Sabbath
law?'
(B) *The Reply of R. Ishmael*:
(1) *Preamble to the Argument*:
R. Ishmael answered and said, 'Behold [Scripture] states, *If a thief is
found breaking in and is struck so that he dies, there shall be no blood
guilt for him* [that is, the occupant of the building who has killed the thief
is *not* considered guilty of murder] (Exod 22:1).
Now of what does this speak? [It speaks of] a case where there is doubt
(ספק) whether the thief came [merely] to steal, [or] doubt (ספק) that he
came [also] to kill.'
(2) *Argument of R. Ishmael*:
From this [verse therefore an answer to the opening question] can be
deduced by an argument *kal va-chomer*:
If the shedding of blood [= murder], which defiles the land and causes the
Presence of God to be removed, is allowed to override Sabbath law,
is it not logical to assume that
[action in any situation of] danger to life (פיקוח נפש) overrides Sabbath
law![25]

The different sources of the phrase פיקוח נפש in the text above—first
in the editorial question and then in the body of the argument—are
potentially significant, because while the technical vocabulary of the
editor of a text probably reflects the terminology of the school of the
editor, terms used within a cited text may or may not represent the school
of the sage who is cited by the editor of the text.[26]

25. Lauterbach, *Mekilta*, 3:197–8. This text is repeated at b. Yom 85a. The use
of the term 'Sabbath' to refer symbolically to *all* Jewish law is discussed in Chapter
11.
26. When citing the text of a different school, the editor of an ancient text may
substitute the technical terminology of his own school, rather than use the technical
terminology of the different (perhaps rival) school. This is discussed by Kahana,
'The Halakhic Midrashim', in *The Literature of the Sages: Second Part* (Amsterdam: Fortress, 2006) 35 and 39 n. 161. For example, according to the *Mekilta*

The reply of R. Ishmael (section B above) begins with R. Akiva's interpretation of Exod 22:1, which claims that the occupant of the building is not guilty of murder in order to save (his own) life, because the biblical identification of the intruder as a *thief* (גנב), rather than a *murderer* (רוצח), means that there is doubt whether or not this intruder entered the building intending to steal or intending both to steal and to kill (see the above discussion on t. Shab 15.17). There is no hint of R. Ishmael's comparatively circuitous interpretation of Exod 22:2, which leads to the same understanding of Exod 22:1, via his interpretation of Exod 22:2 (see the discussion above on the *Mekhilta de-Rabbi Shimon bar Yochai* 22.2). Nevertheless, the dramatic imagery in this argument, which first refers to 'murder which defiles the land' and then to 'the removal of the presence of God' may be the contribution of R. Ishmael, thus accounting for the attribution of this argument to R. Ishmael, rather than to R. Akiva, to whom this interpretation probably originally belongs.

Based on the understanding that the thief-intruder may be killed with impunity because there is doubt whether he came to kill the occupant of the house or whether he came merely to steal, R. Ishmael then claims that if killing the thief in order to save (one's own) life is allowed on the Sabbath when there is doubt, so also it is allowed to save life on the Sabbath, because this also is an action which must be taken when in doubt.[27] The subject of 'doubt' is thus essential to the argument, and without this assumption in the final section of the argument, the same conclusion could not be made. This is the reason that the term 'doubt' occurs in each part of the argument *kal va-chomer* of R. Akiva (see t. Shab 15.17, discussed above), first in a direct reference to the interpretation of Exod 22:1 which is based on the assumption of doubt, and subsequently in the conclusion of the argument in the terminology used for the saving of life, namely להחיות נפש בספק. However, the above argument of R. Ishmael does not refer to the aspect of doubt. In particular, in contrast with the final part of the argument of R. Akiva (הבא מן הדין, *ha-ba min ha-din*, 'what can be deduced from the law', see Chapter 2) in which R. Akiva uses the phrase להחיות נפש בספק, R. Ishmael instead uses the expression פיקוח נפש. The conclusion of the argument of

---

de-Rabbi Ishmael Nez 17 (Lauterbach, *Mekilta*, 3:130) R. Akiva used the Ishmalean phrase מופנה להקיש ולדון גזירה שוה (literally, 'an expression free to be used as the basis for a *gezerah shaveh*') when opposing R. Yose, who argued that this hermeneutical method may also be used for two words that have already been put to other exegetical use. See also J. N. Epstein, *Prolegomena Ad Litteras Tannaiticas* (Jerusalem: Magnes, 1957) 511(ב)-23 (in Hebrew).

27. Assuming that the phrase דין הוא, *din hu*, is synonymous with the phrase קל וחומר, *kal va-chomer*.

R. Ishmael thus relies only on an implied allusion to 'doubt', which suggests that this is not the earliest articulation of this argument itself. Accordingly, in view of the use here of R. Akiva's understanding of Exod 22:1 without reference to Exod 22:2 (the latter being used by R. Ishmael to arrive as the same understanding of Exod 22:1—see the discussion above on the *Mekhilta de-Rabbi Shimon bar Yochai* 22.2), it can be assumed that the more complex argument of R. Ishmael is based on the argument of R. Akiva, but has been rephrased. The argument now includes imagery presumably composed by R. Ishmael, and also the terminology פיקוח נפש which refers to any situation of healing and/or danger to life, which—as will be seen—is repeatedly associated with R. Ishmael.

Moreover, since it is reasonable to suppose that the synonymous phrases associated with R. Akiva—ספק נפשות and להחיות נפש בספק— were also known to the editor of the *Mekilta* from contemporary tannaitic sources, then the fact the editor chose to use the expression פיקוח נפש (in the editorial question that opens this debate) suggests an informed preference for the latter phrase. It cannot be argued that terminology used in the question reflects and follows the terminology of the subsequent debate. This can be seen from the text from the Tosefta printed below, which shows that it was acceptable to open a debate on the subject of healing and/or the saving of life using one phrase, in this case, פיקוח נפש, while the alternative expressions of R. Akiva, ספק נפשות and להחיות נפש בספק, are used within the body of the text of the response:

תוספתא מסכת שבת פרק טו הלכה טז-טח

אמ' ר' יוסה מנין לפיקוח נפש שדוחה את השבת?

שנ' את שבתתי תשמרו...

יכול מילה ועבודה ופיקוח נפש ת"ל אך—חלק פעמים שאתה שובת ופעמים שאי אתה שובת. ...

אמ' ר' עקיבא וכי במה החמירה תורה בעבודה או בשבת החמירה בעבודה יותר מבשבת שעבודה דוחה את השבת ואין שבת דוחה אותה והרי דברים קל וחומר:

ומה עבודה שדוחה את השבת ספק נפשות דוחה אותה שבת שעבודה דוחה אותה

אינו דין

שספק נפשות דוחה אותה הא למדת שספק נפשות דוחה את השבת.

ר' אחא אמ' משם ר' עקיבא הרי הוא אומ' אם במחתרת ימצא הגנב וג' בעל הבית מהו ודיי או ספק?

הוי או' ספק.

אם הורגין נפש להחיות נפש בספק,

דין הוא

שידחו את השבת להחיות נפש בספק. ...

אין כל דבר עומד בפני פקוח נפש חוץ מע"ז וגלוי עריות ושפיכות דמים.

Tosefta Shabbat 15.16-17

Said R. Yose, 'How do we know that [a situation of] danger to life (פיקוח
נפש) overrides Sabbath law?…'

Said R. Akiva, 'Now in what respect did the Torah impose a more strict
rule, in the case of Temple service or in the case of Sabbath law? It was
stricter in the case of Temple service than in the case of Sabbath law'.

From this it is possible to construct an argument *kal va-chomer*:

If Temple service overrides Sabbath law, and [a situation of] doubt
[concerning] the saving of life (נפשות) ספק overrides it (that is, overrides
the Sabbath), which Temple service overrides,

is it not reasonable to assume

that [in a situation of] doubt [concerning] the saving of life (ספק נפשות)
overrides it (that is, overrides the Sabbath).

Tosefta Shabbat 15.17

R. Aha says in the same of R. Akiva, 'Behold, Scripture says, If a thief is
found breaking in and he is struck so that he dies, there shall no blood be
shed for him (Exod 22:1).

Now the [life of the] occupant of the building—is it [a matter of]
certainty or doubt?

You [must] say it is [a matter of] doubt (since it cannot be known for sure
if the man labelled as a thief will kill the occupant of the house].

If they kill a person [in a situation] to cause a life to live [when] in doubt
(להחיות נפש בספק),

surely it is logical to assume

they override [the laws of] the Sabbath [in a situation] to cause a life to
live [when] in doubt

(להחיות נפש בספק)…

Nothing in the world is more important than the duty to heal and/or save
life (פיקוח נפש) apart from [avoiding the sins of] idolatry, incest and
murder.'

(2) *Mekilta de-Rabbi Ishmael, Nezikin 13.*

מכילתא דרבי ישמעאל משפטים—מס' דנזיקין פרשה יג ד'ה אם במחתרת

אם במחתרת ימצא הגנב...

ומה זה, ספק שבא לגנוב ספק שבא להרוג.

אתה אומר ספק שהוא בא לגנוב וספק להרוג, או אינו אלא ספק וספק
שלא לגנוב.

אמרת, אם כשיגנוב ודאי והרגו הרי זה חייב, ק'ו זה שספק בא לגנוב ספק לא
בא לגנוב.

מכאן אתה דן על פקוח נפש [שספיקו דוחה את השבת]

ומה שפיכות דמים שמטמאה את הארץ ומסלקת את השכינה היא דוחה את
הספק,

[ק'ו לפיקוח נפש שידחה את הספק] הא אין עליך לומר כלשון האחרון אלא
כלשון הראשון, ספק בא לגנוב ספק בא להרוג.

<u>Mekilta de-Rabbi Ishmael Nezikin 13</u>
(A) *Introduction*
If a thief is found breaking in and he is struck so that he dies, no blood shall be shed for him (Exod 22:1). With what case does this law deal? [It deals] with a case where there is doubt whether (a) he came to steal, [or] doubt that (b) he came to kill. Or perhaps there is doubt only that (a) he came to steal or doubt that (b) he did not come to steal.
[In order to understand Exod 22:1] you must reason as follows: If even in the case when he definitely comes to steal and [the occupant of the building] is guilty of murder if he kills him, is it not reasonable to assume that the occupant [of the building] is guilty if he kills him in the case where there is doubt whether he came to steal or not?
From this you can draw a conclusion with regard to [a situation which involves] a danger to life.
(B) *The Argument*
Since even shedding of blood which defiles the land and causes the Shekinah to remove, is permitted in disregard of doubt,
it is not logical to assume that
[a situation which involves] a danger to life should override any doubt].
(D) Hence you must not interpret it (namely, Exod 22:1) as in the latter version, but you must interpret it (namely, Exod 22:1) as in the former version—it deals with a case where there is doubt whether the thief came merely to steal or also to kill.[28]

The phrase פיקוח נפש is used in this text, both in the introduction and within the argument itself. The fact that it occurs in the introduction is likely to be due to the preference of the editor of this text for the terminology of R. Ishmael, rather than that of R. Akiva, which the editor of this text must surely also have known. This is confirmed when we consider that the introduction to the argument (section [A] above) justifies the killing of the thief-intruder because of 'doubt', without referring to Exod 22:2, the latter which is used by R. Ishmael (but *not* by R. Akiva) to arrive at the conclusion that Exod 22:1 justifies the killing of the thief-intruder by the occupant of the house, in order to save the latter's own life. The lack of reference to Exod 22:2 thus suggests that the argument here is based wholly on R. Akiva's interpretation of Exod 22:1 (rather than R. Ishmael's more circuitous argument which begins with an argument based on Exod 22:2 (see the above discussion on the *Mekhilta de-Rabbi Shimon bar Yochai* 22.2), although the editor of the text has replaced the terminology of R. Akiva in his argument, להחיות נפש בספק, with the terminology of R. Ishmael, פיקוח נפש.

---

28. Lauterbach, *Mekilta*, 3:101-2.

(3) *Mekilta de-Rabbi Ishmael Nezikin 4.*

מכילתא דרבי ישמעאל משפטים—מס' דנזיקין פרשה ד ד'ה מעם מזבחי
אמר תלמיד אחד מתלמידי ר' ישמעאל, הרי הוא אומר ...
רציחה דוחה את העבודה ואין פקוח נפש דוחה את העבודה.
שהיה בדין, ומה אם שבת שאין רציחה דוחתה, פקוח נפש דוחתה,
עבודה שרציחה דוחתה,
אינו דין שיהא פקוח נפש דוחה את העבודה, [ת'ל מעם מזבחי תקחנו למות, בא
הכתוב ללמדך על העבודה, שאין פקוח נפש דוחה את העבודה].

Mekilta de-Rabbi Ishmael Nezikin 4
A certain student of R. Ishmael states that…
[We know that according to Exod 21:14] punishment for murder (רציחה)
overrides Temple service, but [an act] of healing and/or saving of life
(פיקוח נפש) does not override Temple service!
For [if this were so, it could be argued]: If the Sabbath, which is not
overridden by the punishment for murder (רציחה), [but] is overridden by
an act of healing and/or the saving of life (פיקוח נפש) [according to the
midrashic interpretation of Exod 21:14 by R. Akiva]
then surely [it is logical to argue that] an act of healing and/or the saving
of life overrides Temple service. But Scripture states: *Thou shalt take
him from my altar that he may die*. Scripture thus teaches that regarding
Temple service, [a situation regarding] the saving of life (פיקוח נפש) does
not override Temple service.[29]

In the passage above, an apparently sceptical, unnamed student from
the school of R. Ishmael finds fault with R. Akiva's midrashic understanding of Exod 21:14, which for R. Akiva meant that the man labelled
as a murderer in this biblical verse might live, although the biblical text
states that the murderer must die (see the discussion above on t. Shab
15.17). No source is given for this interpretation, but since the argument
of R. Akiva is the only source in which this argument has been preserved, it can be assumed that the unnamed author of this text based his
complaint on the sorite of R. Akiva now preserved in the Tosefta (at
t. Shab 15.16, see above), which proved (presumably to the satisfaction
of R. Akiva) that acts of healing and/or saving of life override Sabbath
law. Nevertheless, the terminology of R. Akiva (which can be assumed
was known to the author of this text because he alludes to the midrashic
understanding of R. Akiva on which the argument is based) has been
replaced with the expression פיקוח נפש. This is no surprise. As noted
above, the study of rabbinic texts has shown that although the technical
terminology of the rabbinic schools may differ, the opinions of the sages
are generally recorded in the terminology of the school of the redactor of

29. For an alternative translation, see Lauterbach, *Mekilta*, 3:39-40.

a text.[30] In this case, therefore, the editor from the school of R. Ishmael uses the terminology of R. Ishmael when recording an opinion of R. Akiva.

(4) *R. Akiva in Mekilta de-Rabbi Ishmael Shab 1.*

מכילתא דרבי ישמעאל כי תשא—מס' דשבתא פרשה א ד'ה פרשת כי
מנין לפיקוח נפש שדוחה את השבת...
רבי עקיבא אומר, אם דוחה רציחה את העבודה שהיא דוחה שבת, קל וחומר
לפיקוח נפש שדוחה השבת.

Mekilta de-Rabbi Ishmael Shabbatta 1

From where [in Scripture] do we know that [a situation of] saving life
(פיקוח נפש) overrides Sabbath law?
...Says R. Akiva:
If [punishment for] murder (רחיצה) overrides Temple service, which overrides the Sabbath,
is it not reasonable to assume that [a situation of] the saving of life
(פיקוח נפש) overrides Sabbath law![31]

As the direct attribution to R. Akiva suggests, the above argument is based on R. Akiva's midrashic interpretation of Exod 21:14, which (as discussed above) suggests that Temple law may be violated by removing a priest who is in the process of serving at the Temple altar, in order that this priest should serve as a witness for the defence of a man charged for premeditated murder, for which the penalty is death, so that the latter may be acquitted, and his life thereby saved. This is the single instance in a tannaitic text in which R. Akiva is directly attributed with the expression פיקוח נפש, a phrase which is otherwise always associated with R. Ishmael. As noted in the discussion above on the text from the *Mekilta de-Rabbi Ishmael* Shab 1, this can be explained by the ancient practice of the editor of a rabbinic text who replaced the technical terminology of a rival school with that of his own. In this case the terminology of the school of R. Akiva has been replaced with that of R. Ishmael.

(5) *R. Simon b. Menasia in the Mekilta de-Rabbi Ishmael, Nezikin 4.* The following argument on the subject of healing and/or saving life is attributed to Rabbi Simon b. Menasia, a tannaitic sage who flourished around 165–200 CE:

30. See n. 26.
31. For text and English translation, see Lauterbach, *Mekilta*, 3:39-40.

מכילתא דרבי ישמעאל משפטים—מס' דנזיקין פרשה ד ד'ה מעם מזבחי
וכי יזד איש על רעהו להרגו בערמה מעם מזבחי תקחנו למות.
... ר' שמעון בן מנסיא אומר ויהא פקוח נפש דוחה את השבת והדין נותן:
אם דוחה רציחה את העבודה
שהיא דוחה את השבת
פקוח נפש שהוא דוחה את העבודה
לא כל שכן.

Mekilta de-Rabbi Ishmael Nezikin 4
*But if a man comes wilfully upon his neighbour, to slay him treacher-
ously, you shall take him from my altar, that he may die* (Exod 21:14)...
R. Simon b. Menasia says, 'A situation of danger to life (פיקוח נפש)
should override the Sabbath, as the following reasoning proves:
If [according to a midrashic interpretation of Exod 21:14], (A) saving the
life of a man accused of murder overrides (B) Temple service,
which [that is, Temple service] overrides (C) [the laws of] the Sabbath,
then (A) a situation of danger to life (פיקוח נפש) which overrides (B)
Temple service
should (C) [override the laws of] the Sabbath!'[32]

This argument is presented as a sorite, whose basic argument can be
stated: If subject (A) overrides subject (B), and if subject (B) overrides
subject (C), it can then be assumed that subject (A) overrides subject (C).
In the argument above, (A) stands for healing and/or the saving of life,
(B) stands for Temple law (expressed as 'Temple service', עבודה) and
(C) stands for Sabbath law. This argument thus repeats the earlier
argument of R. Akiva preserved in the Tosefta (t. Shab 15.16), which is
not surprising as R. Menasia was a pupil of R. Meir, who was a pupil of
R. Akiva. The above text thus suggests that R. Menasia was familiar with
the argument and terminology of R. Akiva. This being the case, the use
in this context for the terminology of R. Ishmael can again be attributed
to the preference of the redactor of the *Mekilta de-Rabbi Ishmael* who—
we can reasonably assume—was from the school of R. Ishmael. He thus
recorded the argument of R. Menasia, using the terminology of R.
Ishmael.

B. *The Phrase* פיקוח נפש *in the Tosefta*
The text of the Tosefta uses the expression פיקוח נפש in (1) two editorial-
type comments and in (2) two attributed passages.

(1) *Editorial-type additions with the phrase* פיקוח נפש. The two editorial
comments in the Tosefta which include the phrase פיקוח נפש are almost
certainly later additions to the original text. One of these comments

---

32. For text and translation, see Lauterbach, *Mekilta*, 3:38, 40.

follows two directives which deal with the permitted source of breast milk for a child (see t. Shab 9.22). This text has been cited above, in relation to the two ancient definitions of the phrase פיקוח נפש. As was noted in the discussion on this text, the additional nature of the final comment to these directives is evident from the fact that it has little direct connection with either of the preceding texts. It is probable that the first directive which prohibits the expressing of breast milk into an open receptacle deals with a basic problem of hygiene, while the second, which forbids the employment of a gentile woman to breastfeed a child, is probably motivated by a wish to prevent the exposure of a Jewish child to non-Jewish practices.[33] The editorial, additional nature of the final comment in the Tosefta is also indicated by the fact that unlike the text of t. Shab 9.22, neither the text in the Mishnah, which also deals with the subject of the breastfeeding of a child by a gentile (m. AZ 2.1), nor the similar decree in the Tosefta, which permits a Samaritan woman to breastfeed a child (t. AZ 3.1), is followed with a comment on acts of healing and/or the saving of life.

It is thus reasonable to assume that the final comment that follows the two directives at t. Shab. 9.22, which includes the phrase פיקוח נפש, is a later addition to these directives by an editor who was probably aware of the phrases להחיות נפש בספק and ספק נפשות used by R. Akiva, especially the latter, because this phrase occurs in the Tosefta itself (see t. Shab 15.16 and 17 discussed above). This suggests, therefore, that the editor responsible for the addition deliberately chose the expression פיקוח נפש, *pikkuach nefesh*, the terminology associated with R. Ishmael, in preference to the terminology of R. Akiva.

The same conclusion follows from the comment in the Tosefta which is placed after a discussion of second-century Jewish sages in which they provide biblical proofs that acts of healing and/or the saving of lives may override Jewish law:

תוספתא מסכת שבת פרק טו הלכה טח

אין כל דבר עומד בפני פקוח נפש חוץ מע׳׳ז, וגלוי עריות ושפיכות דמים.

Tosefta Shabbat 15.17
Nothing prevents action for the saving of life, except for idolatry, forbidden sexual acts and the shedding of blood.

---

33. This accounts for the exception to this rule, stated at m. AZ 2.1, which notes that a gentile woman may breastfeed a (Jewish) child if she feeds the child in the mother's house, where, we assume, non-Jewish practices do not take place.

There is little doubt that this text is a later addition to an earlier completed section of the Tosefta. In contrast with the replies to the opening section of this text which state how it can be known that acts of healing and/or saving life are allowed to take place at the expense of Jewish law (as the opening question asks), this final statement lists the situations when action to heal and/or save life *may not* take place. The additional nature of this comment is also evident from the fact that the text is absent from the similar discussion preserved in the *Mekilta de-Rabbi Ishmael* Shab 1.

Once again, we must conclude that the phrase פיקוח נפש, rather than one of the synonymous expressions associated with R. Akiva, was used because of the personal preference of an editor who added this comment to an earlier text.

(2) *Attributed arguments with the phrase* פיקוח נפש—*the question and argument of R. Yose in the Tosefta, Shabbat 15.16.* Two other examples of the phrase פיקוח נפש in the Tosefta occur at t. Shab 15.16:

תוספתא מסכת שבת פרק טו הלכה טז

אמ' ר' יוסה מנין לפיקוח נפש שדוחה את השבת?

שנ' את שבתתי תשמרו—יכול מילה ועבודה ופיקוח נפש

ת'ל אך חלק פעמים שאתה שובת ופעמים שאי אתה שובת.

Tosefta Shabbat 15.16
(A) Said R. Yose: How do we know that a situation of danger to life (פיקוח נפש) overrides Sabbath law?
(B) Because it says *But* (אך) *My Sabbaths should you observe* (Exod 13:13).
(C) Might one think that circumcision or Temple service or a situation of danger to life(פיקוח נפש) [are subject to Sabbath law?].
(D) Scripture says, *but* (אך) by way of imposing a distinction. [This means that] there are Sabbaths that you must rest and Sabbaths that you should not rest [in order to save life].[34]

The first example of the phrase פיקוח נפש in the question of R. Yose clearly indicates his preference for the phrase, especially as the stories of his frequent clashes with R. Akiva mean that he would almost definitely have been familiar with the Akivan terms.[35]

---

34. t. Shab 15:16.
35. For example, it is claimed that R. Yose said to R. Akiva, 'Although you interpret for the whole day I shall not listen to you' (b. Zev 82a).

The argument presented immediately after the opening question of R. Yose—probably R. Yose the Galilean who is attributed with this same interpretation in the *Mekilta d'Rabbi Ishmael* Shab 1—is interrupted by section (C), which identifies three situations which are allowed to violate Sabbath law—Temple service, circumcision and actions of healing and/or the saving of life. These stated exceptions interrupt R. Yose's midrashic interpretation of Exod 13:13. This interruption is not found in an unattributed version of R. Yose's argument in the Jerusalem Talmud (see y. Yom 8.5). It is probable, therefore, that the original words of R. Yose, expressed above by sections (A) and (B), are probably more accurately preserved in the *Mekilta de-Rabbi Ishmael* (which is repeated verbatim in the Babylonian Talmud at b. Yom 85a), and which does not include a similar remark, as can be seen from the text and translation below:

מכילתא דרבי ישמעאל כי תשא—מס' דשבתא פרשה א ד'ה פרשת כי

רבי יוסי הגלילי אומר, כשהוא אומר, אך את שבתותי תשמורו, אך חלק, ויש
שבתות שאתה דוחה, ויש שבתות שאתה שובת.

Mekilta de-Rabbi Ishmael Shabbatta 1

R. Yose the Galilean says: When [Scripture] says, *But* (אך) *My Sabbaths you shall keep*...the word 'but' (אך) implies a distinction [between one Sabbath and another]. [This means that] there are Sabbaths on which you must keep and there are Sabbaths on which you must override [and must violate in order to perform acts which save life].[36]

It is likely, therefore, that the interpolation יכול מילה ועבודה ופיקוח נפש, 'Might one think that circumcision or Temple service or a situation of danger to life [are subject to Sabbath law?]', was added to R. Yose's reply by the editor of the Tosefta, who again shows a preference for the Ishmaelean phrase פיקוח נפש rather than one of the synonymous expressions associated with R. Akiva, which the editor of the Tosefta must have known, since they are used in the continuation of this passage in the Tosefta. This later chronological relationship to the basic text is also suggested by the specific situations to which the interpolation refers. The first two situations mentioned in the interpolation—namely, circumcision and Temple law—are both Pentateuchal injunctions that override Sabbath law. On the other hand, the fact that action necessitated by the saving of life also overrides Sabbath law could only have been claimed after acceptable proofs had been found via the tradition of oral law, which is the subject of the question of R. Yose. The reference to saving

---

36. Lauterbach, *Mekilta*, 3:198.

life in the interpolation is thus effectively the conclusion of the proofs
that had been found, rather than the actual proofs themselves, which is
the subject of the opening question of this text.[37]

(3) *The phrase* פיקוח נפש *in Sifra.* The expression פיקוח נפש occurs in the
course of a discussion on Lev 5:17-19 in *Sifra*, a tannaitic commentary
on Leviticus:

ספרא ויקרא—דבורא דחובה פרשה יב ד'ה פרשה יב

רבי אומר הרי הוא אומר: ואשר יבוא את רעהו ביער לחטוב עצים ונדחה ידו
בגרזן לכרות העץ ונשל הברזל מן העץ ומצא רעהו ומת הוא ינוס. קבע הכתוב
פיקוח נפש למי שבא לידו ספק נפש ולא ידע.

Sifra Vayikra Dibura Dehobah Parasha 12
Rabbi says, 'Behold Scripture says, "For example, a man goes with his
neighbour into a grove to cut wood. As his hand swings the axe to cut
down a tree, the axe-head flies off the handle and strikes his neighbour
who dies. The man will flee [to save his life in a city of refuge]" (Deut
19:5). Scripture has fixed the saving of life for whoever happens to kill,
and there is doubt that this was intentional, and he did not intend [to
kill].'[38]

The commentary *Sifra* was originally edited by the school of R.
Akiva. Scholarly opinion, however, suggests that several lengthy passages from the school of R. Ishmael were later added to the text.[39] The
expression פיקוח נפש appears in a passage which comments on Lev 5:17-
19, which has not been thought to show the influence of the school of R.
Ishmael. Nevertheless, there is reason to believe that this passage is not
part of the original text of the school of R. Akiva.

As can be seen, this section of *Sifra* is attributed to 'Rabbi', the
familiar name of R. Judah ha-Nasi. This attribution is probably incorrect.
R. Judah ha-Nasi was probably the editor of the Mishnah. Yet the
expression פיקוח נפש does not appear in the Mishnah although this work

37. Remarks of the sages in the *halachic* midrashim are ranked according to their
schools, and precedence is given to the sages and opinions of the school of the
redactor, see Kahana, 'The Halakhic Midrashim', 35.

38. *Sifra* Vayikra Dibura Dehobah, Parasha 12 (twice). Similarly, *Yalkut Shimoni
Torah* 479. For a translation of *Sifra*, see J. Neusner, *Sifra: An Analytical Translation*, vol. 1 (Brown Judaic Series 139; Atlanta: Scholars Press, 1988) 328, who
translates the phrase פיקוח נפש loosely as 'loss of life'.

39. For the background of *Sifra*, see Strack and Stemberger, *Introduction to the
Talmud and Midrash*, 285-7. For a discussion of different editions and the Ishmael-
ian sections of *Sifra*, see Kahana, 'The Halakhic Midrashim', 78, 84-7.

includes directives which deal with the problems in Jewish law caused by acts of healing and/or the saving of life (which will be listed in Chapter 11) and although R. Ishmael (who is repeatedly associated with the phrase פיקוח נפש in the *Mekilta*) is mentioned in the Mishnah over seventy times, so that it is reasonable to assume that R. Judah ha-Nasi was familiar with the terminology of R. Ishmael in relation to acts of healing and/or saving life. Similarly unrecorded in the Mishnah is the phrase in *Sifra* 'scripture has fixed', קבע הכתוב, which introduces the words of R. Judah in the above text, although the Mishnah includes seventy-two occurrences of the verb קבע, none of which are used in this way.[40] It is therefore unlikely that the phrase פיקוח נפש in the citation above should be attributed to R. Judah ha-Nasi, but is more likely to be an addition to the original, basic text of *Sifra* by a scribe from the school of R. Ishmael.

(4) *Pikkuach Nefesh and Safeq Nefashot in Amoraic texts*. The amoraic sages enthusiastically embraced both the phrases associated with R. Akiva and R. Ishmael. Thus, in contrast with the Mishnah where only the terminology of R. Akiva appears (see m. Yom 8.6, and possibly also m. Yom 8.7), the Jerusalem Talmud uses the terminology of both R. Akiva and R. Ishmael, and correctly links these phrase with each sage. The expression פיקוח נפש, which is associated with R. Ishmael, thus appears in a context which cites R. Ishmael's interpretation of Exod 22:2, although his argument also includes unacknowledged allusions to R. Akiva's reference to 'doubt'.[41] Similarly, the expression of R. Akiva, ספק נפשות, appears twice, in close proximity to the discussion on the mishnaic directive of m. Yom 8.6 in which this expression is also used in a directive attributed to Mattithiah b. Heresh, a disciple of the school of

---

40.   Rabbinic deductions from Scripture in the Mishnah which do not include a scriptural text are introduced with a variety of phrases, including: מעלה הכתוב, literally, 'Scripture brings up' (e.g. m. San 4.5), אמר הכתובת ('Scripture has said', e.g. m. San 7.4); פרט הבתוב ('Scripture has detailed', e.g. m. Makk 1.7); הכתוב ענש ('Scripture has punished', e.g. m. Makk 1:7); ריבה הכתוב ('Scripture has extended [the law]', e.g. m. Shevu 3.5); הכתוב מדבר ('Scripture speaks', e.g. m. Zev 11.1); תלמוד לומר ('Scripture states/teaches, e.g. m. Makk 1.7). The questionable attribution of the phrase קבע הכתוב to R. Judah ha-Nasi may also be the opinion of Neusner, whose translation of this text labels the latter as 'B', whereas the words of Rabbi are marked 'A'; see Neusner, *Sifra*, 328.

41.   y. San 8.8, trans. Neusner, *Talmud of the Land of Israel: Sanhedrin and Makkot*, vol. 31 (Chicago: University of Chicago Press, 1984) 277-8.

R. Akiva.[42] R. Abbahu also states in the name of R. Yohanan, '[The problem of healing a sick person on the Sabbath] is dealt with as a case of doubt concerning life (ספק נפשות), and in any case of doubt concerning life (ספק נפשות), the needs of the sick person override Sabbath law'.[43] It seems that R. Yohanan, the (presumed) editor of the Jerusalem Talmud, uses this expression preferentially, rather than because he is accurately citing the text of m. Yom 8.6 in which this phrase appears, because the editorial question 'How do we know that the duty to save life overrides Sabbath law? (מניין שספק נפשות דוחה את ה שבת?)[44] includes the expression ספק נפשות, rather than the expression פיקוח מפש, which R. Yohanan must also have known. (As noted above, the deliberate choice of terminology is implied by a comparison between this question and the similar question of R. Yose in the Tosefta at t. Shab 15.16, and the *Mekilta de-Rabbi Ishmael* Shab 1, which both use the term פיקוח נפש. In any case, for obvious reasons, any editorial question is likely to show the preference of an editor of a text.) This suggest that the editor of the Jerusalem Talmud preferred the terminology of R. Akiva rather than that of R. Ishmael, although he was prepared to acknowledge the existence of both. In contrast, the editor of the tannaitic *Mekilta de-Rabbi Ishmael* uses only the terminology of R. Ishmael, and R. Judah ha-Nasi, who probably edited the Mishnah, does not use the terminology of R. Ishmael at all.

The Babylonian Talmud also uses a mixture of terms. The expression פיקוח נפש appears fifteen times, while ספק נפשות appears fourteen times (in addition to the four mishnaic quotations, two at b. Yom 83a and two at b. Yom 84b). However, this phrase appears mainly in a modified form, either in association with, or more commonly, with the addition of, the term להקל, thus producing the expanded phrase ספק נפשות להקל (which is not found in the Jerusalem Talmud). Moreover, unlike the phrase פיקוח נפש, the phrase ספק נפשות or its variants are *never* interpolated into the words of the tannaim who are cited in an amoraic text.

The apparent parity of numbers with respect to the phrases ספק נפשות and פיקוח נפש in the Babylonian Talmud does not however indicate a similar preference for each. As noted above, the expression פיקוח נפש does *not* appear in the Mishnah, which is the rabbinic text on which the

42. y. Yom 8.4, 5, trans. Neusner, *The Talmud of the Land of Israel: Yoma*, 14:221-2.

43. y. Yom 8.4.

44. y. Yom 8.5, trans. Neusner, *The Talmud of the Land of Israel: Yoma*, 14:223.

commentary of the Talmud is most obviously based. This means that when the amoraic sages use the term פיקוח נפש, they are not citing a phrase from the Mishnah, but have imported this term from another source, probably from the toseftan *baraitot*, which are also the subject of commentary in the Talmud. The term פיקוח נפש is thus used in the Babylonian Talmud *despite* its absence from the Mishnah. This suggests an amoraic preference for the term of R. Ishmael, פיקוח נפש, in comparison with the alternative expressions that can be attributed to R. Akiva. In fact, the terminology of R. Akiva would be comparatively poorly represented in the Babylonian Talmud were it not for the addition of the term להקל to his phrase ספק נפשות, thus producing the idiomatic expression, ספק נפשות להקל, which appears nine times in all, and which may indicate a perceived inadequacy by the Babylonian amoraim for the original Akivan phrase.[45]

The greater popularity of the expression פיקוח נפש is also indicated by the addition of this phrase—rather than any of the expressions associated with R. Akiva—in passages in the Babylonian Talmud which cite tannaitic texts, and in which lack any special terminology relating to acts of healing and/or saving life. For example, neither of the two versions of the argument of the first-century R. Eleazar in the Tosefta and the *Mekilta de-Rabbi Ishmael* (which are based on the need to perform the act of circumcision on the Sabbath when a male child is born on the Sabbath) include the phrase פיקוח נפש. The Tosefta thus states:

תוספתא מסכת שבת פרק טו הלכה טז

ר' ליעזר או' מילה דוחין עליה את השבת מפני מה מפני שחייבין עליה כרת
לאחר זמן והרי דברים קל וחומר ומה על אבר אחד ממנו דוחין את השבת דין
הוא שידחה שבת על כולו.

Tosefta Shabbat 15.16
R. Eleazar [b. Azariah] says, 'As to circumcision, why does it override the Sabbath? It is because they are liable to [the punishment of] *karet* if it is not done on time. Now the matter can be argued logically: If on account of a single limb of a person they override the prohibitions of the Sabbath, is it not logical that they should override the prohibitions of the Sabbath on account of [saving] the whole of him!'

---

45. b. Shab 129a; b. Yom 83a, 84b; b. Ket 15a; b BK 44b (× 2), 90a; b. BB 50b; b. San 79a. It seems that only R. Safra, a Babylonian sage from the first half of the fourth century CE, uses the phrase ספק נפשות, without the addition להקל; see b. Yom 83a. But R. Safra may only be citing R. Mattithiah b. Heresh, by whom the phrase ספק נפשות is used.

Similarly without the phrase פיקוח נפש, the *Mekilta de-Rabbi Ishmael* states:

מכילתא דרבי ישמעאל כי תשא—מס' דשבתא פרשה א ד'ה פרשת כי
נענה רבי אלעזר בן עזריה ואמר, מה מילה שאינה אלא אחד מאיבריו של אדם
דוחה שבת, קל וחומר לשאר כל גופו.

Mekilta de-Rabbi Ishmael Ki Tisa Shabbat 1
R. Eleazar b. Azariah answered and said, 'If in the performing of the ceremony of circumcision, which affects only one member of the body, one overrides Sabbath law, how much more one should do so for the whole body when it [= the whole body] is in danger'.[46]

In contrast, the phrase פיקוח נפש has been added to the later report of this argument in the Babylonian Talmud:

תלמוד בבלי מסכת שבת דף קלב עמוד א
רבי אלעזר בן עזריה אומר: מה מילה שהיא אחת מאיבריו של אדם—דוחה את
השבת, קל וחומר לפיקוח נפש שדוחה את השבת.

Babylonian Talmud Shabbat 132a
R. Eleazar b. Azariah said, 'If circumcision, which is performed on [only] one of the limbs of a man supersedes the Sabbath, is it not logical that the duty of saving of life (פיקוח נפש) overrides the Sabbath!'

R. Eleazar b. Azariah came from the second generation of tannaitic sages, which flourished in the early part of the second half of the first century CE. He was a junior contemporary of Rabban Gamaliel II, R. Eliezer b. Hurcanus and R. Yoshua b. Hananiah, and thus an older contemporary of R. Akiva and R. Ishmael.[47] It is thus unlikely that he himself employed a phrase whose earliest use can probably be attributed to R. Ishmael, which helps to confirm that the phrase פיקוח נפש was added to the later, amoraic report of his (tannaitic) words.

The relative popularity of the phrase פיקוח נפש in the Babylonian Talmud can also be observed in the discussion in this text of the directives in the Mishnah and Tosefta which call for the Sabbath removal of fallen debris which has caused danger to life. This tannaitic directive includes the term ספק, which suggests that this version of the text was probably framed no earlier than the time of R. Akiva. The Mishnah thus declares:

---

46. For the text and an English translation, see Lauterbach, *Mekilta*, 3:198.
47. *Sifre* to Deuteronomy 32; b. San 101a. R. Eleazar b. Azariah was an older contemporary of R. Akiva.

משנה מסכת יומא פרק ח משנה ז

מי שנפלה עליו מפולת ספק הוא שם ספק אינו שם ספק חי ספק מת ספק עובד
כוכבים ספק ישראל מפקחין עליו את הגל מצאוהו חי מפקחין עליו ואם מת
יניחוהו.

Mishnah Yoma 8.7

If a building fell down on a person and there is doubt (ספק) whether anyone
is there or doubt (ספק) anyone is not, or doubt (ספק) whether anyone is
alive or doubt (ספק) anyone is dead, or doubt (ספק) whether the individual
is a gentile or doubt (ספק) the individual is an Israelite, they may clear
away the ruin from above the individual. If they find someone alive they
may clear away from above the individual; but if dead, they leave the
individual [until after the Sabbath].

The phrase ספק נפש also appears in the similar directive in the Tosefta:

תוספתא מסכת שבת פרק טו הלכה יא

מפקחין על ספק נפש בשבת והזריז הרי זה משובח ואין צריך ליטול רשות מבית
דין.

Tosefta Shabbat 15.11

They remove debris for a person whose life is in doubt (ספק נפש) on the
Sabbath, and a person who is prompt in this matter, behold, this person is to
be praised. And there is no need to ask permission from a [Jewish] court.

On the other hand, there is no reference to 'doubt' in either of the two
later repetitions of these directives in the Babylonian Talmud cited
below. Both repetitions, however, include the expression פיקוח נפש, even
though the amoraic words of introduction to this text, the phrase תנו רבנן,
meaning 'our tannaitic masters taught', suggests an accurate repetition of
its original, tannaitic source:

תלמוד בבלי מסכת יומא דף פד עמוד ב

תנו רבנן: מפקחין פקוח נפש בשבת והזריז הרי זה משובח, ואין צריך ליטול רשות
מבית דין.

Babylonian Talmud Yoma 84b

Our rabbis taught [that] one must remove debris to save life (פיקוח נפש) on
the Sabbath, and the more eager one is the more praiseworthy and one need
not seek permission from the Beth Din.

תלמוד בבלי מסכת כתובות דף ה עמוד א

ואמר רבי רבי יעקב בר אידי אמר רבי יוחנן : מפקחין פיקוח נפש בשבת.

Babylonian Talmud Ketuboth 5a

And R. Yacob, the son of Idi said that R. Yohanan said, 'One may remove
debris to save life (פיקוח נפש) on the Sabbath'.[48]

48.   The phrase פיקוח נפש is translated in a general way by Daiches, *The Babylonian Talmud: Seder Nashim: Ketuboth* (London: Soncino, 1936) 14, 'One may do
any work to save life on the Sabbath'.

The last section of the directive in the Mishnah at m. Yoma 8.7—*If they find someone alive they may clear away from above the individual; but if dead, they leave the individual [until after the Sabbath]*—gives rise to a discussion in the Babylonian Talmud on the problem of the detection of signs of life. A solution to this problem is offered by an anonymous speaker who cites the words of the tannaitic sage, Abba Saul (110–135 CE). When introducing the words of Abba Saul, the speaker refers to a mishnaic directive with the phrase פיקוח נפש, and thus confirms that the situation of a man buried under rubble should be considered as a humanitarian situation which can be defined by the phrase פיקוח נפש, for which it is permitted to violate Sabbath law:

תלמוד בבלי מסכת יומא דף פה עמוד א

... אבל לענין פקוח נפש—אפילו אבא שאול מודי דעקר חיותא באפיה הוא,
דכתיב +בראשית ז+ כל אשר נשמת רוח חיים באפיו.

Babylonian Talmud Yoma 85a
...but regarding a situation in which life must be saved (פיקוח נפש) [Abba Saul] would agree that life manifests itself through the nose especially, as it is written, *In whose nostrils was the breath of the spirit of life* (Gen 7:22).

In summary, therefore, it is clear that the special terminology of both R. Akiva and R. Ishmael was used frequently by the amoraim, without the arguments in which they were originally expressed, as a kind of lexical shorthand for an argument that permits any action to heal and/or save life, even though such action would cause a violation of Jewish law. The Babylonian Talmud, however, reveals the beginnings of the greater popularity of the phrase associated with R. Ishmael. This trend continued in later times, as can be seen from a simple word search in the *Responsa Project of the University of Bar Ilan* (version 14), which shows 2,725 occurrences of the phrase *pikkuach nefesh* in post-amoraic texts, but only 593 instances of the phrase *safeq nefashot* (there are no examples of the expression לחיות נפש בספק). It is clear that, as far as the frequency of its usage is concerned, the expression associated with R. Ishmael triumphed over the expressions associated with R. Akiva. This is certainly the personal experience of the author of this book, which suggests that the phrase פיקוח נפש is the phrase of choice used by Jewish people today to refer to the necessity to perform a humanitarian act which causes a violation not only of Jewish law, but the violation of *any* law.

V. *Conclusions*

(1) Either R. Eleazar b. Azariah or R. Akiva was responsible for the innovative use of the verb דחה to refer to a secular act of healing and/or saving life which would override Jewish law. This phrase is implied in the conclusion of the underlying Hebrew text of the argument used by Jesus in the story when he meets the Pharisees in the Galilean fields (see the discussion in Chapter 3 on Mark 2:28, Luke 6:5 and Matt 12:8), which suggests that it was *first* used in this way around 70 CE, a date which accords with the early public life of R. Eleazar b. Azariah. This suggests that the argument in which this phrase was used was composed well after the life of the historical Jesus (around forty or so years after the crucifixion) and thus could not have been composed or voiced by the historical Jesus himself.

(2) The composition of the phrase ספק נפשות, *safeq nefashot*, and its derivatives, which refers to *any* act or *any* situation of healing and/or saving life that overrides Jewish law, can be attributed to R. Akiva. These phrases could not therefore have been used before his time. Their presence in a tannaitic directive need not, however, fix the *terminus a quo* of composition of a directive, but may indicate only the earliest date for the addition of this phrase to a directive, the latter which was composed at an earlier time.

(3) It was probably R. Akiva who formally introduced the concept of ספק, *safeq* ('doubt'), into directives on healing and/or saving life. As for the expression ספק נפשות, the presence of this term in a tannaitic directive does not establish the original date of composition of the directive, but indicates only the *earliest* date for the addition of this phrase which could have been added to a far earlier composed text.

(4) The composition and earliest use of the phrase פיקוח נפש, *pikkuach nefesh*, which refers to *any* act or *any* situation of healing and/or saving life, can be attributed to R. Ishmael.

(5) The phrase פיקוח נפש does not appear in the Mishnah. Both the phrases פיקוח נפש and ספק נפשות appear in the Tosefta, although the editor of this text shows a preference for the phrase פיקוח נפש. The phrases in the Tosefta are probably correctly attributed. The *Mekilta de-Rabbi Ishmael* uses only the phrase פיקוח נפש, which it attributes both to R. Akiva and R. Ishmael. Both the Babylonian and Jerusalem Talmud use both phrases. The Babylonian Talmud, however, shows a preference for פיקוח נפש. This trend has continued in modern times.

(6) Both the Jerusalem and Babylonian Talmuds tend to add the phrase פיקוח נפש to citations of tannaitic sages, even though this phrase does not occur in the cited tannaitic text. This will be further discussed in Chapter 8.

(7) The term סכנה, *sakanah*, in a *tannaitic* text refers *only* to a situation of healing and/or danger to life in which the necessary action does *not* violate Jewish law. In contrast, this term in an amoraic text also refers to situations of healing and/or danger to life in which the necessary action may or may not cause a violation of Jewish law. For further discussion of this term, see Chapter 8.

(8) The definition of פיקוח נפש by the term סכנה in the Tosefta at t. Shab 9.22 is probably an amoraic addition to this tannaitic text.

Chapter 6

DIRECT INTERACTION BETWEEN R. AKIVA AND MATTHEW?
THE SORITES OF MATTHEW AND R. AKIVA COMPARED

I. *The Sorites of R. Akiva and His School*

The discussion in Chapters 3 and 5 have shown that both R. Akiva and Matthew are attributed with one or more sorites that justify an act of healing and/or saving life. What however has not been noted so far is that these sorites are remarkably alike in their content, in their method of argumentation and in their conclusion. To show this similarity, let us begin with a brief review of four sorites preserved in the tannaitic texts that can be directly attributed to R. Akiva and his school. These have all been discussed in Chapter 5, but for the sake of convenience two of these texts are described again here. These sorites all follow the same schematic pattern, which can be symbolically expressed in the following way: If subject (A) overrides subject (B), and if subject (B) overrides subject (C), it can then be assumed that subject (A) overrides subject (C). In the sorites of R. Akiva, (A) refers to healing and/or the saving of life, (B) refers to Temple law (expressed as 'Temple service') and (C) refers to Sabbath law.

The simplest version of these sorites is attributed directly to R. Akiva and provides one of the answers to the question of R. Yose, probably R. Yose the Galilean, *From where (in Scripture) do we know that the saving of life overrides Sabbath law?*:

תוספתא מסכת שבת <u>פרק טו הלכה טז</u>

אמ' ר' יוסה מנין לפיקוח נפש שדוחה את השבת?

אמ' ר' עקיבא וכי במה החמירה תורה בעבודה או בשבת? החמירה בעבודה
יותר מבשבת שעבודה דוחה את השבת ואין שבת דוחה אותה. והרי דברים קל
וחומר.

ומה עבודה שדוחה את השבת ספק נפשות דוחה אותה שבת שעבודה דוחה
אותה אינו דין שספק נפשות דוחה אותה.

הא למדת שספק נפשות דוחה את השבת!

270

Tosefta Shabbat 15.16

Said R. Yose, 'From where [in the holy Jewish texts] do we know that the saving of life overrides the Sabbath law?'
Said R. Akiva:
'Now in what regard did the Torah impose a stricter rule? Was it for Temple service or for the Sabbath? It was more strict for Temple service than for the Sabbath.
For (B) Temple service overrides (c) [the laws of] the Sabbath, but the [laws of] Sabbath do not override it [= the Temple service].
From this it can be deduced:
If (B) Temple service overrides (C) [the laws of] the Sabbath
and (A) a [situation concerning] doubt of the saving lives (ספק נפשות) overrides (B) it [= Temple service], then, if (C) [the laws of] the Sabbath, which (B) Temple service overrides,
is it not logical that a [situation which involves] (A) the doubt of saving lives (ספק נפשות), that is, healing and/or the saving of life) overrides (C) it [= the laws of the Sabbath]!'

Summary of the argument:
Thus you have learned that (A) [a situation of] doubt of the saving of lives (ספק נפשות) overrides (C) [the laws] of the Sabbath![1]

The second claim in this sorite, that '(B) Temple law overrides (C) Sabbath law', is based on the fact that Temple law overrode Sabbath law in the vicinity of the Temple. This statement needs no proof, as it would have been known to all especially in Temple and near post-Temple times (see Chapter 3 on *The Relationship Between Sabbath and Temple Law*). The basis for the opening claim '(A) the saving of life overrides (B) Temple law' is, however, less obvious, and needs acceptable proof. As was discussed in Chapter 3, in both the versions of the argument used by Jesus to the Pharisees in the Galilean fields—whether phrased as an argument *kal va-chomer* by Mark and Luke, or as a sorite by Matthew— this proof is provided by a reference to the midrashic version of the story of David and the sacred bread. There is, however, no reference to any proof for the basis of the opening statement in the sorite of R. Akiva cited above. As a result, the audience of this text must accept without proof that, as the argument claims, an act of healing/and or saving life (A) overrides Temple law (B). The argument then continues in a predictable way: since Temple law (B), overrides Sabbath law (C), (on the Sabbath within the vicinity of the Temple), it can then be concluded that an act of healing and/or saving life (A) overrides Sabbath law (C).

---

1. For a translation, see Neusner, *The Tosefta: Translated from the Hebrew: Second Division Moed*, 62.

The lack of a proof text in the sorite of R. Akiva is, however, rectified in the three other versions. These all include term רציחה (*retsichah*), literally 'murder', but in this case meaning 'punishment for murder'. This term alludes to R. Akiva's midrashic interpretation of Exod 21:14, the proof text on which the argument is based, although the term רציחה does not appear in the biblical text.[2] As was noted in Chapter 5, the midrashic interpretation of this biblical verse claims in effect that the biblical priest is innocent of murder and may be removed from the altar of the Temple even while performing his duties (an act which violates Temple law), in order that he might act as a witness for the defence of a person who is accused of murder, and thus—it is claimed—will save the life of this (other) person who is accused. The underlying thought in this midrash may therefore be expressed in rabbinic style: an act of healing and/or the saving of life overrides Temple law. Consequently, if (A), an act of healing and/or saving life, overrides (B), Temple law, and if (B), Temple law, overrides (C), Sabbath law, it may then be concluded that (A), an act of healing and/or saving life, overrides (C), Sabbath law. This argument is expressed in the sorite below, which is again attributed directly to R. Akiva:

מכילתא דרבי ישמעאל כי תשא—מסכתא דשבתא פרשה א
כבר היה רבי ישמעאל ורבי אלעזר בן עזריה ורבי עקיבא מהלכין בדרך, ולוי
הסדר ורבי ישמעאל בנו של רבי אלעזר בן עזריה מהלכין בדרך אחריהם,
ונשאלה שאלה זו בפניהם, מנין לפיקוח נפש שדוחה את השבת? רבי עקיבא
אומר, אם דוחה רציחה את העבודה שהיא דוחה שבת, קל וחומר לפיקוח נפש
שדוחה השבת!

Mekilta de-Rabbi Ishmael Shabbatta 1
R. Ishmael, R. Akiva and R. Eleazar b. Azariah were once on a journey, with Levi ha-Saddar and R. Ishmael, the son of R. Eleazar b. Azariah who were following them. Then this question was asked, 'How do we know that danger to life overrides [the laws of] the Sabbath?'... R. Akiva said, 'If (A) [saving the life of a man accused of] murder (רציחה) overrides (B) Temple law [because the priest who is a witness for the defence has to be removed from his duties] which (B) [= and if Temple law] overrides (C) the Sabbath, is it not logical to conclude (קל וחומר) that the saving of life (פיקוח נפש) overrides (C) Sabbath law!'[3]

---

2. R. Akiva's interpretation of Exod 21:14 is found in b. Yom 85a–b, which is cited and discussed in Chapter 5.
3. For the Hebrew text and parallel English translation, see Lauterbach, *Mekilta*, 3:198.

The other two versions of this sorite again include a reference to R. Akiva's midrashic interpretation of Exod 21:14 as proof that the saving of life overrides Temple law. They are preserved at *Mekhilta de-Rabbi Shimon bar Yochai* 22.2 (which is attributed to R. Yose the Galilean, a student, and subsequently a colleague, of R. Akiva) and at *Mekilta de-Rabbi Ishmael* Nez 4 (which is attributed to R. Simon b. Menasia, but again can be attributed to the influence of R. Akiva as R. Simon b. Menasia was a pupil of R. Meir, who was one of the five famous students of R. Akiva, and one of the two students whom he ordained). These texts present the same argument as the two other sorites above, and have been cited and discussed in Chapter 5.

To summarise therefore: four sorites exist in the tannaitic texts, two of which are attributed directly to R. Akiva, and two of which can be attributed to the influence of R. Akiva. These all use the same basic argument to 'prove' that healing and/or the saving of life may override Sabbath law. The main difference between the four is that one (t. Shab 15.16) makes no reference to any proof text, while the three others are based on R. Akiva's midrashic version of Exod 21:14.

II. *The Sorite of Matthew 12:5-6, 8 Compared with the Sorites of R. Akiva*

As noted above, the four tannaitic sorites of R. Akiva begin with the following two consecutive statements: (1) acts of healing and/or the saving of life override Temple law, and (2) Temple law overrides Sabbath law. This leads to the final conclusion, in effect the third and final line of the sorite, that acts of healing and/or the saving of life must override Sabbath law. A moment's reflection will confirm that these are exactly the same basic statements and the same basic conclusion as the sorite of Matthew. The only significant difference between them is that whenever the proof text in the sorites of R. Akiva is identified (as in three of the four sorites discussed above), it is based on a midrashic interpretation of Exod 21:14, whereas the proof text of the sorite of Matthew is based on a midrashic interpretation of 1 Sam 21:1-6. Thus:

1. Matt 12:3-4 states that David and his companions violated Temple law by illegally eating the sacred Temple bread because they were hungry and thus in danger of death. Or, as this would be expressed rabbinic-style, 'the saving of life from hunger overrides Temple law';

2. Matt 12:5 notes that although the Temple priests violate Sabbath law, they are innocent ('guiltless'). This can be expressed in rabbinic style as: 'Temple law overrides Sabbath law'. Then follow Matt 12:6 and 12:7, which interrupt the logic of the main argument and need not therefore be considered within the logic of this text (as was discussed in Chapter 3);

3. Matt 12:8 repeats the ingenious translation of the probable underlying, original Hebrew argument *kal va-chomer* from which his sorite is derived, which has obscured the meaning of the original argument. This probably originally stated that in order to heal and/or save life from starvation, man in general was allowed to override Sabbath law. (For discussion on this understanding of Matthew's text, see on Mark 2:28 in Chapter 3.)

Apart from the fact that the last section of the sorite of Matthew deals specifically with the 'cure' of starvation (an inevitable consequence of the use of the proof text of a story which features starvation as a cause of danger to life that overrides Temple law), the logic and the conclusion of the sorites of R. Akiva and his school and the sorite of Matthew are essentially the same. They differ only with regard to the different proof texts on which their opening statements are based, *whenever each is identified*—as noted above, the sorite of Matthew is based on a midrashic understanding of the biblical story of David at 1 Sam 21:1-6, whereas the sorites of R. Akiva and his school are based on a midrashic understanding of Exod 21:14. This similarly is of course a result of the fact that the midrashic interpretation of each of the biblical texts has been contrived to serve as an example of a situation in which an act that heals and/or saves life causes a violation of Temple law.

There is probably only one possible explanation for this similarity. In view of the fact that R. Akiva is attributed with the midrashic interpretation of Exod 21:14, it is reasonable to assume that R. Akiva substituted the proof text of his midrashic interpretation of Exod 21:14 for that of the midrashic interpretation of 1 Sam 21:1-6, in a sorite that he originally wrote, which was essentially a re-phrasing of an argument *kal va-chomer* that was composed probably by a Pharisee, before around 70 CE, and is now preserved only in a Christianised version in the synoptic gospels of Mark and Luke (Mark 2:23-26, 28; Luke 6:1-5).

It is, however, obvious that the midrashic story of David and the sacred bread is far more attractive and thus far more acceptable as the basis for an argument *kal va-chomer* than the midrashic story of the priest at Exod 21:14 used in the other sorites that can ultimately be attributed to R. Akiva. Even if many of the original Jewish audience of the argument *kal va-chomer* in the texts of Mark and Luke, and the audience of the rephrased version of the argument in the sorite in Matthew, which were all based on the midrashic story of David, were aware that the Temple was built *after* David had died, the intrinsic anonymity of the term 'house of God' in the midrashic tale of David and the sacred bread makes it easy to accept that the future King David was at the Temple at Jerusalem, rather than the shrine at Nob, when he ate the sacred bread. It is also easy to accept that the midrashic David *il*legally consumed the sacred bread, because only priests were allowed the sacred bread in the Temple at Jerusalem, which thus excluded David and his men from this privilege because were *not* priests. Similarly, David's request to the priest for provisions makes it easy to accept that he was starving to death, although this is not stated in the biblical text. Moreover, although the biblical David arrived at Nob alone, it is not difficult to accept (as the synoptists suggest) that the companions of David were equally starving and similarly also in danger of their lives. In any case, the whole midrashic story is neatly summarised in the argument used by Jesus, and needs no extra knowledge from the audience of this text.

In contrast, however, a similar ease of acceptance cannot be claimed for the midrashic interpretation of Exod 21:14. Even without an accurate knowledge of the Hebrew content of Exod 21:14, it is reasonable to assume that a story which features a charismatic future king is far more attractive than the story of an unnamed priest who must leave his work on the altar of the Temple to act as a witness for the defence of a person on a capital charge. It is moreover obvious that for those familiar with the biblical text, the midrashic changes made to the biblical story suggested by Exod 21:14 are far more difficult to accept than the changes made to the biblical story of David at Nob. Thus instead of the simple biblical statement that the priest who has committed deliberate murder must be removed from his work at the altar and must be put to death, the midrashic interpretation of Exod 21:14 claims that this priest is innocent of any crime and must be removed from his work on the Temple altar (which causes the violation of Temple law necessary for the argument) in order to serve as witness for the defence at the trial of an individual who is accused of murder, so that the testimony of this priest will save the accused's life. Moreover, although it could be argued that action taken to prevent a judicial sentence of death (in this case, a punishment for the crime of murder) results in the saving of life, actions associated with acts of healing and/or saving life are more usually associated with events from an outside, usually uncontrollable, source, such as an illness or accident, or acts of war, rather than the man-made, controllable proceedings of a court of law. A situation of starvation which threatened the lives of David and his men is thus a typical example of a situation which requires action in order to heal and/or save life, but this is less likely to be said of a situation in which action must be taken by a witness who gives evidence for the defence of the accused in a capital trial. Finally, it must be noted that in contrast with the midrashic story of David which is summarised in the argument used by Jesus so that the audience of this text needs no further information, no similar summary occurs of the midrashic interpretation of Exod 21:14, which must be identified only by the term רציחה, literally 'murder' rather than the meaning given by R. Akiva, 'punishment for murder'. The term רציהה does not even appear in the biblical verse on which R. Akiva's midrash is based. The precise significance of this term in the argument is thus difficult to ascertain, and its midrashic significance is therefore probably understood only by those familiar with R. Akiva's interpretation of Exod 21:14, which is now preserved in the Babylonian Talmud (at b. Yom 85a–b, cited in Chapter 5). Unless a person was familiar with R. Akiva's midrashic interpretation of Exod 21:14, how then would he (or she) know that murder overrode Temple law? It is moreover interesting to note that the term רציחה is not used for 'murder' in the three actions which the later sages stated should never be performed, even for acts of healing and/or the saving of life— namely idolatry, sexual sins and the shedding of blood, for which the term שחיטה is used.

There is thus little doubt that the midrashic tale of David is a far more attractive and suitable text to use as the basis for the argument *kal va-chomer* or sorite featured in the gospels, compared with R. Akiva's difficult midrashic interpretation of Exod 21:14. Why then, we must ask, was it replaced with the relatively *un*attractive interpretation of Exod 21:14? It is unlikely that this was done because of a preference by the Jewish sages for proof texts from the Pentateuch, because proof texts from other sacred sources are frequently used in the rabbinic texts. It is, however, possible that the Jewish sages wished to avoid the use of an argument which had been originally composed by a Jewish sage, but had subsequently been used (one might claim that it has been taken over) in a story in the gospel texts, whose popularity can be gauged by the fact that Luke and Matthew had been forced to make probably unwanted amendments to the tale because of the genuine defects that were perceived when it originally appeared in the gospel of Mark (e.g. could the disciples have eaten raw grain?—see the discussion on the hunger of the disciples in Chapter 3). On the other hand, the Jewish sages wished to retain the basic structure of the argument which 'proved' action to solve the problem of starvation was permitted to override Sabbath law. They therefore searched the accepted holy Hebrew texts, particularly the Pentateuch, the holiest of these sources, for material which could be used in some way to illustrate the principle that acts of healing and/or saving life were permitted to override Temple law. Such a text, suitably midrashically interpreted, could then replace the midrashic story of David, while still preserving the basic structure of the original argument (because it relayed the same message of an action that overrode Temple law). On the other hand, the rabbinic argument would now differ significantly from the argument in the gospel texts.[4] One text which may have been discussed in the course of such a search was Hos 6:6, which could be interpreted to mean that 'mercy' overrode Temple law, and this may account for the citation of this verse by Matthew at Matt 12:7. Hosea 6:6 is, however, unsuitable for the argument of R. Akiva's sorite because if the statement that 'mercy overrode Temple law' was used as the first premise of a sorite based on the pattern outlined above, the final section of the sorite would end with the declaration that 'mercy overrides Sabbath law'. Such a conclusion not only fails to prove the main intention of the sorite (namely that acts of healing and/or saving life override Sabbath law), but makes little sense as it would imply that God-given Sabbath law is not merciful, which would certainly cause offence among 'the Jews' and would be totally unacceptable in Jewish thought.

Whatever texts were proposed by the Jewish sages as substitutes for the biblical verse that served as a basis for the midrashic account of David at Nob, the text finally chosen was Exod 21:14, which was midrashically interpreted by R. Akiva to prove the same basic conclusion, namely that Temple law could be overridden by an action to save life. It is clear, moreover, that R. Akiva's midrashic interpretation of Exod 21:14 is most suitable for the construction of a short circular sorite or an argument *kal va-chomer* (as it was later used by R. Yose the Galilean in *the Mekhilta de-Rabbi Shimon bar Yochai* 21.14), whereas this is not the case for his midrashic interpretation of Exod 22:1-2, which

---

4. The Mishnah records a discussion of the third-generation tannaitic sages, Rabbis Eliezer, Joshua and Akiva, concerning what could be 'greater', or could override, the Sabbath; see m. Pes. 6.2.

was also midrashically interpreted by R. Akiva and which is more suitable for use in an argument *kal va-chomer*. The midrashic story of David was thus replaced in the argument with this midrashic interpretation of Exod 21:14. As a result of this, the new argument preserved the structure of the original argument *kal va-chomer* of the Pharisees and led to the same basic conclusion, while echoes of the argument used in the gospels were now significantly reduced. This substitution was successful—it seems that until now, no one has noticed the similarity between the sorites of R. Akiva based on Exod 21:14 and Matthew's sorite in the story of Jesus in the Galilean fields. The subsequent attributions to R. Yose and R. Menasia of the sorite of R. Akiva with its substituted proof text also show that the substitution which was made originally probably by R. Akiva was accepted by the later sages. The comparatively unsuitable nature of Exod 21:14 for its role in the argument, compared with the story of David and the sacred bread, thus means that Exod 21:14 can be regarded as a kind of rabbinic compromise which was probably composed in view of the popularity in the late first century CE of the story in the gospels of Jesus and the Pharisees in the Galilean fields. This also suggests that in spite of a ban on even reading the gospels (which can be assumed from the command that 'the portions of the sacred books and the scrolls of the *minin* should not be saved from a fire but should be allowed to burn where they are', t. Shab 13.5), it seems that R. Akiva and probably others had read or at least discussed one story from these writings, namely the story of Jesus in the Galilean fields.

This understanding of the use of Exod 21:14 in the three sorites of R. Akiva and his school may help account for the complete absence of any reference to a proof text in the sorite of R. Akiva at t. Shab 15.16, the first of the four sorites cited above. Rabbinic sources usually indicate the proof text on which an argument is based, as is the case for the three other versions of the sorite associated with R. Akiva. The absence of any reference to a proof text in t. Shab 15.16 is all the more strange when we consider that it was R. Akiva, the attributed author of the sorite, who was also the author of the midrashic understanding of Exod 21:14, to which reference is made in the other sorites cited above. The missing reference to a proof text may, however, be explained on the assumption that this reference once existed, but was later removed, perhaps by R. Akiva himself or even perhaps by the editor of the Tosefta, because the sorite based on the midrashic understanding of the story of David and the sacred bread would have echoed the argument used by the synoptic authors in their Galilean tale, especially the version in Matthew's text. Some evidence that the midrashic story of David was known to R. Akiva is provided by the fact that the debate on the legality of David's act in eating the sacred bread was known to R. Shimon b. Yochai, who was one of the five famous students ('disciples') of R. Akiva, and one of only two students whom R. Akiva ordained.[5] R. Shimon b. Yochai may thus have learnt of this midrash directly from R. Akiva.

In summary therefore, it is possible that the sorite of R. Akiva at t. Shab 15.16 was originally based on a *stated* midrashic interpretation of the biblical story of David and the sacred bread, and this sorite was echoed by Matthew at Matt 12:3-5, 8. This sorite survived orally even after R. Akiva had replaced its proof text with his midrashic version of Exod 21:14, and the sorite with its new proof text also circulated among the Jewish sages. The similarity of Matthew's sorite with that of R. Akiva's original sorite was, however, noted perhaps by the editor of the Tosefta or perhaps even by R. Akiva. Whoever was responsible removed the proof text based on the story of David to avoid any kind of allusion to gospel text. In other words, the *stated* reference to the proof text in the sorite of R. Akiva was removed for the same reason that R. Akiva replaced the midrashic version of the story of David at Nob in his sorite with his midrashic version of Exod 21:14. The reference to the story of David was *not*, however, replaced by a reference to the midrashic version of Exod 21:14, perhaps because there was no allusion to this midrash in the original soritic text—it was sufficient to remove the reference that was already there.

III. *When Did the Substitution of Midrashic Stories Take Place?*

The timing of the substitution of the midrashic stories may be indicated by Josephus' account of the biblical story of David at Nob, which is translated below:

Josephus, Jewish Antiquities VI.242-43
But David, fleeing from the king [Saul] and death at his hands, now came to the city of Naba, to Abimelech the high priest, who was astonished to see him arrive alone with neither friend nor servant in attendance, and desired to know the reason why no man accompanied him. He replied

---

5. Leviticus Rabbah XXI.8, 'Simon b. Yochai went to study Torah at the school of R. Akiva at Bene Berak and stayed there for thirteen years'.

that he had been charged by the king with a secret matter for which he required no escort since he wished to remain unknown. 'Howbeit' he added, 'I have ordered my servant to join me at this place'.[6]

The above account shows that Josephus was familiar with the biblical tale of David at Nob. Thus he uses the name 'Nob', and he repeats the biblical David's claim that he was alone because he was on a secret mission from King Saul (see 1 Sam 21:2). Josephus also refers to the enquiry of the biblical priest concerning the fact that David arrived alone (1 Sam 21:1-2) and he correctly records the name of the priest Abimelech who met David at Nob. These details are absent from the midrashic tale used in the gospels. With such familiarity with the biblical tale, why then does Josephus remove the two probably most memorable features of the story in the Bible, namely the hunger of David and his consumption of the sacred bread? In addition, although Josephus claims that David was accompanied by a servant, he does not refer to the companions of David, who are mentioned twice in the biblical account (see 1 Sam 21:2, 5).[7] It is possible however that these changes were made, along with the specific reference to Nob (which removes any possibility of the midrashic assumption that David arrived at the Temple in Jerusalem) in order to ensure that even if the account of Josephus was midrashically interpreted, the story *could never be used in the argument in the gospels to claim that David and his companions illegally ate the sacred bread in the Temple of Jerusalem.* In other words, the story told by Josephus could never suggest that David and his starving companions violated Temple law in order to prevent them starving to death. Josephus has thus effectively discredited and invalidated the argument used by Jesus in the Galilean tale. He thereby has supported, albeit indirectly, the change of proof text in the sorites of R. Akiva.

IV. *A Possible Chronology for the Changes in the Argument*

The *Jewish Antiquities* was published around 93 or 94 CE, which overlaps the early public career of R. Akiva. This dating helps provide a chronology for R. Akiva's midrashic change. Thus it is possible that at an earlier time, close to, and preceding the composition of Matthew's

6.   Trans. H. St. J. Thackeray and R. Marcus, *Josephus, Jewish Antiquities, Books V–VII* (Cambridge, Mass.: Harvard University Press; London: Heinemann, 1958), 287-8.
7.   Josephus also changes the biblical role of Abimelech the priest to that of a *high* priest.

gospel, R. Akiva composed a sorite in Hebrew based on an argument *kal va-chomer* which had earlier been composed by a Jewish sage, perhaps by himself or by R. Eleazar b. Azariah (see Chapter 5). R. Akiva's sorite reused the midrashic interpretation of the biblical tale of David and the sacred bread on which the Hebrew (and later Greek) argument *kal va-chomer* was based. The sorite of R. Akiva subsequently inspired Matthew to rephrase the argument *kal va-chomer* of Mark 2:25-26, 28 (or Luke 6:3-5) as a sorite, which is now preserved at Matt 12:3-5, 8. Subsequently, attempting to avoid an echo of the argument in the gospels, R. Akiva replaced the midrashic story of David and the sacred bread in his sorite with his midrashic interpretation of Exod 21:14. Josephus learnt and approved of this change which he supported by deliberately suppressing significant details in his account of the biblical story of David and the sacred bread, so that the story could no longer be used either in the argument in the gospels or in R. Akiva's original (first) sorite. Josephus thus effectively discredited the argument used by Jesus in the gospel texts and indirectly supported R. Akiva's substitution of the story of David in the sorite with a midrashic interpretation of Exod 21:14. Finally, sometime before around 230 CE (when the Tosefta was finally edited), the reference to the proof text based on the story of David which was used in the earliest version of R. Akiva's sorite was removed from this version of the sorite, and the latter was published in this depleted form.

The following diagram summarises the proposed relationships between (a) the original argument *kal va-chomer*, composed in Hebrew by a Jewish sage, probably sometime around 70 CE, which was based on a midrashic version of 1 Sam 21:1-6; (b) the translation of this argument into Greek in the gospels of Mark and Luke; (c) the sorite of R. Akiva which rephrased the Hebrew argument; (d) the sorite of Matthew in his version of the argument of Jesus; (e) the later sorite of R. Akiva which replaced the midrashic interpretation of 1 Sam 21:1-6 with the midrashic interpretation of Exod 21:14; (f) the removal of a reference to the proof text in R. Akiva's original sorite, and the publication of the sorite without any proof text in the Tosefta:

An argument *kal va-chomer* based on a midrashic version of 1 Sam 21:1-6
was composed in Hebrew by a Jewish sage around 70 CE, close to,
but before the time that Mark's gospel was composed

⇗   ⇩

The Hebrew argument was translated into a Greek, ⇩
Christianised version and cited at Mark 2:25-26, 28 ⇩

⇩   ⇩

The Greek argument was repeated at Luke 6:3-5 ⇩

⇩   ⇩

   ⇩ R. Akiva expressed the argument based on 1 Sam 21:1-6
   ⇩ as a sorite. This was before Matthew's gospel appeared
   ⇩ ⇗ ⇩

Matthew, inspired by R. Akiva's sorite, rephrased ⇩
the argument of Mark (or Luke) as a sorite, ⇩
which is preserved at Matt 12:3-5, 8 ⇩
       ⇩

After Matthew's gospel appeared, R. Akiva substituted
the midrashic interpretation of 1 Sam 21:16 with his own midrashic
interpretation of Exod 21:14

⇩

⇩

Publication by Josephus of *The Jewish Antiquities* in 93–94 CE,
which discredited the argument used by Jesus in the gospels
by an giving an account of David at Nob that could not be used
midrashically in the argument

⇩

⇩

Around 230 CE, the proof text based on 1 Sam 21:1-6 was removed
from R. Akiva's sorite, and this sorite was published without a proof
text in the Tosefta (t. Shab 15.16)

V. *Did the Sorite of R. Akiva Inspire the Sorite of Matthew?*

It is unlikely that Matthew's sorite at Matt 12:3-5, 8 inspired the sorite of
R. Akiva at t. Shab. 15.16. This can be assumed from the dependence of
early Christianity on the texts of Judaism, especially on the Septuagint,
rather than Jewish dependence on the early Christian texts. It is also
indicated by the antagonism of the tannaitic Jewish sages to the texts of
the early Jewish followers of Jesus who, as noted above, advised that the
'portions of the books and the scrolls of the *minin* should not be saved
from a fire, from a ruin or a flood' (t. Shab 13.5). This suggests that even
if R. Akiva had heard or read the text of Matt 12:3-5, 8 (as is possible) he

would not have re-used any of the material that he found.[8] On this basis alone, it is thus more likely that the sorite of Matthew was inspired by R. Akiva, directly or indirectly, rather than the other way around.

R. Akiva was almost certainly a contemporary of Matthew, who may therefore have been directly in contact with this Jewish sage. After the destruction of the Temple in 70 CE, the future R. Akiva studied at the academy at Yavneh, and was noted as a prominent scholar by 95–96 CE.[9] R. Akiva was thus active before this time (reputations are not instantaneously achieved!), which was around the time that Matthew's gospel was composed, probably in the last quarter of the first century CE.[10] If, therefore, the sorite of R. Akiva (now cited without its proof text in the Tosefta at t. Shab 15.16) was composed early in his career, it may have provided the model which was subsequently adapted by Matthew for his version of the argument of Jesus in the story of Jesus in the Galilean fields. The ingenuity of Matthew is thus seen in the simple way that he expressed the rabbinic principle that 'Temple law overrides Sabbath law', which conforms with the stylistic informality of the rest of the argument, thus, *Or have you not read in the law how on the Sabbath the priests in the Temple violate the Sabbath, and are guiltless* (Matt 12:5).

VI. *A Comparable Reaction of the Jewish Sages*

It seems most strange that the Jewish sages should abandon the use of a proof text in one of their arguments, merely because the same proof text was re-used in a popular story in the synoptic texts. A comparable

8.   The Tosefta makes the negative attitude of the tannaitic sages to the Christian texts very clear, see t. Shab 13.5: The portions of the sacred books and the scrolls of the *minin* they do not save from a fire, but they are allowed to burn where they are. R. Yose the Galilean says, "On ordinary days, one cuts out the references to the Divine Name which are in them and stores them away, and the rest burns". Said R. Tarfon, 'May I bury my sons if such things come into my hands, and I do not burn them, and even the references to the Divine Name which are in them. And if someone was running after me, I should go into a temple of idolatry, but I should not go into their houses [of worship]. For idolaters do not recognize the Divinity in denying him, but these recognize the Divinity and deny him. And about them Scripture states, *Behind the door and the doorpost you have set up your symbol [for deserting me you have uncovered your bed]* (Isa 57:8)'. See also b. Shab 116a.

9.   For the active life of R. Akiva, see H. Freedman, 'Akiva', in *Encyclopaedia Judaica*, vol. 2 (Jerusalem: Keter, 1971), 488-92.

10.   For the date of composition of Matthew's Gospel, see W. D. Davies and D. C. Allison, *The Gospel According to Saint Matthew*, vol. 1 (Edinburgh: T. & T. Clark, 1988), 128.

precedent however exists, which also took place in tannaitic times. This is the reaction of the Jewish sages when they discontinued the recitation in the Temple of the Ten Commandments during daily Jewish prayers which, according to the Mishnah (m. Tam 5.1), was recited by the priests every morning before their recitation of the daily *Shema*. The recitation of the Ten Commandments in the daily prayers of individual Jews in tannaitic times is also suggested by the inclusion of the Ten Commandments in the Nash papyrus (from the second century BCE) and also within phylacteries from Qumran. The Jerusalem Talmud, however, relates that the practice of reading the Ten Commandments every day in the Temple—and presumably also the practice of binding the Ten Commandments into phylacteries and reciting them every day— was brought to an end because of the 'impure thought of the heretics' (טינת המינין, *tinat ha-minin*), lest they say, 'These alone were given to Moses at Sinai' (y. Ber 1.5). Similarly, the Babylonian Talmud notes that '[the recitation of the Ten Commandments was] abolished because of the murmuring of the heretics' (תרעומת המינין, *taromet ha-minin*, b. Ber 12a).[11] The cessation of the recitation of the daily prayers in the Temple must have ceased by 70 CE (when the Temple was destroyed) and the evidence from the *Antiquities* of Josephus above suggests that the substitution of proof texts in the sorites attributed to R. Akiva and his school probably took place towards the end of the first century, when, it is reasonable to assume, both those responsible for the cessation of the recitation of the commandments, or their close students, and those responsible for agreeing with the substitution of the proof text, were still alive. It is thus possible therefore that just as the action of 'heretics' (מינין) caused Judaism to decide to discontinue a traditional practice of oral law, so also the earlier followers of Jesus (perhaps the same 'heretics', who were not yet called 'Christians' according to Acts 11:26) caused the Jewish sages to discontinue their use of a proof text that had become popular in a story in the disparaged synoptic tales.[12]

11. For the discontinuation of reading the Ten Commandments in the Temple, see Urbach, *From the World of the Sages* (Jerusalem: Hebrew University, Magnes Press, 1988 [Hebrew]), 578-96, esp. 582-4, and Urbach, *The Sages: Their Concepts and Beliefs* (Cambridge, Mass.: Harvard University Press, 1987), 361.

12. The change of proof text in R. Akiva's sorite as a reaction to the use of this proof text by 'the *minin*' (t. Shab 13.3), may help to identify the people, whose remarks seem to have brought about the cessation of the daily recitation of the Ten Commandments.

VII. *When Did the Activity of R. Akiva and R. Ishmael Begin?*

Most conservative estimates suggest that R. Akiva was active by around 90 CE.[13] This dating is, however, challenged by the discussion above which suggests that the sorite of Matthew was inspired by the sorite of R. Akiva (now preserved at t. Shab 15.16), which suggests that R. Akiva was active before the publication of the gospel of Matthew. If so, R. Akiva was active before 80 CE (probably the earliest date that Matthew's gospel was composed) and thus perhaps as early as 75 CE.[14] If, however, it was R. Akiva, rather than R. Eleazar b. Azariah, who was responsible for this innovative use of the verb דחה (see Chapter 5), then R. Akiva, a younger contemporary of R. Eleazar, might also have been active before the publication of the gospel of Mark, which probably took place around 70 CE.

VIII. *Conclusions*

(1) Assuming that Mark's gospel was composed around 70 CE, an argument *kal va-chomer* was composed in Hebrew, perhaps by R. Eleazar b. Azariah or by R. Akiva, before around 70 CE. This argument was based on a midrashic interpretation of 1 Sam 21:1-6. It was translated into a Christianised Greek version and used by Mark in his midrashic story of Jesus and the Pharisees in the Galilean fields (Mark 2:25-26, 28). The argument was repeated by Luke in his version of the same tale (Luke 6:3-5).

(2) It is probable that R. Akiva rephrased the Hebrew argument *kal va-chomer* based on the midrashic interpretation of 1 Sam 21:1-6 as a sorite, still using the midrashic interpretation of 1 Sam 21:1-6.

(3) The sorite of R. Akiva inspired Matthew to replace the earlier arguments of Mark and Luke (Mark 2:25-26, 28 and Luke 6:3-5) in the story of Jesus and the Pharisees in the Galilean fields, as a sorite. This now appears at Matt 12:3-5, 8. Matthew thus re-phrased the argument *kal va-chomer* used earlier by Mark and Luke.

(4) Perhaps in reaction to the popularity in the synoptic gospel texts of the story of Jesus in the Galilean fields, which includes the argument used by Jesus in this tale, especially in the version of Matthew, R. Akiva

13. H. L. Strack and G. Stemberger, *Introduction to the Talmud and Midrash* (Edinburgh: T. & T. Clark, 1991), 76, 79.
14. L. Ginsberg, 'Akiba ben Joseph', in *The Jewish Encyclopedia*, vol. 1 (New York: Funk & Wagnalls, 1807), 304.

replaced the midrashic interpretation of 1 Sam 21:1-6 in his sorite with his midrashic interpretation of Exod 21:14.

(5) R. Akiva's original sorite based on the midrashic interpretation of 1 Sam 21:1-6 was published in the Tosefta (t. Shab 15.16), but without any midrashic proof text. In view of the problem surrounding this proof text (which can be assumed from R. Akiva's substitution by his mid-rashic interpretation of Exod 21:14) it is possible that the original proof text in the sorite of R. Akiva, which was based on the midrashic interpretation of 1 Sam 21:1-6, was deliberately removed.

(6) Sorites using and citing the midrashic proof text of R. Akiva based on Exod 21:14 are attributed directly to R. Akiva or to those from his school and are preserved in three tannaitic texts, *The Mekilta de-Rabbi Ishmael* Shab 1, *The Mekilta de-Rabbi Ishmael* Nez 4 and *The Mekhilta de-Rabbi Shimon bar Yochai* 22:2.

(7) The biblical story of David at Nob (1 Sam 21:1-6) described by Josephus (Ant VI.242-43) refers to the fact that David arrived at Nob, rather than 'the House of God', and does not include any reference to the fact that David ate the sacred bread. The account by Josephus could not, therefore, be used to claim that David overrode Temple law by eating the sacred bread in the Temple at Jerusalem. The story of David by Josephus was published in *The Jewish Antiquities*, which appeared in 93 CE.

Josephus thus discredits the argument in the gospels, because his story cannot be used to 'prove' that David overrode Temple law, as the gospel argument claims. It seems, therefore, that Josephus lent support to R. Akiva who, perhaps in an effort to destroy the argument used in the synoptic gospels, substituted the original midrashic story of David in the argument (originally perhaps composed by R. Eleazar b. Azariah, see [1] above) with his—R. Akiva's—midrashic interpretation of Exod 21:14.

The evidence of Josephus thus also suggests that the substitution of proof texts was made towards the end of the first century CE.

(8) A comparable precedent for ceasing to use a probably popular midrashic story of David and the sacred bread in an originally Jewish rhetorical *halachic* argument can be seen in the cessation of the daily recitation of the Ten Commandments in the Temple and probably also in daily private prayer. The ending of this practice is attributed in rabbinic texts to the 'impure thoughts of heretics' and their 'murmur-ings'. These 'heretics' (מינין) may possibly be identified with the readers of the gospels, that is, with the early followers of Jesus, whose enthusi-asm for the story of Jesus and the Pharisees in the Galilean fields, especially for the argument used by Jesus in this story, as recorded by

Matthew, may have led R. Akiva to change the biblical proof text in the original argument which was based on the story of David at 1 Sam 21:1-6.

(9) Assuming a close link between R. Akiva and Matthew, which may have inspired Matthew to use a sorite inspired by R. Akiva, it is possible that the public activity of R. Akiva, and perhaps also that of his contemporary R. Ishmael, was established by 75 CE, before the publication of Matthew's gospel around 80 CE. If, however, R. Akiva was also responsible for the innovative use of the verb דחה in order to refer to a secular action of healing and/or saving life, which underlies the final section of the argument used by Jesus to the Pharisees in the Galilean fields, we can then conclude that the public life of R. Akiva began around 70 CE, that is, before the publication of the gospel of Mark, in whose gospel the Greek translation of the Hebrew argument first appeared.

Chapter 7

SECOND-CENTURY INTERPRETATIONS OF BIBLICAL VERSES BASED ON PENTATEUCHAL JEWISH LAW

I. *Background to the Interpretations*

The earlier chapters of this book have shown that the Jewish sages in the first century CE justified acts of healing and/or saving life that violate Jewish law by means of arguments *kal va-chomer*, rephrased in one case as a sorite. As was discussed in Chapter 4, the earliest of these arguments are specific for their cure and could not be used to justify any other cure. These are the arguments which first appear, or which only appear, in the gospels of Mark and Luke (Mark 2:25-26, 28; Luke 13:15b-16; 14:5). In contrast, the later arguments that were composed can be used to justify any action for any cure and/or for the saving of life. These are the general arguments preserved by Matthew and John (Matt 12:11-12; John 7:23), and the arguments and special vocabulary of R. Akiva and R. Ishmael and the argument of R. Eleazar b. Azariah, discussed in Chapter 5.

The characteristic of generality in arguments *kal va-chomer* to justify acts of healing and/or saving life was (and *is*) of course clearly preferable to the specificity of the arguments composed in earlier times and only general arguments have survived from the second century CE. It seems, moreover, that no other arguments *kal va-chomer* which dealt with the problem of acts of healing and/or saving life, either specific or general, were composed after the first century CE. Apparently also abandoned was the search of the Jewish sages to find biblical incidents to serve as a basis on which future arguments could be composed. The reason for these changes is not difficult to surmise. The lack of incidents in the holy texts whose simple meaning showed that acts of healing and/or saving life were allowed to violate Jewish law (which was undoubtedly the kind of material for which the Jewish sages must originally have searched) meant that the biblical verses that were eventually found and which were finally used could not be employed without extensive midrashic modifi-cations, which could completely change the simple meaning of the biblical

288

text. Of all the biblical incidents used in the first century CE, only R. Akiva's interpretation of Exod 22:1-2 managed to keep closely to the original meaning of the text. In contrast, the incident described at 1 Sam 21:1-6 was distorted by making the midrashic David a violator of Temple law, which was a complete reversal of his behaviour in the biblical account, and also by placing him in the Temple in Jerusalem, which did not exist while the historical David was alive. Similarly distorting was the midrashic account of the conduct of the priest who had deliberately committed murder in Exod 21:14, who was now midrashically exonerated and transformed into an innocent witness who witnessed in the defence of a person on a capital charge. Subsequently, moreover, it was necessary to incorporate each of these distorted midrashic interpretations into a sophisticated rhetorical argument—a rabbinic argument *kal va-chomer*— which was undoubtedly understood by the Jewish sages themselves, but was probably less easy to grasp by ordinary Jewish people, who could not have been familiar with such rhetorical speech. The opposition of ordinary Jewish people to at least four of Jesus' Sabbath cures shows, however, that it was especially these ordinary people who needed to be convinced that acts of healing and/or saving life should always be performed on the Sabbath day (see Chapter 4).

It is therefore no surprise that the Jewish sources have not preserved any evidence from the second century CE that any other biblical incidents were used to prove the legality of healing on the Sabbath day and it seems that no further arguments *kal va-chomer* were composed after the first century CE.[1] Instead, the second-century Jewish sages tried

---

1. An argument *kal va-chomer* that *might* also have been used in tannaitic times to justify the violation of Jewish law to heal and/or save life in the specific situation of starvation but which has not survived is hinted in two tannaitic directives which both cite a biblical phrase found only at 1 Sam 14:24-45, namely, 'his eyes were enlightened', ותארנה עיניו (1 Sam 14:27, 29; see m. Yom 8.6 and t. Yom 4.4). This text describes how Jonathan (a son of King Saul) saved his own life from starvation by violating a command of the king, and thus, in effect, violated his own oath. (For the importance in Judaism of keeping an oath, see, e.g., Deut 6:13-14 and 10:20.) Unlike the story of David at Nob (1 Sam 21:1-6), the story of Jonathan needs only the minimum midrashic manipulation to show that Jonathan violated holy law. Thus on the assumption that the keeping of an oath was considered less important ('lighter') than keeping Sabbath law, it could be argued: If life can be saved from starvation by breaking an oath (a relatively 'light' violation of Jewish law) then surely (*kal va-chomer*) life can also be saved from starvation by violating Sabbath law (a relatively 'heavy' violation of Sabbath law)!

It is, however, strange that in view of the undoubted search of the Jewish sages, at least from after around 167 BCE, to find incidents in the holy texts that could be used to justify acts of healing and/or the saving of life that violated Jewish law, the

a different approach. Those who were interested in finding a solution to the problem of healing and/or saving life within Jewish law abandoned their search for suitable biblical events on which arguments could be based, and turned instead to texts in the holy writings concerned with Jewish law, especially those which could be interpreted in a simple way. This was surely logical because the basic aim of their quest was concerned with the subject of Jewish law. Their approach was successful. As will be seen from the discussion below, four named Jewish sages from the second century CE 'discovered' four biblical, Pentateuchal texts, each basically concerned with Jewish law, which could be interpreted in a simple and memorable way to yield the message for which the Jewish sages had sought, namely that the Jewish God indeed intended that His people should perform acts of healing and/or saving life even at the cost of violating His law. There is little doubt that these interpretations were easily understood by ordinary Jews. The texts that they found and the interpretations that they proposed will now be discussed.

II. *Exodus 31:13: The Interpretation of R. Yose the Galilean*

The following midrashic interpretation of Exod 31:13 is attributed in the *Mekilta de-Rabbi Ishmael* to R. Yose the Galilean, a younger pupil and subsequently a colleague of R. Akiva, who was active between the years 110 and 135 CE:

only two stories in the Hebrew Bible which perhaps best illustrate this principle were apparently never used. One is the story of the siege of Jericho, which continued for seven days (Josh 6:15), and the other is the story of the Jewish Queen Esther, who, against all Jewish tradition, married a gentile (Est 2:2-9; for the Jewish tradition against marrying with gentiles, see, e.g., Gen 26:34-35; Ezra 10:3, 10-12) and thereby saved the lives of her people by thwarting an order for their genocide which was ultimately sanctioned by her gentile husband, the king (although this could not have been known when she married the king). The non-use of this story in an argument to prove the paradoxical legality of violating Jewish law in cases of healing and/or saving life, can however be explained if the book of Esther was added to the canon only *after* the first century (see b. Meg 7a and b. Shab 14a), that is, it was added in the second century CE, by which time it seems that the Jewish sages had abandoned the search to find incidents in the then-agreed holy texts that could be used to illustrate the principle that acts of healing and/or saving life permitted a violation of Jewish law. In other words, the non-use of the story of Esther in arguments to justify healing and/or saving life at the expense of Jewish law suggests that the book of Esther was not considered as a holy text by the first-century sages and thus the story was not considered suitable as the basis of an argument *kal va-chomer* which proved that acts of healing and/or saving life are permitted to violate Jewish law. But why the story of Joshua was not used for this purpose remains to be explained.

מכילתא דרבי ישמעאל כי תשא—מס' דשבתא פרשה א
רבי יוסי הגלילי אומר, כשהוא אומר, אך את שבתותי תשמורו, אך חלק, ויש
שבתות שאתה דוחה, ויש שבתות שאתה שובת.

Mekilta de-Rabbi Ishmael Shabbatta 1

R. Yose the Galilean says: When it says *But* (אך) *My Sabbaths you shall keep* (Exod 31:13) [the word] 'but' implies a distinction [between some Sabbaths and other Sabbaths]. [It means] there are some Sabbaths that you should override [= heal and/or save life] and other Sabbaths on which you should rest [that is, you must cease from work, if it is not necessary to 'work' on these Sabbaths by healing and/or saving life].[2]

This interpretation is inspired by the rabbinic belief that the Torah is perfect, because it records the words of God, so that any apparent blemish, such as a repetition or a seemingly superfluous term, must be further interpreted, even if this understanding goes beyond the simple meaning of the text. It is moreover the duty of the Jewish sages to reveal this understanding, which can then be added to the body of Jewish oral law.[3] Using one of the methods of exegesis attributed to his older contemporary and colleague R. Akiva, R. Yose the Galilean thus claims that the particle 'but' (אך) in Exod 31:13 is superfluous to the sense of the sentence, and that this superfluity indicates that some Sabbaths should be excluded from the general rule that forbids any work on the Sabbath day. As a result, according to R. Yose, acts of healing and/or saving of life are permitted to take place on the Sabbath day.

It is evident that this interpretation of a biblical text, although contrived, is far more accessible and easy to understand than any of the complex rhetorical arguments from the first century CE. Moreover, unlike any of the arguments in the gospels of Mark and Luke, it does not define or limit in any way the situation which necessitates action of

---

2. Lauterbach, *Mekilta*, 3:198. The same interpretation is attributed simply to 'R. Yose' at t. Shab 15.16, which was discussed in Chapter 5. The Babylonian Talmud also attributes this interpretation of Exod 31:13 to R. Yose the son of R. Judah, a late second-century tannaitic sage (b. Yom 85b), and the Jerusalem Talmud attributes it to the third-century amoraic sage R. Yohanan (y. Yom 8.5). The preservation of this interpretation in two tannaitic texts—the *Mekhilta de-Rabbi Ishmael* and the Tosefta—however, suggests that it is a tannaitic composition, and is probably correctly attributed to the second-century R. Yose the Galilean.

3. The claim that perceived superfluous words in the Torah bring an added significance to the text is attributed to R. Ishmael; see H. L. Strack and G. Stemberger, *Introduction to the Talmud and Midrash* (Edinburgh: T. & T. Clark, 1991) 270, citing David Hoffmann, *Zur Einleitung in die halachischen Midraschim* (Berlin: M. Driesner, 1887). For the exegetical methods of R. Akiva, see Kahana, 'The Halakhic Midrashim', 17-26.

healing and/or saving life, for which this argument might be used. In other words, it is a *general* directive which could be used to justify *any* action in *any* situation that requires an act of healing and/or saving life.

III. *Exodus 31:16: The Interpretation of R. Nathan the Babylonian*

The earliest Jewish sage who is attributed with the following interpretation of Exod 31:16 is R. Nathan, a contemporary of R. Yose the Galilean (who was probably responsible for the interpretation of Exod 31:13, see above), who was active between the years 110 and 135 CE:

מכילתא דרבי ישמעאל כי תשא—מס' דשבתא פרשה א ד.ה פרשת כי

רבי נתן אומר, הרי הוא אומר, ושמרו בני ישראל את השבת לעשות את השבת
לדורותם, חלל עליו שבת אחת, כדי שישמור שבתות הרבה.

Mekilta de-Rabbi Ishmael Shabbatta 1

R. Nathan says, 'Behold it [= Scripture] says, *And the children of Israel will keep the Sabbath to observe the Sabbath throughout their generations* (Exod 31:16). [This implies that] we should violate one Sabbath for the sake of [saving the life of] a person so that he will observe many Sabbaths [in the future].'[4]

This interpretation by R. Nathan extends the meaning of the biblical verse in a quasi-logical way—if the children of Israel must always keep and observe Sabbath law, as is commanded at Exod 31:16, then, according to the understanding of this verse by R. Nathan, they must heal and/or save life on one Sabbath, so that they will continue to be alive and thus be able to keep and observe all future Sabbath days.

This same interpretation of Exod 31:14 is attributed in the Babylonian Talmud to the tannaitic sage R. Simon b. Menasia, who was active in the late second century, 170–200 CE:

תלמוד בבלי מסכת יומא דף פה עמוד ב

רבי שמעון בן מנסיא אומר: +שמות לא+ ושמרו בני ישראל את השבת, אמרה
תורה: חלל עליו שבת אחת, כדי שישמור שבתות הרבה.

Babylonian Talmud Yoma 85b

R. Simon b. Menasia said: *And the children of Israel shall keep the Sabbath* (Exod 31:14). [This means that] the Torah said: [This implies that] we should violate one Sabbath for the sake of [saving the life of] a person so that he will observe many Sabbaths [in the future].

---

4.   Lauterbach, *Mekilta*, 3:198–200. See also b. Yom 84b, which also cites this interpretation of Exod 31:13, but without any reference to R. Nathan or to the biblical verse on which it is based.

The attribution of this interpretation to R. Nathan in a tannaitic text, compared with its attribution to R. Menasia in a later amoraic work, however, suggests that the former attribution is probably correct. This may be confirmed by the allusion to R. Nathan's interpretation of Exod 31:16 in the Tosefta, which follows a directive on the necessity to provide warm water for a sick person on the Sabbath, in spite of the fact that such action causes a violation of Sabbath law:

תוספתא מסכת שבת פרק טו הלכה טו

מחמין חמין לחולה בשבת בין להשקותו בין לרפאותו. ואין אומ' המתינו לו שמא
יחיה.

אלא ספיקו דוחה את השבת ולא ספק שבת זו אלא ספק שבת אחרת ...

Tosefta Shabbat 15.15
They heat water for a sick person on the Sabbath, whether to give him to drink or to heal him with it. And they do not say, Wait on him, perhaps he will live [without any action that violates Sabbath law].
But a matter of doubt concerning him overrides [the prohibitions of] the Sabbath.
And the doubt need not be about this Sabbath, but it may be about another Sabbath...

Although lacking both an attribution and proof text, this allusion to R. Nathan's interpretation of Exod 31:16 helps to confirms that his understanding of the verse was composed in tannaitic times. It is also clear that, like the interpretation of Exod 31:13 by R. Yose the Galilean (discussed above), the understanding of Exod 31:16 also provides a general rule that justifies *any* action on the Sabbath in *any* situation of healing and/or saving life.

R. Nathan is also credited with the interpretation of the biblical verse Ps 119:126, *It is time to work for the Lord; they have made void Your Law*, which he understood as an indication for the legal suspension of Jewish law:

משנה מסכת ברכות פרק ט משנה ה

ואומר עת לעשות לה' הפרו תורתך (תהלים קיט). ר' נתן אומר הפרו תורתך עת
לעשות לה'.

Mishnah Berachoth 9.5
And it says [in Scripture], *it is a time to work for the Lords; they have made void Thy Law* (Ps 119:126). R. Nathan says, '[This means that] they have made void Thy Law because it was a time to work for the Lord'.

According this understanding of Ps 119:126, it may sometimes be right to set aside God-given law, in order that God may best be served. This may seem an excellent justification for the permitted violation of Jewish law by acts of healing and/or saving life, and the fact that it is never used for this purpose in any Jewish text remains unexplained.

IV. *Exodus 31:14: The Interpretation of R. Simon b. Menasia*

The following midrashic interpretation of Exod 31:14 in the *Mekilta de-Rabbi Ishmael* is attributed to R. Simon b. Menasia, a tannaitic sage who was active between the years 170 and 200 CE:

מכילתא דרבי ישמעאל כי תשא—מס' דשבתא פרשה א

רבי שמעון בן מנסיא אומר, הרי הוא אומר, ושמרתם את השבת כי קדש היא
לכם. לכם שבת מסורה, ואי אתם מסורין לשבת. ...
ושמרתם את השבת. זה הוא שהיה ר' שמעון בן מנסיא אומר, לכם שבת
מסורה, ואי אתם מסורין לשבת.

Mekilta de-Rabbi Ishmael Shabbatta 1

R. Simon b. Menasia says: Behold it says *And you [= the children of Israel] shall keep the Sabbath for it is holy to you* (לכם) (Exod 31:14). [The superfluous term] 'to-you' (לכם) [is present in the biblical text in order to show that] the Sabbath is handed down 'to you', that is, the Sabbath is handed down to the children of Israel, and you—the children of Israel—are not handed down to the Sabbath [so that *you*, the children of Israel, can decide if it is necessary on the Sabbath to violate holy law in order to heal and/or save life]. ...

And you shall keep the Sabbath for it is holy unto you...

This is [the verse which] R. Simon the son of Menasia interpreted as saying, 'The Sabbath is handed down to you [so that you are now in charge of it], but you are not handed down to the Sabbath [so that the Sabbath is not in charge of you]'.[5]

Like the interpretation of Exod 31:13 by R. Yose (discussed above), this interpretation is also inspired by the rabbinic belief that the Torah is perfect because it records the words of God, so that any apparent imperfection—in this case a repetition—must be assumed to convey an added significance to the text which goes beyond the simple meaning of the words and which must be revealed by the Jewish sages to add to the body of Jewish oral law. In the case of Exod 31:14, R. Menasia notes a repetition of the term 'you'. The first 'you' is the subject of the verb 'keep' (שמרתם—'you' is indicated by the suffix of the verb תם-) and, according to R. Menasia, refers to the children of Israel, that is, it refers

5. Lauterbach, *Mekilta*, 3:198, 199.

to the Jewish people (as can be assumed from the simple meaning of the text). The second 'you' (in the term לכם, 'to-you', 'you' is indicated by the suffix כם-) cannot therefore refer simply to the Jewish people (because this would mean that God repeated himself), but has a further, deeper significance. In this case (claims R. Menasia) the second 'you' refers to the fact that the Sabbath has been given to the children of Israel (that is, 'given to *you*, the Jewish people'), rather than that the Children of Israel have been given to the Sabbath. The Jewish people, who are the children of Israel, are therefore guardians of the Sabbath (which they have been given), and thus may behave on the Sabbath as they wish, which means in this case by allowing the performance of deeds of healing and/or saving life.

It is clear that, just as the interpretations discussed above, this interpretation of Exod 31:14 is again simple to understand, and justifies *any* action in *any* situation of healing and/or danger to life.

The Babylonian Talmud links the same interpretation with R. Jonathan b. Joseph, a tannaitic sage who flourished around 135 to 170 CE, in the generation before R. Menasia:

תלמוד בבלי מסכת יומא דף פה עמוד א״ב

נשאלה שאלה זו בפניהם, מניין לפקוח נפש שדוחה את השבת? ...
רבי יונתן בן יוסף אומר, "כי קדש היא לכם—היא מסורה בידכם, ולא אתם
מסורים בידה".

Babylonian Talmud Yoma 85a-b
The question was asked, 'From where [in holy text] do we know that danger to life overrides Sabbath law?'…
R. Jonathan b. Joseph said, 'For it is holy *to you* … (Exod 31:14). [That is] it (= the Sabbath) is passed down into your charge (יד, literally, "hand") and not you into its [that is, the Sabbath's] charge [that is, "the hand of the Sabbath").'

In this version of the interpretation, the term 'hand' (יד) serves as a synonym for the two references to 'you' in Exod 31:14. This echoes the frequent biblical use of the singular term יד meaning 'power' or 'ownership', and thus, like the interpretation attributed to R. Menasia, also conveys the thought that the laws of the Sabbath are in the 'power' or 'charge' of the Jewish people, rather than the reverse.[6] The fact that the comment of R. Jonathan is preserved in an amoraic, rather than in an earlier tannaitic text (as is the case for the remark of the tannaitic sage R. Menasia), however, suggests that R. Menasia, rather than R. Jonathan b. Joseph, should probably rightly be credited with the interpretation of this verse.

6. BDB, s.v. יד, 5.

V. *Leviticus 18:5: The Interpretation of Samuel of Nehardea*

At Lev 18:5, God instructs the Jewish people *You shall therefore keep my statutes, and my judgments; which if a man does, he shall live in them...* This is clearly a command to follow the laws of the Jewish God, as is confirmed in the ancient interpretations at Ezek 20:11 and Neh 9:29. However, an unattributed interpretation of this verse in the Tosefta claims that the phrase 'to live by them' indicates that the Jewish God has commanded His people to perform any acts of healing and/or the saving of life at any time, and in spite of any violation of this law, in order that they should stay alive and will thus be able to continue to obey His law:

תוספתא מסכת שבת פרק טו הלכה יז

הא לא נתנו מצות לישראל אלא לחיות בהן, שנ' אשר יעשה אותם האדם וחי בהם. וחי בהן ולא שימות בהן.

Tosefta Shabbat 15.17
Behold, were not the religious requirements given to Israel so that they may live by them, since it says, w*hich a man will do and live by them* (Lev 18:5). [This means] he will *live* by them and he will *not die* by them.[7]

The Babylonian Talmud attributes this interpretation of Lev 18:5 to R. Ishmael:

Babylonian Talmud Avodah Zarah 27b
R. Ishmael used to say: Whence can we deduce that if a man was commanded, 'Worship the idol and thou wilt not be killed', that he may worship it so as not to be killed? Because Scripture says, *He shall live by them* (Lev 18:5)—[this means] that he will not die by them (ולא שימות בהם)!

However, according to R. Judah, a Babylonian amora from the second half of the third century, this understanding of Lev 18.5 should be attributed to Samuel, probably Samuel of Nehardea (also known simply as Samuel, or Samuel bar Abba or Samuel Yarchinah, who is frequently cited by R. Judah) who was born towards the end of the tannaitic era around 165 CE and died around 257 CE:

---

7. A different tannaitic interpretation of Lev 18:5 is attributed to R. Simeon, probably R. Shimon b. Yochai (135–170), who claimed that this verse refers to the fact that a person is rewarded for *not* committing a transgression, including *no* transgression of Jewish law (m. Makk 3.15). The same interpretation is attributed to R. Ishmael in the Jerusalem Talmud (y. AZ 2.2), but does not appear in the earlier tannaitic account of the story to which R. Ishmael refers (see t. Hull 2.22).

תלמוד בבלי מסכת יומא דף פה עמוד ב
אמר רב יהודה אמר שמואל: אי הואי התם הוה אמינא: דידי עדיפא מדידהו,
+ויקרא יח+ וחי בהם—ולא שימות בהם. אמר רבא: לכולהו אית להו פירכא,
בר מדשמואל דלית ליה פרכא.

Babylonian Talmud Yoma 85b
R. Judah said in the name of Samuel, 'If I had been there, I should have
told them something better than what they said. [I would have cited the
text] *You shall therefore keep my statutes, and my judgments; which if a
man does, he shall live in them* (Lev 18:5). [This means] he shall live by
them, but he shall not die because of them!' Raba said: [The exposition]
of all of them [that is, all the arguments to justify the violation of Jewish
law by acts of healing and/or saving life] could be refuted, except that of
Samuel, which cannot be refuted.

The fact that the tannaitic sage R. Ishmael is never credited with this
understanding in a tannaitic text, although (confusingly) the interpretation itself appears first in the Tosefta (which is a tannaitic text), where it
is *not* attributed to any sage, suggests that it should *not* be attributed to
R. Ishmael, but was indeed composed by Samuel of Nehardea, as the
Talmud claims. It is, however, clear that this understanding of the verse
is not linked to anyone earlier than R. Ishmael. This conforms with the
dating of the three other second-century interpretations discussed above—
they are all products of the second century CE. Like these other interpretations, this interpretation of Lev 18:5 also implies the basic principle
that *any* action is permitted in *any* situation of healing and/or danger
to life to violate Sabbath law. In other words, like the three other interpretations discussed above, this interpretation of Lev 18:5 is a *general*
justification for acts of healing and/or saving life that violated Jewish
law. It is clear moreover that none of these arguments emerged before
the second century CE.[8]

The technique of interpretation used for this understanding of Lev
18:5 which assumes that if a text does not state a particular exclusion,
this exclusion may be assumed, goes back at least to the turn of the
millennium, to Shammai the Elder who assumed that because Deut
20:19-20 does not exclude the Sabbath, the permit granted in this biblical
text can be extended to the Sabbath (see Chapters 1 and 11). This
technique is also evident in R. Akiva's interpretation of Exod 22:1-2
(see Chapter 5).

8. In the personal experience of the author of this book, whenever Jewish
religious leaders are asked how they justify acts of healing and/or saving life that
violate Jewish law, they cite only Lev 18:5, often together with the phrase פיקוח נפש,
the expression associated with R. Ishmael, although used in an argument *kal
va-chomer* that was probably composed by R. Akiva.

VI. *Further Evidence for the Second-Century Date of Composition of Mark 2:27*

The four interpretations discussed above which justify acts of healing and/or saving life on the Sabbath are based on biblical statements concerned with Jewish law, rather than on specific biblical incidents, or laws based on such incidents, as was the case for arguments *kal va-chomer* composed in the first century CE. Moreover, unlike the earlier arguments, these interpretations do not require an extensive midrashic interpretation of the biblical verses on which they are based. They are thus free of the rhetorical complexity of the earlier arguments composed in the first century CE. As a result, they are easier to understand, to remember and to recite. Most importantly, unlike the specific arguments that are first preserved, or only preserved in the gospels of Mark and Luke which justify actions of healing and/or saving life only in specific situations, the second-century interpretations of biblical legal texts can be used to justify *any* action in *any* situation of healing and/or saving life that violates Jewish law.

This last observation adds further confirmation to the conclusion that the comment recorded at Mark 2:27 could not have been composed in the first half of the first century while Jesus was alive. For it is clear, even out of context, and however it is translated and understood, that unlike the arguments that are first recorded, or only in the gospels of Mark and Luke, which are specific for the situations with which each of them deals (Mark 2:23-26, 28 justifies the 'cure' of hunger, Luke 13:15b-16 justifies the cure of a woman with a bent back and Luke 14:5 justifies the cure of dropsy), Mark 2:27 provides a general comment that justifies any act in any situation of healing and/or saving life, thus *The Sabbath was made for man and not man for the Sabbath* (see the discussion on R. Simon b. Menasia's interpretation of Exod 31:14 above). Mark 2:27 therefore shares the characteristic of generality which is typical of the arguments that were composed only *after* the second half of the first century and in the second century CE. Even if it was not possible to link Mark 2:27 specifically with R. Menasia, the fact that this verse is phrased in this *general* way is thus evidence enough to show that it was unlikely to have been composed before the second half of the first century CE, and was probably composed in the second century CE. This characteristic of Mark 2:27 may therefore be added to the reasons discussed in Chapter 3 which indicate that Mark 2:27 is a later addition to Mark's text, namely: (1) the similarity of the thought and structure of Mark 2:27 with the interpretation of Exod 31:14 by R. Menasia, even though they are now preserved in two different languages; (2) the disruption of the logic of the argument *kal va-chomer* articulated at Mark 2:25-26, 28; (3) the curious and unique use of the term ἐγένετο in Mark 2:27, which can only be explained as an attempt to provide a translation equivalent of the Hebrew verb מסר, 'to transmit', the verb used in R. Menasia's interpretation of Exod 31:14 to refer to the transmission through the generations of Jewish oral law, but is unsuitable for the context in which Mark 2:27was placed; (4) the fact that Mark 2:27 appears only in Mark but is absent from the other gospels; and (5) the absence of Mark 2:27 from the 'western' family of manuscripts of Mark.

The cumulative evidence thus suggests that Mark 2:27 is a fairly accurate translation from Hebrew into Greek of the interpretation of Exod 31:13 by the late second-century Jewish sage R. Menasia, and thus was originally composed over a century after Mark's gospel appeared. It was therefore interpolated into Mark's gospel no earlier than the late second century CE. This fact should be made clear to readers of Mark's text who surely expect to read the words of Mark, rather than the interpolated comment of a second-century Jewish sage.

VII. *Conclusions*

(1) The second-century Jewish sages ceased to use arguments *kal va-chomer* to justify acts of healing and/or the saving of life and also—it seems—abandoned their efforts to find incidents in the holy Jewish texts on which these or any other type of arguments for healing and/or saving life could be based.

(2) Instead, they 'discovered' four passages from the Pentateuch, the holiest of the religious Jewish texts which dealt with Jewish law, which could each be interpreted in a relatively simple and memorable way to prove—to the satisfaction of the Jewish sages—that *any* action could be performed in *any* situation in order to heal and/or save life. Thus, R. Yose the Galilean 'discovered' Exod 31:13, R. Nathan 'discovered' Exod 31:16, R. Simon b. Menasia 'discovered' Exod 31:14 and probably Samuel of Nehardea 'discovered' Lev 18:5.

(3) The interpretation of these biblical texts continued the trend which began in the second half of the first century for *general* (rather than *specific*) arguments that justified *any* act in *any* situation of healing and/or saving life that violated Jewish law.

(4) The Greek text of Mark 2:27, when removed from the argument *kal va-chomer* in which it now lies, is a close literal translation of the Hebrew text of R. Menasia's interpretation of Exod 31:14, which

provides a general justification for acts of healing and/or saving life. It is thus clear that this justification depends on an understanding of Exod 31:14, which provides its *raison d'être*. For obvious reasons, however, Exod 31:14 could not be repeated in Mark's gospel text, and the lack of such a basis is further proof that R. Menasia's interpretation has been interpolated into Mark's text. The generality of the tone of Mark 2:27 also means that it is unlikely that this comment was composed before the second half of the first century CE, which is a further reason that Mark 2:27 could never have been composed or voiced by the historical Jesus, who died before such general arguments were composed.

Chapter 8

TWO SYMBOLIC SEALS OF APPROVAL FROM THE AMORAIM

This chapter will discuss how the amoraic sages of the Talmud show that they accepted the policy and proofs of their tannaitic predecessors concerning the necessity always to perform acts of healing and/or saving life. Thus in addition to the many specific situations that they discuss and permit, the latter often without any reference to any of the proofs 'discovered' by the tannaim, the amoraic sages make their approval known by an amendment that they added to the basic principle of the necessity always to heal and/or save life, and by their extended use of the term *sakanah* (סכנה). These two more indirect, but very positive, signs of their approval will now be discussed.

I. *A Legal Amendment to the Basic Policy of the Amoraim*

In any civilised society amendments may be added to an earlier estab-lished law. These amendments often deal with aspects of a law that were not anticipated when a given law was first accepted or passed. In general, therefore, the existence of a later amendment shows the original accep-tance by a society of the law or custom to which the amendment is attached. The amoraic Jewish sages thus show their approval for the necessity to perform deeds of healing and/or saving life, even at the cost of a violation of Jewish law, by an amendment that they added to this basic rule—in effect, a kind of legal rider—which prohibits any actions of healing and/or saving life if it is necessary to perform acts of idolatry or sexual sins or the shedding of blood. As can be seen in the text below, the initiative for this addition is attributed to R. Simeon b. Yehozadak, an amoraic sage who was active between 250 and 220 CE:

301

תלמוד ירושלמי מסכת שביעית פרק ד הלכה ב=תלמוד בבלי מסכת סנהדרין דף
עד עמוד א
א'ר זעירא רבי יוחנן בשם רבי ינאי ר' ירמיה רבי יוחנן בשם ר' שמעון בן יוצדק
בלוד, על כל התורה מניי' אם יאמר גוי לישראל לעבור ¹נמנו בעליית בית לבזה
על אחת מכל מצות האמורות בתורה חוץ מן העבודה זרה וגילוי עריות ושפיכות
דמים יעבור ולא ייהרג.

Jerusalem Talmud Sheviit 4.2 = Babylonian Talmud Sanhedrin 74a
Did not R. Zeira and R. Yohanan in the name of R. Yannai, R. Jeremiah,
R. Yohanan in the name of R. Simeon b. Yehozadak, say, 'They took a
vote in the upper room of the house of Nithzah in Lod [which concluded
that] in the case of all the commandments of the Torah if a non-Jew says
to an Israelite to violate one of all the commandments that are stated in
the Torah except for idolatry, sexual sins and the shedding of blood, one
should violate the commandment and not be put to death'.[2]

If the attribution is correct, it seems that the three totally prohibited
offences—idolatry, sexual sins and the shedding of blood—were first
linked with deeds of healing and/or the saving of life in amoraic times,
sometime around 250 CE. Some confirmation that this remark is *not* a
product of tannaitic times may be found in the following text from the
Babylonian Talmud in which the amendment is not cited by the second-
century tannaitic Jewish sage R. Meir (who was active between 135 and
170 CE). However, the amendment appears in the paraphrase of his
words by the amora Raba (who was active around 270 to 350 CE), who
thus supplies what R. Meir might have said, had the amendment been
framed in his time:

תלמוד בבלי מסכת כתובות דף יט עמוד א
אמר רב חסדא, קסבר ר'מ: עדים, שאמרו להם חתמו שקר ואל תהרגו—יהרגו
ואל יחתמו שקר. אמר ליה רבא: השתא אילו אתו לקמן לאמלוכי, אמרינן להו:
זילו חתומו ולא תתקטלון, דאמר מר: אין לך דבר שעומד בפני פיקוח נפש אלא
עבודת כוכבים וגלוי עריות ושפיכות דמים בלבד.

Babylonian Talmud Ketubot 19a
Said R. Hisda [who was active around 250 to 320 CE], 'R. Meir is of the
opinion that if one said to witnesses, "Sign a falsehood and you will not
be killed", they should rather be killed and not sign a falsehood'. Raba
said to him, 'Now, if they would come to us to ask [our] advice, we

---

1.   The Responsa Project of Bar Ilan, Version 18 at y. San 3.5 reads נתזה, which
is the usually accepted name of the owner of the upper chamber where this discussion took place.
2.   The same amendment to the basic acceptance of the necessity always to
perform acts of healing and/or saving life is also preserved in the Jerusalem Talmud
at y. Shab 14.4; y. San 3.5 and y. AZ 2.2 and in the Babylonian Talmud at b. Yom
82a-b; b. Ket 19a and b. Pes 25a (although 'murder' is not mentioned in this latter
text).

would say unto them, Go [and] sign and do not be killed, for a Master said, "There is nothing that comes before the saving of life except idolatry, sexual sins and the shedding of blood"'.

If then the link between acts of healing and/or saving life and the three prohibited offences can be attributed to the amora R. Simeon b. Yehozadak, this suggests that, just as the definition of the phrase פיקוח נפש in the Tosefta at t. Shab 9.22 (discussed in Chapter 5), the following declaration of this principle is also an amoraic addition to the toseftan text:

תוספתא מסכת שבת פרק טו הלכה יז

אין כל דבר עומד בפני פקוח נפש חוץ מע"ז, וגלוי עריות ושפיכות דמים.

Tosefta Shabbat 15.17

Nothing prevents action for healing and/or the saving of life, except for idolatry, forbidden sexual sins and the shedding of blood.[3]

The popularity of the above directive, with its implied re-affirmation of the basic principle that acts of healing and/or saving life must always otherwise take place, can be seen in the fifteen or so times that it is repeated in different ways in the amoraic texts.[4] The three prohibited actions are in fact three of the seven Noahide laws first listed in the Tosefta, which, according to Jewish thought, are incumbent on every civilised society to adopt.[5]

II. *The Extended Amoraic Use of the Tannaitic Term* סכנה *(sakanah), 'Danger'*

A second revealing indication of the acceptance by the amoraim that acts of healing and/or saving life that violate Jewish law must always be performed can be seen in their ubiquitous use of the term סכנה (*sakanah*), 'danger'. In amoraic texts (although *not* in tannaitic texts) this term refers to *any* situation of healing and/or saving life, *whether or not* the action that must be taken causes a violation of Jewish law. For example, in the following passage, the amora R. Joshua b. Levi uses the term סכנה to refer to the fact that all illnesses must be treated on the Sabbath day:

---

3. It is a matter for speculation why the same basic statement at t. Shab 9.22, which is also probably amoraic (see Chapter 5), has no reference to the three exemptions of idolatry, sexual sins and the shedding of blood.

4. y. Shiv 4.2; y. Shab 14.4; y. San 3.5; y. AZ 2.2; 3.5, אל יירהג for שפיכות דמים, b. Pes 25a; b. Yom 82a; b. Gitt 6a; b. Ket 19a, לא תתקטלון, b. San 56a; 57a; 74a, אל תהרג, Kallah Rabbati 5.1.

5. The seven Noahide laws (thirty according to y. AZ 2.1) are listed at t. AZ 8.4, and discussed at b. San 56a.

תלמוד ירושלמי מסכת ברכות פרק ד דף ח טור ב /ה'ד
רבי חנינא בריה דרבי אבהו רבי שמעון בר אבא בשם רבי יהושע בן לוי כל
החולי בחזקת הסכנה.

Jerusalem Talmud Berachoth 4.4
R. Haninah b. R. Abbahu, R. Simeon b. Abba in the name of R. Joshua b.
Levi, '*All* illnesses imply (the) danger (הסכנה)'.

Similarly, R. Mana, probably a fifth-century amora, uses the term סכנה
to stress that *all* illnesses, *even those that are apparently not serious*,
must be considered as a danger to life, and thus must always be treated
on the Sabbath day:

תלמוד ירושלמי מסכת סוכה פרק ב דף נג טור א /ה'ה
אמר רבי מנא לא סוף דבר חולין של סכנה אלא אפילו חולין שאינן של סכנה.

Jerusalem Talmud Sukkah 2.5
Said R. Mana, 'It is not the end of the matter [for deciding who is allowed
to stay outside a *sukkah*] that those who are sick and in danger (סכנה) [of
their lives are exempt from the requirements of the *sukkah*]. But even
those who are sick and [apparently] not [also incurring] danger (סכנה) [of
their lives are exempt].'

Likewise, the following text from the Jerusalem Talmud uses the term
סכנה in relation to several illnesses in order to imply that they may cause
a danger to life and must therefore be treated on the Sabbath despite an
inevitable violation of Sabbath law:

תלמוד ירושלמי מסכת עבודה זרה פרק ב הלכה ב
תמן אמרין בשם רבי יוחנן גבות ידים ורגלים סכנה. רבי אבהו בשם יוחנן אהן
סומקא סכנה... רבי אבין לוקטין לו עוקץ עקרב בשבת... רבנן דקיסרי אמרי
הדא עורדענא סכנה. רבי חזקיה אמר בשם רבנין דקיסרין הדא עכשבוניתא
סכנה. רבי שמואל בר רב יצחק הדא גומרתא סכנה... רבי אבהו בשם רבי יוחנן
אהן צפדונא סכנתא... תלת שמע מינה אהן צופדנה סכנה.

Jerusalem Talmud Avodah Zarah 2.2
There [in Babylon] they say in the name of R. Yohanan, '[Any injuries]
to hands and feet are a danger (סכנה) [to life]'. R. Abbahu [said] in the
name of Yohanan, 'Reddening [that is, the inflammation of the skin] is a
danger (סכנה) [to life]'. Said R. Abin, 'They remove the sting of a
scorpion on the Sabbath'…. Rabbis of Caesarea say this, '[A wound] in
the shape of a frog is a danger (סכנה) [to life]'. R. Hezekiah says in the
name of the rabbis of Caesarea, 'A wound from a spider's bite is danger
(סכנה) [to life]'. R. Samuel b. R. Isaac, 'Any burn is a danger (סכנה) [to
life]. …R. Abbahu in the name of R. Yohanan, 'Scurvy is a danger [to
life] (סכנתא)… From this story you learn three lessons: You learn that
scurvy is a danger [to life] (סכנה)…'

The term סכנה is used similarly in the Babylonian Talmud:

תלמוד בבלי מסכת פסחים דף כה עמוד
אמר רבי יעקב אמר רבי יוחנן: בכל מתרפאין, חוץ מעצי אשירה. היכי דמי? אי
נימא דאיכא סכנה—אפילו עצי אשירה נמי! ואי דליכא סכנה—אפילו כל
איסורין שבתורה נמי לא!—לעולם דאיכא סכנה, ואפילו הכי—עצי אשירה לא.
... כי אתא רבין אמר רבי יוחנן, בכל מתרפאין, חוץ מעבודה זרה וגילוי עריות.

Babylonian Talmud Pesahim 25a
R. Jacob said in the name of R. Yohanan, 'We may cure ourselves with all things, save with the wood of the Asherah. How is this meant? If we say that there is danger (סכנה) [to life] even the wood of the Asherah too [is permitted]; while if there is no danger (סכנה) [to life] even all [the other] forbidden things of the Torah too are not [permitted]. After all [it means] that there is danger (סכנה), yet even so the wood of the Asherah [must] not be used...' When Rabin came, he said in the name of R. Yohanan, 'We may cure [or save] ourselves with all [forbidden] things [even by violating Jewish law], except [by acts of] idolatry and sexual sins'.

On the other hand, as was briefly noted above, the term סכנה is also used in the amoraic texts for situations in which the action that is necessary does *not* violate Jewish law. Four examples from many are cited below:

(1) y. Peah 4.1: I can include [as *peah*] those [types of produce] that pose no threat of danger to the poor [when gathering the *peah*] and exclude those [types of produce] that pose a danger (סכנה) [to the poor] such as fruit high up on a trellis or a palm tree].

(2) y. MS 1.1: If one had [illegal] coins [which caused him to face] danger (סכנה) [on their account] — [such a] case came before R. Immi, who said, 'He must dispose of the [illegal] coins in the Dead Sea'.

(3) y. Gitt 6.5: Said R. Mana, 'It is not the end of the matter [that we are discussing] that if he goes out in chains because of danger to life (סכנה) but even if he goes out in chains because of a monetary claim [we should do the same].

(4) b. Shab 61a: What is an approved amulet? One that has healed [once], a second time and a third time; whether it is an amulet in writing or an amulet of roots, whether it is for an invalid [in] danger (סכנה) [of his life], or for an invalid whose life is not in danger (סכנה).

It is however the case that in complete contrast with its use in the amoraic texts, the term סכנה in the tannaitic texts (where it appears forty-five times, mostly in the Tosefta and the Mishnah) is, with one exception, used *only* for situations in which the necessary action does *not* violate Jewish law. That is, with one exception, this term is *never* used for situations of healing and/or saving life where the necessary action violates Jewish law. For example, the following tannaitic text deals with the problem of danger to life while walking in a dangerous place, in which the advised action does not violate Jewish law:

משנה מסכת ברכות פרק ד משנה ד
רבי יהושע אומר המהלך במקום סכנה מתפלל תפלה קצרה אומר הושע השם
את עמך את שארית ישראל בכל פרשת העבור יהיו צרכיהם לפניך בא"י שומע
תפלה.

Mishnah Berachoth 4.4
R. Joshua says, 'He that journeys in a place of danger (סכנה) should pray a short prayer, saying "Save O Lord, the remnant of Israel at their every cross road let their needs come before Thee. Blessed art Thou, O Lord, that hearest prayer!"'

Similarly, the phrase סכנת נפשות in the text below refers to the possible danger to life by eating meat from an animal which may be permitted by Jewish law, but which must not be consumed because it is contaminated with poison, which is a situation that does not cause a violation of any Jewish law:

משנה מסכת חולין פרק ג משנה ה
... אכלה סם המות או שהכישה נחש מותרת משום טרפה ואסורה משום סכנת
נפשות.

Mishnah Hullin 3.5
... [an animal that] has eaten poison, or if a snake has bitten it, although it is not forbidden because it is *terefa* (that is, food forbidden by Jewish law). It is forbidden because it is a danger to life (סכנות נפשות).

The single exception in the tannaitic texts in which the term סכנה is used for a situation of healing and/or danger to life, and in which the necessary action violates Jewish law, is preserved in the Tosefta where it serves as a definition of the phrase פיקוח נפש (see the discussion on t. Shab 9.22 in Chapter 5). As was discussed at length in Chapter 5, this expression is associated with R. Ishmael and refers only to an action or situation of healing and/or saving life in which it is necessary to violate Jewish law.[6] In view of this single use in the tannaitic texts and in view

---

6. The only other possible tannaitic example of סכנה used for a situation in which action to deal with the danger to life overrides Jewish law occurs in the *Mekilta de-Rabbi Ishmael*, Amalek 3: 'R. Jose says, God forbid! – to think that this righteous man [Moses] neglected the duty of circumcision even for one hour! But if he should perform the circumcision and immediately go on his journey, there is danger (סכנה) [to life]' (Lauterbach, *Mekilta*, 2:170). This text, however, stresses

of the frequent usage of this term in the amoraic texts for situations of healing and/or saving life that violate Jewish law, it is thus difficult to avoid the conclusion that this definition of סכנה in the Tosefta is an amoraic addition to the toseftan text.

The fact that the term סכנה is used in the amoraic texts for both situations in which the necessary action involves a violation of Jewish law, and for situations in which it does not, can only mean that with the proviso that any violation of Jewish law must be as minimal as possible (which is usually unexpressed), then, according to the amoraic sages, all situations that require acts of healing and/or saving life should be considered in the same way, *whether or not* they involve a violation of Jewish law.

III. *The Amoraic Preference for the Term* סכנה

The popularity of the term סכנה among the amoraim can be seen from the fact that the amoraic commentators frequently add this term to their citations of tannaitic texts on healing and/or saving life, rather than either of the terms composed by R. Akiva and R. Ishmael, פיקוח נפש or ספק נפשות, which more accurately refer only to situations in which the necessary action causes a violation of Jewish law. Thus in the above cited text of b. Pes 25a, the statement of the amoraic sage R. Yohanan (who died in 279 CE), *We may cure ourselves with all things, save with the wood of the Asherah* (b. Pes 25a), is cited by R. Jacob (who was active between 290 and 320 CE) and is discussed by the amoraic sages R. Jacob and Rabin (the latter was active between 320 and 375 CE). R. Jacob and Rabin both introduce the term סכנה into the discussion, although this term is not used in the earlier report of R. Yohanan. The following texts provide further examples of this tendency in amoraic texts:

1. Permission to attend to the wound of circumcision on the Sabbath is stated in the following three tannaitic directives, in which *no* special vocabulary is used, either the special vocabulary of R. Akiva or of R. Ishmael. Neither is the term סכנה used:

the danger if Moses makes the journey after circumcising his son, which would not cause a violation of Jewish law, rather than the danger caused by the neglect of circumcision, which would indeed violate Jewish law.

(1)

משנה מסכת שבת פרק ט משנה ג

מניין שמרחיצין את המילה ביום השלישי שחל להיות בשבת שנאמר (בראשית
לד) ויהי ביום השלישי בהיותם כואבים...

Mishnah Shabbat 9.3

From where do we learn that they may bathe a circumcised child on the
third day that falls on a Sabbath? Because it is written, *And it came to
pass on the third day when they were sore* (Gen 34:25)...

(2)

משנה מסכת שבת פרק יט משנה ג מרחיצין את הקטן בין לפני המילה ובין
לאחר המילה ומזלפין עליו ביד אבל לא בכלי ר' אליעזר בן עזריה אומר, מרחיצין
את הקטן ביום השלישי שחל להיות בשבת שנא' (בראשית לד) 'ויהי ביום
השלישי בהיותם כואבים.

Mishnah Shabbat 19.3

[On the Sabbath] they may wash the child either before or after the
circumcision and sprinkle it [on the Sabbath] by means of the hand, but
not by means of a vessel. R. Eleazar b. Azariah says, 'They may wash the
child on the third day if this falls on a Sabbath, for it is written, *And it
came to pass on the third day when they were sore* (Gen 34:25)'.

(3)

תוספתא מסכת שבת פרק טו הלכה ד

ומזלף עליה חמין.

Tosefta Shabbat 15.4

And one sprinkles warm water on it [that is, one sprinkles warm water on
the wound of circumcision on the Sabbath].

In contrast, the sages of the Babylonian Talmud justify this on the
grounds that the wound of circumcision is a 'danger' (סכנה), which
implies for the amoraic sages that it is one of innumerable situations
which can be treated on the Sabbath, as would be done on any other non-
Sabbath day. The final section of this discussion also alludes to a
tannaitic directive of R. Eleazar b. Azariah (see m. Shab 19.3), which
does not use the term סכנה in the tannaitic record of this argument,
although this term now appears in the amoraic commentary on his text:

תלמוד בבלי מסכת שבת דף קלד עמוד ב

דאמר רב, אין מונעין חמין ושמן מעל גבי מכה בשבת. מתקיף לה רב יוסף, ולא
שני לך בין חמין שהוחמו בשבת לחמין שהוחמו מערב שבת? מתקיף לה רב
דימי, וממאי דהכא בחמין שהוחמו בשבת פליגי, דילמא בחמין שהוחמו בערב
שבת פליגי? אמר אביי, אנא בעאי דאישני ליה, וקדם ושני ליה רב יוסף, מפני
שסכנה הוא לו. איתמר נמי: כי אתא רבין אמר רבי אבהו אמר רבי אלעזר,
ואמרי לה אמר רבי אבהו אמר רבי יוחנן, הלכה כרבי אלעזר בן עזריה, בין
בחמין שהוחמו בשבת בין בחמין שהוחמו מערב שבת, בין הרחצת כל גופו, בין
הרחצת מילה, מפני שסכנה היא לו.

Babylonian Talmud Shabbat 134b

For Rab said, 'One does not withhold hot water and oil from a wound on the Sabbath'. R. Joseph demurred, 'And do you not admit a distinction between hot water heated on the Sabbath and hot water heated on the eve of the Sabbath?' To this R. Dimi demurred, 'And whence [does it follow] that they differ here in respect of hot water heated on the Sabbath? Perhaps they differ in respect of hot water heated on the eve of the Sabbath?' Said Abaye, 'I wanted to answer him, but R. Joseph anticipated [me] and answered him, "Because it is a danger (סכנה) for him [with regard for this life]"'. It was also stated: When Rabin came, he said in R. Abbahu's name in R. Eleazar's name, [but] others state, R. Abbahu said in R. Johanan's name, 'The halachah is as R. Eleazar b. Azariah in respect of both hot water heated on the Sabbath and hot water heated on the eve of (that is, *before*) the Sabbath, whether for the bathing of the whole body or for the bathing of the membrum, because it is a danger (סכנה) for him [with regard to his life]'.

2. The term סכנה is *not* used in the following text in the Tosefta:

תוספתא מסכת שבת פרק טו הלכה טו
מחמין חמין לחולה בשבת בין להשקותו בין לרפאותו ואין אומ' 'המתינו לו שמא
יחיה', אלא ספיקו דוחה את השבת.

Tosefta Shabbat 15.15

They heat water for a sick person on the Sabbath, whether to give it to him to drink or to heal him with it. And they do not say, 'Wait [to see] if he will live without it', but doubt [of his life] overrides the Sabbath.

In contrast, the Jerusalem Talmud cites this directive using the term סכנה:

תלמוד ירושלמי מסכת שבת פרק ט הלכה ג
רבי יעקב בר אחא אמ' ר' אלעזר ורבי יוחנן מפקדין לחייתא כל שיקויין דאתון
עבדין בחולא עבדין בשובתא לכן צריכה אפילו ביום השלישי שחל להיות
בשבת. שמואל אמר מפני הסכנה. רבי יוסה בעי אם מפני סכנה מחמין לו חמין.
רבי יוסי בי רבי בון בשם רבנן תמן מחמין לו חמין בשבת.

Jerusalem Talmud Shabbat 9.3

R. Jacob b. Aha said R. Eleazar and R. Yohanan instructed the midwives, 'Any kind of potions which you administer on an ordinary day, you may [also] administer on the Sabbath'. It was necessary to give this instruction [not for the day of the circumcision, but rather] for the third day when it coincided with the Sabbath. Samuel said, 'It is because of danger (סכנה) to life'. R. Yose asked, 'If it is because of danger (סכנה) to life, may they then heat water for him?' R. Yose b. R. Bun said in the name of rabbis over there [in Babylon], 'They may heat water for him on the Sabbath'.

3. The following discussion in the Jerusalem Talmud implies the earlier existence of a tannaitic directive on which this amoraic discussion is based, which stated that 'they wash, press and steam vegetables [on the Day of Atonement] from *minhah* onwards', that is, this directive was expressed without the term סכנה. The term סכנה is, however, used in the subsequent amoraic discussion by the amoraic sage R. Jacob b. Aha, who was active between 305 and 335 CE. R. Aha thereby makes explicit the implication of the tannaim, namely that the neglect of this directive may result in danger to life:

תלמוד ירושלמי מסכת פסחים פרק ד הלכה ד

רבי יעקב בר אחא בשם רבי אלעזר מה טעם אמרו מדיחין כבשים ושלקות מן
המנחה ולמעלן מפני סכנה סכנה שנייא היא סכנת יום הכיפורים שחל להיות בשבת
שנייא היא יום הכיפורים שחל להיות בחול התיב.

Jerusalem Talmud Pesahim 4.4

R. Jacob b. Aha [said] in the name of R. Eleazar, 'Why did they say [that] they wash, press and steam vegetables [on the Day of Atonement] from *minhah* onwards? [They said this] because of danger (סכנה) [to life from hunger if one has to delay breaking one's fast for the additional time needed to wash food]. Is the danger (סכנה) of the Day of Atonement that falls on the Sabbath distinct and is the [danger] of the Day of Atonement that falls on a weekday distinct? [Because the danger is the same if washing is permitted in the latter case, it should also be permitted in the former case].'

4. The following passage in the Mishnah allows a lamp to be extinguished on the Sabbath (which is normally forbidden by Sabbath law, see m. Shab 7.2), whenever this action is performed for a person who is ill:

משנה מסכת שבת פרק ב משנה ה

המכבה את הנר מפני שהוא מתירא מפני עובדי כוכבים מפני לסטים מפני רוח
רעה ואם בשביל החולה שיישן פטור.

Mishnah Shabbat 2.5

If a man puts out the lamp [on Friday night, the night of the Sabbath] from fear of gentiles or of thieves or of an evil spirit, or to allow a sick person to sleep, he is free from any blame.

In contrast, the amoraic commentary in the Babylonian Talmud uses the term סכנה to indicate that the illness of this invalid is a danger to his life which must be treated on the Sabbath, irrespective of any violation of Sabbath law:

תלמוד בבלי מסכת שבת דף ל עמוד א

מדקתני סיפא חייב—שמע מינה רבי יהודה היא. רישא במאי עסיקנא? אי
בחולה שיש בו סכנה—מותר מיבעי ליה! ואי בחולה שאין בו סכנה—חייב
חטאת מיבעי ליה! לעולם בחולה שיש בו סכנה, ובדין הוא דליתני מותר, ואיידי
דבעי למתני סיפא חייב—תנא נמי רישא פטור. והדתני רבי אושעיא אם בשביל
החולה שיישן—לא יכבה, ואם כבה—פטור אבל אסור—ההיא בחולה שאין בו
סכנה, ורבי שמעון היא.

Babylonian Talmud Shabbat 30a

Since the second clause [of the Mishnah] teaches *he is free from any
blame*, it may be inferred that it is R. Judah [who teaches that the work of
extinguishing is not needed *per se* but merely for some ulterior purpose,
for example, to spare the oil]. Then to what does the first clause [in the
Mishnah] refer? If [it refers] to an invalid [in] danger (סכנה) [of his life]
should [the tannaitic sage] have stated, 'It is permitted'? On the other
hand, if [it refers] to an invalid who is not [in] danger (סכנה) [of his life],
should [the tannaitic sage] have stated, He is liable to a sin-offering?
After all, [it refers] to an invalid [in] danger (סכנה) [of his life], and
logically he should teach, it is permitted; but because he wishes to teach
he is culpable in the second clause, he also teaches *he is free from any
blame* in the first. And as for what R. Oshaiah taught, 'If it is for the sake
of a sick person, that he should sleep, he must not extinguish it; but if he
extinguishes it, he is not liable, though it is forbidden'—that refers to one
who is not [in] danger (סכנה) [of his life], and agrees with [the opinion
of] R. Simeon.

R. Oshaiah can be identified as R. Oshaiah, one of the editors of the
Tosefta, who flourished in the first half of the third century between 220
and 250 CE.

5. The following two tannaitic directives from the Mishnah and Tosefta
allow a violation of Pentateuchal law by exempting ill persons from the
religious requirement to stay in a *sukkah* during the festival of Sukkot
(see Lev 23:42):

משנה מסכת סוכה פרק ב משנה ד

חולין ומשמשיהן פטורין מן הסוכה

Mishnah Sukkah 2.4

The sick, and their attendants are exempt [from the law of staying in] the
sukkah.

תוספתא מסכת סוכה פרק ב הלכה ב

חולין ומשמשיהן פטורין מן הסוכה. ולא חולה מסכן אלא אפי' חש בראשו אפי'
חש בעינו.
אמ' רבן שמעון בן גמליאל מעשה וחשתי בעיני בקיסריון והתיר לי ר' יוסה בי ר'
לישן אני ושמשי חוץ לסוכה. אמ' ר' כשהיינו באין אני ור' לעזר בי ר' צדוק אצל
ר' יוחנן בן נורי לבית שערים והיינו אוכלין תאנים וענבים חוץ לסוכה.

Tosefta Sukkah 2.2

The sick, and their attendants are exempt [from the law of staying in] the *sukkah*. And [this is the case] [only for a person who is] seriously ill, but even [for someone who] feels ill in his head, or feels [something] in his eye.

   Rabban Simeon b. Gamaliel told [the following] story, 'I was suffering with my eyes in Caesarea and R. Yose Berebi permitted me and my attendant to sleep outside the *sukkah*'. Said Rabbi, 'When we were going—I and R. Eleazar b. R. Sadoq—to visit R. Yose b. Nur in Beit Shearim, we would eat figs and grapes outside the *sukkah*'.

In contrast, R. Mana, an amoraic sage from the land of Israel (who was active around 350–375 CE), adds the term סכנה to his citation of the above text, using this term in its extended amoraic sense to refer to the same situation in which it is necessary to violate Jewish law:

תלמוד ירושלמי מסכת סוכה פרק ב דף נג טור א /ה'ה

אמר רבי מנא, לא סוף דבר חולין של סכנה אלא אפילו חולין שאינן של סכנה.

Jerusalem Talmud Sukkah 2.5

Said R. Mana, 'It is not the end of the matter [for deciding who is allowed to stay outside a *sukkah*] that those who are sick and in danger (סכנה) [of their lives are exempt from the requirement of staying in the *sukkah*]'.

The commentary of the Babylonian Talmud also uses the term סכנה:

תלמוד בבלי מסכת סוכה דף כו עמוד א

תנו רבנן: חולה שאמרו—לא חולה, שיש בו סכנה, אלא אפילו חולה שאין בו סכנה, אפילו חש בעיניו, ואפילו חש בראשו.

Babylonian Talmud Sukkah 26a

Our Rabbis taught, 'The invalid spoken of here is not [only] an invalid who is in danger (סכנה) but also one who is not in danger (סכנה) even one who suffers from eye ache or headache'.

6. In the following example, two similar directives in the Mishnah and Tosefta deal with the treatment of a pregnant woman who craves and is allowed a particular food which (it is implied) is prohibited by Jewish law:

משנה מסכת יומא פרק ח משנה ה

עוברה שהריחה מאכילין אותה עד שתשיב נפשה

Mishnah Yoma 8.5

If a pregnant woman smelled [food which she craved] they may give her food until she recovers herself.

תוספתא מסכת יומא (כפורים) פרק ד הלכה ד
ר' יהודה או' עוברה שהריחה שביעית תוחבין לה בכוש. הריחה תרומה תוחבין
לה ברוטב.

Tosefta Yoma 4.4
R. Judah says, 'A pregnant woman who smells and craves produce of the
Seventh Year, they hand over to her a reed-full. [If] she smells [and
craves] food in the status of heave-offering, they hand over to her the
juice.

In contrast, the corresponding amoraic discussion classifies the state of
the pregnant woman under the general term סכנה, which justifies action
to heal and/or save her life, whether or not the action would cause a
violation of Jewish law:

תלמוד בבלי מסכת כריתות דף יג עמוד א
התירו לה לעוברה לאכול פחות מכשיעור מפני הסכנה. מפני הסכנה, אפילו
טובא נמי תיכול! אמר רב פפא, הכי קתני: הותרו לה לעוברה פחות מכשיעור
אפילו טובא מפני הסכנה.

Babylonian Talmud Kerithoth 13a
It is stated, 'A pregnant woman is permitted to eat a quantity smaller than
the standard size, because of danger (סכנה) [to her life]. If by reason of
danger (סכנה) [to her life] she should be permitted to eat even more! Said
R. Papa: "Read thus, 'A pregnant woman is permitted to eat even more,
yet in quantities smaller than the standard size, because of danger (סכנה)
[to her life]'"'.

7. Parallel directives in the Mishnah and Tosefta both state that the
violation of Jewish law for humanitarian reasons by Jewish people must
not be avoided by requesting the services of those who have less, or no
responsibility for observing Jewish law, for example, children or non-
Jews. The Mishnah thus notes:

משנה מסכת שבת פרק טז משנה ו
עובד כוכבים שבא לכבות אין אומרים לו כבה ואל תכבה מפני שאין שביתתו
עליהן. אבל קטן שבא לכבות אין שומעין לו מפני ששביתתו עליהן.

Mishnah Shabbat 16.6
If a gentile came to put out the fire [on the Sabbath] they may not say
to him, 'Put it out' or 'Do not put it out', since they are not answerable
for his keeping the Sabbath. But if it was a minor that came to put it out
they may not permit him, since they are answerable for his keeping the
Sabbath. [That is, it is the responsibility of adult Jews to extinguish a fire
that causes damage on the Sabbath, although they then violate Sabbath
law].

Similarly, in the Tosefta:

תוספתא מסכת שבת פרק טו הלכה טו
ואין אום' יעשו דברים בגוים ובקטנים אלא בגדולים שבישראל אין אום' ייעשו
דברים הללו על פי נשים על פי כותים אלא מצרפין דעת ישראל עמהן

Tosefta Shabbat 15.15
And they do not say, 'Let the matters [of healing and saving life at the
expense of Jewish law] be done by gentiles or [Jewish] children [who are
too young to have assumed responsibility for Jewish law], but they should
be done by adult Israelites'. And they do not say, 'Let these matters be
done by the testimony of women, by Samaritans, but they join the opinion
of Israelites with them [to act to heal or save life by overriding the
Sabbath].

In contrast, this principle is restated twice in the Jerusalem Talmud
with the addition of the term סכנה:

תלמוד ירושלמי מסכת יומא פרק ח הלכה ה / תלמוד ירושלמי מסכת נדרים
פרק ד דף לח טור ד /ה'ט
תני כל דבר שהוא של סכנה אין או' יעשו דברי' בגוי' ובקטני' אלא אפי' בגדולי'
בישר'.

Jerusalem Talmud Yoma 8.5 / Jerusalem Talmud Nedarim 4.9
It has been taught [by a tannaitic sage], 'In any matter involving danger
(סכנה) [to life], they do not say, "Let the matters be done by gentiles or
children". But they should be done by adult Israelites.'

Similarly again in the Jerusalem Talmud:

תלמוד ירושלמי מסכת שבת פרק טז דף טו טור ד /ה'ז
בימי רבי אמי נפלה דליקה בכפר אפיק רבי אימי כרוז בשוקי דארמאי ומר מאן
דעבד לא מפסיד אמר רבי אלעזר בי רבי יוסה קומי רבי יוסה סכנה הייתה אם
היתה סכנה אפילו רבי אמי יטפי ולא כן תני כל דבר שיש בו סכנה אין אומרין
ייעשו דברים הללו בנשים ובקטנים אלא אפילו בגדולים אפילו בישראל.

Jerusalem Talmud Shabbat 16.7
In the time of R. Immi, a fire broke out in the village. R. Immi issued a
proclamation in the market place of the Arameans, saying 'Whoever does
[something to put out the fire] will not lose out!'
    Said R. Eleazar b. R. Yose, '[It was all right to do this, for] it was a
matter of danger (סכנה). If it was a matter of danger (סכנה) then even R.
Immi should have put the fire out. Is it not taught [that] in a matter of
danger (סכנה) they do not say, "Let the matter be done by gentiles or
minors, but [it must be done] even by the adult Israelites".'

Contrary to what might be expected, the commentary on m. Shab 16.6
in the Babylonian Talmud (b. Shab 121a) provides an exception and does
not include the term סכנה.

8. The three directives in the Mishnah and Tosefta cited below permit extinguishing a fire and making barriers on the Sabbath day. The corresponding discussion in the Babylonian Talmud refers to these situations with the term סכנה:

(1)

משנה מסכת ראש השנה פרק ב משנה ה

בראשונה לא היו זזין משם כל היום. התקין רבן גמליאל הזקן שיהו מהלכין אלפים אמה לכל רוח ולא אלו בלבד אלא אף ... והבא להציל מן הדליקה ... הרי אלו כאנשי העיר ויש להם אלפים אמה לכל רוח:

Mishnah Rosh Ha-Shanah 2.5
Before they could not move from there [= Beth Yaazek, the court in the Temple where witnesses gathered to witness the New Moon]. But Rabban Gamaliel the Elder ordained that they [= the witnesses] might walk within two thousand cubits in any direction. And not only these [people] but… whoever came to rescue from a burning house…are deemed to be people of the city and may move within two thousand cubits.

(2)

משנה מסכת שבת פרק טז משנה ה ...ועושין מחיצה בכל הכלים בין מלאים בין ריקנים בשביל שלא תעבור הדליקה...

Mishnah Shabbat 16.5
…and they make a partition wall of all the vessels, whether filled [with water] or empty, so that the fire shall not spread.

(3)

תוספתא מסכת שבת (ליברמן) פרק טו הלכה יג

... מכבין ומפסיקין לדליקה בשבת והזריז הרי זה משובח ואין צריך ליטול רשות בית דין.

Tosefta Shabbat 15.13
…they (may) put out a fire and make a barrier against a fire on the Sabbath, and the one who is prompt, behold, this one is to be praised, and it is not necessary to get permission from a court.

The commentary on this text in the Babylonian Talmud uses the generalising term סכנה:

תלמוד בבלי מסכת ביצה דף כב עמוד א

בעא מיניה אביי מרבה: מהו לכבות את הדלקה ביום טוב? היכא דאיכא סכנת נפשות לא קא מבעיא לי, דאפילו בשבת שרי.

Babylonian Talmud Betzah 22a
Abbaye asked Rabbah, 'May one extinguish a fire on a Festival? When the duty to save life (סכנת נפשות) is involved, I do not ask, for this is permitted even on a Sabbath.'

There are many other examples in the amoraic texts in which the term סכנה is used *without* the special additional meaning of danger to life *which necessitates a violation of Jewish law*, and which arise in discussions that are not directly based on a tannaitic text. This further underlines the popularity of this term and adds evidence to the fact that the amoraic sages used the use of the term סכנה for situations in which it is necessary to violate Jewish law (which has been demonstrated above), and considered that there was no essential difference between the action that must be taken in situations of healing and/or saving life that violate Jewish law, and comparable situations in which there is no violation of Jewish law.

IV. *Conclusions*

(1) Unlike the sages of tannaitic times, the amoraic sages used the term סכנה with the added religious meaning of the tannaitic expressions פיקוח נפש and ספק נפשות, the latter in the Babylonian Talmud with the addition of the term להקל. The amoraic sages thus used the term סכנה both for situations that required action that does *not* violate Jewish law (the sole tannaitic usage) and also for situations in which action inevitably violates Jewish law.

(2) This means that, with the proviso (usually unexpressed) that there should be a minimal violation of Jewish law, the amoraic sages considered that in relation to the action that must be taken to heal and/or save life, situations in which Jewish law must be violated, and those in which it is *not* violated must be considered in the same way.

(3) The amoraic sages thus fully accepted the conclusions of the tannaim, especially those of R. Akiva, R. Ishmael and the second-century sages responsible for the interpretations discussed in Chapter 7, that action should always be taken in *any* situation that required an act of healing and/or saving life, *whether or not* this action caused a violation of Jewish law. This is also indicated by the legal rider that was added by the amoraim to the basic principle that acts of healing and/or saving life must always be performed, unless it is necessary to commit either the sin of idolatry, sexual sins or the shedding of blood.

(4) This analysis of the amoraic use of the term סכנה also helps to confirm that the definition of the phrase פיקוח נפש in the Tosefta at t. Shab 9.22 is probably an amoraic addition to the tannaitic text and the same can be said for the legal rider that forbids the sins of idolatry, sexual sins and the shedding of blood, which had been added to the text of t. Shab 15.17.

Chapter 9

SPECIFICITY VERSUS GENERALITY:
TEST CASES FOR DATING EARLY *SPECIFIC* TANNAITIC
DIRECTIVES IN RELATION TO LATER *GENERAL* DIRECTIVES

I. *General Considerations*

The three arguments *kal va-chomer* which first appear or which only
appear in the gospels of Mark and Luke are essentially permits to violate
Sabbath law only in *specific* situations of healing and/or saving life,
Thus, the argument *kal va-chomer* that first appears in Mark allows a
violation of Sabbath law to 'cure' severe hunger (Mark 2:25-26, 28), and
one of the two arguments *kal va-chomer* which only appear in Luke
allows a violation of the Sabbath only to heal the condition of a bent
back, while the other permits the Sabbath cure of dropsy (Luke 13:15b-
16 and 14:5). These directives can be grouped with others that were
composed before around 80 CE, which are also only specific for the
action they allow, and thus which similarly give no impression that the
specific action they allow could be extended to include action in any
other situation of healing and/or saving life. These texts include the texts
which were discussed in Chapter 1, namely the edict of Mattathias issued
in 167 BCE, which allowed a violation of Sabbath law only by fighting
in self-defence, the two directives from Qumran which allowed a
violation of the Sabbath only to save a person who had fallen in a pit,
and the edict of Shammai issued around the turn of the millennium,
which allowed a violation of the Sabbath only by permitting siege to be
continued on the Sabbath day.

In contrast, as has been shown in the discussions above, the tannaitic
Jewish sages who were active towards the end of the first century and in
the second century CE composed *general* arguments and used special
vocabulary which justified *any* action that violated Jewish law in *any*
situation of healing and/or saving life. These include a general argument
kal va-chomer based on animal husbandry preserved in Matthew's gospel
(Matt 12:11-12, discussed in Chapter 3), an argument *kal va-chomer*

composed by R. Eleazar b. Azariah (t. Shab 15.16, see the discussion on John 7:23 in Chapter 3), an argument *kal va-chomer* and a sorite, both composed by R. Akiva, the former which was adapted by R. Ishmael (see Chapter 5), and the four general arguments of the second-century Jewish sages based on relatively simple interpretations of Pentateuchal texts (see Chapter 7).

The fact that the specific arguments and permits were composed, at the earliest, in the early part of the second half of the first century CE, while the general arguments and the special vocabulary of R. Akiva and R. Ishmael were composed around and after that time suggest that a significant change took place in the approach of the Jewish sages who were active towards the end of the first century concerning directives and arguments that justified actions of healing and/or saving life. In contrast with the specific permits and the specific arguments which justify specific actions of healing and/or saving life, the subsequent arguments and innovative vocabulary of the tannaitic sages suggest that the Jewish sages now pursued a conscious policy to allow *general* arguments and directives that could be used to justify *any* action in *any* situation of healing and/or saving life that violated Jewish law.

Evidence for this change can be expanded and confirmed by the tannaitic texts that allow acts of healing and/or saving life that violate Jewish law, whose compositions can be objectively dated to a time *before* around 80 CE. The attitude shown in these texts can then be compared with the general approach of other rabbinic directives—both tannaitic and amoraic—whose historical details reveal that they were composed *after* this time. This comparison will help to confirm the change in the approach of the Jewish sages towards the end of the first century with regard to the type of permits they issued for acts of healing and/or saving life, which was briefly summarised above.

II. *Specificity in Directives Composed Before Around 80 CE*

A. *A Permit Which Allowed a Pregnant Woman to Eat Terumah, Tosefta Yoma 4.4*

The Tosefta has preserved the following ruling which allowed a pregnant woman to be given the juice of the particular meat for which she craved, presumably on a day when fasting was decreed (although this is not stated in the text):

תוספתא מסכת יומא (כפורים) פרק ד הלכה ד:

ר' יהודה או' עוברה שהריחה שביעית תוחבין לה בכוש. הריחה תרומה תוחבין
לה ברוטב.

Tosefta Yoma 4.4
R. Judah says, 'A pregnant woman who smelt [and desperately craved]
produce of the Seventh Year, they hand over to her a reed-full. [If] she
smelt [and desperately craved] food of the status of] a heave-offering
(תרומה) they let her taste the juice (רוטב) [of the *terumah*].'

To date this text it is necessary to know the meaning of *rotev* and
terumah. In Second Temple times, the term *terumah* referred either to an
offering of agricultural produce which was brought to the Temple; or
else it referred to a part of an animal sacrifice (specifically, the right
thigh of the priestly ordination offering and well-being offering), which
only a priest and his family were allowed to eat.[1] As far as agricultural
produce is concerned, although biblical law states that the agricultural
produce used for offerings of *terumoth* (the plural of *terumah*) should
consist of 'grain, wine and oil', the later Jewish sages decreed that whatever was considered as food and whatever was 'guarded' (that is, food
that does not grow wild) and grows from the earth, is liable to tithes and
should be considered as *terumah*.[2] On the other hand, agricultural *rotev*
refers only to fresh dates.[3] If, then, the pregnant woman in t. Yom 4.4
craved for a kind of agricultural *terumah* other than that of fresh dates,
and, according to the above directive, she was given fresh dates in order
to satisfy her craving, it is highly unlikely that she would be cured
(because she craved for another kind of agricultural *terumah*), and
Jewish law would have been violated for no achieved aim. It is therefore
unlikely that the *terumah* in this directive refers to agricultural produce
of any kind.

This means that *terumah* in this text must refer to the meat from a
sacrifice which could be eaten only by the priest and his family, so that
the term רוטב—the food that the Tosefta allows the pregnant woman to
eat—must refer to the 'juice' which can be derived from such meat. The
pregnant woman was thus allowed a food that was appropriate for the
craving which had caused her to be ill. This relationship between *rotev*,
'meat juice', and *terumah* results from the simple fact that *terumah* itself
is essentially meat, in Hebrew *basar* (בשר), from which *rotev* (רוטב), that
is, 'juice', may be derived. This can be seen in the following tannaitic
texts, two examples from many, which show clearly that *rotev* refers to
juice which is derived from meat:

1. Lev 27:32; Num 18:27-28; m. Ter 7.2.
2. A. Oppenheimer, 'Terumot and Ma'aserot', in *Encyclopedia Judaica*, 15:1026.
3. For agricultural רוטב, see Jastrow, *Dictionary of the Targumim*, ad loc.

משנה מסכת זבחים פרק ג משנה ד

השוחט את הזבח לאכול כזית מן העור מן הרוטב מן הקיפה מן האלל מן
העצמות מן הגידים מן הטלפים מן הקרנים חוץ לזמנו או חוץ למקומו כשר ואין
חייבים עליהם משום פגול ונותר וטמא.

Mishnah Zevachim 3.4

If a man slaughtered the offering purposing to eat an olive's bulk of the
hide or juice (רוטב) or sediment or flayed-off flesh or bones or sinews or
hoofs or horns outside the proper time or outside the proper place, the
offering remains valid and none becomes liable thereby through [trans-
gression of the laws of] Refuse or Remnant or Uncleanness.

Similarly:

תוספתא מסכת תרומות פרק ח הלכה כ

חתכה אסורה שנתערבה בחתכות אפלו הן אלף כולן אסורות. הרוטב בנותן
טעם אם נמחה הרי זה בנותן טעם.

Tosefta Terumoth 8.20

A forbidden piece of [meat] which was mixed with [other] pieces, even if
they are a thousand in number, all of them are forbidden. [In the case of
forbidden] juice (רוטב) [which was mixed with pieces of forbidden
meat]—the meat was prohibited if it is flavoured by the juice.

It is thus safe to conclude that the *terumah* which was craved by the
pregnant woman in the directive above (t. Yom 4.4) was the meat from
a sacrifice that was reserved for a priest or for his family. This is confirmed by the later Jewish sages. The Jerusalem Talmud directs that
the pregnant woman may be cured with something roasted 'on a spit'
(תוחבה ברוטב, y. Yom 8.4), which must refer to meat, while the Babylonian Talmud states clearly that the craving of the pregnant woman was
for 'holy meat or the meat of pork' (בשר קודש או בשר חזיר, b. Yom 82a).
These amoraic commentaries also confirm the implication of the Tosefta
that the craving of the pregnant woman was considered as an illness that
threatened her life, whose treatment would cause a violation of Jewish
law.

Since sacrifice in the Temple ceased in 70 CE, when the Temple was
destroyed, *terumah* could not have been available after 70 CE. Even
allowing for the fact that references to Temple practice were made
in the tannaitic texts well after the Temple itself was destroyed, this suggests that the above directive from the Tosefta was probably originally
composed before 70 CE.[4] If, then, the R. Judah who is cited in this

---

4.   It seems that *terumah* from agriculture—but *not* from meat—continued to be
offered to individual priests after 70 CE. Thus t. Hag 3.33 notes that R. Tarfon
received heave-offering, which he justified with a ruling from R. Yohanan b. Zakkai.

directive is R. Judah b. Ilai, known in Jewish sources simply as R. Judah, who was active between 135 to 170 CE, the remark of this sage is a later addition to the toseftan text. This is confirmed by the parallel text in the Mishnah which does not report R. Judah's remark, but which uses the same phrase as the Tosefta to refer to 'a pregnant woman who smelled [food]', עוברה ההריחה. This suggests that the texts of the Mishnah and Tosefta are both derived from the same source. The text of the Mishnah is cited below:

משנה מסכת יומא פרק ח משנה ה

עוברה שהריחה מאכילין אותה עד שתשיב נפשה.

Mishnah Yoma 8.5
If a pregnant woman smelled [and craved food] they may give her the food until she recovers herself (literally, 'until her life will return').

An older, perhaps original version of the toseftan directive—without the remark of R. Judah—was thus probably expressed in the following way. The additional words of R. Judah are enclosed in square brackets and printed in small font:

תוספתא מסכת יומא (כפורים) פרק ד הלכה ד

[ר' יהודה או'] עוברה שהריחה [שביעית תוחבין לה בכוש]. [הריחה] תרומה תוחבין לה ברוטב.

Tosefta Yoma 4.4
[R. Judah says] A pregnant woman who smelt [produce of the Seventh Year, they hand over to her a reed-full] heave-offering, they hand over some juice.

It seems therefore that before 70 CE there existed a directive that allowed meat juice (רוטב) to be given to a pregnant woman in order to cure her craving for *terumah* on a day when fasting was decreed. There is, however, no hint in this directive that this permit could be extended to allow action in any other situation of healing and/or saving life—for example, it could not be extended to cure a pregnant woman who craved food other than *terumah*. This directive thus provides an example of the specificity that is typical of directives that were composed before the early part of the second half of the first century CE.

The later, additional comment of R. Judah will be discussed in Chapter 10.

This is also implied at t. Shab 15.14. According to J. Neusner, *Development of a Legend: Studies on the Traditions Concerning Yohanan Ben Zakkai* (Leiden: Brill, 1970) 68–9, R. Tarfon was probably about 12 or 13 years old around 70 CE; see y. Yom 3.7; b. Kidd 71a; b. San 101a.

B. *The Edict of Rabban Gamaliel ha-Zaken, Mishnah Rosh Hashanah 2.5*
A date of composition before 50 CE can be assumed for the directive at
m. RH 2.5 which is attributed to Rabban Gamaliel the Elder, who was
probably a Pharisee (according to Acts 5:34) and one of the teachers of
Paul (according to Acts 22:3), and who died around 50 CE.[5] His edict
first deals with those who have travelled to Jerusalem on the Sabbath to
witness the sighting of the new moon (the astronomical sign for the
beginning of the first calendar day of the Jewish month), to whom
Rabban Gamaliel allowed the full limit of the Sabbath *eruv*, irrespective
of the distance they had already traversed. He then extends this specific
leniency to those who had performed five separately specified actions on
the Sabbath, in order to heal and/or save life, namely: (1) a midwife who
had assisted at a birth, (2) those who had extinguished a fire, (3) those
who had fought against ravaging troops, (4) those who had saved people
from drowning in a river, and (5) those who were involved in saving the
life of a person buried beneath debris. The directive of Rabban Gamaliel
is cited below:

משנה מסכת ראש השנה פרק ב משנה ה

חצר גדולה היתה בירושלים ובית יעזק היתה נקראת ולשם כל העדים מתכנסים
ובית דין בודקין אותם שם וסעודות גדולות עושין להם בשביל שיהו רגילין לבא
[ו] בראשונה לא היו זזין משם כל היום. התקין רבן גמליאל הזקן שיהו מהלכין
אלפים אמה לכל רוח. ולא אלו בלבד אלא אף
החכמה הבאה לילד
והבא להציל מן הדליקה
ומן הגייס
ומן הנהר
ומן המפולת.
הרי אלו כאנשי העיר ויש להם אלפים אמה לכל רוח.

Mishnah Rosh Hashanah 2.5
There was a large courtyard in Jerusalem called Beth Yaazek, where all
the witnesses [for the new moon] assembled, and there the Court questioned them. And they prepared large meals for them so that they might
come regularly. [And] at first, [when they came on the Sabbath] they
were not allowed to move from there the whole day. [But] Rabban
Gamaliel the Elder ordained that they might walk two thousand cubits in
any direction. And not only these, but also

---

5. This approximate date is derived from b. Shab 15a, which notes that Hillel the
Elder became head of the Patriarchate a hundred years before the destruction of the
Temple, and was followed briefly by Simeon, his son, then Rabban Gamaliel II and
then Simeon, all direct descendants of Hillel the Elder, their lives spanning the
century.

(1) a midwife that comes to [deliver] a child,
(2) or anyone that come to rescue [someone] from a fire,
(3) or ravaging troops,
(4) or from a river,
(5) or from collapsed debris,[6]
who are [also] considered as the people of the city and may move within two thousand cubits in any direction.

As can be seen, Rabban Gamaliel takes for granted that five specified activities were permitted to violate Sabbath law. Those engaged in these activities were then granted a further leniency with regard to the Sabbath *eruv*. It is significant that Rabban Gamaliel does not allow a collective group leniency to *anyone* who was involved in these humanitarian tasks but instead refers to each activity that had previously been separately allowed. This directive thus provides a further example of the specificity of permits composed by the end of the first century, in this case before 50 CE. This helps to confirm that the Jewish sages before the end of the first century considered that it was necessary to issue only *specific* permits for acts of healing and or saving life, rather than allowing all such actions to take place by providing a directive that was expressed in a general way.

C. *A Directive of R. Yohanan b. Zakkai Issued Before 70 CE, Mishnah Shabbat 16.7*

According to the Mishnah, while R. Yohanan b. Zakkai lived in Galilee he was asked a question concerning the penalty for a violation of the Sabbath law by an act of healing and/or saving life. We know that R. Yohanan lived in Galilee before 70 CE, which thus fixes the latest

---

6. The antiquity of the date of composition of the reference to saving people from fallen debris reflects the fact that because of the shortage of materials to stoke a kiln (such as wood), houses in the ancient east were not usually built from permanent materials, such as fired bricks, but from bricks made from a mixture of clay, mud and sand, combined with water and a binding material such as rice husks or straw. This produced a stiff mixture that was shaped and dried in the sun for about twenty-five days. The resulting material required the constant application of some kind of plaster to keep out damp. In any case, these kinds of buildings collapsed after twenty-five to thirty years and new buildings were erected on the resulting debris. This accounts for the mounds ('tells') on which many ancient cities are built, which are silent witnesses to the countless accidents that probably occurred when buildings collapsed and buried the people inside. For a description of ancient brick-making, see R. G. Blakemore, *History of Interior Design and Furniture: From Ancient Egypt to Nineteenth-Century Europe* (New York: John Wiley & Sons, 1996) 100.

possible date of this event.[7] This dating is confirmed in the following text by R. Yohanan's cautious suggestion (חוששני) that the penalty for the stated violation of Sabbath law was a sin-offering, which could not have been brought to the Temple after 70 CE:

משנה מסכת שבת פרק טז משנה ז

כופין קערה על גבי הנר בשביל שלא תאחוז בקורה ועל צואה של קטן ועל ערב שלא תישך.

אמר רבי יהודה, 'מעשה בא לפני רבן יוחנן בן זכאי בערב ואמר 'חוששני לו מחטאת.

Mishnah Shabbat 16.7
They may cover a lamp with a dish so that it shall not scorch a rafter and [they may cover] animal droppings to protect a child [from harm], or a scorpion so that it will not bite [anyone].[8] R. Judah said, 'Such a case once came before R. Yohanan b. Zakkai in Arab [in Galilee, near Sepphoris] and he said, "I doubt whether he is not liable to a sin offering"'.

The dating of the composition of this directive before the end of the first century—in fact, before 70 CE—is confirmed by its specificity, which does not give the impression that the permit it allows for the three specifically identified actions could be extended to include any other actions in any other situation on the Sabbath when it might also be necessary to perform an act of healing and/or saving life. The suggestion of culpability for performing an act of healing and/or saving life further confirms this early date. Culpability for performing a deed of healing and/or saving life would surely also have been less likely after around 70 CE, when it seems that R. Eleazar b. Azariah or R. Akiva first used the verb דחה in the phrase דחה את השבת to suggest the suspension, or the overriding, of the Sabbath when performing an act of healing and/or saving life (see the discussion in Chapter 5). Used in a directive that allows an act of healing and or saving life to violate Sabbath law, this phrase implies that the Sabbath does not exist while the act of healing and/or saving life is taking place, in which case no violation of Sabbath law can occur, which further suggests that no punishment should be imposed.

---

7. The life of R. Yohanan b. Zakkai is traditionally divided into three forty-year periods: in the first he was a merchant; in the second he studied; and in the third he taught (see b. RH 31b). According to *Sifre Devarim* 357, he was a leader of Israel in the last forty years. If this is approximately correct, and if he lived at the latest one decade after the destruction of Jerusalem, his public activity began in Galilee, sometime between 30 and 40 CE.

8. The amoraic sages considered this offence as a violation of the prohibition of hunting on the Sabbath, the twenty-fifth of the thirty-nine main prohibited Sabbath actions (m. Shab 7.2); see y. Shab 14.1 and b. Shab 121b.

There is thus little doubt that this directive was composed before the end of the first century CE; in fact, as its historical details suggest, it was composed before 70 CE.

III. *The Generalising Character of Post-First-Century Directives*

Let us now examine three of many other directives which involve acts of healing and/or saving life and which are enclosed in accounts of events whose historical details indicate a date of composition after the end of the first century CE. As will be seen, typical of such texts is the fact that they are phrased in a way that suggests that the specific permits they allow are only representative of the many other actions of this kind. In other words, the specific action that is permitted is generalised in some way. This may be achieved by the use of generalising terminology, most commonly the expressions פיקוח נפש and ספק נפשות (the special technical vocabulary of R. Ishmael and R. Akiva, which symbolise their general arguments, see Chapter 5), and, also in amoraic texts, by the extended amoraic use of the term סכנה (see Chapter 8), although, in order to show other possibilities, only one of the following examples uses these terms.

A. *Healing and/or Saving Life That Violates Jewish Law Is 'a Mitzvah', Tosefta Betzah 2.6*
The story below features the tannaitic sages R. Judah b. Baba and Simon of Teman, who were both active around 110 to 135 CE:

תוספתא מסכת ביצה (יום טוב) פרק ב הלכה ו
אין עושין לא לאכילת גוים... ביום טוב. מעשה—בשמעון התימני שלא יצא בלילי
יום טוב לבית המדרש. לשחרי' מצאו ר' יהודה בן בבא. אמ' לו, מפני מה לא
באתה אמש לבית המדרש? אמ' לו, מצוה אחת אירע לי ועשיתיה. בלשת של
מתיראין שמא יצחיבו את בני העיר. עשינו להם עגל ⁹גוים נכנסה לעיר והינו
והאכלנום והשקינום וסכנום כדי שלא יצחיבו את בני העיר.

Tosefta Betzah 2.6
Food is not prepared for gentiles...on the [first] festival day [of Shavuot]. A story [is told that] on the [first] night of the festival [of Shavuot], Simeon of Teman did not go to the House of Study. He met R. Judah b. Baba at dawn. He [= R. Judah] said to him, 'Why did you not come last night to the House of Study?' He [= Simeon of Teman] said to him

---

9. Reading הינו with *Mekhilta de-Rabbi Shimon bar Yochai* 12.16; see Nelson, *Mekhilta de-Rabbi Shimon Bar Yoḥai*, 35. The same incident is recorded at b. Betz 21a.

[= R. Judah b. Baba], 'A certain religious duty (מצוה אחת) came my way so I went and did it. A troop [of Roman soldiers] came to town, and we were afraid that they might cause trouble for the people of the town. So we prepared a calf for them and gave them food and drink and made a place for them to stay so that they would not make trouble for the people of the town.'

According to this tale, Simon of Teman justified his absence from the customary session of study in the *beit ha-midrash* on the first night of the festival of Shavuot (the Festival of Weeks) because he needed to prepare accommodation and food (including the killing and cooking of a calf, a soft, delicate meat), in order to satisfy the demands of Roman soldiers who had unexpectedly arrived. The introduction to this account and continuation of this text (the latter is not cited above) notes that these actions on a festival day cause a violation of Jewish law. Simon of Teman, however, justifies his actions with the claim that the Roman soldiers would otherwise have 'caused trouble' for the people, which is unquestionably a euphemistic description of the havoc and the danger to life which the soldiers would have wrought. Simon of Teman justifies and generalises his specific violation of Jewish law by calling it 'a certain (Jewish) religious duty' (מצוה אחת), that is, his specific violation of Jewish law in order to save life was 'a customary Jewish law'—the basic meaning of the term מצוה—which must always be performed.

Simon of Teman was probably a younger contemporary of R. Akiva, whom he knew and thus was active in the early second century CE.[10] The fact that he justifies his action with the *general* term מצוה אחת also confirms that this event took place after the end of the first century CE. The evidence examined so far in this book suggests that it is most unlikely that a deed of healing and/or saving life that violated Jewish law would have been described in this generalised way much before the end of the first century CE.

B. *Feeding the Army of Ursicinus, Jerusalem Talmud Sheviit 4.2*
The presence of the fourth-century sages in the following text strongly suggests that—unless they have been retroverted into an earlier composed tale, which is unlikely—this narrative could not have been composed before the fourth century CE. This accords with the fact that the specific act that it permits to heal and/or save life is generalised by the legal rider (discussed above in Chapter 8) which takes for granted

10. For example, Simon of Teman disputes with R. Akiva at t. Ber 4.18 and b. BK 90b.

that acts of healing and/or saving life must always be performed, and refers merely to the three exceptions to this basic rule:

תלמוד ירושלמי מסכת שביעית פרק ד דף לה טור א /ה'ב

ר' יונה ורבי יוסה הורון מפי לארסקינס בשובתא. אמר רבי מנא קשיתה קומי רבי יונה, אבא לא כן א'ר זעירא רבי יוחנן בשם רבי ינאי ר' ירמיה רבי יוחנן בשם ר' שמעון בן יוצדק נמנו בעליית בית לבזה בלוד על כל התורה מניי' אם יאמר גוי לישראל לעבור על אחת מכל מצות האמורות בתורה חוץ מן העבודה זרה וגילוי עריות ושפיכות דמים יעבור ולא ייהרג.

Jerusalem Talmud Sheviit 4.2

R. Jonah and R. Yose rule that the Israelites might bake bread for the army of Ursicinus on the Sabbath. Said R. Mana, asking a question in the presence of R. Jonah, 'Father, did not R. Zeira and R. Yohanan in the name of R. Yannai, R. Jeremiah, R. Yohanan in the name of R. Simeon b. Yosedeq say, "They took a vote in the upper room of the house of Nitzah in Lud [and decided that] in the case of all the commandments of the Torah, if a gentile asks an Israelite to violate (לעבור) one of all the commandments that are stated in the Torah except for idolatry, sexual offences, and the shedding of blood, one should violate the commandment and not be put to death"'.

This discussion of the Jewish sages concerns the command of Ursicinus to bake bread on the Sabbath, which would have caused a gross violation of Jewish law, as 'baking' is one of the thirty-nine *main* activities (the eleventh) which are otherwise prohibited on the Sabbath day (see m. Shab 7.2). The sages, however, note that it was permitted to transgress (לעבור) Sabbath law, in this case by baking bread on the Sabbath, because this was not one of three offences which are totally forbidden in all circumstances, namely, idolatry, sexual sins and the shedding of blood. It is clear, therefore, that these sages accepted the basic principle that acts of healing and/or saving life must always take place, which they justify by listing the three violations which are *not* allowed. The sages thus accept that apart from these exceptions, the situation in which it was necessary to bake bread for Ursicinus fell into the *general* category of the innumerable situations in which action must be taken to heal and/or save life. As a result, even without the identification of the fourth-century sages R. Jonah, R. Yose and R. Mana, and even without the reference to Ursicinus, a Roman general who fought under the emperor Constantius Gallus (c. 325/326–354), this general attitude helps to confirm that this particular discussion took place *after* the end of the first century CE.

C. *Healing and/or Saving Life Is Halachah, Babylonian Talmud Shabbat 128b-29a*

A third example of this generalised attitude after the first century CE in relation to acts of healing and/or saving life can be seen in the following words of Meremar, a Babylonian sage who was active in the late fourth century and fifth century CE:

תלמוד בבלי מסכת שבת דף קכח ב—קכט א

מר רב יהודה אמר שמואל, חיה כל זמן שהקבר פתוח, בין אמרה צריכה אני בין
לא אמרה צריכה אני, מחללין עליה את השבת. נסתם הקבר, בין אמרה. צריכה
אני בין בין לא אמרה צריכה אני, אין מחללין עליה את השבת. רב אשי מתני הכי.
מר זוטרא מתני הכי. אמר רב יהודה אמר שמואל, חיה כל זמן שהקבר פתוח, בין
אמרה צריכה אני ובין אמרה אין צריכה אני, מחללין עליה את השבת. נסתם
הקבר, אמרה צריכה אני, מחללין עליה את השבת לא אמרה צריכה אני, אין
מחללין עליה את השבת. אמר ליה רבינא למרימר, מר זוטרא מתני לקולא, ורב
אשי מתני לחומרא, הלכתא כמאן? אמר ליה: הלכה כמר זוטרא, ספק נפשות
להקל.

<u>Babylonian Talmud Shabbat 128b-29a</u>
Rab Judah said in Samuel's name, 'If a woman is in labour, as long as the uterus is open, whether she states, "I need it", or "I do not need it", we must desecrate the Sabbath on her behalf. If the uterus is closed, whether she says, "I need it" or "I do not need it", we may not violate the Sabbath for her. That is how it was interpreted by R. Ashi.' Mar Zutra interpreted saying, 'Rab Judah said in Samuel's name, "If a woman is in labour, as long as the uterus is open, whether she says, 'I need it' or 'I do not need it', we violate the Sabbath for her. If the uterus is closed, if she says, 'I need it', we violate the Sabbath for her. If she does not say, 'I need it', we do not violate the Sabbath for her."' Rabina asked Meremar, 'Mar Zutra decided it in the direction of leniency, [while] R. Ashi decided it in the direction of stringency. What is the *halachah* (הלכתא)?' 'The *halachah* (הלכה) is as Mar Zutra [decided]', he replied, 'When life is in doubt, we are lenient (ספק נפשות להקל)'.

The sages in this text discuss the violation of Sabbath law caused by assisting in childbirth on the Sabbath day. Meremar states finally that this action must be considered as a *halachah* (הלכה), that is, it must be considered as a basic and established *general* Jewish law, and this is further emphasised by his use of the emended expression of R. Akiva that anonymises the permitted action in any situation of healing and/or saving life, namely, ספק נפשות להקל, 'When life is in doubt, we are lenient [with regard to the violation of any Jewish law]'. It is safe to say that even if this passage was not dated by the identity of the participants in the story, or by the preservation of the story in an amoraic text, this permit to violate the Sabbath could not have been expressed with such generalised terminology before around the end of the first century CE.

IV. *Amoraic Comments at Babylonian Talmud Yoma 84b on the Tannaitic Text of Tosefta Shabbat 15.11-13*

The change in the attitude of the post-second-century Jewish sages revealed by the change from the early specific directives to those in which the specific action allowed was generalised in some way can also be seen in the commentary of the amoraic sages on the seven separate specific directives in the Tosefta at t. Shab 15.11-13, which is cited below. (The Hebrew text of this passage is cited in Chapter 11):

Tosefta Shabbat 15.11-13
(1) They remove debris from one whose life is in doubt on the Sabbath, and he who is prompt in the matter, behold, this person should be praised. And it is not necessary to obtain permission from a [Jewish] court. How so?
(2) [If] someone fell into the sea and cannot climb up,
(3) [or if] his ship is sinking in the sea and he cannot climb up, they go down and bring him up from there.
And it is not necessary to seek permission from a [Jewish] court.
(4) [If] a person fell into a pit and could not get out, they let down a chain to him and go down and raise him out from there.
And it is not necessary to seek permission from a [Jewish] court.
(5) A young child who went into a building and cannot get out, they break down the doors of the building for him, even if they are [made] of stone, and they get him out of there.
And it is not necessary to seek permission from a [Jewish] court.
(6) They (may) put out a fire
(7) and they make a barrier [against a fire] on the Sabbath.
And he who is prompt, behold, this person should be praised, and it is not necessary to obtain permission from a [Jewish] court.[11]

The amoraic commentary on the above text is cited and translated below:

תלמוד בבלי מסכת יומא דף פד עמוד ב

ואף על גב דקא ממכיך מכוכי. וצריכא, דאי אשמועינן ים - משום דאדהכי והכי אזל ליה, אבל בור דקא יתיב - אימא לא, צריכא. ואי אשמועינן בור - משום דקא מיבעית, אבל נגעלה דלת - אפשר דיתיב בהאי גיסא ומשביש ליה באמגוזי, צריכא. מכבין ומפסיקין למה לי? דאפילו לחצר אחרת.

Babylonian Talmud Yoma 84b
... Now all these situations [listed in the Tosefta at t. Shab 15.11-13] must be mentioned separately. For if only the situation of [the child falling into] the sea had been mentioned [one would have said, it is permitted] because meantime the child might be swept away by the water,

11. For further on t. Shab 15.11-13, see Chapter 11.

but that does not apply in the case [of its falling into] the pit, because since it stays therein [rather than being swept away, as in the previous edict, so that] one might have thought that one may not [save it before obtaining permission], therefore it is necessary [also] to refer [separately] to that [situation]. And if the teaching [of the tannaim] had confined itself to the case of the pit, [one might have thought it was] because the child is terrified [and must therefore be saved although this may cause a violation of Jewish law]. But in the case of a door closing upon it [that is, if a child is confined in a building], one might sit outside and [amuse the child] by making a noise with nuts, therefore it was necessary [to include that instance too, since even if the terror of the child is placated, this does not mean that the child should remain in the building]. [And] for why is it necessary [to mention] the 'extinguishing' and 'isolating' [from a fire]? [These things must be mentioned] even for the benefit of another [different] courtyard.

The commentary of the amoraic sages indicates that they did not understand why the tannaitic directives are each separately allowed, rather than permitted in a general way. They therefore attempted to link the separate situations, as if they could be expressed as one *general* permit that allowed most of the acts of healing and/or saving life that are mentioned in the Tosefta. Thereby the situations in the tannaitic list could be considered as a single generalised list of situations in which it might be necessary to violate Jewish law. In respect, however, to the tannaitic sages, the amoraic commentators do not criticise the list of separate specific directives but begin with the claim that *all these situations must be mentioned separately.* Accordingly, beginning with the fifth directive in the toseftan list (which allowed the doors of a house to be broken down on the Sabbath in order to remove a child confined inside), this directive is linked to the preceding four by assuming that they all relate to the situation of the child, thus suggesting that each follows logically from the one that precedes, and that they are in fact one single decree. Finally, the amoraic commentators suggest that the sixth and seventh directives (extinguishing a fire and making a barrier to prevent the spread of a fire) are mentioned together *for the benefit of another [different] courtyard*, that is, one may violate the Sabbath to save lives even if a fire rages in a different courtyard.

These amoraic comments are clearly contrived and, viewed with the benefit of historical hindsight, can be explained by the change of attitude that took place regarding the necessity to give separate permits for each separate situation, as in the toseftan list above, which the evidence discussed above suggests was the policy of the tannaim who lived before the beginning of the second half of the first century CE. It seems, however, that after this time, although the Jewish sages of course continued to discuss specific instances which necessitated an act of healing and/or saving life, these permits were expressed in a general way. The list of separate directives of the tannaitic sages in the Tosefta thus suggests that at the time each was issued there was no way to indicate that each separate situation was in effect a paradigm for all situations which needed an act of healing and/or saving life.

V. *Conclusions*

(1) An examination of directives that allow acts of healing and/or saving life that were composed before around 80 CE suggests that their authors permitted only specific acts of healing and/or saving life, and did not consider that the specific permission they allowed could be extended to include any other of the innumerable situations in which it is necessary to heal and/or save life. These directives thus add to the evidence of the other seven similarly datable texts listed at the beginning of the chapter—the edict of Mattathias issued in 167 BCE, the two directives from Qumran, the edict of Shammai issued around the turn of the millennium, and the three arguments *kal va-chomer* which first appear or which only appear in the gospels of Mark and Luke, making ten in all— that tannaitic directives that allow acts of healing and/or saving life that were composed soon after the start of the second half of the first century CE are wholly specific for the action that they allow.

(2) In contrast, the last three directives discussed above, the historical details of which reveal that they were composed *after* the end of the first century, are generalised in a way that shows that their authors considered that each of the specific acts of healing and/or saving life that they allowed are merely examples of the innumerable actions that must be performed in the many situations when such deeds must take place. These texts thus add to and confirm the evidence of the *halachic* arguments which appear only in the gospels of Matthew and John (the latter a version of the argument composed by R. Eleazar b. Azariah, recorded at t. Shab 15.16 and in the *Mekhilta de-Rabbi Ishmael* Shab 1), the arguments and special vocabulary of R. Akiva and R. Ishmael, the second-century interpretations of Pentateuchal texts, and the confirmation provided by the amoraic sages (discussed in Chapter 8).

Chapter 10

OTHER INDICATIONS FOR DATING:
THE MODIFICATION OF TANNAITIC DIRECTIVES ON
HEALING AND/OR SAVING LIFE AND VOCABULARY
OF CULPABILITY

I. *The Modifications of Restrictions*

About twenty or so of the directives which are preserved in Jewish
sources from tannaitic and earlier times that permit an act of healing
and/or saving life also include details that dictate in some way how the
permitted act may and/or may not be performed. In contrast, however,
unless during a debate on a tannaitic text in which such instructions are
included, these details are never mentioned in discussions of situations
of healing and/or saving life in comparable amoraic texts. Thus, for
example, the amoraic discussion in the Jerusalem Talmud at y. AZ 2.2,
which refers to fifteen or so different situations that require an act of
healing and/or saving life (including a lesion within the lips, the removal
of swollen glands in the throat, the treatment of an inflamed eye, the
treatment of injuries to the hands and feet and a wound that is inflamed,
the removal of the sting of a scorpion, the treatment of a wound in the
shape of a frog and the treatment of burn, chills and a fever), makes no
reference at all to a particular method that must or must not be used
when treating these ills. This raises the question: if such details are
absent from comparable amoraic sources, why are they present in the
tannaitic texts?

The answer to this question seems to depend on the nature of the
instructions that are found in these texts. Two types occur. One is
restrictive, for example the instruction in a tannaitic ruling which states
that a wound on the leg may be treated on the Sabbath only if a sponge is
placed over the wound and water is dripped down the legs of the
wounded person on to the sponge (t. Shab 12.14). Similarly, another
directive, also preserved in the Tosefta, allows a sick person to be given
an oral medicine provided it is delivered by means of a siphon and

a perforated vessel (see t. Shab 2.7). This kind of restrictive detail can also be seen in the directive from Qumran, which forbids the use of 'a ladder, a rope or a utensil'.[1] These restrictions on the methods that may be used can be explained as a result of the effort of the Jewish sages to limit the inevitable violation of Jewish law that was caused when or however the permitted action was performed. Thus, for example, the restriction imposed by the directive of t. Yom 4.4 ensured that the pregnant woman received a minimal amount of the food that she craved, and the restrictions imposed in the directive from Qumran prevents the carrying of any implements to the site of the accident, that is, from one domain to another, which is the last of the thirty-nine *main* prohibited activities on the Sabbath day (see m. Shab 7.2, cited in Chapter 1).

In contrast with these restrictive instructions, the second type of instruction found in tannaitic texts that deal with acts of healing and/or saving life is permissive. For example, a permit in the Tosefta allows rescuers to go into a sinking ship if an individual on the ship cannot climb out (t. Shab 15.11). Another allows leeks to be gathered on the Sabbath and a chicken to be killed in order to cure a bite from a snake (t. Shab 15.14). The existence of such details is more difficult to explain because they may be so obvious that they hardly need to be said. Why, for example, after giving permission to save a person from a sinking ship, was it also necessary to state that the rescuers might climb down and remove the endangered individual when this kind of action could be anticipated as a part of the action that was needed for the individual to be saved (see t. Shab 15.11)? Similarly, having allowed someone to be removed from a pit on the Sabbath, why was it also necessary to state that it was permitted to let down a chain, presumably in order to remove the individual from the pit (see t. Shab 15.[12]13)?

These permissive details may, however, be explained as the response of later tannaitic sages to the existence of restrictive details in earlier directives which were seen as potential impediments to the intention of a directive to allow a deed of healing and/or saving of life, an action which the arguments of R. Akiva and R. Ishmael, and the sages of the second century, had clearly exposed was the will of the Jewish God. These texts thus give the impression of leniency in comparison with earlier versions of the same permit. For example, the woman who craved *terumah* (at t. Yom 4.4) may not have been cured if she was allowed only to consume the juice of the *terumah*, as this directive commands. If, then, the remedy for her illness was restricted in this way, not only would Jewish law have been violated by giving her the juice (probably on the day of a religious

---

1. CD 11:16-17, see Chapter 1.

fast), but the woman who was ill would not have been cured, so that the intention of the directive would not have been achieved and Jewish law would have been violated in vain. It is clear that such problems were recognised by the amoraic sages, who therefore allowed the sick woman to eat the meat itself, even if it was pork (see below on b. Yom 82a), in order to ensure that she was successfully cured. Similarly, it may not have been possible to provide an oral medicine on the Sabbath in exactly the manner prescribed in t. Shab 2.7, with resulting dire effects for the person who was ill. Earlier restrictive details which might have prevented the success of an action of healing and/or saving life were therefore modified in such a way that they were neutralised and thus effectively removed and now appear as permissive, often unnecessary details in the relevant tannaitic texts. For example, the permissive detail in the directive at m. Yom 8.7, which states that the debris of a building that had fallen on the Sabbath may be removed on the Sabbath, whether or not it was known if someone was buried by the debris, may suggest that an earlier directive had imposed a restriction that forbade the action of removing debris on the Sabbath unless there was clear evidence that someone had been buried. Alternatively, rather than modifying an earlier restriction, such restrictions may have been removed; see, for example, the directive m. Yom 8.6, which omits some of the restrictions imposed on the giving of an oral medicament on the Sabbath, in the probably earlier text of t. Shab 2.7. It can however be assumed that the apparent leniency of such directives is an illusion, and is merely the result of the desire of the later tannaitic sages to ensure—as far as possible—a successful outcome of the action that was permitted, it being assumed that an attempt would always be made to limit the inevitable violation of Jewish law that would be caused, so that restrictions were not needed to achieve this result.

It is possible, therefore, that a tannaitic directive which allows an action of healing and/or saving life that violates Jewish law (the latter can of course be assumed for all directives of this kind, for otherwise there would be no reason for such actions to be allowed) and which also includes apparently unnecessary permissive details which seem to suggest leniency in the way that the permitted action is performed or achieved, are later versions of directives in which corresponding restrictive instructions were originally imposed. In other words, it is possible that any permissive-type detail on the way a permitted action of healing and/or the saving of life could be performed or achieved counteracts a restriction that was originally imposed in an earlier version of this directive, whether or not this earlier directive now exists. It is possible also that a directive preserved in a tannaitic text which includes no restrictive or permissive instructions is a later version of an earlier, perhaps unrecorded text in which the same action is allowed.

This theory will now be tested by comparing pairs of directives that can be independently dated in a relative way, and which allow the same actions of healing and/or saving life. As will be seen, the earlier of these texts includes restrictions on the method that may be used, while the later text includes permissive details that counteract the earlier restrictions, or perhaps such directives include no details at all. The relative dating of such directives may be indicated by the reference to a named Jewish sage, or by the fact that one version of a directive appears in a tannaitic text, while a second version of the same permit appears in an amoraic text. It also makes sense to accept the conclusions of Chapter 9, and thus to assume that unless there are indications to the contrary, a tannaitic directive which is specific for the permit that it allows and which includes no generalising vocabulary is probably older than the version of the same permit in which generalising vocabulary is found. Relative dates may also be indicated by a later addition to a directive which modifies the directive itself, or by a comparison of the content of similar directives in different rabbinic texts, particularly the Mishnah and Tosefta. These directives are compared in the paragraphs below.

A. *The Craving of a Pregnant Woman—Tosefta Yoma 4.4 in Comparison with Mishnah Yoma 8.5 and Babylonian Talmud Yoma 82a*
The directive preserved at t. Yom 4.4 allows a pregnant woman from the family of a priest to eat the juice from sacrificial *terumah*, presumably on the day of a religious fast. The discussion on this text in Chapter 9 has shown that an early version of this decree was almost certainly composed before 70 CE, and was later expanded with the insertion of the comment of R. Judah, probably R. Judah b. Ilai, who was active in the second century, around the years 135–170 CE. The present version of the directive in the Tosefta is cited below and the probably earlier version and the words of R. Judah are separated in the following translation of the text:

תוספתא מסכת יומא (כפורים) פרק ד הלכה ד

עוברה שהריחה שביעית תוחבין לה בכוש. ר' יהודה או' עוברה שהריחה
שביעית תוחבין לה ברוטב.

Tosefta Yoma 4.4
(A) R. Judah says: A pregnant woman who smelt produce of the seventh year, they hand over a spindle-full.
(B) A pregnant woman who smelt *terumah*, they hand over juice.

332336 *Jesus, the Sabbath and the Jewish Debate*

It is clear that the earliest version of this directive (labelled B above), is particularly restrictive—it applies only to a pregnant woman from the family of a priest, and thus excludes the majority of pregnant women who—in any case—were ineligible for *terumah*, and who might also have suffered in a similar way. Even if this directive relates to the craving for *terumah* by a pregnant woman who was *not* from the family of a priest (perhaps a servant of the family of a priest who somehow had access to *terumah*), the number of women to whom it could apply would be small. Moreover, the directive limits the craving to the food called *terumah*, ignoring the possibility for a craving for any other types of foods. Both these restrictions—the small number of women to whom the directive could apply, and the craving for one particular, very restricted food—are, however, modified by R. Judah b. Ilai, who increased the number of women who might benefit from such a permit, while at the same time conceding the possibility for a different kind of food. The latter is achieved by an ingenious exploitation of the theoretical ambiguity of the term *terumah*. As was noted in Chapter 9, this term may refer either to the meat from a sacrifice which was reserved for a priest and his family, as in the earliest version of the directive,[2] or else it could refer to agricultural produce. R. Judah chose to relate it to its alternative meaning, namely agricultural *terumah*, which he then linked with *sheviit*, that is, agricultural produce from the land of Israel whose use is forbidden by Pentateuchal law every seventh year, and thus—although forbidden—is potentially a food that was available to all.[3] The decree in the Tosefta was thus widened to include all pregnant Jewish women, and relates to a freely available, although forbidden, food. The Mishnah further widens the original directive by removing both the reference to a particular food, and the restricted quantity that was allowed (which the toseftan addition of R. Judah limited to a 'spindle-full'), thus allowing a craving for any kind of food, and allowing as much of it as was necessary for the woman to be cured, the latter expressed with the ingenious added rider 'until she recovers herself', עד שתשיב נפשה:

משנה מסכת יומא פרק ח משנה ה
עוברה שהריחה מאכילין אותה עד שתשיב נפשה.

2. Lev 27:32; Num 18:27-28; m. Ter 7.2. See Oppenheimer, 'Terumot and Ma'aserot', 1026.
  3. Exod 23:10-11; Lev 25:1-7, 20-22; Deut 31:10-13.

Mishnah Yoma 8.5

If a pregnant woman smelled [and craved any type of food] they may give her the food until she recovers herself.

It is clear, therefore, that the second-century sage R. Judah b. Ilai modified an early, very restrictive directive that was probably composed before 70 CE in such a way that it was far less restrictive, thus confirming the theory proposed above. In comparison with R. Judah b. Ilai's modification in the Tosefta, the comparable directive in the Mishnah is further modified in a way that further widens its application, which suggests that it was composed at a later date than the toseftan decree.

The version of this directive in the Babylonian Talmud is based on the present version in the Tosefta (which includes the comment of R. Judah). In common with the Mishnah, the amoraic commentary also continues the apparent trend towards leniency, noting that even if the pregnant woman craved for pork—a totally forbidden food in normal circumstances for all Jewish people—she would be allowed to eat this meat if other remedies had failed. As can be seen from the text below, the amoraic commentary also notes that if a small quantity of the juice of the meat does not cure, the woman is allowed to eat the meat itself, without any limitation of the quantity she is allowed:

תלמוד בבלי מסכת יומא דף פב עמוד א

תנו רבנן: עוברה שהריחה בשר קודש או בשר חזיר - תוחבין לה כוש ברוטב,
ומניחין לה על פיה. אם נתיישבה דעתה - מוטב, ואם לאו - מאכילין אותה רוטב
עצמה, ואם נתיישבה דעתה - מוטב, ואם לאו - מאכילין אותה שומן עצמו.

Babylonian Talmud Yoma 82a

Our tannaitic sages taught that if a pregnant woman smelt the flesh of holy flesh, or of pork, we put for her a reed into the juice and place it upon her mouth. If she then feels that her craving has been satisfied, it is well. If not, we feed her with the juice itself. If her craving is satisfied it is well. If not, we feed her with the fat meat itself, for there is nothing that can stand before [the duty of] saving life, with the exception of idolatry, incest and bloodshed (which are prohibited in all situations).

The increasingly apparently more lenient versions of this directive in the Tosefta, then in the Mishnah and finally in the Babylonian Talmud thus illustrate the gradual lifting of the restrictions imposed in the probably earliest version of the decree, of which no simple record exists.

B. *Feeding a Starving Person on the Day of a Fast, Mishnah Yoma 8.5 in Comparison with Babylonian Talmud Yoma 83a*

Another example of the modification of an earlier directive which similarly widens the application of this directive can be seen by comparing the mishnaic directive at m. Yom 8.5 and the amoraic later commentary on this text. The mishnaic directive allows a starving person to be given food (presumably at a time when fasting was decreed), but only on the advice of 'experts', rather than on the 'advice' of the starving person himself. It is reasonable to assume that the person who was starving would be more generous and thus more lenient towards himself in relation to the quantity of food that he might ingest, compared with the more objective approach of 'experts', who can be expected to adopt an impartial, probably stricter approach. This suggests that the original tannaitic restriction was imposed in order to minimise the violation of Jewish law when the permit was performed. The Mishnah thus states that 'experts' must be present to ensure the starving individual receives a minimum amount of food, and that he (or she) may decide on the amount only if no 'experts' are at hand:

משנה מסכת יומא פרק ח משנה ה

...חולה מאכילין אותו על פי בקיאין. ואם אין שם בקיאין מאכילין אותו על פי
עצמו עד שיאמר די.

Mishnah Yoma 8.5
...He that is sick may be given food according to the advice of experts. And if no experts are there, he may be given food at his own wish, until he says 'Enough'.

The restriction in the Mishnah concerning the amount of food that may be given is, however, removed in the later version of this directive in the Babylonian Talmud, which gives preference to the wish of the starving patient over the opinion of the (presumably) more objective and conservative 'experts', in this case defined as a doctor (רופא). Thus, according to the Talmud, it is obvious (פשיטא!) that even when the doctor wishes the patient to eat, but when the patient does not, the wishes of the doctor are followed only because the patient is asleep. Otherwise the wishes of the patient take precedence over the doctor's (or expert's) advice:

תלמוד בבלי מסכת יומא דף פג עמוד א

מר רבי ינאי: חולה אומר צריך, ורופא אומר אינו צריך, שומעין לחולה. מאי
טעמא? +משלי יד+ לב יודע מרת נפשו. פשיטא! מהו דתימא: רופא קים ליה
טפי, קא משמע לן. רופא אומר צריך וחולה אומר אינו צריך. שומעין לרופא.
מאי טעמא ? תונבא הוא דנקיט ליה.

Babylonian Talmud Yoma 83a
R. Yannai said, 'If the patient says, "I need [food]", whilst the physician says, "He does not need it", we listen to the patient. Why is this so? [We listen because it is written], "The heart knows its own bitterness" (Prov 14:10). But is that not obvious (פשיטא!)! You might have said, "The physician's knowledge is more established", [and] therefore the information [that we prefer the patient's opinion is incorrect]. [This is correct but only] if the physician says, "He needs it", while the patient says that he does not need it. [If so], we listen to the physician. Why? Because sleep overcame him [that is, sleep overcame the patient, so that he was not aware of his lack of food].'

It is clear, therefore, that in comparison with the earlier tannaitic directive at m. Yom 8.5, the later amoraic directive at b. Yom 83a shows greater leniency by the almost complete removal of an earlier restriction, and thus adds evidence to the claim that the theory proposed above is probably correct.

C. *Delivering Oral Medicine on the Sabbath, Tosefta Shabbat 2.7 in Comparison with Mishnah Yoma 8.6*
The following directive in the Tosefta stipulates that a siphon and a perforated vessel must be used when administering an oral medicine to a sick person on the Sabbath. Presumably these conditions were imposed in order to minimise the violation of Sabbath law:

תוספתא מסכת שבת פרק ב הלכה ז
... מעלין בדיופי ומטיפין מן הארק לחולה בשבת.

Tosefta Shabbat 2.7
...They bring up [liquid] with a siphon (דיופי) and drip [drops of the liquid] from a perforated vessel (ארק) to [heal] a sick person on the Sabbath.

A date of composition for this version of the directive before the end of the first century CE is suggested by its specificity, as was discussed in Chapter 9. In contrast to the specific nature of the toseftan decree, the comparable mishnaic text includes the generalising vocabulary of R. Akiva (ספק נפשות) which suggests a later date of composition compared with the totally specific directive of t. Shab 2.7. Moreover, the fact that the toseftan directive is unattractive *may* also suggest an earlier date of composition in comparison with the mishnaic decree, which is attributed to a second-century sage. Most significantly, although this mishnaic directive allows the same action, it omits the demand for a siphon or a perforated vessel, and is thus more permissive in the way that it allows the permitted action to be performed:

משנה מסכת יומא פרק ח משנה ו
... ועוד אמר רבי מתיא בן חרש החושש בגרונו מטילין לו סם בתוך פיו בשבת
מפני שהוא ספק נפשות וכל ספק נפשות דוחה את השבת.

Mishnah Yoma 8.6
...Moreover, R. Mattithiah b. Heresh said, 'If a person has pain in his throat they drip medicine [into the patient's mouth] on the Sabbath because it is a case of danger to life (ספק נפשות), and all [situations of] danger to life (וכל ספק נפשות) override the Sabbath'.

A second-century date of composition for the above version in the Mishnah is indicated by its attribution to the second-century sage R. Mattithiah b. Heresh, who was active around 135–170 CE, and also by R. Mattithiah's use of the generalising phrase ספק נפשות, which (as shown in Chapter 5) suggests that the permit that allowed for this action could also be allowed for all other acts of healing and/or saving life. As noted above, this suggests a later date of composition in comparison with the specific directive at t. Shab 2.7. It is probable therefore that m. Yom 8.6 is a later version of the directive at t. Shab 2.7. This being the case, the fact that the probably second-century version of this directive has simplified the restrictions that were imposed for the same action in a directive that was probably composed before the end of the first century CE, helps to confirm the theory proposed above.

D. *A Prohibited Cure for Rabies is Now Allowed, Mishnah Yoma 8.6*
R. Mattithiah b. Heresh is also credited with reversing an earlier restriction on the consumption of the liver of a rabid dog as a cure for rabies:

משנה מסכת יומא פרק ח משנה ו
...מי שנשכו כלב שוטה אין מאכילין אותו מחצר כבד שלו ורבי מתיא בן חרש
מתיר...

Mishnah Yoma 8.6
Whoever was bitten by a mad dog, he may not be given the lobe of its liver to eat. But R. Mattithiah b. Heresh allows [it].

No directive which prohibited the consumption of the rabid liver of a dog to cure rabies has been preserved. Its prior existence is, however, implied by the first part of the above directive. This restriction in this earlier directive is, however, negated by R. Mattithiah, who thereby again demonstrates the tendency of the second-century sages to lighten, and here to remove completely, an earlier restriction on an action which could heal and/or save life.

E. *A Modification of a Prohibition to Use Vinegar, Mishnah Shabbat 14.4 Versus Tosefta Shabbat 12.9*

The Mishnah prohibits the *deliberate* use of vinegar in order to cure toothache on the Sabbath, because this commonly consumed substance would then have been *deliberately* used on the Sabbath for healing, (rather than for food) in violation of Sabbath law:

משנה מסכת שבת פרק יד משנה ד

החושש בשיניו לא יגמע בהן את החומץ. אבל מטבל הוא כדרכו ואם נתרפא נתרפא.

Mishnah Shabbat 14.4
The [person who] is worried about his teeth [because he has toothache must] not [deliberately] suck vinegar through them [to cure his tooth-ache]. But if he dips [his food in vinegar] according to his custom, and he is healed, then he is healed.

The Tosefta, while apparently agreeing with the Mishnah, ingeniously reverses the mishnaic prohibition by allowing vinegar to be *swallowed*, but not *spat* out. This procedure is considered to make possible the *deliberate* use of vinegar to cure toothache on the Sabbath, without contravening Sabbath law:

תוספתא מסכת שבת פרק יב הלכה ט

חושש בשיניו לא יגמע בהן יין וחומץ ופולט. אבל מגמע ובולע ומטביל כדרכו ואינו חושש.

Tosefta Shabbat 12.9
The [person who] is worried about his teeth [because he has toothache must] not [deliberately] suck wine and vinegar through them [to cure his toothache] and spit out. [But if] he sucks and swallows (ובולע) and dips [his food in vinegar] according to his custom, he [need] not worry [about violating Sabbath law].

The addition of the reference to swallowing suggests that this version of this directive in the Tosefta is a later version of the mishnaic decree. The addition in the Tosefta of the words 'and swallows' (ובולע) modifies the restriction in the Mishnah in such a way that this restriction is effectively removed—it is now possible to take vinegar as a deliberate medicament on the Sabbath without a violation of Sabbath law. The Tosefta thus illustrates the later modification of an earlier restriction to allow a Sabbath act of healing and/or saving life.

F. *The Use of Rose Oil for Healing and/or Saving Life, Mishnah Shabbat 14.4*

In the following directive, R. Simon, probably the second-century sage R. Simon b. Yochai, dismisses an earlier claim that a certain substance—here, rose oil—should only be used by royalty as a medicament on the Sabbath because its curative effect for those by whom it was used in a routine way would be an accidental by-product of its routine use (as for vinegar in the directives above). For ordinary people, however, for whom the use of this substance was comparatively rare, its use on the Sabbath was considered as equivalent to a medicament for healing, which is not permitted on the Sabbath day:

משנה מסכת שבת פרק יד משנה ד

החושש במתניו לא יסוך יין וחומץ אבל סך הוא את השמן ולא שמן ורד. בני
מלכים סכין שמן ורד על מכותיהן שכן דרכם לסוך בחול. רבי שמעון אומר כל
ישראל בני מלכים הם.

Mishnah Shabbat 14.4

He [who] is concerned [with pain] in his loins [must] not rub [them] with wine and vinegar, but he rubs [them] with oil but not [with] rose oil. The children of kings may anoint their wounds [with rose oil] for thus it is their custom on ordinary [non-Sabbath] days. R. Shimon says, 'All Israelites are children of kings'.

The leniency of R. Simon has clearly been added to an earlier directive which restricted the use of rose oil as a medicament to 'the children of kings'. The specificity of the earlier statement, which relates only to a wound on the loins, and which restricts the treatment that is allowed, suggests a date of composition well before the end of the first century CE (see Chapter 9). The comment of R. Shimon, however, ingeniously removes the earlier restriction which forbade rose oil to be used as a medicament by those by whom this substance was not generally used. This again adds evidence to the claim that earlier restrictions imposed in directives that allowed acts of healing and/or saving life, were modified in later times.[4]

G. *The Edict of Mattathias Cited by Josephus, War 1.146 in Comparison with Jewish Antiquities XII.276-77*

The commentary of Josephus in *The Jewish War*, which was published between 75 and 79 CE, notes that the Jews were allowed to fight on

---

4. The similar permit is allowed by Rabban Simon b. Gamaliel: 'A woman may wash her child in wine, even though this is intended for healing'. On the basis of the argument here, this should be attributed to Rabban Simon b. Gamaliel II rather than Rabban Simon b. Gamaliel I, as identified in the Bar Ilan Responsa, version 20.

the Sabbath only in self-defence. Josephus thus repeats the restriction originally issued in the edict of Mattathias in 167 BCE.[5] A translation of his report follows below:

The Jewish War I.146
Indeed the labours of the Romans would have been endless had not Pompey taken advantage of the seventh day of the week, on which the Jews, from religious scruples, refrain from all manual work, and then proceeded to raise the earth works, while forbidding his troops to engage in hostilities. For on the Sabbaths *the Jews only fight in self-defence* (γὰρ τοῦ σώματος ἀμύνονται τοῖς σαββάτοις).

In contrast, however, almost twenty-five years later, in 93 CE, a more lenient version of Mattathias' edict was published by Josephus in *The Jewish Antiquities* which states that the Jews are allowed to violate Sabbath law by fighting on the Sabbath 'whenever it is necessary':

Jewish Antiquities XII.276-77
And [Mattathias] instructed them [the Jews] to fight even on the Sabbath, saying that if for the sake of observing the law they failed to do so, they would be their own enemies, for their foes would attack them on that day, and unless they resisted, nothing would prevent them from all perishing without striking a blow. These words persuaded them, *and to this day we continue the practice of fighting even on the Sabbath whenever it becomes necessary* (καὶ ἄχρι δεῦρο μένει παρ' ἡμῖν τὸ καὶ σαββάτοις, εἴ ποτε δρήσειε, μάχεσθαι).

Although it could be claimed that fighting in self-defence (according to Mattathias' version of this directive) could include a pre-emptive attack, and thus could also allow fighting 'whenever it is necessary', the later report of Josephus removes any ambiguity, making it clear that any kind of fighting on the Sabbath is now officially allowed. The restrictive demand of the earlier directive has thus been removed.[6]

The relative date of the publications of Josephus, moreover, suggest the time when this change to the edict of Mattathias was made, namely, sometime between 75 and 93 CE.

---

5. 1 Macc 2.41, cited in Chapter 1; also 2 Macc 6.11.

6. A further directive in the Tosefta which includes permissive details allows (1) a doctor to be called from a distance further than the Sabbath *eruv*, (2) a chicken to be killed and (3) leeks to be gathered, in order to treat a snake bite on the Sabbath day, see t. Shab 15.15. On the basis of the discussion in this chapter, the presence of these permits suggests the existence of an earlier directive that forbade these procedures. No such directive, however, has been preserved.

H. *Reversal to Earlier Restrictions, Tosefta Shabbat 12.12*

This text shows that before the time of R. Meir, whose active life began around 140 CE, it was not permitted to mix a medicine on the Sabbath. This ruling was rescinded by R. Meir, although he refused this leniency for himself:

תוספתא מסכת שבת פרק יב הלכה יב

... עושין אלנתית לחולה בשבת. אימתי? בזמן שטרפ' מערב_שבת שלא טרפה
מערב שבת אסורה שאין טורפין בתחלה בשבת אין טורפין יין ושמן לחולה
בשבת.
רבי שמעון בן אלעזר אומר משום רבי מאיר טורפין יין ושמן לחולה בשבת אמ'
ר' שמעון בן לעזר פעם אחת חלה ר' מאיר ובקשנו לעשות לו ולא הניחני אמ' לו
רבינו תבטל דבריך בחייך אמ' לנו אף על פי שאני אומ' כן לא מלאני לבי מימי
לעבור על דברי חביריי.

Tosefta Shabbat 12.12
...They prepare a wine-potion for an invalid on the Sabbath only when (literally, When?) it was prepared on the eve of the Sabbath [that is, prepared on Friday afternoon before sunset when the Sabbath began]. But if it was not mixed on the eve of the Sabbath, it is prohibited to do so. For they do not begin to mix on the Sabbath [itself]. They do not mix wine and oil for a sick person on the Sabbath.
[But] R. Simeon b. Eleazar says in the name of R. Meir, 'They *do* mix wine and oil for a sick person on the Sabbath'. Said R. Simeon b. Eleazar, 'Once R. Meir fell ill [on the Sabbath], and we wanted to prepare it for him, but he did not let me do so. I said to him "Our master, will you nullify your opinion during your own lifetime?" He said to us, "Even though that happens to be my opinion, my heart has never been so puffed up in my whole life as to let me violate the opinion of my colleagues"'.

I. *An Application of the Theory Proposed Above*

The texts discussed above help to confirm that the apparently more lenient version of a directive which allows the same or very similar action of healing and/or saving life is probably a later composed version of the earlier, similar decree. This may help to establish the relative dates of composition of the following three pairs of directives, which probably cannot otherwise be dated in a relative way.

(1) *Mishnah Yoma 8.7 Compared with t. Shab 15.11*. Each of these directives allows debris to be moved on the Sabbath in order to save a person who is buried beneath. Both include the concept of doubt, which was probably first officially introduced into directives on healing and/or saving life by R. Akiva (see Chapter 5) and thus suggests that both versions were composed after the activity of R. Akiva which, as discussed

above, probably began in the second half of the second century CE. The version in the Mishnah follows below:

משנה מסכת יומא פרק ח משנה ז

מי שנפלה עליו מפולת ספק הוא שם ספק אינו שם ספק חי ספק מת ספק עובד כוכבים ספק ישראל מפקחין עליו את הגל. מצאוהו חי מפקחין עליו ואם מת יניחוהו.

Mishnah Yoma 8.7
If debris fell on a person and there is doubt (ספק) that he is there [or] doubt (ספק) that he is not there, or doubt (ספק) if he is alive or doubt (ספק) that he is dead, or doubt (ספק) that he is a gentile or doubt (ספק) that he is an Israelite, they may remove the mound [that has fallen] on [top of] him. [But if] they find him alive, they may [continue] clearing away [the debris lying] on him and if dead, they leave him [so that he/she can be buried after the Sabbath].

As can be seen, this directive contains three *permissive* details, namely (1) that there is *no need* to know for certain before even beginning the removal of debris if someone is buried beneath, (2) that there is *no need* to know whether or not the person buried beneath the debris is alive, (3) that there is *no need* to know if this person was an 'Israelite'. It is thus difficult to avoid the conclusion that a likely reason for referring to and for allowing such obvious particulars (especially the first two) is that they each counteract specific restrictions in an earlier directive. This being the case, it can be assumed that the mishnaic directive is a later version of an earlier directive which forbade the removal of debris unless it was known for certain that someone was buried beneath and until it was known whether he (or she) was alive.

The corresponding directive in the Tosefta does not include any of the permissive details of the mishnaic decree:

תוספתא מסכת שבת פרק טו הלכה יא

מפקחין על ספק נפש בשבת ...

Tosefta Shabbat 15.11
They remove debris for [one for whom there is] doubt of [his] life (על ספק נפש) on the Sabbath ...

This version of the directive thus resembles the simplicity of directives on healing and/or saving life preserved in the relevant discussions in the Jerusalem and Babylonian Talmuds, which do not include any restrictive or permissive details on the way that the permitted action may be performed. It is possible therefore that the directive in the Tosefta may be a later version of the mishnaic decree.

(2) *Mishnah Shabbat 16.5 Compared with t. Shab 15.(12)13*. The same
relationship may be seen between the directives of m. Shab 16.5 and
t. Shab 15.(12)13. The details in the first, m. Shab 16.5, which allow a
chest, box or cupboard to be covered with the hide of a kid, and the use
of vessels, all in order to prevent the spread of a fire, may suggest that
such permissive actions were forbidden in an earlier version of this
decree. On this basis, therefore, this directive which is attributed to the
second-century sage R. Simeon b. Nanos, is a later version of an earlier
directive which has not been preserved, in which restrictions were
imposed concerning the way that a barrier could be built on the Sabbath
to prevent the spread of a fire:

משנה מסכת שבת פרק טז משנה ה

רבי שמעון בן ננס אומר פורסין עור של גדי על גבי שידה תיבה ומגדל שאחז בהן
את האור מפני שהוא מחרך ועושין מחיצה בכל הכלים בין מלאים בין ריקנים
בשביל שלא תעבור הדליקה ...

Mishnah Shabbat 16.5
Rabbi Simeon b. Nanos says: They may spread the hide of a kid over a
chest, a box or a cupboard that has caught fire, since it will [only] scorch
[and not light another fire, which is forbidden on the Sabbath, even if it
results from an inadvertent action], and they may make a partition wall of
the vessels, whether filled [with water] or empty, so that the fire shall not
spread...[7]

The comparable directive in the Tosefta simply states that a barrier may
be built:

תוספתא מסכת שבת פרק טו הלכה יג

... ומפסיקין לדליקה בשבת ...

Tosefta Shabbat 15.(12)13
...and they make a barrier against the fire on the Sabbath...

The simplicity of this directive again resembles the simplicity of the
statements which allow specific acts of healing and/or saving life in the
amoraic texts, and thus suggests total leniency in the way that a barrier
may be built, which suggests that it is a later version of the comparable
mishnaic decree.

(3) *The Directives from Qumran Compared with t. Shab 15.13*. The
directives from Qumran (cited in Chapter 1) allow a person to be saved
from a pit on the Sabbath but severely restrict how this might be done.
They can be compared with the clearly more lenient directive in the

7. For commentary on this text, see b. Shab 120b.

Tosefta which also allows someone to be saved from a pit. Thus, as can be seen, the directive 4Q265 Frag. 6 6-7 restricts any device that could be used for the rescue to a garment and also specifically forbids the use of 'an implement'. Similarly, the directive CD 11:16-17 forbids the use of 'a ladder, a rope or an implement'. In contrast, the decree in the Tosefta not only allows the rescuer to climb down into the pit, to pull out the fallen individual, but also specifically notes that a chain, that is, 'an implement' (כלי), may be lowered to the person in the pit. This stated permit not only directly counteracts the specified prohibition in Qumran that 'an implement' may not be used, but also—we must assume—counteracts the implied prohibition in these directives against carrying on the Sabbath day, for why and how else would a chain be brought to the site?:

תוספתא מסכת שבת פרק טו הלכה יג

נפל לבור ואין יכול לעלות עוקרין לו חוליה ויורדין ומעלין אותו משם ...

Tosefta Shabbat 15.13
[If a person] fell into a pit, and cannot climb out, they remove him with a chain and go down [into the pit] and raise him up from there...

In view of the evidence discussed above which shows the relaxation of restrictions in earlier expressed texts, it is thus possible that a version of a directive that allowed a person to be rescued from a pit on the Sabbath which was as similarly restrictive as those in Qumran existed in the normative Jewish community in Maccabean times, and continued to be part of the *halachah* of Qumran when this community broke away. The restrictions in the normative community were, however, later removed, producing the above modified version in the Tosefta, in which the reference to 'doubt' (the concept introduced into directives on healing and/or saving life probably by R. Akiva) suggests that it was composed after around 70 CE.

To conclude: it is clear that the above three pairs of directives do not prove the theory suggested at the beginning of the chapter, but the fact that they exist and seem to fall into the suggested pattern helps to confirm that this theory is correct.

J. *When Did the Change in Directives Take Place?*

The directives cited above are few in number because there are very few directives in the tannaitic texts that allow the same or similar action of healing and/or saving life, and which can also be dated in a relative way. Those that exist, however, help to confirm the suggestion that the restrictions imposed in early directives that permitted a specific deed of healing and/or saving life were relaxed or even completely removed in later versions of these decrees. For how otherwise are such changes to be explained? Moreover, as can be seen from the examples above, the few tannaitic directives on healing and/or saving life which include *permissive* details and which are attributed to named Jewish sages, are linked only with Jewish sages from the second century CE, namely R. Simeon b. Nanos (m. Shab 16.5), R. Simon b. Yochai (m. Shab 14.4), R. Mattithiah b. Heresh (m. Yom 8.6) and R. Judah b. Halafta (t. Yom 4.4). None are linked with Jewish sages from before the second century CE. There are, moreover, no tannaitic directives with *restrictive* details that are linked with a second-century Jewish sage. This helps to confirm that the modifications to earlier directives resulting in permissive details are a later aspect of the Jewish debate. These modifications may thus be a further aspect of the change in the approach of the tannaitic sages in the latter half of the first century, probably after 70 CE, from permits that allowed only a specific action of healing and/or saving life to those that allowed action in *any* situation of healing and/or saving life (discussed in Chapter 9). This may be confirmed by the dates of the references to the edict of Mattathias by Josephus, cited above, who refers in a work published between 75 and 79 CE to the restrictive directive of Mattathias. Subsequently, about twenty-five years later in a work published in 93 CE, Josephus refers to a modified, apparently more lenient version of this decree. It is possible, therefore, that the modification of earlier restrictive directives began between the publication of these works, in the last two decades of the first century CE.

II. *Culpability for Dating Early Tannaitic Directives on Healing and/or Saving Life*

A further indication of a directive that was composed *before* around 70 CE is the presence of vocabulary which suggests culpability, in particular the verb חלל, 'to violate', and the terms פטור and its antonym חייב, the former indicating that a person is 'free from potential culpability for a violation of Jewish law', the latter indicating that a person is 'liable for a penalty for a violation of Jewish law'. Unless in discussion on tannaitic texts on healing and/or saving life in which these terms appear, these terms are not used in comparable amoraic discussions. Moreover, as will be seen in Chapter 11, these terms are often used in directives whose other features, especially their lack of generality, also strongly indicate a date of composition before the activity of R. Akiva and R. Ishmael, which may have begun around 70 CE.

The last datable evidence that those who performed a deed of healing and/or saving life were verbally identified as culpable in some way is the remark R. Yocahan b. Zakkai made when he lived in Galilee before 70 CE, when he hesitantly suggested that a person who had violated Sabbath law by a deed of healing and/or saving life should present a sin-offering in the Temple (see on m. Shab 16.7 in Chapter 11). It is, however, difficult to believe that culpability of any kind continued to be attributed to a person performing a deed of healing and/or saving life after the popularity of the verb דחה in the phrase דחה (את) (ה)שבת, 'to override the Sabbath', which it seems was used in relation to an act of healing and/or saving life after around 70 CE (see Chapter 5). This is because the phrase 'to override the Sabbath' used in relation to a deed of healing and/or saving life implies hypothetically the Sabbath was suspended when the deed was performed, so that no Sabbath offence could be attributed to the performer of this deed. It is also unlikely that a term suggesting culpability continued to be used in the composition of directives that permitted a deed of healing and/or saving life which were composed after the composition of the arguments and special vocabulary of R. Akiva and R. Ishmael towards the end of the first century (see Chapter 5), which justified in general all acts of healing and/or saving life. Although, therefore, it seems that at least two of the second-century tannaitic Jewish sages could not tolerate the thought that a violation of Jewish law by an act of healing and/or saving life should be euphemistically obscured with the verb דחה—namely, Simon of Teman, who referred to such a violation with the more direct verb לעבור, 'to transgress' (see t. Betz 2.6), and R. Simeon b. Eleazar, who used the verb חלל to emphasise that *even* (אפילו) the healing and/or the saving of life of a one-day-old child must be allowed to violate (מחללין) Sabbath law (see t. Shab 17.19)—unless when discussing tannaitic passages in which blame is implied (see, e.g., in the amoraic discussion at b. Shab 128b which is based on the text of m. Shab 18.3), the second-century Jewish sages and the amoraim avoided the use of terms which suggest blame or culpability in relation to acts of healing and/or saving life. It is thus reasonable to assume in general that tannaitic directives which include terms that imply culpability for an act of healing and/or saving life were probably composed before around 70 CE, especially when this dating is confirmed by other details in a text.

An illustration of the terminology of culpability is provided by the text of m. Shab 18.3:

משנה מסכת שבת פרק יח משנה ג

(1) ...ומילדין את האשה בשבת.

(2) וקורין לה חכמה ממקום למקום. ומחללין עליה את השבת.

(3) וקושרין את הטבור. רבי יוסי אומר אף חותכין...

Mishnah Shabbat 18.3

(1) …And they may deliver a woman [of her child] on the Sabbath.

(2) And [they may] call a midwife for her from anywhere [that is, even from a distance that exceeds the *eruv*]. And [= so that] one may violate (מחללין) the Sabbath on her behalf.

(3) And they tie (קושרין) the umbilical cord [on the Sabbath]. R. Yose says they also cut (חותחין) [it on the Sabbath]…

The three sections of this directive allow actions that are essential for childbirth and thus state the assumption of Rabban Gamaliel the Elder at m. RH 2.5 (discussed in Chapter 9) who refers to one or more permits that allowed the work of a midwife on the Sabbath day. Thus, since Rabban Gamaliel died around 50 CE, it can be assumed that it was officially permitted before 50 CE to violate Sabbath law in the ways described above in order to deliver a child on the Sabbath day.

The first of the above directives allows the *specific* action of delivering a child. It does not allow for any other medical act.

The second directive *specifically* allows a midwife to violate the Sabbath *eruv*.[8] The verb חלל used in the phrase מחללין את השבת, literally, 'one violates the Sabbath', which confirms the permitted action, repeats the verb used in the biblical prohibition against the violation of Sabbath law voiced at Exod 31:14, thus ושמרתם את השבת ... מחלליה מות יומת, 'and you will keep the Sabbath…those who violate it (מחלליה) shall surely be put to death'. The use of this verb thus implies the serious culpability of the person violating the Sabbath law.

The third of the directives in m. Shab 18.3 is repeated verbatim in the Tosefta:

תוספתא מסכת שבת פרק טו הלכה ג

קושרין את הטבור. רבי יוסי אומר אף חותכין [את הטבור בשבת].

Tosefta Shabbat 15.3

They tie (קושרין) the umbilical cord [on the Sabbath]. R. Yose says they also cut (חותחין) [it on the Sabbath]…

The verb קשר, 'to tie', which is used in both the Mishnah and Tosefta, is one of the thirty-nine *main* classes of work (the twenty-first) listed at m. Shab 7.2 which is prohibited on the Sabbath day. As was noted in

8. The Jerusalem Talmud, y. Shab 18.3, justifies this leniency on the basis of m. RH 2.5, although leniency is allowed in the latter only *after* the midwife has completed her task, rather than *before*, as in m. Shab 18.3.

Chapter 3, there is good reason to assume that a directive that repeats a term used in this mishnaic list for the specific permit of healing and/or saving life was composed before the Maccabean composition of m. Shab 7.2. A date of composition before 50 CE is in any case suggested by the allusion to the work of a midwife in the edict of Rabban Gamaliel (at m. RH 2.5), because separating the child from the umbilical cord is an essential part of her work.

The additional remark of R. Yose, probably the second-century R. Yose b. Halafta, who was active from around 135 to 170 CE, uses an imperfect tense to state that it was also common to cut the umbilical cord, thus חותכין נוהגין היינו, *we used to cut.* This helps to confirm that the action of cutting the umbilical cord was also officially sanctioned on the Sabbath before his time. It may also be significant that R. Yose uses the *Kal* (*Paal*) conjugation to refer to the cutting of the umbilical cord (חותכין), rather than the *Piel* conjugation of the verb חתך, 'to cut', which is used in the list of the thirty-nine main prohibited actions (the thirty-first) at m. Shab 7.2 (המחתך), as this may imply that R. Yose avoided close repetition of the one of the thirty-nine main activities prohibited on the Sabbath, thereby suggesting—even if only euphemistically—a lesser violation of Sabbath law.

To conclude, therefore, it is reasonable to assume that the three directives preserved at m. Shab 18.3 were composed well before 50 CE, and perhaps even before the composition of m. Shab 7.2, the latter probably in Maccabean times. These directives include the implication of culpability which never appears in directives whose date of composition can be assumed after around 70 CE.

III. *Cumulative Evidence for a Flurry of Activity After 70 CE*

Listed below are the possible reasons for assuming that changes in the approach of the Jewish sages to directives that allowed acts of healing and/or saving life, including the modifications made to earlier texts which are discussed above, probably began around 70 CE.

(1) Before around 70 CE, the datable directives which allowed an act of healing and/or saving life in Jewish texts—the edict of Mattathias in 176 BCE, the declaration of Shammai at the turn of the millennium (see t. Eruv 3.7 and *Sifre Devarim* 203), the assumptions of Rabban Gamaliel the Elder at m. RH 2.5 and the comment of R. Yohanan b. Zakkai made in Galilee before 70 CE (m. Shab 16.7)—are all solely *specific* for the permits that they allow. After around this time, there are no datable directives that do not *generalise* in some way the specific actions that they allow.

(2) This is corroborated by the gospels of Mark and Luke, the earliest of the four gospels (the gospel of Luke is thought to have been composed around 75 CE, and that of Mark before the gospel of Luke), which include permits (expressed as arguments *kal va-chomer*) that allow only *specific* acts of healing and/or saving life. In contrast, the later gospels of Matthew and John (that of Matthew was probably published around 80 CE, and the gospel of John after this time) contain general permits (again expressed as arguments *kal va-chomer*) which could be used to allow *any* action in *any* situation of healing and/or saving life. This suggests that these general arguments were first composed sometime between around 75 CE and 80 CE—the time between the publication of the gospels of Matthew and Luke.

(3) It is likely that the verb דחה, used in the phrase דחה (את) (ה)שבת, was used in the underlying Hebrew text of the conclusion of the argument voiced by Jesus to the Pharisees in the midrashic-type story of their meeting in the Galilean fields (Mark 2:28, see the discussion in Chapter 3). This argument is first recorded in Mark's gospel which was probably published around 70 CE. This being the case, Mark's gospel records the earliest innovative use of the verb דחה, used to refer to a secular (rather than religious) act of healing and/or saving life that overrode Pentateuchal Jewish law. The earliest Jewish sages to whom this innovative use of the verb דחה can be attributed are R. Eleazar b. Azariah, who was probably active in 70 CE, or else his younger contemporary R. Akiva. The publication of Mark's gospel thus indicates the earliest date of composition of the *general* arguments *kal va-chomer* of R. Akiva in which this phrase is used.

(4) *The Jewish War*, a work published by Josephus between 75 and 79 CE, reports that the edict of Mattathias allowed fighting on the Sabbath only in the specific case of self-defence. However, almost twenty-five years later in *The Jewish Antiquities* published in 93 CE, Josephus reports a modified, apparently more lenient version of the edict of Matthias which allowed fighting 'whenever it is necessary', that is, this directive now allows fighting *in general* on the Sabbath, not only in cases of self-defence. This suggests that a change from specific to general permits along with the modifications that were necessary to bring older directives in line with the newer, apparently more lenient and general approach, took place between around the years 75 and 93 CE.

(5) If Matthew was inspired by the sorite of R. Akiva to rephrase the argument *kal va-chomer* apparently used by Jesus to the Pharisees in the Galilean fields, then R. Akiva must have re-phrased the earlier composed argument *kal va-chomer* before the publication of Matthew's gospel, which is thought to have been published around 80 CE.

(6) It seems that R. Akiva changed the proof text of an argument *kal va-chomer* (which he re-phrased as a sorite) from a midrashic account of David at Nob which was based on 1 Sam 21:1-6, to a midrashic interpretation of Exod 21:14 (see Chapter 6). This may have been done in response to the popularity of the story of Jesus and the Pharisees in the Galilean fields, especially in the account of Matthew in his gospel which was published around 80 CE (see [5] above). On this basis, therefore, the change of proof text in R. Akiva's sorite probably took place sometime around 80 CE.

(7) The change in proof text around 80 CE (discussed briefly in the paragraph above) is corroborated by Josephus's account of the biblical David's visit to Nob in *The Jewish Antiquities*, which relates the biblical story in such a way that it could not be used as a proof text in the sorite of Matthew (and neither, of course, in the corresponding argument *kal va-chomer* in the gospels of Mark and Luke). The version of the story of David at Nob by Josephus thus discredits the logic of the sorite of Matthew (and also, of course, the logic of the argument in Mark and Luke). This suggests that Josephus supported the change of proof text made to the argument by R. Akiva. Otherwise, it is difficult to explain why Josephus tells the biblical story in a way that not only omits two of its main features, namely the hunger of David, and his consumption of the sacred bread, but also makes sure that his readers know that David arrived at the shrine of Nob, rather than the Temple in Jerusalem. This being the case, the fact that the story of David at Nob was published by Josephus in *The Jewish Antiquities* in 93 CE, suggests that that R. Akiva had changed the proof text before 93 CE.

(8) The arguments *kal va-chomer* in the gospel texts suggest the popularity of these arguments in the first century CE. In contrast, it seems that only arguments which are based on relatively simple interpretations of biblical texts were composed in the second century CE (see Chapter 7). The arguments *kal va-chomer,* with their special vocabulary which are attributed to R. Akiva and R. Ishmael, were probably composed between these two different types of argument, and the cumulative evidence suggests that this happened towards the end of the first century, rather than in the second century CE.

(9) The directive in the Mishnah at m. Yom 8.7 (which allows the removal of debris on the Sabbath, see the discussion above) contains permissive details of a kind that suggest that this version of the directive is a later version of an earlier decree in which corresponding restrictions were imposed. The date of composition of this later directive is suggested by its references to 'doubt' (ספק), an aspect of directives on healing and/ or saving life which was probably introduced by R. Akiva. This being

the case, it seems that the modification to the earlier (now unrecorded decree) took place after the activity of R. Akiva had begun, which was probably after 70 CE. As second-century Jewish sages are associated with modifications of probably earlier texts which allowed acts of healing and/or saving life, it can be assumed that such modifications continued in the second century CE.

(10) Terms which suggest culpability for the performance of an act of healing and/or saving life that violates Jewish law are not used in directives which were probably composed well into the second half of the first century CE. The last evidence of any culpability attributed to the person who performed an act of healing and/or saving life is the directive attributed to R. Yocahan b. Zakkai, which can be dated before 70 CE (m. Shab 16.7). The popular use of the term דחה in the phrase דחה (את) (ה)שבת after around 70 CE 'to override the Sabbath', which effectively removes culpability when used in relation to a deed of healing and/or saving life may help to explain why no terms of culpability are used in directives that allow acts of healing and/or saving life that were originally composed after around 70 CE.

The conclusions expressed in the paragraphs above are only tentative. There is moreover little doubt that the changes in arguments and permits suggested above did not occur in a systematic, smooth way. Nevertheless, it seems reasonable to conclude that what may be regarded as a flurry of activity among the Jewish sages regarding the search for ways in which to justify acts of healing and/or the saving of life that violated Jewish law, began around the watershed date of 70 CE, and continued into the second century CE. It was probably initially inspired by R. Akiva and R. Ishmael, This activity eventually allowed the Jewish sages to claim with great certainty that, with the later added rider that deeds of idolatry, sexual sins and the shedding of blood should *never* be performed, acts of healing and/or saving life must always take place in spite of the fact that they might violate Jewish law, as is consistently confirmed in the amoraic texts (see Chapter 8).

IV. *Conclusions*

(1) Some early tannaitic directives include restrictions in the way that the permitted acts of healing and/or saving life were allowed to take place. It is probable that these restrictions were imposed in order to help ensure the minimum violation of Jewish law when the permitted deed of healing and/or saving life took place.

(2) In the absence of any indications to the contrary, it is probable that tannaitic directives which include such restrictions were composed—at the very least—before the end of the first century. This is especially the case if the directive is *specific* for its cure and thus includes no hint that it may serve as a *general* paradigm for the other innumerable situations that necessitate acts of healing and/or saving life.

(3) Although these imposed restrictions in tannaitic directives on healing and/or saving life would have prevented a greater than minimal violation of Jewish law, they might also have thwarted the action that was permitted to heal and/or save life. This would account for their later modification or even removal by rabbinic activity which probably began around the last two decades of the first century and continued into the second century CE.

(4) It is possible that permissive details in tannaitic directives on healing and/or saving life directly counteract the restrictions imposed in earlier directives, although there may now be no written evidence of such earlier texts. This may allow us to speculate on the probable content of earlier, although now unrecorded, texts.

(5) Terms in directives on healing and/or saving life that suggest culpability for the action performed may indicate that such directives were probably not composed after around 70 CE.

Chapter 11

ESTIMATED EARLIEST DATES OF COMPOSITION OF
TANNAITIC DIRECTIVES ON HEALING AND/OR SAVING LIFE

I. *General Considerations*

In spite of prolonged and intense scholarly debate on healing on the
Sabbath, especially in relation to the gospel texts, it seems that no simple
list of directives that allow acts of healing and/or saving life on the
Sabbath which are recorded in the Jewish texts (some of which definitely
pre-date or are contemporary with Jesus) has ever been compiled. This
may be due to the fact that even if they are recorded without regard to
their possible date of composition, a list of such directives is not easy to
compile. These directives are not arranged in a systematic way—
although most are preserved in the Mishnah and Tosefta, in the order
Moed, they are scattered throughout the tractates, occurring mostly
in *Shabbat* and *Yoma*, but also in *Eruvin, Pesahim, Sukkah, Rosh
ha-Shanah* and *Taanith*. Moreover, even when they are identified, it is
clear that many of them are predicated on earlier, often now-unrecorded,
texts. For example, the edict of Rabban Gamaliel issued before 50 CE
assumes that five actions of healing and/or saving life already existed
(see Chapter 9), although none of these earlier permits have been
preserved. Similarly, a directive which allows specific violations of
Jewish law in order to treat the bite of a snake (see t. Shab 15.14) is
clearly based on the assumption that a permit exists for a snake bite to be
cured, which means that this earlier permit must be assumed, although—
once again—it no longer exists. Another difficulty in compiling a list of
tannaitic directives is caused by the similarity of many of the directives
that now exist. For example, should the two consecutive statements in
the Tosefta, one which allows a person to be saved *from the sea*, while
the second permits a person to be saved *from a ship which is sinking in
the sea* (t. Shab 15.11), be counted as one directive or as two, since both
of them relate to the saving of a drowning individual on the Sabbath
day? Does the fact that these directives are listed separately suggest that
they were originally expressed in relation to two different situations,

356

and must therefore be considered as two separate decrees? Or are they alternative wordings of the same decree? For the list compiled below, it has generally been assumed that even with such similarities, such directives were originally separate permits, which means that each should be separately recorded. Those who disagree with this decision may then make the necessary adjustment(s) to the final list. Similar considerations relate to directives which are not consecutive, but which allow the same action, although this action is expressed in a different way. For example, there seems little essential difference between an action described as 'the saving of life from a flame', להציל מן הדליקה (as in m. RH 2.5 and m. Pes 3.7), and those that allow the extinguishing of a fire, using the verb כבה (as in m. Shab 2.5; 16.6 and t. Shab 15.13). In such cases, however, since these details suggest only the modification of earlier, more restrictive directives (as discussed in Chapter 10), and since it is these earlier directives that are of interest here, differently expressed versions of similar permits will not here be considered as separate decrees. Again readers are free to adjust the final count. Another problem is posed by the grouping together of several permits which are allowed to violate the same Jewish law—should each separately listed action be considered as a separate directive or should the whole group of permits be considered as one? For example, m. Taan 3.7 allows the blowing of the *shofar* on the Sabbath because of three separate emergencies (see below). In such cases, it has been decided in this book that each permitted action must be considered as a directive which was used separately; otherwise, a permit to allow the blowing of the *shofar* would be stated in a general way, and there would be no need to state the occasions when such an action was allowed. Such permits are thus in effect short lists of directives that have probably been gathered together by editorial activity, partly, at least, because they involve a violation of the same Jewish law.

In view of such problems, it is therefore unrealistic to assume that the number of tannaitic directives listed below even approaches the number that actually existed before the end of the second century (the 'cut-off' point for tannaitic texts), and although the historical details of some of these texts strongly suggest that they were composed before 50 CE or even 70 CE, the probable dates of composition of other directives are more doubtful and open to subjective debate. Assuming, however, the basic validity of the criteria which have been discussed, which is summarised briefly in the guidelines below, absolute accuracy is less essential at this stage of research than an appreciation of the *likely* approximate numbers of tannaitic directives on healing and/or saving life that were composed before and after the end of the first century CE. If, for example, it seems that there are probably *significantly* more directives in the tannaitic texts which permitted actions of healing and/or the saving of life which were composed *before* the end of the first century CE, compared with those which were originally composed after this time, then, even if the final numbers of directives listed below is not correct, the difference between them would strongly suggest that the majority of directives in tannaitic texts that deal with situations of healing and/or saving life were probably composed before the end of the first century CE.

II. *Guidelines for Estimating the Earliest Dates of Composition of Tannaitic Directives on Healing and/or Saving Life*

Historical details (such as the attribution to a named Jewish sage, or an allusion to a practice that could not have taken place after 70 CE) are undoubtedly helpful in estimating the date of composition of a directive. Absolute reliance cannot however be placed on such information, and any estimated dates must take into account one or more of the following guidelines:

(1) In the absence of any indications to the contrary, it is probable that directives on healing and/or saving life which were composed before the end of the first century allow a violation of Jewish law *only* for a *specific* situation and give no indication that this permit may be extended in a *general* way to allow a similar action in any situation in which it is necessary to heal and/or save life. Such *specific* directives may include arguments *kal va-chomer* which justify the specific actions of healing and/or saving life, as these arguments are basically simple permits for specific actions which are also justified according to Jewish law. As will be seen, most specific permits are not justified in any way. It should also be noted that the end of the first century is a convenient and generous 'cut off' date for such directives, many of which were probably composed at significantly earlier times.

Specific permits preserved in a tannaitic text may however be generalised in a way that suggests that the specific action which is allowed is only one of many for which it is similarly permitted to heal and/or save life. This generality in a tannaitic text is often indicated with an additional comment which includes the special vocabulary of R. Akiva and R. Ishmael, especially the phrases ספק נפשות or פיקוח נפש, although other generalising terms may also be used (see Chapter 9). In any case, the version of a directive which includes the special vocabulary of R. Akiva or R. Ishmael could not have been composed before the activity of these sages had begun in the second half of the first century, perhaps as early as 70 CE. This, however, is an approximate date, and such directives were probably composed much later in the first century or second century CE, the latter especially if they are attributed to a second-century sage. It is also important to consider whether such generalising terms have been added to an earlier composed version of a directive, or whether the directive was originally expressed in the way it is now preserved (see Chapter 9).

(2) It is unlikely that after the compilation of the mishnaic list of the thirty-nine *main* prohibited actions on the Sabbath day (m. Shab 7.2), the Jewish sages would have issued permits that used one of the same verbs to identify the permitted action. Instead, it is reasonable to surmise that they would express their permits with a *subcategory* of one of the *main* verbs, in order to allow—even if only euphemistically—a lesser violation of Jewish law. Accordingly, and in the absence of any contra-indications, it is probable that a directive that permits an action of healing and/or saving life that violates Jewish law which repeats one of the terms used in the list of at m. Shab 7.2, may have been composed before or around the time of the composition of this mishnaic list. If indeed the latter was composed in Maccabean times (see Chapter 1), it is therefore probable that such a directive was also originally composed in earlier Maccabean times.

The corollary of this assumption is that those directives that indicate a permitted action with a term that can be assumed to be a sub-category of one of the *main* prohibitions that are expressed in m. Shab 7.2 (in Hebrew, 'descendants', תולדות of the '*main* actions', אבות מלאכות) and thereby permit a lesser violations of Jewish law, were probably composed after this Maccabean list.

However, if (a) directives that may have been originally composed before the Maccabean list included restrictions which were expressed with a term that repeats one of the thirty-nine *main* prohibitions, and if (b) it can be assumed that these restrictions were later modified (in order to minimise the possibility that the act of healing and/or saving life may fail, see Chapter 10), thus giving the impression of a later directive, then the later modification *may* include the same term used in the earlier restriction (see, e.g., on m. Shab 16.5 and t. Shab 15.4 discussed below). In short, *permissive* modifications that include a term which repeats, or which is derived from the list at m. Shab 7.2, may indicate that the original directive was originally composed in early Maccabean times.

(3) Restrictive details in a directive on healing and/or saving life, which closely prescribe the way in which the permitted action may be taken, may suggest that this directive was first composed before the end of the first century CE, perhaps even before 70 CE, when the activity of

R. Akiva and R. Ishmael, and also probably R. Eleazar b. Azariah, may have begun (see Chapter 10). On the other hand, permissive details in a directive may suggest a later version of an earlier decree with corresponding restrictions that was composed before around 70 CE and almost certainly before 100 CE.

(4) A further indication of a directive that was composed *before* around 70 CE, and possibly as early as Maccabean times, is the presence of vocabulary which suggests culpability for the performance of a deed of healing and/or saving life. The terms most commonly used are the verb חלל, 'to violate', and the terms פטור and חייב, the former indicating that a person is free from potential culpability in relation to Jewish law, and the latter indicating that a person is 'liable for a penalty for a violation of Jewish law' (see Chapter 10).

III. *A List of Tannaitic Directives on Healing and/or Saving Life*

Before the earliest dates of composition of tannaitic directives can be evaluated, it is necessary to provide a list of those that now exist. A provisional list thus follows below. Each of these directives is followed by a short discussion on the approximate dating of the version that is now recorded, together with any information that may be relevant in the estimation of the approximate date of issue of the *earliest* version of a directive in which the specific action is allowed.

As noted above, most of tannaitic texts dealing with acts of healing and/or saving life are found in the Mishnah and Tosefta. Some appear in groups, while others are stated singly, although some of the latter also allow actions that are allowed among directives which are grouped. The main groups can be loosely classified as Focused Lists and Collected Lists. The Focused Lists group together actions of healing and/or saving life which are allowed to violate the *same* Jewish law, for example, the violation of the Sabbath *eruv*, or the violation of Sabbath law that forbids the extinguishing of a fire. They can be further divided into (1) mixed focused lists, which contain directives which deal both with situations of healing and/or saving life and with other kinds of situations, all of which violate the same Jewish law, and (2) directives dealing *only* with situations of healing and/or saving life, which all violate the same Jewish law. Some directives in these lists also occur singly (that is, they are not part of any list, but also appear elsewhere) and, for the sake of convenience, are discussed together with the relevant directives in the Focused Lists.

In contrast with the Focused Lists, the Collected Lists give permission for actions that are necessary to heal and/or save life, each of which violates a *different* Jewish law. As is the case for some of the directives in the Focused Lists, some situations in the Collected Lists also occur on their own, but for the sake of convenience are also discussed with the relevant directives in the Collected Lists.

The third category of directives on healing and/or saving can be considered as Scattered Directives, that is, they are not found in either the Focused or Collected lists.

A. *The Focused Lists*

(1) *Focused directives implied by Rabban Gamaliel the Elder, m. RH 2.5.* The text of the edict of Rabban Gamaliel the Elder has been cited in Chapter 9. According to this decree, those who had travelled to Jerusalem on the Sabbath to witness the sighting of the new moon (the astronomical sign for the beginning of the new Jewish month) were additionally allowed to travel the full extent of the Sabbath *eruv*. This leniency was also granted to those who had performed one of five specific acts of healing and/or saving life, namely, (1) acting as a mid-wife, (2) rescuing people from a fire, (3) fighting against ravaging troops, that is, those fighting in self-defence, (4) rescuing a person from drowning in a river, and (5) rescuing a person from beneath collapsed debris. The edict of Rabban Gamaliel is thus based on the *prior* assumption that these five actions were already officially allowed to violate Jewish law, especially Sabbath law. This being the case, it can be assumed that individual permits for these five specific actions were in existence before 50 CE (approximately when Rabban Gamaliel died). The edict of Rabban Gamaliel thus adds to the evidence that directives composed before around 70 CE were specific for their action, and did not give any indication that the permits they allow could be extended to allow the performance of any other act of healing and/or saving life. Otherwise, it is likely that Rabban Gamaliel would have referred collectively or generally to these permitted actions—for example, he could have permitted '*anyone* who has travelled further than the Sabbath *eruv* to witness the new moon to perform an action of healing and/or saving life'. It is significant moreover that no generalising vocabulary is used in his edict, which helps to confirm that it was composed before the activity of R. Akiva and R. Ishmael had begun.

Separate tannaitic directives relating to all five of the activities assumed by Rabban Gamaliel exist in the Mishnah and Tosefta. As will be seen, none include any generalising terminology, which again suggests that they were all probably originally composed before the activity of R. Akiva and R. Ishmael, and certainly before the end of the first century CE. Any other indications of an early composition will be noted as each directive is discussed.

(a) *Permits for Sabbath acts of healing and/or saving life for childbirth.*

משנה מסכת שבת פרק יח משנה ג

(1) ...ומילדין את האשה בשבת.

(2) וקורין לה חכמה ממקום למקום. ומחללין עליה את השבת.

(3) וקושרין את הטבור. רבי יוסי אומר אף חותכין.

(4) וכל צרכי מילה עושין בשבת.

Mishnah Shabbat 18.3

(1) ...And they may deliver a woman [of her child] on the Sabbath.

(2) And [they may] call a midwife for her from anywhere [that is, even from a distance that exceeds the *eruv*]. And [= so that] one may violate (מחללין) the Sabbath on her behalf.

(3) And they tie (קושרין) the umbilical cord [on the Sabbath]. R. Yose says they also cut (חותחין) [it on the Sabbath].

(4) And they may perform on the Sabbath all things that are needed for circumcision.

The probable early date—before 70 CE and perhaps during Maccabean times—of the first of these three directives has been discussed in Chapter 10. As the second and third of these directives are also necessary procedures in childbirth, it is probable that they were also permitted at around the same time. In any case, these permits are assumed in Rabban Gamaliel's edict that refers to the work of midwives on the Sabbath, so that it is reasonable to assume they were first composed before 50 CE, around which time Rabban Gamaliel died.

The final (fourth) section of the above text allows everything necessary for circumcision to be performed on the Sabbath day. The change of subject suggests that this is a later general addition which was added to this list (perhaps before the addition of R. Yose) in order to cover all details of the ritual, which was issued after the earliest versions of the specific directives in relation to the act of circumcision recorded at m. Shab 9.3, 19.3 and t. Shab 15.4 (see below).

(b) *Saving life from a fire on the Sabbath.*

This is the second of the permitted Sabbath activities which is assumed by Rabban Gamaliel the Elder at m. RH 2.5. The reference to this activity by Rabban Gamaliel clearly implies that an official directive, which allowed the extinguishing a fire on the Sabbath, was originally composed before 50 CE.

(c) *Saving life by fighting in self-defence on the Sabbath.*

Those who save life from 'the ravaging troops' (הגייס) on the Sabbath are the third group of people who Rabban Gamaliel the Elder assumes were allowed to violate Sabbath law. The reference to 'ravaging troops' suggests a surprise attack which necessitates actions of self-defence in order to save life.[1] In fact, as was discussed in Chapter 1, official permission to violate the Sabbath by fighting in self-defence is the earliest datable directive which permits an act of healing and/or saving life on the Sabbath, which was probably issued around 167 BCE.[2] If indeed Rabban Gamaliel the Elder was a Pharisee (according to Acts 5:34), his allusion to this permit thus confirms the existence of this Maccabean edict in Pharisaic oral law. The permit to violate Sabbath law for the purpose of self-defence is again mentioned by R. Judah b. Bathyra, a sage from before 70 CE.[3]

The following directive in the Tosefta also assumes that fighting is allowed on the Sabbath day:

תוספתא מסכת עירובין פרק ג הלכה ה

גוים שבאו על עיירות ישראל יוצאין עליהן בזיין ומחללין עליהן את השבת. אימתי? בזמן שבאו על עסקי נפשות. לא באו על עסקי נפשות אין יוצאין עליה בזיין ואין מחללין עליהן את השבת. באו לעיירות הסמוכות לספר אפי' ליטול את התבן ואפי' ליטול את הפת יוצאין עליהן בזיין ומחללין עליהן את השבת

Tosefta Eruvin 3.5

(1) Gentiles who came against Israelite towns they go forth to do battle against them carrying weapons and they violate the Sabbath on their account. When? When they came to take human life. [But if] they did not come to take human life, they do not go out against them carrying weapons, and they do not violate (אין מחללין) the Sabbath on their account.

(2) [But if] they came against towns near the frontier, even to take straw, even to take bread, they go out (יוצאין) against them carrying weapons and they violate (ומחללין) the Sabbath on their account.[4]

The first part of this directive echoes the edict of Mattathias that allows fighting on the Sabbath, with the restriction that this is allowed only in self-defence, or, as this is phrased, only 'on concerns of lives' (עסקי נפשות). As was discussed in points 1 and 4 of the guidelines above, the specificity of this directive and the use of the verb חלל, 'to violate',

1. For גייס, literally, 'ravaging troops', that is, those who attack and thus necessitate a reaction of self-defence, see Jastrow, *Dictionary of the Targumim*, ad loc. Note, for example, t. Yeb 14.10, נפל עלינו גייס ונתלה הוא בייחור של תאנה ופשחו והחזיר את הגייס לאחוריו, 'attackers fell on us, and he grabbed the branch of a fig-tree and tore it off and drove the attackers away'.

2. 1 Macc 2:39-41 and 2 Macc 6:11.

3. *Mekilta de-Rabbi Ishmael* Shab 1, Lauterbach, *Mekilta*, 3:200-1.

4. For other tannaitic decrees on war on the Sabbath, which focus more on the conduct of war rather than the saving of life, see M. D. Herr, 'The Problem of War on the Sabbath in the Days of the Second Temple and the Mishnah and Talmud', *Tarbiz* 30 (1961) 242-56, 341-56 (Hebrew).

rather than perhaps דחה, 'to override', suggests a date of composition well before the end of the first century, probably before 70 CE, and perhaps as early as Maccabean times.[5]

Vocabulary from the compilation of the mishnaic list at m. Shab 7.2 can also be observed in the second part of the directive, which repeats the verb הוציא (in the form יוציאין, 'they carry out'), the last of the thirty-nine *main* prohibited activities listed in m. Shab 7.2. As was discussed in the guidelines above, this repetition, along with the use of the verb חלל (in the form ומחללין) which implies culpability suggests an early date of composition for this directive, perhaps as early as Maccabean times, as they are terms that are avoided by the Jewish sages after around 70 CE, when granting a permit to heal and/or save life. This being the case, it is possible that this second part of directive of t. Eruv 3.5 also predates the composition of m. Shab 7.2, and was also composed in Maccabean times. It is, however, clear that this second part of the directive has widened the permit to include fighting to prevent damage to property, in addition to that of self-defence.

It seems, moreover, that in addition to re-stating the edict of Mattathias, the directive at t. Eruv 3.5 is the earliest of our recorded directives which officially permits an act of carrying on the Sabbath, although only for the specific purpose of carrying weapons. The similar directive at t. Eruv 3.6 also permits the carrying of weapons but does not repeat the verb הוציא, which may imply that in contrast with the date of composition of t. Eruv 3.6, the directive at t. Eruv 3.6 was composed later than the list of the thirty-nine prohibited actions at m. Shab 7.2:

תוספתא מסכת עירובין פרק ג הלכה ו

בראשנה היו מניחין זינן בבית הסמוך לחומה. פעם אחת חזרו עליהן והיו נדחקין
ליטול את זינן והרגו זה את זה. התקינו שיהא כל אחד ואחד מחזיר לביתו.

Tosefta Eruvin 3.6
At first they would leave their weapons in the house nearest the wall. One time they ran about and were in a haste to grab their weapons and they ended up killing each other. They [therefore] decreed that each one should return home [to get his weapon(s)].

This text suggests that weapons for the defence of a walled city were originally stored centrally, near the city wall (a suitable location as this is the place where an enemy would attack), perhaps in order to reduce the violation of Sabbath law by minimising the distance that weapons were carried on the Sabbath day. But due to a fatal confusion among the

---

5. A date of composition in Maccabean times for t. Eruv 3.7 is suggested by Herr, 'The Problem of War on the Sabbath', pp. 247-8.

defenders, perhaps during an attack at night, the practice was abandoned, and weapons were subsequently stored at home. The absence of the verb הוציא in this directive is comparable to t. Eruv 3.5, and again suggests that this directive was composed later than t. Eruv 3.5, although perhaps still in Maccabean times.

In any case, as was discussed in point 1 of the guidelines above, a date of composition before the end of the first century is confirmed by the specificity of both the above directives, neither of which give the impression that the permits they allow are merely examples of the *general* necessity always to heal and/or save life in spite of the violation of Sabbath law.

(d) *Saving the life of a person drowning in a river*. This directive is also assumed in the Focused Lists at m. Pes 3.7, m. Taan 3.7, t. Eruv 3.8 and t. Taan 2.12, which will be discussed below. (Another watery location from which people may be saved on the Sabbath is the sea, to which reference is made in the Collected List at t. Shab 15.11, which will also be discussed).

(e) *Saving life on the Sabbath by removing debris that has fallen over a person*. As noted above, since Rabban Gamaliel died around 50 CE, his edict which assumes official permission on the Sabbath to remove debris that has buried a person on the Sabbath indicates that by the first half of the first century CE, it was officially permitted to save life on the Sabbath in this specified way. No simple directive on these lines now exists, but other more elaborate directives that allow the performance of this action are preserved at m. Yom 8.7 and t. Shab 15.11. The text from the Mishnah follows below:

משנה מסכת יומא פרק ח משנה ז

מי שנפלה עליו מפולת ספק הוא שם ספק אינו שם ספק חי ספק מת ספק עובד כוכבים ספק ישראל מפקחין עליו את הגל. מצאוהו חי מפקחין עליו ואם מת יניחוהו.

Mishnah Yoma 8.7
If debris fell on a person and there is doubt (ספק) that he is there [or] doubt (ספק) that he is not there, or doubt (ספק) if he is alive or doubt (ספק) that he is dead, or doubt (ספק) that he is a gentile or doubt (ספק) that he is an Israelite, they may remove the mound [that has fallen] on [top of] him. [If] they found him alive, they may [continue] clearing away [the debris lying] on him, and if dead, they leave him [for burial after the Sabbath].

As noted in Chapter 10, the references to 'doubt' (ספק) in this directive suggest the influence of R. Akiva, who was probably the first officially to introduce this aspect into directives on healing and/or the saving of life (see Chapter 5), probably sometime between 70 CE and the end of the first century CE. This being the case, the above version of this directive was probably composed after the activity of R. Akiva had begun—that is, sometime after 70 CE—and may even be a product of the activity of R. Akiva himself. In view of the tendency for later versions of directives to modify earlier restrictions (as briefly discussed in point 3 of the guidelines above), it is possible that the stated permits in this directive counteract restrictions that were originally imposed in an earlier, now-unpreserved directive on the actions that could be taken when performing the same task. In other words, an earlier oral directive allowed the removal of fallen debris on the Sabbath in order to save the life of a person who was buried beneath, on condition that it was known (1) that a person was buried beneath the debris, (2) that this person was still alive, and perhaps also (3) that this person was an 'Israelite'.[6] This being the case, the present version of the directive in the Mishnah is probably a late first-century or second-century version of an earlier oral directive whose basic intention was to save the life of anyone buried beneath debris. This is separately implied in the edict of Rabban Gamaliel the Elder, and means that this permit was officially recognised in Pharisaic oral law *before* 50 CE.

This dating can also be assumed for the corresponding directive in the Tosefta:

6. The directive now preserved thus stresses that in matters of healing and/or the saving of life, gentiles and Jews must be treated in exactly the same way. It is possible that the reference to gentiles in m. Yom 8.7 was added at the time of the Maccabean persecutions, just as (probably) chapter 9 was probably added to the biblical book of Esther at this time. No differentiation between the treatment of Jews and gentiles, however, exists today. Thus, for example, after the catastrophic earthquake in Haiti in 2010, an Israeli rescue team of orthodox Jews (called ZAKA, the initial letters of the words זיהוי קורבני אסון, *zihuy korbany ason*, literally, 'The Identification of the Victims of a Disaster') went to Haiti on their own initiative and expense, and reported that 'We did everything to save lives, *despite Shabbat*. People asked, "Why are you here? There are no Jews here [that is, no Jews live in Haiti]". But we are here because the Torah orders us to save lives... *We are desecrating Shabbat with pride*...'; see http://www.ynetnews.com/articles/0,7340, L-3835327,00.html.

תוספתא מסכת שבת פרק טו הלכה יא
מפקחין על ספק נפש בשבת.

Tosefta Shabbat 15.11
They remove debris for [one for whom there is] doubt of life (על ספק נפש)
on the Sabbath.

In contrast with the redactor of the text of m. Yom 8.7, who may
have modified the restrictions of an earlier version of this directive,
it is possible that the redactor of the above-cited version in the Tosefta
chose instead to remove the original restrictions imposed in an earlier,
unpreserved oral decree. The reference to 'doubt' (ספק) in the phrase
על ספק נפש again indicates the influence of R. Akiva, and, especially in
the absence of any generalising terminology, again suggests that this
version of the directive was also composed sometime in the second half
of the first century CE.

(2) *A focused list at m. Pes 3.7.* The text of m. Pes 3.7 is cited below:

משנה מסכת פסחים פרק ג משנה ז
ההולך לשחוט את פסחו ולמול את בנו ולאכול סעודת אירוסין בבית חמיו ונזכר
שיש לו חמץ בתוך ביתו אם יכול לחזור ולבער ולחזור למצותו יחזור ויבער. ואם
לאו מבטלו בלבו. להציל מן הנכרים [ס"א הגייס] ומן הנהר ומן הלסטים ומן
הדליקה ומן המפולת יבטל בלבו...

Mishnah Pesahim 3.7
If a man was on the way to offer his Passover-sacrifice or to circumcise
his son, or to eat the betrothal meal at his father-in-law's house, and he
remembered that he had left *hametz** in his house, if he has yet time to go
back and remove it and return to fulfil his religious duty, let him go back
and remove it. But if not, he may annul it in his heart. [If he was on the
way] to help against ravaging troops, and from a river and from robbers,
and from a fire, and from collapsed debris, he may [also] annul the
*hametz** in his heart...

**hametz*—anything containing leavened material, which is forbidden
during the Passover week, see Exod 13:7

Like the edict of Rabban Gamaliel at m. RH 2.5, this directive also
assumes the prior existence of five directives which officially permitted
acts of healing and/or saving life while violating Sabbath law, namely,
(1) fighting against 'ravaging troops' (גייסים), that is, fighting in self-
defence, (2) rescuing a person (or persons) from a river, (3) rescuing a
person (or persons) from robbers, (4) rescuing a person (or persons) from
a fire and (5) rescuing a person (or persons) from beneath fallen debris.
The action permitted in each of these situations is then allowed to violate

the Pentateuchal law that requires the removal of all leavened material from a place of habitation before the start of the Passover week.

Apart from the reference to the rescue of a person (or persons) from robbers, the same situations of healing and/or saving life are also assumed in the edict of Rabban Gamaliel. This suggests that m. Pes 3.7 was composed at around the same time as the edict of Rabban Gamaliel, that is, it was composed sometime before 50 CE. If so, it can again be assumed that the five permitted assumptions were also issued before 50 CE. In any case, the specificity and lack of any generalisation in this decree (which could have been shown, for example, by the use of the arguments or special terminology of R. Akiva or R. Ishmael), suggests that this directive was composed before around 70 CE, and almost certainly before the end of the first century CE.

(3) *A focused list at m. Shab 17.2.* The following directive permits the Sabbath use of eight different, specified instruments for a purpose for which they were *not* originally designed. This concept in Jewish law is called *muktsa* (מוקצה, literally, 'set aside' or 'excluded') and was originally conceived by the Jewish sages in order to 'place a wall around the Torah', an idiom which expresses the thought that an individual should not be placed inadvertently in a position in which it was possible to violate Sabbath law.[7] One of the instruments mentioned in this decree is related to an act of healing and/or saving life, namely, a sewing needle, which this permit allows to be used on the Sabbath in order to remove a thorn or a splinter:

משנה מסכת שבת פרק יז משנה ב

נוטל אדם קורנס לפצע בו את האגוזים, וקרדום לחתוך את הדבילה, מגירה לגרור בה את הגבינה, מגריפה לגרוף בה את הגרוגרות, את הרחת, את המזלג לתת עליו לקטן, את הכוש, ואת הכרכר לתחוב בו, מחט של יד ליטול בו את הקוץ, ושל סקאים לפתוח בו את הדלת.

Mishnah Shabbat 17.2

A man may take up a hammer to crush walnuts, or a hatchet to split a fig cake, or a saw to cut through a cheese, or a shovel to scoop up dried figs, or a winnowing shovel or a fork to give something to a child, or a

---

7. *Muktsa* (מוקצה) is essentially a restriction imposed on the use of objects that were not 'prepared' for use before the Sabbath. According to the fifth-century amoraic sage R. Hanina, the law of *muktsa* in relation to particular implements originated under the prophet Nehemiah (b. Shab 123b). The earliest recorded direct reference to this concept is preserved at m. Shab 21.3, which is further discussed at b. Shab 124a. For a brief discussion on *muktsa*, see P. Birnbaum, *A Book of Jewish Concepts* (New York: Hebrew Publishing, 1975) 392.

reed-spindle or a whorl to thrust into something, or a hand sewing needle to take out a thorn (מחט של יד ליטול בו את הקוץ), or a sackmaker's needle with which to open a door.

Once again, there is prior assumption in this list of a specific earlier, oral permit, in this case which allowed the removal of a thorn on the Sabbath. This directive now additionally notes that an instrument whose use was prohibited for one of the thirty-nine *main* prohibited actions in m. Shab 7.2, namely, 'sewing' (the twenty-third), may now be used for removing a thorn (or a splinter) although it was not originally designed for this task. The extreme specificity of this decree, which not allows for only one particular implement but also notes the specific purpose for which it might be used, provides a strong indication that it was composed before 70 CE and certainly before the end of the first century CE.

(4) *Specific situations that are allowed to violate Sabbath law, t. Eruv 3.8.* The following directive specifies six different situations that are allowed to violate (any) Sabbath law:

תוספתא מסכת עירובין פרק ג הלכה ח

עיר שהקיפוה גוים או נהר וכן ספינה המטורפת בים וכן היחיד שהיה נרדף מפני
גוים ומפני ליסטים ומפני רוח רעה הרי אילו מחללין את השבת ומצילין את
עצמן.

Tosefta Eruvin 3.8
(1) [People in] a town which gentiles surrounded, or (2) [saving people from] a river and also (3) [those saving] a ship sinking in the sea, and also (4) an individual who was pursued by gentiles and (5) [was pursued] by robbers and (6) [was pursued] by an evil spirit, these people [may] violate (מחללין) the Sabbath and [thus may] save themselves.

The term מחללין (from חלל, 'to violate'), suggests that this directive dates originally from Maccabean times (see point 4 of the guidelines above). In any case, a date of composition before around 70 CE and certainly before the end of the first century is indicated by the specificity of the situations that are included in this list, and the lack of any generalising arguments or terms.

The individual permits which allow the violation of Sabbath law in this directive are all stated or assumed in other directives. Thus the edict of Rabban Gamaliel the Elder at m. RH 2.5 assumes that it is permitted to save oneself on the Sabbath from 'gentiles that surround a town', that is, to act in self-defence in the face of an attacking force. Similarly, one of the basic assumptions of m. Pes 3.7 (see above), m. Taan 3.7 and t. Taan 2.12 (see below) gives permission to violate Jewish law by saving someone from a river. A permit to save a ship sinking at sea on the

Sabbath is also assumed at m. Taan 3.7 and t. Taan 2.12 (see below) and is stated with permissive modifications at t. Shab 15.11. Finally, permits to allow the violation of the Sabbath by an individual who was pursued by gentiles and/or by robbers and/or by an evil spirit are assumed at m. Shab 2.5 (again see below), which also adds that such people may extinguish the fire of a lamp. As will be seen in the commentary on these texts, there is good evidence to suggest that they all were composed before 70 CE, particularly m. Shab 2.5, which may well be Maccabean (see below). In the case of t. Eruv 3.8, it is also reasonable to assume, especially in view of the use of the term מחללין (see point 4 of the guidelines above) that this directive may also have been composed in Maccabean times.

Unlike the mixture of situations in the texts discussed above, the situations featured in the following directives deal *only* with acts of healing and/or saving life.

(5) *A focused list at m. Taan 3.7.* The same specific permits as t. Eruv 3.8 are allowed at m. Taan 3.7, which allows (1) fighting on the Sabbath, expressed euphemistically as 'when a city is surrounded by gentiles', (2) rescuing people from a river on the Sabbath, and (3) rescuing a ship floundering at sea on the Sabbath, as can be seen from the text below:

משנה מסכת תענית פרק ג משנה ז

על אלו מתריעין בשבת: על עיר שהקיפוה גוים, או נהר ועל הספינה המטרפת בים...

Mishnah Taanith 3.7
Because of the following [situations] they [are permitted to] sound the *shofar* [even] on the Sabbath: (1) When a city is surrounded by gentiles, or (2) when [people are drowning in] a river, or (3) when a ship is floundering at sea...

However, in contrast with t. Eruv 3.8, the text of m. Taan 3.7 allows the above actions only in relation to sounding the shofar on the Sabbath. It is thus more restrictive than t. Eruv 3.8, which allows the violation of any Sabbath law. For this reason therefore, it is likely that m. Taan 3.7 was composed before t. Eruv 3.8, that is, well before the end of the first century CE.

(6) *A focused list at t. Taan 2.12.* The same assumptions can be made for the comparable text in the Tosefta at t. Taan 2.12, which lists six situations of healing and/or saving life in which permission to act was officially allowed, three of which repeat those assumed in m. Taan 3.7. In

contrast, however, with the mishnaic decree, which is expressed in relation to a violation of Sabbath law by blowing a *shofar*, these permits are expressed in relation to the violation of a religious fast:

תוספתא מסכת תענית פרק ב משנה יב

עיר שהקיפו גוים או נהר וכן ספינה המטרפת בים וכן יחיד הנדרף מפני גוים
ומפני לסטין ומפני רוח רעה אין רשאין לסנף עצמן בתענית שלא לשבר את כחן.
וכן היה אומר רבי יוסי אומ' אין היחיד רשאי לסנף את עצמו בתענית, שלא יפול
כל הצבור ויהיו צריכין לפרנסו.

Tosefta Taanith 2.12
(1) [People in] a town which gentiles besieged, or (2) [those saving people from drowning in] a river and so too (3) [those saving people from] a ship floundering at sea, and so too (4) an individual pursued by gentiles or (5) by robbers or (6) by an evil spirit, they are not permitted to afflict themselves in a fast, so as not to sap their strength.

And thus R. Yose said, 'An individual is not permitted to afflict himself in a fast lest he fall on to the public charity and [the community] must support him'.

The situations in the above list are all assumed elsewhere, either in the Mishnah or Tosefta, although in relation to the violation of a different Jewish law. On the assumption that different permits would be needed for a permit to violate different laws, the fact that the violations listed in t. Taan 2.12 are replicated elsewhere in relation to different laws suggests that these permits must be considered as *separately* composed, and are therefore counted separately in the final list below. Readers may of course make whatever adjustments they wish. However, it is difficult to argue for example that a permit which specifically allows the sounding of a *shofar* on the Sabbath when saving people from a ship (see m. Taan 3.7) can be considered as the same permit as one which allows a specific violation of a law requiring a religious fast by those who are saving people from a sinking ship (as at t. Taan 2.12). Otherwise, these directives would simply state that it is always permitted to violate Jewish law when dealing with any situation of danger to life. Similarly, an allusion to a directive that permits fighting in self-defence and the saving of people who are drowning in a river cannot be the same permit as Rabban Gamaliel's edict at m. RH 2.5, in which fighting in self-defence and saving people from a river is linked with a violation of the Sabbath *eruv*.

The specificity of these decrees gives no impression that the situations to which they refer fall under a general heading of situations in which any Jewish law may be violated in order to heal and/or in order to save life, which suggests that both the above lists were composed before around 70 CE and certainly before the end of the first century CE (see point 1 in the guidelines above).

It can be assumed that the remark of R. Yose in the Tosefta is a later addition to the directive, as it lies outside the textual framework of the main directive, and is absent from the comparable version in the Mishnah. This remark is not concerned with an act of healing and/or saving life, and therefore suggests only a relative date for the composition of the text which permits acts of healing and/or saving life. Assuming that R. Yose is R. Yose b. Halafta, who was active around the years 135 to 170 CE, it can be assumed that the text of the directive concerned with acts of healing and/or saving life was composed before the mid-second century. This accords with the conclusion of the paragraph above that the original decree was composed before the end of the first century CE.

(7) *Focused situations in m. Shab 2.5.* This Focused List is also composed *only* of situations of healing and/or saving life. Three of these permits repeat specific permits that are listed at t. Taan 2.12 (discussed above). In contrast however, rather than causing a violation of Sabbath law by blowing a *shofar*, the permitted situations in m. Shab 2.5 relate to the violation of Sabbath law caused by extinguishing a fire, the thirty-sixth of the thirty-nine *main* prohibited activities on the Sabbath day (see m. Shab 7.2 cited in Chapter 1). In this case, moreover, the fire to be extinguished is further specified as the *fire of a lamp*:

משנה מסכת שבת פרק ב משנה ה

המכבה את הנר מפני שהוא מתירא מפני עובדי כוכבים מפני לסטים מפני רוח רעה ואם בשביל (ונ"א מפני) החולה שיישן פטור. כחס על הנר כחס על השמן כחס על הפתילה חייב.

ורבי יוסי פוטר בכולן חוץ מן הפתילה מפני שהוא עושה פחם.

Mishnah Shabbat 2.5

If one extinguishes (המכבה) the lamp because he is afraid of gentiles, robbers, or an evil spirit, or for the sake of an invalid, so that he should sleep, he is not liable for any punishment [for the violation of holy law] (פטור). [But] if [it was because] he wanted to spare the lamp, the oil, or the wick, he is [held] liable [for the violation of holy law] (חייב).

R. Yose exempts him [that is, exempts the perpetrator of these actions] from blame in all cases, except in respect of the wick, because [thereby] he makes charcoal.[8]

This Focused List permits a violation of Sabbath law by the act of extinguishing a lamp in the following four situations: (1) a fear of gentiles, (2) a fear of robbers, (3) a fear of an evil spirit and (4) the care of an invalid who cannot otherwise sleep.

---

8. The prohibition for extinguishing a fire on the Sabbath is not Pentateuchal, but is noted at m. Shab 7.2 and t. Shab 11.4.

The verb כבה (in the form המכבה, 'the one that extinguishes [a fire]') which is used in this directive for the above permitted action, repeats the verb used to refer to the extinguishing of a fire in the thirty-nine *main* actions (it is the thirty-sixth) that are prohibited on the Sabbath, according to m. Shab 7.2. However, as was discussed in point 2 of the guidelines above, in order to minimise the violation of Sabbath law (even if only euphemistically), it is unlikely that after the compilation of the list of m. Shab 7.2 the Jewish sages would repeat a verb that was used for one of the thirty-nine *main* prohibited activities when permitting any action that violates Sabbath law, but would instead refer to the permitted activity with a sub-category of one of these main actions. The use of the verb כבה for the situations that are mentioned in m. Shab 2.5 thus suggests that this directive was composed before the composition of m. Shab 7.2, which itself may have been composed in Maccabean times.

An early date for this directive is also implied by the use of the terms פטור, 'to be exempt from punishment for violating Jewish law', and חייב, 'to be liable for punishment for the violation of Jewish law', expressions which imply either the potential culpability (פטור) or the real culpability (חייב) of whoever performed the permitted act of healing and/or saving life. As noted in point 4 of the guidelines above, tannaitic directives in which these terms appear may have been composed in Maccabean times and were almost certainly composed by around 70 CE. In any case, as none of the directives in this list give any impression of a *general* attitude that would allow *any* act of healing and/or saving life to violate any Jewish law (which could be shown, for example, by reference to the arguments or special vocabulary associated with R. Akiva and R. Ishmael), it is probably safe to assume that none were composed after around 70 CE. This accords with the fact that, as for the directive at t. Taan 2.12 (discussed above) the remark of R. Yose (probably R. Yose b. Halafta, a tannaitic sage who was active around 135 to 170 CE) lies outside the framework of the decree, and is therefore a later addition to this text, which means that the earlier directive to which his words are attached was composed before around 135 CE.

(8) *Focused situations at t. Yoma 4.4.* Both the directives in this list focus on specific situations when it is necessary to violate a religiously decreed fast in order to heal and/or save life. The first allows food to be given in a situation of starvation, and the second allows a pregnant woman to eat:

תוספתא מסכת יומא כפורים פרק ד הלכה ד
מי שאחזו בולמוס מאכילין אותו הקל הקל. כציד? היו לפניו טבל ושביעית
מאכילין אותו שביעית טבל ונבלה מאכילין אותו נבלה נבלה ותרומה מאכילי'
אותו תרומה תרומה ושביעית מאכילין אותו שביעית עד שיאורו עיניו. מניין היו
יודעין שיאורו עיניו? כדי שיכיר בין יפה לרע. ר' יהודה או' עוברה שהריחה
שביעית תוחבין לה בכוש הריחה תרומה תוחבין לה ברוטב.

Tosefta Yoma 4.4

(1) Whoever was seized by a ravenous ox-hunger (בולמוס) they feed him
a minimum amount [to limit the violation of Jewish law]. How [can this
be done]? If there was before him untithed produce, and [otherwise
prohibited produce] of the Seventh year, they feed him [otherwise
prohibited] produce of the Seventh year? [This can be justified with the
following sorite]: [If there is] untithed produce and carrion, [they feed
him] carrion.[9] [If there is] carrion and heave-offering, [they feed him]
heave-offering. [If there is] heave-offering) and [produce] of the Seventh
year, [they feed him] produce of the Seventh year until his eyes are
enlightened.
How do we know when 'his eyes are enlightened'? [We know] when he
knows the difference between good and evil.
(2) R. Judah says, 'A pregnant woman who smells produce of the Seventh
Year, they hand over to her a reed-full. [If] she smelled [and craved]
heave-offering they hand over the juice.

As was discussed in Chapter 9, a permit which allowed a pregnant
woman who craved *terumah* to be given the juice of the *terumah*, presumably on the day of an official religious fast, was probably originally
composed before 70 CE. On the other hand, as was discussed in Chapter
10, the additional remark of R. Judah (probably R. Judah b. Ilai) in the
second part of the above directive probably dates from the mid-second
century (135–170 CE). The corresponding version in the Mishnah at
m. Yom 8.5 was probably composed at an even later date, although (of
course) before the end of the second century CE.

An early date before the end of the first century for the composition
of the *original* version of these two decrees is also suggested by their
specificity combined with the lack of any hint that the permits allowed
are merely examples of a further innumerable number of situations which
also require acts of healing and/or the saving of life.

---

9. Untithed food brings a punishment of death (*karet*), should God decide (see
b. San 83a), whereas the eating of carrion involves only the relatively more lenient
punishment of lashing (b. Yom 36b).

B. *Dating of the Focused Lists and the Directives They Contain*
The first three of the Focused Lists above are compiled from two kinds of situations, namely, those that necessitate acts of healing and/or saving life and also other situations of everyday life. In contrast, the last six of the Focused Lists are concerned *only* with situations of healing and/or saving life. The mixed composition of the first three lists—m. RH 2.5, m. Pes 3.7 and m. Shab 17.2—suggests *that at the time that these lists were compiled*, acts of healing and/or saving life were not considered as a discrete, separate group which required its own particular religious law, but each situation was considered only in relation to whatever offence in Jewish law that the permitted action might cause. However, by the time of the compilation of the last six of these lists—m. Shab 2.5, m. Taan 3.7, t. Eruv 3.5 and 3.8, t. Yom 4.4 and t. Taan 2.12—it seems that although these situations were still classified according to the violation of one particular specific Jewish law, the Jewish sages had accepted that situations of healing and/or saving life should be considered as a separate category of their own. This suggests, therefore, that the first three of these lists discussed above were compiled before the last six. All of them, however, were assembled at a time when situations of healing and/or saving life were still considered in relation to the violation of the specific Jewish law that they would cause. This probably ceased to be the case in later times, perhaps as early as around 70 CE, due, at least in part, to the use of the verb דחה in the phrase דחה (את) (ה)שבת used in relation to acts of healing and/or saving life, which may be attributed to R. Eleazar b. Azariah and/or to the activity of R. Akiva and R. Ishmael (see Chapter 5), who provided general justifications for the violation of any Jewish law. If, then, the Focused Lists were composed before around 70 CE, and certainly by the end of the first century, this suggests that the individual directives that are included in these lists were composed at an even earlier time.

Let us now turn to the Collected Lists which group together directives on healing and/or saving life that, in contrast with the Focused Lists, violate *different* Jewish laws.

C. *The Collected Lists*
(1) *A collected list in the Mishnah, m. Shab 16.7.* The following list includes three directives. The third was considered by the amoraim as an example of hunting, a *main* forbidden act on the Sabbath day.[10] This

---

10. Hunting is the twenty-fifth of the thirty-nine main forbidden acts at m. Shab 7.2. For the amoraic commentary, see y. Shab 16.8 and b. Shab 121b.

same violation cannot, however, be linked logically with the two other permits. This short list thus groups together directives which violate different Jewish laws, and for this reason has been placed among the Collected, rather than the Focused Lists:

משנה מסכת שבת פרק טז משנה ז

כופין קערה על גבי הנר בשביל שלא תאחוז בקורה, ועל צואה של קטן ועל ערב שלא תישך.

אמר רבי יהודה: מעשה - בא לפני רבן יוחנן בן זכאי בערב ואמר 'חוששני לו מחטאת'.

Mishnah Shabbat 16.7

They may (1) cover a lamp with a dish so that it shall not scorch a rafter and (2) [they may cover] animal droppings to protect a child, and (3) [they may cover] a scorpion so that it will not bite [anyone]. R. Judah said, '[Here is a story—[the last of these cases] came before R. Yohanan b. Zakkai in Arav [near Sepphoris in Galilee] and he said, "I doubt whether he is not liable to a sin offering"'.

The specificity of each of the permits in the above list indicates a date of composition before around 70 CE and certainly by the end of the first century CE. This is confirmed for the third of the permits, which is the subject of a comment of R. Yohanan b. Zakkai when he lived in Galilee, before he moved to Jerusalem where he lived during the Roman siege of the city in 70 CE.[11] This timing may also be confirmed by the nature of the penalty suggested by R. Yohanan for the person who covered a scorpion with a dish on the Sabbath, namely, a sin offering, a sacrifice performed in the Temple in Jerusalem, which could not have been offered after the Temple was destroyed in 70 CE.[12]

(2) *Six directives in the collected list at m. Yom 8.5-7.* This list consists of six directives which permit actions in situations of healing and/or saving life which violate four kinds of Jewish law, namely, (a) law which prohibits the consumption of food on the day of a religious fast, see (1), (2) and (5) in the text below, (b) law which prohibits the consumption of certain types of food, see (3) and (4) below, (c) law which prohibits healing on the Sabbath, see (5) below, and (d) law which forbids the removal of debris on the Sabbath, see (6) below:

11. R. Yohanan b. Zakkai's escape from Jerusalem is told at b. Gitt 56a.
12. A sin offering was the punishment prescribed for an unintentional sin, see J. Milgrom, *Leviticus 1–16* (AB 3; New York: Doubleday, 1991) 228-9, 256, 331-63. For the life of R. Yohanan b. Zakkai, see n. 7, Chapter 9.

משנה מסכת יומא פרק ח משנה ה

(1) עוברה שהריחה מאכילין אותה עד שתשיב נפשה.

(2) חולה מאכילין אותו על פי בקיאין ואם אין שם בקיאין מאכילין אותו על פי
עצמו עד שיאמר די.

משנה מסכת יומא פרק ח משנה ו

(3) מי שאחזו בולמוס מאכילין אותו אפילו דברים טמאים עד שיאורו עיניו.

(4) מי שנשכו כלב שוטה אין מאכילין אותו מחצר כבד שלו ורבי מתיא בן חרש
מתיר.

(5) ועוד אמר רבי מתיא בן חרש החושש בגרונו מטילין לו סם בתוך פיו בשבת
מפני שהוא ספק נפשות וכל ספק נפשות דוחה את השבת.

משנה מסכת יומא פרק ח משנה ז

(6) מי שנפלה עליו מפולת ספק הוא שם ספק אינו שם ספק חי ספק מת ספק
עובד כוכבים ספק ישראל מפקחין עליו את הגל מצאוהו חי מפקחין עליו ואם
מת יניחוהו:

Mishnah Yoma 8.5

(1) If a pregnant woman smelled [and craved food] they may give her the food until she recovers herself.

(2) A person that is sick may be given food at the word of skilled persons.

And if there are no skilled persons, a person may be given food at his own wish, till he says, 'Enough!'

Mishnah Yoma 8.6

(3) If ravenous ox-hunger seized a person, he/she may be given even unclean things to eat until his/her eyes are enlightened.

(4) If a mad dog bit a person he/she may not be given the lobe of its liver to eat. But R. Mattithiah b. Heresh permits it.

(5) Moreover R. Mattithiah b. Heresh said, 'If a person has pain in his throat they may drop medicine into his mouth on the Sabbath, since there is doubt whether his/her life is in danger, and whenever there is doubt whether life is in danger this overrides the Sabbath.

Mishnah Yoma 8.7

(6) If debris fell on a person and there is doubt that he is there [or] doubt that he is not there, or doubt if he is alive or doubt that he is dead, or doubt that he is a gentile or doubt that he is an Israelite, they may remove the mound [that has fallen] on [top of] him. [But if] they find him alive, they may [continue] clearing away [the debris lying] on him and if dead, they leave him [so that he/she can be buried after the Sabbath].

These directives will now be separately discussed.

(a) *Allowing a pregnant woman to eat food on a day of a fast, m. Yoma 8.5.* The relevant text for this directive is displayed above and in Chapter 10, where it has been discussed in detail in relation to t. Yom 4.4. There is little doubt that an early version of this toseftan decree existed before 70 CE and that the above version in the Mishnah was probably composed after the addition of the modification of R. Judah bar Ilai to the

version in the Tosefta (t. Yom 4.4). The above mishnaic version of this
directive was thus perhaps composed towards the end of the second
century CE.

(b) *Feeding a sick person on the day of a decreed religious fast, m. Yom
8.5.* The relevant text for this directive is displayed above and also in
Chapter 10, where it was discussed in detail in relation to the later
version expressed at b. Yom 83a. As was noted in this discussion, the
exclamation 'Enough!' (די) in the second part of the text of m. Yom 8.5
suggests a concern that an excess of food might be given to the person
who is fed, thereby causing a greater violation of Jewish law than was
necessary for the purpose of healing and/or saving the sick person's life.
It is thus assumed that the person who is starving would be more
generous with himself than the 'experts', who would be more objective
and therefore more sparing with the amount of food that they allowed the
sick individual to eat. This being the case, the required presence of
'experts' is effectively a restriction imposed in order to limit the amount
of food that is given (in order to minimise the permitted violation of
Jewish law), which suggests that a directive with this restriction was
composed probably before around 70 CE. On the other hand, the final
instruction in the Mishnah—that the starving person may decide on the
quantity of food that is eaten—suggests a modification of the earlier
restriction, which was probably added after 70 CE (see point 3 of the
guidelines above). Only this later modified version of the directive has,
however, been preserved.

(c) *Feeding 'unclean' food to a ravenous person, m. Yom 8.6.*

משנה מסכת יומא פרק ח משנה ו

מי שאחזו בולמוס מאכילין אותו אפילו דברים טמאים עד שיאורו עיניו.

Mishnah Yoma 8.6
Whoever was seized by a ravenous ox-hunger they feed him even
unclean things to eat until his eyes are enlightened.

The comparable directive in the Tosefta does not include the phrase
'even unclean things to eat', which suggests that this phrase is a later
addition to the words in the Mishnah, 'Whoever was seized by a
ravenous ox-hunger they feed him until his eyes are enlightened'. This
directive is specific, giving no impression that the state of 'ravenous ox-
hunger' is only one of innumerable situations when it is necessary to
perform an act of healing and/or saving life that violates Jewish law. On
this basis alone—as briefly indicated in point 1 of the guidelines above—
it is probably safe to assume that it was probably originally composed

before around 70 CE and definitely before the end of the first century CE. The expansion of the directive with the permissive detail that 'even things that are ritually unclean' (אפילו דברים טמאים) may therefore suggest an even earlier date of composition for a now-unrecorded directive which allowed the same action but which included a restriction that the present mishnaic version has removed.

This early dating is confirmed by a comparison of this directive with that of the comparable directive in the Tosefta cited below. The words of the Tosefta which repeat those in the Mishnah are underlined in the Hebrew text. The sorite (which has been discussed in Chapter 4) is clearly a later addition to the text, and is printed in small font in square brackets in the English translation:

תוספתא מסכת יומא (כפורים) פרק ד הלכה ד
<u>מי שאחזו בולמוס מאכילין אותו</u> הקל הקל.
[כיצד היו לפניו טבל ושביעית מאכילין אותו שביעית? טבל ונבלה מאכילין אותו נבלה.
נבלה ותרומה מאכילי' אותו תרומה. תרומה ושביעית מאכילין שביעית].
<u>עד שיאורו עיניו.</u>
מניין היו יודעין שיאורו עיניו? כדי שיכיר בין יפה לרע.

Tosefta Yoma 4.4
Whoever was seized by ravenous ox-hunger they feed him a minimum amount [to limit the violation of Jewish law]. [How can this be done]?

If there was before him untithed produce, and [otherwise prohibited produce] of the Seventh year, they feed him [otherwise prohibited] produce of the Seventh year? [This can be proved in the following way]:

[[If there is] untithed produce and carrion, [they feed him] carrion.[13]

[If there is] carrion and heave-offering, [they feed him] heave-offering.

[If there is] heave-offering) and [produce] of the Seventh year, [they feed him] produce of the Seventh year] *until his eyes are enlightened*].

How do we know when 'his eyes are enlightened'? [We know] when [the sick person] knows the difference between good and evil.

The earliest version of the above decree that may now be recovered is printed below. A comparison with the corresponding text in the Mishnah suggests that just as the mishnaic expression אפילו דברים טמאים ('even things that are ritually unclean') is probably a later addition, so also is the expression הקל הקל in the Tosefta. This phrase is thus printed with small font and enclosed in square brackets:

---

13.   Untithed food may bring a punishment of death by God, but only *if* and only *when* God (rather than any human judgment) decides (b. San 83a), whereas the eating of carrion involves a (human) punishment of lashing (b. Yom 36b).

תוספתא מסכת יומא (כפורים) פרק ד הלכה ד
מי שאחזו בולמוס מאכילין אותו [הקל הקל] עד שיאורו עיניו.

Tosefta Yoma 4.4

He that was seized by ravenous ox-hunger, they feed him [that which least violates Jewish law] until his eyes are enlightened.

It is likely that the phrase in the Tosefta, הקל הקל, here indicating food which least violates Jewish law, was added in order to introduce and to justify the addition of the sorite to the directive. The addition in the Mishnah, אפילו דברים טמאים ('even things that are ritually unclean'), does not identify any forbidden food, and allows the maximum leniency regarding the type of food that the starving person may be given to eat. This phrase thus both subsumes and expands the four otherwise forbidden foods listed in the toseftan sorite, which suggests that it was added to the basic directive *after* the addition of the sorite to t. Yom 4.4 (see point 3 of the guidelines above). The version of the directive preserved in the Mishnah was thus probably composed no earlier than the late first century CE.

(d) *Allowing 'unclean' food—the liver of a dog—to cure rabies, m. Yom 8.6.*

משנה מסכת יומא פרק ח משנה ו
מי שנשכו כלב שוטה אין מאכילין אותו מחצר כבד שלו ורבי מתיא בן חרש
מתיר ... ועוד אמר רבי מתיא בן חרש ... וכל ספק נפשות דוחה את השבת.

Mishnah Yoma 8.6

If a mad dog bit him he may not be given the lobe of its liver to eat. But R. Mattithiah b. Heresh permits it. ... And even more said R. Mattithiah b. Heresh '...all [actions performed] when life is in danger override the Sabbath'.

The biblical command of Lev 11:3-8 forbids consumption of the flesh of any animal which does not chew the cud and does not possess a cloven hoof. As neither of these features is found in a dog, the flesh of a dog is declared 'unclean', and therefore prohibited from consumption according to Jewish law. The above directive suggests that this prohibition was upheld even though the consumption of the liver of a rabid dog was thought to cure rabies (a disease which in ancient times, if correctly diagnosed, inevitably led to death). The prohibition is, however, rescinded by R. Mattithiah who thus permitted this specific example of 'unclean food'. It is however interesting to note that 'unclean' food is allowed for the purpose of healing and/or saving life in the early, pre-second-century directives of m. Yom 8.6 and t. Yom 4.4. Were these directives known to R. Mattithiah? Whatever the case, this Jewish sage then generalised the leniency he allowed with the expression דוחה את השבת, which he used in conjunction with the special vocabulary of R. Akiva, namely ספק נפשות, thereby implying that the permit he allowed is merely one example from many when Jewish law must be violated to heal and/or save life (see Chapter 5). The use of this terminology along with the attribution to R. Mattithiah, who was active in the first third of the second century (110–135 CE), thus indicates strongly that this directive was composed well after the composition of merely specific permits had ceased in the second half of the first century, and, because it was sanctioned by R. Mattithiah, probably in the second century CE.

(e) *Giving oral medicine on the Sabbath, t. Shab 2.7 and m. Yom 8.6.*

משנה מסכת יומא פרק ח משנה ו

ועוד אמר רבי מתיא בן חרש החושש בגרונו מטילין לו סם בתוך פיו בשבת ...
מפני שהוא ספק נפשות וכל ספק נפשות דוחה את השבת.

Mishnah Yoma 8.6
...Moreover R. Mattithiah b. Heresh said, 'If a man has a pain in his throat they may drop medicine into his mouth on the Sabbath, because there is doubt whether his life is in danger, and whenever there is doubt whether life is in danger this overrides the Sabbath'.

The discussion above has suggested that the date of composition of the present version of m. Yom 8.6 lies between the years 110 and 135, a time which spans the active life of R. Mattithiah. This does *not*, however, mean that R. Mattithiah was *originally* responsible for a permit which allowed a person with a pain in the throat to be healed with an oral medicine that was administered on the Sabbath day. As was discussed in Chapter 10 (and briefly summarised in point 3 of the guidelines above), there is evidence to suggest that the second-century Jewish sages modified the restrictions imposed on acts of healing and/or saving life, which were originally included in order to limit the violation of Jewish law, but which might have prevented the success of whatever action the permit allowed. This kind of modification can be assumed for the above permit by the existence of a comparable directive in the Tosefta which allows the same action, but places restrictions on the way that the action is performed. According to this text, the medicament must be administered with a siphon and the fluid must be dropped into a sick person's mouth using a perforated vessel, in order, we must assume, to limit the violation of Jewish law:

תוספתא מסכת שבת פרק ב הלכה ז
...מעלין בדיופי ומטיפין מן הארק לחולה בשבת.

Tosefta Shabbat 2.7
...They bring up [a liquid medicament] with a siphon (דיפוי) and drip
[drops of the liquid] from a perforated vessel (ארק) to [heal] a sick person
on the Sabbath.

This restrictions imposed suggest that the above toseftan version of the
permit was composed before around 70 CE, while the removal of these
restrictions, combined with the attribution to R. Mattithiah, suggest that
his version of the directive was produced well after this time and probably in the second century CE. It seems, therefore, that the statement in
the Mishnah beginning 'because' (מפני ש־) links the later addition to an
older directive that originally permitted the treatment of a sick person
with medicine on the Sabbath, on condition that the medicament was
given in a specified, restricted way.

(f) *Moving debris from over a person on the Sabbath, m. Yom 8.7,
t. Shab 15.11.*
The directives at m. Yom 8.7 and t. Shab 15.11 which allow the removal
of debris on the Sabbath which may have fallen over a person have been
discussed in Chapter 9. This permit is also the sixth of the assumptions
of Rabban Gamaliel in his edict at m. RH 2.5, and therefore, as was
discussed in Chapter 9, it can be assumed that official permission for this
action on the Sabbath existed in oral Jewish law before 50 CE. This early
permit may have included restrictions which are counteracted by the
permissive modifications in the present version of the text. The version
of this directive with its modifications and references to 'doubt' (ספק)
in the Mishnah can, however, be dated to a time after the activity of
R. Akiva, and the date of composition of the corresponding directive in
the Tosefta, t. Shab 15.11, which consists of a simple statement with no
permissive details, and thus resembles the directives in the amoraic texts,
can probably be dated to a later time, although of course before the end
of the tannaitic period at the end of the second century CE.

D. *Seven Directives in the Collected List at Tosefta Shabbat 15.11-13*
The following collected list in the Tosefta is composed of seven
directives that allow actions of healing and/or saving life which violate
different Jewish laws:

תוספתא מסכת שבת פרק טו הלכות יא-יג

(1) מפקחין על ספק נפש בשבת והזריז הרי זה משובח. ואין צריך ליטול רשות מבית דין. כיצד?

(2) נפל לים ואין יכול לעלות.

(3) טבע' ספינתו בים ואין יכול לעלות, יורדין ומעלין אותו משם. ואין צריך ליטול רשות בית דין.

תוספתא מסכת שבת פרק טו הלכה (יב) יג

(4) נפל לבור ואין יכול לעלות עוקרין לו חוליה ויורדין ומעלין אותו משם. ואין צריך ליטול רשות בית דין.

(5) תינוק שנכנס לבית ואין יכול לצאת שוברין לו דלתות הבית ואפי' היו של אבן ומוציאין אותו משם. ואין צריך ליטול רשות בית דין.

(6) מכבין

(7) ומפסיקין לדליקה בשבת והזריז הרי זה משובח. ואין צריך ליטול רשות בית דין.

Tosefta Shabbat 15.11-13
Tosefta Shabbat 15.11
(1) They remove debris from one whose life is in doubt on the Sabbath, and he who is prompt in the matter, behold, this person should be praised. And it is not necessary to obtain permission from a [Jewish] court. How so?
(2) [If] someone fell into the sea and cannot climb up,
(3) [or if] his ship is sinking in the sea and he cannot climb up, they go down and bring him up from there. And it is not necessary to seek permission from a [Jewish] court.
Tosefta Shabbat 15.(12)13
(4) [If] a person fell into a pit and could not get out, they let down a chain to him and go down and raise him out from there. And it is not necessary to seek permission from a [Jewish] court.
(5) A young child who went into a building and cannot get out, they break down the doors of the building for him, even if they are [made] of stone, and they get him out of there. And it is not necessary to seek permission from a [Jewish] court.
(6) They extinguish a fire
(7) and they make a barrier [against a fire] on the Sabbath. And he who is prompt, behold, this person should be praised, and it is not necessary to obtain permission from a [Jewish] court.

E. *When Was the Above List Compiled?*

The individual directives in the list above are bound verbally both externally, by the twice-repeated refrain after the first and last directive—*And he who is prompt, behold, this person should be praised*—and internally, by the five-times repeated refrain after the first, third, fourth, fifth and seventh directives—*And it is not necessary to obtain permission from a [Jewish] court.* These verbal links suggest that this list was deliberately compiled as a whole. A date of composition for the list itself may be indicated from the statement in the external refrain which stresses that an individual who was 'prompt' (הזריז) to cause violation of Jewish law with an act of healing and/or saving life, must be 'praised' (משובח). This suggests that this list was compiled at a time when the Jewish sages had decided that although they wished to preserve earlier directives that had been issued by the earlier tannaitic Jewish sages, there was now no need to issue official permission for each of the future deeds of healing and/or saving life that might be needed to be performed. It seems, therefore, that this list was compiled at a time when it was expected that pious individuals would decide for themselves whether to perform an act of healing and/or saving life, rather than seeking official permission before such an act was performed. This being the case, it is possible that this list was compiled after the arguments and special vocabulary of R. Akiva and R. Ishmael had been composed which justi-fied any act in any situation of healing and/or saving life (see Chapter 5), perhaps even after the second-century interpretations of biblical texts had justified any action in any situation of healing and/or saving life with interpretations that were simple for ordinary people to understand (see Chapter 7). This being the case, the above list in the Tosefta was com-piled in the late second century, when perhaps ordinary pious Jews who had originally opposed acts of healing and/or saving life that violated Jewish law, especially when there was no obvious perception of an immediate threat to life (see Chapter 4), were now prepared to reverse their opposition, and on their own initiative to violate Jewish law by an act of healing and/or saving life, whenever the need for such a violation might arise. This, however, does not of course indicate the date of composition of the individual directives in the list, which will now be discussed.

(1) *Moving debris which has fallen over a person on the Sabbath, t. Shab 15.11.* This directive has already been discussed above and in Chapter 9, along with the comparable directive at m. Yom 8.7. There is little doubt that a directive to this effect was assumed by Rabban Gamaliel (at m. RH 2.5). Thus, as Rabban Gamaliel died around 50 CE, this means that a permit that allowed this action on the Sabbath was definitely in force before 50 CE. The references to 'doubt' (ספק) in this directive and m. Yom 8.7, however, suggest that this version of the permit was composed after the activity of R. Akiva, that is—at the earliest—after around 70 CE.

(2) *Saving the life of someone who has fallen in the sea on the Sabbath, t. Shab 15.11.*

תוספתא מסכת שבת פרק טו הלכה יא

...נפל לים ואין יכול לעלות ... יורדין ומעלין אותו משם.

Tosefta Shabbat 15.11
...[If] someone fell into the sea and cannot get up...they go down and
bring him up from there.

A similar decree is assumed in the Focused List at m. Pes 7.3 and in the
Focused Lists at m. Taan 3.7 and t. Taan 2.12 (although both the latter
allow the rescue from a river, rather than the sea). This suggests that, as
for all the directives in the Focused Lists, an official directive that
permitted the violation of Sabbath law to save someone who had fallen
into the sea existed before around 70 CE, and certainly by the end of the
first century CE. This may be confirmed by the permissive details in
t. Shab 15.11 (above), which allow rescuers to 'go down' and to 'bring
up'. As was discussed in Chapter 10, the inclusion of these apparently
lenient details can be explained as modifications of corresponding
restrictions imposed in an earlier version of the directive which probably
existed before the 70 CE, in which such permissive actions were specifically *not* allowed.

(3) *Saving a person from a sinking ship on the Sabbath, t. Shab 15.11.*

תוספתא מסכת שבת פרק טו הלכה יא

... טבע' ספינתו בים ואין יכול לעלות, יורדין ומעלין אותו משם.

Tosefta Shabbat 15.11
...[if] his ship is sinking in the sea and he cannot climb up, they go down
and bring him up from there.

The above permit allows the rescue of a person from a ship floundering
at sea. The similar decree in the Focused Lists at m. Taan 3.7 and t. Taan
2.12 (see above) suggests that, as for all the directives in the Focused
Lists, an official directive that permitted the violation of Sabbath law to
save a ship floundering at sea existed before around 70 CE, and certainly
by the end of the first century CE. This may again be confirmed by
the permissive details in the above decree, which allow rescuers to 'go
down' and to 'bring up'. As was discussed in Chapter 10, the presence
of such details can be explained as modifications of the corresponding
restrictions in an earlier version of the directive which probably existed
before the 70 CE, in which such actions were specifically *not* allowed.

(4) *Rescuing someone from a pit on the Sabbath, t. Shab 15.13.*

תוספתא מסכת שבת פרק טו הלכה יג
נפל לבור ואין יכול לעלות, עוקרין לו חוליה ויורדין ומעלין אותו משם.

Tosefta Shabbat 15.(12)13
[If] a person fell into a pit and could not get out, they let down a chain to
him and they go down and raise him out from there.

The permissive actions allowed in this permit, which sanctions a rescuer
to 'let down a chain', 'to go down' and 'to raise up', in order to save a
man who had fallen in a pit, again suggest the existence of an earlier
decree in which such actions were in some way not allowed (see point 3
of the guidelines above). Otherwise, we must explain why official permission was needed for such obvious actions to be performed. In this
case, therefore, it is probable that an earlier directive allowed the rescue
of an individual from a pit, but effectively prohibited the lowering of a
chain and 'going down' and 'bringing up'. In fact, restrictions of this
kind exist in the two directives from Qumran which permit a person to be
saved from a pit (or a well) on the Sabbath, but which prohibit the use of
an 'implement' for the task.[14] It is possible, therefore, that the directives
from Qumran are earlier, restrictive versions of the above directive,
which were part of the official *halachah* of the Hasmonean Jews and
which were taken over and used by those in Qumran when those in this
community broke away. This being the case, the restrictions in the directives from Qumran are less a reflection of the strict laws in Qumran and
more probably an illustration of the kind of restrictive directive that was
issued in Hasmonean times which allowed a specific act of healing
and/or saving life while also attempting to minimise the permitted violation of Sabbath law.

(5) *Releasing a child locked in a building on the Sabbath, t. Shab 15.13.*

תוספתא מסכת שבת פרק טו הלכה יג
תינוק שנכנס לבית ואין יכול לצאת שוברין לו דלתות הבית ואפילו היו של אבן
ומוציאין אותו משם.

Tosefta Shabbat 15.13
[If] a young child went into a building and cannot get out, they break
down the doors of the building for him, even if they are [made] of stone,
and they bring him out from there.

14.   See on 4Q265 Frag 7, CD 11:16-17 in Chapter 1.

This directive gives the impression of an historical incident when a young child was trapped alone in a house on a Sabbath day. As briefly discussed in point 3 of the guidelines above, the permissive detail that *even* (אפילו) *stone doors* may be broken to rescue the child *may* suggest that an earlier version of this directive, composed before around 70 CE, included a restriction to the effect that stone doors should *not* be broken down. The use of the verb שבר, 'to break down', moreover suggests that the author of this directive was aware that action described by the verb סתר, 'to tear down', was one of the thirty-nine *main* activities that are prohibited on the Sabbath (the thirty-fifth, see on m. Shab 7.2 in Chapter 1), and thus used the verb שבר as a subcategory (תולדה) of סתר, in order to minimise, even if only verbally and euphemistically, the permitted violation of Jewish law. This suggests that the earliest version of this directive was composed *after* the compilation of the list of thirty-nine *main* Sabbath prohibitions recorded at m. Shab 7.2. The specificity of the above decree, which allows no suggestion that the permit is merely one of many examples of situations in which there is a need for action to heal and/or save life, moreover suggests that it was originally composed before around 70 CE and certainly before the end of the first century CE.

(6) *Extinguishing a fire on the Sabbath, t. Shab 15.13.*

תוספתא מסכת שבת פרק טו הלכה יג
מכבין ... דליקה בשבת.

Tosefta Shabbat 15:13
They extinguish…a fire on the Sabbath [in order to heal and/or save life].[15]

The purpose of this directive is implied by Rabban Gamaliel at m. RH 2.5 when he assumes a permit to save life from a fire, which he expresses with the euphemistic phrase הבא להציל מן הדליקה. As was briefly noted

---

15. In contrast with the biblical prohibition against lighting a fire on the Sabbath (Exod 35:3), there is no *biblical* prohibition against *extinguishing* a fire on the Sabbath. Both lighting and extinguishing are, however, specifically forbidden at m. Shab 7.2 (cited in Chapter 1) and t. Shab 11.4:

תוספתא מסכת שבת פרק יא הלכה ד
... המכבה והמבעיר הרי זה חייב

Tosefta Shabbat 11.4
One who extinguishes [a fire] and one who lights [a fire], behold this person is liable [to be punished for a violation of Sabbath law].

in point 2 of the above guidelines, the use of the verb כבה in the above directive (in the form מכבין, 'they extinguish'), which repeats the term used in the list of thirty-nine *main* prohibited Sabbath actions at m. Shab 7.2 (the thirty-sixth) suggests that this now unrecorded early directive was originally composed *before* the composition of the mishnaic list, which was probably compiled in Maccabean times.

The early existence of this permit is also assumed in the following tannaitic text, which identifies 'adult Israelites' as those who are *obliged* to extinguish a fire on the Sabbath:

משנה מסכת שבת פרק טז משנה ו

עובד כוכבים שבא לכבות אין אומרים לו, כבה ואל תכבה, מפני שאין שביתתו עליהן. אבל קטן שבא לכבות אין שומעין לו מפני ששביתתו עליהן.

Mishnah Shabbat 16.6
[If] a gentile came to extinguish a fire [on the Sabbath] they may not say to him, 'Put it out' or 'Do not put it out' (תכבה או אל תכבה), since they are not responsible for his keeping the Sabbath. But if a [Jewish] minor came to put it out, they may not permit him, since they are responsible for him keeping the Sabbath.

It is clear that a text which identifies the people by whom a fire must be extinguished on the Sabbath is based on the prior assumption that a Sabbath fire must be put out. This directive repeats the term כבה which is used to prohibit the extinguishing a fire in the list of thirty-nine *main* prohibitions at m. Shab 7.2, which again suggests that the permit to allow the extinguishing of a fire on the Sabbath was composed before the composition of the mishnaic list. The fact that this (probably) Maccabean permit is assumed in the above directive means, however, that the present version of the text was composed *after* the composition of this mishnaic list, and probably also after the directive at t. Shab 15.13. It seems, however, that the term כבה in the original text (which allowed the extinguishing of a fire) was retained when t. Shab 15.13 was composed. The same retention of the terminology of m. Shab 7.2 will be seen again in the permissive details expressed at t. Shab 15.14, in this case the terms שחת and גזז (see below)

(7) *Building a barrier on the Sabbath to stop a fire spreading, t. Shab 15.13.*

תוספתא מסכת שבת פרק טו הלכה יג

...ומפסיקין לדליקה בשבת.

Tosefta Shabbat 15.13
...and they make a barrier [against a fire] on the Sabbath.

As was discussed in Chapter 10, a directive in the Mishnah for the same basic action includes *permissive* instructions for the methods that may be used:

משנה מסכת שבת פרק טז משנה ה

רבי שמעון בן ננס אומר פורסין עור של גדי על גבי, שידה, תיבה ומגדל, שאחז
בהן את האור מפני שהוא מחרך ועושין מחיצה בכל הכלים בין מלאים בין
ריקנים בשביל שלא תעבור הדליקה...

Mishnah Shabbat 16.5
R. Simeon b. Nanos says, 'They may spread the hide of a kid over a chest, a box or a cupboard that has caught fire, since it will [only] scorch [and will not light another fire, which is forbidden on the Sabbath], and they may make a partition wall of the vessels, whether filled [with water] or empty, so that the fire shall not spread...'

The life of R. Simeon b. Nanos, the attributed author of this directive, probably overlapped the period of the second- and third-generation tannaim, which suggests that he died sometime between 110 and 135 CE. It is possible therefore that the above version of the directive was composed sometime in the early second century. The permissive details it includes may however suggest that an earlier, now unrecorded version of this directive was composed before around 70 CE. This earlier version, which specifically allowed a barrier to be built on the Sabbath to stop a fire, included restrictions which are countered by the permissive instructions of R. Simeon. The directive of R. Simon, with its permissive details, may thus be a second-century version of an earlier directive which included restrictions that R. Simon's directive have effectively removed.

F. *Two Directives in the Collected List at Tosefta Shabbat 15.14-15*
The following two directives are located immediately after the list in the Tosefta at t. Shab 15.11-13 (discussed above), but are clearly not part of the original toseftan list:

תוספתא מסכת שבת פרק טו הלכה יד-טו

לו תרנגול, וגוזזין לו (יד)[16] מי שנשכו נחש קורין לו רופא ממקום למקום, ושוחטין
כרישין. אוכל ואין צריך לעשר דברי ר' רבן שמעון בן גמליאל [אומר] צריך
לעשר.
(טו) מחמין חמין לחולה בשבת, בין להשקותו בין לרפאותו. ואין אומ' המתינו לו
שמא יחיה אלא ספיקו דוחה את השבת. ולא ספק שבת זו אלא ספק שבת
אחרת. ואין אומ' יעשו דברים בגוים ובקטנים אלא בגדולים שבישראל אין אומ'
ייעשו דברים הללו על פי נשים על פי כותים אלא מצרפין דעת ישראל עמהן.

---

16. According to b. Yom 83b, the chicken is 'torn'—מקרעין—rather than 'slaughtered'— שוחטין.

Tosefta Shabbat 15.14-15

(14) He who was bitten by a snake, they call a doctor for him from one place to another, and they slaughter (ושוחטין) a chicken for him, and they cut (וגוזזין) leeks for him. 'He eats [them] and does not have to tithe them'. [These are] the words of Rabbi. [But] Rabban Simeon b. Gamaliel says, 'He must tithe'.

(15) They heat (מחמין חמין) water for a sick person on the Sabbath, either to give him to drink or to heal him. And they do not say, 'Wait for him [to get better], perhaps he will live [without treatment, and we shall thus avoid violating Sabbath law]'.

But a matter of doubt concerning him overrides [Sabbath law].

And the doubt need not be about this Sabbath, but may be about another Sabbath.

And they do not say, 'Let these matters be done by the testimony of women, by Samaritans, but they join the opinion of Israelites with them [to save life by overriding Sabbath law].

(1) *Curing a Snake Bite on the Sabbath, t. Shab 15.14*. This directive is based on the *prior* assumption of a permit that specifically allowed a snake bite to be treated on the Sabbath and focuses instead on the permissive methods that may be used so that the action of curing a snake bite may be performed. The permitted actions in this directive allow (1) a doctor to be called even if he must travel further than the Sabbath *eruv* (ממקום למקום, literally, 'from place to place'), (2) a chicken to be slaughtered and (3) leeks to be cut, all actions that are otherwise forbidden on the Sabbath. As was discussed in Chapter 10, these permissive details suggest that an earlier, now unpreserved text included restrictions which these permits now counteract. That is, an earlier, now unpreserved text specifically allowed the treatment of a snake bite on the Sabbath, but included restrictions which effectively forbade the slaughtering of a chicken, the gathering of leeks, and the summoning of a healer who was located further than the Sabbath *eruv*. The fact that the permits in the present version of this text at t. Shab 15.14 are expressed with verbs that are used in the list of the thirty-nine *main* prohibited Sabbath activities expressed at m. Shab 7.2 (rather than terms that could be considered as 'subcategories' of the *main* actions) can be explained on the assumption that these verbs were present in the original restrictions. It is possible, therefore, that the original, earlier now-unpreserved directive was composed in Maccabean times, *before* the list of the thirty-nine *main* prohibited activities on the Sabbath (see point 2 in the guidelines above). If so, the present version of this directive, with its permissive details, was composed after around 70 CE. At an even later time, in the late second century, the words of Rabbi (probably R. Judah ha-Nasi) and Rabban Gamaliel II were added to the earlier established oral text.

(2) *Using a fire to warm water for a sick person on the Sabbath, t. Shab 15.15*. The use of warm water implies the action of heating water which further implies the use of fire, an action which is prohibited on the Sabbath by the Pentateuchal law, *You shall kindle no fire* (לא תבערו אש) *throughout your habitations on the Sabbath* (Exod 35:3, see above on t. Shab 15.[12]13). This prohibition is repeated in the list at m. Shab 7.2 in which the act of 'burning' is one of the thirty-nine *main* actions (the thirty-seventh) which are prohibited on the Sabbath. Nevertheless, the toseftan decree permits this violation in order to treat a person who is sick. It is, however, significant that t. Shab 15.15 avoids the use of the verb העביר, which is used in m. Shab 7.2 to refer to the burning of a fire, and uses instead the verb חמם, 'to warm', which is *not* one of the thirty-nine *main* categories of activity that are prohibited on the Sabbath. This suggests that the act represented by the verb חמם was considered in this context as a sub-category (תולדה) of the verb הבעיר, and was therefore used in order to minimise—even if only euphemistically—the inevitable violation of Sabbath law which was caused by the permit that was allowed.

The specificity of this decree, which does not indicate in any way that it was considered only one of innumerable incidents when it is necessary to perform an act of healing and/or saving life, suggests that it was probably *originally* composed before around 70 CE and certainly by the end of the first century CE.[17] It seems, however, that this directive was subsequently updated, perhaps in two stages, first with a reference to 'doubt', an aspect of any situation of healing and/or saving life, which was probably first articulated in contexts of healing and/or saving life by R. Akiva, probably after 70 CE (see on t. Shab 15.16-17 in Chapter 5), and secondly, with the remark, 'And the doubt need not be about this Sabbath...' The latter is almost certainly an allusion to the midrashic exegesis of Exod 31:16, which is attributed to R. Nathan, a tannaitic sage who was active between the years 135 and 170 CE (see Chapter 7).[18] This suggests that this allusion to his interpretation was added sometime in the second century to an earlier version of t. Shab 15.15 which was probably originally composed—at the latest—before the end of the first century CE.

17. See the discussion below on the story of Hillel (b. Yom 35b) which uses the euphemistic phrase והושיבוהו כנגד המדורה, 'they placed him opposite the fire', to refer to the fact that a fire was used on the Sabbath to save the life of Hillel, thereby violating the law not to burn on the Sabbath, the thirty-seventh of the thirty-nine main prohibitions at m. Shab 7.2, and thus illustrating the directive of t. Shab 15.15.
18. *Mekilta de-Rabbi Ishmael* Shab 1, Lauterbach, *Mekilta*, 3:198-200; the interpretation is also attributed to R. Menasia at b. Yom 85b (see Chapter 7).

G. *Dating of the Collected Lists and Their Contents*

In contrast with the Focused Lists in which each of the situations of healing and/or saving life allow a violation of the *same* Jewish law, the permits for action in the situations in each of the Collective Lists allow the violation of *different* Jewish laws. This suggests that these lists were compiled at a time when the Jewish sages no longer considered that acts of healing and/or saving life should be grouped in relation to the violation of one specific Jewish law, but that these acts should be considered as a separate group of their own, irrespective of the particular law that each one transgressed. This suggests, therefore, that the Collected Lists were compiled at a time later than the Focused Lists, probably after the work of R. Akiva and R. Ishmael at the end of the first century, whose arguments and special vocabulary had shown that *all* acts of healing and/or saving life could be justified according to Jewish law in exactly the same way and were permitted to violate *any* Jewish law. Acts of healing and/or saving life were thus grouped together, whatever violation of Jewish law they caused. But this of course does not date the composition of each of the individual directives in the Focused Lists.

IV. *Single Tannaitic Directives Not Found in the Focused or Collected Lists*

A. *Permission to Continue a Siege on the Sabbath, Sifre Devarim 203*

This is the earliest recorded example of a biblical text which was used as proof that allowed an act of healing and/or saving life on the Sabbath. It is attributed to Shammai the Elder, who was active between the years 50 BCE and 30 CE:

תוספתא מסכת עירובין פרק ג הלכה ז / ספרי דברים פרשת שופטים פיסקא רג
מחנה היוצאה למלחמת הרשות אין צרין על גוים של עיר פחות משלשה ימים
קודם לשבת. ואם התחילו. אפי' בשבת אין מפסיקין. וכך היה שמיי הזקן דורש
'עד רדתה' - ואפי' בשבת.

Tosefta Eruvin 3.7 / Sifre Devarim 203

A camp [of soldiers] that goes out to fight an optional war does not besiege a gentile town less than three days before the Sabbath. But if one begins [a siege, it may continue]. Even on the Sabbath we do not stop. And thus did Shammai the Elder interpret [regarding Deut 20:19-20], *When thou shalt besiege a city...and you shall build siege works against the city that makes war with you until it falls*—[this means that you can continue a siege] even on the Sabbath.

The text of Deut 20:19-20 does not exclude Sabbath activity from the act of conducting a siege. This enables the claim that a siege may be conducted on the Sabbath day. Even apart from the attribution to Shammai, the specificity of this decree confirms that this text was composed before the end of the first century CE.

B. *Permission to Straighten the Back of an Adult on the Sabbath, Mishnah Shabbat 22.6*

משנה מסכת שבת פרק כב משנה ו

ואין מעצבין את הקטן ואין מחזירין את השבר.

Mishnah Shabbat 22.6
They may not straighten (מעצבין) [the body] of a child (קטן) and they may not straighten a [broken] limb (שבר) [on the Sabbath].

Assuming that the noun שבר refers to a limb of a human body, and that the verb מעצבין refers to 'straightening' the human body, this prohibition against straightening the body of a child (קטן) on the Sabbath can only mean that it was permitted only to straighten the body of an adult. Otherwise there is no significance in the reference to a child. The restriction preventing straightening the body of a child, along with the specificity of this directive, suggests that it was composed before 70 CE and certainly by the end of the first century CE.

This text provides the only true echo in a tannaitic source of one of the Sabbath healing incidents in the gospels, when Jesus straightened the back of a woman who had been ill for eighteen years. She was therefore an adult, at least eighteen years old (see on Luke 13:10-17 in Chapter 3), and thus eligible, according to the above directive, to be cured on the Sabbath. This echo of the gospel cure in this directive is not proof of an early date of composition, but does not dispel the impression that it was probably issued before 70 CE.

C. *Violation of the Requirement to Stay in a Sukkah, Mishnah Sukkah 2.4 and Tosefta Sukkah 2.2*

The following two directives exempt sick people and their attendants from the Pentateuchal command of living in a temporary building (in Hebrew, a *sukkah*) during the seven days of the festival of Sukkot, as commanded at Lev 33:34-36. The Mishnah has preserved the simplest version of this decree:

משנה מסכת סוכה פרק ב משנה ד

חולין ומשמשיהן פטורין מן הסוכה.

Mishnah Sukkah 2.4
The sick, and their attendants are exempt from [the requirement to stay in] the *sukkah*.

This permit is repeated and elaborated in the Tosefta, along with the permissive additions of two late second-century Jewish sages:

תוספתא מסכת סוכה פרק ב הלכה ב

חולין ומשמשיהן פטורין מן הסוכה. ולא חולה מסכן אלא אפי' חש בראשו אפי'
חש בעינו.

אמ' רבן שמעון בן גמליאל, מעשה וחששתי בעיני בקיסריון והתיר לי ר' יוסה בי ר'
לישן אני ושמשי חוץ לסוכה.

אמ' ר' כשהיינו באין אני ור' לעזר בי ר' צדוק אצל ר' יוחנן בן נורי לבית שערים,
והיינו אוכלין תאנים וענבים חוץ לסוכה. ...

Tosefta Sukkah 2.2
The sick, and their attendants are exempt from [the requirement to stay in] the *sukkah*. And not [only] an ill person [whose life is] endangered, but even if someone has [a pain] in his head, or even [a pain] in his eye. Said Rabban Simon b. Gamaliel, '[Here is] a story—I had a pain in my eye [when I was] in Caesarion, and R. Yose b. Rabbi permitted me and my servant to sleep outside the *sukkah*'.
Said Rabbi (= R. Judah ha-Nasi), 'When we were going—I and R. Eleazar b. R. Sadok—to visit R. Yohanan b. Nuri in Beit Shearim,[19] we would eat figs and grapes outside the *sukkah*'.

In comparison with m. Sukk 2.4, the text of the Tosefta extends the permit to stay outside the *sukkah* to those with a pain in the head, or in the eye, and the subsequent *aggadah* includes even the attendant and visitors of the sick person. These toseftan extensions suggest that the Mishnah has preserved the earliest written version of this decree, and its specificity suggests that it was probably composed before 70 CE and almost certainly by the end of the first century CE. The names of the sages to whom the final toseftan *aggadah* is attributed suggest that this story was added to the mishnaic directive in the late second century CE.

D. *The Sabbath Care of a Wound on the Leg and Body, Tosefta Shabbat 12.14*

תוספתא מסכת שבת פרק יב הלכה יד

לא יתן מים על גבי ספוג ויתן על גבי מכתו. אבל נותן הוא על גבי רגליו והן יורדין
לספוג.

נותן אדם מוך יבש וספוג יבש על גבי מכתו אבל לא גמי יבש ולא כתותין יבשין
על גבי מכתו.

19. R. Yohanan b. Nuri was an older contemporary of R. Akiva (*Sifra* Kedoshim 4.9; b. Arak 13b). If he was visited by R. Judah ha Nasi, as t. Sukk 2.2 suggests, he may have been very old at the time, and thus perhaps ill. This may explain why he and perhaps also his visitors sought and gained permission not to enter the *sukkah*.

<u>Tosefta Shabbat 12.14</u>
One may not put water on a sponge and place it on his wound. But he
may put [water] on his legs and let it go down onto the sponge [which is
on the wound].
A person may put a dry cloth or a dry sponge on his wound, but not dry
reed-grass or a dry compress of rags on his wound.

These two permits, presented in a single directive, which appears only in
the Tosefta, permit (1) the Sabbath cleaning of a wound on the leg, and
(2) the Sabbath treatment of a wound in an unspecified location on the
body. The former may only be washed in an indirect way, using a sponge.
A wound on the body (the location is unspecified) may be covered with
'a dry cloth or 'a dry sponge', but not with 'dry reed-grass or a dry compress of rags'. The extreme specificity and strict restrictive instructions
of this directive, which were undoubtedly imposed in order to limit the
violation of Sabbath law (and which, incidentally, seem of comparable
severity with the restrictions issued in Qumran, see Chapter 1) suggest
that this permit was composed well before 70 CE.

E. *Lancing an Abscess on the Sabbath, Mishnah Eduyoth 2.5 and Tosefta
Eduyoth 1.8*
The following mishnaic text deals with the treatment of an abscess on the
Sabbath, stating that if this action is to be performed on the Sabbath, it
must be described as 'bringing out pus', להוציא לחה, rather than 'making
a mouth' (that is, 'making an opening'), לעשות פה:

משנה מסכת עדויות פרק ב משנה ה
המפיס מורסא בשבת אם לעשות לה פה חייב. ואם להוציא ממנו לחה פטור.

<u>Mishnah Eduyoth 2.5</u>
The one who cuts open an abscess on the Sabbath in order to make a
mouth (לעשות פה) [for the pus to come out] is [held] liable [for a violation
of Jewish law]. [But] if it was to let out pus (להוציא לחה), the individual is
not liable [for a violation of Jewish law].

The clearly later version of this text in Tosefta expands the directive in
the Mishnah, explaining that the phrase 'to make a mouth' refers to 'the
way that doctors work':

תוספתא מסכת עדויות פרק א הלכה ח
... המיפיס מורסא בשבת אם לקולפה או לעשות לה פה כדרך שהרופאים עושין
חייב. אם להוציא ממנה לחה פטור.

<u>Tosefta Eduyoth 1.8</u>
...He who cuts open an abscess on the Sabbath, either to scrape it or to
make a mouth (לעשות פה) in the way that doctors work (כדרך שהרופאים
עושין), is [held] liable [for a violation of Jewish law]. [But] if it was to
bring out pus (להוציא לחה), he is not liable [for a violation of Jewish law].

The phase לעשות פה, 'to make a mouth', is explained by the later Jewish sages as an act of 'building' (in particular, building an opening to a building, בונה פתח), which is one of the thirty-nine *main* activities (the thirty-fourth) which is totally forbidden on the Sabbath day.[20] The substitution of the phrase 'to let out pus', in place of the phrase 'to make a mouth', suggests an underlying background discussion among the tannaitic sages of the possibility that alternative terminology could be used for a permitted act of healing and/or saving life which caused a violation of Jewish law, which might help solve the problem posed by the frequent clash of such deeds with Jewish law. This being the case, it is likely that such a discussion ceased after the use of the special vocabulary of R. Akiva and R. Ishmael, ספק נפשות and פיקוח נפש, which, when used in permits for specific violations, generalised all actions of healing and/or saving life so that alternative terminology no longer needed to be considered. If so, it can then be assumed that m. Eduy 2.5 was composed *before* the work of R. Akiva and R. Ishmael in relation to acts of healing and/or saving life, that is, probably before 70 CE. An early date of composition, perhaps in Maccabean times, is also implied by the terms חייב and פטור. As briefly mentioned in point 4 of the guidelines above, these terms imply culpability for an act of healing and/or saving life, which is an aspect in the Jewish perception of such deeds that is absent from comparable texts composed after 70 CE (except of course when the amoraic sages discuss tannaitic directives in which culpability is implied).

F. *Circumcision and Washing the Wound of Circumcision on the Sabbath, Mishnah Shabbat 9.3, 19.3 and Tosefta Shabbat 15.4*

According to Pentateuchal law, a male Jewish child must be circumcised on the eighth (inclusive) day after birth (Gen 17:13-14). In practice, therefore, although the ritual of circumcision involves actions considered in Jewish law as 'work', and therefore actions which cause a violation of Sabbath law, every male child born on the Sabbath must be circumcised on the following Sabbath day. Moreover, as can be assumed from the following mishnaic directive, it was customary to wash, in effect, 'to heal', the wound of circumcision on the third (inclusive) day after the ritual had been performed. It is thus again necessary to violate the Sabbath by washing the wound of circumcision of a male Jewish child who is born on the fourth day of the Jewish week, as can be seen from the directive below:

20. m. Shab 7.2, see Chapter 1. For the definition by Rashi of לעשות פה see b. Shab 107a.

משנה מסכת שבת פרק יט משנה ג
מרחיצין את הקטן בין לפני המילה ובין לאחר המילה ומזלפין עליו ביד אבל לא
בכלי. ר' אליעזר בן עזריה אומר מרחיצין את הקטן ביום השלישי שחל להיות
בשבת שנא' (בראשית לד ויהי ביום השלישי בהיותם כואבים...

Mishnah Shabbat 19.3

They may wash the [part of the] child [to be circumcised] either before or
after the circumcision and sprinkle it by means of the hand, but not by
means of a vessel. R. Eleazar b. Azariah says they may wash the child on
the third day if this falls on the Sabbath, for it is written, *And it came to
pass on the third day when they were sore* (Gen 34:25)...

The above permit to wash the wound of circumcision includes the
restriction that the wound may be sprinkled 'by means of the hand, but
not by means of a vessel'. This specific restriction suggests that the permit was originally issued before 70 CE (see Chapter 10). This being the
case, the proof text which is attributed to R. Eleazar, who lived at the
time of the destruction of the Temple, was probably added after 70 CE.[21]
Although the similar directive in the Mishnah at m. Shab 9.3 refers to the
same biblical proof text, the latter is not attributed and neither is there
any reference in the directive itself to 'sprinkling with the hand':

משנה מסכת שבת פרק ט משנה ג
... מנין שמרחיצין את המילה ביום השלישי שחל להיות בשבת שנאמר
(בראשית לד) ויהי ביום השלישי בהיותם כואבים...

Mishnah Shabbat 9.3

...From where do we learn that they might bathe a circumcised child on
the third [inclusive] day [after circumcision] when this falls on the
Sabbath? Because it is written *And it came to pass on the third day when
they were sore* (Gen 34:25).

The removal and consequent lack of any restrictive details in this mishnaic version of the directive suggests that it is a later version of m. Shab
19.3 in which the original restriction was removed, and was composed
perhaps in the late first century or second century CE. It remains to be
explained why the attribution to R. Eleazar was also removed.

The similar lack of any restriction in the toseftan version of this decree,
combined with the *permissive* instruction that water that is warmed may
be sprinkled on a wound, which obliquely indicates the otherwise
forbidden use of fire, suggests that the toseftan version of this directive
was composed after m. Shab 9.3:

---

21. See *Sifre*, Deut. 32 and b. San 101a. R. Eleazar b. Azariah was a younger
contemporary of Gamaliel II, Eliezer b. Hurcanus and Joshua b. Hananiah, and an
older contemporary of R. Akiva.

תוספתא מסכת שבת פרק טו הלכה ד

... ומזלף עליה את החמין ... ולא עוד אלא שאדם מזלף את החמין על גבי
מכתו...

Tosefta Shabbat 15.4

...And one sprinkles warm water on it [= the wound of circumcision].
And not only [on the wound of [circumcision], but a man sprinkles hot
water on his wound...

G. *Pregnant and Nursing Women Exempted from Religious Fasts, Tosefta Taanith 2.14*

תוספתא מסכת תענית פרק ב הלכה יד

העוברות והמניקות מתענות בתשעה באב וביום הכפורים ובשלש תעניות
השניות של צבור, ושאר תעניות לא היו מתענות. ולא שינהגו את עצמן
בתפנוקין אלא שאוכלות ושותות כדי קיום הולד.

Tosefta Taanith 2.14

Pregnant and nursing women fast on the ninth of Av, the Day of Atonement, and the second sequence of the three public fasts. But on other
fasts, they do not fast. And it is not that they should indulge themselves,
but that they should eat and drink for the benefit of the [unborn and
young] child.

The lack of any generalising terminology in this directive indicates a date
of composition before 70 CE, and definitely before the end of the first
century CE.

H. *Exemption from the Ritual of Circumcision, Tosefta Shabbat 15.8*

תוספתא מסכת שבת פרק טו הלכה ח

... היתה יולדת זכרים והן נמולין ומתין, מלה ראשון ומת שני ומת שלישי תמול
רביעי לא תמול.

Tosefta Shabbat 15.8

...if she [a wife] produces [three] male children, and they were circumcised and died, [that is,] if the first was circumcised and died, and the
second [was circumcised] and died, and the third [was circumcised and
died], she [must] not circumcise the fourth.

The specificity and lack of any terminology which could have general-
ised this directive—such as the special terminology of R. Akiva and
R. Ishmael—strongly suggests that it was originally composed before 70
CE and definitely before the end of the first century CE.

I. *Medicaments that May and May Not Be Used on the Sabbath, Mishnah Shabbat 14.4 and Tosefta Shabbat 12.12*

Both the following directives record that restrictions were imposed concerning the medicaments that could be used in earlier versions of these decrees. Thus the Mishnah allowed vinegar to be used for a pain in the mouth, but only if this was an accidental effect of its normal use. Oil is, however, allowed as a cure for a wound on the thighs on the Sabbath, providing that rose oil was not used. This is because it is not usual for ordinary people to use rose oil, so that for ordinary people it would be classed as a medicament, whose use would indicate a deliberate act of healing on the Sabbath, which would violate Sabbath law. This restriction is, however, ingeniously removed by the remark of R. Simon, probably R. Simon b. Yochai, that 'all Israelites (that is, all Jewish people) are the children of kings!':

משנה מסכת שבת פרק יד משנה ד
החושש בשיניו לא יגמע בהן את החומץ אבל מטבל הוא כדרכו ואם נתרפא
נתרפא החושש במתניו לא יסוך יין וחומץ אבל סך הוא את השמן ולא שמן ורד
בני מלכים סכין שמן ורד על מכותיהן שכן דרכם לסוך בחול רבי שמעון אומר כל
ישראל בני מלכים הם:

Mishnah Shabbat 14.4
If his teeth pain him, he may not suck vinegar through them, but he may take vinegar after his usual fashion, and if he is healed, he is healed...
He [who] is concerned [with pain] in his loins [must] not rub [them] with wine and vinegar, but he rubs [them] with oil but not [with] rose oil.
The children of kings may anoint their wounds with rose oil since it is their custom to do so on ordinary days. R. Simeon says, 'All Israelites are the children of kings!'

The specificity of this directive, along with its restriction against using rose oil, suggests that it was originally composed before 70 CE. It is however reasonable to assume that the remark of R. Simon is a later, second-century addition. Unusually however, the restriction has been retained, perhaps so that the reason for R. Simon's addition may be clearly understood.

The corresponding directive in the Tosefta seems to be both permissive regarding the use of oil, which may be rubbed on *any* wound (מכה) rather than only on the loins (מתניים, as in the Mishnah) and also restrictive with its prohibition of the use of a cloth or rag:

תוספתא מסכת שבת פרק יב הלכה יב

סך אדם שמן על גבי מכתו ובלבד שלא יטול במוך ובמטלית.

Tosefta Shabbat 12.12
A person may rub oil on his wound, providing that he does not take a cloth or a rag.

The restriction that is imposed suggests an original date of composition well before 70 CE (see Chapter 10).

J. *Permission to Hunt a Snake on the Sabbath, Mishnah Eduyoth 2.5*
The following directive permits the hunting of a snake on the Sabbath:

משנה מסכת עדויות פרק ב משנה ה

הצד נחש בשבת אם מתעסק שלא ישכנו פטור. ואם לרפואה חייב ...:

Mishnah Eduyoth 2.5
If someone hunts a snake on the Sabbath [in order to prevent loss of life], if he is engaged [in catching] it so that it should not bite him, he is exempt [from punishment] (פטור). [But] if [in order] to [make] a remedy, he is liable [for a punishment] (חייב)...[22]

The use of the term צד repeats the verb used for the twenty-fifth prohibition in the list of thirty-nine *main* prohibited actions on the Sabbath preserved at m. Shab 7.2. This suggests that this directive was composed in Maccabean times (see point 2 of the guidelines above), before the composition of the mishnaic list. An early date of composition is also suggested by the terms פטור and חייה, the former suggesting potential, although excused culpability for the action that is permitted, and the latter suggesting culpability for the action performed (see point 4 of the guidelines above).

K. *Permission to Treat Asphyxia on the Sabbath, Babylonian Talmud Yoma 84b*
According to the Babylonian Talmud, in addition to allowing medicine to be dripped into the mouth of a sick person, and permitting the consumption of the liver of a rabid dog (see m. Yom 8.6, discussed above), R. Mattithiah b. Heresh also approved the treatment of asphyxia on the Sabbath:

תלמוד בבלי מסכת יומא דף פד עמוד א

רבי ישמעאל ברבי יוסי ששמע משום רבי מתיא בן חרש: מקיזין דם לסרונכי
בשבת, ומי שנשכו כלב שוטה מאכילין אותו מחצר כבד שלו, והחושש בפיו
מטילין לו סם בשבת.

---

22.   Amoraic commentary at b. Shab 107a.

Babylonian Talmud Yoma 84a

R. Ishmael son of R. Yose reported three things in the name of R. Mattithiah b. Heresh: One may let blood in the case of asphyxia on the Sabbath, and one whom a mad dog has bitten may be given to eat the lobe of its liver, and one who has pains in his mouth may be given medicine on the Sabbath.

The above permits are expressed in a simple, factual way, without instructions of any kind, which is typical of such statements in the amoraic texts.

V. *A Provisional List of the Earliest Versions of Tannaitic Directives Listed Above*

The directives discussed above are listed below, according to the earliest time that they were probably first composed, and as far as our existing sources allow. Directives marked with an asterisk are those whose *earliest* dates of composition can be assumed on historical grounds (that is, without reference to the discussion in this book) before 50 CE or 70 CE.

A. *Directives Composed Before 50 CE*

*(1) It seems that official permission to violate the Sabbath by fighting in self-defence was issued in by Mattathias the Maccabean priest in 167 BCE, and is the earliest datable official directive that permits an act of healing and/or saving life on the Sabbath day.[23] The first part of the directive at t. Eruv 3.5 repeats the essence of the decree of Mattathias which allowed fighting in self-defence. The second part of t. Eruv 3.5 also allows fighting on the Sabbath to defend property. The text of t. Eruv 3.8 also permits this action to violate Sabbath law. The use of the verb חלל in both t. Eruv 3.5 and t. Eruv 3.8 suggests a date of composition in Maccabean times, confirming the date of the edict of Mattathias. An allusion to such a directive can also be found at m. RH 2.5. A permit to violate Sabbath law for the purpose of self-defence is also mentioned by R. Judah b. Bathyra, a sage who was active before 70 CE.[24] This permit is also assumed at m. Pes 3.7 (in relation to the removal of leavened material), at m. Taan 3.7 (in relation to the sounding of the shofar) and at t. Taan 2.12 (in relation to the violation of a religiously ordained fast).

*(2) An official directive allowing the work of a midwife on the Sabbath is assumed by Rabban Gamaliel I at m. RH 2.5. As Rabban Gamaliel died around 50 CE, his assumption indicates that a directive

---

23. 1 Macc 2:39-41 and 2 Macc 6:11.
24. *Mekilta de-Rabbi Ishmael* Shab 1, Lauterbach *Mekilta*, 3:200-1.

402 Jesus, the Sabbath and the Jewish Debate

allowing the work of a midwife on the Sabbath was issued and in force before 50 CE. Rabban Gamaliel may in fact be referring to the first of the three directives at m. Shab 18.3, whose vocabulary of culpability (מחללין) may also indicate a date of composition well before 50 CE.

(3) An official directive that allowed a midwife to travel on the Sabbath further than a distance that exceeds the *eruv*, in order to reach her patient, is stated at m. Shab 18.3. The fact that it is grouped with the permits in m. Shab 18.3 (see [2] above) suggests an early date of composition, well before 50 CE.

(4) An official directive that permits the umbilical cord to be *tied* (rather than *cut*) on the Sabbath is also preserved at m. Shab 18.3. As severing the umbilical cord is one of the essential tasks of a midwife, this action may also be implied by Rabban Gamaliel at m. RH 2.5, which suggests that it was composed before 50 CE.

(5) An allusion to an earlier permit that allows the umbilical cord to be cut (rather than *tied*) on the Sabbath is also preserved at m. Shab 18.3. This is attributed to R. Yose bar Chalafta, a second-century student of R. Akiva. As 'cutting' rather than 'tying' is merely an alternative method for the necessary task of severing the umbilical cord, it is possible that this method was also was allowed in early times.

*(6) A permit to allow a fire to be extinguished on the Sabbath is assumed by Rabban Gamaliel I in his edict recorded at m. RH 2.5, and thus must have been issued and in force before 50 CE. Rabban Gamaliel alludes to such a permit using euphemistic terminology for the action of extinguishing a fire (הבא להציל מן הדליקה, 'the one who comes to save from the flame') (a phrase which also appears at m. Pes 3.7) which indicates that his edict was composed after the list of *main* prohibitions at m. Shab 7.2. The text of t. Shab 15.(12)13 may be the earliest preserved version of such a decree, and the use of the verb כבה in this text (which is the same verb used in the list of *main* prohibitions at m. Shab 7.2) suggests that this directive may date from Maccabean times. The text of m. Shab 2.5 (which specifically allows the extinguishing of a lamp, rather than a—presumably—otherwise uncontrollable fire) also uses the term כבה, which may thus also indicate a Maccabean date. The story of Shemaiah and Abtalion (preserved at b. Yom 85b, and discussed below) also suggests that a directive to this effect was originally issued and was in force before 50 CE. A later further allusion to this permit, probably composed in the last two thirds of the second century, is preserved at m. Shab 16.6. The directive at t. Shab 15.15 also allows the use of fire— expressed euphemistically as 'warming water'—חמין חמין—to enable the treatment of a sick person on the Sabbath. It seems that this directive has

been modified by the addition of an allusion to the second-century interpretation of Exod 31.16 by R. Nathan. The directive at t. Shab 15.4 also alludes to the permitted use of fire on the Sabbath when it permits warm water—חמין—to be sprinkled on a wound of circumcision.

(7) A violation of Sabbath law for the purpose of saving oneself from robbers is permitted at t. Eruv 3.8. The use of the verb חלל in this permit may indicate a date of composition before 70 CE. The same permit is also assumed at m. Shab 2.5 (in relation to the extinguishing of a lamp), which may date from Maccabean times. It is again assumed at m. Pes 3.7 (in relation to the removal of leavened material), and at t. Taan 2.12 (in relation to the permitted violation of a religious fast).

(8) The text of t. Taan 2.12 allows people in a town who are besieged by gentiles to violate a religious fast. The early dating of this directive is based on the fact that it appears in a Focused List.

(9) The text of t. Taan 2.12 also allows those saving people from drowning in a river to violate a religious fast. The early dating of this directive is again based on the fact that it appears in a Focused List.

(10) Also according to t. Taan 2.12, those saving people from a ship floundering at sea are also permitted to violate a religious fast. The early dating of this directive is based on the fact that it appears in a Focused List.

(11) A general violation of the Sabbath for the purpose of saving oneself from an evil spirit is permitted at t. Eruv 3.8. The verb חלל used in this directive, which suggests culpability, may indicate a date of composition in Maccabean times.

(12) A general violation of the Sabbath for the purpose of saving oneself from pursuing gentiles is permitted at t. Eruv 3.8. The verb חלל used in this directive, which indicates culpability, may again indicate a date of composition in Maccabean times.

(13) A directive which permits saving people from a sinking ship on the Sabbath is preserved at t. Eruv 3.8. The verb חלל used in this directive may again indicate a date of composition in Maccabean times. The rescue of someone from a ship on the Sabbath is also specifically allowed at t. Shab 15.11, along with the permissive detail that the rescuer may climb down and bring people up. The permit may reverse an earlier version of the text which included correcponding restrictions, namely that a person could *only* be rescued from a ship floundering at sea if it was *not* necessary for the rescuer to 'climb down' or 'bring up' (see Chapter 10). The assumption of such a permit is also evident in m. Taan 3.7 (in relation to the sounding of the *shofar*) and in t. Taan 2.12 (in relation to the violation of a religious fast).

*(14) The permit of Rabban Gamaliel I assumes permission to save people from drowning in a river on the Sabbath (m. RH 2.5). As Rabban Gamaliel died around 50 CE, this indicates a date of composition for such a directive before 50 CE. This permit is also found at t. Eruv 3.8, a directive which may also date from Maccabean times (see paragraph [1] above. The same permit is also assumed at m. Pes 3.7 (the latter in relation to the disposal of *hametz*), in the Focused List at m. Taan 3.7 (in relation to a permit that allows the Sabbath blowing of the *shofar*) and also in t. Taan 2.12 (in relation to a permit that allows the violation of a religious fast).

(15) According to m. Taan 3.7 it is permitted to sound the *shofar* on the Sabbath when a city is surrounded by gentiles. The early dating of this directive is based on the fact that it appears in a Focused List.

(16) Similarly, but probably in an earlier-composed permit, m. Taan 3.7 allows the sounding of the *shofar* on the Sabbath when people are drowning in a river. The early dating of this directive is based on the fact that it appears in a Focused List.

(17) Again, probably in a separate permit, m. Taan 3.7 permits the *shofar* to be sounded on the Sabbath when a ship is floundering at sea. The early dating of this directive is based on the fact that it appears in a Focused List.

*(18) A directive which allowed the Sabbath rescue of a person from beneath collapsed debris, and which probably originally included restrictive details on the way that this action was performed, is assumed at m. RH 2.5 and at m. Pes 3.7. As the former was issued by Rabban Gamaliel who died around 50 CE, it can be assumed that the original permit to which he alludes was composed before 50 CE. A later version of the original directive, which contains permissive details and which also includes vocabulary that suggests the activity of R. Akiva in the second half of the first century, is preserved at m. Yom 8.7. A version which does not include any permissive details but which also shows evidence of the work of R. Akiva is preserved at t. Shab 15.11.

(19) A permit which assumes that people may be rescued from robbers on the Sabbath is stated at t. Eruv 3.8 and at m. Shab 2.5, which both may date from Maccabean times (see paragraphs [7] and [11] above). The permit is also assumed at m. Pes 3.7 in relation to the removal of *hametz*, at t. Eruv 3.8 in relation to Sabbath law, and at t. Taan 2.12 in relation to the violation of a religious fast.

*(20) A person (or persons) may be saved from a pit on the Sabbath. Early versions of this directive, expressed with strict restrictions on the way the rescue may be performed, may be preserved in Qumran at 4Q265 Frag. 7 and CD 11:16-17. These permits may be derived from the

law of the normative Jewish community which continued to be used by those who settled in Qumran in Maccabean times. A later, perhaps second-century version of the permit, which includes permissive details that specifically counteracted the restrictions preserved in the directives from Qumran, is preserved at t. Shab 15.(12)13.

(21) Those fighting in self-defence are permitted to violate the Pentateuchal law that all leavened material (*hametz*) must be removed from a place of habitation before the start of the Passover week. This is stated at m. Pes 3.7, in a list that resembles the list of Rabban Gamaliel at m. RH 2.5, and may therefore also have been issued before 50 CE, around which time Rabban Gamaliel died.

(22) Those helping to save people drowning in a river are permitted to violate the Pentateuchal law that requires the removal of all leavened material (*hametz*) from a house before the start of the Passover week. This is stated at m. Pes 3.7, in a list that resembles the list of Rabban Gamaliel at m. RH 2.5. Like this latter list, m. Pes 3.7 may therefore also have been issued before 50 CE, around which time Rabban Gamaliel died.

(23) Those helping to save people from robbers are permitted to violate the Pentateuchal law that requires the removal of all leavened material (*hametz*) from a house before the start of the Passover week. This is stated at m. Pes 3.7, in a list that resembles the list of Rabban Gamaliel at m. RH 2.5, and may therefore also have been issued before 50 CE.

(24) Those helping to save people from a fire are permitted to violate the Pentateuchal law that requires the removal of all leavened material (*hametz*) from a house before the start of the Passover week. This is stated at m. Pes 3.7, in a list that resembles the list of Rabban Gamaliel at m. RH 2.5, and may therefore also have been issued before 50 CE.

(25) Those helping to save life from beneath fallen debris are permitted to violate the Pentateuchal law that all leavened material (*hametz*) must be removed from a house before the start of the Passover week. This is stated at m. Pes 3.7, in a list that resembles the list of Rabban Gamaliel at m. RH 2.5, and may therefore also have been issued before 50 CE.

(26) The text of m. Shab 2.5 permits a person to extinguish (המכבה) a lamp on the Sabbath because of a fear of gentiles. The term כבה, which repeats a verb in the list of thirty-nine *main* prohibited activities preserved at m. Shab 7.2, along with the terms פטור and חייב, which indicate culpability and potential culpability, suggests that this permit was issued in early Maccabean times.

(27) The directive at m. Shab 2.5 permits the extinguishing (המכבה) of a lamp on the Sabbath for fear of robbers. For reasons elaborated in paragraph (26) above, there is good reason to believe that this permit was issued in early Maccabean times.

(28) The text of m. Shab 2.5. also permits an individual to extinguish (המכבה) a lamp on the Sabbath for fear of an evil spirit. For reasons elaborated in paragraph (26) above, there is good reason to believe that this permit was issued in early Maccabean times.

(29) The text of m. Shab 2.5 permits an individual to extinguish (המכבה) a lamp on the Sabbath for the sake of allowing an invalid to sleep. For reasons elaborated in paragraph (26) above, there is good reason to believe that this permit was issued in early Maccabean times.

(30) A directive preserved at t. Eruv 3.5, which was probably composed in Maccabean times (see paragraph [1] above), permits the carrying of weapons on the Sabbath. This permit is also assumed at t. Eruv 3.6.

(31) The directive at t. Shab 15.14 is based on the prior assumption of a directive that permitted a snake bite to be cured on the Sabbath day. The permissive details in the present version of this directive suggest that an earlier, now-unpreserved directive, specifically forbade the slaughter of a chicken or the gathering of leeks in order to provide a cure for the bite, and also may have forbidden a potential healer to travel further than the Sabbath *eruv*. The vocabulary of these permissive details in the present version of this text—in particular the verbs שחת and גזז, which repeat terms used in the list of thirty-nine *main* prohibited actions on the Sabbath—suggests that this earlier directive may have been originally issued in early Maccabean times.

(32) It is permitted to slaughter a chicken on the Sabbath in order to cure the bite of a snake. The use of the verb שחת in this directive suggests that this permit repeats the verb used in a restriction imposed in an earlier version of the directive, which may therefore have been composed in early Maccabean times, before the list of thirty-nine prohibited Sabbath activities preserved at m. Shab 7.2, the latter including the action suggested by the verb שחת.

(33) It is permitted to cut leeks on the Sabbath in order to cure the bite of a snake. The use of the verb גזז for this action suggests that this permit repeats the vocabulary used in a restriction imposed in an earlier directive that was originally composed in early Maccabean times, before the list of thirty-nine *main* prohibited Sabbath activities preserved at m. Shab 7.2, the latter including the action suggested by the verb גזז.

(34) The text of m. Eduy 2.5 permits the hunting of a snake on the Sabbath. The use of the verb צד in this directive, which is the twenty-fifth of the thirty-nine *main* prohibited activities on the Sabbath preserved

in the (probably) Maccabean list at m. Shab 7.2, suggests that this directive was issued in early Maccabean times, before the compilation of the mishnaic list at m. Shab 7.2. The term פטור in this directive, which implies potential culpability, also suggests a time of composition before around 70 CE, see point 4 in the guidelines above.

*(35) The directive at t. Eruv 3.7 (= Sifre Devarim 203) states that Shammai used the text of Deut 20:19-20 both to permit and to justify the continuation of a siege on the Sabbath.

(36) The extreme specificity of t. Shab 12.14 and its very restrictive details on the way that the permitted action of washing a wound on the leg may be performed (which are comparable in their severity and detail with the strict restrictions included in 4Q265 Frag. 7, CD 11:16-17), suggests that this directive was composed well before the end of the first century CE. Thus, according to this directive, water may not be put directly on the wound on a leg, but is allowed to trickle down on to the wound from a sponge. In addition, although it is permitted to place a dry cloth or a dry sponge on a wound, it is not permitted to use dry reed-grass or a dry compress of rags.

(37) The directive at t. Eduy 1.8 permits the lancing of an abscess on the Sabbath day, and suggests an acceptable verbal expression with which this action may be described, in order to legalise this action in the context of Sabbath law. It seems that the standard medical expression for this procedure—'to make a mouth' (לעשות פה)—was considered to imply the action of 'building', which is the thirty-fourth of the thirty-nine *main* prohibited actions listed at m. Shab 7.2. It is likely that such verbal alternatives were discussed before the composition of the arguments and special vocabulary of R. Akiva and R. Ishmael sometime around 70 CE (see Chapter 5).

B. *Directives Composed Before 70 CE*

*(1) The text of t. Yom 4.4 refers to an earlier directive composed before 70 CE that allowed a pregnant woman from the family of a priest who craved *terumah* to be given the juice from *terumah* on a day of religious fasting. This earlier (unrecorded) directive was later widened with an addition attributed to the second-century R. Judah b. Ilai. His addition widened the scope of the directive to include all pregnant woman and to include food that was potentially available to all, in this case a small, stipulated amount of the otherwise forbidden food of *sheviit*. Probably the latest tannaitic version of this directive, which allows a pregnant woman any amount of any food that she craves, is preserved at m. Yom 8.5.

*(2) Official permission to save life from starvation by violating Sabbath law is assumed in the argument *kal va-chomer* based on 1 Sam 21:1-6. This argument is preserved in a christological Greek translation at Mark 2:25-26, 28, which is repeated at Luke 6:3-5, and phrased as a sorite at Matt 12:3-5, 8 (see Chapter 3). (Other directives preserved in Jewish sources which permit a 'cure' for starvation allow the violation of Jewish laws that are related either to fasting or to the eating of 'unclean' foods, rather than to the violation of *Sabbath* law.) A sorite which is based on the original probably Hebrew argument (on which Mark's argument was based) may be preserved at t. Shab 15.16, where it is attributed to R. Akiva (see Chapter 6).

*(3) According to m. Shab 16.7, a scorpion may be covered with a dish to prevent it from biting.

C. *Directives Probably Composed Before 70 CE*
(1) According to m. Shab 16.7, a lamp may be covered with a dish so that it does not scorch a rafter, and thereby cause a fire.

(2) According to m. Shab 16.7, animal droppings may be covered with a dish to protect a child from harm.

D. *Directives Composed by 100 CE*
The following list includes those directives whose specificity and lack of any generalising details suggests that that they were probably composed, at the latest, by around 100 CE. If however we use the date 70 CE as an approximate time for the start of the activity of R. Akiva and probably also R. Ishmael, and we also assume that their work made redundant the issue of specific permits, a date of 100 CE is probably a very conservative estimate, as the specificity of these directives suggests that a significant number were probably composed well before this time.

(1) It is assumed at m. Shab 17.2 that a thorn may be removed on the Sabbath.

(2) It is stated at m. Shab 17.2 that a sack-maker's needle may be used to remove a thorn on the Sabbath.

(3) The text of t. Yom 4.4 states that it is permitted to feed a starving person at the time of a religious fast. A later version of this decree is preserved at m. Yom 8.6.

(4) A directive at m. Sukk 2.4 exempts the sick and their attendants from the requirement to stay in a *sukkah*. A later version of this directive at t. Sukk 2.2 widens the scope of this directive to include someone with a pain in his head, or in his eye and a late second-century *aggadic* addition includes the attendants and friends of the person who is ill.

(5) The body and broken limb of an adult may be straightened on the Sabbath. This is stated at m. Shab 22.6 and is also permitted in an argument *kal va-chomer* probably composed by one of the Jewish sages after 70 CE, which is preserved at Luke 13:15b-16. Apart perhaps from directives which allow the relief from starvation when the method that used would violate Jewish law, this is the only directive dealing with a situation in the Sabbath healing events that is clearly echoed in a gospel text.

(6) A permit which allowed the life of an animal to be saved from a pit may be implied at m. Betz 3.4 (= t. Betz 3.3). Such a directive is assumed in the arguments *kal va-chomer* at Luke 13:15b-16 and 14:5, as well as Matt 12:11-12.

(7) It is permitted to cure dropsy. A specific directive for this permit, presented as an argument *kal va-chomer*, which was probably originally composed by a Jewish sage, is preserved in Greek, at Luke 14:5.

(8) A directive which allows a young child to be freed from a building on the Sabbath is preserved at t. Shab 15.(12)13. The permissive detail that even stone doors may be broken down may suggest the existence of an earlier, now-lost directive which allowed this action on the Sabbath, on condition that it did not entail the demolition of stone doors (see Chapter 10).

(9) A directive preserved at m. Shab 16.5 and attributed to the second-century sage R. Simeon b. Nanos allows a barrier to be erected on the Sabbath. This includes the permissive details that the hide of a kid may be spread over a chest, a box or a cupboard that has caught fire and that a partition may be made with a wall of vessels, either filled with water or empty. These permissive details may suggest that an earlier, now unpreserved permit was issued, probably before 70 CE (see Chapter 10). A permit that allows a barrier to be built, which is expressed with no restrictions or permissive details, is preserved at t. Shab 15.(12)13. In view of the existence of the directive of R. Simon, with its permissive details, this toseftan directive may be a late second-century version of an earlier, restrictive directive, from which any restrictions have been removed, thus resembling the directives on healing and/or saving life in the later amoraic texts.

(10) The directive at m. Shab 19.3 allows the wound of circumcision to be washed on the Sabbath, although with the restrictive detail that it must be sprinkled with water from the hand, but not from a vessel. The antiquity of the ritual of circumcision, for which such a permit would be urgently needed, and the restrictive detail of this directive, suggests that it was issued well before 70 CE. The text of Gen 34:25, which justifies the basic procedure (although not any restrictive detail) is provided by the later addition of R. Eleazar b. Azariah.

(11) The directive preserved at m. Yom 8.5 assumes that a starving person may violate a religious fast provided that he (or she) was given a supervised minimum quantity of food. The present version of this directive removes the restriction and allows the starving person to decide on the amount of food that he (or she) might need.

(12) A second directive preserved at t. Yom 4.4 (see on t. Yom 4.4 above, for the first directive listed under this heading) allowed a starving person to eat a minimum quantity of 'unclean' food (that is, food otherwise not allowed for consumption by Jewish law). A similar directive preserved at m. Yom 8.6 further modified the earlier restriction by allowing the starving person to eat as much of the 'unclean' food as he (or she) wished. This modification towards apparent leniency suggests that the mishnaic directive was probably composed at an even later time.

(13) A directive which allowed an oral medicine to be given to an invalid, but which imposed restrictions on the way the medicine could be delivered, is preserved at t. Shab 2.7. A later version of this directive, from which the restrictions are removed, was probably composed in the second century, and is attributed to R. Mattithiah b. Heresh at m. Yom 8.6.

(14) According to t. Shab 15.14, it is permitted for a doctor to travel further than the Sabbath *eruv* to treat a bite from a snake.

(15) A directive at t. Taan 2.14 exempts pregnant and nursing women from all fasts, except those on the ninth of Av, the Day of Atonement, and the second sequence of the three public fasts.

(16) A directive at t. Shab 15.8 exempts a male child from circumcision if the procedure has caused three earlier-born siblings to die.

(17) A directive at m. Shab 14.4 allows pain in the loins to be rubbed with oil, but adds the restriction that it must not be rubbed with vinegar. A later addition to this directive attributed to R. Simon b. Yochai allows rose oil to be used. These restrictions suggest an original date of composition well before 70 CE.

(18) A directive in the Tosefta at t. Shab 12.12 allows oil to be used on any wound, providing it is not applied with a cloth or a rag. These restrictions suggest an original date of composition well before 70 CE.

E. *Directives Probably First Composed in the Second Century CE*
(1) The second-century sage R. Mattithiah b. Heresh allowed the liver of a rabid dog to be used as medicine to cure rabies. This is stated at m. Yom 8.6 (and repeated at b. Yom 84a). Rather than a new permit, this, however, may however be considered as the specific application of

earlier directives that allow the consumption of material that is forbidden by Jewish law, which were probably composed before the end of the first century (see above on m. Yom 8.6 and t. Yom 4.4). These texts, however, give permission to eat 'unclean' food only in a case of starvation, rather than in a case of a sickness such as rabies, which suggests that the directive of R. Mattithiah was indeed new.

(2) The text of b. Yom 84a records that the second-century sage R. Mattithiah b. Heresh also allowed blood to be let in the case of asphyxia on the Sabbath.

VI. *Some Implications of the Dates of Composition of the Above Directives*

As has already been noted above, but must be stressed once again, the above list is only provisional regarding both the identification of the directives themselves and their dates of composition, and no doubt in the future will be considerably improved. For example, even if all the relevant recorded permits have been identified above (which is unlikely), they cannot include the many oral permits which must also have been issued in tannaitic times, a fact which is evident merely because Jewish oral law before the end of the second century was indeed truly oral, so that it is most unlikely that *all* the existing directives on healing and/or saving life were committed to writing at the end of the second century, and were thereby preserved. These lost, unrecorded directives must surely have included the inevitably large number of permits that allowed the performance of ancillary actions which accompany any action of healing and/or saving life, and which also cause violations of Jewish law. Thus, for example, it can be assumed that those who were permitted to rescue people from a fire (according to the implication of m. RH 2.5 and m. Pes 3.7, and the permit stated at t. Shab 15.[12]13) were also permitted to carry equipment from one domain to another, in spite of the fact that this action is one of the *main* prohibited actions (the thirty-ninth) in the directive of m. Shab 7.2, and although it appears that there was particular sensitivity to the violation caused by this prohibition. This is evident in the directives from Qumran, which not only forbid such an action, but also pre-empt it by prohibiting the use of 'implements' which could be carried to the site (see Chapter 1). It seems that such ancillary actions were officially permitted in a general way only in the time of R. Akiva, which suggests that such permits for the violation of Jewish law also once existed and could therefore be added to the above officially permitted list.[25] All in all, therefore, there is thus little doubt that far more specifically permitted violations of Jewish law allowing an act of healing and/or saving life were granted than are now preserved in the tannaitic texts.

It is, however, likely that the editors of the Mishnah and Tosefta, in which the majority of relevant tannaitic directives are found, preserved those directives that they considered were the most important. It is also likely that most of these directives have been listed above and that a significant percentage of their original dates of composition have been correctly estimated (even if only in a relative way), especially in relation to those whose historical details suggest that they were composed before 70 CE, the period of greatest interest to those who deal with the gospel texts. On this basis, therefore, it seems that at least around thirty-seven *specific* directives were first composed and officially in force before 50 CE, over half of these (twenty-one in the above list) probably in Maccabean times. At least another five *specific* directives were probably first composed before 70 CE, and another eighteen or so, also *specific*, before the end of the first century, although many of these probably in earlier times. It seems that only two of the directives listed above were probably first composed after the first century CE.

Even on the very conservative estimate of the dates assumed above, and taking into account the above caveats, these numbers suggest that most of the recorded tannaitic directives issued by the Jewish sages which permitted acts of healing and/or saving life that violated Jewish law were probably first composed before 50 CE—according to the numbers collected above, thirty-seven out of sixty-two. The preponderance of early directives should in fact be no surprise. It can be expected that from the time that the problem caused by acts of healing and/or saving life in Jewish law was first noted by pious Jews, which apparently happened in Maccabean times sometime around 167 BCE, permission would be sought by pious individuals to perform acts of healing and/or saving life that violated Jewish law. As a result, the majority of permits for commonly recurring situations, especially if they were *urgent*—such as the five situations assumed in the edict of Rabban Gamaliel at m. RH 2.5, namely childbirth, fires, a situation of war, saving people from drowning

---

25. m. Shab 19.1, m. Pes 6.2 and m. Men 11.3: R. Akiva laid down a general rule: Any act of work that can be done on the eve of the Sabbath does not override the Sabbath, but what cannot be done on the eve of the Sabbath overrides the Sabbath. Was this—partly at least—a response to requests for permits for such ancillary actions by pious Jews?

in a river and saving people from beneath fallen debris, especially, no doubt, saving those beneath the debris of a collapsed mud-built house[26]—date from that time. This accounts for the fact that according to the directives listed above, it seems that only two out of sixty were issued after the first century CE. This may have been due primarily to the pioneering efforts of R. Akiva and R. Ishmael, whose activities probably began after 70 CE. As noted above in Chapter 5, these sages produced general arguments to justify any action in any situation of healing and/or saving life, and thus obviated the need for pious Jews 'to get permission for such actions from a Jewish court' (t. Shab 15.11-13).

The greater number of directives issued at the latest before 100 CE is significant for both the history of Christianity and Judaism. As far as the history of Christianity is concerned, the high number of directives that were probably composed before the end of the first century, especially the number composed before 50 CE, helps to confirm that Jesus was not alone among first-century Jewish healers in performing acts of healing and/or saving life that violated Jewish law. This is especially the case when we consider that of the permits that were probably first issued before 50 CE (thirty-seven are listed above) there is only one—the permit to straighten the bone of an adult on the Sabbath—that echoes a Sabbath deed of healing that Jesus performed (see on Luke 13:10-17 and m. Shab 22.6). It is likely therefore, that apart from those who may have healed without permission from the Jewish sages (for example, probably the disciples of Jesus, see Mark 6:7, Luke 9:1 and Matt 10:1) there were also other Jewish healers in the first century who also put into practice the thirty-six other permits listed above that heal and/or save life, while violating Jewish law.

As far as concerns the Jewish history traced in this book—namely, the accommodation of the often mutually exclusive conflicting demands of acts of healing and/or saving life when set against the requirements of Jewish law—the fact that most of the directives discussed above were probably composed by the end of the first century suggests—as was briefly noted above—that many of the commonly recurring situations which needed acts of healing and/or saving life were already officially permitted by this time. In addition, it seems that by the end of the first century, a majority of those pious Jews who had earlier questioned the religious legality of such acts (whose opposition in the second century BCE is implied by the edict of Mattathias, and in the first half of the first

---

26. See n. 6 in Chapter 9 for the necessity of this directive, based on historical-archeological grounds.

century is recorded in the synoptic gospels, see Chapter 4) were now persuaded that such acts should take place, even in apparently non-urgent situations. There is little doubt that this was due, at least in part, to the activity of R. Akiva and R. Ishmael who, sometime around 70 CE, composed *general* arguments *kal va-chomer* using special vocabulary that proved that all acts of healing and/or saving life must be allowed to violate Jewish law (as was discussed in Chapter 5). But until such general justifications had been found, it seems that the Jewish sages responded to the numerous requests of pious Jewish individuals by issuing separate specific permits for each situation of healing and/or saving life about which they were approached. The work of R. Akiva and R. Ishmael, however, obviated the need for such a piecemeal approach, although—as can be seen from the few directives that were probably composed in the second century CE—their solutions to the problems caused by acts of healing and/or saving life was not accepted by all.

Moreover, the fact that Jesus was a Jewish healer who healed on the Sabbath in the first half of the first century, when the problem of healing and/or saving life in Jewish law had still not been resolved, while the activity of R. Akiva and R. Ishmael must be dated to a time *after* the life of Jesus in the second half of the first century, accounts for the recurring gospel references to the problem in Judaism caused by acts of healing and/or saving life, which took the shape of stories of Jesus' Sabbath cures. If, however, Jesus had lived after around 70 CE, it is doubtful that the Sabbath would have featured in any accounts of his cures, even those he performed on the Sabbath day, still less that Jesus would have been given any arguments to justify such deeds. In short, the stories of the Sabbath cures that Jesus performed are simply an expression of Jewish history and debate in the first half of the first century CE that came to a conclusion after Jesus had died.

VII. *The 'Sabbath' as a Symbol for All Jewish Law*

The centrality of the Sabbath in Jewish life—whose laws were described by R. Judah ha-Nasi as 'equal in weight to all of the commandments of the Torah' (y. Ber 1.5)—accounts for the fact that over 80 percent of the tannaitic directives listed above, which deal with acts of healing and/or saving life, are concerned with the violation of Sabbath law rather than with any other aspect of Jewish law. (The second most numerous category is linked in different ways with food, including the violation of a religious fast, law relating to 'unclean' and forbidden foods, and law relating to food that must not be consumed during the Passover week.)

It is thus no surprise that the term 'Sabbath' became a symbol for the totality of all Jewish law especially in relation to acts of healing and/or saving life. This symbolic use of the term 'Sabbath' can first be observed in a tannaitic directive attributed to the second-century R. Mattithiah b. Heresh which is expressed in relation to the Sabbath, although its topic— the administration of an oral medicine—is relevant both to Sabbath law (because healing, which is 'work', is not allowed on the Sabbath) and to law which forbids food at the time of a religious fast. The relevance of this directive to a day of fasting is however only indirectly acknowledged in this directive by the fact that it is preserved in the tractate 'Yoma' which deals mainly with the laws of the fast of the Day of Atonement, rather than in the tractate 'Shabbat', as can be seen from the text below:

משנה מסכת יומא פרק ח משנה ו

ורבי מתיא בן חרש מתיר ועוד אמר רבי מתיא בן חרש החושש בגרונו מטילין לו
סם בתוך פיו בשבת מפני שהוא ספק נפשות וכל ספק נפשות דוחה את השבת.

Mishnah Yoma 8.6
Moreover R. Mattithiah b. Heresh said, 'If a man has a pain in his throat they may drop medicine into his mouth on the *Sabbath*, since there is doubt whether life is in danger, and whenever there is doubt whether life is in danger, this overrides the *Sabbath* [law] (דוחה את השבת).

The symbolic use of the term 'Sabbath' to represent all Jewish law is echoed in the amoraic commentary on the above text, when R. Yohanan, probably the late third-century sage R. Yohanan b. Naphtha, again justifies feeding a sick person on the Day of Atonement with the other-wise nonsensical remark that the saving of life overrides *Sabbath* law:

תלמוד ירושלמי מסכת יומא פרק ח הלכה ד

רבי אבהו בשם רבי יוחנן נעשה כספק נפשות וכל ספק נפשות דוחה את השבת.

Jerusalem Talmud Yoma 8.4
[On the problem of treating a sick person on the Day of Atonement], R. Abbahu said in the name of R. Yohanan, 'This is dealt with as a case of the saving of life, and each situation that involves the saving of life overrides the *Sabbath* (דוחה את השבת)'.

This understanding of the term 'Sabbath' considerably extends the literal meaning of the term, and has caused some confusion, especially among commentators of the gospel texts. This can be seen particularly in relation to a passage in the medieval commentary, the *Yalkut*, which repeats the story of David and the sacred bread (1 Sam 21:1-6) used by the midrashic Jesus in his argument to the midrashic Pharisees in the Galilean fields (see on Mark 2:25-26, 28; Luke 6:3-5; Matt 12:3-5, 8 in Chapter 3). Significantly however there is no repetition in the *Yalkut* of the argument itself.[27] Instead, after recounting the story, this source apparently illogically notes that the starvation of David, which was a danger to his life, gave him authority to override *Sabbath* law. The *Yalkut* also claims that David arrived at the shrine on the Sabbath day. The relevant text follows below:

ילקוט שמעוני שמואל א רמז קל

והיה שבת וראה אותם דוד שהיו אופין לחם הפנים בשבת שהורה להם דואג,
אמר להם מה אתם עושין אפייתו אין דוחה שבת כי אם עריכתו שנאמר ביום
השבת יערכנו. כיון שלא מצא שם כי אם לחם הפנים, אמר לו דוד תן לי שלא
נמות ברעב שספק נפשות דוחה שבת.

Yalkut Shimoni Neviim 130

And it was the Sabbath (והיה שבת) and David saw them, that they were baking the sacred Temple bread on the Sabbath that Doeg taught to them. He (= David) said to them, 'What are you doing? Baking [the sacred Temple bread] does not override the Sabbath [that is, the sacred bread must not be baked on the Sabbath], but [the bread may be] arranged [in the Temple on the Sabbath], as it is said, *on the day of the Sabbath you will arrange it*' (Lev 24:8). Since he [= David] only found there Sacred Bread, David said to him [= the priest], 'Give [it] to me, so that we shall not die of hunger, *for actions to save life override Sabbath [law]*'.

The claim in the *Yalkut* that David arrived at Nob on the Sabbath is based on a short digression at the end of the story in the biblical text which notes that the sacred bread in the shrine at Nob was 'removed from before the Lord, to be replaced by hot bread on the day it is taken away' (1 Sam 21:6). The editor of the *Yalkut* thus assumed that because the sacred bread in the Temple in Jerusalem was replaced on the Sabbath (Lev 24:8), so also the replacement of the holy bread in the ritual at Nob also took place on the Sabbath day. Thus, as the biblical account seems to imply that David arrived at Nob when the bread was replaced, it was assumed by the editor of the *Yalkut* that David arrived on the Sabbath day.[28] But the day that David arrived at the shrine in the *Yalkut* has no connection with the way that he justified his consumption of the sacred bread with the words 'for actions to save life override Jewish law'. Assuming with the editor of the *Yalkut* that David was in the Temple in Jerusalem *rather than at the shrine of Nob*, David violated Jewish law *not* because it was the Sabbath, but because only priests in the Temple at

---

27. For the problem caused by a lack of understanding of the symbolic use of the term 'Sabbath' in Jewish sources that deal with acts of healing and/or saving life, see, e.g., Casey, *Aramaic Sources of Mark's Gospel*, 155-6.

28. Lev 24:8; Josephus, Ant III.255.

Jerusalem were allowed to eat the Temple bread and David was not a priest. The author of the *Yalkut* thus uses the midrashic story of David *not* as the basis for an argument *kal va-chomer* to justify the violation of Jewish law (as in the gospels), but as a free-standing tale in which the behaviour of David illustrates the fact that in a situation of danger to life (in this case, caused by starvation) it was permissible to violate (any) Jewish law, which happened in this case to be Temple law. The term 'Sabbath' in the words of David 'for actions to save life override Sabbath law' thus functions as a symbol for *all* Jewish law and is wholly irrelevant to the day of the week that he arrived. In short, David's remark in the text of the *Yalkut*, namely, that '*safeq nefashot [= actions to save life] override Sabbath [law]*', merely exploits the fact that the Sabbath had become a symbol for all Jewish law.

The loss of the use of the midrashic story of David as the basis for an argument *kal va-chomer* in Jewish texts is almost certainly the result of the substitution by R. Akiva of the midrashic story of David, which R. Akiva replaced with his own midrashic interpretation of Exod 21:14 (see Chapter 6). As a result the midrashic story of David was now no longer used by the Jewish sages as the basis for an argument *kal va-chomer* in the Jewish sources, but—as can be seen from the text of the *Yalkut*—served only as a free-standing story that illustrated the fact that an act of healing and/or saving life was permitted to override any Jewish law. Without the preservation of the argument in the gospels which is based on the midrashic story of David, we would therefore be unaware that in the first half of the first century, this midrashic story was once the basis for the first part of an argument *kal va-chomer*, which 'proved' the legality of violating Sabbath law, in order to ensure that starving people did not die.

VIII. *Saving the Life of Hillel on the Sabbath, Babylonian Talmud Yoma 35b—When Was this Story Composed?*

Conclusions from the discussions above can be used to clarify and to establish the date of composition of a story about the great sage Hillel in relation to the end of the first century CE. This story describes how Hillel was saved from near death on the Sabbath by Shemaiah and Abtalion, the heads of the Sanhedrin in the mid-first century BCE. Although Hillel himself was an early tannaitic sage, active between the years 110 BCE and 10 CE, the story is not preserved in a tannaitic text, but first appears in the Babylonian Talmud, which was edited sometime in the fifth century CE. The absence of this story in a tannaitic text and its presence in an amoraic text that was edited about three hundred years after tannaitic times, thus implies that the story was composed in amoraic times. The following discussion will, however, suggest that, whether or not the event itself took place, the story itself was probably composed before the end of the first century and thus is probably a product of tannaitic times.

The story is preserved in Hebrew and is cited and translated below:

תלמוד בבלי מסכת יומא דף לה עמוד ב

אמרו עליו על הלל הזקן שבכל יום ויום היה עושה ומשתכר בטרפעיק, חציו היה נותן לשומר בית המדרש, וחציו לפרנסתו ולפרנסת אנשי ביתו. פעם אחת לא מצא להשתכר, ולא הניחו שומר בית המדרש להכנס. עלה ונתלה וישב על פי ארובה כדי שישמע דברי אלהים חיים מפי שמעיה ואבטליון. אמרו: אותו היום ערב שבת היה, ותקופת טבת היתה, וירד עליו שלג מן השמים. כשעלה עמוד השחר אמר לו שמעיה לאבטליון, אבטליון אחי! בכל יום הבית מאיר, והיום אפל, שמא יום המעונן הוא? הציצו עיניהן וראו דמות אדם בארובה, עלו ומצאו עליו רום שלש אמות שלג. פרקוהו, והרחיצוהו, וסיכוהו, והושיבוהו כנגד המדורה. אמרו, ראוי זה לחלל עליו את השבת.

<u>Babylonian Talmud Yoma 35b</u>
It was reported that Hillel the Elder used to work every day and earn one tropaik, half of which he gave to the guard at the House of Learning, and the other half he spent on the living expenses of himself and his family. One day he found nothing to earn and the guard at the House of Learning would not let him come in. [So] he climbed up [on the roof] and sat on the skylight, in order to hear the words of the living God from the mouth[s] of Shemaiah and Abtalion. They say that day was the eve of Sabbath in the winter solstice and snow fell down upon him from heaven. In the morning at dawn, Shemaiah said to Abtalion, 'Brother Abtalion, every day this house is light [at dawn] but today it is dark. Is it perhaps a cloudy day?' They looked up and saw the shape of a person on the skylight (דמות אדם בארובה). They went up and found him covered by three cubits of snow. They moved him, and bathed him and anointed him and placed him opposite the fire (והושיבוהו כנגד המדורה) and they said, 'It is proper that the Sabbath be violated on his behalf (ראוי זה לחלל עליו את השבת)'.[29]

According to this tale, one Friday afternoon/evening, before the beginning of the Sabbath, the young Hillel found that he did not have enough money to attend the School of Learning on the Sabbath (which began on Friday evening and continued for around twenty-four hours until the following Saturday evening). Anxious to hear the discussion of the sages

---

29. Trans. Leo Jung, *The Babylonian Talmud Seder Mo'ed* (London: Soncino Press, 1938), 163. An alternative translation for the final declaration of the sages is discussed below in the main text.

that took place on Friday evening within the school, Hillel climbed up to the skylight of the building, from where—we must assume—he was able to hear the debate below. It was winter and snowing and, while he was on the skylight, he was covered with snow. The following Sabbath morning the sages Shemaiah and Abtalion noticed a 'shape of a person' on the skylight. They then climbed onto the roof and brought the frozen 'shape' down. Then they 'bathed and anointed' the frozen person which, when performed on the Sabbath for the purpose of healing, are actions that result in a violation of Sabbath law. A further violation of Sabbath law took place when the frozen Hillel was warmed 'opposite the fire', because the use of fire of the Sabbath is one of the thirty-nine *main* violations of Sabbath law (the thirty-seventh, see m. Shab 7.2, cited in Chapter 1). Shemaiah and Abtalion however justified their deed with a remark which is translated in the popular English (Soncino) translation of this text, 'This man deserves (ראוי זה) that the Sabbath be violated on his (that is, on Hillel's) behalf'. The term ראוי is thus here understood as 'fit' or 'worthy'.[30]

If this translation is correct, the sages justified their action because Hillel was meritorious in some way. This implies that the Jewish sages would *not* have saved a person of lesser worth, which makes little sense, either morally or according to the details of the story itself. The story depends on the fact that Hillel had no money to attend the School of Learning, which suggests that when this event occurred, Hillel had not yet proven or revealed his adult-type 'worth', so that the sages could not have known if he was 'worthy' in any way. In any case, when Shemaiah and Abtalion noticed that the light from the skylight was obscured by 'the image of a person' (דמות אדם), they could not have known who was there. Their decision to save the 'image' on the roof was thus made in total ignorance of the worth of the person on the roof. It is, moreover, difficult to believe that Shemaiah and Abtalion would have left the frozen person to die, because, in their opinion, he (or she) was not worthy to be saved.

This means that the phrase ראוי זה in the final sentence of the story cannot refer personally to Hillel, but must be translated impersonally, for example, 'it is authorised' or 'it is fitting', which makes far better sense in the context of the story than the translation above. The impersonal use of the phrase ראוי זה is more common in amoraic than in tannaitic texts, but nevertheless occurs, for example in the following tannaitic commentary on Deut 22:8:

---

30. Jastrow, *Dictionary of the Targumim*, 1435, s.v. part. pass. ראוי.

ספרי דברים פרשת כי תצא פיסקא רכט ד"ה כי יפול
כי יפול הנופל ממנו, ראוי זה שיפול אלא מגלגלים זכות על ידי זכיי וחובה על ידי
חייב...

Sifre Devarim 229
If he who falls should fall from there (Deut 22:8) [means that] it is fitting/
appropriate (ראוי זה) for him to fall from there, nevertheless merit is
brought about by the meritorious and guilt by the guilty...[31]

Similarly, the impersonal use of the phrase ראוי זה occurs in the tannaitic
text of *The Fathers of Rabbi Nathan*:

סכתות קטנות מסכת אבות דרבי נתן הוספה ב לנוסחא א פרק ח
אמרו בן מ' שנה היה ורועה של בן כלבא שבוע היה. ראתהו בתו שהיה צנוע
מכל רועי של בית אביה אמרה ראוי זה שיהא מורה הוראה בישר'.

The Fathers According to Rabbi Nathan, A 8
They said that he [Rabbi Akiva] was forty years old and a shepherd for
Ben Kalba Shevuah. His daughter saw him and he was more modest than
all the shepherds of the household of her father. She said, 'It is fitting/
appropriate (ראוי זה) that he will be a teacher of Torah in Israel'.

The sages in the story of Hillel thus justified their violation of Sabbath
law with the impersonal comment that 'it is fitting to violate the Sabbath
on his behalf'. This declaration does not show any indication of a
justification that was composed after the first century CE. For example,
it does not use any of the special vocabulary of R. Akiva or R. Ishmael,
and neither does it use the term סכנה, *sakanah*, which is often used in
amoraic discussions on healing and/or saving life and is even introduced
into amoraic citations of tannaitic texts (see Chapter 8). It is unlikely that
such terms were deliberately excluded from the story in order to give an
impression that it was written in tannaitic times, even if only because (as
was shown in Chapter 8) the amoraic sages did not hesitate to add such
terminology to words of the tannaitic sages that they cited in the amoraic
texts, although they undoubtedly knew that these terms were not used
originally. A further indication of a pre-second-century date of composition of this story is provided by the use of the verb חלל in the phrase
לחלל את השבת, 'to violate the Sabbath', which in the contexts of permits
that allow a violation of Jewish law to heal and/or save life, suggests the
culpability of those by whom such acts were performed. As was noted in
point 4 of the guidelines above, this kind of reference to the violation of
Jewish law probably ceased after the use of the verb דחה, in the phrase
דחה את השבת, 'to suspend the Sabbath', in relation to acts of healing

31. Based on the translation of Reuven Hammer, *Sifre: A Tannaitic Commentary
on the Book of Deuteronomy* (New Haven: Yale University Press, 1986), 239.

and/or saving life, which probably occurred around 70 CE, and was certainly the case by the end of the first century CE. In any case, the phrase חלל את השבת is never used by the amoraic sages in relation to acts of healing and/or saving life, unless in a discussion on a tannaitic text in which this phrase occurs (e.g. the amoraic commentary at b. Shab 128b-29a on m. Shab 18.3). The cumulative evidence thus suggests that, on the reasonable assumption that the final section of the story of Hillel was composed at the same time as the main story itself, the story of Hillel was probably composed before the end of the first century, and (because of the use of חלל rather than דחה) perhaps even before 70 CE. Although it first appears in an amoraic text, there is thus evidence to suggest that the story of the young Hillel was composed in tannaitic times.[32] The reference to Hillel as 'the Elder' in the opening of the tale is thus merely a reflection of how Hillel was remembered by the unidentified amora who included this story in the talmudic text.

32. The story of the revival of Hillel at b. Yom 35b is the longest of the rabbinic *aggadic* stories which describe an event when Jewish law was violated by an act of healing and/or saving life. Other *aggadot* which describe such acts include: (1) m. Shab 16.7, in which R. Yohanan b. Zakkai suggested that a person who covered a scorpion with a vessel on the Sabbath might be liable for a sin offering; (2) t. Shab 12.12, in which R. Meir forbade mixing a medicament on the Sabbath for himself because it was prohibited by his colleagues, but permitted it for others; (3) t. Shab 13.9, the story of a fire which broke out on the Sabbath in the courtyard of Yoseph b. Simai of Sihin, which was finally extinguished by rain, but not before a detachment of Roman soldiers came to extinguish it, who Yosef b. Simai rewarded with money; (4) t. Shab 15.8, the story of the second-century R. Nathan the Babylonian, who permitted the postponement of the ritual of circumcision for a jaundiced child; (5) y. Shab 16.7, the story of R. Immi, who tried to avoid a violation of Sabbath law by asking gentiles, in an indirect way, to put out a fire on the Sabbath; (6) t. Suk 2.2 which notes that R. Yose b. Rabbi permitted Rabban Simon b. Gamaliel to sleep outside a *sukkah*; (7) t. Betz 2.6, the story of Simon of Teman who violated the first day of the festival of Shevuot in order to prevent a potentially violent disturbance by Roman soldiers; (8) t. Shab 12.12, in which R. Meir refused to allow for himself the leniency he allowed to others regarding the application on the Sabbath of a medicament for the eyes; (9) y. Yom 8.4 which records the story of two pregnant woman who wanted to eat on the Day of Atonement—one was persuaded to desist, but the other was not; (10) b. Pes 25b, the story of Rabina, who justified his attempt to save the life of his daughter by rubbing her skin with olives taken from a tree that was less than three years old (*orlah*) on the grounds that her condition was a *sakanah*; (11) b. Sot 21b, the brief, perhaps apocryphal story of a 'foolish pietist' (חסיד שוטה) who did not rescue a drowning woman because he felt it was improper to look at her.

IX. *Minimal References to the Roles of R. Akiva and R. Ishmael in the Jewish Debate*

It has long been recognised that the Mishnah transmits the teaching of R. Akiva, often through his students who are cited more frequently than any others in this text, and with whom the *halachah* most often agrees. This being the case, why then is there no acknowledgement in the Mishnah of the unique contribution of R. Akiva to the Jewish debate on the problem caused in Judaism by acts of healing and/or saving life?[33] The only possible traces in the Mishnah of his contribution can be seen in two examples of his special terminology, namely, the phrase ספק נפשות (*safeq nefashot*, literally, 'doubt of lives') and the single term ספק. The former appears at m. Yom 8.6, where it is not linked with R. Akiva but with R. Mattithiah b. Heresh and the latter at m. Yom 8.7, which is stated anonymously, as is also the case for the parallel directive in the Tosefta, t. Shab 15.11. Otherwise, the only direct link with R. Akiva seems to be his ruling that *Any act of work that can be done on the eve of the Sabbath does not override the Sabbath, but what cannot be done on the eve of the Sabbath overrides the Sabbath.*[34] However although this text is attributed to R. Akiva, it is not specifically linked with acts of healing and/or saving life. Similarly, there is no direct acknowledgement of the work of R. Akiva on the legality of an act of healing and/or saving life in the *Mekhilta de-Rabbi Shimon bar Yochai*, a text which was also composed under his influence, in which the phrase ספק נפשות occurs twice, but each time anonymously, giving no indication of its author or source.[35] Also missing from this text and the Mishnah is any acknowledgement of the contributions of the three students associated with the school of Akiva, who composed three of the four second-century interpretations of biblical texts that justify acts of healing and/or saving life, namely, R. Yose the Galilean, R. Nathan and R. Simon b. Menasia, although the fact that these interpretations are preserved and attributed in the Tosefta suggests that, along with the arguments and special terminology of R. Akiva, they were known to the editors of the tannaitic works.

It is also strange that although the Mishnah includes numerous references to R. Ishmael, there are no references in this work to his contribution to the Jewish debate on healing and/or saving life, and neither

33. For the origins of the Mishnah, see Strack and Stemberger, *Introduction to the Talmud and Midrash*, 138-41.
34. m. Shab 19.1, m. Pes 6.2 and m. Men 11.3.
35. *Mekhilta de-Rabbi Shimon bar Yochai* 22.2.

are there any in the *Mekhilta de-Rabbi Shimon b. Yochai*, in which R. Ishmael also appears. It is moreover astonishing that the special terminology of R. Ishmael, namely the phrase פיקוח נפש, which became so popular among the amoraim especially in the Babylonian Talmud (it appears only twice in the Jerusalem Talmud), does not even appear in the Mishnah, and although it appears in the Tosefta, it is not directly linked with R. Ishmael. Only in the *Mekilta de-Rabbi Ishmael* is this phrase directly linked with R. Ishmael, which is thus the only tannaitic work that directly recognises his role in the Jewish debate.

There is, however, little doubt that the omission of any direct reference to the work of R. Akiva, especially in the Mishnah—which must surely be deliberate—was noted and perhaps even criticised by the editors of the Tosefta (which was published around 230 CE, about thirty years after the Mishnah), who attribute to R. Akiva his arguments and special terminology, and also—as noted above—cite the interpretation of Pentateuchal verses by the second-century Jewish sages from the school of R. Akiva (as does also the *Mekilta de-Rabbi Ishmael*). The Tosefta, however, does not attribute R. Ishmael with any arguments, although the phrase פיקוח נפש appears twice in this text.

The lack of attribution to the work of R. Akiva in the Mishnah and the *Mekhilta de-Rabbi Shimon b. Yochai*, and the absence of any attribution, even oblique, to the contribution of R. Ishmael in these works, thus remains to be explained.

Chapter 12

A Very Brief Summary of the History of the Early Jewish Debate on Acts of Healing and/or Saving Life and the Contribution of the Gospels and the Historical Jesus to this Jewish Debate

I. *A Very Brief Summary of the History of the Jewish Debate*

The discussion in this book has traced the early history of the Jewish *halachic* debate which sought to solve the problem caused by Jewish written law which, when strictly observed, often functions in a way that would prevent the humanitarian actions of healing and/or saving life. The roots of this problem lie in the fact that Judaism considers that words of the Pentateuch record the words of the Jewish God. Consequently, because the written laws in the Pentateuch are stated in an absolute way, with no mitigating exceptions made for the possible violation of this law, actions of healing and/or saving life may necessitate actions that violate this law. The problem occurs most frequently on the Sabbath because, according to Jewish rabbinic *oral* law, acts of healing and/or saving life are considered as 'work', which according to the *written* and divine Pentateuchal law, is totally prohibited on the Sabbath day. In practice therefore it seems that no acts of healing and/or saving life may legally take place for twenty-four hours every seven days, a long and frequent duration of time. It seems, however, that in spite of the antiquity of Judaism, whose origins stretch back far before the second century BCE, the clash between the performance of acts of healing and/or saving life and the resulting violation of Jewish law, especially on the Sabbath, only became of practical concern in the second century BCE, in Maccabean times, in 167 BCE, when around one thousand pious Maccabean Jews refused to violate Sabbath law by fighting in self-defence. As a result, when attacked by their enemies on the Sabbath day, all of them were killed (see Chapter 1). The Jewish sages of the time reacted to this event by issuing an edict which allowed the violation of Sabbath law when fighting in self-defence. The reason they gave for this permitted violation

424

of holy law was wholly rational and pragmatic—if the Jews refused to fight their attackers on the Sabbath, this was the day that they would always be attacked. They would then soon be annihilated and would cease to exist. But while such sensible realism would probably satisfy a society in which laws of this kind are passed with little or no reference to any revered texts, this Maccabean justification for a violation of holy law, which permitted actions that were forbidden by the words of God Himself—actions which openly flouted His law—cannot have been comfortable for the Jewish sages of the time. Neither can it have been comfortable for those ordinary pious Jews from later times who held the same religious opinion about violating Sabbath law as the unfortunate Maccabeans who died because they would not fight on the Sabbath day. It must therefore be assumed that at least from the time of the Maccabean decree, the Jewish sages officially recognised the problem caused by acts of healing and/or saving life and began to investigate how the problem could be solved. They thus set about to discover how actions of healing and/or saving life could always be justified within Jewish law. Until however a solution emerged, it is clear that—to their credit—the Jewish sages responded positively to requests from pious individual Jews to violate Jewish law when performing an action of healing and/or saving life. For example, it was permitted by the sages to eat food that was otherwise forbidden by Jewish law; it was also permitted to violate Jewish festival law; and above all, it was permitted to violate the sanctity of the Sabbath day (see Chapter 11). It seems that the disquiet that these practical permits must have caused was dissipated in part by attempts to minimise the permitted violation of Jewish law while performing a permitted action of healing and/or saving life. Thus, just as the edict of Mattathias in 167 BCE was restricted to self-defence, some—if not all—of these early permits were issued with strict instructions on the way that the permitted actions could be performed (see Chapter 10). Nevertheless, as noted above, the fact that these and no doubt other early permits were not justified according to Jewish law, either in the written or the oral law, must have caused continuing grave disquiet, both among the Jewish sages of the time, and also among ordinary pious Jews. As a result, it is safe to assume that from this time and until an acceptable solution had been found the subject of healing and/or saving life in relation to Jewish law was discussed by the Jewish sages in order to discover how the Jewish God intended His people to perform acts of healing and/or the saving of life that violated His law. The Jewish sages—the Pharisees in the time of Jesus—were thus ultimately responsible for the development of this Jewish *oral* law, which was the only way that the problem could be solved, there being no simple solution in the holy *written* texts.

An initial breakthrough to this problem, which challenged Judaism itself—for how can the laws of any civilised society prevent actions of healing and/or saving life?—came around the turn of the millennium when Shammai the Elder used the Pentateuchal text of Deut 20:19-20 to 'prove' that a siege could be continued on the Sabbath day. This is the first recorded use of a Pentateuchal text to justify an act of healing and/or saving life which violated any Jewish law and the first recorded justification of such a permit; it showed that a careful interpretation of God's holy words could reveal a hidden message to His people, the Jews. It is thus significant that Shammai did not live at a time when the Jewish people were conducting sieges of any kind, so that, unlike the edict of Mattathias, Shammai's permit to conduct a Sabbath siege was not a response to a contemporary need. A likely reason therefore for the issue of this directive is thus the ongoing discussion of the Jewish sages which—as noted briefly above—probably began around 167 BCE to find a way (or ways) to show that acts of healing and/or saving life were permitted to violate Jewish law. This unresolved question in the first half of the first century accounts for the content of two *halachic* questions which are now preserved only in the gospels, one at Mark 3:4 (which is repeated almost verbatim at Luke 6:9), and a second at Luke 14:3. These questions, which were almost certainly derived from a Jewish source, appear to open a *halachic* debate, and are worded in a way that expects a positive reply—in this case, 'Yes—it is permitted on the Sabbath to heal and/or save life' (see Chapter 3). It seems that the Jewish sages who debated the problem expected to find that it was the intention of the Jewish God that acts of healing and/or saving life should violate His law, rather than finding that the opposite was the case. These questions show that they were composed before the problem of healing and/or saving life in Jewish law had been solved.

The synoptic gospel texts have also preserved the discovery of the Jewish sages, at first probably by the Pharisees and then by their rabbinic successors, that rhetorical rabbinic arguments *kal va-chomer* could be composed to prove that acts of healing and/or saving life were allowed to violate Jewish, especially Sabbath, law. Five of these arguments have been preserved in the gospels, all of them probably derived from a Jewish source (for a discussion of these arguments, see Chapters 3 and 4). The earliest of the arguments in the gospel texts was probably composed around 70 CE and is based on a midrashic interpretation of the biblical story of David at Nob (1 Sam 21:1-6). According to this midrash, David violated Jewish Temple law because he was starving and thus in danger of his life. This midrash was then used in an argument *kal va-chomer* which justified the specific 'cure' of starvation by the violation of Sabbath law. Thus—according to the argument—if the starving David was allowed to violate Jewish (Temple) law, so also the starving disciples must be allowed to violate Jewish (Sabbath) law, which, in the confines of the Temple, overrides Sabbath law. This argument with this proof text, although almost certainly of Jewish origin, is now preserved only in a Christianised version in the synoptic gospel texts (Mark 2:25-26, 28; Luke 6:3-5; Matt 12:3-5, the latter expressed as a sorite, a variant of an argument *kal va-chomer*). Three other arguments *kal va-chomer* preserved in the gospels, which were probably composed soon after 70 CE, are based on an anomaly in Jewish oral law which allowed the life of an animal—although *not* a human being—to be healed and/or saved on the Sabbath day. Thus according to this argument, if on the Sabbath it was permitted to save the life of a relatively low valued animal, so also, it could be argued, was it permitted to save the life of a relatively higher valued man ('man' understood in a universal way). Two examples of such arguments have been preserved in Luke's gospel, one which justifies the specific Sabbath cure of an adult with a bent back (Luke 13:15b-16), and the other which justifies the specific Sabbath cure of a man with dropsy (Luke 14:5). The third of these animal-based arguments *kal va-chomer* is preserved in the later gospel of Matthew which was probably composed around 80 CE. It differs from Luke's arguments because although voiced in relation to a *specific* cure (the cure of a man with a withered hand, Matt 12:9-14) it provides a *general*, rather than a *specific* justification, that is, it permits *any* action of healing and/or saving life. However although only three arguments of this kind exist (as will be noted, none are found in the rabbinic sources), it is obvious that because the basic pattern of this argument could be easily modified by the addition of specific details—in particular, the situation of the animal which was saved could be made comparable with that of the man—it is very likely that many more were composed. The fifth argument *kal va-chomer* preserved in the gospels is recorded in the last of these works, in the gospel of John, at John 7:23. Like the argument in Matthew this again is a *general* argument, justifying *any* action in *any* situation of healing and/or saving life. The argument was almost certainly derived by John from an argument composed by R. Eleazar b. Azariah, probably in the late first century CE (when John's gospel was composed), which John must have heard and which he cited in his text.

In addition to the argument *kal va-chomer* of R. Eleazar, the Jewish sources have preserved two other arguments that justify the violation of Jewish law. One of these replicates the logic of the argument preserved in the gospels which is based on the midrashic story of David at Nob. It has however been modified in such a way that its similarity is difficult to detect. This newly phrased argument is attributed to R. Akiva who, it appears, removed the midrash of David from the argument now preserved in the gospels, and replaced it with his own midrashic interpretation of Exod 21:14. This midrash 'proved' the same 'fact' as the midrash of David, namely that the saving of life could override Jewish (Temple) law, and thus, when incorporated in the same argument *kal va-chomer*, proved that Jewish law could be violated in order to save life, which was the same conclusion as the argument now preserved in the gospel texts (see Chapter 6). The midrashic story of David used in the gospel argument did not however disappear entirely from Jewish circles, but survived in the Jewish texts as a free-standing tale which—it was claimed—showed that Jewish law could be violated for the sake of healing and/or saving life (see Chapter 11).

The original rabbinic argument *kal va-chomer* which was based on the midrashic story of David, was probably composed soon after 70 CE, probably by R. Eleazar b. Azariah, or perhaps by R. Akiva. A second argument *kal va-chomer* preserved in the Jewish sources which justified a violation of Jewish law for the sake of healing and/or saving life was also almost certainly composed by R. Akiva. This argument was based on a midrashic understanding of Exod 22:1-2, which may possibly be attributed to R. Ishmael (see Chapter 5), although the way that it was incorporated into an argument *kal va-chomer* was almost certainly the work of R. Akiva. Whatever the case, each of these sages is attributed with the same basic argument and each of them stamped their own seal on the argument by incorporating their own special vocabulary. For R. Akiva, the most frequent of these phrases was ספק נפשות (*safeq nefashot*) and for R. Ishmael it was פיקוח נפש (*pikkuach nefesh*). The literal meaning of these phrases is almost irrelevant—in practice each of them refers to *any* action or any situation of healing and/or saving life. As a result, like the arguments in the later gospels of Matthew and John (the latter citing the argument of R. Eleazar), the arguments of R. Akiva and R. Ishmael also provided *general* justifications for *any* specific action in *any* specific situation that requires an act of healing and/or saving life. In other words, the special vocabulary of these sages transformed *specific* arguments that permitted a *specific* act of healing and/or saving life into *general* permits, because they could be understood to refer both to the specific action that was permitted and also to any other situation that necessitated an act of healing and/or saving life. The phrases of these sages were subsequently used both in the tannaitic and the amoraic texts, as symbolic terms for the arguments themselves.

It seems that the special vocabulary of R. Akiva and R. Ishmael was formulated at the end of a discussion of the Jewish sages which

considered whether the terminology itself that was used for permits that
allowed an act of healing and/or saving life could at least help to solve
the problem in Judaism caused by such acts. Crucial to this line of
thought was the issue of the (probably) Maccabean list of thirty-nine
main prohibited actions on the Sabbath day (see the discussion on
m. Shab 7.2 in Chapter 1). It seems that after the appearance of this
Maccabean list, permits issued by the Jewish sages which gave permission for specific acts of healing and/or saving life generally avoided
the use of any of the thirty-nine *main* terms and instead used a verbal
sub-category of the *main* prohibitions for the action that was permitted
to violate Jewish law (see Chapter 10). For example, the edict of
Rabban Gamaliel the Elder (preserved at m. RH 2.5) does not use the
term המכבה for 'a person who extinguishes a fire', which is the thirty-
sixth of the main prohibition at m. Shab 7.2, and instead substitutes the
phrase הבא להציל מן הדליקה, literally, 'the one who comes to save from
a flame'. Similarly, the verb τίλλειν, which is used for the action of the
disciples in the gospel story of their violation of the Sabbath in the
Galilean fields is probably the Hellenistic Greek equivalent in Hellenistic
Jewish law of the Hebrew verb תלש, which is a sub-category of the verb
גזז, the twelfth of the *main* prohibited actions in the list at m. Shab 7.2
(see Chapter 3). Another example of such euphemistic terminology can
be seen in the tannaitic instruction to avoid לעשות פה, literally, 'to make
an opening/mouth' when giving permission to lance an abscess on the
Sabbath day. This was because the phrase 'opening a mouth' was considered as synonymous with one of the *main* prohibited actions, namely
the verb בנה, meaning 'to build', the thirty-fourth of the thirty-nine *main*
actions which were forbidden on the Sabbath day. Thus—according to
the Jewish sages—the phrase should not be used by healers for the action
of lancing an abscess on the Sabbath, and instead it was deemed
acceptable to use the alternative terminology להוציא לחה, 'to bring out
moisture' (see on m. Eduy 2.5 in Chapter 11). Clearly however, although
alternative terminology might be found for some actions which would
ensure—even if only euphemistically—a lesser violation of Jewish law,
the difficulty in finding alternative terminology for all actions of healing
and/or the saving of life for which permission might be sought meant
that it was not a practical way to solve the problem of healing and/or
saving life within Jewish law.

In contrast, the innovative terminology of R. Akiva and R. Ishmael
cited above still continues to be used today. Another phrase which
became a fixture in Jewish legal terminology, especially in permits on
healing and/or saving life, was the phrase דחה (את) (ה)שבת, 'to push
aside (or, to override) Sabbath law'. This phrase was probably first used

for Jewish ritual situations (that is, when it was necessary for one prescribed ritual to override another), at least from the beginning of the first century CE (see Chapter 5). It seems, however, that probably around 70 CE this phrase was also used for the non-religious activity of actions of healing and/or saving life. The phrase can thus be detected in the underlying Hebrew argument *kal va-chomer* that lies behind the words of Jesus when he justifies the behaviour of his disciples in the Galilean fields. In particular, it probably underlies the famous last section of the argument 'For the son of man is Lord of the Sabbath', which should almost certainly have been translated literally into Greek in a way that means, 'men may override Sabbath law' (see on this text in Chapter 3). The phrase 'overrides Sabbath law' was also used by R. Akiva and R. Ishmael, along with their special vocabulary in the arguments *kal va-chomer* that they composed, and continued to be used by the later tannaitic and amoraic sages in permits that allowed acts of healing and/or saving life.

It seems, however, that arguments *kal va-chomer*, which were apparently so popular in the first century CE, were no longer composed in the second century CE. Several reasons probably lie behind this fact. Thus, in spite of the probable Jewish origin of the arguments *kal va-chomer* that are preserved in the gospels and are based on the fact that animals could be healed and their lives saved on the Sabbath day, these arguments have left no trace in the Jewish texts, perhaps because they were based on oral law, rather than on written Pentateuchal law. As far as concerns arguments *kal va-chomer* based on biblical texts, the total absence in the Jewish holy *written* sources, especially the Pentateuch, of any plain indication that acts of healing and/or saving life were allowed to violate Jewish law meant that any biblical texts that were used in these arguments required a complex, midrashic interpretation, which could completely distort the plain meaning of the text. In addition, it was then necessary to insert the midrashic interpretation into a rhetorical argument *kal va-chomer* that was probably not easy for ordinary people to understand. It is also the case that these tannaitic arguments were probably always composed in Hebrew, rather than in the common vernacular of Aramaic (see Chapter 2), although the evidence from the gospels shows that it was the ordinary people who spoke Aramaic, who needed to be convinced of the necessity of deeds of healing and/or saving life that violated Jewish law (see Chapter 4). Whatever the reasons for the demise of arguments *kal va-chomer*, it is however clear that the Jewish sages of the second century abandoned their use for justifying acts of healing and/or saving life and searched instead for deeper meanings of biblical texts in which the basic principle of healing and/or saving life might be expressed, without the need for its subsequent insertion into a rhetorical argument which would then expose the message the Jewish sages sought. The search for such texts resulted in the discovery of the type of evidence for which the Jewish sages had probably originally tried to find, namely, Pentateuchal texts on the subject of Jewish law whose relatively simple interpretation, *without* subsequent insertion into an argument *kal va-chomer*, could be understood to indicate that the Jewish God always expected His people to perform acts of healing and/or saving life, even when causing a violation of His holy law. Thus in the mid-second century CE, R. Yose the Galilean 'discovered' Exod 31:13, R. Nathan 'discovered' Exod 31:16 and towards the end of the century R. Menasia 'discovered' Exod 31:14. Finally, in the late second-century, Samuel of Nehardea 'discovered' the text of Lev 18:5, which became the most popular of all of the proofs (for these interpretations, see Chapter 7).

Once the principle of healing and/or saving life in all situations, even at the expense of Jewish law, had been proven and accepted at least by the second-century Jewish sages, it seems that some of these sages, not wishing to abandon the directives of their predecessors, modified earlier directives composed by their predecessors in a way which effectively removed any restrictions that had been imposed. This especially affected the methods that had been forbidden while performing actions of healing and/or saving life. It is probable that these were originally included in order to minimise the violation of Jewish law. Such restrictions were however now probably seen as impediments which might prevent the success of any permitted action that the Jewish sages now agreed was proven according to Jewish law and thus was now known to be divinely allowed.

The opinion of the tannaitic Jewish sages regarding the necessity always to perform acts of healing and/or saving life and the evidence for this principle was subsequently endorsed by the later amoraic Jewish sages whose discussions feature in the Talmudic texts. This can be seen especially by their innovative use of the term סכנה, 'danger', a term never used by the tannaitic sages for situations of danger in which the necessary action violated Jewish law. In contrast however the term סכנה was used by the amoraic sages for *any* situation of healing and/or saving life, *whether or not* that action caused a violation of Jewish law. The amoraic sages thus implicitly denied that there was any significant religious difference between situations of healing and/or saving life that necessitated a violation of Jewish law, and those that did not. They also, moreover realised that while accepting the basic principle of healing and/or saving life, there were exceptions to this rule. This problem was solved with the addition of a legal rider to the basic principle which stated that acts of healing and/or saving life should never be performed if they entailed a deed of idolatry, sexual sins or the shedding of blood. It is thus clear that through a process of discussion and argument over about two and a half centuries, the tannaitic Jewish sages had finally solved the seemingly intractable problem of healing and/or saving life within Jewish law, which the amoraic sages wholly endorsed. In this way, the initial, rational and pragmatic reaction to the tragic event of 167 BCE, when it seems that the problem in Jewish law was first formally exposed by a group of pious Jews who refused to fight on the Sabbath day, was solved.

II. *The Contribution of the Gospels and the Historical Jesus to the Jewish Debate*

As Chapters 3 and 4 of this book have shown, our knowledge of the history of the Jewish debate on acts of healing and/or saving life, particularly the debate in the first century CE, would be severely impoverished without the evidence preserved in the gospel texts. For example, the preceding paragraphs have shown that only *general* arguments *kal va-chomer* have been preserved in the Jewish texts. Thus without the evidence of the gospel texts we would be unaware of the variety of the *specific* rabbinic arguments *kal va-chomer* that were almost certainly used by the Jewish sages from around 70 CE in order to justify specific acts of healing and/or saving life. In particular, we would never have known that a midrashic version of the biblical story of David at Nob (based on 1 Sam 21:1-6) was used by the Jewish sages as the basis of an argument *kal va-chomer* since the argument itself has not been preserved in any Jewish source, and only the midrashic story itself has survived in any of the Jewish texts (see on b. Men 95b-96a in Chapter 3 and the discussion on *Yalkut Shimoni Neviim* 130 in Chapter 11).

Similarly, without the evidence of the gospels, we would not know of the probable existence in Jewish circles of arguments *kal va-chomer* to justify actions of healing and/or saving life which were based on Jewish oral law that permitted an animal (although not a human being) to be saved on the Sabbath day; we would probably not even be aware that Jewish oral law of the first century CE permitted animals to be saved on the Sabbath day. Similarly, without the evidence from the gospels we would also not have known of the Socratic-type questions that probably opened discussions of the Jewish sages in the first century CE, in the course of their quest to discover how to justify actions of healing and/or saving life. We would also be less aware that when the post-Maccabean Jewish sages gave permission for acts of healing and/or saving life, they expressed their permission, whenever it was appropriate, with *sub*-categories of the thirty-nine *main* prohibited actions on the Sabbath day, rather than with the same terms as the *main* categories themselves. This is shown in the gospels by the use of the verb τίλλω to describe the actions of the disciples in Mark's account of the meeting between Jesus and the Pharisees in the Galilean fields (Mark 2:23). Careful investigation shows that this verb is probably a subcategory of a term in Greek that corresponds with the Hebrew verb תלש, which itself is a subcategory of the verb גזז, the twelfth *main* action that is prohibited in the list at m. Shab 7.2. The use of a subcategory of one of the *main* prohibited actions may also account for the presence of the comparatively rare verb ψώχω, 'to thresh', rather than the more common λικμάω in Luke's account of the Galilean tale (Luke 6:1, see on these texts in Chapter 3). Without the evidence of the gospels there would also be no evidence that the phrase דחה (את) (ה)שבת was probably used in relation to a non-religious, effectively *secular* act of healing and/or saving life as early as around 70 CE, rather than exclusively for a Jewish ritual that overrode another Jewish ritual law as it was used at the beginning of the first century CE (see Chapter 5).

Moreover, although the general opposition of ordinary pious Jews to acts that saved life at the cost of violating Sabbath law might be suspected from the account of the Maccabean incident in 167 BCE when it was ordinary Jews who chose to die rather than violate Sabbath law by fighting in self-defence (and were, in effect, immediately criticised by the Jewish leaders who issued an edict which allowed fighting on the Sabbath in self-defence), only the gospels provide definite evidence of the first-century opposition from ordinary people, usually Galileans, to the violation of the Sabbath by acts of healing and/or saving life. The clearest indication of this strict religious attitude of ordinary people is the event described in Mark 6:1-6, when Jesus was criticised by his family and other Galileans for performing Sabbath cures, and this criticism is confirmed by careful reading of Luke 4:16-30 with Matt 13:53-58 (see Chapter 3). The opposition of ordinary people to Sabbath healing can also be seen from a close reading of the synoptic descriptions of the Sabbath cure of a man with a withered hand, especially in the account of Matthew (Matt 12:9-14, whose evidence is confirmed by Mark 3:1-6 and Luke 6:6-11). The same opposition is similarly evident from an analysis of Luke's description of the cure of a woman with a bent back (Luke 13:19-17) and his description of the cure of a man with dropsy (Luke 14:1-6).

The same critical attitude of some ordinary Jews to the performance of Sabbath cures is also implied in the synoptic gospels by an incident when a group of Galileans waited until after the end of the Sabbath to bring their sick to Jesus to be cured, as there is no other reason for a Sabbath-related delay (see the discussion on Mark 6:1-6 with Luke 4:16-30 in Chapter 3). The same avoidance of Sabbath healing is also indicated by the fact that in contrast with the invariable requests for cures on non-Sabbath days, both direct and indirect, there is only one incident when ordinary people (in this case, his own disciples) ask Jesus to perform a Sabbath cure (see the discussion on Mark 1:29-31 and Luke 4:38-39 along with Matt 8:14-15). As was noted in Chapter 3 in the discussion on this text, this exceptional request can, however, be explained by details in the story that suggest that in the opinion of the onlookers (the disciples in this case), the woman Jesus cured was seriously ill, and without Jesus' intervention, would probably have died. Although therefore at least some pious Jews in the first half of the first century opposed acts of healing on the Sabbath, this incident suggests they had modified their attitude to the extent that they accepted the necessity for the performance of such deeds whenever they considered that there was a clear risk of death. With this one modification it is however clear that the gospels have preserved evidence of the opposition of ordinary pious Jews to the performance of Sabbath cures in the first half of the first century CE, which has not been preserved in the rabbinic texts. Luke may also hint that the Sadducees similarly opposed the performance of Sabbath cures (see the discussion on the identity of the leader of the synagogue at Luke 13:14), which—if this was the case—confirms the evidence of Josephus regarding the rejection by the Sadducees of Jewish oral law, although Jewish oral law was the only possible route through which the problem of healing on the Sabbath could be justified and thus permitted within the tradition of Jewish law. The fact that apart from the Galilean incident described by Mark (at Mark 6:1-6), the people's opposition to Sabbath cures performed by a Jewish healer—who happened in this case to be Jesus—is only obliquely intimated in the gospel texts is therefore simply a reflection of the reluctance of the gospel writers to describe a reality that—for obvious reasons—they would probably have preferred to suppress. Their verbal camouflage does not however detract from the historical veracity of the information they provide.

Without the evidence of the gospels, there would also be less evidence for the significant change in the nature of permits used by the Jewish sages in the first century to allow acts of healing and/or saving life. According to the gospels these permits (expressed as arguments *kal va-chomer*) were at first *specific* for their cures, and only later, towards the end of the first century, were they expressed in a *general* way that allowed *any* action of healing and/or saving life to override *any* Jewish law. As a result, arguments which justify and only permit *specific* cures first occur, or *only* occur, in the two probably earliest gospels of Mark and Luke, while *general* arguments that effectively permit *any* act in *any* situation of healing and/or saving life are found only in the two later gospels of Matthew and John. In contrast to the mixture of specific and general arguments found in the gospels, only the general arguments *kal va-chomer* of R. Akiva and R. Ishmael have been preserved in the Jewish texts. It could of course be argued on logical grounds that the use of specific arguments (in particular, arguments *kal va-chomer* that justified a specific cure) probably preceded those of general arguments, and that specific permits to heal and/or save life preceded the composition of those that are expressed in a general way. It is however clear that without the evidence of the gospels there would be no solid evidence on which to base such a claim, which would probably rest only on the specific permits in Jewish sources whose historical details show that they were originally composed before 70 CE, namely: (1) the permit of Mattathias issued in 167 BCE which allowed fighting on the Sabbath only in self-defence, (2) the permit of Shammai issued at the turn of the millennium which only allowed a siege to be continued on the Sabbath, (3) the edict of Rabban Gamaliel at m. RH 2.5 issued before 50 CE which referred only to specific actions of healing and/or saving life permitted on the Sabbath, and (4) the permit in the Tosefta at t. Yom 4.4 issued before 70 CE, which allowed only women from the close family of a priest to eat one specific food on the day of a fast. Consequently, there would be less evidence to claim that the majority of tannaitic directives with no date-revealing historical details, and which permit *specific* acts of heal ing and/or saving life, but do not generalise their permits in any way, were probably composed before around 70 CE, and certainly by the end of the first century CE (see Chapter 11). Moreover, there would be no evidence at all to suggest that any rhetorical arguments were constructed that allowed specific actions of healing to be performed.

A close examination of the Sabbath healing accounts in the gospels that takes into account their many anomalies and which appreciates the Jewish background in which these incidents took place, also refutes the bitter accusations that have been made against the Pharisees, and clarifies the activity and character of the historical Jesus himself. This review of the evidence thus strongly suggests that no Pharisees or any other Jewish officials were ever even present at any of Jesus' Sabbath cures, and neither is there any convincing evidence that they subsequently discussed these events. These facts completely exonerate the Pharisees from the long-held accusation that they watched, opposed and criticised Jesus, and even planned for his death because of his performance of Sabbath cures (the evidence for this claim is summarised in Chapter 4). In other words, according to evidence of the gospels themselves (the only source of this long-trumpeted claim), neither the Pharisees nor any other Jewish officials ever opposed any of the acts of healing and/or saving life that Jesus performed on the Sabbath day.

Evidence from the gospels also suggests that those sections of the Sabbath stories which are directly relevant to the Jewish debate on acts of healing and/or saving life, namely, the *halachic* (legal) sections of these tales—the *halachic* arguments and the *halachic* questions—although spoken by Jesus in the gospel accounts, were probably neither composed nor voiced by the historical Jesus himself. Instead, there is evidence to suggest that this *halachic* material was derived from the first-century debates of the Jewish sages who were probably contemporary with the gospel writers (rather than with Jesus), on the problem of healing and/or saving life in Jewish law. This *halachic* material has, however, been removed from its original Jewish context, that is, removed from the debate of the Jewish sages which probably took place in the synagogues and Schools of Learning, and has been transferred into the alien environment of the stories of Jesus' Sabbath cures. (The one exception is the argument now expressed by Jesus at John 5:17, which was probably composed by early Jewish followers of Jesus who were not part of the official religious establishment, rather than by any of the Jewish sages, see on this text in Chapter 3.) If, then, the historical Jesus never debated with the Pharisees on the subject of healing and/or saving life on the Sabbath (because no Pharisees were present at any of his Sabbath cures), and as there are no other occasions described in the gospels when such exchanges on *halachah* might have taken place, this can only mean that the historical Jesus never challenged the Pharisees with regard to Sabbath healing and that (as was noted above) the historical Pharisees never criticised the historical Jesus for performing Sabbath cures. A probable reason for the addition of this Jewish *halachic* material to the gospels has been discussed in Chapter 4.

In fact, Jesus has never been promoted as a *halachist*—an expert in Jewish law—either in the New Testament or in the many extensive commentaries on these texts. But in the same way that any intelligent individual has an opinion on the main issues of his day, especially on a subject in which he (or she) is involved—as must be assumed for Jesus as a healer—Jesus held an opinion on the performance of Sabbath cures, which was undoubtedly an important topic in the first century CE. His opinion, however, was not demonstrated by his verbal participation in legalistic debate, but by the open and extremely public performance of Sabbath cures. The importance of these *public* demonstrations cannot be over stressed. The greater significance in Judaism of an act performed in public rather than in private is stated in the Mishnah by the second-century tannaitic sage R. Eleazar of Modi'im, who expressed this thought in the following trenchant way: *If a man profanes Hallowed things and despises set feasts and puts his fellow to shame in public* (ברבים)...*even though (he has) a knowledge of (Jewish) law and (he performs) good deeds, he has no share in the world to come.*[1] The same sentiment is again stated in the following amoraic text:

תלמוד ירושלמי מסכת שביעית פרק ד הלכה ב

על כל התורה כולה מניין אם יאמר עכו"ם לישראל לעבור על אחת מכל מצות

האמורות בתורה חוץ מן העבודה זרה וגילוי עריות ושפיכת דמים יעבור ולא

יהרג. הדא דתימא בינו לבין עצמו. אבל ברבים אפילו מצוה קלה לא ישמע לו.

Jerusalem Talmud Sheviit 4.2
...in the case of all the commandments of the Torah, if a gentile tells an Israelite to violate one of all the commandments that are stated in the Torah except for idolatry, sexual sins, and bloodshed, one should violate the commandment and not be put to death. That which you say applies if the Israelite is alone. But in public he should *not* obey him [namely, the gentile] even for the most trivial of commandments.[2]

As far as Jesus' Sabbath cures are concerned, only the cure of the mother-in-law of one of his disciples was performed in private, and this was at the request of the disciples themselves. Otherwise, it is clear that the opposite was the case. On two occasions, Jesus even cured in a synagogue (the cure of a man with an evil spirit in Mark 1:21-28 and Luke 4:31-37, and the cure of a man with a withered hand in Mark 3:1-6, Luke 6:6-11 and Matt 12:9-14), which was certainly a most public affirmation of his belief that Sabbath cures should be performed, in a place which was a centre for all classes of Jews. He also even cured on the Sabbath in cases where there was probably no perception of urgency or immediate danger to life, as when the patient had been ill for a long time, and could no doubt have waited to be healed after the close of the Sabbath day. This is emphasised especially by Luke when he notes that

---

1. m. Avot 3.11 (according to the Responsa project of Bar Ilan 18) and m. Avot 3.12 (according to Danby).

2. Similarly, y. San 3.5 and the Babylonian Talmud, e.g., b. Ber 43b: R. Yohanan said it in the name of R. Shimon b. Yohai, 'It is better for a man that he should cast himself into a fiery furnace rather than that he should put his fellow to shame in public'.

Jesus cured a woman on the Sabbath who had already been ill for eighteen years (see on Luke 13:11, discussed in Chapter 3). The cure of the man with an evil spirit and the cure of the mother-in-law of one of his disciples—Mark 1:29-31, Luke 4:38-39 and Matt 8:14-15—are probably the only urgent Sabbath cures that Jesus performed.

Jesus thus challenged the belief of some of the ordinary pious Jews of his time. He may even have helped to convince them that acts of healing and/or saving life should always take place on the Sabbath, whether or not there was a perceived danger to life. It is also even possible that Jesus used his public performance of Sabbath cures to challenge Sadducean objections, as when Luke implies that Jesus publicly challenged the leader of a synagogue whom Luke seems to portray as a Sadducean (see on Luke 13:15 in Chapter 3), although it is unlikely that Luke describes an historical event. Moreover, because Jesus also successfully taught his own disciples to heal and/or save life, and because there is no evidence that he forbade Sabbath cures, we can reasonably assume that they also, like Jesus, healed and/or saved life on the Sabbath day. Jesus can therefore ultimately be held responsible for the relief of much suffering, especially on the Sabbath, when other Jewish healers may have refused to heal. The fact that he probably did not utter any of the *halachic* material with which he is now attributed in the gospel Sabbath healing events thus in no way detracts from the comfort and relief that he and his disciples must have brought to many sick individuals, especially on the Sabbath day. Moreover, the fact that no Pharisees or Jewish officials ever criticised Jesus for performing Sabbath cures is in no way a challenge to basic Christian beliefs.

All in all, the facts that can be gathered from the Sabbath healing events preserved in the synoptic gospels provide and confirm invaluable information, which may not exist or may only be hinted in the rabbinic texts. This information provides important facts concerning the first-century Jewish *halachic* debate which sought to justify acts of healing and/or saving life that violated Jewish law. As far as concerns the historical Jesus himself, it is evident that although he himself was not a part of the *halachic* debate, he fully supported the policy of the Jewish sages, almost certainly the Pharisees, by public acts of healing and/or saving life on the Sabbath day. In other words, as the previous chapters have shown and as the following paragraphs will once again confirm, with regard to acts of healing and/or saving life on the Sabbath, the policy of Jesus and the Jewish officials of his time was exactly the same. It is clear therefore that in spite of nearly two thousand years of bitter accusations by readers of the gospels, with far reaching repercussions in many aspects of Western history and life, the historical Jesus was never criticised or condemned by the Jewish sages for performing Sabbath cures. Why indeed should he have been pilloried for putting into practice what they themselves preached?

III. *Final Conclusions:*
Jewish Leaders Always Allowed Acts of Healing
and/or the Saving of Life

Despite the total absence of any material in the holy Jewish texts, especially in the Pentateuch, which indicates in a simple way that the Jewish God allowed actions of healing and/or saving life to violate His holy law, it is nevertheless clear that, at least from the time when it seems that acts of healing and/or saving life first caused any problem in Jewish law, namely, from around the time of the edict of Mattathias the Maccabean and his colleagues in 167 BCE, the Jewish sages were always prepared to allow acts of healing and/or saving life which violated Jewish law. This can be seen in existence of the many simple, specific permits in the tannaitic texts which were issued by the Jewish sages, some of which almost certainly date back to Maccabean times (see Chapter 11). It seems that at least sixty such specific permits were composed before 100 CE, at the very latest, and there is little doubt that many others were in force, although they have not been recorded in the written texts. In view of the belief that Jewish law, especially Pentateuchal law, is the word of God, it is astonishing to consider that these permits were issued in spite of the fact that in the earliest stages of the Jewish debate, until at least around the early first century CE, the Jewish sages were unable to provide any kind of religious proof to justify their many permits to violate this holy law. They probably thus felt that they were challenging and overriding the law of God Himself, with perhaps serious consequences for their Jewish souls. Yet they continued to act in this permissive way. One of the few possible dissensions (perhaps the *only* dissension) from this otherwise unified opinion of the Jewish sages regarding the necessity always to perform acts of healing and/or saving life, is the apparent prohibition against eating the liver of a rabid dog as a cure for rabies (which can be assumed from m. Yom 8.6). This, however, may have been forbidden only because the disease of rabies was invariably fatal in ancient times, so that eating the liver of dog would have violated Jewish law for no achievable aim, a situation which pious Jews would surely avoid. Other examples of reluctance to allow an act of healing and/or saving life, especially on the Sabbath, can be seen in relation to the Jewish sages themselves, and illustrates the strength of

their adherence to Jewish written law. Thus the second-century sage
R. Meir allowed others to mix oil and wine on the Sabbath for healing
the sick, but forbade it for himself because it was not allowed by 'his
colleagues' (חבירי, t. Shab 12.12). A similar reluctance to permit a
violation of Sabbath law can be seen in the story of R. Yohanan, who
chose to be treated for scurvy by the non-Jewish daughter of the Emperor
Domitian, and thus avoided the possibility that he might ask for healing
from a Jewish healer on the Sabbath day.[3] Yet it was R. Yohanan himself
who declared on behalf of others that וכל ספק נפשות דוחה את השבת, 'all
acts of healing and/or saving life override Sabbath law' (y. Yom 8.4).

Evidence for the underlying belief of the Jewish sages which led to a
policy to allow deeds of healing and/or saving life that violated Jewish
law can be seen not only in the many directives that were issued and
which are not justified in any way (see Chapter 11), but also in the composition and development of the arguments which justified acts of
healing and/or saving life. For how else can we account for the highly
contrived, midrashic interpretations of incidents from the biblical texts
which were used by the Jewish sages as the basis for arguments *kal
va-chomer* in order to justify Sabbath acts of healing and/or saving life,
unless these interpretations were deliberately contrived with the intention
to prove that these actions should take place? Why otherwise, for
example, was it necessary to interpret the biblical story of David at Nob
(1 Sam 21:1-6) as if David had arrived at the Temple in Jerusalem
(which did not exist when David was alive), where he violated Temple
law by eating the holy bread (which would not have been possible at the
shrine of Nob, where he legally ate the sacred bread), unless the author
of this midrash began his interpretation with the conscious intention to
mould the biblical tale to show that David overrode Temple law? As a
result, the story could be used in an argument *kal va-chomer* to show that
the saving of life was allowed to violate Temple law (which itself is an
unwarranted assumption, and shows one of the weaknesses of the
argument), so that what was allowed to violate Temple law should also
be allowed to violate Sabbath law. As was noted in detail in Chapter 3, if
David had not arrived at the Temple in Jerusalem where he illegally ate
the sacred bread, this conclusion to the argument could not have been
made. Similarly, why otherwise did R. Akiva midrashically transform
the biblical murderer at Exod 21:14 into an innocent witness who
overrode Temple law in order to testify for the defence of some other
person accused of murder, unless this Jewish sage intended from the

---

3. y. Shab 14.4 and y. AZ 2.2. The non-Jewish identity of the daughter of
Domitian is emphasised by the story that she later converted to Judaism.

beginning to use his midrashic transformation to show that an act of healing and/or saving life overrode Temple law. Thereby, it could be concluded from an argument *kal va-chomer* that if an act of healing and/or saving life was permitted to override Temple law, so also the same act could override Sabbath law (see on t. Shab 15.16 in Chapter 5). Why again did R. Simon b. Menasia give the term 'to-you' (לכם) in Exod 31:14 a significance in relation to acts of healing and/or saving life that far exceeds the literal meaning of the term, unless this was done in order to make it possible to claim that acts of healing and/or saving life to override Sabbath law were always permitted by the Jewish God (see on R. Menasia's interpretation of Exod 31:14 in Chapter 7)? It is hardly necessary to note that the term לכם, literally 'to-you', could very plausibly have been interpreted in a way that has nothing to do with acts of healing and/or saving life. And why should the simple text of Lev 18:5—*You shall therefore keep My statutes and My ordinances, by doing which a man shall live*—convey any more significance than a command to obey the laws of Judaism, unless the author of this interpretation—Samuel of Nehardea—was genuinely of the opinion that a permit to allow the violation of Jewish law with acts of healing and/or saving life must be drawn out from the Jewish holy texts? We can only conclude that the Jewish tannaitic sages offered these and other arguments to justify acts of healing and/or saving life because they instinctively believed that actions of healing and/or saving life must always be performed, *in spite of the absence of any simple justification for this violation in the holy Jewish texts*. In short, it was not the arguments of the Jewish sages—the first-century arguments *kal va-chomer* and the second-century interpretations of biblical texts—that shaped their opinion regarding the necessity always to perform acts of healing and/or saving life. Rather, it was the basic and united opinion of the Jewish sages that dictated the content of the arguments they composed.

It is therefore no surprise not only that there is perhaps only one possible directive that forbade an act of healing that would violate Jewish law (see the possible prohibition on eating the liver of a rabid dog in m. Yom 8.6, discussed above) but that no Jewish leaders are ever associated with a directive that effectively forbids an action of healing and/or saving life. It is also no surprise that the Jewish sages associated with such permits include many of the most distinguished individuals of their time. A history of the pre-tannaitic and tannaitic period, the time of the Jewish debate on healing and/or saving life which is traced in this book, could be based on their names. This would begin with Mattathias the Maccabean, a priestly leader in the second century BCE, who, together with his colleagues—undoubtedly members of a Sanhedrin—permitted fighting on the Sabbath in self-defence (see on 1 Macc 2:39-41 in Chapter 1). Subsequently, if the story of the saving of the life of Hillel is historical (see on b. Yom 35b, discussed in Chapter 11), the first century BCE saw the activity of Shemaiah and Abtalion, the leaders of the Sanhedrin, who were probably Pharisees, who saved the life of an unidentified person on the Sabbath (described as 'an image on the sky-light') and thus violated Sabbath law. Later, sometime around the turn of the millennium, Shammai, the vice-president of the Sanhedrin, and later its leader, claimed that the text of Deut 20:19-20 proved that a siege could be continued on the Sabbath day (see on t. Eruv 3.7 and *Sifre Devarim* 203, discussed in Chapter 11). Shammai was followed in the first half of the first century by Rabban Gamaliel the Elder, again a leader of the Sanhedrin and probably also a Pharisee, who issued an edict which granted an extension of the Sabbath *eruv* to five groups of people who were already permitted to violate Sabbath law (see the discussion on m. RH 2.5 in Chapters 9 and 11). Later in the first century, before 70 CE, R. Yohanan b. Zakkai, who played a major role in the continuation of Jewish tradition after the destruction of the Temple, reluctantly conceded (חוששני, 'I perhaps think...'—see on m. Shab 16.7, in Chapter 8) that an act of healing and/or saving life on the Sabbath should be considered as a violation of Sabbath law. It can be assumed that his hesitation to pronounce a penalty for the violation of Sabbath law on which he was consulted was nothing to do with his disapproval of the action, but simply a reflection of the fact that the Jewish sages of his time had not yet discovered how to justify such acts within the tradition of Jewish law. It is therefore no surprise that according to a careful reading of the gospels which describe Jesus healing on the Sabbath day, it is clear that the Pharisees, who were the most popular and undoubtedly the most influential of the Jewish religious leaders in their time, never opposed Jesus when he performed Sabbath cures—which adds to the evidence that they were fully in favour of performing such acts. Subsequently, probably around the time of the destruction of the Temple in 70 CE, one of the Jewish sages, probably either R. Eleazar b. Azariah, a popular leader of the Sanhedrin, or perhaps R. Akiva, composed an argument *kal va-chomer* which justified and thus allowed the 'cure' of starvation on the Sabbath by violating Sabbath law. This argument was adapted by Mark for his midrashic story of Jesus and his meeting with Pharisees in the Galilean fields. R. Eleazar may also be responsible for the innovative use of verb דחה, 'to override', used in the phrase דחה (את) (ה)שבת to refer to a secular act of healing and/or saving life that overrode Jewish law (rather than for the overriding of one Jewish ritual for another), which was used by later Jewish sages in later directives on healing and/or saving life. The commitment of R. Eleazar towards solving the problem of healing and/or saving in Jewish law can also be seen from his use of Gen 34:25 to justify the ancient permit that allowed the wound of circumcision to be washed (that is, to be 'healed') on the Sabbath day (see the discussion on m. Shab 19.3 in Chapter 11) and from his ingenious argument *kal va-chomer* based on the alleged 'healing' effect of the act of circumcision on the Sabbath, which—according to his argument— proved that it was permitted to heal and/or save life on the Sabbath (see the discussion on John 7.23 in Chapter 3). The argument of R. Eleazar based on circumcision is one of the earliest of the *general* (rather than *specific*) arguments which justified any action in any situation of healing and/or saving life and thus indicates significant progress in the Jewish debate (see the discussion above).

Probably also around 70 CE came the contributions to the Jewish debate of the two younger contemporaries of R. Eleazar, who are among the greatest of the luminaries of Jewish oral law, namely, R. Akiva and R. Ishmael, Two general arguments *kal va-chomer* which justified any action to heal and/or save life are attributed to R. Akiva. One of these was adapted by R. Ishmael, whose contribution to the Jewish debate is directly acknowledged in the tannaitic work associated with his school, the *Mekilta de-Rabbi Ishmael*. As noted above, both R. Akiva and R. Ishmael also composed special vocabulary which anonymised any action and any situation of healing and/or saving life especially when used in combination with the phrase דחה (את) (ה)שבת, 'to override the Sabbath'. R. Akiva is thus associated with the phrase ספק נפשות, literally, 'doubt of lives', and R. Ishmael is associated with the phrase פיקוח נפש, literally, 'the removal of debris [to save] a life'. In practice however both of these phrases possess the general significance of *any* action or *any* situation in which it is necessary to heal and/or save life. The special vocabulary of both R. Akiva and R. Ishmael was subsequently used in a symbolic way to represent the arguments *kal va-chomer* in which they first appeared, and continues to be cited in Jewish circles today (see Chapter 5).

The work of R. Akiva and R. Ishmael was continued in the first half of the second century by their younger contemporaries, R. Meir (see on t. Shab. 12.12), R. Yose the Galilean, and by R. Nathan, Simon of Teman, and later, towards the end of the second century, by R. Simon b. Menasia, and finally Samuel of Nehardea. As was discussed in Chapter 7, these four Jewish sages abandoned the search for biblical incidents which could be used in arguments *kal va-chomer* that proved (to rabbinic satisfaction) that deeds of healing and/or saving life were allowed to override Jewish law. Instead, they 'discovered' verses from the Pentateuch, the holiest of the Jewish holy texts, which dealt with Jewish law and which could be interpreted simply and memorably to prove the conclusion for which the sages had all sought, namely, that acts of healing and/or saving life must always be allowed to violate Jewish law. The simple interpretation of Lev 18:5 by Samuel of Nehardea (in fact, an apparently logical extension of the meaning of this text), became the most popular way in which to justify such acts, and, in combination with the phrase פיקוח נפש, continues this usage up till today.

Other named Jewish sages from the second century CE widened and effectively removed restrictions which had been imposed in earlier directives. These were probably intended to limit the violation of Jewish law, but, in practice, might thwart the intention of the permit to heal and/or save life. These sages include R. Simeon b. Nanos, who removed restrictions on building a barrier against a fire (see on m. Shab 16.5 in Chapter 10), Rabban Simon b. Gamaliel, the leader of the Sanhedrin in the mid-second century, who extended the permit of m. Sukk 2.4 to remain outside a *sukkah* to include any kind of illness (see on t. Sukk 2.2 in Chapter 11), R. Judah bar Ilai, one of the five famous students of R. Akiva, who ingeniously updated t. Yom 4.4 by exploiting two meanings of the term *terumah* (see on t. Yom 4.4 in Chapter 11), and R. Mattithiah b. Heresh who updated the directive of t. Shab 2.7 using the special terminology of R. Akiva (see on m. Shab 8.6, in Chapter 10), and who also allowed the treatment of asphyxia and decreed that the liver of a rabid dog (a type of 'unclean' food) might be eaten to cure rabies (it seems that 'unclean' food was previously allowed only for the 'cure' of starvation). It is also possible that R. Akiva himself updated the directives which allow the removal of debris on the Sabbath with the addition of the term 'doubt' (see on m. Yom 8.7 and t. Shab 15.11 in Chapter 10, although there is no attribution to his work in these texts). It is also clear that R. Yose b. Halafta, one of the five famous students of R. Akiva, agreed with his colleagues regarding the *halachah* of deeds of healing and/or saving life, because comments in his name that are added to directives on this topic all accept their basic premise (see on m. Shab 2.5 and t. Taan 2.12 in Chapter 11 and on t. Shab 15.3 in Chapter 10). The positive attitude of these named Jewish sages is affirmed yet again by R. Judah ha-Nasi, the formidable editor of the Mishnah, who shows his basic approval of deeds of healing and/or saving life by including directives in the Mishnah that permitted such acts (although, as noted in Chapter 11, there is no direct attribution to the contributions of R. Akiva or R. Ishmael in the Mishnah itself). The same positive attitude is shown by R. Oshaiah and his pupil R. Hiyya, the probable editors of the Tosefta, who also, like R. Judah ha-Nasi, include in the Tosefta unattributed, undoubtedly early, directives that are not justified in any way. Unlike R. Judah however the editors of the Tosefta also directly acknowledge the contribution to the Jewish debate of R. Akiva and the second-century sages (t. Shab 15.16-17).[4] The tannaitic sages of the second century CE also stressed that acts of healing and/or saving life should never be postponed and that it is the responsibility of any Jewish individual to perform these deeds swiftly and independently without recourse to a permit from any Jewish sage (see on t. Shab 15.11-13 in Chapter 11). The sages even decreed that the violation of Jewish law by any individual in order to heal and/or save life should be acclaimed, והזריז הרי זה משובח, *And behold the person who rushes [to violate Jewish law for the sake of healing and/or saving life] should be praised* (t. Shab 15.11-13), which is an astonishing statement in view of the sanctity and centrality in Judaism of Jewish law.

It is also clear that the amoraic (post-tannaitic) Jewish sages carried on the policy of their predecessors, the tannaim. This can be seen especially in rulings in both the Jerusalem and Babylonian Talmuds that accept the basic premise, merely adding the condition that acts of healing and/or saving life must never be performed if they necessitate acts of idolatry, sexual impropriety or the shedding of blood, thus invoking three of the seven laws that Judaism expects the 'sons of Noah' to keep. The approval of all deeds of healing and/or saving life, whether or not they violated Jewish law, by both named and unnamed amoraic sages, can also be seen in their use of the term סכנה, literally, 'danger', which, unlike their tannaitic predecessors, can refer in the amoraic texts to *any* situation of healing and/or danger, whether or not the action resulted in a violation of Jewish law (see Chapter 8). The amoraic sages thus rejected the thought that there was any true religious difference between situations of healing and/or danger to life which necessitated an action that violated Jewish law, and those for which the necessary action did *not* violate Sabbath law.[5] This permissive attitude thus accounts for the

4. For the editors of the Mishnah and Tosefta, see Strack and Stemberger, *Introduction to the Talmud and Midrash*, 138-56, 169.
5. The following is a provisional list of *named* amoraim who use סכנה as a synonym for פיקוח נפש; the many other examples are unattributed. First generation (220–250 CE): R. Joshua b. Levi, from the land of Israel (y. Ber 4.4) and Samuel of Nehardea from Babylon (y. Shab 9.3; 19.3). Second generation (250–290 CE): R. Yohanan, from the land of Israel, one of the editors of the Jerusalem Talmud (y. Shab 14.4); R. Hamnuna from Babylon (b. Shab 129a). Third generation (290–320 CE): R. Abbahu, from the land of Israel (b. Shab 134b); R. Oshaiah, from Babylon (b. Shab 30a); R. Samuel b. R. Isaac, born in Babylon and emigrated to Israel (y. Shab 14.4); R. Yakov, born in Babylon and moved to the land of Israel and

astonishing statement in the Babylonian Talmud that *regulations con-cerning danger to life are more stringent than ritual prohibitions* (b. Hull 10a). In other words, it is more important to heal and/or save life by violating Jewish law than it is to adhere to Jewish law itself.

This attitude of the Jewish sages is, however, no surprise. There is little doubt that Judaism has always treasured human life. Judaism therefore has always focused on the necessity for its preservation in this world, rather than the anticipation of a possible life after death (which traditional Judaism neither confirms nor denies). Acts of healing and/or saving life are thus intrinsic to Judaism and are considered among the most noble of deeds that a Jewish person can perform. Or, as this thought is stated in the Mishnah, the earliest work of rabbinic oral law, in a comment which explains why only one person (Adam) was the ancestor of the whole human race:

משנה מסכת סנהדרין פרק ד משנה ה

לפיכך נברא אדם יחידי ללמדך שכל המאבד נפש אחד מישראל מעלה עליו הכתוב כאילו איבד עולם מלא. וכל המקיים נפש אחת מישראל מעלה עליו הכתוב כאילו קיים עולם מלא

Mishnah Sanhedrin 4.5

Therefore, only a single individual was [originally] created in the world to teach [us] that if any person has caused a single soul to perish, Scripture imputes to this person as though he had caused a whole world to perish. And if any individual saves a single life, Scripture considers that this person has saved the whole world.[6]

studied with R. Yohanan (b. Pes 25a); R. Yosef b. Chaiyya from Babylon (b. Shab 134b). Fifth generation (350–375 CE): R. Papa, from Babylon (b. Shab 133b; b. Ker 13a). Sixth generation (375–425 CE): R. Ashi, from Babylon (b. Betz 22a); Rabina, from Babylon and Mar son of Rav (b. Pes 25b). Seventh-generation (425–460 CE): Mar Ashi, from Babylon (b. Pes 25b).

6. For a brief review of this subject in relation to different aspects of Jewish law, see M. S. Lew, *The Humanity of Jewish Law* (London: Soncino, 1985). In the above Hebrew text of m. San 4.5 the twice-repeated term מישראל is bracketed because it is almost certainly a later addition to the text, as it does not reflect the thought of this text, which refers to the creation of human beings in general, rather than to the Jewish people in particular. A disturbance in the text of the Mishnah is in any case shown by the masculine term אחד, which qualifies the feminine noun נפש. For a discussion of the problem of the phrase מישראל in m. San 4.5, see E. E. Urbach, *From the World of the Sages* (Jerusalem: Magnes Press, 1988) pp. 561-76 (Hebrew), which traces all known manuscripts, printed texts and citations of this passage and thus demonstrates its absence from the earliest manuscripts and printed editions, and its later insertion (both accidental and deliberate) into later versions and citations of this text.

BIBLIOGRAPHY

Abegg, M., Jr, P. Flint and E. Ulrich. *The Dead Sea Scrolls Bible: Translated and with Commentary* (Edinburgh: T. & T. Clark, 1999).

Albeck, H. *The Mishna: Seder Nezikin* (Jerusalem: Dvir, 1988).

Arndt, W. F., and F. W. Gingrich, *A Greek–English Lexicon of the New Testament and Other Early Christian Literature* (2nd edn; Chicago: University of Chicago Press, 1958).

Barrett, C. K. *The Gospel According to St John; An Introduction with Commentary and Notes on the Greek Text* (2nd edn; London: SPCK, 1978).

Basser, H. W. *The Mind Behind the Gospels: A Commentary to Matthew 1–14* (Boston: Academic Studies, 2009).

Baumgarten, J. et al., *Qumran Cave 4, XXV: Halakhic Texts* (Discoveries in the Judaean Desert 35; Oxford: Oxford University Press, 1999).

Beare, F. W. 'The Sabbath Was Made for Man?', *Journal of Biblical Literature* 79 (1960) 130-6.

Beasley-Murray, G. R. *John* (Word Biblical Commentary 36; Dallas: Word, 1991).

Birnbaum, P. *A Book of Jewish Concepts* (New York: Hebrew Publishing, 1975).

Bivin, D. 'Evidence of an Editor's Hand in Two Instances of Mark's Account of Jesus' Last Week?', in *Jesus' Last Week* (ed. R. S. Notley, M. Turnage and B. Becker; Leiden: Brill, 2006) 211-24.

Black, M. *An Aramaic Approach to the Gospels and Acts* (3rd edn; Oxford: Clarendon, 1966).

Blakemore, R. G. *History of Interior Design and Furniture: From Ancient Egypt to Nineteenth-Century Europe* (New York: John Wiley & Sons, 1996).

Broshi, M. *Bread, Wine, Walls and Scrolls* (Sheffield: Sheffield Academic, 2001).

Brown, R. E. *The Gospel According to John (I–XII)* (Garden City: Doubleday, 1966).

Büchler, A. *Types of Jewish-Palestinian Piety: From 70 BCE to 70 CE* (London: Jews' College, 1922).

Büchsel, F. 'krínō [to judge]', *Theological Dictionary of the New Testament Abridged in One Volume* (ed. G. W. Bromiley; Grand Rapids: Eerdmans, 1985) 469-75.

Bultmann, R. *The Gospel of John: A Commentary* (trans. G. R. Beasley-Murray; Oxford: Blackwell, 1971).

———*The History of the Synoptic Tradition* (trans. J. Marsh; Oxford: Blackwell, 1963).

Burer, M. H. *Divine Sabbath Work* (Winona Lake: Eisenbrauns, 2012).

Casey, P. M. *Aramaic Sources of Mark's Gospel* (Cambridge: Cambridge University Press, 1998).

———'Culture and Historicity: The Plucking of the Grain (Mark 2:23-8)', *New Testament Studies* 34 (1988) 1-23.

———*The Solution to the 'Son of Man' Problem* (London: T&T Clark International, 2007).

Chajes, Z. H. *The Student's Guide Through the Talmud* (2nd edn; trans. J. Schachter; New York: Philipp Feldeim, 1960).

Chilton, B., and C. A. Evans, eds. *Authenticating the Words of Jesus* (Leiden: Brill, 2002).

Chilton, B. et al., *A Comparative Handbook to the Gospel of Mark* (Leiden: Brill, 2010).

Cohn-Sherbok, D. *Rabbinic Perspectives on the New Testament* (Studies in the Bible and Early Christianity 28; Lampeter: Edwin Mellen, 1990).

Cohon, S. H. 'The Place of Jesus in the Religious Life of His Day', *Journal of Biblical Literature* 48 (1929) 82-108.

Collins, N. L. 'The Jewish Source of Rom 5:17, 16, 10, 9: The Verses of Paul in Relation to a Comment in the Mishnah at m. Macc 3:15', *Revue Biblique* 112.1 (2005) 27-45.

———'Review: Aramaic Sources of Mark's Gospel (Cambridge, 1998)', *Novum Testamentum* 42/3 (2000) 286-91.

Cranfield, E. B. *The Gospel According to Mark* (Cambridge: Cambridge University Press, 1959).

Creed, J. M. *The Gospel According to St. Luke* (London: Macmillan, 1960).

Daiches, S. *The Babylonian Talmud: Seder Nashim: Ketuboth* (London: Soncino, 1936).

Danby, H. *The Mishnah: Translated from the Hebrew with Introduction and Brief Explanatory Notes* (Oxford: Oxford University Press, 1933).

Daube, D. 'Rabbinic Methods of Interpretation and Hellenistic Rhetoric', *Hebrew Union College Annual* 22 (1949) 239-64.

———'Responsibilities of Master and Disciples in the Gospels', *New Testament Studies* 19 (1972–73) 1-15.

Davies, W., and D. C. Allison, *A Critical and Exegetical Commentary on the Gospel According to Saint Matthew*, vols. 1–3 (Edinburgh: T. & T. Clark, 1988, 1991, 1997).

Davila, J. A. '(How) Can We Tell if a Greek Apocryphon or Pseudepigraphon Has Been Translated from Hebrew or Aramaic?', *Journal for the Study of the Pseudepigrapha* 15.1 (2005), 3-16.

Doering, L. 'Much Ado About Nothing? Jesus' Sabbath Healings and Their Halakhic Implications Revisited', in *Judaistik und Neutestamtliche Wissenschaft* (ed. L. Doering, H.-G. Waubke and F. Wolk; Göttingen: Vandenhoeck & Ruprecht, 2008) 217-41.

Doeve, J. W. 'Jewish Hermeneutics in the Synoptic Gospels and Acts', in *Jewish Hermeneutics in the Synoptic Gospels and Acts* (trans. G. E. Van Baaren-Pape; Assen: Van Gorcum, 1954).

Donahue, J. R., SJ, and D. J. Harrington, SJ, *Sacra Pagina the Gospel of Mark* (College-ville: Liturgical, 2002).

Donaldson, J. 'The Title Rabbi in the Gospels: Some Reflections on the Evidence of the Synoptics', *Jewish Quarerly Review* 59 (1972–73) 287-91.

Dunn, J. D. G. *Jesus Remembered* (Grand Rapids: Eerdmans, 2003).

Elon, M. *Jewish Law, History, Sources, Principles*, vol. 1 (Philadelphia: JPS, 1994).

Eltester, W. *Judentum, Urchristentum, Kirche: Festschrift für Joachim Jeremias* (Beifte zur Zeitschrift für die Neutestammentliche Wissenschaft und die Kunde der Älteren Kirche 26; Berlin: Töpelmann, 1960).

Ensor, P. W. *Jesus and His 'Works': The Johannine Sayings in Historical Perspective* (Tübingen: J. C. B. Mohr, 1996).

Epstein, E. J., and E. Z. Melamed, *Mekhilta de-Rabbi Shimon b. Yochai* (Jerusalem: Mekitze Nirdamim, 1955).

Epstein, I. *The Babylonian Talmud, Seder Kodashim* (London: Soncino, 1948).

Epstein, J. N. *Prolegomena Ad Litteras Tannaiticas* (Jerusalem: Magnes, 1957 [Hebrew]).

Fernandez, M. P. *An Introductory Grammar of Rabbinic Hebrew* (Leiden: Brill, 1997).

Fischel, H. A. 'The Uses of Sorites *(Climax, Gradatio)* in the Tannaitic Period', *Hebrew Union College Annual* 44 (1973) 119-51.

Fitzmyer, J. A. *The Genesis Apocryphon of Qumran Cave 1* (Rome: Pontifical Biblical Institute, 1966).

———*The Gospel According to Luke I–IX* (AB 28; New York: Doubleday, 1981).

———*The Gospel According to Luke X–XXIV* (AB 28A; New York: Doubleday, 1985).

Flusser, D. 'Healing through the Laying-on of Hands in a Dead Sea Scroll', *Israel Exploration Journal* 7 (1957) 107-8.

Freedman, H. 'Akiva R.', in *The Encyclopaedia Judaica*, vol. 2 (Jerusalem: Keter, 1971) 488-92.

Freedman, I. *The Babylonian Talmud, Seder Moed, Sabbath*, vol. 2 (London: Soncino, 1938).

Freeman, H., and M. Simon. *Midrash Rabbah Genesis*, vol. 1 (London: Soncino, 1939).

Funk, R. W., R. W. Hoover and the Jesus Seminar, *The Five Gospels: The Search for the Authentic Words of Jesus* (San Francisco: HarperSanFrancisco, 1993).

García Martínez, F., and E. J. C. Tigchelaar, eds. *The Dead Sea Scrolls: Study Edition* (Leiden: Brill, 1997).

Ginsberg, L. 'Akiba ben Joseph', in *The Jewish Encyclopedia*, vol. 1 (New York: Funk & Wagnalls, 1807) 304-10.

Goldin, J. *The Fathers According to Rabbi Nathan* (New Haven: Yale University Press, 1955).

Goldstein, J. A. *1 Maccabees: A New Translation with Introduction and Commentary* (AB 41; New York: Doubleday, 1976).

Goulder, M. *Luke A New Paradigm* (Sheffield: Sheffield Academic, 1989).

Green, J. B. *The Gospel of Luke* (Michigan: Eerdmans, 1997).

———'Jesus and a Daughter of Abraham (Luke 13:10–17)', *Catholic Biblical Quarterly* 51 (1989) 643-54.

Gryson, R., and P.-A. Deproost, *Commentaires de Jérôme sur le prophète Isaïe* (Freiburg: Herder, 1993).

Guelich, R. A. *Mark 1–8:26* (Word Biblical Commentary 34A; Dallas, Texas: Word Books, 1989).

Gundry, R. H. *A Commentary on His Apology for the Cross* (Michigan: Eerdmans, 1993).

Haenchen, E. *John: A Commentary on the Gospel of John.* Vol 1, *Chapters 1–6* (trans. R. W. Funk; Philadelphia: Fortress, 1984).

Hammer, R. *Sifre: A Tannaitic Commentary on the Book of Deuteronomy* (New Haven: Yale, 1986).

Harrington, D., SJ. *The Gospel of Matthew* (Collegeville: Liturgical, 1991).

Herr, M. D. 'The Problem of War on the Sabbath in the Days of the Second Temple and the Mishnah and Talmud', *Tarbiz* 30 (1961) 242-56, 341-56 (Hebrew; English summary, p. VII).

Hobart, W. K. *The Medical Language of Luke* (Dublin, London: Hodges, Figgs & Co.; Longmans Green & Co., 1882).

Horovitz, H. S. *Siphre d'BeRab* (Jerusalem: Wahrmann, 1966).

Horovitz, H. S., and I. A. Rabin, *Mechilta D'Rabbi Ismael* (Jerusalem: Wahrmann, 1970).

Hultgren, A. J. 'The Formation of the Sabbath Pericope in Mark 2:23-28', *Journal of Biblical Literature* 91 (1972) 38-43.

Iersel, Bas M. F. van. *Mark: A Reader-Response Commentary* (trans. W. H. Bisscheroux; Sheffield: Sheffied Academic, 1998).

Israelstam, J. *Midrash Rabbah: Leviticus* (London: Soncino, 1939).

Jacobs, L. 'Hermeneutics', in *The Encyclopaedia Judaica*, vol. 8 (Jerusalem: Keter, 1971).

———'The *qal va-ḥomer* Argument in the Old Testament', *Bulletin of the School of Oriental and African Studies* 35.2 (1972), 221-7.

Jastrow, M. *A Dictionary of the Targumim, the Talmud Babli and the Yerushalmi, and the Midrashic Literature* (Israel: n.p., 1972).

Jeremias, J. '’Abba as an Address to God', in *The Historical Jesus in Recent Research* (ed. J. D. G. Dunn and S. McKnight; Winona Lake: Eisenbrauns, 2005) 201-6.

Johns, A. F. 'The Military Strategy of Sabbath Attacks on the Jews', *Vetus Testamentum* 13 (1963) 482-6.

Josephus, *Josephus, Jewish Antiquities, Books V–VII* (trans. H. St. J. Thackeray and R. Marcus; Cambridge, Mass.; Harvard University Press; London Heinemann, 1958).

———*Josephus, Jewish Antiquities, Books XII–XIV* (trans. R. Marcus; Cambridge, Mass.: Harvard University Press; London Heinemann, 1961).

———*Josephus, Jewish Antiquities, Books XVII–XX* (trans. L. H. Feldman; London, Cambridge, Mass.: Harvard University Press; London Heinemann, 1961).

———*Josephus, The Jewish War, Books IV–VII* (trans. H. St. J. Thackeray and R. Marcus; Cambridge, Mass.: Harvard University Press; London Heinemann, 1961).

Jung, L. *The Babylonian Talmud, Seder Moed, Yoma* (London: Soncino, 1938).

Kahana, M. I. *The Genizah Fragments of the Halakhic Midrashim, Part I* (Jerusalem: Magnes, 2005).

———'The Halakhic Midrashim', in *The Literature of the Sages: Second Part* (Amsterdam: Fortress, 2006), 3-106,

Katsh, A. I., 'Unpublished Geniza Fragments of Pirke Aboth in the Anonin Geniza Collection in Leningrad', *The Jewish Quarterly Review* 61 (1970–71) 1-14.

Keener, C. S. *The Gospel of John: A Commentary*, vol. 1 (Massachusetts: Hendrickson, 2003).

Kister, M. 'Plucking of Grain on the Sabbath and the Christian Jewish Debate', in *Jerusalem Studies in Jewish Thought*, vol. 3 (Jerusalem: Magnes, 1983–84) 349-66, English summary vii-ix.

Lachs, S. T. *A Rabbinic Commentary on the New Testament* (Hoboken: Ktav, 1987).

Lauterbach, J. Z. *Mekilta de-Rabbi Ishmael*, vols. 1–3 (Philadelphia: The Jewish Publication Society of America, 1976).

Leiberman, S. *Tosefet Rishonim*, vol. 1 (Jerusalem: Reuben Mass, 1999).

Levine, A.-J. *The Misunderstood Jew: The Church and the Scandal of the Jewish Jesus* (New York: HarperOne, 2007).

Lew, M. S. *The Humanity of Jewish Law* (London: Soncino, 1985).

Liddell, H. G., R. Scott and H. S. Jones, *A Greek–English Lexicon* (Oxford: Clarendon, 1968).

Liddell, H. G., R. Scott, P. G. W. Glare and A. A. Thompson, *Greek–English Lexicon Revised Supplement* (Oxford: Clarendon, 1996).

Lindars, B. *The Gospel of John* (London: Marshall, Morgan & Scott, 1972).

Lohse, E. 'Huiós David', in *Theological Dictionary of the New Testament Abridged in one Volume* (ed. G. Kittel and G. Friedrich; trans. G. W. Bromiley; Grand Rapids: Eerdmans, 1985) 1224-5.

———'σάββατον', in *Theological Dictionary of the New Testament*, vol. 7 (ed. G. Kittel and G. Friedrich; trans. G. W. Bromiley; Grand Rapids: Eerdmans, 1971).

Luz, U. *Matthew 8–20: A Commentary* (trans. J. E. Crouch; Minneapolis: Augsburg Fortress, 2001).

Maccoby, H. *The Myth-maker: Paul and the Invention of Christianity* (San Francisco: Harper & Row, 1986).

Mann, C. S. *Mark: A New Translation Introduction and Commentary* (Anchor Bible 27; Garden City: Doubleday, 1986).

Marcus, J. *Mark 1–8: A New Translation with Introduction and Commentary* (Anchor Bible 27; New York: Doubleday, 2000).

Margaliot, M. *Encyclopaedia for the Sages of the Talmud and the Geonim* (2 vols.; Tel Aviv: Yavneh, 2000 [Hebrew]).

Marshall, I. H. *The Gospel of Luke* (Exeter: Paternoster, 1978).

Martyn, J. L. M. *History and Theology in the Fourth Gospel* (New York: Harper & Row, 1968).

McNeile, A. H. *The Gospel According to St. Matthew* (London: Macmillan, 1928).

Meier, J. P. *A Marginal Jew*. Vol. 1, *Rethinking the Historical Jesus: The Roots of the Problem and the Person* (New York: Doubleday, 1987).

———*A Marginal Jew*. Vol. 2, *Rethinking the Historical Jesus: Mentor, Message and Miracles* (New York: Doubleday, 1994).

———*A Marginal Jew*. Vol. 3, *Companions and Competitors* (New York: Doubleday, 2001).

———*A Marginal Jew*. Vol. 4, *Law and Love* (New Haven: Yale University Press, 2009).

Mielziner, M. *Introduction to the Talmud* (5th edn; New York: Bloch, 1968).

Milgrom, J. *Leviticus 1–16* (AB 3; New York: Doubleday, 1991).

Moles, J. 'Jesus the Healer in the Gospels, the Acts of the Apostles, and Early Christianity', *Histos* 5 (2011) 117-82.

Nelson, D. W. *Mekhilta de-Rabbi Shimon Bar Yoḥai* (Philadelphia: The Jewish Publication Society, 2006).

Neusner, J. *Development of a Legend: Studies on the Traditions Concerning Yoḥanan Ben Zakkai* (Leiden: Brill, 1970).

———*The Talmud of the Land of Israel*. Vol. 11, *Shabbat* (Chicago: University of Chicago Press, 1991).

———*The Talmud of the Land of Israel*. Vol. 14, *Yoma* (Chicago: University of Chicago Press, 1990).

———*The Talmud of the Land of Israel*. Vol. 17, *Sukkah* (Chicago: University of Chicago Press, 1988).

———*The Talmud of the Land of Israel*. Vol. 22, *Ketubot* (Chicago: University of Chicago Press, 1985).

―――*The Talmud of the Land of Israel*. Vol. 23, *Nedarim* (Chicago: University of Chicago Press, 1985).

―――*The Talmud of the Land of Israel*. Vol. 31, *Sanhedrin and Makkot* (Chicago: University of Chicago Press, 1984).

―――*The Talmud of the Land of Israel*. Vol. 32, *Shevuot* (Chicago: University of Chicago Press, 1983).

―――*The Talmud of the Land of Israel*. Vol. 33, *Abodah Zarah* (Chicago: University of Chicago Press, 1982).

―――*The Tosefta Translated from the Hebrew: Second Division Moed* (New York: Ktav, 1981).

―――*Siphré to Numbers* (2 vols.; Providence: Brown University Press, 1986).

Nicholson, P. T., and I. Shaw. *Ancient Egyptian Materials and Technology* (Cambridge: Cambridge University Press, 1999).

Nolland, J. *Luke 9:21–18:34* (Word Biblical Commentary 35B; Dallas: Word, 1993).

Oppenheimer, A. *The ʾAm Ha-Aretz* (Leiden: Brill, 1977).

―――'Terumot and Maʾaserot', in *The Encyclopedia Judaica*, vol. 15 (Keter: Jerusalem, 1971) 1026.

Oswalt, J. N. *The Book of Isaiah: Chapters 1–39* (Grand Rapids: Eerdmans, 1986).

Peck, A. J. *The Priestly Gift in the Mishnah: A Study of Tractate Terumot* (Chicago: Scholars Press, 1981).

Pietersma, A., and B. G. Wright, eds. *A New English Translation of the Septuagint* (New York: Oxford University Press, 2007).

Piovanelli, P. 'Jesus' Charismatic Authority: On the Historical Applicability of a Sociological Model', *Journal of the American Academy of Religion* 73.2 (2005) 395-427.

Plummer, A. *A Critical and Exegetical Commentary on the Gospel According to S. Luke* (Edinburgh: T. & T. Clark, 1896).

Porton, G. P. *Understanding Rabbinic Midrash: Text and Commentary* (New Jersey: Ktav, 1985).

Pryke, E. J. *Redactional Style in the Marcan Gospel* (Cambridge: Cambridge University Press, 1978).

Rabbinowitz, J. 'Kallah Rabbati', in *The Minor Tractates of the Talmud*, vol, 2 (London: Soncino, 1965) 415-528.

Safrai, S. 'Eleazar ben Azariah', in *The Encyclopaedia Judaica*, vol. 6 (Jerusalem: Keter, 1971) 586-87.

Safrai, Z. *The Economy of Roman Palestine* (London: Routledge, 1994).

Sanders, E. P. *Jesus and Judaism* (London: SCM, 1985)

―――*Jewish Law from Jesus to the Mishnah* (London: SCM, 1990).

―――*Judaism, Practice and Belief 63BCE–66CE* (London: SCM, 1992).

Sanders, J. N., and B. A. Mastin. *The Gospel According to St John* (London: A. & C. Black, 1968).

Sarfatti, G. 'Pious Men, Men of Deeds and the Early Prophets', *Tarbiz* 26 (1956–57) 126-53 (Hebrew), II-IV English summary.

Schiffman, L. H. *Reclaiming the Dead Sea Scrolls* (Philadelphia: The Jewish Publication Society, 1994)

Schürer, E. *The History of the Jewish People in the Age of Jesus Christ*, vol. 2 (ed. G. Vermes, F. Millar, M. Black and P. Vermes; Edinburgh: T. & T. Clark, 1979).

Shanks, H. 'Origins of the Title "Rabbi"', *Jewish Quarterly Review* NS 59 (1968) 152-7.

Sibley Towner, W. 'Hermeneutical Systems of Hillel and the Tannaim: A Fresh Look', *Hebrew Union College Annual* 53 (1982) 101-35.

Sigal, P. *The Halakah of Jesus of Nazareth According to the Gospel of Matthew* (Lanham: University Press of America, 1986).

Sion, A. *Judaic Logic* (Geneva: Slatkine, 1997).

Slotki, I. W. *Eruvin* (2 vols.; London: Soncino, 1938).

Sperber, *Sidrah* (סידרא) 25-27, Minora (זוטא), 473-84 (475-78), and *Jewish Studies, an Internet Journal* (2012) 1-18 (18), http://www.biu.ac.il/JS/JSIJ/11-2012/Sperber.pdf (Hebrew)

Steinsaltz, A. *The Babylonian Talmud: Masechet Yoma* (Jerusalem: The Institute for Talmud Publications, 1977), in Hebrew.

Strack, H. L., and P. Billerbeck. *Kommentar zum Neuen Testament aus Talmud und Midrasch. Bd.2, Das Evangelium Nach Markus, Lukas und Johannes und die Apostelgeschichte*, vol. 2.5 (Munich: Beck'sche, 1926–28).

Strack, H. L., and G. Stemberger. *Introduction to the Talmud and Midrash* (trans. M. Boekmuehl; Edinburgh: T. & T. Clark, 1991).

Swete, H. B. *The Gospel According to St Mark* (3rd edn; London: Macmillan, 1909).

Taylor, V. *The Gospel According to Mark: The Greek Text with Introduction, Notes and Indexes* (2nd edn; Grand Rapids: Baker Book House, 1981).

Urbach, E. E. *From the World of the Sages* (Jerusalem: Hebrew University, Magnes Press, 1988 [Hebrew]).

———*The Sages: Their Concepts and Beliefs* (Cambridge, Mass.: Harvard University Press, 1987).

Van der Loos, H. *The Miracles of Jesus* (Leiden: Brill, 1965).

Vermes, G. *The Authentic Gospel of Jesus* (London: Allen Lane/Penguin, 2003).

———*The Complete Dead Sea Scrolls in English* (London: Allen Lane/ Penguin, 1997).

———*Jesus in His Jewish Context* (Minneapolis: Fortress, 2003).

———*Jesus the Jew: A Historian's Reading of the Gospels* (London: SCM, 1983).

———*The Religion of Jesus the Jew* (London: SCM, 1993).

Weisenberg, E. J. 'Calendar', in *The Encyclopaedia Judaica*, vol. 5 (Jerusalem: Keter, 1971) 43-53.

Westcott, B. F. *The Gospel According to St. John: The Greek Text with Introduction and Notes*, vol 1 (London: John Murray, 1908).

Wikamp, L. T. 'The Use of Traditions in John 5.1–18', *Journal for the Study of the New Testament* 25 (1983) 19-47.

Wintermute, O. 'Jubilees', in *OTP* 2:35-142.

Yadin, A. *Scripture as Logos* (Pennsylvania: University of Pennsylvania Press, 2004).

Yarbro Collins, A. *Mark A Commentary* (Minneapolis: Augsburg Fortress, 2007).

Zahavy, T. *The Talmud of the Land of Israel*. Vol. 1, *Berakot* (Chicago: University of Chicago Press, 1989).

Zeitlin, S. 'The Title Rabbi in the Gospels is Anachronistic', *Jewish Quarterly Review* 59 (1968) 158-60.

INDEX OF SUBJECTS

The entries in the following index are not exhaustive, but are meant merely to indicate the main aspects of the subjects discussed.

* indicates a Sabbath-related healing event recorded in the gospels.
Rabbinic titles are indicated with 'R.' after the main entries.
Numbers in normal print indicate page numbers.
Numbers in italics indicate a reference in the notes.
Numbers in bold print indicate the full citation of a text.

INDEX OF SOURCES

Index of Sources

5:17	7, 178, 179, 183, 185, 187- 9, 208, 217, 220, 436	9:17	180	5:14	47
		9:18-23	193	7:5	47
		9:24	192	22:12	47
		11:44	116	23:3	47
		17:23	162	23:9	47
		18:20	181	24:7	47
5:18	164, 177, 178, 189			34:9	47
		Acts			
5:19-47	183	1:43	209	*2 Corinthians*	
5:46-53	171	3:1-8	209	3:8	22
6:27	7	3:8	193	3:9	22
6:28	7	3:10	165	3:11	22
6:30	7	5:15	209		
6:59	181	5:16	209	*Philippians*	
7:14-25	18, 159, 175, 201	5:34	215, 224, 322, 363	2:12	22
7:14	181	6:8	209	*Philemon*	
7:15	211	8:7	209	16	22
7:18	184	9:6	165		
7:19	164, 166	9:34	209	*James*	
7:21	7, 163-6, 201, 204	9:40-41	209	5:13-16	174
		11:26	284		
7:22	159	14:3	209	JOSEPHUS	
7:23	120, 159, 162, 164- 6, 175, 218, 222, 232, 288, 318, 427	14:8-10	209	*Antiquities*	
		16:16-18	209	III.255	416
		19:11-12	209	VI.242-43	279, 286
		20:9-12	209	VI.242	47
		21:27	138	VII.110	47
		22:3	322	VIII.48	193
		24:12	126	XII.276-77	342, 343
7:24	21, 216	28:8-9	209	XII.4	10
7:25	166			XII.6	10
7:41-42	210			XIII.288	212
7:52	210	*Romans*		XIII.297-98	140, 212
9:1-17	18, 190, 201	5:3-4	91	XIII.297	8
		5:9	22, 23	XIII.372	119
9:1-14	125, 179, 204	5:10	22, 23	XV.3	224
		5:15	22	XVIII.15	212
9:2	174	5:16	23	XVIII.17	212
9:4	7	5:17	22, 23		
9:6	100, 194	8:29-30	91	*War*	
9:7	116	10:14-15	91	I.146	342, 343
9:8-12	191	11:12	22	IV.281	47
9:13-17	204	11:24	22	V.426-27	64
9:14	183, 194, 196				
		1 Corinthians			
9:16	190, 191, 194	3:3	47		
		4:11	47